WOMEN AND MIGRATION
IN THE U.S.-MEXICO BORDERLANDS

A book in the series
LATIN AMERICA OTHERWISE:
LANGUAGES, EMPIRES, NATIONS
Series editors:
Walter D. Mignolo, Duke University
Irene Silverblatt, Duke University
Sonia Saldívar-Hull, University
of Texas, San Antonio

WOMEN AND MIGRATION IN THE U.S.-MEXICO BORDERLANDS

A READER

EDITED BY DENISE A. SEGURA
AND PATRICIA ZAVELLA

Duke University Press
DURHAM AND LONDON
2007

© 2007 Duke University Press
All rights reserved
Printed in the United States
of America on acid-free paper ∞
Designed by Amy Ruth Buchanan
Typeset in Minion by Tseng
Information Systems, Inc.
Library of Congress Cataloging-in-
Publication Data and republication
acknowledgments appear on the last
printed pages of this book.

Contents

About the Series ix
Acknowledgments xi
Introduction 1

PART 1. *Borderlands as Sites of Struggle*

ROSA LINDA FREGOSO
Toward a Planetary Civil Society 35

LEO R. CHAVEZ
A Glass Half Empty: Latina Reproduction and Public Discourse 67

ADELAIDA R. DEL CASTILLO
Illegal Status and Social Citizenship: Thoughts on Mexican Immigrants in a Postnational World 92

EITHNE LUIBHEID
"Looking Like a Lesbian": The Organization of Sexual Monitoring at the United States-Mexican Border 106

JONATHAN XAVIER INDA
The Value of Immigrant Life 134

PART 2. *The Topography of Violence*

LESLIE SALZINGER
Manufacturing Sexual Subjects: "Harassment," Desire, and Discipline on a Maquiladora Shopfloor 161

MELISSA W. WRIGHT
The Dialectics of Still Life: Murder, Women, and Maquiladoras 184

SYLVANNA M. FALCÓN
Rape as a Weapon of War: Militarized Rape at the U.S.-Mexico Border 203

GLORIA GONZÁLEZ-LÓPEZ
"Nunca he dejado de tener terror": Sexual Violence in the Lives of Mexican Immigrant Women 224

PART 3. *Flexible Accumulation and Resistance*

XÓCHITL CASTAÑEDA AND PATRICIA ZAVELLA
Changing Constructions of Sexuality and Risk: Migrant Mexican Women Farmworkers in California 249

FARANAK MIRAFTAB
Space, Gender, and Work: Home-Based Workers in Mexico 269

MARÍA DE LA LUZ IBARRA
Mexican Immigrant Women and the New Domestic Labor 286

CYNTHIA CRANFORD
"¡Aquí estamos y no nos vamos!" Justice for Janitors in Los Angeles and New Citizenship Claims 306

PART 4. *Family Formations and Transnational Social Networks*

NORMA OJEDA DE LA PEÑA
Transborder Families and Gendered Trajectories of Migration and Work 327

LAURA VELASCO ORTIZ
Women, Migration, and Household Survival Strategies: Mixtec Women in Tijuana 341

SYLVIA CHANT
Single-Parent Families: Choice or Constraint? The Formation of Female-Headed Households in Mexican Shanty Towns 360

DENISE A. SEGURA
Working at Motherhood: Chicana and Mexican Immigrant Mothers and Employment 368

PIERRETTE HONDAGNEU-SOTELO AND ERNESTINE AVILA
"I'm Here, but I'm There": The Meanings of Latina Transnational Motherhood 388

PART 5. *Transculturation and Identity in Daily Life*

VICTORIA MALKIN
Reproduction of Gender Relations in the Mexican Migrant Community of New Rochelle, New York 415

JENNIFER S. HIRSCH
"En el norte la mujer manda": Gender, Generation, and Geography in a Mexican Transnational Community 438

OLGA NÁJERA-RAMÍREZ
Unruly Passions: Poetics, Performance, and Gender in the Ranchera Song 456

DEBORAH PAREDEZ
Becoming Selena, Becoming Latina 477

FELICITY SCHAEFFER-GRABIEL
Cyberbrides and Global Imaginaries: Mexican Women's Turn from the National to the Foreign 503

Bibliography 521
Contributors 585
Index 587

About the Series

Latin America Otherwise: Languages, Empires, Nations is a critical series. It aims to explore the emergence and consequences of concepts used to define "Latin America" while at the same time exploring the broad interplay of political, economic, and cultural practices that have shaped Latin American worlds. Latin America, at the crossroads of competing imperial designs and local responses, has been construed as a geocultural and geopolitical entity since the nineteenth century. This series provides a starting point to redefine Latin America as a configuration of political, linguistic, cultural, and economic intersections that demands a continuous reappraisal of the role of the Americas in history, and of the ongoing process of globalization and the relocation of people and cultures that have characterized Latin America's experience. Latin America Otherwise: Languages, Empires, Nations is a forum that confronts established geocultural constructions, rethinks area studies and disciplinary boundaries, assesses convictions of the academy and of public policy, and correspondingly demands that the practices through which we produce knowledge and understanding about and from Latin America be subject to rigorous and critical scrutiny.

In recent years the number of women migrating to the United States from Mexico has increased to the point that they now nearly equal the number of men. The strength of this migration has caused large transformations in the economic, political, social, and cultural spheres of both countries. The United States is becoming increasingly Mexicanized, while Mexico is now flooded with North American products, firms, and settlers. These transformations are characterized by what Paul Farmer calls "structural violence," that is, "a series of large-scale forces—ranging from gender inequality to racism and power—which structure unequal access to goods and services. *Women and Migration in the U.S.-Mexico Borderlands* presents a collection of highly influential essays on how women adapt to such structural transformations and challenges, and how they contest or create representations of their identities in light of their marginality and give voice to their own agency.

Reflecting both social science and cultural studies approaches, this collection addresses questions about (1) how decisions are made within households regarding who migrates and who remains behind, (2) under what circumstances women migrate alone, with children, or with other family members, (3) how new identities and social formations are being reconstructed on either side of the border by Mexican women, and (4) how these reconfigured identities and social formations are being represented in cultural expressions in the United States and Mexico. The volume is divided into five parts. The first part examines how nativist discourses in the United States have affected the representation and treatment of Mexican women—discourses especially virulent through the 1990s—whose effects are most dramatically evidenced in the apparently systematic murder of women in northern Mexico. In the second part, contributors study how structural violence is intertwined with interpersonal, psychic, spiritual, and institutional violence. Essays in this part examine misogynist discourses in Mexico and the United States and their relationship to the organization of work as well as to the forms of sexual debasement and sexual violence prevalent on both sides of the border. The third part focuses on changes in the division of labor and how these changes articulate with issues of sexuality, domesticity, and economic security. Part IV analyzes how the global economy disrupts the traditional rhythms of daily life and draws women into the migrant stream, often resulting in the erosion of patriarchal privilege. This part deals with the problem of transborder families. A final part analyzes women's cultural expressions that span the U.S.-Mexico border; it includes discussions about women settling far north of the border region as well as studies of women performers such as Selena, music styles such as the ranchero, and Internet relationships.

This volume addresses comprehensively the sea change of social transformations that affect women in the borderlands between Mexico and the United States.

Acknowledgments

We are deeply grateful to the University of California Institute for Mexico and the United States (UC MEXUS) and El Consejo Nacional de Ciencia y Tecnología (CONACYT), which funded the two binational *encuentros* (conferences or symposia) that significantly influenced our thinking and the production of this anthology.

Our first faculty symposium, "Mexican Women in Transnational Context: Labor, Family, and Migration," was held on 23–24 April 1999 at the University of California, Santa Cruz (UCSC). Thanks to the Chicano/Latino Research Center at UCSC and the Chicano Studies Center at the University of California, Santa Barbara (UCSB), both funded by the University of California Committee on Latino Research (UCCLR), which provided support for this project and helped organize the encuentro. The participants included Claudia Bambrila-Gonzales, Maylei Blackwell, Socorro Castañeda-Liles, Xóchitl Castañeda, Leo Chavez, María de la O Martínez, Rosa Linda Fregoso, Lorena García, Aída Hurtado, María Ibarra, Jonathan Inda, Norma Klahn, Veronica Lopez-Duran, Guadalupe Montes de Oca, Olga Nájera-Ramírez, June Nash, Sylvia Ortega-Salazar, Juan-Vicente Palerm, Beatríz M. Pesquera, María Josefina Saldaña, Martha Judith Sánchez, Denise Segura, Laura Velasco Ortiz, Patricia Zavella, and Christian Zlolniski.

The research symposium "Mujeres Migrantes Mexicanas en Contextos Transnacionales: Trabajo, Familia y Actividades Políticos-Comunitarias," sponsored by El Centro de Investigaciónes y Estudios Superiores en Antropología Social de Occidente (CIESAS) in Guadalajara, the Center for Chicano Studies at UCSB, and the Chicano/Latino Research Center at UCSC, was held in Chapala, Mexico, on 22 March 2001. María Eugénia de la O Martínez (CIESAS Guadalajara) and Christian Zlolniski (University of Texas, Arlington) took the lead in organizing this encuentro. The participants included Gabriela Arredondo, Alejandro Canales, Cynthia Cranford, María Eugenia de la O, Guillermo de la Peña, Orlandina de Oliveira, Agustín Escobar, Rosa-linda Fregoso, Mercedes González de la Rocha, María Ibarra, Jonathan Inda, Norma Klahn, Sara María Lara, Olga Nájera-Ramírez, Beatríz M. Pesquera, María Angela Rodríguez, María Josefina Saldaña, Vania Salles, Martha Judith Sánchez, Denise Segura, Paola Sesia, José Manuel Valenzuela, Laura Velasco, Ofelia Woo Morales, Patricia Zamudio, Patricia Zavella, and Christian Zlolniski. Gracias a todos/as.

We appreciate the superb research assistance of Maria Socorro Castañeda-Liles, Joseph Manuel Castañeda-Liles, Gladys García-López, and Catherine Medrano from UCSB, and Marisol Castañeda, Adrian Flores, and Sandra Mata from UCSC. Rebecca Gámez from the University of Texas, Austin provided helpful initial translations of some articles. Thanks to Jonathan Fox, Francisco A. Lomelí, Juan-Vicente Palerm, and Manuel Pastor for help with translation of technical terms and general scholarly input. We are grateful to two anonymous reviewers whose insightful suggestions greatly improved the manuscript. Thanks to Reynolds Smith for his support throughout this project. Pam Morrison, the assistant managing editor, and Tricia Mickelberry, the copy editor, did a tremendous job synchronizing text and language. Finally, we thank Carl Gutiérrez-Jones, Director of the Center for Chicano Studies at UCSB, Theresa Peña, and Zenaida Perez, whose consistent support helped make this volume a reality. Mil gracias a todos/as!

Introduction

A borderland is in ... a constant state of transition.
—Gloria Anzaldúa, *Borderlands*

※ In 1999 the anthropologist Leo Chavez presented a slide show on magazine covers to a symposium of scholars from the United States and Mexico at the University of California, Santa Cruz. The slides vividly illustrated U.S. nativist discourse on Mexican immigration, including regimes of representation that posited invasion of the nation through women's fertility (Chavez 2001). The ensuing, lively discussion centered on how women's bodies served as sites for mapping transnational relations of social inequality, but Mexican and U.S. scholars differed in their approaches to migration vis-à-vis questions asked and theoretical models engaged. The Mexican scholars focused by and large on how structural processes pushed women northward into the migrant stream and acknowledged that until recently, discourse about migrants had considered them lost to the nation. The U.S. scholars, on the other hand, focused more on migrant agency in negotiating survival, resistance, and even empowerment in the face of marginalization and discrimination toward Mexican migrants in the United States. In what we characterized as "a lightbulb moment" (or, as we say in Spanish, "se prendió el foco"), we realized we had been proceeding on parallel tracks.

The differences in assumptions and approaches articulated at this seminar may not be representative of the larger population of Chicana and Mexican scholars involved in research on Mexican women in the U.S.-Mexico borderlands or on immigration. However, the diversity of the participants' respective disciplinary training (anthropology, sociology, economics, literature, women's studies, and ethnic studies) pointed to the need to interrogate and move beyond a nation-bound discourse. We therefore committed ourselves to work on developing a binational approach that would include structural forces and women's agency as well as incorporate U.S. and Mexican perspectives on women on either side of the U.S.-Mexico border.[1]

This anthology is a step in that direction, presenting some of the resources we used to develop binational, collaborative conversations on Mexican women in the U.S.-Mexico borderlands. For the seminar, each participant had selected one article that she or he found to be central on questions of Mexican women in transnational context, focusing on women's participation in processes that transcend the actual geopolitical boundary or are shaped by transnational migration. Some of those articles are included here alongside others that deepen a transborder conversation regarding Mexican women in what Anzaldúa (1987) referred to as the "borderlands."

Throughout history the United States and Mexico have been economically, socially, and culturally intertwined, with migration to the United States being predominantly male. Now, at the beginning of the twenty-first century, however, women are just about as likely to migrate as men. Internal economic development polices within Mexico, the North American Free Trade Agreement (NAFTA), and a huge buildup of "free enterprise" zones have increasingly drawn women from different regions to the border area and even, in many cases, to the United States. These developments coupled with the need for low-wage, flexible labor and the growth of numerous informal-economy jobs, particularly in the service sector in both countries, have further strengthened the economic integration of Mexico and the United States and the feminization of transnational migration.

The magnitude and intensity of transnational migration has created tremendous transformations in the economic, political, social, and cultural spheres. The United States is becoming increasingly Mexicanized as migrants settle in disparate sites that replenish traditional Mexican communities (e.g., California and Texas) and create new migrant communities (e.g., Georgia). At the same time, Mexico is coping with the increased presence of North American products, firms, and settlers. In the current period of global integration, these transformations are rooted in growing economic polarization or what Paul Farmer calls structural violence: "a series of large-scale forces—ranging from gender inequality to racism and power—which structure unequal access to goods and social services" (1996, 369).[2] While this term is often used in relation to developing countries, we agree with Mary K. Anglin, who argues that structural violence is manifest in developed countries as well and often affects women differently: "Through structural forms of violence persons are socially and culturally marginalized in ways that deny them the opportunity for emotional and physical well-being, or expose them to assault or rape, or subject them to hazards that can cause sickness and death" (1998, 145). Despite the need to understand the multifaceted ways in which women experience structural violence, women remain underrepresented in the vast literature on migration from Mexico or the social changes occurring related to U.S.-Mexico integration.[3]

In this volume, we explore how women adapt to structural transformations, contest or create representations of their identities in light of their marginality, and give voice to their complex human agency, or "subjective transnationalism," as we refer to it. Drawing on the work on transnationalism and Chicana/o Studies, we argue that women are constructing their identities in spaces "located in the interstices between the dominant national and cultural systems of both the United States and Mexico" (David G. Gutiérrez 1999, 488) as they live, work, and play in communities on both sides of the border. Women in the U.S.-Mexico borderlands construct a new diasporic subjectivity that may be oppositional and transformative (Emma Pérez 1999) as they reflect on their experiences of migration, settlement, work, or social reproduction that are affected by globalization and structural violence. Subjective transnationalism reflects the experience of feeling "at home" in more than one geographic location where identity construction is deterritorialized as part of a borderlands mixture of shifting race and ethnic boundaries and gendered transitions in a global economy. Conversely, subjective transnationalism includes feelings that one is neither from "here" nor from "there," that is, not at home anywhere. As women's market activities increase, so do their negotiations for an enhanced social space in households, local communities, and the state. These negotiation processes often contest patriarchal ways of being as women increasingly engage in productive as well as reproductive labor. Even if this labor is viewed by more privileged "first world" inhabitants as "low value" and "semi-skilled," women's participation in the peripheral sectors of the economy can facilitate a critique of the exploitative processes that characterize global economic transactions, as vividly demonstrated by the rise of labor activism, the increase in the numbers of women utilizing social services, the growing participation of women's involvement in their children's schooling, and the development of economic strategies associated with the rise of female-headed households. While households headed by women are typically characterized by economic marginality, women increasingly demonstrate a preference for reliance on the fruits of their own labor when a partnership (either male or female) lowers the quality of their lives, creating a heightened subjectivity about their constraints and options. The essays in this volume reflect a sea change of social transformations that affect women in the borderlands between Mexico and the United States.

Notions of borderlands are complex and have been used by writers and theorists in widely disparate ways (Klahn 1997).[4] One of the most influential thinkers about borderlands, the Chicana feminist lesbian poet and theorist Gloria Anzaldúa, argues that borderlands have multiple meanings (1987). Literally, the borderlands include the geopolitical space around the U.S.-Mexico border, where there is a great deal of movement of people, products, and ideas. Borderlands also refer to how subjects cope with social inequalities based on racial, gender, class, and/or sexual differences, as well as with spiritual transformation and psychic processes of exclusion and identification—of feeling "in between" cultures, languages, or places. And borderlands are spaces where the marginalized voice their identities and resistance. All of these social, political, spiritual, and emotional transitions transcend geopolitical space. In an often-cited statement, Anzaldúa writes, "The U.S.-Mexico border *es una herida abierta* (an open wound) where the Third World grates against the first and bleeds. And before a scab forms it hemorrhages again, the lifeblood of two worlds merging to form a third country—a border culture. Borders are set up to define the places that are safe and unsafe, to distinguish us from them" (1987, 3).

Borderland studies within the social sciences focus on transnational social formations, on how migrants engage in economic, political, or sociocultural activities that transcend national borders and "deterritorialize," or span international boundaries (Levitt 2003; Portes, Guarnizo, and Landolt 1999).[5] Increasingly, ethnographers who use this approach conduct field research in multiple sites—"sending" and "receiving" communities—so as to concretize how sustained deterritorialized processes unfold. A second approach to borderlands within cultural studies "emphasize[s] the ways in which identity formation is linked to multiple sites, both real and imagined, such that new hybridized and creolized identity forms emerge. According to this perspective, identities shift and are negotiated in responses to forces from above and below and therefore are never fixed or bounded" (Levitt 2001, 237–38).[6] This anthology includes work from both of these approaches to provide insight on the multifaceted changes that Mexican women negotiate daily in the borderlands.

U.S.-Mexico Integration

The borderlands between the United States and Mexico are rooted in the intertwined processes of neoliberal policies and economic restructuring in the United States and in Mexico that create structural violence. The integration of the U.S. and Mexican economies, which pre-dated the passage of NAFTA in 1994 but accelerated once the two countries became formally allied, reflects the long-standing, complex relations between both societies. Historically, production has been binational, with Mexico serving as the reserve army of labor for U.S. agriculture, manufacturing, and service sectors.[7] Over time, however, this relationship changed. Increasingly, social reproduction is taking place in the United States as more women migrate and form families here, whereas production is relocating south, as U.S. jobs are "outsourced." These changing economic relations frame the context for the emergence of borderlands politics facilitated by dual nationality, in social formations (such as binational families), and through transculturation—cultural expressions and identities that transcend the border (Paredes 1993).

At the macro level, the increasing interdependence of world economies, communications systems, and popular cultures are reshaping local and global political and economic dynamics. Remittances sent by U.S.-based Latinas/os to Latin America—principally to Mexico and the Caribbean, but also to the entire region—now constitute one of the area's largest sources of capital.[8] Under NAFTA and other trade agreements, economic, social, environmental, and agricultural policies carried out by the United States now affect Mexico much more directly than in the past. At the same time, Mexico's economic and political strategies, particularly those related to migration, affect the United States. That the border is porous is evident in recent transformations in biomedical-environmental policies that have resulted in greater availability of more affordable AIDS treatments and additional regulation of genetically modified agricultural and medicinal products. The binational dialogue from these transformations is becoming even more challenging in the post-9/11 era, where calls for border controls and greater regulation of international migration are restructuring relations of scientific and cultural exchange between the United States and Mexico.

A key feature of contemporary U.S.-Mexico economic interdependence is women's increasing mobility. More and more women migrate within Mexico and from Mexico to the United States, a development that exacts particular regional effects in both countries, including women's incorporation into the labor market and the feminization of specific occupations on both sides of the border. With these changes come a number of contradictions, such as limited occupational mobility for women despite their higher educational attainment. This development, coupled with the growth of households headed by women, enlarges their numbers among the working poor. These global, regional, and local changes have far-reaching consequences for women's work experiences, their family lives, their social identities, and their cultural expressions.

The sociologist Shawn Kanaiaupuni argues that "migration as a response to macro level conditions is shaped by the relative opportunity structures for men and women in places of origin and destination" (2000, 1316). She suggests that migration from Mexico has been predominantly male because of three factors: patriarchal social norms, the presence of children, and occupational segregation. Patriarchal norms deem men to be breadwinners, so if the local employment structure does not provide adequate wages, the conditions favor male migration. This situation is mitigated by local gender considerations; for example, when there are significant local employment opportunities for women, male partners tend not to migrate. The interplay between marital status, the presence of children, and the local opportunity structure vary by gender as well. The presence of children influences men to migrate if they do not earn enough income to support their families in Mexico, whereas the effect is not that direct among women. In general, the presence of children often makes geographical mobility difficult, and the cost of raising a family is lower in Mexico than in the United States; both factors discourage women from migrating. "Hence married women with children are more likely to remain in the sending communities while male family members migrate" (1318). More important predictors of women's migration include level of education, prior marital status, and the strength of their social networks in the United States. Women who are no longer in conjugal relationships are more likely to migrate even if they have children and particularly if they have strong social ties in the United States. Women with higher levels of education also tend to migrate, given the low returns on their human capital investments in Mexico vis-à-vis men (Belinda Reyes 1997).

In addition to these economic and social considerations in Mexico, U.S. immigration policies have strongly influenced gendered migration patterns, beginning with the Bracero Program (1942–1964), which constructed social networks for sharing knowledge about and resources for migration but did not provide opportunities for women to work in the United States. The 1965 Immigration Law emphasized family reunification, which usually meant that wives and children of male migrants could legally join them. The Immigration Reform and Control Act of 1986 (IRCA), which offered amnesty to migrants who could document their residency and employment, presented disadvantages to women, who largely worked in the informal sector, and favored men, who were more likely to have formal employment and thus were able to document their status.

Despite such formidable barriers, migration by women (both documented and undocumented) has grown steadily. Between 1910 and 1939—an era that included both the Mexican Revolution and the Great Depression, which were characterized by significant Mexican repatriations—women constituted 5 percent of migrants from Mexico; that figure increased to 7 percent in the period between 1940 and 1964 (the era of the Bracero Program), and climbed to 20 percent after 1965, following the implementation of the 1965 Immigration Reform Act (Durand 1992, 121). During these same periods, the percentage of women who migrated within Mexico—one indicator of possible future transnational migration—increased from 15 percent to 16 percent to 27 percent, respectively (121). Thus, women were part of larger demographic changes in the migrant stream and in the political-economic forces that pushed Mexicans to leave their home regions, attracted to jobs elsewhere (Durand 1992; Cardenas and Flores 1986).

More recently, migration to the United States has included even higher proportions of women. Since 1970, at least 6.8 million Mexican migrants have entered the United States with or without documents: "The percentage of women among documented migrants fluctuated around 46 percent before IRCA (1980–1986), during the post IRCA transition period (1987–1992), and after IRCA (1993 onward)" (Massey, Durand, and Malone 2002, 134). Other sources estimate that 57 percent of authorized Mexican migrants were women (Cerrutti and Massey 2001). Alongside the growth of documented female migration was an increase in the propensity for undocumented women to migrate. Prior to IRCA, undocumented women comprised about one quarter of all migrants. During the transition and post-IRCA periods, that figure rose to one third (Massey, Durand, and Malone 2002, 134). At the same time, more indigenous Mexicans, including women, joined the migrant stream (Fox and Rivera-Salgado 2004). These demographic changes suggest a feminization of migration from Mexico. Indeed, Kanaiaupuni's analysis of demographic changes in migration finds that "migration is a profoundly gendered process and . . . conventional explanations of men's migration in many cases do not apply to women" (2000, 1312).

Clearly, we need to understand better the nature of this shift in the gender composition of transnational migrants and what it means for women's work and family experiences as well as women's identities and cultural expressions in the United States and in Mexico. Once women enter the migrant stream, they find themselves in the borderlands between the United States and Mexico, with important political implications.

The Politics of Transnational Migration

In the political realm, migration from Latin America has been a flashpoint in the United States, particularly visible in California, where 40 percent of all migrant Mexicans reside (Fry 2002). Anti-immigrant proponents often assume that all Latinos—whether citizens or authorized permanent residents—are migrants and therefore "illegal" (De Genova 2002). A series of propositions have been passed or proposed to control the effects of a growing Latino presence: Proposition 63, "English as the Official Language of California," passed in 1986, was intended to preserve, protect, and strengthen the English language; Proposition 187, "Save Our State," passed in 1994, aimed to disallow "illegal aliens'" use of education and health services, but it was nullified by the courts as unconstitutional; Proposition 209, "End Racial Preference and Affirmative Action," passed in 1996, requires state-university systems to dismantle race-specific practices even though they are required to meet federal affirmative-action laws; Proposition 227, "English Only" (the Unz initiative), passed in 1998, requires a one-year transition to English-language instruction for all schoolchildren; Proposition 54, the "Color Blind" initiative, defeated on 7 October 2003, would have disallowed the collecting of official statistics about racial groups, since that practice supposedly perpetuates racism. (The defeat was seen as a major victory for those who value monitoring discrimination against racial groups and their institutional underrepresentation.) These propositions mobilized citizens who felt they were defending the state, as well as Latinos and progressive voters who opposed racist exclusionary legislation.

At the national level, Congress ultimately passed legislation that enforced some of the restrictionist sentiments in Proposition 187. The Illegal Immigration Reform and Immigrant Responsibility Act, passed in 1996, restricted access to healthcare, except for emergency care, for undocumented migrants and further entrenched the border as a militarized zone with increased border patrols and technology. In addition, labor policy became integrally linked to migration issues and patterns of investment. This relationship was evident in the 2004 U.S. electoral season, during which various candidates promoted or opposed support for "offshore" investment in Latin America by U.S. corporations, for a guest-worker program, or for making driver's licenses available to undocumented immigrants (Vieth and Chen 2004). The negotiations between President George W. Bush and Vicente Fox over new migration policies, delayed by the terrorist attacks of 9/11, have been watched closely on both sides of the border.[9]

For politically underrepresented and racially subordinated groups like Mexicans, cultural expressions—literature or film, popular music, visual arts such as murals or folk art, performance arts like dance or theater—provide essential social spaces and a sense of belonging within their local communities and in the larger, dominant society (Aparicio 2004; Iglesias and Fregoso 1998). In particular, popular culture provides important sites for contesting nativism and exploring issues such as bilingualism, immigration, and racism. In the context of globalization, migration, and marginalization as experienced by many Mexicans—both migrants and citizens—cultural expressions are often key sites for expressing language, rituals, and cultural memories, and for affirming their identities.

All of these developments have an impact in the United States, leading to significant social, economic, and cultural transformations, including the growth in the Chicana/o and Latina/o populations.[10] The 2000 census recorded 37.4 million Latinos in the United States. Mexicans constituted 67 percent of those Latinos, who made up 13.7 percent of the total population. According to those numbers, Latinos had become the largest racial-ethnic minority group in the United States (U.S. Bureau of the Census 2003), exceeding the projections of the previous census, which had indicated that Latinos would not overtake African Americans as the largest minority group until 2010.[11] The increase in the numbers of Chicanos/Latinos in the United States was most pronounced in California, where they comprised nearly one-third of that most populous state in the nation, and in Texas, which was 31 percent Chicano/Latino (Texas State Data Center 1998).

In tandem with increased migration to the United States, policies have shifted in Mexico toward what Jorge Durand (2004) calls "shared responsibility." Vicente Fox, while a presidential candidate, made several highly publicized trips to campaign in the United States. After he was elected president, Fox created the short-lived Presidential Office for Mexicans Abroad and promulgated a discourse about migrants being heroes to the nation, a discourse that, while controversial, signaled a change in how Mexicans regard those who leave. Several legislators in the Mexican congress had migrant experiences and represent those who migrate back and forth. Mexico extended dual nationality to Mexicans who become American citizens as well as to their children (Levitt and de la Dehesa 2003). Clearing the first hurdle in changing the constitution, the Mexican congress passed legislation that enabled those living abroad to vote in Mexican elections, thus joining sixty other nations that allow migrants to vote in their former countries' elections (Thompson 2005). The Mexican government has also increased funding to hometown associations that channel U.S.-based resources in economic-development projects in Mexico and often matches what they contribute through a program called Three for One. Some of the federations of hometown associations, especially those formed by indigenous migrants, are active in the United States and Mexico and provide a source of identity and political activity (Fox and Rivera-Salgado 2004). And feminists contribute to debates about politics, ethnic groups, classes, and party affiliations in Mexico (Biron 1996).

One important consequence of increased migration to the United States is growing attention to Mexican women's fertility. Overall, Latinas have higher fertility rates than Caucasians, African Americans, or Asians and Pacific Islanders (Johnson, Hill, and Heim 2001). In part, this reflects the larger number of Latina women in their childbearing years, with 51 percent of all Latinas being between fourteen and forty-four years old, compared to 42 percent of white women (U.S. Bureau of the Census 2000). Furthermore, foreign-born Latinas have higher fertility rates than Latinas born in the United States, a disparity that the demographer Hans Johnson and colleagues (2001) attribute partially to IRCA, which provided amnesty predominately for young men, who then brought over their spouses and began families. Family reunification thus created a baby boom, which is predicted to be of short duration. Indeed, fertility rates for foreign-born Latinas declined between 1990 and 1997. What is critical for the quality of life of Mexicans in the United States is that women's reproduction is disparaged as a threat to the racial purity and well-being of the nation (Chavez essay in this volume).[12]

Surprisingly, little attention has been paid to the *decline* in Mexican women's fertility (Chavez essay in this volume). In the early 1970s the size of Mexican American families averaged 4.4 persons, as opposed to 3.5 persons for non-Latinos (Chavez essay in this volume). In order to examine whether Mexican women's fertility continued to decline, Leo Chavez undertook a survey in 1992–93 of 803 Latinas and 422 white women that revealed that the fertility rate for U.S.-born Mexicans was 1.81 and for Anglos was 1.27. Because reproduction is 2.0, these rates represent zero population growth for both groups. Fertility has also been declining in Mexico for several decades. In 1970 the lifetime number of children per woman was 7.5; that figure declined to 4.4 by 1980, to 3.4 by 1990, and to 2.4 by 2000 (Hirsch 1998a, 540–41; Chavez essay in this volume). "Clearly Mexico has experienced dramatic decline in fertility rates over the last few decades" (Chavez essay in this volume). Jennifer Hirsch (2003) attributes this decline to changing beliefs about marriage, delays in bearing children, the spacing of births, and increased contraceptive use—processes found in the United States as well. Moreover, U.S.-born, second- and third-generation women of Mexican origin have lower fertility rates than either migrants or U.S. white women. Despite these shifts in fertility, Mexican women's reproduction is often represented as "out of control" and largely responsible for Mexicans' low socioeconomic status (Chavez essay in this volume).

Changes in the political, economic, and social environments in both countries alongside the changing character of fertility, employment, and migration have led to polarized debates about the appropriate constitution of national communities, as well as the role of migrants in both nations (Chavez 2001; Chavez essay in this volume). "The nation is imagined in such a way as to suppress the heterogeneity and routine border crossings of everyday life, as well as the knowledge that different peoples with different and often opposing histories exist within the boundaries of the same territory" (Chapin 1998, 405–6).

Mexican women are at the center of such immigration debates. Their reproductive bodies are represented as hostile and foreign, threatening the social safety net and thus the well-being of the nation. Such representations constitute a form of social violence (Chavez 1997; Inda 2002; also see the essays by Chavez and Inda in this volume). As Renato Rosaldo suggests, "Social analysts need to recognize the centrality of actual violence and the symbolics that shape that violence" (1997, 3). Negative representations of Mexican migrants, women in particular, mask the state-sanctioned structural violence that pushes subjects into the migrant stream, as well as the social violence that migrants negotiate in everyday life (Flores and Valdez Curiel forthcoming). Further, women's economic contributions, creative adaptation strategies, cultural expressions, and everyday contestations remain largely unrecognized in scholarship and in the media.

Mexican women have become key contributors to the new economy, which is characterized by flexible accumulation, borderless organizations of work, and the expansion of low-wage jobs, all of which are consequences of structural violence. Disruptions in family life, brought on by migration and participation in the labor market, present challenges for women who have come to the United States in search of better lives and who cope with social violence in migrant communities and even within families. These changes have contributed to the development of new social identities and cultural formations that span national borders. Mexican women thus are situated within intersections of significant political, economic, and social transformations that the discourses on immigration, globalization, and Latin American and Chicano studies have approached in different ways.

Parallel Conversations on Mexican Women

Along with the feminization of migrant streams, the increased incorporation of women into the labor force has been assessed using different analytical frameworks in Mexico and the United States. Current research on women workers in Mexico demonstrates that the labor market is becoming feminized, particularly in the agricultural sector, as more women are recruited for seasonal jobs such as weeding, planting, and occasionally even harvesting.[13] Growing sources of women's employment include industrial homework in electronics (expanding as firms outsource production), manufacturing of textiles or other products, and street vending. Women's employment in these sectors is changing household dynamics as women age or support families on their own.[14] Sex work remains highly stigmatized even as women attempt to gain more control over the conditions of such work (Lamas 1996; Castañeda et al. 1996).

The Border Industrialization Program (BIP), initiated in the 1960s, attracted more women to the U.S.-Mexico border, one of the largest crossing points in the world, and was based on gendered dynamics. The BIP accelerated the development of *maquiladoras* (factories that produce for export), which targeted women as workers for "women's work" that required "nimble fingers" and docility as well as participation in gendered social activities such as beauty pageants (Salzinger 2003; Cravey 1998). Since the factories at first predominantly employed women, they stimulated men's migration to the United States (Fernández-Kelly 1983a, 1983b, 1983c). After restructuring in the 1980s, the factories employed more men as well (de la O Martínez 1995). The BIP stimulated urbanization in border "twin cities"—Juarez and El Paso, San Diego and Tijuana, for example—which grew tremendously. The BIP furthered the integration of the U.S. and Mexican economies and the fluidity of the border, generating frequent crossings for visiting, shopping, entertainment, and the like (Ojeda de la Peña essay in this volume). In the late 1980s the Reagan administration launched the War against Drugs to counter the national-security threat presented by the flow of drugs, particularly cocaine, heroin, and marijuana, across the U.S.-Mexico border through personal possession or as cargo. Increasing attention to narcotrafficking stimulated violence within the border region.

The border is a region where power structures of capitalism, patriarchy, and racialization intersect, generating structural violence that is most visible in the deaths of migrants who cross the border and in the rise of *colonias*, communities characterized by underdeveloped or substandard housing, which can be found on either side of the border. Structural violence is also apparent in the increase of female-headed households that live in conditions of poverty despite employment and in exploitative working conditions on either side of the border. Chant (1991; essay in this volume) finds that households and labor markets are linked and that women are more likely to enter the labor market after becoming heads of households and when there is increased labor demand.[15]

Excellent case studies of women working in the maquiladoras indicate that profound changes are occurring as women face the challenges of physically taxing, gendered work and polluted work sites where women are subject to sexual harassment and surveillance.[16] Not unlike processes occurring in the United States, women's incorporation into the labor force in Mexico draws on and often reinforces traditional ideological notions that a woman's place should be within the home despite her contributions to household income (Fowler-Salamini and Vaughan 1994; González de la Rocha 1984).[17] Furthermore, Mexican families are adapting varied forms, ranging from extended households to single-parent families, to cope with women's labor-market participation (González Montes and Tuñon 1997). Similar to women workers elsewhere, Mexican women living in poverty construct complicated survival strategies through the use of social exchange among social networks and fictive kin, including what the anthropologist Carlos Vélez-Ibañez (1983) calls "rituals of marginality," whereby they confront the conditions of poverty through organized resistance at work sites or within their communities.[18]

Within labor markets and work sites segregated by race and gender in the United States, Mexican women are also concentrated in "women's jobs," with migrants at the bottom of the occupational structure in the secondary labor market.[19] These jobs are often nonunion, pay minimum wages, have few benefits, are seasonal and/or subject to displacement (e.g., in agriculture or garments), and often require relatively low training or educational levels although the work itself may be quite difficult.[20] Those working in the informal sector (e.g., domestic workers or day-care providers) are subject to irregular work hours, little oversight over the conditions of work, and few recourses if their employers do not pay or underpay.[21] Even workers who are located in unionized sectors (e.g., food processing) find that unions are often unresponsive to their particular needs, and union democracy struggles have been waged over translating contracts and union meetings into Spanish and electing representatives who understand the needs of the Mexican workers.[22]

Despite the passage of equal-employment-opportunity laws and increases in educational attainment by Mexican women born in the United States, patterns of occupational segregation continue. Analysts suggest that this is due to a combination of structural changes and vulnerabilities in human capital.

Mexicans often reside in regions where economic restructuring has dismantled industries such as steel or auto manufacturing which provided well-paying, stable jobs and shifted to other manufacturing sectors (garments, electronics) that hire predominantly migrant women at low wages (Ortiz 1996). Indeed, some argue that migrant labor, particularly that of women, is a central feature of a flexible, global economy.[23] Like electronics, the garment and food-processing industries have undergone outsourcing to the Third World, and to the extent that they remain in the United States, these industries increasingly rely on migrant labor forces, especially women.[24] When downsizing occurs, those who have recently moved into jobs or up the job ladder (particularly women) are vulnerable to lay offs, long-term unemployment, and stress.[25] These structural processes are fueled by increased immigration and by employers who prefer to hire migrants, who often do not speak English, have few skills that are marketable here (although they may be well trained in their home country), or are undocumented.

There is a clear relationship between occupational segregation in low-wage jobs and poverty. Mexicans have disproportionately high rates of poverty, and contrary to expectations of upward mobility through successive generations born in the United States, Mexican poverty rates remain disproportionately high even by the third generation.[26] Generally, Mexicans make up the working poor, where at least one member of the household has a low-wage job (Moore and Pinderhughes 1993; Pastor forthcoming). Mexicans in the Southwest for the most part experience structural forces which produce poverty differently than forces that affect other racial groups, notably African Americans in the Midwest and on the East Coast, where deindustrialization, white flight, inner-city residential segregation, employer perceptions of blacks vs. migrants, and declining infrastructures create formidable barriers to job creation. Particularly in the Southwest, Mexicans living in poverty are likely to be located in suburban or rural areas. Like other racial groups, Mexicans have experienced a feminization of poverty: Mexican women consistently have higher poverty rates than men within each generation, and the percentage of women heading households below the poverty level has increased (Treviño et al. 1988; Amott and Matthei 1996).

Mexican women in the United States (whether migrants or not) often rely on their own resources and nurture intense social networks that help them get through the vicissitudes of poverty and social isolation.[27] Grassroots, community-based organizations are another venue through which women struggle to change the daily conditions of their lives, and Mexican women are increasingly organizing *encuentros* (conferences or symposia) that bring together activists from both sides of the border.[28] Regarding family life, there are important differences between migrant Mexican women and second- and third-generation women of Mexican heritage who work in secondary labor-market jobs, particularly in how they perceive themselves as working mothers (Segura essay in this volume).[29] Some women migrate independently, while others rely on direct sponsorship or are accompanied by men.[30] Furthermore, women "consolidate settlement" after immigration differently than men: through community-wide social networks that originate in women's wage work, through women's relatively stable jobs, and through the utilization of private and public institutional forms of assistance, including credit (Hondagneu-Sotelo 1994). There is growing evidence that some transnational migrants retain close ties with families, extended kin, social networks, or communities in Mexico through the construction of binational households or families.[31] When speaking of poor Mexican women workers, then, one must often refer to processes occurring on both sides of the border, which are integral to women's daily life experiences.

Paradigm Shifts

Debates about Mexican women are at the center of four main paradigm shifts in immigration studies, Chicana/o Studies, Latin American Studies, and global and international studies.

Immigration has been the dominant paradigm for analyzing mobility across national boundaries and the dilemmas of settlement. Research in this field typically examines linear processes, characterized by identifying the impetus to immigrate, the receptivity or availability of jobs in the host nation, and processes of adaptation and assimilation. Alejandro Portes and Rubén Rumbaut, however, argue that "while assimilation may still represent the master concept in the study of today's immigrants, the process is subject to too many contingencies and affected by too many variables to render the image of a relatively uniform and straightforward path credible" (2001, 45). With the integration of gender and globalization, the portrait becomes more complicated, with processes of adaptation becoming sites of cultural transformation and human agency that have been little explored for Mexican women in the United States (notable exceptions include Hondagneu-Sotelo 1994, 2001; Fernández-Kelly and García 1990).

Through rigorous critique of assimilationist perspectives, Chicana/o Studies scholars demolished the cultural-deficiency arguments that had rationalized Mexican subordination through internal cultural or social mechanisms when they did not assimilate. Until recently, research within Chicana/o Studies has been nationally or regionally based, with uneven attention to the diversity of experiences among people of Mexican origin (Rodolfo Acuña 1981; Barrera 1979). The two major ideological frameworks that guided the Chicano Movement and Chicano Studies—*El Plan Espiritual de Aztlán* and *El Plan de Santa Bárbara*—articulated an agenda of self-determination and empowerment that was fundamentally nationalistic and male-centered (Fregoso and Chabram 1990).

The early framework of Chicano Studies relied on actualizing a series of categorical opposites: a racialized class of colonized Chicanos (men) versus a superordinate class of Anglo colonizers; Chicano (male) activists versus Mexican American assimilationists; and Chicana loyalists versus Chicana feminists. Chicana feminism was highly contested terrain where men challenged women activists as disloyal sell-outs if they strayed too far from the nationalist agenda. According to the undifferentiated nationalist text, racial oppression is primary, and all Chicanos are victims of white racism and have been oppressed more or less equally by all Anglo-Americans. This principle predominated within the earliest Chicano texts that informed the first generation of Chicano scholarship (see, for example, Rodolfo Acuña's often-cited *Occupied America*). Thus, the earliest blueprints for Chicano Studies did not situate women at the center of the intellectual or political paradigm (Alma García 1989, 1997; Segura 2001). The growth of Chicana feminism led to a fundamental shift in the analytic, male-centered core of "Chicano" discourse toward an ever more inclusionary "Chicana/o" Studies framework.

The economic and cultural impacts of globalization, however, are challenging Chicana/o Studies and scholars of Latina/o populations to incorporate the local effects of global processes such as continuing migration from Mexican and Latin America, in particular with regard to their gendered character. Scholars working within a Chicana/o Studies approach who research the effects of migration from Mexico find significant tensions between Mexican migrants and U.S.-born Chicanos and Mexican Americans regarding political agendas, ethnic identification, and cultural knowledge.[32] In addition, U.S.-born Mexican Americans experience competition with Latino migrants in the labor market (Ruiz 1998; Segura 1992; Zavella 1987) and with African Americans (Cranford essay in this volume; Mindiola, Flores Niemann, and Rodriguez 2002). Scholars are diversifying the one-dimensional portrait of Mexican-origin populations by emphasizing the challenges facing Mexican migrants who speak Spanish or indigenous languages, as well as English-speaking, U.S.-born Chicanos.[33] Yvette Flores-Ortiz (1993) finds that the many tensions generated by migration may exacerbate domestic violence in dysfunctional families through "cultural freezing," where "tradition" and control are imposed as a means to cope with distressing disruptions. Lourdes Argüelles and Ann

Rivero (1993) suggest that violence or homophobia forces some women to leave Latin American countries for the north in order to escape the abuse and to construct their lives on their own terms.

Latin American Studies has traditionally been concerned with the analysis of specific countries as well as with internal migration south of the U.S.-Mexico border. However, with migrant populations strongly influencing the emergence of new social, political, and ethnic identities, Latin Americanists have become increasingly concerned with global processes, including migration to the United States. Largely utilizing ethnographic research, theorists of the "new transnationalism" have shifted scholarly thinking from immigration to migration (Glick Schiller, Basch, and Blanc-Szanton 1992, 1995; Kearney 1995a, 1995b). These theorists suggest the necessity of examining transnational circuits, spaces, networks, or identities as people move from one nation to another yet retain ties to "sending communities." While the great "waves" of immigrants to the United States often maintained ties with their countries of origin, Nina Glick Schiller, Linda Basch, and Cristina Blanc-Szanton argue, the current connections between migrants and home societies are of a different order than those of previous generations. They draw on Saskia Sassen's analyses (1988, 1998) of the global mobility of labor, wherein she recommends examining "the particular historical and political context of the current migration phase," which shifts over time and involves subjects from multiple social locations (1988, 3). Thus, new circuits of capital, transformations in technologies of transportation and communication, and the inability of migrants to become fully incorporated into countries in which they settle help sustain transnational ties. Transnational theorists also advocate cultivating a "bifocal" orientation and examining "the processes by which immigrants build social fields that link together their country of origin and their country of settlement," including familial, economic, social, organizational, religious, and political relations that span national borders (Glick Schiller, Basch, and Blanc-Szanton 1992, ix).[34] They suggest use of the term *migrants* (as opposed to *immigrants*) to connote transnational ties when people migrate from one country to another (Rouse 1992, 1995a, 1995b). However, only recently has the transnational approach come to incorporate a gender analysis that includes women (Glick Schiller and Fouron 2001; Hirsch 2003; Levitt 2001).

Research in globalization literature has typically focused on processes of economic integration that occur irrespective of national boundaries. This literature is characterized by macrolevel analysis of the increasing interdependence of world economies, communications systems, and popular cultures, but gives inadequate attention to everyday resistance, cultural changes, or strategies for creating social meaning (Wallerstein 1976). Women's labor tends to be situated within larger analysis of the fragmentation and deterritorialization of production processes, internal migration flows, and commodity chains (Applebaum and Bonacich 2000). Increasingly, scholars, policy makers, and social activists have to cope with processes that transcend international borders and transform work sites, worker cultures, and family lives; for example, the fact that women must contend with continuing state-sanctioned violence along the U.S.-Mexico border and elsewhere (Fregoso 2003; Mohanty 1997; Schmidt Camacho 2004a, 2004b; Wright essay in this volume). Scholarly work on the transnational division of labor has theorized how social reproduction in daily life is represented in the political economy of nations and in the global economy (Wright 2006; Sassen 1998; Nash and Fernández-Kelly 1983). At the microlevel, how people negotiate these larger social processes provides insight for understanding how culture is created and communities are transformed. In this sense, transnational social networks, cultural expressions, and identities enhance survival in daily life and can promote contestation of global processes (Velasco Ortiz essay in this volume; Malkin 1997; Hurtado 1997).

Placing Women at the Center

Despite the magnitude of these economic and social transformations, little research has included the voices and experiences of Mexican women. Indeed, much of the research on men's experiences has failed to include gender analysis that integrates ideologies of masculinity and femininity alongside of structural variations that generate unequal outcomes for men and women. This volume is part of the larger effort to make gender and gender oppression central to studies of migration, Chicana/o studies, Latin American studies, and studies of globalization. To initiate a cross-border dialogue that would examine women's life chances at the systemic, cultural, and individual levels, we convened two binational symposia with the purposes of facilitating intellectual exchanges between scholars from Mexico and California, interrogating the state of the field, sharing research findings, and developing a research agenda that put women at the center. The first symposium, "Mexican Women in Transnational Context: Labor, Family and Migration," held at the University of California, Santa Cruz, on 23–24 April 1999, focused on dominant paradigms within studies of globalization, migration, Chicana and Mexican women's social identities, and cultural transformations in a transnational context. These studies included intersections between family and work, new family forms, the role of social networks, resistance and empowerment, and different modes of women's cultural expressions.

During the second symposium, "Migrantes Mexicanas en Contextos Transnacionales: Trabajo, Familia y Actividades Políticos-Comunitarias," held in Chapala, Mexico, on 22 March 2001, the participants presented research relevant to such questions. Two critical needs became clear: the need for a text on Mexican women that spanned the border; and the need to develop binational research teams to pursue scholarly work on Mexican women. Perhaps the most disturbing outcome of the symposium was its revelation of the many layers of violence that originate in structural dislocation and permeate family life, work sites, and interpersonal relations. Moreover, other key questions emerged: How are decisions made within households regarding who migrates and who remains behind? Under which circumstances do women migrate alone, with children, or other family members? In view of global interpenetration, how are new identities and social formations being reconstructed on either side of the border by Mexican women? How are these reconfigured identities and social formations being represented in cultural expressions and imaginaries in the United States and Mexico?

When women become the center of the analysis, questions change and previously held assumptions become subjects of inquiry. This anthology focuses on Mexican women, compiling recent research that incorporates important paradigm shifts. The essays herein explore a range of women's experiences, from reconstructions of "tradition" to contestations of racist, patriarchal, and/or heteronormative structures in work sites, families, popular culture, and the state. The selections also explore women's abilities to maneuver within structures of power that are often brutal, whether it be by contesting personal or political abuse or by resisting discourses of state or social violence. This anthology utilizes an interdisciplinary approach to reveal the poetics and performance of Mexican women's agency, crafting a tapestry of voice and resistance that speaks to their multiple realities.

The Ojeda de la Peña and Velasco Ortiz essays have been translated from Spanish to English. These articles, along with the binational focus of some of the U.S. scholars, deepen our analysis of women in Mexico and the United States. Both pieces, originally published in Spanish, contain information spanning the 1980s and 1990s, a key decade in that the migration of Mexican women began to increase dramatically. Hence, both essays interrogate the forces that pushed women into the migrant stream, such as the gendered construction of social networks that facilitated the migration of women, including indigenous women, and frequent border crossings prior to increased militarization of the border. Other essays discuss the promulgation of nativist discourses and practices that focused on women and families, as well as how racialization and sexualization profoundly affected how Mexican women constructed new lives in the United States or through migration to the northern border region in Mexico.

Overview

Part I, "Borderlands as Sites of Struggle," presents critical perspectives on the ways in which globalization and nativist discourses in U.S. politics and the state have influenced how Mexican women are treated and represented. Although these discourses became especially virulent in the 1990s, when the presence of Mexican women migrants became more noticeable, they have a long history. As racial-ethnic "others," Mexican women bear the brunt of nationalist, patriarchal, and heteronormative views that proliferate in the context of border economic development and migration from Mexico to the United States. Several essays discuss California, which is often ground zero for contradictory anti-immigrant discourses.

In "Toward a Planetary Civil Society," Rosa Linda Fregoso explores the politics of gender extermination in northern Mexico, as seen within the "apparently random yet seemingly systematic appearance of brutally murdered women's bodies and the equally horrific disappearance of many more women." She situates this feminicide in the context of globalization along the U.S.-Mexico border, which, despite increased enforcement following 9/11, is a site of tremendous economic and social exchange among businesses, people, and goods, as well as of cooperative law enforcement for control of the drug trade. Fregoso argues that cultural representations informed by discourses of globalization and misogyny deflect attention from the complicity of the United States and Mexican states in creating this climate of violence. She reveals the competing narratives of the causes of gendered violence and the "*ni una más*" (not one more murdered woman) transnational campaigns organized to counter negative representations of the disappeared and demand social justice for the crimes against them.

Leo R. Chavez effectively dismantles nativist arguments that would blame women for social problems that originate in binational social structures. In "A Glass Half Empty" he reports on a survey of 803 Latinas and 422 white women that reveals that for both U.S.-born Mexican women and Anglos, fertility rates indicate zero population growth. Concurrently, fertility has been declining in Mexico for several decades and U.S.-born, second- and third-generation women of Mexican origin have lower fertility rates than either immigrants or white American women. Chavez questions why despite these shifts in fertility, Mexican women's reproduction is represented as "out of control" and as largely responsible for Mexicans' low socioeconomic status.

How undocumented migrant communities challenge conventional understanding of legitimacy and citizenship forms the subject of Adelaida Del Castillo's "Illegal Status and Social Citizenship." Del Castillo argues that the traditional definition of citizenship by birthright contradicts the principle of honoring free individual choice celebrated by the founders of the U.S. nation-state. She highlights the role of women migrants in the adaptation process, as they both utilize and contribute to the resources and benefits associated with legal citizenship. Noting that the persecution of undocumented immigrants denies their human rights and therefore violates a moral and political authority that transcends that of any one nation-state, she predicts more and more challenges to conventional citizenship definitions as transnational migration increases across the globe.

In " 'Looking Like a Lesbian' " Eithne Luibheid presents a history of women's border crossings as subject to sexualization and homophobic surveillance. She argues that the Immigration and Naturalization Service (renamed the U.S. Citizenship and Immigration Services after 9/11) takes great pains to identify and exclude foreign-born women believed to be lesbians. She illustrates how sexuality functions as a "dense transfer point for relations of power" at the border and how Mexican migrants—in some cases permanent U.S. residents—contest and negotiate assessments of their deportment, clothing, and bodies.

As perhaps the most repressive legislation monitoring Mexican migration, Proposition 187 (passed in 1994, then nullified in the courts) was a turning point on the political scene, with thousands of U.S. citizens mobilizing in support of the act, which would purportedly "Save Our State" from the negative effects of "illegal aliens," mainly Latinos. In "The Value of Immigrant Life" Jonathan Xavier Inda illuminates the exclusionary discourse that blames migrants for the effects of globalization—especially rising unemployment and taxes—often with deadly consequences for the migrants. He argues that the logic of biopolitics simultaneously protects the social body of the nation while authorizing a holocaust against the lives of those seen as a threat. In particular, the policy measures that would make border crossing more dangerous and deny migrant women access to prenatal healthcare illustrate the power of the state to render some subjects expendable, members of an "unworthy population." By this logic, Mexican women's fertility must be regulated so as to discourage their reproduction, whereas other women can access state support for their reproductive health needs.

Collectively, the essays in part I illustrate the structural and symbolic violence perpetrated against Mexican women, which constitutes violations of individual and collective human rights. Nativist discourses that foster highly polarized debates about the impact of development and immigration justify the misogyny and poor treatment that women experience in their daily lives. Increasing mobility across and within the political and social borderlands not only disrupts conventional notions of legitimacy and citizenship but also highlights women's adaptation and agency.

Part II explores "The Topography of Violence," illustrating how structural violence leads to and is intertwined with multifaceted interpersonal, psychic, spiritual, or institutional violence perpetrated against Mexican women. In charting this landscape of pain and survival, the essays in this section render graphic stories of women's resilience and organization against misogynist discourses in Mexico, the United States, and the institutions that regulate their integration. They also point out that abuses are too often unseen or unnoticed, so women must find their own ways to cope, resist, and tell their stories, inspiring others with their strength and courage.

Leslie Salzinger interrogates how the organization of work structures unequal gender relations in "Manufacturing Sexual Subjects." With a keen eye for detail, she illustrates the ways in which women workers are held accountable to an idealized notion of femininity, which includes dressing to accentuate their physical features and flirting. The male gaze of supervisors is legitimated as essential for monitoring quality and efficiency in production but typically intrudes into women's private spaces through touching, teasing, and overt sexual overtones. Although such behaviors are typically categorized as sexual harassment, Salzinger argues against using that particular framework. Rather, she asserts an analysis of sexuality and desire as key organizing principles within the maquiladoras, which turns the focus away from individual actors—victim and victimizer—toward a structure that produces both goods and "docile and dexterous" women workers.

Melissa W. Wright explores gendered discourse at the border from another perspective in "The Dialectics of Still Life." She deploys the concept "dialectical image," an image whose apparent stillness obscures the clashing forces that create the "Mexican woman." Further, she presents a turnover story, told by maquila administrators, whereby the Mexican woman is characterized as uncommitted to the job, nervous, and "untrainable," thereby losing value to the firm. Eventually, her life is stilled, as she becomes waste to be discarded through job departure. When maquila workers exercise their agency by seeking better jobs, they are represented as adventure-seeking and heedless of danger, a depiction that deflects attention away from the multiple causes of women's deaths and the fact that few victims are actually maquila workers.

The tensions associated with maintaining this image reverberate with the contradictions of gender, class, and location when the master narratives are contested; that is, corporate leaders deny any connection to feminicide along the border, thereby erasing the women even as their families and activists dispute these representations in their counterstories.

In "Rape as a Weapon of War" Sylvanna Falcón analyzes women's stories and testimonies. She finds multiple instances of abuse by members of the Immigration and Naturalization Service (INS), where women are intimidated, harassed, and sexually assaulted. She argues that sexual violence is the outcome of the militarization of the U.S.-Mexico border, a war zone where colonialism, patriarchy, and hypermasculinity are interconnected in the perpetration of militarized rape. She charts the deployment of low-intensity-conflict policies and lax hiring practices that allow repeat abusers and rogue mercenaries to find employment in the INS. Analyzing formal complaints filed by women, she argues that militarized rapes are integral to maintaining control at the border—a form of state violence against women.

In "Nunca he dejado de tener terror" (I have never been without terror), Gloria González-López analyzes the psychological effects of the violence experienced by women in Mexico and the United States. She explores the interpersonal and emotional violence—kidnapping, sexual assault, sexual harassment, date rape, and incest perpetrated by men, as well as silencing mechanisms within families—as factors contributing to women's migration. Moreover, González-López asserts, Mexican women often endure interpersonal assaults and their long-term effects on both sides of the border. She also discusses the discursive notions that blame women for their "failures" to retain their "virtue"—such as the availability of reconstructive surgery to reinstate intact hymens in order to restore cultural "purity"—as forms of power and control. Ultimately, González-López recognizes women's struggles to reclaim their lives from the terror, establish support groups, socialize their daughters and sons to value nonviolent ways of being, and form healthy relationships.

The essays in this part resonate with those in part I that explored gendered discourses at the national and state level, particularly analyses of gendered violence toward women workers and border crossers. Collectively, they illustrate the multiple divides that Mexican women must negotiate, whether in Mexico, the United States, or in transit between the two nations.

Part III, "Flexible Accumulation and Resistance," reveals shifts in agricultural fields, industrial homework, domestic work, janitorial labor organizing, and the division of labor. Key themes in this section include the gendered and sexualized organization of work, the political economy of risk among working-class subjects, Mexican women's participation in the reorganization of social reproduction, and workers' resistance to labor exploitation and objectification of their bodies. Employers' strategies to refine labor processes to maximize output while minimizing workers' agency pose critical challenges for women workers, labor organizers, and employers.

The centrality of sexuality to labor control and workplace relations is not specific to any one country or occupation, as Xóchitl Castañeda and Patricia Zavella vividly demonstrate in "Changing Constructions of Sexuality and Risk." The authors illustrate how Mexican women constantly negotiate between the contradictory discourses of gendered sexuality and feminine modesty. Women wear clothes to cover themselves from the male gaze and sexual abuse by co-workers and supervisors as they bend over in front of men to pick the crops. Women also express a sexuality that is silent on the subject of condom use due to the cultural dictum that "decent" women do not raise such questions, and they thereby become subject to the "political economy of risk." Ultimately, women develop survival mechanisms that increasingly transgress traditional gendered boundaries and challenge restrictive sexual discourses, creating their own poetics of desire and new subjectivities regarding their work and their bodies.

Women's crucial work in alleviating economic pressures within low-income households also initiates spatial and social dynamics that challenge patriarchal restrictions on their mobility. Faranak Miraftab, in "Space, Gender, and Work," argues that the integration of informal production into the homes of low-income families (i.e., maquila subcontracting) changes the organization of space and the gender-based division of labor. Miraftab observes that installing a sewing machine, for example, alongside other components necessary for labor subcontracting requires the entire family to modify space utilization and that leads in turn to other changes in the household division of labor to facilitate women's economic output. Men's increasing participation in social reproduction within the family-workshop environment provides an important albeit understudied avenue of social change.

Mexican women express agency in various ways in informal-sector work. María de la Luz Ibarra, in "Mexican Immigrant Women and the New Domestic Labor," argues that Mexican women are reorganizing social reproduction. Global and national economic processes have led to a huge demand for new forms of domestic labor centered on human care, including adult or elder care as well as childcare. The new domestic labor positions human care on one side of the desirability scale and independent housekeeping work at the other end. Both are forms of socially necessary labor that Mexican migrant women engage in and increasingly redefine to assert boundaries and better working conditions. This assertion often puts them at odds with employers, who often seek greater flexibility in job definitions, working conditions, and pay.

The drive for flexible organization of work through the expansion of contract, temporary, and informal employment is a key feature of global capitalism. How employers seek and workers resist job "flexibility" forms the core of Cynthia Cranford's analysis of community unionism among janitorial workers in Los Angeles. Cranford argues that the growth of precarious jobs characterized by low wages, few benefits, little job security, and poor working conditions has led to the development of oppositional politics contesting unequal relations of gender and citizenship as well as class. Well aware of the dilemmas faced by migrant workers, in particular undocumented workers, Cranford attributes the success of Justice for Janitors to strategic legal action, direct action, and symbolic action. Women are well represented in the union, lending further weight to Cranford's assertion that the janitors' entitlement claims have a strong potential to disrupt a gendered and racialized hegemony of flexibility operating in the increasingly diverse city.

As narratives of struggle and resistance, the essays in part III reveal how women's work across formal and informal settings intersects with state-sanctioned hegemonic narratives of appropriate versus inappropriate spaces and activities. When women transgress these definitions, they become objectified and subject to a broad spectrum of violence at work as well as in the home. Their resistance identifies holes in the exploitative organization of work and offers new ways to effectively organize the so-called "unorganizable."

Part IV, "Family Formations and Transnational Social Networks," presents research by Mexican scholars based in Mexico and scholars based in the United States. The articles analyze how the effects of global economic transactions in the cities and rural areas of Mexico and the United States disrupt the traditional rhythms of daily life or draw women into the migrant stream. The intersection of the social organization of a woman's home and family economic need provides the context for women's migration and sets the stage for eroding patriarchal privilege. Familism emerges as a key dynamic that can justify women's migration, employment, and redefinition of motherhood to incorporate a transborder and transnational structure.

One of the most significant developments of migration within Mexico and to the United States is the emergence of transborder families, argues Norma Ojeda de la Peña in "Transborder Families and Gendered Trajectories of Migration and Work." Ojeda de la Peña is one of the first Mexican scholars to situate migration within the context of the family life course. Her analysis reveals the impact of marriage, the birth of children, the departure of children, and divorce on migration and work. She illustrates the importance of migration and transmigration on the formation and reproduction of "transborder" families who reside in Tijuana, Mexico. That is, internal and international migration have converged in a "unique crossing zone" where migrants help shape the local, social, and demographic environment as family members work both in the United States and Mexico.

Presenting migration through the voice of indigenous women is a growing concern of Mexican and U.S.-based scholars. Laura Velasco Ortiz, in "Women's Migration and Household Survival Strategies," demonstrates that migration within Mexico—for example, from Oaxaca to Tijuana, or circular migration—is a household strategy driven by global macroeconomic disruptions in rural life in southern Mexico. The decision to migrate reflects power relations among household members. Velasco Ortiz finds that women are more likely than men to migrate to urban cities in Mexico, where they can more easily find work as street vendors and domestic workers. Gendered preferences for urban migration are bound, however, to the life cycle, since women can easily reconcile childrearing with street vending and different types of domestic work. Thus, gendered strategies for survival fuel migration in ways that allow a degree of autonomy for women.

Women's increasing desire for autonomy is part of a larger social phenomenon reflected in the growth of single-parent families, argues Sylvia Chant in "Single-Parent Families: Choice or Constraint?" While many female-headed families are a result of male abandonment, Chant's research points to a rise in women electing to leave untenable marriages and *uniones libres*. These women quickly stabilize their incomes to a level close to those of households headed by men that do not have other income earners. Most important, children in female-headed households are being socialized to engage in the work associated with running a household, which has significant implications for the future, including changes to the patriarchal division of labor and the ideology of family solidarity or familism.

In "Working at Motherhood" Denise Segura examines how women deploy familism to carve greater economic decision-making authority in family and employment decisions in the United States. Segura argues that women's attachment to their jobs and feelings about being employed mothers is not negatively affected by so-called traditional (i.e., rural) Mexican culture. Chicanas' and Mexican immigrant women's constructions of motherhood reflect two different systems of patriarchy. For Mexican immigrant women, patriarchy takes the form of a corporate family model in which all members are expected to contribute to the common good. This form of familism allows women to work outside the home without feeling the guilt and ambivalence expressed by U.S.-born (or long-term-resident) Chicanas whose patriarchal structure is fundamentally classed and centers on the desirability of stay-at-home motherhood. This finding suggests that a number of employment problems (e.g., unemployment, underemployment) are related less to "traditional" Mexican cultural configurations than to such factors as language, labor-market structure, and policies.

Pierrette Hondagneu-Sotelo and Ernestine Avila, in "'I'm Here, but I'm There,'" extend the range of analysis of the articles in this section to consider how immigrant women mother across national borders while working "for" the family. They illustrate how migration creates new family forms, including alternate constructions of motherhood that contradict dominant white, middle-class American models, as well as Latinas' ideological notions of motherhood. Although transnational mothers work in occupations segregated by gender, race, class, nationality, and citizenship, their wages are critical for the well-being of their families in their countries of origin.

The essays in this part demonstrate that as women develop strategies to redress economic need, they challenge deeply gendered boundaries of family and work in both Mexico and the United States, and deploy familism in ways that extend their economic and social agency. Moreover, idealized notions of family and motherhood are constantly being recrafted to maximize women's survival and mobility.

"Transculturation and Identity in Daily Life," the final part of this volume, presents analyses about women's cultural expressions and social identities that span the U.S.-Mexico border and other social divides, including the Internet. The essays in this section reflect on the multiple changes that Mexican women negotiate while migrating, settling in new sites, or creating cultural visions of community and family.

In "Reproduction of Gender Relations in the Mexican Community of New Rochelle, New York," Victoria Malkin illustrates the process of Mexican settlement outside the Southwest. Mexican women are late to settle in rural New York relative to other regions and "are arriving in uncharted territory: no substantial cohort of women preceded them to help their passage." Drawing on field research in New York and Mexico, she argues that men have assumed positions of power they often held in Mexico and that women situate their lives in relation to families, reproducing gender relations in the new site. She illustrates how Mexicans construct transnational social networks and a sense of community with one another, fellow residents, and staff in social agencies. Navigating a veritable "minefield of contradictory practices," Mexican women construct viable social identities attentive to the discursive and material constraints within local spaces. Malkin argues that contradictions in women's lives actually form part of their multiple subject positions and, hence, complex identities.

In "En el norte la mujer manda" Jennifer Hirsch suggests that changes in marriage and daily life comes from multiple sources. Based on field research and the life histories of thirteen women in Atlanta, Georgia, and of their mothers and sisters or sisters-in-law in two communities in Jalisco, Hirsch finds important generational shifts in cultural values and normative practices. In general, older women adhere to notions of *respeto* (respect) and deference to males in marriage, which limits their openness and closeness with spouses. Young women are more likely to embrace and work out an ethos of *confianza* (trust), sexual intimacy, and emotional closeness and to view their spouses as peers. Further, *el norte* provides options unavailable to women in rural Mexico and thus provides a context for a shift to greater egalitarianism in gender relations.

In "Unruly Passions" Olga Nájera-Ramírez considers women's performances of the Mexican ranchera, "an expressive musical form intimately associated with Mexican cultural identity on both sides of the U.S.-Mexico border." Attentive to the dismissal of rancheras as sentimental, she views them as an evocative form of melodrama, perhaps akin to the blues, whose popularity surged with the urbanization of Mexico and migration to the United States. She argues that rancheras are "discursive spaces in which topics of emotional weight may be addressed in culturally appropriate ways." Female participants in rancheras, whether as skilled performers expressing nuances of identity through lyrics or body language, or as members of the audience attuned to the performances, are often oriented toward Mexico in their yearnings. Simultaneously, rancheras express the multiple poetics and feelings—nostalgia, regret, and wonder—that migration and settlement produces, revealing women's stories and identities in the United States.

In "Becoming Selena, Becoming Latina" Deborah Paredez analyzes how young Latinas "become" the popular performance artist Selena, all the while revealing processes of racialized sexuality and sociopolitical identification that respond to hostile nativist projects and override the constraints on individual constructions of identity. Prior to her death at the age of twenty-three, Selena had received worldwide acclaim for her interventions in the male-dominated Tejano music scene and for her invention of herself as a good girl who negotiated family, community, and sexuality with grace and charm. Popular in the United States and Latin America, Selena became an icon of independence and sexuality. Paredez suggests that Selena's simultaneous maintenance of her Tejana identity and her claims to the space of Latinidad (Latina/o identities) through her musical style and body are compelling to young Latinas who have "created imaginative cartographies of identification through their participation in the Selena phenomenon." Paredez situates Latinas' subjectivity in the emotionally laden and fraught context of Latinidad within popular culture, arguing that Latinas perform Selena as a means of self-discovery and collective articulation of Latina identity within the contested terrains of Latinidad and larger transnational imaginaries. She points to the fact that Mexican women are in dialogue with racial-ethnic others from diverse Latin American heritages and construct occasional nationalist moments as well as pan-Latina affiliations.

In "Cyberbrides and Global Imaginaries" Felicity Schaeffer-Grabiel focuses on the cyber-expressions of middle-class, professional women in Mexico seeking to realize fantasies about "the American way of life" through international matchmaking industries. Her interviews with women reveal their strong desire to escape from traditional value systems in families, a corrupt and unstable government, and confining notions of gender and womanhood. Women in her study represent Mexican men as macho and therefore unappealing, which leads her to consider the uneven and contradictory global imagination of women and men through the lens of "two countries whose differences mark the site of desire." By shifting their imaginary to transnational citizenship, Mexican women construct fluid identities and enhance their prospects for intimacy, self-improvement, and social and material opportunities.

By exploring multiple sites of gendered control and contestation, the essays in this volume reveal the complex representations, experiences, and identities that Mexican women construct in the context established by globalization, transnational migration, and social formations and imaginaries that span national borders. They explore women's complex yearnings in light of nativist politics in the United States and silencing discourse in Mexico, as well as traditional gendered expectations that would constrain women's live. Within these structural and socially violent discourses, Mexican women enact the full range of human agency and challenge narrow notions of citizenship and community in the borderlands.

Notes

1. Members of the Transborder Consortium, which includes scholars and activists from the Southwest Institute for Research on Women, University of Arizona, Colegio de la Frontera Norte, Tijuana, and El Colegio de Sonora, went through a similar process. See Denman, Monk, and Ojeda de la Peña 2004.
2. While Farmer is most interested in how structural violence impedes access to health care, we argue that structural violence has broader consequences, such as impeding

participation in the labor market or through negative representations of Mexican women.

3 For exceptions, see Barrera and Oehmichen Bazán 2000; Mummert 1999; and Stephen 2005.

4 Also see Michaelsen and Johnson 1997.

5 According to Portes, Guarnizo, and Landolt, "It is preferable to limit the concept of transnationalism to occupations and activities that require regular and sustained social contacts over time across national borders for their implementation" (1999, 219).

6 A third approach, centered in European scholarship, views transnationalism as a shift beyond the nation-state to political claims based on universal rights, memberships in political organizations that include multiple states (e.g., the European Union), or pan-religious affiliations such as Muslims (Levitt 2001). There are very few texts that take this approach and focus on Mexican women, so we have not included any here.

7 For a discussion of this traditional U.S. production–Mexico–social reproduction nexus, see Palerm and Urquiola 1993.

8 Marcelo Suarez-Orozco notes that in 1996 remittances were the largest sources of foreign exchanges in Mexico (1998, 10). He further estimates that remittances to Mexico were "equivalent to 57 percent of the foreign exchange available through direct investment in 1995, and 5 percent of the total income supplied by exports" (1998, 10).

9 President Bush's announcement about a guest-worker program for undocumented migrants sparked a dramatic increase in migration to the United States. In the first seven months of the fiscal year beginning in fall of 2003, detentions increased 30 percent overall on the U.S.-Mexico border and increased 56 percent in the Tucson sector, which includes most of the Arizona-Mexico border and is the busiest route for undocumented migration (Gold 2004).

10 The term *Chicana/o* refers to people of Mexican descent in the United States. *Latina/o* is a broader term that typically refers to people of Latin American heritage, which also includes Mexicans. Latino is often used interchangeably with the term *Hispanic*. Chicanas and Latinas are women.

11 According to the 2000 Census, African Americans constituted 13 percent of the population. Latinos were undoubtedly undercounted by the census, which often missed migrants and the undocumented.

12 The Sierra Club, for example, debated advocating limits on immigration because of their stance on population control (Werbach 2004). Eventually the group broke into two factions over this issue.

13 For a discussion of the feminization of the agricultural labor force in Latin America, see Sara María Lara Flores 1995; González Montes and Salles 1995.

14 Arias and Wilson 1997; Behar 1993; Benería and Roldán 1987; Chant 1994; González Marín 1998; Latin American Data Base 2004; Miraftab 1996 essay in this volume; Stephen 2005.

15 González de la Rocha 1994; López Estrada 2002; Tabuenca Córdoba 1998; Tuñon Pablos 2001.

16 For research on the BIP and its complex effects on the border region, see de la O Mar-

tínez 1995; Fernández-Kelly 1983a, 1983b, 1983c; Peña 1997; Iglesias-Prieto 1997; Ruiz and Tiano 1987; Salzinger 2003.

17 At one time, Mexican law required women to have formal written permission from their husbands as a precondition for employment. In the 1970s about two-thirds of Mexican husbands had the final say on whether their wives took a job (Elmendorf 1977).

18 Also see Teresa Carrillo 1998; de Oliveira 2000; Diaz Barriga 1996; González de la Rocha 1994; González Montes 1993; Hernández-Castillo 2001; Peña 1997; Tirado 1994.

19 For discussions of Latina/os and occupational segregation in the labor market, see Catanzarite 2000; Lamphere et al. 1993; Mauricio Gastón Institute 1994; Ortiz 1994; Segura 1989a, 1991; Zavella 1984, 1987.

20 For research on agricultural labor, including women's struggles, see Buss 1993; Griffith et al. 1994; Herr Harthorn 2003.

21 Ruiz 1987; Romero 1992; Salzinger 1991; Ibarra 2002, 2003a, 2003b, and essay in this volume; Hondagneu-Sotelo 1994, 2001.

22 William V. Flores 1997; Friaz 1991; Lamphere and Zavella 1997; Soldatenko 1991; Zavella 1987, 1988.

23 Sassen 1988; Morales and Bonilla 1993; Morales and Ong 1991.

24 Fernández-Kelly and García 1997; Hossfeld 1994; Lamphere, Stepick, and Grenier 1994.

25 For research on the effects of plant closures on Latina/o workers, see Borrego and Zavella 2000; Castro, Romero, and Cervantes 1987; Romero, Castro, and Cervantes 1988; Zavella 2002.

26 Hayes-Bautista, Schink, and Chapa 1992; Hurtado et al. 1992; Pérez and Martínez 1993; Pastor 2003 and forthcoming.

27 For research on adaptation to poverty, see Vélez-Ibañez and Greenberg 1992; Vélez-Ibañez 1993; Edin and Lein 1997; Chavez 1992; Hondagneu-Sotelo 1994; Palerm 1991; Zabin et al. 1993. Also see Hurtado 1994.

28 For research on grassroots organizing, see Hondagneu-Sotelo 1998; Pardo 1990, 1998a, 1998b. For works on binational encuentros by women activists, see Teresa Carrillo 1998; Sampaio 2002, 2004.

29 For research comparing Chicanas' and Mexicanas' self-perceptions about combining work and motherhood, see Segura 1991 and essay in this volume; Hirsch 2003. Guendelman et al. 2001 compares Mexican immigrants with those living in Mexico regarding their orientations toward motherhood. For other studies on Mexican immigrant women, see Cardenas and Flores 1986; Decierdo 1991; Melville 1978; Solórzano-Torres 1987; Ruiz 1987; Ibarra essay in this volume.

30 For circumstances where most women migrated only with male sponsorship, see Chavira-Prado 1992.

31 Goodson-Lawes 1992, 1993; Hondagneu-Sotelo and Avila essay in this volume; Palerm 1991.

32 Browning and de la Garza 1986; David G. Gutiérrez 1995; Keefe and Padilla 1987; Ortiz 1996; Rocco 1997.

33 For research on indigenous Mexican migrants, see Fox and Rivera-Salgado 2004; Nagengast and Kearney 1990; Zabin et al. 1993. For works on Chicano students, see Fry 2002; Gándara 1996; Stanton-Salazar 2001; Delgado-Gaitan 2001; Rumberger and Arrellano forthcoming.

34 For ethnographic work deploying a transnational framework, also see Glick Schiller and Fouron 2001; Hirsch 2003; Levitt 2001; Gina Pérez 2004; Rouse 1992, 1995a, 1995b.

BORDERLANDS AS SITES OF STRUGGLE

PART 1

Toward a Planetary Civil Society
ROSA LINDA FREGOSO

Cruelty has no unearthly punishment and often no earthly reason.
—Jean Franco, *The Decline and Fall of the Lettered State*

✷ The campaign to end the killing of women in Ciudad Juárez took the name Ni Una Más. Ni una más en Ciudad Juárez. Not one more murdered woman in Ciudad Juárez. Mothers and grandmothers, women's rights and human-rights groups, and friends from both sides of the border joined in a movement of denunciation, demanding an end to the most sordid and barbarous series of gender killings in Mexico's history. By mid-2002, there were 282 victims of feminicide in this city across the border from El Paso, Texas, and more than four hundred disappeared women.[1] Ni Una Más staged women's visibility and invisibility in the nation as well as a confrontation with the historical and social trauma in the region.

The politics of gender extermination in this region took the form of the apparently random yet seemingly systematic appearance of brutally murdered women's bodies and the equally horrific disappearance of many more women. What is now understood as various forms of feminicide started in 1993, a year after the signing of the North Atlantic Free Trade Agreement (NAFTA), and persisted through the tenure of three Mexican heads of state: Carlos Salinas, Ernesto Zedillo, and Vicente Fox.[2] As the numbers of dead and missing women grew, the state continued to turn a blind eye to the violence afflicting women.

In spring 2001 a number of nongovernmental organizations (NGOS) involved in human-rights work, including Grupo 8 de Marzo, Comité Independiente de Chihuahua de Derechos Humanos, and Taller de Género de la Universidad Autónoma de Juárez, delivered a report, "Cases of Murdered Women in Ciudad Juárez, Chihuahua," to the special rapporteur for human rights for the United Nations, Dato' Param Cumaraswamy. The authors of the report had compiled files for 189 women murdered between January 1993 and April 2001.[3] By early 2002, according to a report prepared by La Red Ciudadana contra la Violencia, the number of murdered women had increased to 269, with an additional 450 disappeared.[4] Between 1985 and 1992, by contrast, thirty-seven women were murdered in Ciudad Juárez.

Grupo 8 de Marzo of Ciudad Juárez keeps records of the identities of the assassinated and disappeared women.[5] All were poor, most were dark skinned, and many of them had been mutilated, tortured, and sexually violated.[6] Although there have been random appearances of dead bodies in public places throughout the city, most of them were found on the outskirts of Juárez, in the desert, near poor *colonias* (shantytowns) like Anapra, Valle de Juárez, Lomas de Poleo, and Lote Bravo. Ranging in age from eleven to fifty, the murdered and disappeared women shared humble origins and, in many instances, the experience of migrating to these borderlands.

Sensationalistic media accounts of these murders have exploited the stereotype of single or multiple serial killers violently and systematically exterminating young women. However, in a highly perceptive study, Julia Estela Monárrez (2000) suggests that the murder and disappearance of women in Juárez cannot be considered simply as the work of psychopaths. Rather than the aberration of a single individual or group, she argues, the murders of women are "politically motivated sexual violence" rooted in a system of patriarchy (Monárrez 2000, 94). In fact, the various feminicides in Mexico make evident the exercise of power across the social spectrum: the power of the state over civil society; the rich over the poor; the white elite over racialized people; the old over the young; men over women. The feminicides constitute a novel kind of "dirty war," one waged by multiple forces against disposable female bodies. The women targeted in these unprecedented border feminicides represent the "stigmatized bodies," those "marked for death in drug wars and urban violence" (Franco 2002, 16). Feminicide in Juárez exposes the reality of overlapping power relations on gendered and racialized bodies as much as it clarifies the degree to which violence against women has been naturalized as a method of social control.

"Yet another massacre, another mass grave," writes Jean Franco. "In our time, only too often we are given the image of the mass of bodies—the massacres of Rwanda or Kosovo—out of which it is difficult for those of us watching the television screen or looking at news photographs to construct a meaningful narrative" (2002, 234). This difficulty is often compounded by the competing discourses used to construct a narrative. In September 1999 I attended the "Burials on the Border" conference, held at New Mexico State University, Las Cruces, where I witnessed a struggle over the meanings of these gender murders. There, before an audience of activists, researchers, and family members, representatives of the Mexican state publicly blamed the victims of feminicide in Juárez. The heated exchange I witnessed between representatives of the state and civil society derived in large measure from competing interpretive frameworks. For the purpose of my own study, the public debate about the social identities of the victims and the meaning of their deaths raises broader issues of cultural representation and its role in our efforts to construct a meaningful narrative. In this chapter I intend to examine competing and often overlapping narratives that have been used to interpret the murders of women and, in the process, expose the subject that is constructed within each account.

From Negation to Disaggregation

One would expect the modern state to intervene on behalf of its citizens and limit extreme expressions of gender violence such as those unfolding in Ciudad Juárez, but the Mexican government has failed dismally. It has justified its failure through a rhetorical strategy of defection that has taken two narrative forms: negation and disaggregation. Early on, state officials repeatedly framed their interpretation of the killings within a discourse of negation, refusing to acknowledge the reality of systemic and calculated acts of violence against women.

The state's early response, negation, involved at first a denial that the killings were systematic. Then, when the state could no longer deny this reality, officials shifted the blame onto the victims, committing further sacrilege against already violated bodies.[7] In many instances the state emphasized women's nonnormative behaviors, accusing them of transgressing sexual norms—either of lesbianism or of leading a *doble vida* (double life), that is, engaging in respectable work by day and sex work by night—as though nontraditional sexual behavior justified their killings.[8] Indeed, the Comisión Nacional de Derechos Humanos (National Human-Rights Commission) found that police authorities had violated the victims' rights by making declarations such as the following to members of the commission: "Many of the murdered women worked in factories during the week and as prostitutes during the weekend in order to make more money" (Benítez et al. 1999, 61).[9]

The discourse of negation thus tended to discredit the murdered women by emphasizing their alleged transgressive sexual behavior: "She visited a place where homosexuals and lesbians gathered"; "She liked dating different men and was an avid patron of dance halls" (Benítez et al. 1999, 36).[10] Such expressions of nonnormative sexuality were so relentless that the mother of murder victim Adriana Torres Márquez responded indignantly, "Don't they have anything else to invent? They have said the same in every case: that it's the way women dressed or their alleged double life" (128).[11] Nonnormative sexuality was central to the causal chain that went from transgression of patriarchal norms to murder.

To establish legitimacy for this narrative of negation, the state enlisted the testimony of scientific "experts" whose testimony linked transgressive sexual behavior to newfound independence. A Spanish criminologist echoed the by now standard "moral panic" about the dangers of modernization: "As a result of the influence of the United States, women are joining the workforce at an earlier age and therefore discovering independence. This means young women could become more promiscuous. Some of these independent women have maintained sexual relations with more than one person. This behavior leads to danger."[12]

Again, nonnormativity became the lens through which the killings were interpreted, although the criminologist's comments also laid bare the patriarchal nostalgia for an earlier era of male authority in which women remain wedded to the private sphere of domesticity and motherhood. Like those who championed the conservative "family values" campaign in the United States in the 1990s, Mexican State officials blamed women's growing independence and mothers entering the workforce for the "disintegration" of the family and for the loss of male authority in the domestic sphere.[13]

It bears emphasizing that the subject constructed within the state's discourse is an "immoral" one. The patriarchal state's initial preoccupation with women's morality and decency is a form of institutional violence that makes women primarily responsible for the violence directed against them. Thus, those women who do not conform to the mother/wife model of womanhood (lesbians, workingwomen, women who express sexual desire, and so forth) are suitably punished. Women are thus transformed into subjects of surveillance; their decency and morality become the objects of social control. What's more, shifting the blame toward the victims' moral character in effect naturalizes violence against women.

By the end of 2001, both the state's investigation of the murders and its dubious interpretive framework had been placed in question after a series of events galvanized the public during that year: the assassination of human-rights lawyer Digna Ochoa, the unearthing of the bodies of eight women in an empty lot adjacent to the headquarters of the Maquiladora Association, and the police assassination of a defense lawyer in Juárez. A broad-scale social force emerged within civil society. Hundreds of NGOs—feminist, civil, and human-rights groups from both sides of the border—joined the existing network of local grassroots activists and women's groups that had been denouncing the killings for several years. Media coverage of the killings zeroed in on state corruption and indifference.

Negating the reality of widespread violence against poor and dark-skinned women proved to be not just a transparent but an obscene interpretive strategy. To counter the growing national and international movement of outrage and denunciation, the state adopted a less ideological strategy, this time enlisting the techniques of science to transform its narrative of interpretation from outright denial to disaggregation.

In December 2001 the office of the governor of the State of Chihuahua released the document "Homicidio de mujer en Ciudad Juárez, enero 1993–noviembre 2001" (Homicide of woman in Ciudad Juárez, January 1993–November 2001).[14] Although a month earlier Zulema Bolívar, special prosecutor for Juárez, had acknowledged the murder of 259 poor women, "Homicidio de mujer" in essence disassociated the individual cases, undermining the idea of the Juárez feminicides as a phenomenon by reformulating most of the murders as discrete and unrelated.

The state authenticated its new narrative through technologies of statistics and forensic evidence, thus shifting the discussion away from broader social issues and isolating each "case" from the more general and systemic phenomenon of violence against women. In other words, the state now conceded the fact of the murders, but it refused to accept their interconnection, claiming that only 76 of the 261 murders exhibited traces of sexual violence or were related as "multiple homicides."[15] As the months passed, the discourse of disaggregation served the state in several ways. First, it provided the state with a veneer of "scientific" authority and professionalism to counter its image as a corrupt "Third World" police force, especially in meetings with representatives of international organizations and media. Second, disaggregation bolstered the scientific claims of the state, especially regarding the universal aspect of the crimes, with similar crimes being cited as a "common" occurrence in any major city; in claiming the Juárez murders to be a normal part of urban life, for example, state officials cited the recent serial killing of fifty women in Canada. Finally, the state used disaggregation in a discursive war, a campaign to discredit women's-rights and human-rights activists meeting with representatives from the United Nations and the Organization of American States by accusing the activists of "politicizing" the murders (Villalpando and Breach 2002a, 47). To some extent, the discourse of disaggregation has proven to be an effective strategy, providing the Mexican State a certain legitimacy with U.S. officials and international media, which report the new narrative uncritically.[16] Ironically, the state's disaggregation of "the rest" of the murders as "crimes of passion, drug traffic, theft, sexual, intrafamilial violence, vengeance, [and] imprudence" does not preclude linking violence against women to gender hierarchies within a patriarchal state (Gustavo Castillo García 2001, 17).

Globalism on the Borderlands

Whereas the state's narrative anchored the meanings of the murders of women at the microlevel of the individual, other accounts of feminicide constructed a narrative out of macroprocesses, as is evident in the discourse of globalism.[17] Unlike the state's narrative, this discourse grew out of a progressive impulse, one critical of the expansion of transnational capitalism and global neoliberalism under the coordination of the International Monetary Fund (IMF), the World Trade Organization (WTO), and the World Bank. Established as a major interpretive framework during the mid-1990s, the discourse of globalism equated *exploitation* with the *extermination* of gendered bodies, tracing both conditions to a single process: economic globalization. And, on the Mexico-U.S. border, globalism was most visibly embodied in the maquiladora industry.[18]

The Juárez feminicides came to be seen as part of the "more insidious—and far more widespread—violence of work on the global assembly line" (Nathan 1997, 22). Given the geopolitics of the region, connecting feminicide to the maquiladora industry proved to be a compelling narrative, especially since the murders of poor and dark-skinned women began in 1993, a year after NAFTA solidified the project of neoliberalism and economic globalization in the region. One feature of global capitalism is the creation of export-processing zones throughout the Third World. During the 1990s, Ciudad Juárez was the largest export-processing zone on the border, host to roughly 350 manufacturing plants owned primarily by U.S. transnational corporations. These plants employed roughly 180,000 workers who were paid around $23 per week in take-home pay, a little less than $4 per day, or fifty cents per hour.[19]

In many respects, the geopolitical and economic characteristics of the region lent legitimacy to arguments that the exploitation of bodies on the "global assembly line" and the extermination of bodies in the public sphere were part of a single process. In studies of the worldwide grid of export-processing zones, researchers like Saskia Sassen have contributed important insights about the role of women as laboring bodies for global capitalism, documenting the "incorporation of Third World women into wage employment on a scale that can be seen as representing a new phase in the history of women."[20] It is precisely this body of work on the "feminization of the proletariat" that is used to construct a narrative about the murders of women in Juárez, to make claims about how their "lives and deaths centered around the global assembly line" (Nathan 1997, 18). In other words, since both "exploited female bodies" and "exterminated female bodies" are expressions of the exercise of power and gender hierarchies, the cause of one condition (exploitation of gendered bodies) has served handily to explain the other (extermination of gendered bodies).

Critical theories of globalization remain valuable, especially since they help to explain structural transformations in export-processing zones like Ciudad Juárez. Under current conditions of capitalist expansion, transnational corporations function as "the masters of a 'new imperial age' . . . spreading an inhumane model of development . . . with islands of enormous privilege in a sea of misery and despair" (Chomsky 1998, 13–20). Antiglobalization perspectives provide valuable insight into how Juárez figures as the "local" embodiment of the wave of global neoliberalism (market-based development) under the coordination and direction of the Group of Eight (G8), the IMF, the WTO, and the World Bank; of the concentration of economic power in transnational corporations; of the internationalization of social divisions; and of the subordination of national economies to global forces. Without doubt, global and transnational dynamics implode into the geography of Ciudad Juárez.

To be sure, the effects of this newly constituted global economic order impact the most vulnerable communities—the bodies of the poor and Third World women, who are its disposable targets of labor exploitation.[21] Critical globalization theories have astutely noted the unevenness of development in Ciudad Juárez, the further exploitation of the poor, and the lack of infrastructural development (housing, sewage, electricity, health and other basic services) to accommodate the many poor immigrants recruited from southern Mexico and Central America by the maquiladora industry. And, although the process of economic globalization is "out of control," globalism is a monolithic, top-down analysis that neither captures nor explains the complexity of feminicide.[22] Nor does conflating the exploitation of gendered bodies with their extermination offer us the nuanced account of violence that feminicide demands.

Attributing the murders of women to processes of globalization has created the enduring myth of "maquiladora killings," one in which the killers allegedly target maquiladora workers—a cliché that continues to this day.[23] For a Left drawn to critiques of global injustice, the maquila-murder narrative is certainly alluring.[24] As convincing as this narrative may be, there is ample evidence disputing the myth of "maquiladora killings," especially the research of independent journalists and academics in Mexico. A study of murders between 1993 and 1998 identifies only 15 maquiladora workers among 137 victims (Benítez et. al 1999).[25] Drawing from a larger sample—162 murdered women between 1993 and 1999—the research of Julia Estela Monárrez corroborates the figure of 15 murdered maquiladora workers and cites various occupations for the other victims: students, housewives, sales clerks, sex workers, domestics, and drug traffickers (2000, 110). Since the publication of these two studies, several more maquiladora workers have been murdered, but they are still in the minority. Rather than targeting "actual" maquiladora workers, it is much more accurate to say that the misogynist and racist killers are targeting members of the maquiladora industry's urban reserve of wage labor, namely, a pool of female workers migrating from southern Mexico and Central America and living in the poor surrounding colonias of Juárez.

The Subject of Globalism

In positioning the maquiladora industry as its unifying trope, the discourse of globalism elides the multiple structures of oppression in the lives of women as well as providing an insular explanation for the killings. In other ways, the discourse of globalism focuses a synoptic gaze primarily on women outside domestic spaces—in work or leisure activities—as consequences of processes of globalization. Often its gaze is explicit; sometimes the focus proceeds by inference. But in each case, the subject of the discourse of globalism is an abject one: a subject in need of regulation; a subject as passive victim; or a subject as fetish of the masculinist gaze.

The documentary by Saul Landau and Sonia Angulo, *Maquila: A Tale of Two Mexicos* (2000), participates in this narrative by linking feminicide to globalization. The film treats the issue of global justice, providing a critique of globalization as a "new world disorder" (Bauman 1998, 59). Filmmakers provide a generally persuasive account of unfair labor practices, gender and labor exploitation, health and safety violations, and environmental degradation through the dumping of toxic waste, chemical emissions, and toxic leaks. The film renders the "story of the struggle of a nation / deep in the midst of globalization," as the rap lyrics by Manny Martinez and Greg Landau put it.[26] The documentary is notable for its attention to the growing unionization movement among maquiladora workers, especially in light of the claims made by certain researchers on the Left regarding the impossibility of organizing workers from export-processing zones into a "coherent oppositional politics to capitalism."²⁷ Even though the filmmakers emphasize the agency of transnational activists and labor organizers, *Maquila* adopts a masculinist point of view in rendering feminicide intelligible to viewers.

The film portrays maquila women as alluring victims. The killings of women in Juárez are shown midway into the narrative, opening on the comments of a local economist and member of the opposition party, Victor Quintana, who characterizes "globalization" as a process that "tears apart the social fabric." A montage of women in various public sites follows his commentary: images of women in the maquila industry; images of women hanging out in discos and on the streets; images of women working in the sex industry. Women's visibility in public, nondomestic spaces—as laboring bodies and dead bodies—thus provides the visual evidence for the "tear[ing] apart of the social fabric." The accompanying soundtrack of "El Corrido de la Maquila," by Greg Landau and Francisco Herrera, suggests how to interpret the images, which point to the dangers inherent in women's visibility and expression of nonnormativity, especially in spaces outside the private sphere of the home. "The dangers in the maquila," as the song's lyrics express it, demand parental (masculine) "protection" (regulation and surveillance) of young women outside the private sphere. And if viewers failed to grasp this message, the next segment in the film drives the point home: a graphic scene of police examining the body of a woman murdered in Juárez. The segment ends with the words of Zapatista leader Subcomandante Marcos, who led the popular uprising in Chiapas in the 1990s, describing globalization as a project designed to "eliminate a part of that population; erase them from the face of the earth." But this fails to undo the logic of association established in the film through complementary visual images and song lyrics, namely, that women are killed for engaging in activities that exceed patriarchal gendered norms: hanging out in bars or on the streets, working in the sex industry. In establishing this montage, *Maquila* characterizes women not simply as victims of globalization but as subjects in need of patriarchal regulation.

Early on, journalist Debbie Nathan (1999, 27) also associated feminicide with forms of sexuality engendered under conditions of globalization. Drawing from ethnographic research on sexual practices in the maquiladora industry, Nathan wrote about "a rigid version of femininity" and "the sexualization of factory life" in the maquilas. Evidence for the maquila industry's promotion of hypersexualization included heavy flirting on assembly lines; Mexican male supervisors soliciting dates from assembly workers; competition among women for the supervisors' attention; the grooming of the youngest and prettiest girls for the "annual industrywide 'Señorita Maquiladora' beauty contest, complete with evening gown and swimsuit competition" (1999, 27).

Nathan further described the hyperfemininity of "maquila girls" in this manner: "Unlike their North American sisters, who dress for assembly line in no nonsense T-shirts and sneakers, most maquila girls don miniskirts, heels, gobs of lipstick and eye shadow" (1999, 20)—a hypersexuality that according to Nathan spills over into the weekend and after-hours.[28]

Besides reporting on how maquila workers adopt the hyperfeminine forms of sexuality introduced into "traditional" societies like Mexico by global forces, Nathan uncritically embraces the state's framing of the victims as leading "la doble vida—the double life of assembly work by day and casual prostitution by night" (1997, 20). During the "Burials on the Border" conference, victims' family members were visibly distressed by Nathan's public remarks, in which she drew the following analogy (later published in the NACLA Report) about the rapes: "Oddly, the Spanish word for 'double life,' *la doble vida*, sounds a good deal like *las dos vías*, sex per the vagina and anus" (1999, 26).

Nathan's discussion of the sexualization of maquila life is based on a selective and partial interpretation of the research of sociologist Leslie Salzinger. Although Salzinger does study the "sexualization of factory life" in the maquiladora industry, this reference applies to only one of the three sites in her study; she concludes that representations of gender "vary between localized areas of domination, even those sharing elements of a common discursive framework" (1997, 570). Salzinger focuses on the "constitution of gendered meanings in a set of three work places" and on the ways in which gendered meanings and subjectivities conform or diverge from "public narratives" about the "archetypical nature of Mexican 'sex roles'" (568). One of the factories, Panoptimex (the factory that animates Nathan's argument), exhibits an "objectifying modality of control" and reinforces "gendered meanings and subjectivities [that] appear to echo those crystallized in public discussions about maquilas" (567). However, Nathan ignores Salzinger's findings about the shop floors in the other two factories (Anarchomex and Androgymex): as Salzinger notes, "The differences that emerge here are particularly striking" (568). Unlike in Panoptimex, gender in these two other examples is not a significant category, nor are women's identities "defined around objectification" (562). Salzinger's work on the maquiladora industry in Ciudad Juárez calls attention to "the palpable heterogeneity and fluctuating significance" (570) of gender representations on the borderlands, especially in terms of how these differences are lived out in women's daily lives on the shop floors.

Ignoring this complex variability in gendered meanings and subjectivities, Nathan unwittingly echoes what is in fact the "managerial narrative" of the female Mexican employee, one that has served to describe the dress style of

Mexican female workers through references to prostitution. In large measure, the stereotype of maquila workers as "prostitutes" is part of a much longer history of othering practices derived from colonialist fantasies about the border as a zone of "sexual excess" and border women as "culturally bound to sexual chaos."[29] It is an old colonialist (and now neocolonialist) narrative indeed, this construction of Mexicanas on the border in terms of sexual excess and chaos.

Nathan's reference to the "hyperfemininity" found on the Mexican shop floor and the differences in dress style between U.S. and Mexican factory workers is surely in part related to a narrative of objectification prevalent about workers in Mexican factories in general. But it is also symptomatic of a broader problem in public discourses on femininity that needs to be amended to include the role of national and global culture, for example, the role of Mexican cinema and television in circulating highly sexualized images of femininity, as well as the articulation of class and culture in elements of fashion and dress style. In a study of managers in the maquiladora industry Melissa Wright observes, "Throughout the maquilas, attention to women's dress style is continually articulated as an American or Mexican affect, and often in reference to cultural representation rather than to a national divide. The difference is generally discussed as one of length; fit, in terms of degree of snugness; color (bright or subdued); shoe style; make-up applications and hairstyle" (1998, 130n9).

To a great extent, the links Nathan forges between dress style (what by North American puritanical standards is highly sexualized) and "engaging in casual prostitution" echo managerial narratives about maquiladora workers on the border. As Wright notes, "When I asked one of the production managers, Roger, to describe the labor force, he said, 'Some of these girls have second jobs. You know, I've heard that some work the bars.' The message that you cannot tell the difference between a prostitute and a maquiladora worker was common in my interviews" (1998, 119–20).

The devaluation of border female sexuality, as Nathan has noted, is part of a more generalized narrative about the border as a place of excess, violence, prostitution, drugs, and contraband that circulates in the Mexican popular imaginary. Nathan dates these images of the border to the early twentieth century. One can also trace regional identity differentiation back to the colonial era, especially with metropolitan locations like Mexico City stigmatizing the northern (frontier) regions as sites of vice and degeneracy. Expressed in popular cultural forms such as *corridos, canciones rancheras,* and much later in films and telenovelas, the earlier stigma of the frontier and of its inhabitants contributes to the ongoing othering of border femininity within Mexico, to what Nathan calls "this demonized yet casual throw-away view of border women" within the national imaginary (1999, 30).

According to Nathan, the complexities of identity in Mexico have to do not only with the regional differences in constructions of border women as other but also with patriarchal forms of domination, including "the fact that Juárez also registers the highest levels of reported domestic violence in México" (1999, 30). Nathan unfortunately lapses once again into uncritical acceptance of the narrative of nonnormative sexuality engendered by processes of globalization, positing a link "between maquila development, which has encouraged 'la doble vida,' and the sexualization of violence against women that appears to be a backlash against their changing economic and social roles on Mexico's northern border" (26).

A more nuanced understanding of the regulation of women's bodies under economic processes of globalization is offered by Ursula Biemenn's 1999 documentary, *Performing the Border*. The film focuses on women's bodies, rendered through experimental techniques: nonsynchronized sound and images, time-lapse filming to uncouple the image from real time, image enhancement, and a meditative voice-over. The effect of these nonrealist techniques is to distance and disturb the viewer's relation to reality and to force one to contemplate the links between the exploitation and alienation of laboring bodies in various sites within global capitalism, as exemplified by workers in the maquiladora industry and the sex industry. Informed as it is by a committed feminist politics, *Performing the Border* portrays women not as being in need of regulation and surveillance, but rather as the very objects of regulation and surveillance—an emphasis supported by interviews of the journalist Isabel Velásquez and the writer-filmmaker Bertha Jotar.

Ultimately, though, *Performing the Border* is unable to escape the logic that associates the Juárez feminicides with the nonnormative practices of the victims. Like *Maquila*, Biemenn's film visually equates exploited bodies with exterminated bodies through a linear sequence of narrative elements that creates a chain of associations: maquila workers-sex workers-victims of feminicide. The segment portraying female workers in the maquila industry is followed by the testimony of a Juárez sex worker and immediately afterward by a segment on the murdered women. In its metonymic association of globalization-nonnormative sexuality-feminicide, *Performing the Border* fails to disrupt the premise of the discourse of globalism, especially the notion that the extermination of women's bodies proceeds from the same logic as their exploitation: global capitalism. Like *Maquila*, *Performing the Border* is complicit with "Eurocentric victimology" (Shohat 1998, 9), a discourse that produces the murdered women of Ciudad Juárez solely as objects of global capitalism. In many ways, *Performing the Border* evidences an "imperially charged agenda," the power of First World feminists to define Third World women as "objects of capital" and "traces of patriarchy," failing to record the ways in which "women resist despite huge constraints and penalties" (Nesiah 2000, 48).

Although such film and journalistic representations are limited, they are much less egregious than the literary writings of Charles Bowden.[30] Crossing the line from "titillation and information," his essays warrant close examination for the discursive production of border woman as fetish. Bowden adopts the narrative of globalism to explain the realities of Mexico in colonialist terms, claiming that "the only cheap thing in Mexico is flesh, human bodies you can fornicate with or work to death" (1999, 114). His view of Ciudad Juárez as a "city of violence" supports the emphasis on nonnormativity as the cause of feminicide as well (1998, 58). Bowden similarly reiterates the myth of maquiladora killings, focusing on the sexual behaviors of maquila workers, whom he describes as "mostly young, often living free of family, with their own money and desires" (1999, 114). For Bowden, feminicide represents the "blood price" the nation pays for globalization, and he attributes violence to male backlash. "Killing girls," Bowden argues, "has in effect become what men of Juárez do with the frustrations of living in a town with less than one percent unemployment but with abundant poverty. It is the local language of rage, a blood price exacted for what Juárez is: the world's largest border community, with 300 maquila plants, and the highest concentration of maquila workers in the country" (ibid.).

Although there is no doubt that feminicide embodies the most deadly logic of masculinity, that its perpetrators are misogynist and racist killers, Bowden's focus on working-class men deflects attention away from the multiple structures of violence in the lives of women. However, Bowden's own explanatory logic is also in many ways a form of male rage, of symbolic violence against women. In "I Want to Dance with the Strawberry Girl," his most recent essay on the murders of women in Ciudad Juárez, for example, Bowden borrows the title of a popular *banda* tune ("Quiero bailar con la niña fresa") to stage his own desires and symbolic male rage. He ends his article as follows.

> The faces with the darkened lips and highlighted eyes, the cool young faces all say the same thing: Every man in this building wants me.... Her blouse is rich with red, her long white skirt erupts with roses. Her hair rises on her head in the crown of a contessa and then trails down her slender back. Worship me. The face is blank, no smile. A few hours ago she was a cog in a machine for 40 bucks a week. Tomorrow morning

> she will be scurrying round El Centro for a week's supplies and then to the Mercado publico, where cheap restaurants beckon and old men play the music of Chiapas. Outside, the city is spiked with painted poles and black crosses. El Paso glows across the river, as distant and cold as a star. But now, in here, hips smear against the bass line, the body heat rises. (1999, 118)

The masculine gaze this passage enacts is perverse and disturbing. Bowden assumes to know the desires and thoughts of a working-class woman in Juárez ("Every man in this building wants me"). Bowden conjures up images about the border familiar to U.S. audiences, images that portray the border as a space of "excess." The female body and the territorial body of Juárez are presented as libidinal in a hot-tempered, close-up way, while El Paso is depicted as the icy, distant North American counterpart. With his focus on border/sexual excess, Bowden does not simply reproduce globalism's emphasis on nonnormativity as an explanation for the murders; rather, he adopts a misogynist gaze, enacting the symbolic violence of male rage.

Symbolic violence appears elsewhere in the work of Charles Bowden. In *Juárez: The Laboratory of Our Future* Bowden again crosses the line between titillation and information, recounting his fantasies about Adriana, a "whore" and former maquila worker with two children.

> In my fantasy, Adriana and I do the right thing and follow the instructions of our time. We build a small casa by the sea. Actually, she has wrapped up her graduate studies at the National Autonomous University of Mexico, UNAM. She has an MA in romance languages and, of course an MBA, plus a doctorate in anthropology awarded for her groundbreaking study, "Sexual Surrogates: Free Trade, Multi-Culturalism and the Feminist Perspective." She is now preparing a dictionary of industrial argot in her own work for the journal of linguistics and is contemplating study of dialogues with clients using the full French critical apparatus.... The children will play on the beach. I'll keep an eye on them because the undertow here is terrific. Each morning she and I will jog up and down and the pounds will melt off and restore her girlish figure. We will live on locust, wild honey, young goat, fresh fruit, vitamin supplements, garlic tablets, and various salsas. (1998, 103)

I imagine myself as the interlocutor of this passage. Is Bowden anticipating the feminist, antiracist critique of his writing, explicitly mocking, after constructing, a feminist poststructuralist reading of his literary fantasy? I take the bait, for this brutally senseless parody of yuppie lifestyle à la mexicana heralds the by now classic "rescue fantasy" of Western masculinity—one fixated on saving Third World women from the excesses of their own cultures. Written in the context of his account of feminicide in Ciudad Juárez, Bowden's ironic humor affronts common civility, revealing the perverse logic of his racist and colonialist gaze. The abjection of poor and working women in Juárez is nowhere more flagrant than in the "intimacy" he conjures up with the young women on the border, for example, the "fresa" who animates his voyeuristic gaze, the "whore" who serves as muse for his literary fantasies. Bowden's perversity, his racist and colonialist gaze, constructs border women as abject. What's more, Bowden links these abject bodies to a third one he summons in his text: the mimetic image of one of the murdered border women.

The photograph published on page 66 of *Juárez* depicts the body of a kidnapped, raped, and murdered sixteen-year-old girl found in a park that is located literally on the border between Ciudad Juárez and El Paso and that is "dedicated to friendship between both nations" (Bowden 1998, 67). The photographer, Jaime Bailleres, told Bowden that a newspaper refused to publish the image because, according to Bowden, "the lips of the girl pull back, revealing her white teeth. Sounds pour forth from her mouth. She is screaming and screaming and screaming" (1998, 103).

What logic would venture to further deface this image of a border woman's horrified expression, this face of terror that Bowden initially mistook for a "carved wooden mask" (1998, 105)? "Something," as he writes, "made by one of those quaint tribes far away in the Mexican south." The mask, as Walter Benjamin asserts, allows one to "get ahold of an object at very close range by way of its likeness, its reproduction" (1969c, 223). Bowden continues, "I keep a copy of it in a folder right next to where I work and from time to time I open the clean manila folder and look into her face. And then I close it like the lid of a coffin. She haunts me, and I deal with this fact by avoiding it" (1998, 105).

Bowden did not avoid the face/mask: he published it. By reproducing it both in his first article in *Harper's* and later in his book on Ciudad Juárez, he defaced it, thereby unleashing the magical power of defacement, which is, according to Michael Taussig, "the most common form of magical art" (1999, 25).[31] What if in actuality the editors of the newspaper that refused to publish the picture understood the logic of mimesis? Perhaps in Mexican political culture they are well aware of the enchanting qualities of defacement, and the newspaper's decision represents not a refusal to commodify the image through publication, but instead a refusal to practice a form of defacement, a disfiguration of the copy of her face, because it would in all likelihood summon "a strange surplus of negative energy" (1).[32]

In the hands of Bowden, a literary writer and journalist from the United States, the face of horror belonging to the body of a woman on the border is aestheticized and transformed into a fetish, "a horror made beautiful and primitivism eroticized" (Taussig 1987, 10). Bowden's urge to get "ahold of an object at very close range by way of its likeness" grows stronger every day. "The skin is smooth," Bowden writes, "almost carved and sanded, but much too dark. And the screams are simply too deafening" (1998, 105). Perhaps in Mexico ancient knowledges bespeak the mimetic magic of representation, its ability to animate what it copies. In a "culture of masks," as Subcommandante Marcos refers to Mexican political culture, this face/mask may well trigger "a strange surplus of negative energy."

Rethinking State Terrorism

Cultural representations informed by the discourse of globalism have played a crucial role in deflecting attention away from the complicity of the state in creating a climate of violence. Although liberal and sympathetic to the women murdered in Juárez, the discourse of globalism often reifies the "global economy" as a "thing operating transhistorically and driven by its own laws and motion" (Michael Peter Smith 2001, 98). In other ways, globalism posits an isomorphism between the local and the global, which has led to grand generalizations about the demise of the state.[33] This failure to provide a more nuanced assessment of the interplay of "global and transnational" *as well as* of the "national and local dynamics implod[ing] simultaneously into the everyday experiences of members of urban households" has worked to absolve the state of its complicity and perhaps even direct involvement in the murders of poor and dark-skinned women in Ciudad Juárez (Michael Peter Smith 2001, 148).[34] As the master narrative for the Left, globalism generates a problem of interpretation that is unable to account for the consolidation of a new form of state-sanctioned terrorism in Mexico. The state, however, is in many ways directly implicated in the culture of feminicide in the region. In February 2002, for example, state agents ambushed and assassinated Mario César Escobedo Anaya, a defense attorney for one of the suspects in the killings, who was leading charges against police for their use of torture in extracting confessions. There have been numerous death threats against activists and journalists in Ciudad Juárez, including those against Esther Chávez Cano, the head of the NGO Casa Amiga, and against Samira Izaguirre, a radio journalist and founder of the NGO Luz y Justica. At least a dozen activists, including Izaguirre, have filed petitions for asylum in the United States.[35]

In order to comprehend how the problem of interpretation is complicit with state-sanctioned terrorism one must first examine how "the state is implicated in the construction of gender regimes" (Jacobs, Jacobson, and Marchbank 2000, 7). The absurdly outdated Roman and Napoleonic codes informing Mexico's legal system have in fact ratified and promoted violence against women, especially in the private sphere, where male violence is normalized as "a mechanism of punishment and control."[36] Mexico's regulatory and judicial systems, strengthened by traditional cultural values, support "the idea of masculine authority and ownership" over the lives of women and grant male impunity in the exercise of violence against women (United Nations 1990, 22). Few Latin American countries have legislation against violence in the private sphere. Under current Mexican law, if injuries inflicted during interfamilial violence heal within fifteen days, the woman cannot file charges against her domestic partner; if the injuries heal after fifteen days but are not permanent, the aggressor is merely fined (Cruz 2002; Neft and Levine 1997, 154).

For years, feminist grassroots activists and NGOs have sought legal and judicial redress, aiming to extend full citizenship rights to women. Yet in the struggle to eliminate violence against women, activists are waging an uphill battle. Recently, members of the conservative Partido Acción Nacional (PAN) blocked senate ratification of an international human-rights instrument, the Convention to Eliminate All Forms of Discrimination against Women (CEDAW), a nonbinding document that would at least have signaled the state's support for the prevention of gender violence in Mexico.[37]

The movement to extend rights to women in Mexico is of utmost importance because, as in many other Latin American nations, "violence against women and sexual assault are typified in law as crimes against the honor of the family, rather than as crimes against the personal, physical integrity and human rights of the woman victim" (Macaulay 200, 149).[38] This interpretation of gender violence as "crimes against the honor of the family" has lethal consequences for women, since Mexican laws "still consider the honesty, honor, and good name of the woman to be relevant to the characterization of certain sexual crimes and to determine their punishment" (Macaulay 200, 149).[39] The state in effect tolerates violence against women, especially in the legal and juridical realm, depoliticizing and relegating violence to the domestic private sphere and narrowly portraying it as personal in nature, rather than as a "systematic historical and political event" (Steifert 1994, 68). This same dynamic also depoliticizes other forms of family violence, such as incest and pedophilia, which often go unreported and/or ignored. Reinforcing these manifestations of family violence is a discourse that discourages women from leaving the private sphere, the purported site of patriarchal protection and authority: public space is imagined as inherently dangerous.[40]

Given its failure to extend citizenship rights to women, Mexico's legal and judicial system is part of "the state machineries for the exercise of violence" (Jacobs, Jacobson, and Marchbank 2000, 8). Recognizing state complicity, the United Nations Declaration on the Elimination of Violence against Women "points to areas of state negligence, as opposed to direct responsibility. It notes that states are obliged to exercise 'due diligence' in preventing all acts of violence against women" (Macauley 2000, 147).

Much of the problem with the discourse of globalism stems from its portrayal of sexual violence as primarily an effect of global capitalism without accounting for the ways in which global manifestations of power differ from as much as they intensify earlier and more traditional forms of patriarchy within the nation-state. A more nuanced understanding of sexual violence in Juárez identifies the multiple sites where women experience violence, within domestic and public spaces that are local and national as well as global and transnational. And this leads to another way in which globalism is complicitous with the state.

The meanings surrounding the deaths are elusive. Are they committed by a single or multiple sex serial killers? By the police- and state-sponsored paramilitary groups? By the "Juniors" (sons of the elite)? By traffickers of illegal human organs? By an underground economy of pornography and snuff-films? By a satanic cult? By narcotraffickers? By unemployed men envious of women workers? By men expressing rage against poverty? By men threatened by changing sex roles? By abusive spouses or boyfriends? The multiplicity of contrary interpretations and competing narratives has created a "problem of interpretation" that is "decisive for terror, not only making effective counterdiscourse so difficult but also making the terribleness of death squads, disappearances, and torture all the more effective in the crippling of people's capacity to resist" (Taussig 1987, 128).

Fifty years ago, Walter Benjamin wrote, "The tradition of the oppressed teaches us that the 'state of emergency' is not the exception but the rule. We must attain to a conception of history that is in keeping with this insight" (1969b, 257). These insights permit understanding about the role of the Mexican State in creating the "state of emergency." Mexico's neoliberal policies—its disinvestments in the public sphere, instituted by the shift from a welfare state to a state that facilitated globalization—has produced the very culture of violence that it purports to police.[41] As Giorgio Agamben so aptly points out, "Power no longer has today any form of legitimation other than emergency.... power everywhere and continuously refers and appeals to emergency as well as laboring secretly to produce it" (2000, 4). In Mexico the "state of exception ... has now become the norm."[42]

It is thus important to recognize how violence—not only in Ciudad Juárez but also in Mexico City—is not simply a problem *for* the state but is in fact endemic to it, a "state of exception" produced by an authoritarian government that has cultivated extreme forms of violence, corruption, and even death, in order to cripple people's capacity to resist, to smother effective counterdiscourse, and to overpower the revitalized democratic opposition.

As the uprising of the Zapatistas in Chiapas made clear, the Mexican government has been waging a "dirty war" of terror, violence, and extermination against all forms of dissidence, including the poor women and indigenous communities. The state hides behind the mask of democracy, its appearance a subterfuge for the repressive, authoritarian government which, until the 2000 presidential election of PAN candidate Vicente Fox, had been dominated by a single ruling party, the Partido Revolucionario Internacional (PRI). Feminicide in Ciudad Juárez should be considered a part of the scenario of state-sponsored terrorism because it is situated in the "space of death," which "is important in the creation of meaning and consciousness nowhere more so than in societies where torture is endemic and where the culture of terror flourishes" (Taussig 1987, 4). As Taussig so poignantly writes about the complicity of the state in generating a climate of terror, "There is also the need to control massive populations, entire social classes, and even nations through the cultural elaboration of fear" (8).

If the subject "woman" under the patriarchal state figures as the embodiment of the nation, the "space of death" occupied by these poor and dark-skinned women, embodiments of the nation, creates "meaning and consciousness" around the role of the state in creating the conditions of possibility for feminicide. The fact that all of the victims were members of the most vulnerable and oppressed group in Mexican society—dark-skinned women—underscores the extent to which in Mexico "women's relationship to the state is racialized and ethnicized as well as gendered" (Crawley 2000, 88). One way to politicize violence against women of intersecting identities is by highlighting the role of the patriarchal state in creating the conditions of possibility for the proliferation of gender violence.

Another way to politicize violence is to think about it in broader terms, not just as isolated or personal in nature, but as a form of state-sanctioned terrorism, a tool of political repression sanctioned by an undemocratic patriarchal state in its crusade against poor and racialized citizens: "The choice of particular women as targets of rape is almost inevitably determined by their identities ... [as] members of an ethnic group, race or class" (Human Rights Watch 1995b, 3). The murders of poor and dark-skinned women in Ciudad Juárez, situated as they are in a nexus of violence that spans from the state to the home, are thus connected to broader questions of power and gender inequality within a patriarchal state. The consideration of gender violence as "social feminicide" implicates "the role of an existing social order in practices that result in the death and devaluation of female lives" (Hom 2000, 257n5).

Transnational Activism on the Border

In March 1999 the crosses started appearing. Black crosses on pink backgrounds, painted in protest on electrical poles throughout Juárez by Voces sin Eco (Voices without Echo), a grassroots group of families of the murdered women (fig. 1). Eerily barren crosses, silent witnesses to symbolic and experiential instances of violence, suggestive of what local poet Micaela Solís calls "the language of the abyss: the cries for help we never heard / the screams of their voices."[43] The fusion of traditional secular and religious iconography—pink for woman, cross for mourning—contravenes against epistemic and real violence. Women are the protagonists of this grassroots movement.[44] In painting the crosses in public spaces, Voces sin Eco forged a new public identity for women, claiming public space for them as citizens of the nation.

As in other places in Latin America, in Juárez women used religiosity subversively to stage a confrontation with the historical and social trauma in the region. The use of religiosity—crosses, luminaries, vigils—is a form of indirection and nonliteralness for healing the trauma of the unrepresentable: death as the ultimate other. As a political and discursive strategy, religiosity gives voice to a new consciousness, one that recognizes the contradictions in the interface between woman's visibility as abject subject (murder victim) and the invisibility of woman in the public sphere (citizen).

Woman's visibility as abject is a subject-effect produced by the intersection of experiential violence and symbolic violence: the violence of racist misogynists, the violence of state-sanctioned terrorism, the violence of discursive frameworks of interpretation, but also the violence of representation. The hypervisibility of the feminine body in audiovisual media, as in the commodification of gruesome photographs depicting tortured and dismembered bodies, heightens the invisibility of the disposable body of the poor, dark-skinned woman on the border.[45] Faced with such literalness and explicitness, religiosity is a mode for reimagining the murdered, violate body otherwise: as a subject undeserving of annihilation.[46] In other ways, the discursive strategies of religiosity contemplate visibility for a new subject: the cross marks the intersectional identities of the targeted feminine subject, the feminine body of the poor and dark-skinned woman.

As in other parts of Mexico, in this northern region, certain bodies (white)

1. Black cross on pink background painted on telephone pole in Ciudad Juárez. Photo by Celeste Carrasco. Courtesy of Lourdes Portillo.

are held in higher esteem than others are.[47] Although the murdered women were indeed targeted for their gender, perhaps even more significant are the racial and class hierarchies that constitute their identities as women. As one of the mothers, Mrs. González, so aptly phrases it, "For the poor there's no justice. If they'd murder a rich person's girl, they'd kill half the world to find the murderer. But since they've only murdered poor people, they treat us like dirt."[48]

Three years after the crosses were first painted on the telephone poles, the local coalition of grassroots groups and NGOs extended its reach beyond Juárez, growing into a broad-based national and international movement to end violence against women in Mexico. By early 2002, a new coalition of feminist activists from hundreds of organizations came together under the Ni Una Más campaign. In December 2001, thirty thousand protesters from both sides of the border gathered in Juárez. And in March 2002, hundreds of women dressed in black (elderly women, campesinas, housewives, factory workers, students, and professionals) marched for 370 kilometers, from Chihuahua City to the Juárez-El Paso border, in the Exodus for Life campaign. Staging demonstrations to publicize the murders, the transnational Ni Una Más campaign worked to extend citizenship rights to women in Mexico.

Horrific forms of violence against women have had an unintended and spiraling effect. In the wake of the Juárez feminicides, the emergence of feminist and cross-border activism is part of the new space of planetary civil society, of the movement for global justice, of the challenge to global capitalism, neoliberal state policies, and the rise of the global police state. Women's activism on the borderlands constitutes an identity formation that intersects with the transnational drive for women's human rights that gained momentum in the decade of the nineties, after the 1993 "United National World Conference of Human Rights" in Vienna (Macaulay 2000, 144–62). However, the transnational movement for women's rights poses unique challenges. For example, is it possible to locate women's oppression within the human-rights framework developed by feminists in the First World? Is it possible to evoke a transnational subject identity within a planetary civil society? The writings of Third World feminists provide a cautionary tale.

Claiming a singular transnational identity for women ignores the profound differences among women across the globe, but especially within specific national localities, as Vasuki Nesiah points out: "A discourse about universally shared oppression can obfuscate global contradictions" (2000, 45). Although First World feminists have contributed significantly to "the theoretical and practical revision of international rights law," especially in their redefinition of women's rights as human rights, the challenge today involves framing women's international human rights within very complex and specific cultural contexts. For this reason, Celina Romany writes, "an integrated and more coherent use of international instruments"—such as the coupling of the Women's Convention with the Race Convention in international law, as has been accomplished in South Africa—is an important step in the right direction (2000, 60). "The constitutional agenda had to recognize how a gender-essentialist critique fell short and did not adequately conceptualize a regime of rights and protections responsive to the realities of Black women" (ibid.). In this manner, Romany's "intersectional methodology directs us to ask the woman/race question" and, in the case of Juárez, the class question as well.

Grassroots activists in Juárez are well aware of the limitations of basing a human-rights framework on a singular transnational identity or "shared international subject class." For as Mrs. González makes clear, it is their intersectional identities as specific class, race, and gender subjects which makes women in Mexico particularly vulnerable to feminicide and state terrorism.

In many ways, the murder and disappearance of women in Ciudad Juárez have strengthened the resolve of feminist and human-rights activists in the campaign to eliminate multiple forms of violence in the lives of women and children. In the short term, women's-rights groups are seeking legal and juridical redress, lobbying for reforms to the penal code, including a law covering violence in the private sphere.[49]

The eloquent *El silencio que la voz de todas quiebra*, written by a group of courageous journalists and creative writers, ends with these words: "What makes anyone (random or premeditated killer, individual or serial, alone or accompanied, Mexican or Foreigner) think that in Ciudad Juárez one can rape or kill a woman without fear of retribution?" (Benítez et al. 1999, 144). A rhetorical question, no doubt, but its spirit of denunciation challenges public and private patriarchies in Mexico.

At the national level, the state continues to produce the very "state of exception" it aims to police, combining rhetoric with inaction and nonintervention in eliminating violence against women.[50] In November 2001 President Vicente Fox directed the attorney-general of Mexico to assist in the investigation of feminicide. However, as of this writing, the cultural elaboration of fear continues in Chihuahua. So, too, does the struggle to eradicate all forms of violence in the lives of excluded citizens, disenfranchised subjects of the patriarchal state, women, indigenous people, dark-skinned and poor women, gays, the urban and rural poor, and children. In this newly constituted planetary civil society, human-rights activists on the borderlands hold onto a vision of a future in which no person can "rape or kill a woman without fear of retribution."

Conclusion

This study of the cultural representations of feminicide grew out of my ongoing collaboration with the filmmaker Lourdes Portillo. In September 1999 I joined Lourdes at the "Burials on the Border" conference after she had spent two harrowing weeks in Ciudad Juárez filming for a documentary that was eventually released as *Señorita extraviada* (2001). My current analysis of cultural discourses is informed by the dialogic relationship we cultivated in the course of the production of her documentary. Just as the investigation has influenced my thinking, so, too, has my study influenced her framing of feminicide in Juárez. In the course of our projects, both of us have constituted frameworks of intelligibility that are mutually influenced by our ongoing discussions about the continuing violence against women. I have listened to her theories about the murders and commented on several versions of the film;

she has similarly impacted my study and clarified my understanding about the murders of women.

Lourdes maintained daily contact with the mothers and local women's-rights activists. I drew strength and inspiration from the generosity she exhibited toward family members and activists and from the passion and commitment that drove her documentation of the murder of their loved ones. In the months that followed the release of *Señorita extraviada*, I accompanied Lourdes on several occasions during screenings of the film throughout the United States and abroad. Often we spoke in public forums to audiences who were generally unaware of the murder and disappearance of women in Juárez.

During these public presentations, my work has been to provide a framework for the film and to discuss its political and aesthetic merits. I situate this film within its activist tradition, as a film that refuses to withdraw from political action, that expresses moral outrage, and that seizes terror through confrontation. *Señorita extraviada* is an activist film in large measure because of its crucial role in the formation of what I have termed a planetary civil society. Lourdes has made video copies of the film available to grassroots groups throughout the Southwest, the U.S.-Mexico border, and Mexico City, to help them raise public awareness and participate in fundraising campaigns for families of the murdered women. The film has served women's-rights activists in their appeals beyond the state to international forums. It has also served to publicize the murders of women in European, U.S., and Latin American contexts through its exhibition at major international film festivals, where it has won numerous awards, including the prestigious Nestor Almendros Award from Human Rights Watch.

As an activist film in the tradition of radical cinema, *Señorita extraviada* is driven by a project of social transformation and *concientización*, aiming to move its viewers into political action. The film poignantly echoes the strategies of grassroots activists, mothers, sisters, and relatives of the disappeared in their ongoing struggle against state-sanctioned terrorism, reflecting the struggle of those who continue to demand justice despite threats against their lives and the use of disappearance as a mechanism of social control. *Señorita extraviada* is undoubtedly an issue-oriented film, yet its mode of delivery is eloquent and groundbreaking.

Making a film about an event that continues to unfold is inherently challenging—even more so when the subject matter is as horrid and terrifying as widespread violence, murder, and disappearances. Given the absolute abjection of women through death, as well as the desecration of their bodies in public discourse, Lourdes confronted an enormous problem of representation.

In the course of several trips to Ciudad Juárez, Lourdes not only experienced firsthand the social trauma that these murders have produced throughout the region but also bore witness to the psychic trauma that family members were living with and that they relived with each new report of a murder or disappearance. The film was thus motivated by the inextricably related conditions of problems of representation and of social and psychic trauma. How does one represent the dead in a respectful manner, in a way that does not further sacralize their bodies, but honors the memory of their former existence? How does one represent the dead in a way that is respectful of the families and that honors their grief?

Drawing from the discursive strategies of grassroots groups like Voces sin Eco, Lourdes employs religious symbolism and iconography subversively. She enshrouds her film in the discourse of religiosity. The strategic placement of images of crosses, montages of crucifixes and home altars, along with a musical score of Gregorian chants, including the solemn chant for the dead ("Kyrie Eleison"), all work to establish a meditative, hieratic rhythm in the film. Lourdes describes *Señorita extraviada* as a "requiem." She has in effect resignified the requiem into an artistic composition for the dead. To her credit, not a single dead body appears in the film; nonetheless the haunting presence of the victims is summoned both literally, through the placement of photographs, and figuratively, through her reworking of the requiem form.

Like her earlier film, *Las Madres*, *Señorita extraviada* emphasizes the process of radicalization rather than victimization. The narrative gives voice to women's agency, to the mothers and sisters who have emerged as protagonists in grassroots movements. Through their agency and determination, poor women have shouldered the work of detection and forensic investigation, searching for missing daughters or sisters, combing the desert for bodies, and identifying remains.

The film portrays women on the border neither as passive victims nor as hapless dependents of the patriarchal state, the family, or international human-rights groups. Instead, the film underscores the agency of mothers and women activists on the border, women who affirm the continuity of life, grieving and mourning, while acting as politically motivated citizens demanding the rights of women within the nation-state. It is the mothers and women activists, not secondary sources or experts, who are the film's ultimate guarantors of truth.

Informed as it is by a women's-rights framework, *Señorita extraviada* avoids positing a singular identity for women in Mexico. It emphasizes an intersectional methodology which among Mexican intellectuals has generated a new understanding of feminicide not simply as class and gender motivated but as *racially* motivated as well. Since the release of *Señorita extraviada*, references to the "racial" nature of the killings have appeared on the editorial pages of *La Jornada*, a national daily based in Mexico City, where emphasis on the "misogyny," "classism," and "racism" of the killings has now become common.[51]

Although Lourdes draws from experimental and realist techniques unlike conventional documentaries, *Señorita extraviada* suggests neither a single cause for feminicide nor a contrived resolution. Lourdes draws attention to a confluence of intersecting and overlapping forces including but not limited to broader structural processes of economic globalization and the neoliberal policies of the patriarchal state, as well as more localized virulent forms of patriarchal domination. Ultimately, Lourdes turns her critical gaze onto the patriarchal state, a feature that some audience members have criticized for deemphasizing the role of global capitalism. But it is also clear from Lourdes's investigation that, in the words of one women's-rights activist in the film, "The state is ultimately responsible." The film draws attention to the role of state agents as actual perpetrators of the murders, as well as the state's role in creating the conditions of possibility (the state of exception) for the patriarchal expression of a sexual politics of extermination in the region.

If Lourdes's critical gaze on the state bothers some audiences, even more disturbing is how she ultimately turns the critical gaze back onto the viewers.[52] The film's ending points to our own complicity, not as a literal implication of responsibility for the murders, but as an ethical one. The film ends on the tone of moral outrage and in so doing calls for our ethical political engagement, summoning us to take action. I also like to think about the film's ethics as summoning the "space of death," a space "of immorality, communal memory, of connections between generations," a space "particularly important as a site of struggle in the colonized areas of the world, and this struggle is of necessity ethical" (Franco 1999, 31).

At the "Burials on the Border" conference, I sat next to Guillermina González as she gazed intently at the postcard reproduction of the conference poster (fig. 2). "These are my sister, Sagrario's, eyes," she said. "I took out the photo from my wallet and they are the same eyes." They in fact happened not to be Sagrario's eyes, according to conference organizers, but Guillermina's fixation overwhelmed me. She stared at the image of those almond-shaped indigenous eyes, belonging to a partial face, so photographically enlarged that the pixel dots were visible; a partial face staring through the pink outline of a cross which partially hid this face—or did the cross deface the face? It wasn't Sagrario, but to Guillermina it was. Was I witnessing what Taussig in another context calls "a type of 'release' of the fetish powers of the face in a proliferation of fantasy and of identities, no less so than the very notion of identity itself, a discharge of the powers of representation" (1999, 224)? And

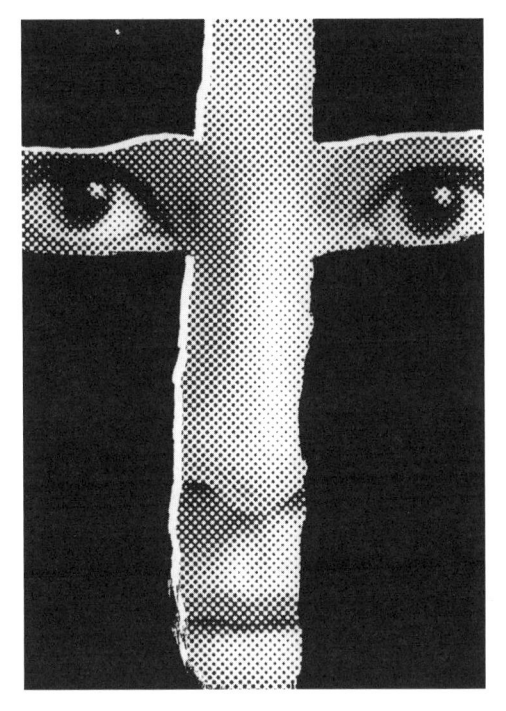

2. Burials on the Border conference poster.

what charge did those almond-shaped eyes with the quality of magic emit? Almond-shaped indigenous eyes, both Sagrario's and not Sagrario's: eyes that return the gaze, transform the object into the subject of the gaze, witnesses for her voice without an echo.

The ghostly, barren black crosses on pink backgrounds, painstakingly emblazoned around Ciudad Juárez, as abrasions in public discourse, as embodiments less of Christ, the man made flesh, than of female flesh made human sacrifice. No literal images of the dead, no identifying names on tombstones, only the symbolism of a cross—the Christian cross, the cross of the Four Cardinal Points—superimposed on the traditional hue for femininity: representations of the unrepresentability of trauma. Hundreds of barren crosses in public spaces, crosses as rearticulations of discursive violence, as recodifications of femininity, as expression of the inability to express terror and trauma: black-crosses-on-pink as figures for the "space of death," so "important in the creation of meaning and consciousness nowhere more so than in societies where torture is endemic and where the culture of terror flourishes." Crosses speaking for justice for eyes that cannot see, for women who can no longer speak, crosses marking the threshold of existence.

Notes

A shorter version of this essay was published in *Emergences* as "Voices without Echo: The Global Gendered Apartheid" (Fregoso 2000).

1 Ciudad Juárez is the fourth-largest city in Mexico. During the 1990s, the city was host to five hundred export-processing factories (maquiladoras) employing three hundred thousand workers. The maquila industry dates back to Mexico's Border Industrialization Program of 1965, when the country created an export-processing zone along the U.S.-Mexico border; the industry was given a boost in 1993 with NAFTA.
2 The term *feminicide* is theorized by Dianna Russell and Jill Radford (1999). Julia Estela Monárrez, in her excellent "La cultura del feminicido en Ciudad Juárez," draws from their work and defines feminicide as "the misogynist murder of women for being women" (2000, 89).
3 In November 2001, seven months after the group's report was released, the bodies of eight slain women were discovered in an area of the city known as the *zona dorada* (see Villalpando 2001; Villalpando and Breach 2001; Deacon 2001; Paterson 2001).
4 This report was presented to Marta Altolaguirre, the special rapporteur for women's rights for the Interamerican Human Rights Commission (see Castañon 2002).
5 Factual information contained in this section has been culled from various sources, including the research of Mexican journalists working independently of the state, who have based their findings on the examination of the files of 137 victims murdered between January 1993 and December 1998. The results were published in Benítez et al. 1999. See also Monárrez 1999.
6 The majority of the victims were dark and thin, with long black hair. Of 137 victims, 5 percent were light skinned, 41 percent dark skinned. Information is not available for the other 54 percent. Many of the murdered women had been gagged, raped, strangled, and mutilated, with nipples and breasts cut off and buttocks lacerated like cattle, or they had been penetrated with objects. The number of murders tabulated as sexual killings is disputed because city authorities don't count penetration as rape when an object is used; for example, a woman found with a blanket in her anus was not recorded in police investigations as having been raped. See Benítez et al. 1999.
7 I am building on my previous characterization of the state's interpretive framework as the "discourse of morality," which I have since modified to draw attention to the state's shifting framework of interpretation (Fregoso 2000).
8 I am indebted to George Lipsitz for bringing to my attention the literature on non-heteronormative sexuality, especially Ferguson 2000 and Shah 2001. See also Benítez et al. 1999, 110.
9 "Muchas de las mujeres asesinadas trabajaban entre semana de obreras y en los fines de semana como prostitutas para hacerse de mayores recursos." Author's translation.
10 "Visitaba un centro en el que se dan cita homosexuales y lesbianas"; "Gustaba salir con diferentes hombres y era asidua asistente a salones de baile." Author's translation.
11 "¿Qué, no tienen otra cosa que inventar? De todos los casos han dicho lo mismo: Que la manera de vestir, su supuesta doble vida." Author's translation.

12 Quoted in Mackler 1998.
13 This point was made at the "Burials on the Border" conference by Ciudad Juárez's chief of police.
14 The document released by the governor of Chihuahua was the first time the state used numbers in a media campaign against activists. See Elizabeth C. Velasco 2001.
15 The state's new numbers were reported in Villalpando and Breach 2002a and in Axtman 2002.
16 This seems mostly to be the case among reporters from the United States (see, for instance, Nieves 2002).
17 My use of the term *globalism* draws from the work of Michael Burawoy, who calls the tendency to explain the local in terms of the global "the fallacy of globalism—namely that one can characterize changes of the whole without examining changes of the parts or, to put the fallacy the other way around, that the secrets of the part can be found in the whole" (2001, 343).
18 In my article "Voices without Echo" (2000) I provide a detailed analysis of antiglobalization discourse as it appears in journalistic writing on feminicide.
19 Researchers in the region, such as the sociologist Victor M. Quintana, are now talking about the "end of the maquila" era. Since 2001, thousands of factory workers have lost their jobs as five hundred foreign-owned maquiladoras have shifted their operations to China. In the state of Chihuahua alone, more than one hundred thousand workers have lost their jobs. See Landau 2002.
20 Quoted in Sassen 1996 (111). See the films *The Global Assembly Line* (1986) and *Love, Women, and Flowers* (1988). See also Fernández-Kelly 1983a.
21 While the incorporation of women into wage employment has been growing in export-processing zones throughout the Third World, the situation in Mexico's border cities differs to some extent. The traditionally female workforce of the maquiladora industry peaked in the 1960s. Due in large measure to Mexico's economic crisis of 1982, border cities like Ciudad Juárez experienced a drop in female participation in the maquiladora labor force, from 68 to 53 percent in the years between 1981 and 1989, with the hiring of men rising in matching proportions. Transnational corporations on the border export zone took advantage of the cheap male labor force produced by high unemployment and inflation during the Mexican recession of the 1980s, creating the phenomenon researchers call "the remasculinization of maquila labor" in Ciudad Juárez. Another factor, according to Maria de la O Martínez (1995), is that maquila technology and organizational structures have become increasingly complex, leading to the perceived need for more highly trained technicians—typically, men. De la O Martínez argues that today "women are marginalized by the hierarchical structures now in place in the maquiladora industry" (261).
22 See Chomsky 1998.
23 See, for example, Laundau 2002.
24 News programs on ABC, CBS, Fox, and UNIVISION—including *20/20*, *60 Minutes*, *Ocurrió así*, and *Primer impacto*—have also assumed the murders to be maquiladora killings.
25 The occupations of the murder victims are listed in Benítez et al. 1999 (11–22).

26 The song "The New World Order Rap" was produced for the film; lyrics by Manny Martinez and Greg Landau; produced and recorded by Greg Landau, copyright 1998–99.
27 See Harvey 2000, 65. Also see Bauman 1998: "One of the most seminal consequences of the new global freedom of movement is that it becomes increasingly difficult, perhaps altogether impossible, to reforge social issues into effective collective action" (69).
28 Nathan characterizes the women workers as "maquila girls," which perpetuates their "infantilization" (1997, 20). With regard to the purported hypersexuality of female maquila workers, Nathan writes, "Downtown Juárez is clotted with bars whose clientele are mostly assembly-line workers. The week-end cover charge and beer are cheap at establishments such as Alive, Noa Noa, and La Tuna Country. U.S. rock, disco, and Mexican music throb from giant speakers by their dance floor, and intermission is punctuated with 'Most Daring Bra' and 'Wet String Bikini' contests for the women customers, as well as performances by handsome young male striptease dancers" (1999, 27).
29 Quoted in Wright 1998, 120. One of Wright's interviewees is Steve, a plant manager who "explained that there were uniform regulations for the Mexican women in administration because 'you should have seen what they used to wear. It looked like one of those cantinas down on Juarez avenue [the red-light district]. It made some of the guys uncomfortable" (119).
30 Quoted in Franco 2002, 244.
31 See Bowden 1996, 44–52.
32 As Taussig adds, "What's more, it's not only as if disfiguring the copy acts on what it is a copy of, but that, associated with this, the defaced copy emits a charge which seems—how else can we say this?—to enter the body of the observer and to extend and to physically overflow, and therewith create an effusion of proliferating defacements" (1).
33 See, for example, Bauman 1998.
34 The same holds true of the discourse which attributes the violence on the Mexican border to narcotrafficking, as with regard to the mass graves discovered in Ciudad Juárez in late November 1999. See Bergman and Golden 1999, 1ff.; Schrader and Smith 1999, 1ff.
35 See Villalpando 2002.
36 I use the phrase "absurdly outdated" because the legal system in Mexico is based on a family model that no longer exists (i.e., male as breadwinner and head of household, female as caretaker); the legal system fails to account for the growing number of female-headed households, working mothers, single and divorced households, and so forth. See Galán 2001, 28.
37 See Gabriela Rodríguez 2001. In addition to CEDAW, adopted for signature in 1979, there are other international instruments that address women's citizenship rights, such as the UN Declaration on the Elimination of Violence against Women (1993) and the Belem do Pará Convention for the Prevention, Punishment and Eradication of Violence against Women of the Organization of American States (1994).

38 See Fiona Macaulay's discussion of Latin American penal codes in "Tackling Violence."
39 According to Macaulay, this is true for the penal codes of all Latin American countries except for Cuba and Nicaragua.
40 I am indebted to George Lipsitz for this important insight.
41 Again, I thank George Lipsitz for pointing me in this direction.
42 According to the translators of *Form of Life*, "In Agamben's passage, 'state of emergency' is translated as 'state of exception'" (2000: 142).
43 A poem read at the "Burials on the Border" gathering.
44 Until Guillermina González announced the "disintegration" of Voces sin Eco in July 2001, its members had gathered every weekend to paint more crosses as a symbol of their struggle for social justice. For an excellent analysis of the political resistance of mothers of the disappeared young women in Juárez see Bejarano 2002.
45 Images of the murdered women were published in Mexican tabloids, newspapers, and television, as well as appearing in a traveling exhibit sponsored by Aperture Press in conjunction with the publication of Charles Bowden's *Juárez: The Laboratory of Our Future*.
46 In some cases family members have unwittingly bought into the patriarchal ideology that justifies murder on the basis of nonnormative behavior. This sentiment can be seen in family members' defensive insistence that their murdered relatives were respectable—innocent, honorable young women who did not lead a doble vida or go to bars, discos, or strip joints. At the "Burials on the Border" gathering, a family member of one of the victims stood up holding a photograph and said, "Esta es mi cuñada. No trabajaba en la maquila. No era prostituta. No más fue víctima inocente" (This is my sister-in-law, one of the victims. She was not a maquila worker. She was not a prostitute. She was just an innocent victim). And Guillermina González—founder of Voces sin Echo, originator of the cross campaign, and sister of murder victim María Sagrario—said to the audience, "No son prostitutas. No son estadísticas. Pero sí tienen historia" (They are not prostitutes. They are not statistics. But they do have a history).
47 Ana María Alonso (1995) notes that Chihuahuans today boast of their collective whiteness. In the north of Mexico "whiteness became central to the creation of a regional sense of community and personhood. This invented tradition of origins is very much alive today and is regularly evoked in the construction of a distinct norteño identity, opposed to that of the Mexicans in the Center, who are subjectively apprehended as 'less white'" (68). Later, she comments on the centrality of whiteness in "the definition of feminine beauty" (98).
48 Interview of Mrs. González in the documentary *Maquila: A Tale of Two Mexicos* (2000).
49 See Gabriela Romero Sánchez 2001; Concha 2001.
50 President Vicente Fox continues government inaction even as he pays lip service to women's groups by speaking on behalf of gender equality and against gender violence. During International Women's Day, at the official ceremony for the appointment of Patricia Espinoza Torres (a feminist ex-PAN deputy) as head of the Instituto Nacional de la Mujer, Fox broached the issue of gender and human rights: "En las ciudades,

las mujeres sufren aún discriminación; en el campo, su situación es muchas veces violatoria de los derechos humanos y clama por una pronta y clara justicia" (In the cities, women still suffer discrimination; in the rural areas, the violation of their human rights is greater and it demands a clear and swift justice) (Cruz and Garduño 2001, 41).

51 For example: "Almost all of them because they are the domestics, the workers, the ones with dark skin, from the working-class neighborhoods, the poor ones, therefore, the exclusive targets of this sexist and classist genocide" (Casi todas porque son las muchachas, las trabajadoras, las de color moreno, las de las colonias populares, las pobres, pues, el blanco exclusivo de este genocidio sexista y clasista) (Quintana 2001b, author's translation; see also Quintana 2001a).

52 I am indebted to my students in a film course I taught during the spring of 2002 at University of California, Santa Cruz, for their insights about how the film's powerfully unsettling and disturbing ending implicates the viewer in responsibility. Nearly forty students in the course "Transnational Cinema and Feminism" wrote critical essays on *Señorita extraviada*.

A Glass Half Empty: Latina Reproduction and Public Discourse

LEO R. CHAVEZ

Issues surrounding reproduction, once considered the most private and taboo of subjects, have become matters of intense public concern.
—Susan Greenhalgh, *Situating Fertility*

✳ Latina reproduction and fertility, especially that of Mexican immigrant women, became ground zero in a political war not just of words but also of public policies and laws in post-1965 America.[1] Perhaps this should come as no surprise to anthropologists, since Faye Ginsburg and Rayna Rapp (1991; 1995a) have argued effectively that scholars need to focus attention on the politics surrounding reproduction, fertility, and women's bodies (Browner 1986; Browner 2000; Greenhalgh 1995; Kanaaneh 2002). Indeed, anti-immigrant sentiment, especially during the 1980s and 1990s, focused specifically on the reproductive capacities of Mexican immigrant and Mexican-origin (U.S.-born) women.[2]

A review of the theoretical and rhetorical issues framing the discussion of Latina reproduction suggests two key questions. First, how have Latina reproduction and fertility been constructed? Latina fertility and reproduction are central, intertwined concepts in a national public discourse on immigration, in a manner suggested by Fraser's and Gordon's (1994) research on the keyword *dependency* in the welfare state. The genealogy of Latina "fertility and reproduction" as "threats to U.S. society" is evident in the visual and textual discourse found in ten national magazines traced over a thirty-five-year period, from 1965 to the end of 1999 (Chavez 2001). As Ginsburg and Rapp observe, "Representations provide the arena in which cultural understandings and hierarchies are produced, contested, and revealed" (1995a, 6).

Discourses that construct people with "dangerous," "pathological," and "abnormal" reproductive behaviors and beliefs are not simply of academic interest, but have real political and economic consequences. In California, for example, the perceived threat of Latina fertility, especially among immigrants, was central to the Save Our State movement that led to Proposition 187, which sought to curb undocumented immigration by denying undocumented immigrants access to social services, particularly prenatal care and education for their children. Bette Hammond, one of the organizers of Proposition 187, characterized Latina immigrants in her hometown in a way that emphasized the threat of reproduction: "They come here, they have their babies, and after that they become citizens and all those children use social services" (Kadetsky 1994, 418). Pete Wilson, governor of California from 1991 to 1999, made denying undocumented immigrant women prenatal care a top priority of his administration (Lesher and McDonnell 1996). The 1996 welfare-reform law also targeted medical services for immigrant women (Fix and Passel 1999). The popular discourse of Latina reproduction is decidedly alarmist in that it becomes part of a discourse of threat and danger to U.S. society and even national security, which is underscored in a post-9/11 world. Thus, because discourses not only filter reality but help construct what is taken for "real," they have important material implications.

Second, is the construction of Latina reproduction and fertility accurate, or is the story more complicated? The doxa, or taken-for-granted beliefs, of Latina reproduction bear analysis from the vantage point of data on Latina reproductive behavior.[3] Questioning the factual bases of the discourse surrounding the politics of Latina reproduction suggests a new way of thinking about reproduction, immigration, and social change.

Anthropology, Reproduction, and Latinas

Faye Ginsburg and Rayna Rapp (1991) argue that "to reproduce" has many connotations. At the very least, it is important to distinguish biological reproduction from social reproduction. Both aspects of reproduction, as well as their intersection, are often sites of political confrontation. In societies with competing and often unequal social groups split along various lines of race, ethnicity, sexuality, and immigration status, the biological and/or social reproduction of one or all of those groups can be the target of public debate and state policies aimed at controlling reproduction (Horn 1994; Lock and Kaufert 1998). As Ginsburg and Rapp note, "Throughout history, state power has depended directly and indirectly on defining normative families and controlling populations" (1991, 314). In the process, regimes of representation can emerge in which particular groups are said to be pathological, even "dangerous" to the larger society.[4] Ginsburg and Rapp (1995a) utilize Shellee Colen's (1990) concept of "stratified reproduction" to describe how for certain groups of women reproduction is characterized positively, while for other groups of women reproduction is "disempowered." As they note, "The concept of stratified reproduction helps us see the arrangements by which some reproductive futures are valued while others are despised" (Ginsburg and Rapp 1995a, 3).

One particularly insidious example of stratified reproduction is the image of the "black welfare mother" used so effectively in political discourse (Fraser and Gordon 1994). As Dorothy Roberts argues, society has blamed poor black mothers for "perpetuating social problems by transmitting defective genes, irreparable crack damage, and a deviant lifestyle to their children" (1997a, 3). African American women pose a "reproductive threat" different from that posed by Mexican immigrant women and their daughters, but both groups have faced the stigma of society's surveillance of their reproductive capacities. As Roberts points out, "Welfare reform measures that cut off assistance for children born to welfare mothers all proclaim the same message: The key to solving America's social problems is to curtail Black women's birth rates" (7).[5]

Ginsburg and Rapp also suggest the importance of examining discourse, noting, "The powerful tools of discourse analysis can be used to analyze 'reproduction' as an aspect of other contests for hegemonic control, such as state eugenic policies, conflicts over Western neocolonial influences in which women's status as childbearers represents national interests, or fundamentalist attacks on abortion rights as a part of a campaign to evangelize the American state" (1991, 331). Ginsburg and Rapp's observations, especially concerning discourse, have implications for Latinas and the politics surrounding their reproduction. As Foucault (1977) argues, discourse produces objects of knowledge and meaning (see also Hall 1977). "Latinas" exist and "reproduction" exists, but "Latina reproduction" as an object of a discourse produces a limited range of meanings, with an emphasis on "over"-reproduction and on a fertility and sexuality depicted as "out of control" in relation to the supposed social norm. Latina biological reproduction combines with its social reproduction to produce fears about the population growth of Latinos in American society, which in turn positions them as a possible threat to the "nation," that is, the "people" as conceived in demographic and racial terms. Reproduction here is an ideological concept that defines normative fertility levels (that of Anglos or non-Latino whites) and their opposite: the nonnormative, stigmatized, "high fertility" level of Latinas and the sexual behavior that produced it.

Not only is Anglo women's fertility considered normative, but Anglo women themselves possess "subject status," which Jürgen Link defines as "an autonomous, responsible, quasi-juridical person of sound mind, as in a legal subject" (1991, 40). In contrast, Latinas do not possess subject status; their behavior is held to be irrational, illogical, chaotic, and, therefore, threatening. The simple dualism inherent in the rendering of a social group as not possessed of subject status works well when constructing images of an enemy that threatens the life and well-being of those with subject status, be they individuals or nations.

Carole Vance (1991) added another important dimension to the politics of reproduction. Because of the increased interest in reproduction and sexuality in the 1980s and early 1990s, Carole Vance titled her article "Anthropology Rediscovers Sexuality." Vance also emphasized the politics surrounding the concept of sexuality: "For researchers in sexuality, the task is not only to study changes in the expression of sexual behavior and attitudes, but to examine the relationship of these changes to more deeply-based shifts in how gender and sexuality were organized and interrelated within larger social relations" (1991, 876). For Latinas, this means their lives as wives and mothers are subject to redefinition by the larger society that views them in comparison to more "modern" U.S. women (Glenn 1994). In particular, Euro-American women's roles are more broadly defined to include education and work outside the home, and their sexuality and reproduction are positively viewed against the "Other" women of the Third World, including Mexican immigrant women and U.S.-born women of Mexican descent, with their "high" reproductive levels.[6]

Complicating what is known about Latina fertility and reproduction is that it has been the subject of social-science interest, and construction, since at least the early 1970s (Elena Rebeca Gutiérrez 1999). For much of this time, the emphasis has been on high fertility levels, especially among Mexican-origin women, with less emphasis on the rapid drop in fertility rates among Mexican and Mexican American women between the 1960s and 1990s. As Hortensia Amaro observed, "The social science literature has often portrayed Mexican-American women as sacrificed to childbearing.... An assumption behind these evaluations of Mexican-American women is that traditional cultural values and religious traditions promote attitudes favorable to continuous childbearing, opposition to contraception, and opposition to abortion" (1988b, 6).

The few studies that have examined actual behavior among Latinas have found some important differences from stereotypical characterizations. For example, Kristen Marchi and Sylvia Guendelman (1994) found that Latina girls had lower rates of sexual activity than non-Latina girls, which they attributed to Latino cultural norms. They noted that with "increasing acculturation to

U.S. norms and values, Latina girls engage in sexual activities at an earlier age and are more likely to have births out of wedlock" (210). Amaro (1988b) also found most of the Mexican American women in her study favored contraceptive use, most had used one or more contraceptive methods, and they sometimes desired smaller families than they actually had. Similarly, Christine Stroup-Benham and Fernando Trevino (1991) found that in 1979, 61 percent of Hispanic women nationwide had used oral contraceptives, a rate almost as high as that of non-Hispanics (68 percent).

Finally, research in Mexico also suggests problems with common characterizations of Mexican women's fertility and reproduction. Carole Browner (1986) found that women in a rural Mexican village generally wanted fewer children than the number promoted by government policies. Jennifer Hirsch (1998a, 540–541) found that, according to Mexico's Consejo Nacional de Población (National Population Council), fertility rates have declined dramatically in Mexico—from 7 to 8 children per woman before 1970, to 4.4 children per woman in 1980, to 3.8 children in 1986, to 3.4 in 1990. In 2002 Mexico's fertility rate had dropped to 2.9 children born to a woman during her lifetime, compared to 2.1 for U.S. women, according to the Population Reference Bureau (2003). The Consejo Nacional de Población (2003) put the fertility rate lower, at 2.4 children per Mexican woman in 2000. Clearly, Mexico has experienced dramatic decline in fertility rates over the last few decades. Among younger Mexican women, such declines are likely greater than these averages indicate. Hirsch attributes the drop in Mexican women's fertility to changing beliefs about marriage, trends toward delaying having children and spacing births out more than in the past, and increased contraceptive use. At the very least, these studies suggest that Latina fertility and reproduction are more complex than generally characterized in the social-science literature.

Latina Fertility and Reproduction in National Magazines

A study of selected issues of ten national magazines published between 1965 and the end of 1999 (Chavez et al. 2001) illuminated characterizations of Latina fertility and reproduction.[7] Magazines were selected if their cover mentioned immigration in image or text or alluded to immigration in some direct way. From a total of seventy-six magazines, along with their covers and pertinent articles, there emerged three primary recurring themes and issues related to Latina fertility and reproduction: high fertility and population growth; reproduction as a "reconquest" of the United States; and immigrant overuse of U.S. social services.

High Fertility and Population Growth

The contribution of Latino immigrants and their children to U.S. population growth was viewed as particularly problematic due to pressure from environmental and population-control groups, such as Zero Population Growth. As Leonard F. Chapman Jr., commissioner of the Immigration and Naturalization Service (INS), commented in a 1974 interview in *U.S. News and World Report*, "We're very close in this country to a zero population growth through births. As we get closer to that zero growth, immigration will become an even larger percentage of the population increase" (1974, 30).

Social-science constructions of the Latina, particularly Mexican American, fertility "problem" often intersected with characterizations found in magazines. For example, David Alvirez and Frank Bean, citing INS Commissioner Chapman's estimates of the growing Mexican American population, noted, "The most noticeable feature of the Mexican American family is its size relative to other groups in America. The fertility of Mexican Americans is substantially higher than other groups" (1976, 271). At the time, the average size of Mexican American families (4.4 persons) was about one person larger than that of all American families (3.5 persons) (Alvirez and Bean 1976, 280–81). Alvirez and Bean also observed that Mexican women's fertility rates were subject to change from urbanization and social mobility, which was substantiated by later empirical findings. As Frank Bean, C. Gray Swicegood, and Ruth Berg (2000) noted, the mean number of children born to Mexican-origin women decreased dramatically between 1970 and 1998. In 1998, all Mexican-origin women in the United States between eighteen and forty-four years of age had 1.81 children, well below zero population growth. Non-Hispanic white women between the same ages, however, had only 1.27 children according to these data, so there still existed a "gap" of 42 percent (Bean, Swicegood, and Berg 2000).

On 4 July 1977 the theme of Mexican women's "high" fertility surfaced on the cover of *U.S. News and World Report*, which carried the headline "TIME BOMB IN MEXICO: Why There'll Be No End to the Invasion of 'Illegals.'" The accompanying article clarified that the "time bomb" was Mexico's population and its expected growth rate, arguing that the fertility of Mexicans and their inability to produce jobs for their population would lead to greater pressure for immigration to the United States. Notably, *U.S. News and World Report* drew attention to the external threat posed by the reproductive capacity of Mexican women, a threat that was also internal since Mexican immigrant women's and their U.S.-born children's high fertility levels were implicated in the rapidly growing U.S. Latino population.

The growth of the U.S. Latino population was often paired with the decline in immigrants from Europe and the declining proportion of whites in the U.S. population. For example, the 17 January 1983 issue of *Newsweek* reported that between 1970 and 1980, the Latino population grew by 61 percent, largely because of Mexican immigration, higher fertility rates among Latinas, and a 46.4 percent decline in European immigration since the mid-1960s. The politics of fertility and reproduction were not limited to immigrant Latinas, but included U.S.-born Latinas, whose high fertility was characterized as partly responsible for demographic changes occurring in the nation's racial composition. A classic example of such claims was written by John Tanton, an ophthalmologist from Michigan, former president of Zero Population Growth, founder of the Federation for American Immigration Reform, and ardent promoter of population control, immigration restrictions, and English as the official language of the United States. In 1988 he wrote a now infamous memorandum about Latina fertility and "the Latin onslaught": "Will Latin American immigrants bring with them the tradition of the *mordida* (bribe), the lack of involvement in public affairs, etc.? Will the present majority peaceably hand over its political power to a group that is simply more fertile? ... On the demographic point: Perhaps this is the first instance in which those with their pants up are going to get caught by those with their pants down!" (Conniff 1993, 24).

The *National Review*'s 22 June 1992 issue featured a cover illustration of the Statue of Liberty standing with a very serious expression on her face and her arm extended in a halting gesture. The text suggested that she was redirecting the flow of immigrants to another country: "Tired? Poor? Huddled? Tempest-Tossed? Try Australia. Rethinking Immigration." In the feature article, "Time to Rethink Immigration?" Peter Brimelow found Hispanics to be particularly troublesome: "Symptomatic of the American Anti-Idea is the emergence of a strange anti-nation inside the U.S.—the so-called Hispanics" (1992, 45). Brimelow used Latinos as a bully pulpit from which to launch a diatribe about bilingualism, multiculturalism, multilingual ballots, citizenship for children of illegal immigrants, the abandonment of English as a prerequisite for citizenship, the erosion of citizenship as the sole qualification for voting, welfare and education for illegal immigrants and their children, and congressional and state legislative apportionment based on populations which include illegal immigrants (ibid.). Latino social and biological reproduction were the basis for Latinos being characterized as a "problem" in the *National Review*.

The alleged high fertility of Latinos informed an apocalyptic vision of the future that appeared in the February 1994 issue of the *Atlantic Monthly*. In "The Coming Anarchy" Robert D. Kaplan foresaw a "new cartography" in which political borders as fixed and abrupt lines were replaced by "buffer entities" (1994, 75). The Latino buffer entity replaced the precise U.S.-Mexico border, with the new map constituting "an ever-mutating representation of chaos" that would change in response to migrations of people, explosions of birth rates, and disease.

Concern about the threat of Mexican fertility to American society continued into the twenty-first century. Samuel Huntington raised the alarm in *Foreign Policy*: "In this new era, the single most immediate and most serious challenge to America's traditional identity comes from the immense and continuing immigration from Latin America, especially from Mexico, and the fertility rates of those immigrants compared to black and white American natives" (2004, 32).

Reconquest

Latino social and biological reproduction was commonly characterized as a taking over, or "reconquest," of the United States. The reconquest theme surfaced in the 13 December 1976 issue of *U.S. News and World Report*, which featured the headline "Crisis across the Borders: Meaning to U.S." The cover image was a map of North America with two arrows, both beginning in the United States, with one pointing to Mexico and the other to Canada. The Canadian problem lay in Quebec, where many French-speaking residents were pushing for greater sovereignty and even separation from the English-speaking provinces (the Quebec model). The crisis in Mexico lay in the potential for increased migration to the United States. The "Quebec problem" would eventually serve as a metaphor, or civic lesson, for the "Mexican problem." On 19 March 1981, for example, *U.S. News and World Report* featured an illustrated map of the North American continent, including Mexico and Canada. The United States was the focal point of the map, and the stars and stripes of the U.S. flag were superimposed on it. To the north was Canada, with the image of a mountie holding the Canadian flag and a French Canadian holding the Quebec flag in one hand and raising his other hand in a defiant, closed-fisted gesture toward the mountie. To the south was Mexico. Given the headline "OUR TROUBLED NEIGHBORS—Dangers for U.S.," the cover's image seemed to suggest that Mexican immigration and the growing Mexican-origin population would pose a problem for the United States much as the Quebecois movement did for Canada.

Reproduction, immigration, and the Quebec threat, or "reconquest," came together on the 19 August 1985 cover of *U.S. News and World Report*: "The Disappearing Border: Will the Mexican Migration Create a New Nation?" The cover image rendered the two nations—the United States and Mexico—through the strategic use of colors. Central to the image were "U" and "S" in large block letters, white in color against a field of green. These rested atop smaller letters forming the word "MEXICO," printed in red against a field of yellow. The red of "MEXICO" bled into the white of "US," which was made possible by the disappearance of the lines (borders) between the letters. Without the borders, a one-way flow moved up (north) in the image, with little figures drawn in stereotypical fashion to suggest Mexicans migrating north. The accompanying article, titled "The Disappearing Border," established the reconquest theme.

> Now sounds the march of new conquistadors in the American Southwest. The heirs of Cortés and Coronado are rising again in the land their forebears took from the Indians and lost to the Americans. By might of numbers and strength of culture, Hispanics are changing the politics, economy and language in the U.S. states that border Mexico.
>
> Their movement is, despite its quiet and largely peaceful nature, both an invasion and a revolt. At the vanguard are those born here, whose roots are generations deep, who long endured Anglo dominance and rule and who are ascending within the U.S. system to take power they consider their birthright. Behind them comes an unstoppable mass—their kin from below the border who also claim ancestral homelands in the Southwest, which was the northern half of Mexico until the U.S. took it away in the mid-1800s. Like conquistadors of centuries past, they come in quest of fabled cities of gold. America's riches are pulling people all along the continent's Hispanic horn on a great migration to the place they call El Norte. (Lang and Thornton 1985, 30)

The often repeated alarm of a Mexican takeover was raised again by Samuel Huntington in 2000, illustrating the persistence of this theme in public discourse: "The invasion of over 1 million Mexican civilians is a comparable threat [as one million Mexican soldiers] to American societal security, and Americans should react against it with comparable vigor. Mexican immigration looms as a unique and disturbing challenge to our cultural integrity, our national identity, and potentially to our future as a country" (Huntington 2000, 22).

Overuse of Medical and Other Social Services
Concern about undocumented immigrants' use of welfare and other social services, displacement of U.S. citizens from jobs, and crime also emerged as a theme in the magazine study. In its 25 April 1977 issue, *U.S. News and World Report* focused on these topics, beginning with the cover headline "Border Crisis: Illegal Aliens Out of Control?" The invasion metaphor raised the specter of a nation under siege, with its national security at stake: "On one point there seems little argument: The U.S. has lost control of its borders" (Kelly 1977, 33).

But the specific "out of control" behavior emphasized in the magazine was the use of welfare and related social services, which purportedly threatened the economic security of the nation.

Themes often become intertwined, especially those of Latina biological and social reproduction, immigration, and the overuse of social services. Both *U.S. News and World Report* (7 March 1983) and *Newsweek* (25 June 1984) published covers typical of such intertwining. *U.S. News and World Report*'s cover announced "Invasion from Mexico: It Just Keeps Growing," emblazoned over a photograph of men and women being carried across a canal. At the head of the line a woman sat on a man's shoulders. *Newsweek* printed a similar cover, using a photograph of a man carrying a woman across a shallow body of water. The woman wore a headscarf and a long shawl. The man carried her handbag, which suggested she was traveling somewhere, moving with a purpose and for an extended amount of time. She held a walking cane. The title read, "Closing the Door? The Angry Debate over Illegal Immigration: Crossing the Rio Grande."

By featuring women so prominently on their covers, these two national magazines, while warning of an "invasion," sent a clear message about fertility and reproduction. Rather than an invading army, or even the stereotypical male migrant worker, the images suggested a more insidious invasion, one that included the capacity of the invaders to reproduce themselves: the women being carried into U.S. territory carried with them the seeds of future generations. These images signaled not simply a concern over undocumented workers but a concern with immigrants who stay and reproduce families and, by extension, communities in the United States. Along with the accompanying articles, these images alluded to issues of population growth, use of prenatal care, children's health services, education, and other social services.

While not exhaustive, this review of national magazines illustrates the issues in a politics of Latina reproduction in popular discourse. The underlying premise of these themes is that U.S.-born Latinas and Latin American immigrants have extreme, even dangerous, levels of fertility relative to an imagined native population. But is this premise accurate?

Latina Fertility and Reproductive Behavior

In the early 1990s, a study was designed to examine beliefs about breast and cervical cancer and the use of cancer-screening examinations (Chavez et al. 2001; Hubbell et al. 1996a; Hubbell et al. 1996b). The data also included information related to fertility and reproduction. While the study did indicate some differences between Latinos and Anglos, they were modest in comparison with the rhetoric surrounding Latina fertility. Moreover, the study pointed to the importance of looking at reproduction and fertility not as something fixed and immutable, but as reflecting differences among Latinas, who were often glossed as homogenous and impervious to change.

Orange County is the third most populous county in California, with 2,846,289 inhabitants according to the 2000 census (U.S. Bureau of the Census 2004). It covers an area of 789 square miles, is largely urban, and contains thirty-four cities and numerous unincorporated communities. Latinos accounted for 30.8 percent of the county's population in 2000. Most Latinos are of Mexican heritage, but Latino immigrants from other nations in Latin America, particularly Central America, also live in the county. Latinos are found in greater concentrations in the northern half of the county, which includes Santa Ana, where about four out of five residents are Latino. The southern half of the county has been an area of rapid growth in new middle-class, upper-middle-class, and exclusive residential communities. Latino immigrants often work in southern county communities but find less expensive housing in the many working-class communities in the northern part of the county.

Data Collection

Trained bilingual women interviewers from the Field Research Corporation in San Francisco conducted a telephone survey from September 1992 to March 1993. Eligible participants were English-speaking or Spanish-speaking women, eighteen years of age or older, who were not institutionalized and who identified themselves as white (Anglo, Caucasian, non-Hispanic white) or Latino (Hispanic, or more specific ethnic identifiers such as Mexican or Mexican American). A larger subsample of Latino respondents was used to examine variation within the population. The telephone survey drew from a cross-sectional sample of random-digit telephone listings to identify eligible subjects. Both listed and unlisted numbers appeared in the listings, avoiding potential bias due to exclusion of households with unlisted numbers (Survey Sampling 1990). Although the findings may not be generalizable to families without phone service, in Orange County approximately 94 percent of Latinos and 99 percent of Anglos have telephones (California State Data Center 1995). The study also would not have found hard-to-reach members of the population, the homeless, and those engaged in street-corner employment and migrant agricultural labor; this may represent more of a bias, however, for male than female Latinas, who are less likely to be homeless or seek daywork by standing on street corners (Chavez 1998).

Our survey randomly selected both households and respondents within households, interviewing the woman eighteen years of age or older who had had the most recent birthday. The cooperation rate was 78.5 percent.[8] Latina respondents could choose to answer the questions in Spanish or English. The questionnaire was pilot tested, its content validity was assessed, and it was translated from English to Spanish to English. The final questionnaire included inquiries about demographic characteristics and questions related to fertility and reproduction. It also included a previously validated five-point "acculturation" scale (Marin et al. 1987) that measured acculturation primarily on the use of Spanish or English (e.g., reads with, speaks with, thinks with, used as child, and speaks with friends). This language-acculturation measure was included because it offered a greater range of variation than the dichotomous foreign-born/U.S.-born variable. Moreover, many people who lack English proficiency face significant obstacles accessing medical services in the United States, including information on reproductive services (Solis et al. 1990).[9]

Since this study was not focused on reproduction and fertility per se, it is limited in the data it provides. For example, there is information on use of birth-control pills, but not on other methods of contraception. Despite this limitation, the data that are available provide interesting information on Latina reproductive behavior.

Interviewee Characteristics

Table 1 presents the nationality of survey respondents. About a third (33.6 percent) of the survey's 803 Latina respondents were born in the United States. Most U.S.-born Latinas were of Mexican descent, but many others traced their heritage to different nations. Most of the Latina immigrants (428, or 80 percent) surveyed were born in Mexico, but the survey also included Latina immigrants from other countries, including twenty-four from El Salvador.

Table 2 provides a summary of respondents' sociodemographic characteristics. The major difference is between Latina immigrants and both U.S.-born Latinas and Anglo women. Latina immigrants (mean age 33) were younger than both U.S.-born Latinas (mean age 37) and Anglo women (mean age 44). Latina immigrants had received fewer years of education (mean 9 years) than U.S.-born Latinas (mean 13 years) and Anglo women (mean 15 years). Latina immigrants had been in Orange County, on average, three-fourths of the time they had been in the United States. Immigrants were also more likely than both U.S.-born Latinas and Anglo women to be married and have at least one child in the household under eighteen years of age. Since Latina immigrants were young, married, and in the early stages of their reproductive cycles, they were more likely than the other women to be homemakers (*amas de casa*). An overwhelming majority of Latina immigrants earned less than $20,000 a year.

Table 1. Survey Respondents

Mexican immigrants	428
Salvadoran immigrants	24
Other Central American immigrants	37
Other Latin American immigrants	44
U.S.-born women of Mexican descent (Chicanas)	168
Other U.S.-born Latinas	102
Anglo women	422

Note: Interviewees $N = 1,225$.

U.S.-born Latinas generally lived in households earning above $20,000 a year, with a quarter of those above $50,000 a year. Almost half of the Anglo women lived in households earning above $50,000 a year.

Scores on the language-acculturation index indicate that immigrant Latinas were much less likely to use English than U.S.-born Latinas. Out of the five points possible, with one point for each question answered in the positive (for example, speaking English at home is one point), Latina immigrants had a 1.6 mean score (standard deviation .83). U.S.-born Latinas, on the other hand, had a mean score of 4.2 (standard deviation .85), which means that most of them used English for much of their communication needs. This score is used as a measure not only of language use but also as an indicator of acculturation (Marin et al. 1987).

Fertility and Reproduction

Before examining the number of children, there are four other factors related to reproduction that deserve attention: age when sexual relations are initiated, number of sexual partners, age at which first child was born, and use of birth control pills. While the discourse on Latina reproduction suggests that Latinas and Anglo women differ significantly in these fertility-related variables, the claims of that discourse—like those of all discourses and ideologies that shape the truth for political ends—are still subject to examination.

Table 3 presents information on the age when the women sampled in Orange County initiated sexual intercourse. Latina immigrants were somewhat less likely than U.S.-born women, both Latinas and Anglos, to begin engaging in sexual intercourse under the age of eighteen. On average, Anglo women (mean age 18.1) began sexual relations about a year younger than all Latinas surveyed (mean age 19.0), a significant difference.[10] The difference is insignificant when U.S.-born Latinas (mean age 17.9) are compared to Anglo

Table 2. Sociodemographic Characteristics of Survey Respondents, by Percent

	Latina immigrants (N = 533)	U.S.-born latinas (N = 270)	Anglo women (N = 422)
Age			
18-30	49.9	40.9	20.0
31-45	39.2	36.1	42.4
46-81	10.9	23.0	37.6
Mean age	33	37	44
Years of schooling			
< 8	39.8	5.6	1.0
9–12	34.7	40.3	24.3
> 12	25.5	54.1	74.8
Years in the U.S.			
5 or less	27.6	NA	NA
6–10	21.1		
11–15	22.6		
> 15	28.6		
Years in Orange County			
5 or less	40.0	20.4	18.3
6–10	21.8	11.9	12.9
11–15	19.2	9.7	12.4
> 15	19.0	58.0	56.4
Married	74.5	63.1	62.8
Child under age 18 in household	80.0	60.8	45.8
Homemaker only	33.6	16.4	17.6
Employed full-time	36.3	53.4	50.5
Employed part-time	12.4	11.9	12.1
Other work status	17.7	18.3	19.8
Income			
< $20,000	70.0	21.2	14.67
$20,000–49,999	25.1	52.4	39.3
> $50,000	4.9	26.4	46.0
Language-Acculturation Index	1.6 SD = .83	4.2 SD = .85	NA

Note: SD = standard deviation.

Table 3. Age at First Sexual Intercourse, by Percent

	Never	Under 18	18-21	22-25	26+
U.S.-born Latinas, not Mexican-origin ($N = 97$)	2.1	40.2	42.3	13.4	2.1
U.S.-born Latinas, Mexican-origin ($N = 157$)	5.7	39.5	38.9	9.6	6.4
Mexican immigrants ($N = 409$)	4.4	31.5	44.3	14.4	5.4
Latina immigrants, not Mexican ($N = 107$)	0.9	26.2	42.1	19.6	11.2
Anglo women ($N = 403$)	2.7	36.0	45.2	11.4	4.7

women, but is significant when Latina immigrants (mean age 19.5) are compared to Anglo women.[11] Latina immigrants were on average about a year-and-a-half older than Anglos when they initiated sexual intercourse.

Latinas and Anglo women also varied on the number of reported sexual partners, as table 4 demonstrates. Latina immigrants were more likely to report having had two or fewer sexual partners. (Another study found that Mexican immigrants were unlikely to have had two or more sexual partners [Harvey et al, 1997].) Anglo women were more likely than Latinas to report having had five or more sexual partners. Latinas generally (mean 2.5 sexual partners) and Anglo women (mean 6.3) differed significantly in the mean number of reported sexual partners.[12] Once again, U.S.-born Latinas (mean 4.3 sexual partners) did not differ significantly from Anglo women, but Latina immigrants (mean 1.8) did.[13]

Table 5 indicates significant differences in the age when women had their first children. Few Anglo women had their first child under the age of eighteen, compared to Mexican immigrants and U.S.-born Chicanas (women of Mexican descent). Anglos were more likely than Latinas to have their first child after the age of twenty-five. The mean age at which Anglo women had their first child (24.3) was significantly older than Latinas generally (21.6), U.S.-born Latinas (21.9), and Latina immigrants (21.4).[14] In contrast to a stereotype of

Table 4. Number of Sexual Partners, by Percent

	0	1	2	3	4	5	6+
U.S.-born Latinas, not Mexican-origin (*N* = 92)	2.2	31.5	18.5	14.1	4.3	9.7	19.6
U.S.-born Latinas, Mexican-origin (*N* = 149)	6.0	38.3	17.4	10.7	10.1	6.0	11.4
Mexican immigrants (*N* = 399)	4.5	64.7	15.8	6.5	4.3	2.5	1.6
Latina immigrants, not Mexican (*N* = 106)	0.9	52.8	22.6	13.2	3.8	0.9	5.7
Anglo women (*N* = 380)	2.9	30.8	13.2	8.7	7.9	8.4	28.2

Table 5. Age at First Child, by Percent

	17 or Younger	18-21	22-25	26+
U.S.-born Latinas, not Mexican-origin (*N* = 73)	11.0	39.7	21.9	27.4
U.S.-born Latinas, Mexican-origin (*N* = 117)	17.1	36.8	18.8	27.4
Mexican immigrants (*N* = 354)	14.7	48.0	25.4	11.7
Latina immigrants, not Mexican (*N* = 89)	10.1	37.1	25.8	6.8
Anglo women (*N* = 308)	5.5	30.8	28.6	35.1

Table 6. Mean Number of Children Ever Born to Latinas and Anglo Women, by Age

Age	No. of Latinas	No. of Children	Mean	No. of Anglos	No. of Children	Mean
18–30	376	469	1.25	82	57	.70*
31–44	289	755	2.61	165	244	1.48*
45+	137	488	3.56	170	431	2.54*
18–44	665	1,224	1.84	247	301	1.22*
All ages	802	1,712	2.13	417	732	1.76*

*t-test: p < .001

rampant fertility among Latinas, all of the women sampled waited, on average, until they were over twenty years old to have their first child.

Finally, the study found that a majority of all the women had used birth-control pills at some point in their lives: Mexican immigrants (64.5 percent), other Latin American immigrants (62.3 percent), Chicanas (72.2 percent), other U.S.-born Latinas (75.3 percent), and Anglo women (85.4 percent). The large proportion of Latinas who were willing to use birth-control pills indicate that Latinas are concerned with family planning and the control of fertility, once again contradicting the discourse on Latina fertility. Although two-thirds of Latinas generally had used birth-control pills, they were still significantly less likely to have done so than Anglo women, most of whom had used the pill.[15]

With regard to the number of children ever born to Latinas and Anglo women in the survey, this variable refers to the number of children a woman had at the moment of the interview, not the total number of children she would have in her lifetime. Table 6 presents the number of children by various age categories to indicate the influence of age and to take into account the different age structures and fertility patterns of Latinas and Anglo women. Examining women only up to forty-four years of age—the convention in most fertility studies—may capture a majority of women during their peak years of fertility, but it leaves out more older women among Anglos than Latinas. About 59 percent of the Anglo women surveyed were between eighteen and forty-four years of age, compared to 83 percent of the Latinas.

Latinas between eighteen and thirty years of age had on average 1.2 children, whereas Anglo women in this age group had .7 children—a significant difference. Given that both groups were still early in their reproductive years,

Table 7. Mean Number of Children Ever Born to Women Ages 18–44 and Fertility Ratio of Non-Anglos to Anglos

	Orange County Study			National Fertility Data[a]	
	N	Children ever born	Ratio to anglos	Children ever born	Ratio to anglos
All Mexican origin	514	1.93	1.58	1.81	1.42
First generation					
Child immigrants	88	1.55	1.27	1.55	1.22
Adult immigrants	301	2.31	1.89	2.45	1.93
Second generation	65	1.17	0.96	1.40	1.10
Third or later generation	60	1.42	1.16	1.71	1.35
Anglos	247	1.22	1.00	1.27	1.00
Other Latin American immigrants	77	1.81	1.48		
Other U.S.-born Latinas	73	1.27	1.04		
All Latin American immigrants	466	2.08	1.70		
All U.S.-born Latinas	199	1.28	1.05		
All Latinas	665	1.84	1.51		

[a] National fertility data provided by Bean, Swicegood, and Berg 2000.

this number is likely to increase, but by how much is difficult to predict. For both Latinas and Anglos, the trend is toward fewer children. With each age category, the number of children increases, but women in their thirties and early forties have fewer children than women forty-five and older. The key age category is eighteen to forty-four years of age. Both Latinas and Anglo women in these prime childbearing years have fewer than the 2.0 children per woman required for population replacement and much fewer than the 2.1 children needed for population growth.

Age is only one factor influencing fertility. How does a Latina's immigration history and generation in the United States influence the number of children she has? Table 7 presents the number of children born to women in the Orange County study between the ages of eighteen and forty-four in relation to immigration and generation patterns. Since Mexican-origin women have been the subject of heightened surveillance and the target of much of the discourse on Latina fertility, the table provides information on them separately. The table includes the national data on all children ever born to Mexican-origin women provided by Bean, Swicegood, and Berg (2000). There are a couple of distinct comparative advantages to using these data, which were obtained by pooling individual records of women of childbearing age from the June 1986 and June 1988 Current Population Surveys (CPS). First, the information on the number of children ever born is broken down into generations in the United States, from immigrants to third and later generations. Second, the CPS data are only a few years earlier than the data collected in the Orange County study.

What is striking about table 7 is the low number of children among almost all the women. Anglo women in Orange County, with 1.22 children per woman, have fewer than the 1.27 children average for Anglo women nationally. Latinas generally also had fewer than 2.0 children per woman. With 1.93 children per woman, Mexican-origin women showed a dramatic decrease from the 4.4 children per woman found in the early 1970s. Mexican immigrants who migrated to the United States as adults (sixteen years old or older) had the highest number of children per woman (2.31), but their rate is lower than that found among their counterparts nationally. But the number of children born to Mexican immigrants who migrated as children (under sixteen years of age) fell to 1.55 per woman, only 22 percent higher than Anglo women.[16] Immigrants from Latin American countries other than Mexico had a mean of 1.81 children per woman. Taken together, immigrants from all Latin American countries, including Mexico, had 2.08 children per women, a rate which demographically replaces the parents but contributes only minimally to growth.

The fertility story is even more dramatic for U.S.-born Latinas. In Orange County second-generation Mexican-origin women (Chicanas) actually had fewer children per woman (1.17) than Anglo women.[17] This is lower than for second-generation Mexican Americans nationally. Third-generation Mexican-origin women had 1.42 children per woman, which is more than second-generation Mexican-origin women but still only 16 percent more than Anglo women in Orange County.[18] Third-generation Mexican-origin women in Orange County had fewer children on average than their counterparts nationally. Together, all U.S.-born Latinas sampled in Orange County had a mean of 1.28 children per woman, only 5 percent more than Anglo women in Orange County and almost equal to Anglo women nationally.

But does the significant difference in the mean number of children born to Latinas and Anglo women hold up in a multivariate analysis, which accounts for the influence of other variables? Table 8 presents the findings from an ordinary least squares regression using the number of children ever born as the dependent variable. The independent variables include Latina/Anglo (values =

Table 8. Ordinary Least Squares Regression: Number of Children Ever Born as the Dependent Variable

	Model 1 Ages 18–30		Model 2 Ages 31–44		Model 3 Ages 18–44		Model 4 All Ages 18+	
	B	SE	B	SE	B	SE	B	SE
Age	.1021	.012*	.0474	.003**	.0859	.006*	.0597	.003*
Years of schooling	−.1117	.013*	−.0442	.013*	−.0681	.009*	−.0581	.009*
Married								
0. No								
1. Yes	.6371	.101*	.7207	.155*	.6502	.091*	.6944	.090*
Ethnicity								
0. Latina								
1. Anglo	−.2322	.144	−.1323	.155	−.2365	.123	−.1618	.127
Language acculturation (5-point scale)	.0156	.038	−.3180	.058*	−.1547	.034*	−.1970	.037*

Note: B = Beta; SE = standard error; *p < .001; **p < .01.

Summary statistics for Model 1: N = 456; multiple R = .64262; R square = .41296; adjusted R square = .40645; standard error = .93705; significance F = <0.0001.

Summary statistics for Model 2: N = 449; multiple R = .52198; R square = .27246; adjusted R square = .26426; standard error = 1.39052; significance F = <0.0001.

Summary statistics for Model 3: N = 908; multiple R = .61087; R square = .37316; adjusted R square = .36968; standard error = 1.20990; significance F = <0.0001.

Summary statistics for Model 4: N = 1210; multiple R = .64262; R square = .41296; adjusted R square = .40605; standard error = .93705; significance F = <0.0001.

0, 1), married (0 = not married, 1 = married), education (total years), age (total years), and the language-acculturation variable (five-point scale). Income was not included because it correlated closely with language-acculturation: Latinas who scored low on their integration into English-speaking U.S. culture and society also generally had lower incomes. A variable indicating U.S. or foreign birth was also not included since it too correlates highly (.9) with the language-acculturation variable (see table 2). In addition, separate regression analyses were run for different age categories to account for Latina and Anglo women's differing age structures.

Table 8 summarizes the results of the regression analyses. In model 1, younger women's (eighteen to thirty years of age) fertility was examined. Age, education, and marital status predicted the number of children women in this age category had. As a woman aged, she was more likely to have children. Married women had more children than unmarried women. The more years of education a woman had, the fewer children she had. Among these relatively young women, language-acculturation did not predict how many children they had. Finally, although Latinas did have more children than Anglos, the difference was not significant when these other variables were taken into consideration.

Model 2 examined fertility among women thirty-one to forty-four years of age. Similar to the younger women, age, education, and marital status were significant predictors of how many children the women had. Also significant, however, was the language-acculturation variable: the more integrated Latinas were into English-language usage and, thus, English-speaking society, the fewer children they had.

Model 3 examined women eighteen to forty-four years of age, the primary reproductive years. All the same variables are predictors of fertility. Ethnicity, at .06, was not a significant predictor of fertility for these women. However, some might argue that at this level of significance, ethnicity must at least be considered an important predictor of fertility for these women.

Model 4 included women of all ages in the analysis. Age, education, marital status, and language acculturation were significant predictors of fertility. Ethnicity, however, was once again not significant for understanding fertility.

Latina Fertility Reconsidered

Dorothy Roberts observes that welfare reform and policies to regulate fertility are propelled by powerful stereotypes: "Myths are more than made-up stories. They are also firmly held beliefs that represent and attempt to explain what we perceive to be the truth. They can become more credible than reality, holding fast even in the face of airtight statistics and rational argument to the contrary" (1997a, 8). The taken-for-granted assumption in the discourse on Latina fertility is that they are a population with "their pants down," and their reproductive behavior thus poses serious threats to the nation. As the discourse in popular magazines underscores, Latina reproduction and fertility threaten the nation's demographic future in terms of size and racial-ethnic composition, provide the basis for a potential takeover or reconquest of U.S. territory, and hasten a destabilization of the nation's medical and other social services.

The data on Latina reproductive behavior examined here cannot possibly refute the deeply held beliefs on which such cataclysmic stories are based. However, the evidence does not support the pejorative view of Latina reproduction-related behavior. Latinas do not begin sexual activities at a relatively early age, nor do they have relatively more sexual partners than Anglo women. While they may have their first child a couple of years younger than

Anglo women, on average they are over twenty years old when they do so.[19] And most Latinas have used birth-control pills at some point in their lives. These findings are not evidence for out-of-control reproductive behavior.

Moreover, Latinas are not static when it comes to fertility. They, like other women in the United States, Mexico, and the world in general, have experienced dramatic declines in fertility. In terms of the number of children ever born to a woman, Latinas in Orange County compare favorably with Latinas nationally. All Latinas have fewer than 2.0 children per woman. Mexicans who immigrated to the United States as adults and second- and third-generation Mexican Americans (U.S.-born) had fewer children, on average, than their counterparts nationally. All U.S.-born Latinas had almost the same number of children as Anglo women nationally, a low 1.28 children per woman. These findings suggest that reproductive behavior can vary among Latinas as their life experiences change. Future research could determine in greater ethnographic detail how context and life experiences influence reproductive behavior among Latinas.

Multivariate analysis suggests that several factors influence the number of children women have, factors that are as, if not more, important than being Latina or Anglo. Age, education, and marital status consistently predict whether women have more or fewer children. In addition, increasing facility with English, perhaps because it increases sources of knowledge about reproduction control, leads to fewer children among Latinas. Ethnicity was an important, but not a statistically significant, variable for understanding fertility differentials in the eighteen to forty-four age group. This is important given the theoretical discussion on stratified reproduction, which emphasizes that Latinas in general are poorer and have less access to health services than Anglos.

How do these empirical findings and their interpretation "speak to" the politics of Latina reproduction? The discourse surrounding Latina reproduction is actually about more than reproduction: it is also about reinforcing a characterization of Anglos as the legitimate Americans who are being supplanted demographically by less legitimate Latinos. A recurring theme in this discourse is the image of Latinas and their "comparatively high" fertility as a threat to the Anglo population, a powerful image that provides fuel for political actions such as California's Proposition 187. As such an image becomes part of "common sense," it makes it difficult to interpret events from different perspectives. For example, the politics of Latina fertility have obscured a rather dramatic story of reproduction over the last thirty years. Latinas and Anglos both have fewer children today than they did three decades ago. This trend toward fewer children is not peculiar to the United States; it is found in most of the world, with the industrialized nations having the lowest birth rates.

In the discourse on Latina fertility, comparisons assume that the extreme decline in birth rates among Anglo women is a positive value against which equally dramatic declines among Latinas inevitably come up short. Latina fertility seems destined to be viewed as a "glass half empty." An unasked question is: at what point do extremely low birth rates become problematic? The implications of falling birth rates was the subject of a recent *Los Angeles Times* headline: "Nation's Birthrate Drops to Its Lowest Level since 1909" (Zitner 2003). The implications have to do with family structure, how communities spend money, how the nation finances retirement, and pressure for immigration.

What are the implications of fertility rates well below zero population growth and the increasingly high value placed on having ever fewer children, especially in industrialized societies? At the present time, a pattern of extreme fertility decline in industrialized nations increases pressure for immigration to satisfy labor demands and to slow down national population declines. Latina fertility levels may be more reasonable from a societal point of view than the continually lower fertility rates among Americans in general and white women in particular.

From an anthropological perspective, comparisons are relative and reflect the taken-for-granted values of the person or society doing the comparison. Shifting assumptions that valorize white women's fertility levels no matter how low they drop would alter the way Latina fertility is represented. Rather than Latinas being characterized as having "comparatively high" birth rates, Anglo women may be characterized as having "comparatively low" birth rates. Would it be just as possible to make the following observation: the abnormally *low* fertility rates of Anglo women are leading to demographic changes and increased pressure for immigration? In Japan, where women have slightly higher fertility rates (1.38 children per woman) than Anglo women in the United States, there are rewards for families who produce more than two children (French 2000; *Newsweek* 2000, "Perspectives" 23). On the other hand, given the fertility rate of some European countries, the U.S. rate is "comparatively high"; for example, it is 19 percent higher than Spain's 1.07 mean children per woman (Wools 2000). Should one therefore describe U.S. fertility as pathologically high in comparison to that of Spanish women?

This shift would refocus the discourse on Latina reproduction. Rather than singling out Latinas and their "fertility problem" as the cause of negative demographic changes (proportionally fewer Anglos), more attention might be paid to understanding the social, economic, and cultural influences on decreasing fertility among all women. It might also spur a societywide discussion about the relationship between fertility and immigration—and the value of children for the reproduction of a nation's population.

Notes

1. With passage of major reforms in the nation's civil-rights and immigration laws, 1965 was a watershed year in U.S. history. It also marked the beginning of the most recent period of large-scale immigration.
2. Chavez 1997; Chock 1996; Elena Rebeca Gutiérrez 1999; Hondagneu-Sotelo 1995; Tamar D. Wilson 2000; Zavella 1997b. In the late nineteenth and early twentieth centuries, the period of the last large wave of immigration, the politics of reproduction were also central to anti-immigrant discourses, most notably in the eugenics movement (Gould 1981; Marks 2002; Roberts 1997a).
3. In essence, I use my research on media representations of immigration-related issues (Chavez 2001) to raise questions that are examined through the use of empirical data collected in another research project I was also involved in (Chavez et al. 1995; Chavez et al. 1997; Chavez et al. 2001). Although the two research projects were independent, the use of one research project to generate research questions for analysis with data from another exemplifies the serendipitous possibilities and even benefits of combining research in this way. The data on Latina fertility and reproduction were collected for a study of cancer and Latinas and not with the thought of refuting a public discourse on Latina fertility. The Orange County data can also be compared to national data to pinpoint differences and similarities between the local and the national.
4. See Elena Rebeca Gutiérrez 1999 for a thorough discussion of the racial politics of Latina reproduction.
5. For research on sterilization of Latinas, see Iris Lopez 1998; Vélez-Ibañez 1980; Vélez-Ibañez 1999.
6. See Tamar D. Wilson 2000 for an in-depth discussion of Latina reproduction in relation to control of immigration from Mexico.
7. The magazines used in the research were *American Heritage, Time, Newsweek, U.S. News and World Report, New Republic, The Nation, National Review, Atlantic Monthly, Business Week*, and *The Progressive*.
8. The cooperation rate is defined as the number of completed interviews divided by the sum of the completed interviews and refusals by eligible women: 1,225/(1,225 + 336).
9. For a detailed discussion of methods and a summary of general findings, see Chavez et al. 1997; Hubbell et al. 1995a; Hubbell et al. 1997.
10. The t-value was -3.71 ($p = <0.001$).
11. The t-value was .63 ($p = .530$) for U.S.-born Latinas and -5.07 ($p = <0.001$) for Latina immigrants.
12. The t-value was 8.78 ($p = <0.001$).
13. The t-value for U.S.-born Latinas was 1.61 ($p = 0.11$) and for Latina immigrants was 10.36 ($p = <0.001$).

14 The t-value was 6.78 (p = <0.001) for Latinas generally, 4.11 (p = <0.001) for U.S.-born Latinas, and 6.90 (p = <0.001) for Latina immigrants.
15 X^2 = <0.0001.
16 This was statistically significant, with a t-value of −2.14 (p = 0.033).
17 This was statistically insignificant, with a t-value of .30 (p = 0.768).
18 This was also statistically insignificant, with a t-value of −1.08 (p = 0.280).
19 This is not to minimize the issue of teenage pregnancies. Latinas have relatively more teen births than Anglo and non-Hispanic African Americans, but here, too, there has been a decline. Pregnancy rates for black and white teenagers between fifteen and nineteen years of age fell 23 and 26 percent respectively from 1990 to 1997. Latina teen pregnancy rates only began falling in 1994, but they fell 11 percent from that time to 1997 (Ventura et al. 2001). These data do not indicate marital status, the father's involvement, or extended family relations for the mother and child, important factors when considering life opportunities.

Illegal Status and Social Citizenship: Thoughts on Mexican Immigrants in a Postnational World

ADELAIDA R. DEL CASTILLO

✳ As a preliminary statement on unauthorized immigrant status and the making and practice of social citizenship in the state, this essay refers to unauthorized or undocumented Mexicans living in the United States as agents of economic, social, and cultural consequence and as individual rights-holders.[1] This approach reconceptualizes the undocumented immigrant as a human person and acknowledges the practice of social citizenship by illegal immigrants through their creation of community in host countries. That undocumented Mexican immigrants have for generations created community and practiced citizenship without consent in the United States questions the fixity of political communities. The unauthorized enactment of social citizenship by those outside the state as well as the application of a human-rights discourse to the situation of undocumented Mexican immigrants remove the latter from the parameters of the state and invite a postnational approach to the challenges posed by undocumented immigrants.

The remaking of civic identity is perhaps what Hannah Arendt (1951) had in mind when she referred to the global conditions of the past century as marked by stateless persons, refugees, and those deprived of rights. Jürgen Habermas (1992) envisions an emergent world citizenship ushered in by a greater human democracy. In Europe notions of a "citizen's Europe" are being used to create a citizenship that extends beyond the nation-state to a European Community. In San Diego, where I live, the constant presence of Mexican immigrants creates my shared community: I eat their food, listen to their music, speak their language, watch their media, know their manners, and hire their labor.

Living on the unitedstatesian side of the border, one is daily reminded of the marks of privilege: legal status, an overprotected political border, and the benefit of social entitlements denied illegal immigrants who help to pay for them through taxes.[2] At times, particularly when the economy is precarious, to live in San Diego is to live on the badlands of a moral geography (Shapiro 1994) where vigilante nativist groups take measures of their own to prevent illegal immigration. This fear of and mobilization against unauthorized immigrants reveals an outside presence within the state that contests territoriality and disrupts normative procedures of membership in the nation-state (Brubaker 1989; Soysal 1994, 1996).[3] For more than a decade, theorists have turned their attention to the theoretical, practical, and unintended consequences of the movement of immigrant populations to the nation-state.[4] Of special interest are the meaning and construction of citizenship status and the possible redundancy of the nation-state to this process (Brubaker 1989; Wallace 1990). Anthropological interest in the human rights of immigrant workers is in part the outcome of the humanitarian concern of social scientists who have lived among them or worked with them, or who are themselves descendants of immigrants from Mexico or other countries. Attention to global interconnectedness and the discourse on borderlands would seem to encourage a global, transnational defense of the undocumented immigrant once this individual is perceived as a human person entitled to rights.

I argue that Mexican immigrants practice a kind of citizenship in the United States that results in an expression of social rights or *social citizenship*. In doing so they defy the state's political and judicial prerogatives and challenge fundamental standards of civil society, nationhood, and national borders by operating on a "postnational" or beyond-the-state level (Kearney 1991; Soysal 1994). Postnational citizenship, or the practice of creating community and the utilization of social rights in the host country, consists mostly of informal, sometimes makeshift, activities at the local level that suggest a civic identity and social citizenship made possible by the benefits and government largesse of the welfare state.[5] That is to say, in a liberal democratic society, where the "citizen" is reproduced through cultural norms, civic education, and cultural resources (Bridges 1994), unauthorized immigrants reproduce cultural and social citizenship primarily through the deployment of survival strategies in the host country. These strategies involve the use of established cultural norms, resources, and institutions, but may also involve informal networks of social service and resources. Such is the outcome of lived life by immigrant populations acting out daily-life aspects of global events and demographic changes often caused by the very nation-states to which they immigrate (Sassen-Koob 1982).

Citizenship

Political citizenship in Western liberal democracies could be described as the modern equivalent of the feudal privilege and inherited status that greatly enhanced one's life chances (Carens 1987). But life chances for outsiders may not be the objective of principles of citizenship that traditionally emphasize politicolegal membership in a community based on ascription (place of birth) or line of descent (ethnic identity).[6] Ethnic homogeneity as a basis of citizenship may have an unsure future as societies become more and more diverse through the influx of guest workers, asylum seekers, refugees, and illegal immigrants, as well as the shifting of national boundaries and, in Germany, postcommunist reunification. Some would argue that the development of a West German identity has resulted in the exclusion of long-term foreign residents as well as ethnic Germans from the former German Democratic Republic (Fulbrook 1996). Ascriptive citizenship, too, is perceived as problematic in a democratic society. Peter Schuck and Rogers Smith, for example, argue that American ascriptive citizenship is contrary to the democratic exercise of choice: "In its purest form, the principle of *ascription* holds that one's political membership is entirely and irrevocably determined by some objective circumstance—in this case, birth within a particular sovereign's allegiance or jurisdiction" (1985, 4).

According to this conception, human preferences do not affect political membership; only the natural, immutable circumstances of one's birth are considered relevant. These authors contend that American citizenship calls for "consensual citizenship" as more faithful to the spirit of choice that inspired the founding of the incipient United States. Schuck and Smith argue that this country's Founding Fathers intended for individual consent to decide political affiliation based on the free choices of individual citizens. This interpretation, they insist, is more consistent with the country's "commitment to consent" and has implications for how citizenship status should be established if the country's pledge to free individual choice is to be honored. Citizenship status, then, should not be based on birthright (which is imposed without the individual's consent), but rather on a process of mutual consent between the national community and the individual. Lastly, Yasemin Soysal (1994, 1996) believes that future conceptualizations of citizenship will have to consider more seriously supranational phenomena such as the growth of international migration, the intervention of international organizations, and the moral weight of universal-human-rights advocacy. Soysal argues, for example, that Turkish guest workers in Europe operate on a postnational level of citizenship rights. My own interpretation of postnational citizenship draws from her work and returns to the question of life chances by addressing the matter of universal human rights for the undocumented immigrant.[7]

Social Citizenship

More than half a century ago, T. H. Marshall (1950) conceptualized citizenship as evolving from a combination of civil, political, and social elements in the eighteenth, nineteenth, and twentieth centuries. All three elements refer to rights: the political element refers to the right to participate in the exercise of political power; the civil element refers to rights considered indispensable for individual freedom, such as freedom of speech, religion, and thought, physical liberty, and the right to own property; and the social element refers to rights associated with the welfare of a people, such as the right to a decent standard of living, leisure, and goods, the right to work, and the right to social services such as education, healthcare, housing, unemployment insurance, pensions, social security, and so on. Social rights address a minimum expectation of standards, goods, and services to be anticipated from the welfare state, that is, the liberal democratic state organized to provide these (Roche 1992). Social citizenship also assumes that individuals have a duty to work in order to generate tax revenues to pay for the benefit of social rights and the welfare state (Marshall 1950; Roche 1992). Illegal immigrants both benefit from the social services of the host country and fulfill the duty of full citizens to create tax revenues through their labor to pay for these services.

Social rights are sensitive to political and economic structural changes, including those caused by industrialization and postindustrialization. As Maurice Roche contends (1992), the global organization of capitalism has undermined social citizenship for full citizens, as is evident in changing quality-of-life standards; however, this same phenomenon presents possibilities for the social rights of noncitizens as well. In less-developed countries with uneven economies such as Mexico's, the postindustrial presence of capital has helped to "push" labor out by making it superfluous. In Mexico's case, much of this labor has sought work, albeit illegally, in the healthier economy of its neighbor, the United States. Illegal residence in the United States has, in turn, made it possible for immigrants to access the services, resources, and higher standard of living of the welfare state, even if procured without consent.

This access to social citizenship by unauthorized immigrants has not escaped the notice of the Right and forms part of its nativist discourses. In 1994 the growing presence of illegal Mexican immigrants in California spurred right-wing groups and their supporters to push for the passage of Proposition 187, denying illegal immigrants access to indispensable social services, including education and healthcare.[8] The measure passed with 59 percent of the vote, reflecting citizens' fears that illegal immigrants were a burden on the state's social-service system despite their economic contributions to the state's economy. A study by RAND Corporation's National Defense Research Institute found that immigrant labor, both legal and illegal, is responsible for the majority of the state's labor-force growth, outpacing the economic growth for the rest of the nation. California's employment growth is directly attributed to the lower cost of immigrant labor relative to the cost of native labor. The same study found that for the period 1991–1993 there were no significant differences between natives and immigrants in their use of public services (McCarthy and Vernez 1998, 29–45).[9] By refusing to acknowledge these economic benefits to the state, California's electorate denies unauthorized immigrants legal access to their social rights, even though they fulfill the social duties of full citizenship by working and paying taxes. Almost two decades ago specialists warned that Mexican immigrant labor to this country would, in effect, constitute a subsidy to the U.S. economy, representing a transfer of human capital and an expansion of this country's reserve army of labor (Bustamante and Cockcroft 1983). These concerns draw attention to the social and moral dimension of universal human rights.

Illegal Immigrants and Postnational Citizenship

Postnational discussions of the nation-state stress a transnational community's relations to institutional, juridical, and spatial notions rather than to bounded political territories.[10] In the late twentieth century, the nation-state in Europe and the Americas took preliminary steps toward open borders and economies to facilitate economic, commercial, labor, and cultural collaboration between nations.[11] Latin America established a common market community that would also allow for cultural exchanges. The Mercado Comun del Sur was established in 1991 by Argentina, Brazil, Paraguay, and Uruguay; its integration offers social, economic, cultural, and political postnational relations and open borders between its member states.[12] In contrast, the North American Free Trade Agreement between the United States, Mexico, and Canada has yet to set provisions for the free movement of labor between its member states.[13] Despite this, illegal Mexican immigrants, through the exercise of social rights in the host country and unauthorized travel across national borders, have unintentionally set a precedent of postnational participation and cultural exchange in North America. Though immigrants' survival strategies must be resilient enough to withstand the pressure of socioeconomic, political, cultural, and moral stigmatization by the broader civic community, postnational citizenship should not be seen as the outcome of premeditated maneuverings by immigrant groups, but rather as the unintended consequence of economic, social, and political phenomena.

This local-level reproduction of citizenship by unauthorized immigrants contributes to a civic identity that does not necessarily assume the equality of the full citizen in the host country, although it does assert the natural freedom of all human persons to pursue and make a living wherever possible. The civilizing cultural practices of undocumented immigrant communities contest civic discourses that privilege only full citizens as special members of society and as free and equal individuals. For the full citizen, this free and equal status is obtained through participation in activities related to the public sphere. For the illegal immigrant, the public sphere is flexible, local, and informal.

Though liberal political theory does not invite conceptualizations of citizenship without a nation-state framework, ethnographic research among undocumented Mexican immigrants shows the generation of what can be considered *social citizenship* patterns by those who fall outside the parameters of the nation-state. How is this possible? Ethnographies are well suited for capturing the meaning and particulars of lived experience over time because of their use of participant observation and extensive periods of field research. The cultures of groups and individuals in Mexico have been the subject of numerous anthropological studies for well over half a century.[14] Their immigrant travels to and settlement in the United States have also generated ethnographic studies. For at least a generation, anthropologists have followed the lives, settlement patterns, and survival strategies of undocumented Mexican immigrants in this country.[15] Ethnographic studies suggest that such immigrants enter the country illegally, secure employment, reunite their families or form new ones, establish and sustain households, and look after the needs and interests of their communities. This settlement process is an important aspect of immigrants' self-perception as community members who have adjusted both socially and emotionally (Chavez 1991).

Tarascans in Southern Illinois

Recruited mainly as temporary migrant workers from Cherán, Michoacán, Mexicans came to southern Illinois in the late 1960s to assist in the labor-intensive harvesting of apples and peaches, the region's principal commodity crops. The recruitment of lone male migrants to the area discouraged permanent settlement until wives and other family members began to migrate in the late 1970s. Now, according to Alicia Chavira-Prado (1992, n.d.), Tarascan immigrants in southern Illinois are predominantly undocumented, Spanish-speaking, and impoverished. The division of labor in migrant camps ranks undocumented immigrant workers below legal migrants and locals, and undocumented immigrant women below everyone else. Most often this means that undocumented Tarascan women assume the lowest paid, most physically demanding jobs in the packing houses and double as a reserve army of labor.

As if to duplicate being-in-the-world in forms reminiscent of sender communities, Tarascans in southern Illinois attempt to buffer the troubles and challenges of newcomer families by forming networks of mutual aid and trust *(confianza)* that make possible loyalties and obligations between kin and ritual kin (Chavira 1988; Chavira-Prado 1992, n.d.). The material assistance, access to services and resources, and exposure to knowledge and information that result from these networks of aid speak to the paramount importance of becoming engaged in community as fictive kin, *compadres* (godparents), *ahijados* (godchildren), and friends, contributing to one's civic responsibility to community.

Though not full members of the body politic, Tarascans nonetheless appropriate rights and services for their communities and participate as individuals in society. They find work, settle, establish viable cultural communities, comply with the law, pay taxes, send their children to public schools, and make use of public and private resources by taking advantage of church, childcare, medical, and welfare services. They are, in effect, practicing social citizenship. Not surprisingly, scholars suggest that social, civic, economic, and even political rights have come to be based on residency and labor, not citizenship status, causing the erosion of distinctions between citizen and alien (Schuck 1989). Adversarial political forces in this country intent on generating anti-immigrant legislation suggest that denial of legal status indeed does not preclude immigrant access to the social rights of full citizens.

Women and the Creation of Community

Studies also describe the impact of gender difference on immigrants' adjustment to the host environment (Hondagneu-Sotelo 1994; Hirsch 1998a; Ibarra in this volume). For more than a generation, women have represented as much as 52 percent of the undocumented immigrant population in the United States (Simon and DeLey 1986). Gender-appropriate norms, their performance and pretense, allow Mexican women in Mexico an inordinate degree of control over the family (Del Castillo 1993). In the United States, Mexican immigrant women make possible access to institutions and agencies that serve the family such as schools, clinics, and religious groups.[16]

Gender difference, for example, is significant to the survival and adaptive strategies of immigrant Tarascan communities in southern Illinois (Chavira 1988; Chavira-Prado 1992). Women assist in the recreation of community through the use and maintenance of sociocultural patterns of interaction based on the social networks of the sending community (Chavira-Prado n.d.).[17] They also enhance the quality of life for family members by making use of community resources such as healthcare for U.S.-born children and pregnant women, church charities, school lunch programs, and day-care centers. Women broker the goods, services, and opportunities that these programs offer to their families by gathering information about them and testing their quality and usefulness through their social networks (Chavira-Prado 1992, n.d.). By the late 1990s, Tarascan undocumented laborers and their families had established communities in or adjacent to Cobden, Murphysboro, and Carbondale by purchasing homes or plots of land. Cobden public schools now offer bilingual programs and a Migrant Head Start program, churches in all three communities offer at least one service in Spanish, healthcare literature is bilingual, Mexican food products are sold in some stores, video stores stock films in Spanish, and Cobden's community park serves as a public space for Mexican families to gather on weekend afternoons (Chavira-Prado n.d.).

The Tarascan data attest to the continued importance of women in a transnational context by showing that (a) immigrant communities without women lack a sociocultural basis for growth, (b) women integrate themselves into male immigrant communities by providing resources and services not readily available to the men, (c) women make use of subsistence work as well as public and private subsidy resources to compensate for diminished male incomes during low employment periods, and (d) women act as mediators of sociocultural conflict (Chavira 1988; Chavira-Prado 1992, n.d.).

The U.S. Constitution ensures the rights of citizens and noncitizens alike, and the state is responsible for enforcing these rights within its territory. Therefore, "citizenship gives rise to no distinctive claim" (Carens 1987).[18] The state is entrusted and expected to enforce the rights that individuals already enjoy by birthright. But human identity is not neutral. The political culture that formally declares human beings as "free and equal" decidedly adheres to a practice of *preferences* that does not encompass everyone. It speaks a moral language that may rank and discriminate according to class, ethnicity, gender (Bridges 1994), and legal status. Excluded from *political citizenship*, illegal immigrant workers have been excluded from a public discourse that erases the value of their lives and makes possible egregious acts of violence against them. One has only to recall the brutal beating of undocumented immigrants by Riverside and Los Angeles police officers caught on television some years ago, the forced detention and enslavement of undocumented farmworkers by growers, and the murder of undocumented immigrants by private U.S. citizens. These and related acts represent a gross violation of the human rights of illegal immigrants. Therefore, advocacy on behalf of undocumented immigrant workers for the defense of their human rights before an international authority seems a rational and necessary step.

Universal Human Rights

Since 1945 the international community has recognized and formally sought to establish human-rights norms as part of customary international law.[19] These rights are considered a birthright because the human person is perceived to be rational, moral, and inherently endowed with dignity, worth, equality, and freedom. By virtue of their humanity, individual persons share equally inalienable and inviolable rights that entitle them to goods, services, and opportunities to be provided by the political community and society in general.[20] The national and international support given human-rights groups and their causes attests to the moral force of these arguments.

It is important to recognize that human-rights norms privilege the individual rights of the person over those of national membership (Soysal 1996) and over the claims of a sovereign people, since these operate within limits set by individual human rights. Not surprisingly, human-rights claims can create tension between the rights of the individual and the will of the people in liberal democracies when the latter violates the human dignity and fundamental freedoms of the human person (Donnelly 2001).

Scholars (Soysal 1994, 1996; Weaver 1988) note that the articulation and elaboration of human rights on a global scale has worked to bestow many citizenship rights and privileges on populations not belonging to a national group, such as immigrants. Undocumented Mexican immigrants in the United States acquire access to the rights and privileges of citizens when they adapt to the host country and create community, even though they do so without consent. Once one frames the plight of undocumented immigrants in the context of universal human rights, one must see them as free and rights-bearing individuals entitled to pursue a life of human dignity through the right of mobility and the right to work in just and favorable conditions (United Nations General Assembly 1948, Article 23).[21] Already the practice of social citizenship without the benefit of political citizenship places the undocumented Mexican immigrant outside the purview of the state, but a human-rights discourse situates the undocumented immigrant within an international community capable of championing his or her rights even though it is the duty of the state to promote, respect, and protect all human rights and freedoms. A human-rights discourse helps to redefine the status and expand the rights of undocumented immigrants. Though rights do not in themselves constitute a legal tradition, human rights speak to a particular moral attitude or notions of "right reason" that apply to all human beings (R. J. Vincent 1992, 252–53). In this sense, immigrants, even if illegal, are rights-holders.

Not surprisingly, the United Nations-sponsored World Conference against Racism (WCAR), held in 1978 and 1983, included "those who are undocumented" on its list of migrant workers in need of human rights protection (Grange 2001). The 1978 WCAR Programme of Action called for migrant workers "to be given treatment no less favourable than nationals," including "contracts, right to reside, trade union activities, access to tribunals, communication in own language, franchise in local elections, right of family reunion, social security, retirement pensions, healthcare, educational opportunities, preservation of cultural identity, acquisition of property within and outside country" (Grange 2001). The 1983 WCAR Programme of Action echoed these requests and also called for migrants to have access to courts and tribunals, remuneration equal to that of nationals, and equal treatment regarding social security and retirement pensions; it further stipulated that children of migrant workers should receive education in their mother tongue and on aspects of their culture. In 1997, however, the U.N. Seminar on Immigration, Racism, and Racial Discrimination noted that a 1990 international convention to protect the human rights of migrant workers was a "near failure" because few states had ratified the agreement. In 2001 the WCAR omitted the term *undocumented* when it listed migrant workers in need of protection (although it did refer to "victims of illegal trafficking").

Still, for more than a generation, nongovernmental organizations have made use of human-rights arguments to question intrastate and cross-border violations of people's rights, even though previously (immediately after World War II) these claims had been the exclusive function of the nation-state. While civic or national rights can only be realized by "a people," one need not belong to a nation to benefit from human rights, since these are not predicated on nationality or territoriality nor based on distinctions of legal or illegal status. Consequently, the growing ability of individuals and non–state agencies to make international claims for the human rights of groups has consequences beyond the state (Jacobson 1996). When immigrant workers and their sympathizers take to the streets to protest violations of their rights and denial of access to social citizenship (as was the intent of California's Proposition 187), they, too, utilize the urban space of the state as an institutional platform from which to address a broader international and constitutional order. In this way, illegal immigrants and their supporters expand the notion of "the people" and challenge the belief that legal citizenship (or nationhood) is vital to the practice of full rights.

Just how international human-rights ethics and institutions are impinging on the nation-state remains a matter of contention. Some scholars believe that, as David Jacobson says, "the state is becoming less constituted by 'the people' in the face of human rights codes and agencies" (1996, 2). That is, the devaluation of citizenship favors the importance of international human rights. Within the nation-state itself, nationality is more and more often reconceptualized to mean *nationality as a human right* and not as a principle that reinforces state sovereignty. There are those who believe that this suggests the nation-state may no longer adequately frame the labor and social parameters of citizenship status in a globally integrated arena.[22] Some theorists have gone so far as to argue that the nation-state has become historically obsolete.[23] Others prefer to speak of rights and obligations "nested" within distinct political communities that challenge exclusive notions of state sovereignty.[24]

Conclusion

I have argued that undocumented Mexican immigrant communities unintentionally undermine the authority of the state to regulate social citizenship status when these communities strive to adapt to life in the United States. They do so by making use of the resources and benefits offered by the welfare state to which they contribute economically with their labor and taxes, helping to keep state economies such as California's afloat. Access to the benefits of social citizenship makes the latter of greater use and value to unauthorized immigrant communities than political citizenship, which remains an exclusionary function of the state.

The concept of a weaker role for the state as arbiter of labor and social citizenship challenges notions of the fixed political boundaries of the state; the United States ultimately cannot contain the undocumented immigration of Mexicans in pursuit of a decent wage and standard of living. This quest by undocumented immigrants raises questions concerning universal human rights. Once again, this contests the power of the state as necessarily the final arbiter of the human rights of unauthorized communities within its boundaries.

With the growing acceptance of human-rights issues as part of international politics in the past thirty years, the displacement of state power by international agencies acting on behalf of a broader international society and a greater good has occurred on several occasions. The presence of unauthorized Mexican immigrants in the United States and their practice of social citizenship have too often been countered with stark violations of their human rights. The protection of undocumented communities is better undertaken by international organizations, given that human rights have increasing moral and political authority that goes beyond that of the nation-state.[25] That is, the state can be held accountable to an international community with the power (however limited) to redress wrongs.

Finally, I have suggested that state sovereignty in the United States has been disrupted by the unauthorized practice of social citizenship by illegal immigrant Mexicans, forcing a rethinking of social, political, and human-rights and nationhood status. This being the case, transnational political entities may in the future have to replace more and more functions of the state in response to the growing number of floating populations who traffic the globe transnationally. The emergent twenty-first century will no doubt see a greater shift from national to transnational institutional standardization and legislation, facilitating the formation of a kind of "world citizenship" to accommodate the rights and dignity of one of the least protected populations: undocumented immigrant workers.

Notes

1. I use *unauthorized*, *undocumented*, and *illegal* as interchangeable designations for immigrants without legal status in the host country.
2. Kearney (1991, 55, 71n9) has coined the term *unitedstatesian* based on the Spanish usage of *estadounidense* to refer to people of the United States. Mexicans have told me that the term *American* includes all peoples who inhabit the Americas, including Mexicans; therefore, they prefer the more accurate *estadounidense* when referring to citizens of the United States.
3. My interest in this topic is based on my experience as an observer of transnationalism on the U.S.-Mexican border, as well as on the growing literature on notions of citizenship and the more recent anthropological interest in the human rights of immigrant workers. See, for example, Downing and Kushner 1988; Weaver 1988; Del Castillo 1997; Nagengast and Vélez-Ibañez 2004; Vélez-Ibañez 2004.
4. This literature grew substantially in the 1990s. For some of the literature prior to this period, see Schmitter 1979; Schuck and Smith 1985; Turner 1986; Carens 1987; Brubaker 1989.
5. Some theorists argue that membership in the welfare state is far more significant than political membership, which they see as declining in importance. See Schuck 1989.
6. Ethnic identity links a community of people integrated geographically or by shared culture and ethnicity, as in the case of Germany.
7. See Cesarani and Fulbrook 1996.
8. Proposition 187 made illegal aliens ineligible for public services, public healthcare (unless an emergency), and public education at the elementary, secondary, and postsecondary levels. In March 1998 a federal judge ruled most of Proposition 187

unconstitutional for several reasons, including a prior Supreme Court decision *(Plyler v. Doe*, 1982) that entitles all children under eighteen to public education regardless of their immigration status. The court cited the general principle that immigration law is a federal, not a state-level, issue. The court did uphold the provision of Proposition 187 that makes the manufacture, distribution, sale, or use of false citizenship or residence documents a felony offense.

9 These services include cash assistance, nutrition, health, and housing programs, with the exception of school lunch and breakfast programs for the children of immigrant parents.

10 Similar notions were anticipated by medieval concepts of civil participation wherein society was not identical with its political organization. G. W. F. Hegel, too, conceptualized civil society as existing beyond the state (Taylor 1990). In contrast, Schuck and Smith (1985) attribute the origins of birthright citizenship to notions of feudal status, sovereignty, and allegiance.

11 For questions of cultural significance and the creation of the European Community see Shore and Black 1996.

12 See Ferrer 1996.

13 A discussion of NAFTA's impact on Mexico's economy is offered by Carolyn Wise (1998). For a comparison between the common market economies of North America and Europe, see Gianaris 1998.

14 See Redfield 1930; Oscar Lewis 1951, 1961; Cancian 1965; Diaz 1966; Foster 1967; Kearney 1972; Chiñas 1973; Romanucci-Ross 1973; Kemper 1977; Lomnitz 1977; Vélez-Ibañez 1983; Chant 1985; Behar 1993; Del Castillo 1993; Gutmann 1996.

15 See Dinerman 1978; Melville 1981; L. Chavez 1985, 1988, 1990, 1991; Kearney 1986; Chavira 1988; Chavira-Prado 1992, n.d.; M. O'Connor 1990; Villar 1990; Goodson-Lawes 1993; Hondagneu-Sotelo 1994; Hirsch 1998a, and in this volume; Pessar 1998; Ibarra in this volume. The recipient of one-third of all immigrants (legal and illegal) to this country, California is an important destination for migrants. Between 1990 and 1995, 1.5 million immigrants entered the state, bringing California's immigrant population to a total of 8 million in 1995. Of the 5 million illegal immigrant residents in this country, an estimated 2 million reside in California. For the past forty years, the influx of Mexican immigrants has represented the single largest immigrant group in California, peaking in the 1980s. Presently, 50 percent of all immigrants to California are Mexican, and Mexico is the primary source of illegal immigration to the United States. See McCarthy and Vernez 1997, 1998.

16 In California, K–12 school enrollment increased by one-third in 1996, with much of this increase attributed to the entry of immigrant children and children born in the United States to immigrant parents. See McCarthy and Vernez 1998.

17 In his study of social networks, *Rituals of Marginality*, Carlos Vélez-Ibañez (1983) documents the importance of these activities in a Mexican context.

18 This is not to deny the body politic where citizenship means political membership or where sovereign people are the source of the supreme authority of the nation in a liberal democracy.

19 In 1945 the Covenant of the League of Nations expressed concern for human rights.

International human-rights instruments adopted by the United Nations include the Universal Declaration of Human Rights adopted by the U.N. General Assembly in 1948; the International Covenant on Economic, Social, and Cultural Rights (1976); the International Covenant on Civil and Political Rights (1976); the Optional Protocol to the International Covenant on Civil and Political Rights (1976); the Second Optional Protocol to the International Covenant on Civil and Political Rights (1991); the Vienna Declaration and Programme of Action (1993); and the human-rights provisions of the Helsinki Final Act (1975).

20 The International Bill of Human Rights opens with: "All human beings are born free and equal in dignity and rights. They are endowed with reason and conscience and should act towards one another in a spirit of brotherhood." The Universal Declaration of Human Rights presents the "inherent dignity and . . . equal and inalienable rights of all members of the human family" as the basis of "freedom, justice and peace in the world."

21 Other human rights relevant to undocumented Mexican immigrants include the rights to self-determination; life; freedom of movement and choice of residence; protection of the family unit; equal access to courts and tribunals; presumption of innocence until proven guilty; equal protection under the law; freedom from torture and cruel, inhumane, or degrading treatment or punishment; freedom from slavery or servitude; liberty and security of person. In addition, there are rights to one's own culture, to leave any country and enter one's own, and so on. See Weaver 1988.

22 This would not apply to declarations of war and hostility by the state toward terrorist groups perceived as a threat to its national security and, by consequence (unintended or not), the persecution of immigrant groups with which terrorists are identified. Such now appears to be the case for Arab Muslims in the United States, thousands of whom are being held without due process since the destruction of the World Trade Center on 11 September 2001.

23 For discussion of the transnational movement of labor in a postnational context, see Soysal 1994; Cesarani and Fulbrook 1996; Jacobson 1996. For discussion of the nation-state as moribund, see Wallace 1990.

24 See Donnelly 2001.

25 See Donnelly 2001, 140–42.

"Looking Like a Lesbian":
The Organization of Sexual Monitoring
at the United States–Mexican Border
EITHNE LUIBHEID

✳ While returning by taxicab from Juarez, Mexico, to El Paso, Texas, on 6 January 1960, Sara Harb Quiroz was stopped for questioning by an immigration-service agent. Quiroz was not a newcomer to the United States. She had acquired permanent U.S. residency in July 1954, at the age of twenty, and lived in El Paso, where she worked as a domestic. It is not known why she traveled to Juarez on that particular occasion. But her parents and her nine-year-old daughter lived there. Other familial, economic, and social ties also drew the residents of El Paso to Juarez.

Documentation that explains why Quiroz was stopped no longer exists. But Albert Armendáriz, the attorney who handled her case, believes she was stopped because of her appearance. "Based on looks. Based on the way she dressed. The way she acted. The way she talked."[1] In the eyes of the immigration inspector who stopped her, Quiroz seemed like a lesbian. Until as recently as 1990, lesbian immigrants were excludable and deportable from the United States.

Quiroz's case provides a window into immigration-service efforts to identify and exclude foreign-born women who were believed to be lesbians. Some scholars date lesbian and gay exclusion from 1917, when "constitutional psychopathic inferiors," including those with "abnormal sexual instincts," became excludable.[2] However, the most extensive records about immigration-service efforts to police the border against lesbians and gay men date from after the passage of the 1952 McCarren-Walter Act. In anticipation of the act, the Senate Committee of the Judiciary recommended in 1950 that "classes of mental defectives [who are excludable] should be enlarged to include homosexuals and other sex perverts" (U.S. Senate 1950, 345). Although the final wording of the McCarren-Walter Act did not explicitly mention homosexuals, homosexual exclusion was rolled into the provision that barred entry by psychopathic personalities. A senate report explained: "The Public Health Service has advised that the provision for the exclusion of aliens afflicted with psychopathic personality or a mental defect ... is sufficiently broad to provide for the exclusion of homosexuals and sex perverts. This change in nomenclature is not to be constructed in any way as modifying the intent to exclude all aliens who are sexual deviants" (U.S. Senate 1952, 46–48). In 1965 lesbian and gay exclusion was recodified, this time under a provision barring entry by "sexual deviates."

Substantive scholarly analysis has been limited to cases involving men who were alleged by the Immigration and Naturalization Service (INS) to be gay. Little is known about the experiences of women.[3] Quiroz's case, which is the only documented case involving a woman that has been uncovered to date, helps renarrate the history of lesbian and gay immigration exclusion in a way that centers, rather than subsumes, specifically female experiences.[4] In addition, Quiroz's case raises questions about the complexities of mapping histories of immigrant, refugee, and transnational women while using sexual categories that substantially derive their meanings from metropolitan centers (Rose 1995, 74).

This essay's methodological and theoretical frameworks are drawn from Michel Foucault's *The History of Sexuality* (vol. 1). Though Foucault never explicitly addressed immigration, his work argues that sex became something for the state to administer and manage. The nineteenth-century multiplication of discourses about sex unquestionably affected the U.S. immigration system, which took up these discourses and developed procedures for regulating sex in relation to multiform objectives (that concerned not only sex but also gender, race, class, and constructions of nation). Foucault's discussion of how homosexual acts became reconstructed as evidence of the existence of homosexual types illustrates the general process whereby the administration of sex enabled relations of power to become organized and extended.[5] It also draws attention to the specific ways that sexual categorizations became "freight[ed] ... with epistemological and power relations," through which immigration monitoring became organized (Sedgwick 1990, 9). The incorporation of sexual categories into exclusion laws, as well as the development of procedures to detect and deter entry by individuals who fit those categories, is key to how the immigration system came to exclude individuals on the basis of sexuality.[6]

That Quiroz encountered difficulties when entering El Paso because an agent suspected that she was a lesbian clearly demonstrated sexuality functioning as a "dense transfer point for relations of power" at the border (Foucault 1990, 103).[7] To determine whether or not she was in fact a lesbian would only participate in power relations that recirculate and naturalize dominant cultural notions of sexual "types."[8] It is more constructive to problematize how mainstream institutions, including the INS, remain invested in constructing fixed boundaries around what homosexuality "is." Such boundary marking involves operations by which mainstream institutions empower and legitimize themselves while producing diverse minoritized populations.

INS monitoring techniques contributed to construction of the very sexualities against which they claimed to guard the nation.[9] This fact becomes clear when one examines how immigrants came to be designated as excludable on the basis of homosexuality. Since there is no easy way to differentiate lesbians and gay men from heterosexuals, what led certain people to be singled out? Case histories suggest that immigrants came to INS attention as possible lesbians or gay men on the basis of "checkpoints" within the immigration process. These checkpoints served as particularly dense sites where dominant institutions constructed (and individuals contested) the possible meanings of lesbian or gay identity and determined who should be included within these categories.

In thinking through the operation of such checkpoints, one must avoid two common and related mistakes. First, one should not assume that coherent, predefined lesbian or gay identities always existed among immigrant applicants and that the checkpoints simply captured these preformed "queer" subjects. To frame the issue in this way would be to miss the myriad ways that these checkpoints regulated the terms by which formation of identity occurred.[10] Second, and conversely, one must conceptualize lesbian and gay identities as being never reducible to these checkpoints. Though the checkpoints were dense power points in the dominant culture's production and policing of homosexuality, not all (potential) lesbian/gay subjects were equally affected, since lesbian and gay identities are also inflected by race, class, gender, cultural, and religious features that defy the idea that there can be any uniform queer identity. The checkpoints themselves also reflected some degree of bias, capturing males more than females and Latin Americans and Europeans more than Asians. Consequently, in looking at who was liable to become ensnared by these checkpoints, one should never imagine that they represented the totality of lesbian, gay, or queer identities that were passing into the United States.[11]

Some of the richest sources of information about these immigration checkpoints are court records. Almost all of the reconstructed court cases concern men. Very striking are the numbers of men who ended up being targeted by the INS because of criminal convictions related to sexual activity. Writing about German-born Horst Nemetz, who had no criminal record connected to his sexual activities with men, Shannon Minter describes the extent to which male-male sexual practices remain heavily criminalized.

> His denial of public activity [for which he could have been convicted] means that he never made love on a beach, in a car, in a park, or in any of the other quasi-public places in which heterosexual couples occasionally engage in sexual relations. His denial of "recruiting" means that he never sexually propositioned a man in a bar, at a party, on the street, or anywhere outside his home. His denial of ever being arrested or questioned by the police means either that he was fortunate, or that he avoided gay bars, gay bathhouses, gay cruising areas in parks and bathrooms, and other places that gay men informally gather and socialize. It also means he never had the misfortune of expressing sexual interest to an undercover police officer posing as a gay man. (1993, 799)

Court cases confirm that significant numbers of immigrant men came to INS attention on the basis of sexual criminalization.

Although lesbian sexuality was not necessarily more socially acceptable than gay male sexuality, a popular disbelief that women could have sex without the presence of a male penis and the fact that gender, in conjunction with race and class, differentially shaped the acquisition and formation of spaces where women come together to have sex meant that lesbian sexuality was not scrutinized and policed in the same ways as gay male sexuality. As a result, INS criminal-record checks were more likely to affect men, rather than women, who engaged in same-sex activities. Given that lesbian sexual activity is not as heavily policed, how can one map lesbians onto this history of immigration exclusion?

One possibility is that lesbians were relatively unaffected by the historic practices of homosexual exclusion. A second possibility is that indicators other than criminal-record checks were used to identify women who might be lesbians, but given the dearth of known lesbian-exclusion cases, it is difficult to know what these indicators might have been.[12] The Quiroz case provides one (possibly unrepresentative) example.[13]

The lawyer who handled Quiroz's case believes she was stopped because she looked, spoke, and acted "like a lesbian." Quiroz was also unlucky enough to encounter an immigration inspector who had undertaken a personal campaign to identify and expel women who he believed were "sexual deviates."

> There was this fellow who was at the International Bridge.... He had a thing for people, especially women ... who were lesbian, or in his mind were deviates, and met the requirements of the statute [for exclusion]. ... They would go to Mexico on a visit, and on the way back he would send them to secondary [inspection] where he would determine they were ineligible to enter. This officer was very, very good at making people admit that they were sexual deviates.[14]

The importance of appearance is confirmed by testimony that was given to the INS by Quiroz's employer, to the effect that "the respondent usually wore trousers and a shirt when she came to work and that her hair was cut shorter than some women's."[15]

The use of visual appearance to monitor the border against possible entry by lesbians connects to a complex history. A 1952 Public Health Service (PHS) report to Congress mentioned visual appearance as one possible index of homosexuality: "In some instances considerable difficulty may be encountered in substantiating a diagnosis of homosexuality or sexual perversion. In other instances, where the action or behavior of the person *is more obvious, as might be noted in the manner of dress* (so called transvestism [sic] or fetishism) the condition may be more easily substantiated" (U.S. House 1952, 47, emphasis added). This passage suggests that monitoring based on visual appearance operated around the notion of gender inversion—that is, homosexuals could be visually identified by the fact that gay men looked effeminate or lesbians looked masculine.[16]

The PHS formulation connects to a broader cultural history of conceptualizing homosexuality as a problem of one gender being trapped in the other gender's body. Linked to that conceptualization were a range of endeavors to scientifically delineate, in a measurable and absolute way, the difference between homosexual and heterosexual bodies. Jennifer Terry (1990) has documented the activities of the Committee for the Study of Sex Variants, which was active in New York City in the 1930s and 1940s and included "psychiatrists, gynecologists, obstetricians, surgeons, radiologists, neurologists, as well as clinical psychologists, an urban sociologist, a criminal anthropologist, and a former Commissioner of the New York City Department of Corrections" (319). This truly impressive array of professionals, scientists, and academics, connected by their efforts to delineate how the homosexual was distinct from the heterosexual, conducted its research under the assumption that "the female sex variant would exhibit traits of the opposite sex. In other words, she would invert her proper gender role" (321).

> Pathologists looked at skin complexion, fat distribution, coarseness of hair, the condition of the teeth, and commented on the overall facial and bodily structure of each subject. Radiologists took x-rays to determine cranial densities of the skull and "carrying angles" of the pelvis in order to identify anomalous gender characteristics. A dense skull was presumed to be masculine. "Graceful" and "delicate" pelvic bones were feminine.
>
> Endocrinologists measured hormonal levels. . . . Sketches of genitals and breasts were drawn in order to document particular characteristics of sex variance. . . . In analyzing the thirty pages of graphic sketches of breasts and genitals, Dr. Dickinson reported on the general genital differences recognizable in the female sex variant population. He identified ten characteristics which he argued set the sex variant apart from "normal women." (323, 332)

These and other studies were formed around and helped to keep alive the notion that lesbians were visibly different from heterosexuals (and that lesbianism and heterosexuality were opposites). Thus, it was not surprising that immigration officers tried to identify immigrants who might be lesbians by using the index of gender-inverted appearance. Men were similarly assessed.

The notion that lesbian and gay immigrants could be identified on the basis of appearance reflects not only commonalities among homophobia, racism, and sexism but also significant differences in terms of an individual's ability to mediate costs associated with looking different. In framing the issue, bell hooks writes, "While we can acknowledge that gay people of all colors are harassed and suffer exploitation and domination, we also recognize there is a significant difference that arises because of the visibility of dark skin" (1989, 125).

Capturing the process of "straightening up" that many lesbians undertake when they expect to deal with immigration officials, Nice Rodriguez describes altering her appearance, with regard to both sexuality and gender, so as to pass official scrutiny during her migration from the Philippines to Canada.

> On the day of her interview [for a visa at the embassy] she wore a tailored suit but she looked like a man and knew she did not stand a chance.
>
> They did not want masculine women in that underpopulated land. They needed babymakers. . . . Her wife got mascara and lipstick and made her look like a babymaker. During her interview with the consular officer she looked ovulating and fertile so she passed it.

Canada had strict immigration laws, but even bugs could sift through a fine mosquito net. (1992, 35–36)

Straightening up includes practices like growing one's hair and nails, buying a dress, accessorizing, and donning makeup. Clearly, there is privilege in that the visual markers of lesbianism, unlike visual markers of race or gender, can usually be altered or toned down in order to pass homophobic border guards.[17] At the same time, the fact that one *has* to straighten up to avoid a penalty emphasizes that lesbianism *is* a difference. Consequently, Rodriguez suggests, her self-presentation as a fertile woman wearing lipstick and mascara did not erase her lesbian difference, but instead confirmed the "bug"-like status of lesbians within the immigration system. Monitoring the border on the basis of visual appearance does lend itself to lesbian and gay male subversion, yet it also marks out an area where the identity that the INS is trying to contain and expel is also reestablished and reinforced.

The experiences of women of color like Quiroz further complicate analysis of visually-based border monitoring. The visual, or that which gets seen, is driven by and redeploys particular cultural knowledges and blindnesses. The inspector who stopped Quiroz for questioning saw something different about her, but what? Was there really anything different about Quiroz to see? Was the difference he claimed to see really a lesbian difference, or was it another kind of difference that simply got defined as "lesbian" through a combination of procedures and expediencies? What cultural knowledges and blindnesses organized this inspector's regime of seeing such that he singled out Quiroz for investigation? What are the connections between the inspector's suspicion that Quiroz was a sexual deviate and the long U.S. history of viewing and treating the bodies of women of color as sexually other? The use of visual judgment to monitor the border involves levels of complexity that have yet to be unraveled with regard to immigrant women of color with diverse sexualities.

In the context of the El Paso-Juarez border where Quiroz was stopped, the regimes through which Mexican immigrants get visually evaluated are further complicated by the historical processes that imposed that border. Timothy Dunn explains that "for many decades, the [U.S.-Mexico] border was a tenuous social construct, established and maintained by force" (1996, 6). The border, which derived from the Texas Revolution of 1836 and the Mexican War of 1846–1848, was "in large part either ignored or actively contested by *Mexicanos* in the region . . . because it was imposed on them and it disrupted their lives. . . . The full pacification of the region required some 70 years, and involved the prominent use of a variety of coercive measures both by the state and by Anglo groups" (ibid.).

The Border Patrol, created by the Immigration Act of 1924, became a key state institution through which the border was maintained. Border-enforcement efforts have continually legitimated the subordination of Mexican-origin peoples in the region, regardless of whether they were citizens, residents, or immigrants. The scrutiny Quiroz received from immigration-service officials derived from and further extended this history.[18] Immigration-service techniques, which involved atomizing and evaluating her appearance, documents, and speech, also echoed and extended the historical processes whereby Latina bodies became racialized and sexualized in the context of imposing the U.S.-Mexico border. As Yvonne Yarboro-Bejarano notes, it is not only "our attitudes about our bodies, but our very bodies themselves" that are constructed within social relations (1991, 46), including the relations Mexican immigrant women negotiate at the southern borders of the United States.

The ways in which lesbians (and gay men) might come to INS attention were not restricted to the visible nor to the existence of police records. Individuals also came under suspicion of homosexuality during required premigration medical inspections; through the timing and location of their arrival (e.g., people coming into San Francisco just before the lesbian, gay, bisexual, transgender parade); because of third-party information supplied to the INS; based on the contents of their suitcases; and as a result of information contained in the forms that all immigrants must complete. Immigration forms included questions about whether or not one was of good moral character, a sexual deviate, or a psychopathic personality, and they also asked the applicant to list all affiliations. Anyone who participated in a lesbian or gay organization potentially had to list that fact. One could, of course, lie or omit information when completing the forms, but only at the risk of incurring a substantial penalty if the INS found out.[19] There were likely other ways in which lesbians and gay men came to INS attention, but those have yet to be uncovered. The impact of methods for identifying women who might be lesbians was undoubtedly differentiated by race, nationality, class, and other features.[20]

Once immigrants came to INS attention as possible lesbians, they were officially excluded by means of a Class A medical-exclusion certificate.[21] This practice perhaps inspired Richard Green's observation that "American immigration policy regarding homosexuals has been a marriage of one government bureaucracy with another: the Immigration and Naturalization Service...and the Public Health Service" (1987, 140).

While it may be tempting to assume the medical-exclusion certification process signals that medical fears motivated the exclusionary treatment of lesbians and gays, such a reading does not take into account the full complexity of how exclusion operated. Exclusion never only involved a simple "failure" of medical knowledge, and although medicine is one key discourse through which the homosexual has been constructed as a threatening type, it is not the only such discourse. Robert Podnanski's analysis notes that fears about "morality, subversion, or destitution may have motivated Congress" to enact lesbian and gay exclusion (1983–1984, 347). A plurality of discourses and institutional practices underpinned exclusion. Furthermore, these discourses and practices were neither necessarily rational nor commensurate with one another.

The workings of exclusion must therefore be grasped not at the level of lack or plenitude of knowledge, but rather at the level of how homophobia is strategically organized and deployed within institutional circuits of power. As David Halperin writes, "Homophobic discourses are not reducible to a set of statements with a specifiable truth-content that can be rationally tested. Rather, homophobic discourses function as part of more general and systemic strategies of delegitimation" (1995, 32–33). Consequently, the practice of issuing Class A medical-exclusion certificates to immigrants who were judged to be lesbian or gay reflected not just that medicine was a key discourse through which lesbians and gay men were constructed as threatening "others," but also that medical practices provided a means through which a larger discourse of homophobia could be mobilized, channeled, and legitimated.[22] The medical-exclusion certification process connected to the drive for rationalized efficiency. Its use required few additional resources, since the PHS already inspected the physical and mental health of aspiring immigrants and had a system whereby "unfit" people could be certified for exclusion.[23] It was easy to add one more group to the list of those already weeded out.[24] The medical-exclusion certification process further fit into the rationality that stressed "scientific" management, since it enabled deployment of disparate homophobic practices under the sign of medical intervention.

Issuance of medical-exclusion certificates to suspected lesbian and gay immigrants was also congruent with the operations of other government apparatuses. During the massive World War II troop mobilizations, the handling of homosexuality in the ranks underwent a shift from criminalization to psychiatrization. Dishonorably discharging homosexuals for mental illness, rather than charging them with a crime, was deemed preferable on various grounds: mental-illness discharges eliminated time-consuming trials and costly imprisonment; they "made it easier for the military to extend its anti-homosexual apparatus to women"; and the process could be conducted in a discretionary manner, without strict evidentiary requirements (Bérubé 1990, 142).

After World War II, these military policies toward homosexuality "served as a model for senators who, in 1950, launched the most aggressive attack on homosexual employees that had ever taken place in the federal government" (Bérubé 1990, 266). Under Eisenhower, the attack widened.

> The government's anti-homosexual policies and procedures, which had originated in the wartime military, expanded to include every agency and department of the federal government, and every private company or corporation with a government contract, such as railroad companies and aircraft plants. This affected the job security of more than six million government workers and armed forces personnel. By the mid-1950s, similar policies had also gone into effect in state and local governments, extending the prohibition on employment of homosexuals to over twelve million workers.... Similar policies were adopted independently by some private companies, and even by such private organizations as the American Red Cross. (269–70)

At the same time, the American Psychiatric Association (APA), "building on the standardized nomenclature developed by the Army in 1945," issued its first *Diagnostic and Statistical Manual of Mental Disorders* in 1952. The manual "firmly established homosexuality as a sociopathic personality disorder" (Bérubé 1990, 259). This APA classification legitimated the PHS practice of issuing Class A medical-exclusion certificates to immigrants who were thought to be lesbian or gay.[25] Class A medical-exclusion certification thus shared significant connections with military and employment apparatuses.

Foucault's *History of Sexuality* further specifies how the PHS certification system organized a circuit of homophobic discourses and practices. Within immigration monitoring, procedures were needed to ensure that "the will to knowledge regarding sex . . . caused the ritual of confession to function within the norms of scientific regularity" (Foucault 1990, 65). Thus, although the sexuality of foreign-born peoples could be investigated at various points within the process, there had to be a way to make the process seem legitimately scientific and to regularize what happened if information such as "I am a lesbian" was revealed. Five procedures, through which these aims could be accomplished, are described by Foucault.

> [First,] a clinical codification of the inducement to speak . . . [second,] the postulate of a general and diffuse causality . . . that endowed sex with an inexhaustible and polymorphous causal power. The most discrete

> event in one's sexual behavior . . . was deemed capable of entailing the most varied consequences throughout one's existence. . . . [Third,] the principle of a latency intrinsic to sexuality . . . made it possible to link the forcing of a difficult confession to scientific practice. . . . [Fourth,] through methods of interpretation . . . [and lastly,] through the medicalization of the effects of confession. (Foucault 1990, 65–67)

The case of Quiroz reveals how these procedures operated together, around the Class A medical-exclusion certification system, to create an integrated circuit of power, knowledge, and homophobic practices.

The first feature of this discursive circuit involves the "clinical codification of the inducement to speak." Inducement to speak conjoins neatly with the third feature, the assumption of a "principle of latency intrinsic to sexuality . . . [that makes] it possible to link the forcing of a difficult confession to scientific practice."

A very basic inducement to speak is built into the immigration system, in that one's ability to gain U.S. entry depends on willingness to respond to any and all questions asked by immigration officials. One risks a substantial penalty for lying or omitting information that the immigration service might consider pertinent to one's application.[26] This substantial inducement to speak is compounded during the experience of being held for secondary inspection, as happened to Quiroz when she attempted to re-enter at El Paso. Secondary inspection is conducted in various ways, but Mr. Armendáriz offers one description of how intimidating the process can be.

> When you go down to the bridge, these people [immigration officials] are kings. And they act like kings. They put them [people detained for secondary inspection] in a little room. And they keep them there for hours and don't feed them. And one comes in and asks a few questions and then leaves them alone. Then another comes in: "We're going to put you in the penitentiary for five years, and we're waiting for them to pick you up and take you to jail. Unless you tell us the truth." And then they end up transcribing what they [the detained] said. . . . In my 45 years, I have come across at least 1,000 people who insisted they did not say [what the INS statement says they said]. Under oath.[27]

One cannot know if this description reflects Quiroz's experience. But at a hearing before a special inquiry officer, she attempted to refute the statements that the INS obtained from her during questioning. The special inquiry officer's decision noted, "The respondent testified in an attempt to impeach her statements (Exhibits 3 and 4). She said that the statements were not read to her and that she cannot read or speak English. She denied that she had ever been a lesbian and stated that she has a 9 year old daughter. She testified that she signed the statements because she was told that everything would be all right."[28] Quiroz thus tried to contest the speech that was attributed to her, for it was primarily on the basis of her *speech* that she was constructed as a lesbian. If the speech could be impeached, the "evidence" of homosexuality would be severely undermined.[29]

How the INS overturned Quiroz's impeachment efforts reveals the connections between inducement to speak, the forcing of a sexual confession, and the use of "scientific practice" to legitimate the whole proceedings. The INS testimony read,

> To rebut the respondent's testimony impeaching the statements, the Government had the two immigration officers who took the statements testify as witnesses. Their testimony was that the statement was read to the respondent at the conclusion, that it was made voluntarily, that she was cooperative, and that her answers were responsive to the questions. Their testimony was also to the effect that there was comprehension between them and the respondent in their speaking with her in the Spanish language during the taking of the statement. In passing it is to be noted that Dr. Coleman [the PHS surgeon who signed the Class A medical exclusion certificate issued to Quiroz] during his testimony, stated that he was present during the taking of the statement (Exhibit 3) and that the respondent replied readily, was relaxed, cooperative, not under duress and did not show hesitancy or embarrassment.
>
> The respondent's attempt to impeach her sworn statements (Exhibits 3 and 4) must fail. Each statement recites at the end thereof that it was read to her. The first statement shows a material correction was made ... and this was initialed by the respondent. ... I shall therefore consider these two statements [signed by Quiroz] as true and correct.[30]

In essence, the INS argued that they followed proper procedures in the Quiroz case, including correct administration of the immigration system, requisite adherence to legal doctrines concerning how evidence may be obtained, and validation by a medical authority.

But procedural propriety is not necessarily the key issue here. More significant, in light of Foucault's description of how an economy of discourses becomes organized to generate confession about sexual practices and feelings, is that there *are* procedures and that they *did* work together to ensure that Quiroz provided explicit statements about her sexuality. It was INS adherence to proper procedures that led Quiroz to "confess" "that she has had homosexual desires for at least a year, that she had homosexual relations on numerous occasions over this period of time with two women whom she named, that she had these relations both in El Paso, Texas, and Juarez, Mexico, and that the relations were had with weekly frequency. She described in detail the manner in which these homosexual relations were performed.... [T]he respondent stated that she enjoyed the sexual relations more with women than with men, and that she had entered into such relations voluntarily."[31]

The very scientific and correct nature of the INS procedures operated as relations of force that induced a certain kind of speaking, or confessing, by this woman. It is difficult to believe that Quiroz would have freely volunteered this information to the INS without being compelled to do so by the procedures. That INS procedures were scientific and proper, however, meant that their operation as relations designed to force sexual confessions become invisible. Consequently, Quiroz's confession, but not the existence of procedures that compelled the confession, became the subject of adjudication in her case. Unfortunately for Quiroz, the alleged "perversity" of lesbians and gay men is often backed up by the claim that they "willingly" talk about their deviant sexual practices so as to "recruit" others into lives of depravity. The erasure of the induced nature of Quiroz's speech subjected her to this derogatory construction, which reconfirmed the government's original assertion about her undesirability. But the fact that her speech about sex was induced surely ranks as a significant perversity, too.[32]

A third feature of the economy of discourses, referred to by Foucault and evident in the Class A medical-exclusion process, was "the postulate of a general and diffuse causality ... that endowed sex with an inexhaustible and polymorphous causal power. The most discrete event in one's sexual behavior ... was deemed capable of entailing the most varied consequences throughout one's existence" (1990, 6). In Quiroz's case, this feature is perhaps clearest in the Board of Immigration Appeals judgment that "her relations with several women on many occasions demonstrated a pattern of behavior which was antisocial, irresponsible, lacking in social judgment and 'without any true judgment of what the results may be.'" To use PHS parlance, she had manifested a disorder of the personality which had brought her into conflict with "the prevailing culture" [according to Dr. Schlenker's testimony].[33] The mere fact that Quiroz testified to having sexual relations with two women was deemed evidence that she was irresponsible, antisocial, and personality disordered. The principle of "diffuse causality" is an ever-present resource on which the dominant culture can draw to justify penalizing lesbian and gay existence.

The fourth and fifth features of the economy, which visibly worked through the medical-exclusion-certificate system, were "methods of interpretation ... [and] medicalization of the effects of confession." In immigration exclusion cases, issues of interpretation play out at every stage of the process. For example, two key interpretive issues (along with many lesser ones) emerged in the course of Quiroz's extended court battle to overturn the deportation order against her: was she a lesbian? If so, did that mean she was necessarily a psychopathic personality? (After all, exclusion was based on a certificate issued to her for being a psychopathic personality, not for lesbianism.) While the law was the key site within which these interpretive battles were fought, medical and psychiatric interpretations powerfully influenced the process.

Quiroz's first line of defense in the preliminary case was to challenge the manner in which her statements were obtained and used as proof of homosexuality. She also bluntly denied that she was a homosexual and invoked the fact that she had a daughter as evidence of her sexual relations with men, thus playing into hegemonic constructions of female heterosexuality. In her second line of defense Quiroz drew on medical and psychiatric testimony to suggest that being a homosexual was not necessarily equivalent to being a psychopathic personality. However, since the government found that Quiroz's statements to the INS were unimpeachable, it thus found her to be a homosexual, despite having had a child. The government did acknowledge a possible gap between homosexuality and psychopathic personality, even including the testimony of one of the PHS surgeons who had signed Quiroz's exclusion certificate: "There are persons who are sexual deviates who are not afflicted with psychopathic personality . . . but [the PHS doctor] is required to certify all homosexuals as psychopathic personalities regardless as to how he privately might feel."[34] Nonetheless, the INS ruled,

> The history of the enactment of Section 212(a)(4) of the Immigration and Nationality Act shows that Congress intended that homosexuals and other sex perverts were to be excluded from admission to the United States and that rather than make a separate class of homosexuals and sex perverts within the excluding provisions, these individuals are to be included within the category of individuals afflicted with psychopathic personality. . . . Notwithstanding the medical opinion of both physician witnesses that a person who is homosexual is not per se afflicted with psychopathic personality and that other character traits must also be considered, Congress has intended that persons who are homosexuals are to be considered as being afflicted with psychopathic personality. It is on the basis of this clear intent of Congress that the United States Public

Health Service, in its manual for the examination of aliens, classifies homosexuals and sexual deviates as being afflicted with psychopathic personality.[35]

Thus, within a legal framework, congressional intent to exclude lesbians and gay men—grounded in Congress's plenary power over immigration, which is not bound by common legal and procedural standards—was affirmed.[36] The order deporting Quiroz stood.

When the case was appealed to the Board of Immigration Appeals (BIA), Quiroz employed essentially the same two lines of defense. But the BIA responded even more harshly than had the special inquiry officer. Regarding the question of whether the evidence established that she was a homosexual, members of the BIA affirmed that Quiroz's original statements were unimpeachable. The BIA also addressed the fact that Quiroz had a daughter. The ruling related the circumstances behind the birth of the daughter: "When she was around sixteen years of age, respondent lived for about two months with a man who then deserted her, apparently when she became pregnant." The board opined that "that affair of ten years ago does not establish that she is not now a homosexual," and it furthermore reconstructed that affair as a possible reason for her (to them, confirmed) present homosexuality. "There may be a causal connection between this earlier incident and her present problems."[37] Quiroz's efforts to reconstruct herself within a heterosexual framework through reference to the birth of her daughter thus backfired, since the BIA used these same facts to advance the common homophobic proposition that unfortunate experiences with a man are the reason why a woman turns to lesbianism.[38]

Regarding the possible gap between homosexuality and psychopathic personality, the BIA tartly ruled: "Each psychiatrist or psychoanalyst may construe the term 'homosexual' and 'psychopathic personality' according to his own perspective, but within the Public Health Service and the Immigration Service, in order to achieve a degree of uniformity and fairness in the interpretation and administration of this law, we are bound to a more rigid system of classification."[39]

Therefore, within this interpretive struggle, the exigencies of uniform administration took precedence over psychiatric opinion. Not only did administrative need require that homosexuality be treated as equivalent to psychopathic personality, but furthermore, the BIA ruled, the two categories actually came together in the person of Quiroz herself. Because Quiroz had engaged in sexual relations with women, "It is our opinion that the respondent falls within the class of [psychopathic] persons defined by the two doctors who testified in this case."[40] Not surprisingly, the BIA concluded that "since

Congress unquestionably intended to include homosexuals within the class of aliens afflicted with psychopathic personality, no finding is possible in this case except that she is subject to deportation."[41]

At the district-court level, to which Quiroz next appealed, her counsel no longer tried to refute the finding that she was a homosexual. Instead, he concentrated on trying to undo the contention that a homosexual is necessarily a psychopathic personality. But the district court merely affirmed the legal overlap between the two, ruling that "since the record shows the plaintiff is a homosexual she is therefore a person of psychopathic personality."[42] The fifth-circuit brief for Quiroz again hinged on the argument that "the court erred in concluding as a matter of law that since the record shows that plaintiff is a homosexual, she is, therefore, a person of psychopathic personality."[43] Various arguments were marshaled to support this contention. Even the government's counter-brief acknowledged that Congress had not defined the term "psychopathic personality" and that there were no cases on which to rely for precedent. Nonetheless, Congress had (and has) the right to decide who shall be excluded from immigrating, and government documents suggested that Congress intended to exclude lesbians and gay men. Quiroz was sent yet another letter that ordered her deportation.

Ultimately, Quiroz's lawyer was unable to drive a wedge between the notion of the equivalence between homosexuality and psychopathic personality, despite engaging in a prolonged interpretive battle within the courts. He was also unable to challenge the evidence that was used to construct her as homosexual.

Quiroz had one last card to play, though. On 23 June 1961 the U.S. Court of Appeals for the Fifth Circuit ruled against her (Re: No. 18724—Sara Harb Quiroz v. Marcus T. Neely) and the INS ordered her deportation by 15 August 1961. On 2 August 1961, she married Edward Escudero and filed a motion to reopen her case. The circumstances surrounding this marriage will probably never be known. Was Quiroz a lesbian engaging in a sham marriage, with Escudero as either a willing participant or a dupe? Or did she enter into the marriage in good faith, perhaps trying to "go straight," or even from honest feelings of love, attraction, and affection? Whatever the circumstances, the motion filed on her behalf requested the right to reopen her case so as to "present evidence of her marriage and full rehabilitation, being new facts which touch upon the issue of deportability . . . [t]hat since the order of deportation was entered herein, your applicant has married Edward Escudero, who joins this application, and that she is prepared to prove that she is, at this time, a normal individual and no longer a psychopathic personality."[44]

Given the timing of the marriage, it certainly seems to constitute an effort to take the charges brought against her and use them to craft a response that satisfied dominant cultural terms regarding women and sexuality. The argument that her marriage offered evidence of "rehabilitation" and of becoming "a normal individual" fits neatly into mainstream assumptions that homosexuality can be "cured" (and even better, that lesbianism can be cured by finding the right man).

It was a brave effort. But marriage, too, failed to prevent Quiroz's deportation. As the INS noted in their "Brief in Opposition": "According to counsel's motion the new facts to be proven at the proposed reopening will show that the respondent has married since the order of deportation was entered, is now a normal individual and no longer a psychopathic personality. Even if all this should be proven, no application is apparent to the matter of the respondent's deportability, *which is based on her condition at entry* on January 6, 1960 and not on circumstances which may have arisen since that time."[45] Both sides thus tried to play on the temporal ambiguity of when one might be said to have "become" homosexual. Quiroz initially tried to deny her homosexuality; then she presented the birth of her daughter as evidence that she had had sexual relations with a man sometime in the past (which might cast doubt on present allegations of homosexuality); then, through marriage, she tried to construct homosexuality as a prior condition that was now "cured." The INS, for its part, refuted her initial denials. The BIA hearing then suggested that the circumstances surrounding birth of her daughter may have "caused" her lesbianism. Finally, they invoked their legal power, by which lesbianism was defined as significant at time of entry, regardless of any changes later. In the interpretive battle over the construction and penalizing of lesbianism, the INS eventually won.

It will never be known with absolute certainty whether Quiroz was a lesbian. After all, lesbianism has no clear, predefined content that indicates a marker between it and other forms of sexuality. But Quiroz's case shows how the immigration service, in conjunction with larger circuits of power and knowledge, established the boundaries of who and what counted as a lesbian, then confined Quiroz within that definition. The effects of Quiroz's battle and its resolution were indeed "medicalized" (the fifth feature mentioned by Foucault): Quiroz's Class A medical exclusion certificate stood, and she was deported.

Quiroz's refusal of the lesbian label was certainly intended to avoid deportation, but other reasons may also have motivated her. Perhaps she did not consider herself a lesbian, despite reporting sexual relations with women. Anthropologists such as Joseph Carrier have documented how the construction of male homosexuality in Mexico differs from dominant U.S. constructions, such that men who have sexual relations with other men are not necessarily stigmatized as homosexual.[46] Carrier's work raises questions about how lesbian identity was constructed in the late 1950s and early 1960s in Mexican and U.S. communities that were familiar to Quiroz. It also raises questions about how Quiroz, who was situated at the intersection of several cultures, communities, and traditions, negotiated her sexual identity, which may have changed over time.[47] Though she reported having sexual relations with women, did this make her a lesbian? If so, according to whose definition?

Even if Quiroz considered herself a lesbian, claiming the label was undoubtedly complicated by being a Mexican immigrant woman living in a U.S. border city. Oliva Espín notes that immigrant lesbians often remain situated within the contradictory space "between the racism of the dominant society and the sexist and heterosexist expectations of [their] own community" (1996, 82). Under those circumstances, female sexuality becomes a site through which cultural contestations are played out. Thus, Cherríe Moraga (1983, 90–142), among others, eloquently documents how declaring oneself a lesbian leaves Latinas vulnerable to the charge of *vendida*, or race traitor. Yolanda Leyva further explains that silence, rather than public admission, enables many Latina lesbians to remain connected to family and community: "Latina lesbians have survived because of that silence, and the protection it has provided, despite the many limits and compromises it has imposed" (1996, 145). The INS charge that Quiroz was a lesbian, whether true or not, shattered the protective silence and jeopardized her access to family and community resources. The lesbian label may also have followed her to Mexico, through the gossip of other returnees, or when she was asked to explain her deportation to family and friends. Resettlement becomes very difficult under those circumstances. Quiroz's efforts to refuse the label of lesbian must be framed, therefore, within the context of multiple jeopardies and competing pressures that she faced as an immigrant woman living in a U.S. border city with an anti-Mexican history, as well as the incommensurabilities between different cultural practices of constructing and naming sexual identities.

For these reasons, and in the absence of documents other than official ones, I have resisted offering a judgment about whether or not Quiroz was a lesbian. I hope to foreground the dangers of reading immigrant women's sexualities within dominant U.S. frameworks (even when the reading is intended to assist in the formation of a counter-history), because unqualified use of the term *lesbian* may arrogate immigrant women's experiences to U.S.-based paradigms that do not allow for theorization of the ways that immigrant status is allied with experiences of racism, cultural difference, and class exploitation, complicate sexual identities. As Quiroz's case shows, this arrogation may occur in conjunction with systemic violence that is imposed by the state (in the form of deportation). But lesbians do cross borders. Immigrant lesbian lives remain little documented or understood, however (Espín 1996, 79).[48]

In 1990 Congress repealed immigration provisions that excluded lesbians and gay men. A congressional report states, "In order to make it clear that the US does not view personal decisions about sexual orientation as a danger to other people in our society, the bill repeals the 'sexual deviation' exclusion ground [in immigration]."[49] The "end" of exclusion based on sexual orientation has received little attention in studies of immigration. However, the congressional report demonstrates one way in which this policy change has been framed and explained: "The law also needs to be updated in its treatment of sexual orientation. The term 'sexual deviation' (INA 212(a)(4)) was included with the other mental health exclusion grounds expressly for the purpose of excluding homosexuals. Not only is this provision out of step with current notions of privacy and personal dignity, it is also inconsistent with contemporary psychiatric theories. . . . To put an end to this unfairness, Congress must repeal the 'sexual deviation' ground [for immigration exclusion]."[50] Tempting as it is to attribute the repeal of exclusion as an outgrowth of "current notions of privacy and personal dignity" and "contemporary psychiatric theories," this explanation is partial at best, for exclusion never hinged solely on medical or psychiatric knowledge; rather, that knowledge was deployed as part of a larger strategic formation of homophobic discourses and practices. Alterations in the composition of that knowledge were not sufficient to generate a repeal without alterations in the discursive economy as a whole.

One of the most significant alterations to the discursive economy that organized exclusion occurred more than a decade before 1990. In 1979 the Surgeon General directed the PHS to stop automatically issuing Class A medical exclusion certificates solely on the basis of homosexuality. Bearing on the Surgeon General's decision was the fact that in 1973 trustees of the American Psychiatric Association (APA) "voted to remove homosexuality *per se* from the categories of mental disorder. In the next year, a referendum upholding the decision was passed by the full APA membership" (Green 1987, 143).[51] Until this APA action, homosexuality was classified as an illness; and even if its exact nature was disputed, its legal status as an illness meant that lesbians and gay men came under PHS purview. After 1974, however, in the absence of an official illness categorization, the PHS no longer had jurisdiction over lesbians or gay men (unless they had other medical or mental conditions).[52] Other factors, too, undoubtedly influenced the Surgeon General's decision.

When the Surgeon General declared that the PHS would no longer automatically issue Class A medical exclusion certificates to lesbians and gay men, John M. Harmon, assistant attorney general for the Department of Justice, responded sharply. In a memorandum to David M. Crosland, acting commissioner of the INS, Harmon excoriated the Surgeon General for his decision and suggested he had overstepped the bounds of his authority. "Congress clearly intended that homosexuality be included in the statutory phrase 'mental defect or disease' and the Surgeon General has no authority to determine that homosexuality is not a 'mental defect or disease' for the purpose of applying the [Immigration] Act," stated the memo.[53] Harmon ruled that the INS remained bound to exclude lesbians and gay men, even without PHS assistance.

In 1980 the INS announced how exclusion would operate: "If an alien made an 'unsolicited, unambiguous admission of homosexuality' to an INS inspector or was identified as homosexual by a 'third party who arrived at the same time,' the alleged homosexual would be subject to a secondary inspection. At that inspection, the person would be asked whether he or she was a homosexual. If the person answered 'no,' entry would be permitted. If the person answered 'yes,' a formal exclusionary hearing would follow" (Green 1987, 143). In some respects, this approach to exclusion was not very different than it had been. Well before 1980, the INS relied on self-disclosure and identification by a third party (though not necessarily a party who arrived at the same time) to pick out immigrants who might be lesbians or gay men. Other identificatory practices, such as criminal-record checks and inclusion of key questions on immigration application forms, operated both pre- and post-1980. Perhaps the main difference was simply the elimination of one step in the exclusion process: whereas before 1980 a suspected lesbian or gay immigrant was sent to the PHS for certification before exclusion, after 1980 the INS skipped the certification process and excluded directly.

The growing questions and criticisms directed toward lesbian and gay exclusion in the 1980s therefore reflect not the implementation of new, egregious forms of border control, but merely the loss of the certification process. An array of practices were suddenly unbound from the legitimation offered by a medical exclusion certificate, in a way that made them available for further questioning and contestation. In addition, new political and social formations, including lesbian and gay legal defense and political advocacy groups, had also emerged, and they directly contested practices like exclusion. During the 1980s,

> the question of how to identify lesbians and gay men had become an increasingly vexed one.... The INS's stated policy of relying on voluntary

> admission drew an openly arbitrary line between lesbians and gay men who, perhaps unaware of the consequences, announced their homosexuality to INS inspectors and those who did not. The enforcement of the procedure was, as even the State Department and some INS officials admitted, uneven and arbitrary. . . . [T]he legal uncertainties [arising from contradictory court rulings in the 1980s] and administrative inconsistencies surrounding the exclusion had made an already controversial provision increasingly difficult to justify. (Minter 1993, 780–81)

Concerns about discrimination against lesbians and gay men was voiced. Some public officials suggested that "a person's sexual orientation should be a private matter that had no relevance to immigration."[54]

The expression of these problematizations continued unchecked, since neither the medical-certification system remained, nor did an equally effective new organization of homophobic discourses emerge. The diversity of problematizations meant that a wide spectrum of groups could find something to support in proposals to repeal the exclusion. "Those who supported [the exclusion's] elimination spanned a broad ideological range, including the Carter, Reagan, and Bush administrations, the Select Commission on Immigration and Refugee Policy, the American Psychiatric Association, and numerous civil rights organizations" (Minter 1993, 781). The Immigration Act of 1990 therefore eliminated all references to lesbian and gay exclusion.

Lesbians and gay men are no longer automatically debarred from emigrating to the United States. While the change is significant, its meanings must be carefully evaluated. After all, although lesbians and gay men are no longer excluded, judicial interpretations of aspects of immigration law remain "heavily influenced by the categoric exclusion of lesbians and gay men under the 1952 Act" and by a heterosexual norm (Minter 1993, 787). Lesbians and gay men are still likely to be excluded for lacking good moral character. They also remain unable to use long-term relationships with U.S. citizens or residents as a basis for gaining U.S. residency (a right that is available to male-female couples). And once they are within the United States, lesbians and gay men must continually contend with homophobia.[55]

These are some of the *effects* of homosexuality that continue to make immigration difficult, even after 1990. To assess how homosexuality is likely to remain salient in immigration in the foreseeable future, one would need to examine the operation of major discourses and practices that are critical to the current production of homosexuality. One would also need to analyze how lesbian and gay identities may be reproduced within new collectivities that are no longer delineated within clear lesbian or gay parameters. For example, HIV has become a significant issue in the administration of the immigration system. And HIV, as Katie King (1992, 80) observes, is both altering the terrain of what counts as the gay and lesbian community and producing new collectivities that cannot be captured within a gay-straight model.[56] In addition to the reconfiguration of identities caused by HIV and AIDS exclusions, the 1990 act also established "a new general category of exclusion based on mental or physical disorders. Although general in nature, this ground is linked carefully to behavior and potentially harmful activities.... [T]wo requirements must be met if an alien is to be excluded because of a mental or physical disorder. The alien must be determined to have a mental or physical disorder and a history of behavior (or current behaviors associated with the disorder) that may pose a threat to the property or the safety of the alien or others.... [T]he standard is based on the behavior of the alien."[57] The standard of "harmful activities" and behaviors has the potential to be unfairly applied to lesbians and gay men in particular, as well as to produce new minoritized collectivities that include but are not limited to lesbians and gay men.

Clearly, despite the 1990 changes, lesbian and gay identities continue to have various kinds of salience in immigration. Nonetheless, the act is a key piece of legislation that makes new social justice strategies possible. Because the act protects foreign-born lesbians, gay men, and "queers" from automatic exclusion, a national movement to secure spousal immigration privileges for same-sex couples, as well as novel ways of publicly linking struggles around homophobia, racism, and anti-immigrant sentiment, have emerged.[58] Before 1990, these political projects were greatly handicapped (if not virtually impossible), since foreign-born people who identified as lesbian, gay, or queer risked exclusion by announcing their presence, publicizing their struggles, or participating in organizing.

Repeal of exclusion based on sexual deviation is intelligible within a framework that is sensitive to the operations of power.

> Power must be understood in the first instance as the multiplicity of force relations immanent in the sphere in which they operate and which constitute their own organization; as the process which, through ceaseless struggles and confrontations, transforms, strengthens, or reverses them; as the support which these force relations find in one another, thus forming a chain or system, or on the contrary, the disjunctions and contradictions which isolate them from one another; and lastly, as the strategies in which they take effect, whose general design or institutional

crystallization is embodied in the state apparatus, in the formulation of the law, in the various social hegemonies. (Foucault 1990, 92–93)

Lesbian and gay exclusion functioned until 1990 not because of its grounding in rational thought, but because of its ability to weave together a range of disparate, sometimes contradictory, and often clearly unreasonable homophobic discourses and practices into a "chain or system." This weaving together found institutional crystallization in the Class A medical exclusion system, which was supported by "the state apparatus, in the formulation of the law, [and] in the various social hegemonies." At the same time, this formation generated its own "disjunctions and contradictions." Contradictions included the ways that the formation contributed to production of the very sexuality against which it claimed to guard the nation. Quiroz's case offers a valuable window into the ways that border monitoring enabled the production of official immigration-service definitions of lesbianism, around which exclusions—that potentially affected not just self-identified lesbians but any woman who did not clearly conform to current heterosexual standards—were organized. Border monitoring, in turn, crucially depended on establishing procedures whereby immigrant sexual confessions could be mandated. Quiroz's case, and her strategies of resistance, also provide information about the ways that sexual monitoring of the border was gender differentiated, even though suspected lesbians and gay men were barred from entry under a shared provision. As the case makes clear, racial and class histories integrally structure how gender and sexual identities are produced, negotiated, oppositionally deployed, and sanctioned at the border. Quiroz's case also raises critical questions about how migrant women negotiate sexual identities and communities when the threat of state-sanctioned exclusion or deportation structures their options. Though an "end" to lesbian and gay exclusion in the broadest sense has not occurred, the transformation of conditions of struggle, and of relations between affected individuals and groups, is beyond question.

Notes

1. Personal interview, El Paso, Texas, 18 March 1996.
2. Cited in *Matter of LaRochelle*, 11 I and N Dec. 436 (Board of Immigration Appeals 1965).
3. A significant amount of information about the history of gay and lesbian exclusion has been reconstructed from the records of court cases. To date, *Quiroz v. Neelly*, 291 F. 2d 906 (5th Cir. Tex. 1961) is the only female court case that has been identified.
4. This essay focuses on the exclusion of lesbians and gay men in U.S. immigration. Though the contemporary notion of "queer" also includes people who are bisexual

and transgendered, as well as various heterosexualities, immigration policing was not organized around these identities. Rather, the historical record suggests that Congress and the immigration service were specifically concerned with a homosexual threat. Court cases indicate that individuals who were sexually involved with both men and women were categorized as homosexual, rather than bi- or heterosexual. Indeed, they were considered to be particularly pernicious homosexuals, who deceitfully tried to hide their "condition" by becoming involved with people of the "opposite sex."

5 Foucault argues that although particular sexual acts had a long history of being forbidden and subject to punishment, it was only in the nineteenth century that these acts became reconstructed as the signs of distinct types of personages, each endowed with a discrete sexual identity that the state needed to monitor and manage. For example, homosexual *acts* became reconstructed as the sign of a homosexual *type*. As a result, "The homosexual became a personage, a past, a case history, and a childhood, in addition to being a type of life, a life form, and a morphology, with an indiscreet anatomy and a possibly mysterious physiology. . . . [T]he homosexual was now a species" (Foucault 1990, 43).

6 The immigration service also excluded those who had committed sexual acts that were forbidden by immigration law, whether or not the person fit within a sexual-identity category. As Janet Halley comments, sexual types and sexual acts "are not mutually exclusive descriptors" (1996, 184), but rather interrelate in the production of categories of people who are marked out for exclusion.

7 For Quiroz, the density of the relations of power also had to do with the fact that she was a Mexican woman and as such was connected to a larger history of strict immigration monitoring directed at people of Mexican origin attempting to enter the United States. See Chavez 1992; Calavita 1992; Rouse 1992; and other writings on Mexican migration.

8 There is a double problem here. Efforts to determine if Quiroz was a lesbian perpetuate sexual categorizations, even if the efforts are motivated by affirmation of resistant and minority sexual subjects. Furthermore, these sexual categorizations substantially derive their meanings from metropolitan centers, which are materially and ideologically implicated in the production of immigrant women as racial or ethnic minorities. Thus, uncritical application of the term *lesbian* to a woman like Quiroz can easily erase her different historical formation and complex positionality, without revealing anything about her sexuality.

9 For a discussion of how the U.S. nation is constituted as heterosexual, see Berlant and Freeman 1992.

10 Thanks to Judith Butler for this succinct formulation. Two examples may help to illustrate how immigration checkpoints can regulate the terms by which identity is formed. I interviewed a woman who had had a sexual relationship with a woman in her country of origin and thought nothing of it—until she was asked by a state-department official, while applying to immigrate, if she was a homosexual. The fact of being asked, and the manner in which she was asked, made her rethink the significance of that sexual experience. A second, rather different example concerns a woman who came to the United States, lived here for several years, and began to think

of herself as a lesbian. But she knew that in order to adjust from immigrant to citizen status, she would one day be asked to account for her activities before immigration officials. Therefore, the woman did not feel free to join lesbian groups or activities until she adjusted to citizen status.

11 The fact that certain forms of queer identities were unlikely to be captured by these checkpoints does not make the fact of policing any less salient for all queer people.

12 One should not treat this dearth of court cases as evidence that lesbians were unaffected by immigration policing; instead, one must remain attuned to the ways in which women were historically excluded/unrepresented within official documents although they were present historically and had an impact. See Leyva 1996.

13 Aside from Quiroz, the only other lesbian immigration case I have ever seen cited is *In re Schmidt*, 56 Misc. 2d 456, 459–60 (N.Y. Sup. Ct. 1961). This case is cited by Minter, who describes the issue: "A New York court applied Judge Hand's standard to a lesbian seeking naturalization after living and working in the United States for fourteen years. The woman testified to having had a series of relationships with women, both before her entry to the country and after. Citing a New Jersey court that found '[f]ew behavioral deviations . . . more offensive to American mores than . . . homosexuality,' the New York court dismissed the woman's petition for citizenship despite the fact that her behavior was private and violated no law" (Minter 1993, 794).

14 Personal interview with Albert Armendáriz, El Paso, Texas, 18 March 1996. He estimates that this officer was single-handedly responsible for the exclusion or deportation of several hundred women for "sexual deviation."

15 Decision of the Special Inquiry Officer concerning case A8 707 653, 25 March 1960, Immigration and Naturalization Service, El Paso, Texas, 3 (on file with the author).

16 Masculinity and femininity are culturally coded in very specific ways, so with respect to culturally different and diverse populations of immigrants, this standard provides only a shaky basis for identifying "deviants."

17 Race and gender are also not reducible to "visible marks," and the "visible" certainly need not provide an accurate index of an individual's gender or race. In terms of race, this point is most thoroughly developed in writings about people with multiracial heritages. See, for example, the essays in *Racially Mixed People in America*, edited by Maria P. P. Root (1992).

18 Since Quiroz crossed the border, U.S.-Mexico border relations have undergone many changes. In the 1980s and 1990s, as part of a renewed war against both drugs and undocumented immigration, the U.S.-Mexico border region has become increasingly militarized. Dunn, among others, has documented the increased deployment of military technology, expansion of Border Patrol powers, involvement of the National Guard, and growth of detention centers in the region since the early 1980s. Civil and human-rights abuses against residents of the region, especially against Latino-origin peoples, have become a significant issue. In addition to Dunn, see Jiménez 1992; Americas Watch Committee 1992.

19 See National Lawyers Guild 1995. This chapter notes that immigrants who willfully and materially misrepresent their cases are excludable.

20 In an April 1995 phone conversation I had with the attorney Ignatius Bau, he related

that in Russia men accused of homosexuality tend to be jailed, while women accused of lesbianism tend to be hospitalized. Consequently, the mark (or at least, the accusation) of homosexuality is visible in gender-differentiated ways in documents that Russian immigrants submit to the INS.

21 When someone seemed potentially lesbian or gay, the INS did not always investigate them thoroughly: it could dispose of them without generating any record at all. Donald C. Knutson, counsel to the National Gay Rights Advocates, explains how this occurred: "If the border guard suspects because of that person's appearance or some other reason [that he or she is gay or lesbian], the normal practice has been to inform that person that he or she is not entitled to enter the country, that he or she has two options. One, get on the plane or boat or train or whatever and go back where you came from and you won't have any more trouble. If you persist, however, you must go before an immigration judge. You must go before a psychiatrist for a psychiatric examination, and then you will be excluded from this country, deported, and never permitted to come back again. Well, it is no wonder that statistics do not indicate that many people have taken that [second] course" (see U.S. House 1984, 193). Consequently, although medical certification provided the means to exclude suspected lesbians and gay men, exclusion could always be implemented more informally, simply by invoking the threat of the medical-certification process.

22 Foucault refers to such organization and deployment as a discursive economy: "The *economy* of discourses—their intrinsic technology, the necessities of their operation, the tactics they employ, the effects of power which underlie them and which they transmit—this, and not the system of representations is what determines the essential features of what they have to say" (Foucault 1990, 68–69, emphasis added).

23 To this day, the PHS remains involved in inspecting the physical and mental health of aspiring immigrants. For more information, see Committee of the Judiciary 1963.

24 As Foucault phrases it, "The exercise of power is not added on from outside, like a rigid, heavy constraint . . . but is so subtly present in them as to increase their efficiency" (1979, 206).

25 I thank Jill Esbenshade for pointing out the fact that there were connections between immigration and military policies during this time period.

26 See n. 22 above.

27 Personal interview, El Paso, Texas, 18 March 1996.

28 Decision of the Special Inquiry Officer concerning case A8 707 653, 25 March 1960, Immigration and Naturalization Service, El Paso, Texas, 3.

29 Once her testimony had been taken, corroborating testimony was also obtained from Celia Rosales, named by Quiroz as one of her lovers during the past fifteen months—so it was not Quiroz's speech alone that constructed her as lesbian. However, in many cases, speech about oneself was sufficient "proof" of homosexuality, even without corroboration, thus making speech and its relation to the self a profoundly contested location. For more on the vexed relationship between self-disclosure and homosexual identity see Sedgwick 1990 (esp. 69–75).

30 Decision of the Special Inquiry Officer concerning case A8 707 653, 25 March 1960, Immigration and Naturalization Service, El Paso, Texas, 3–4.

31 Ibid., 1.
32 The question of using "scientific practice" to "induce" immigrants to speak and to "force a difficult confession" has played out in many ways in monitoring the immigration of lesbians and gay men. The PHS suggested in a 1952 report to Congress that some people might suffer from a "homosexuality of which the individual himself is unaware" and that in such cases "some psychological tests may be helpful in uncovering homosexuality" (U.S. House 1952, 47). Richard Green (1987, 142n7) speculates that the tests in question were Rorschach "inkblot" tests. PHS psychological tests were not the only means used to force a confession about sexuality: a more dramatic example concerns Jaime Chavez, a Mexican who was "held incommunicado under armed guard for over twenty four hours [and] subjected to abusive questioning and an abusive search" (U.S. House 1984, 85). Chavez was treated in this way because he was suspected of homosexuality based on the contents of his luggage.
33 Decision of the Board of Immigration Appeals, Case A-8707653, Washington, D.C., 2 June 1960, 7 (on file with the author).
34 Decision of the Special Inquiry Officer concerning case A8 707 653, 25 March 1960, Immigration and Naturalization Service, El Paso, Texas, 2.
35 Ibid., 5
36 Historically, Congress has enjoyed plenary power over immigration matters, such that "Congress has unbounded power to exclude aliens from admission to the United States; Congress can bar aliens from entering the United States for discriminatory and arbitrary reasons, even those which might be condemned as a denial of equal protection if used for purposes other than immigration" (*Matter of Longstaff*, 716 F 2d 1439 [5th Cir. 1983]). Plenary powers are intended to ensure national sovereignty.
37 Decision of the Board of Immigration Appeals, Case A-8707653, Washington, D.C., 2 June 1960, 4.
38 This argument makes heterosexuality the norm from which all other sexualities are both derivative and deviant; it makes all women's sexual agency derivative of male actions; thus, it implies lesbianism is the result of heterosexuality gone wrong; in this way, it renders impossible the affirmation of women loving women while constructing lesbians as degraded, sick, and inferior.
39 Decision of the Board of Immigration Appeals, Case A-8707653, Washington, D.C., 2 June 1960, 7.
40 Ibid.
41 Ibid.
42 Findings of Fact and Conclusions of Law, United States District Court for the Western District of Texas, El Paso Division, in Civil Action No. 2175, Sara Harb Quiroz v. Marcus T. Neelly, 22 August 1960, 2.
43 United States Court of Appeals for the Fifth Circuit, Case No. 18724, Sara Harb Quiroz v. Richard C. Haberstroh, Brief of the Appellant, March 1961, 2. (A more precise date is not given.)
44 Motion to Reopen, in the Matter of Sara Harb Quiroz, Now Sara Harb Escudero, A8 707 653, to the District Director of Immigration and Naturalization Service of El Paso, Texas, 7 August 1961, 1.

45 U.S. Department of Justice, Immigration and Naturalization Service, "Brief in Opposition," in the Matter of Sara Harb Quiroz, file A8 707 653, 23 August 1961, 2; emphasis added.
46 See Carrier 1995.
47 Tomás Almaguer (1993) documented that Chicano men negotiate sexual identity in the intersections of Mexican/Chicano and dominant U.S. sexuality constructions. How that process of negotiation might have occurred for immigrant Mexican women in the late 1950s is something about which one can only speculate, but immigrant lesbians certainly do not easily fit into what Yolanda Leyva calls "the Anglo lesbian paradigm of the modern lesbian identity" (1996, 149), and other identity formations and traditions must be grasped if one is to theorize the richness of immigrant lesbian history.
48 See also Argüelles and Rich 1984; Argüelles and Rich 1985.
49 U.S. House Report 101–723, Parts 1 and 2, "Family Unity and Employment Opportunity Immigration Act of 1990," 19 September 1990, 101st Cong., 2d sess. (Washington: U.S. Government Printing Office, 1990), 56.
50 Ibid.
51 For a more detailed discussion of the APA's decision, see Bayer 1987. Neil Miller mentions that in an effort to contest the automatic labeling of homosexuality as a mental illness, gay activists "zapped" APA conventions and meetings, and at one panel discussion of the issue, "a psychiatrist . . . created a sensation by announcing that he was gay. It marked the first time that any psychiatrist in the United States had come out publicly; the drama of his revelation was heightened by the fact he found it necessary to wear a mask and speak through a voice altering device" (1995, 256).
52 Thanks to Professor Carolyn (Patty) Blum for her comments on this matter.
53 Memorandum of John M. Harmon, Assistant Attorney General, to David L. Crosland, Acting Commissioner, INS, 10 December 1979, 2.
54 U.S. House Report No. 882, 100th Cong., 2d sess. (Washington: U.S. Government Printing Office), 23–24.
55 There are also difficulties with accessing political asylum, especially for lesbians.
56 In the late 1980s HIV became a grounds for immigration exclusion, although it was not specifically listed in the law. In 1993 Congress voted to officially add HIV to the list of grounds for immigration exclusion.
57 U.S. House Report 101–723, Parts 1 and 2, "Family Unity," 52–53.
58 This is a project which intersects with the more domestically oriented campaign for same-sex marriage.

The Value of Immigrant Life
JONATHAN XAVIER INDA

✳ Over the last two decades, the political right in the United States, particularly in California, has advanced a highly charged political rhetoric in which Third World immigrants are deemed to present a threat to the cultural unity of the nation (see Brimelow 1996). According to the claims of the right, the masses of foreigners, with their plurality of languages, experiences, and histories, are destined to overwhelm the dominant culture of the United States to such an extent as to transform it beyond recognition. Moreover, the general populace has had a propensity to blame immigrants, primarily the undocumented, for many of the socioeconomic ills of the United States: unemployment, crime, deteriorating schools, deficiencies in social services, and so forth. The widespread assumption has been that immigrants generally threaten the social security of the nation.

The political effects of constructing immigrants as a problem have not been insignificant.[1] Such rhetorical fashioning has given rise to and legitimated numerous efforts to exclude immigrants, both legal and "illegal," from the body politic, including Operation Gatekeeper, Proposition 187, and the Illegal Immigration Reform and Immigrant Responsibility Act of 1996. The logic is simple: if immigrants pose a threat to the common good, their exclusion or elimination is necessary in order to guard the well-being of the nation. The repudiation of the immigrant is thus justified in the name of protecting the welfare of the social body.

These practices of exclusion can be interpreted in terms of what Michel Foucault (1980a, 1991a, 1991b) calls biopower. This term describes a technology of power whose main concern is "the welfare of the population, the improvement of its condition, the increase of its wealth, longevity, health, etc." (1991b, 100). The focus of biopower is the control of the species body and its reproduction.[2] It is a regulatory power whose highest function is to thoroughly invest life in order to produce a healthy and vigorous population. There is an underside to biopower, however: as Foucault notes, often "entire populations are mobilized for the purpose of wholesale slaughter in the name of life necessity" (1980, 137). Biopower does not just foster life; it also routinely does away with it in order to preserve it. The counterpart of the power to secure an individual's continued existence is therefore the power to expose an entire population to death (or at least to multiplying its risk of death). Under the rationality of biopower, it is thus possible simultaneously to protect life and to authorize a holocaust.

Contemporary U.S. repudiation of the immigrant, particularly of the undocumented Mexican immigrant, can be situated on the underside of biopower. In order to fortify the well-being of the population, the state and its apparatuses often strive to eliminate those influences deemed harmful to the biological growth of the nation, with certain governmental agents and institutions, as well members of the general populace, codifying the exclusion of the undocumented immigrant as an essential and noble pursuit necessary to ensure the survival of the social body. Two distinct governmental projects have been deployed to this end: the federal government's efforts to police and control the U.S.-Mexico border and former California governor Pete Wilson's repeated attempts to deny undocumented immigrants access to prenatal care. The body of the "illegal" immigrant has served an important terrain of governmental struggle, particularly as it pertains to the regulation of his or her entry into the United States and of his or her capacity to reproduce. Attempts to exclude the immigrant from the body politic imply that illegal lives are expendable—that the lives of undocumented immigrants and their children are not quite worth living.

The Politicization of Life

"For a long time," Foucault notes, "one of the characteristic privileges of sovereign power was the right to decide life and death" (1980a, 135).[3] For instance, if an external enemy sought to overthrow the sovereign, the latter could justly wage war, requiring his subjects to fight in defense of the state. So without directly causing their deaths, the sovereign was sanctioned to risk their lives, thus exercising an indirect power of life and death over his subjects. However, if someone hazarded to rebel against him and violate his laws, the sovereign could exert a direct power over the transgressor's life, such that the latter could be put to death. The right to life and death was thus somewhat asymmetrical, weighted on the side of death: "The sovereign exercised his right to life only by exercising his right to kill, or by refraining from killing; he evidenced his power over life only through the death he was capable of requiring. The right which was formulated as the 'power of life and death' was in reality the right to *take* life or *let* live" (136). As such, this power was wielded mainly as a mechanism of deduction, making it "essentially a right of seizure: of things, time, bodies, and ultimately life itself" (136). That is, sovereign power was fundamentally a right of appropriation—of a portion of the wealth, labor, services, and blood of the sovereign's subjects—that "culminated in the privilege to seize hold of life in order to suppress it" (136).

The power of appropriation or of deduction, Foucault suggests, is no longer the principal form of power in the West. Since the classical age, the mechanisms of power have undergone a radical transformation. Power now works "to incite, reinforce, control, monitor, optimize, and organize the forces under it"; it is "a power bent on generating forces, making them grow, and ordering them, rather than one dedicated to impeding them, making them submit, or destroying them" (1980a, 136). Thus, in contrast to a power organized around the sovereign, modern "power would no longer be dealing simply with legal subjects over whom the ultimate dominion was death, but with living beings, and the mastery it would be able to exercise over them would be applied at the level of life itself; it was the taking charge of life, more than the threat of death, that gave power its access even to the body" (142–43). In short, modern power has assigned itself the duty of managing life. It is now over life that power establishes its hold and on which it seeks to have a positive influence.

The power over life, which Foucault calls biopower, is most apparent in the emergence of "population" as an economic and political problem in the eighteenth century. This population is not simply a collection of individual citizens. One is not dealing with subjects, or even with a "people," but with a composite body "with its specific phenomena and its peculiar variables: birth and death rates, life expectancy, fertility, state of health, frequency of illness, patterns of diet and habitation" (1980a, 25). The population, in other words, has its own form of order, its own energy, traits, and dispositions. The management of this population, principally of its overall well-being, has become a primary commitment as well as a main source of legitimacy of modern forms of government: "It's the body of society which becomes the new principle [of political organization] in the nineteenth century. It is this social body which needs to be protected, in a quasi-medical sense. In place of the rituals that served to restore the corporeal integrity of the monarch, remedies and therapeutic devices are employed such as the segregation of the sick, the monitoring of contagions, the exclusion of delinquents" (1980b, 55).

The concern of government is therefore to produce a healthy and productive citizenry, to protect and enhance the well-being of particular bodies in order to foster the welfare of the composite body of the population. As a result, "biological existence" has come to be "reflected in political existence" (1980a, 142). Biopower ultimately designates "what brought life and its mechanisms into the realm of explicit calculations" (143), its main overall concern being the life of the population, of the species body—the body that functions as the foothold of biological processes pertaining to birth, death, health, and longevity. The species body and the individual as a simple living being have become important stakes in modern forms of government, thus marking the politicization of life and turning politics to some extent into biopolitics.

Foucault argues that the governing of bodies and the calculated management of life has supplanted the old power of death that typified sovereign power. This does not mean, however, that the right of death has altogether disappeared. Rather, it has experienced a shift, or at least "a tendency to align itself with the exigencies of a life-administering power and to define itself accordingly" (1980a, 136). The awesome power of death "now presents itself as the counterpart of a power that exerts a positive influence on life, that endeavors to administer, optimize, and multiply it, subjecting it to precise controls and comprehensive regulations" (137). Wars, for example, are no longer conducted on behalf of the sovereign. They are waged in defense of the population. It is "as managers of life and survival . . . that so many regimes have been able to wage so many wars, causing so many men to be killed" (137). If genocide is an effect of modern power, this is not by virtue of the restitution of the sovereign right to kill, but because power is located and practiced at the level of life. What is at stake in war is not the existence of the sovereign, but the biological well-being of a population. The same thing could be said about the death penalty. Foucault notes,

> Together with war, it was for a long time the other form of the right of the sword; it constituted the reply of the sovereign to those who attacked his will, his law, or his person. Those who died on the scaffold became fewer and fewer, in contrast to those who died in wars. But it was for the same reasons that the latter became more numerous and the former more and more rare. As soon as power gave itself the function of administering life, its reason for being and the logic of its exercise—and not the awakening of humanitarian feelings—made it more and more difficult to apply the death penalty. How could power exercise its highest prerogatives by

putting people to death, when its main role was to ensure, sustain, and multiply life, to put this life in order? For such a power, execution was at the same time a limit, a scandal, and a contradiction. (138)

The only reason, at least according to Foucault, that capital punishment continues to be practiced under modern forms of government is that it calls attention less to the atrocity of the crime itself than to the aberrance and incorrigibility of the criminal—that is, to the danger he or she presents to society. The practice of capital punishment can thus be maintained and justified today only to the extent that its aim is to safeguard the welfare of the population. It is in order to nurture life—the life of the population—that life can be disallowed. As in the case of war, what is of concern is not the existence of the sovereign but the well-being of the population. "The ancient right to *take* life or *let* live," Foucault suggests, "has been replaced by a power to *foster* life or *disallow* it to the point of death" (1980a, 138). This means that while the right to life and death continues to be asymmetrical, it now falls on the side of life. It is to life that power must attend. As such, modern governments can legitimately take life only in the name of life itself.

One important result of the inclusion of man's natural life in the calculations and mechanisms of power is that it becomes possible, according to Foucault (1991a), to simultaneously protect life and authorize a holocaust. The politicization of life, in other words, necessarily implies a judgment regarding the threshold beyond which life stops being politically pertinent and can as such be eliminated without penalty (Agamben 1998). The biopolitical logic of modern forms of government necessitates a decision on the value or nonvalue of life. Every society necessarily makes a distinction between those lives that deserve to be lived and those that do not, the logic being that the death of the other, the death of those lives unworthy of being lived, will make life in general more healthy and pure. This death does not have to be direct (that is, from the literal act of putting to death). It could also be indirect death: the act of exposing to death, of multiplying for some the risk of death, or simply political death, expulsion, rejection, or exclusion. In any case, modern forms of government routinely aim to fortify the welfare of the population through the elimination of those lives that putatively harm the biological growth of the nation. Thus, when life becomes a supreme political value, the logic of war— that one must be capable of killing to keep on living—becomes a predominant principle in governing. The welfare of the population becomes indistinguishable from the fight against (and the necessity of eliminating) the enemy.[4]

An essential characteristic of modern biopolitics is the necessity of establishing a threshold in life that distinguishes what is inside from what is outside, separating those bodily interests that can be represented in the polity from those which cannot, from those adverse to the social order it embodies. The clearest embodiment of this biopolitical rationality is perhaps the Nazi State. The basic goal of the Nazis was to create a new, and better, social order. For them, this meant fostering the life of the species body through the preservation of racial health—that is, through the propagation of those who were considered to be of healthy German stock.[5] The preservation of the health of the social body entailed not only the cultivation of the lives of those of healthy German racial stock, but also the containment, or elimination, of any unhealthy elements. It was only through the systematic selection and elimination of the unhealthy that the propagation of healthy stock could take place (Bauman 1989). It was thus that the Jews came to be designated as enemies of the social body and targeted for elimination.[6] The Nazi State is thus the perfect embodiment of modern biopolitical rationality, for it shows that when the life of the species becomes a political issue, it becomes possible to simultaneously protect life and to authorize a holocaust. It is not just totalitarian states, however, that operate according to biopolitical rationality. Foucault (1991a) argues that the play between the affirmation of life and the right to kill (or at least to disallow life to the point of death) operates to some extent in all modern states. The Nazi State represents only the most radical and horrific extension of a power centered on life. More generally, in modern states biopower works to create a wedge between the normal and the pathological, conferring aberrance on individual or collective bodies and casting certain abnormalities as dangers to the body politic. That is, it functions as a mechanism for distinguishing those bodily interests that can be represented in the polity from those which cannot, from those against whom society must be defended. Biopower thus implies nothing specific about what is to be done with those bodies construed as dangerous. One possibility, of course, is extermination. However, more typical of modern states is the practice of multiplying for some the risk of death or of subjecting dangerous bodies to marginalization, expulsion, and rejection. The logic, in both cases, is the same: the exclusion and/or elimination of certain bodies secures the protection of others. Social death, as much as the literal act of putting to death, serves to safeguard the social body. So whether a modern state practices mass extermination or simply increases the risk of death for certain bodies, it is likely to be operating according to the rationality of biopolitics.

The logic of biopower has played an integral role in the government of "illegal" immigration. Certain popular and governmental discourses have construed undocumented immigrants as dangers to the body politic that need to be eliminated. Indeed, anti-immigrant discourses have constructed illegal immigrants as unsuitable participants in the body politic and thus codified their exclusion as a noble pursuit necessary to ensure the well-being and survival of the social body.

The Threatening Foreigner

In the United States the best place to explore the biopolitical logic of anti-immigrant discourses is the state of California. Over the last four decades, California has undergone a major demographic transformation, changing from overwhelmingly "white" and U.S.-born to increasingly Latino and foreign-born.[7] An important consequence of this metamorphosis has been the notable flourishing of nativism—particularly during the 1990s, but extending into the present—which has produced a political and cultural climate distinctly hostile toward immigrants. This nativism has been very much racialized. Despite the fact that immigrants come to California from all over the world, including Europe, the populations most often stigmatized as a problem are those physically different from the mainstream, white population. More specifically, it is principally Mexican immigrants who are construed as foreign bodies that threaten the welfare of the nation. This racialized nativism, however, does not necessarily resort to crude biologisms in which different racial groups are seen to possess distinct natural endowments. Rather, it emphasizes differences of cultural heritage and their incommensurability. As Etienne Balibar has noted, the dominant theme "is not biological heredity but the insurmountability of cultural differences": it is a nativism that "does not postulate the superiority of certain groups or peoples in relation to others but 'only' the harmfulness of abolishing frontiers, the incompatibility of life-styles and traditions" (1991, 21). Racialized nativism plays out the politics of race on the terrain of culture. It constructs a marked division between the dominant traditions and ways of life of the United States and the cultures of Third World immigrants. Given their cultural difference, the latter populations are often construed as incompatible with and as a threat to the integrity of the national body—the national body "conceived as founded on a bounded and distinct community which mobilizes a shared sense of belonging and loyalty predicated on a common language, cultural traditions, and beliefs" (Stolcke 1995, 8). And since Third World immigrants are seen as cultural threats, they are also customarily relegated to the margins of society, often blamed for the social and economic ills that befall the nation, and exposed to a host of efforts to neutralize their difference.

One of the best articulations of this racialized nativism comes from the nationally recognized conservative politician Patrick Buchanan. In a *Los*

Angeles Times opinion piece published on 28 October 1994, Buchanan expressed a deep concern for the future of the "American" nation. His main anxiety revolved around the possibility that, sometime in the very near future, the majority of Americans would trace their roots not to Europe but to Africa, Asia, Latin America, the Middle East, and the Pacific islands. He thus asked what it would mean for America if, for example, south Texas and Southern California became almost exclusively Latino: "Each will have tens of millions of people whose linguistic, historic and cultural roots are in Mexico," and thus "like Eastern Ukraine, where 10 million Russian-speaking 'Ukrainians' now look impatiently to Moscow, not Kiev, as their cultural capital, America could see, in a decade, demands for Quebec-like status for Southern California" (Buchanan 1994, B11). For Buchanan, this prospect is not very appealing. He notes that the United States is already suffering from the trend toward cultural differentiation: "Crowding together immigrant and minority populations in our major cities [is bringing] greater conflict. We saw that in the 1992 [Los Angeles] riots. Blacks and Latinos have lately collided in Washington's Adams-Morgan neighborhood, supposedly the most tolerant and progressive section of the nation's capital. The issue: bilingual education. Unlike 20 years ago, ethnic conflict is today on almost every front page" (B11).

From Buchanan's perspective, the only solution to the problem of ethnic and cultural conflict is to put a stop to immigration: "If America is to survive as 'one nation, one people,' we need to call a timeout on immigration, to assimilate the tens of millions who have lately arrived. We need to get to know one another, to live together, to learn together America's language, history, culture and traditions of tolerance, to become a new national family, before we add a hundred million more" (B11). He concludes the article by noting that "Americans" must have the courage to make the decisions that affect "our" lives; otherwise, others will "make those decisions for us, not all of whom share our love of the America that seems to be fading away" (B11).

The concern of racialized nativists has not been restricted to the cultural consequences of immigration. Nativist sentiment has also expressed itself in relation to the economic consequences or costs of "illegal" immigration. In 1994, for instance, Governor Pete Wilson filed a series of lawsuits against the federal government in which he sought to have California reimbursed for the cost of providing emergency healthcare, prison facilities, and education for illegal immigrants. According to the claims filed, the economic and political burden of serving the undocumented was so great that California had been denied its sovereign right to shape its own destiny, and thus that the presence of so many illegal immigrants in the state amounted to a foreign invasion the federal government was constitutionally obligated to resist: "The massive and unlawful migration of foreign nationals . . . constitutes an invasion of the state of California against which the United States is obligated to protect California" (Weintraub 1994, A3).[8] What's more, that same year the voters of California approved Proposition 187, a grassroots initiative that sought to deny undocumented immigrants access to welfare, education, and healthcare services.[9] The main assumption behind this proposition was that undocumented immigrants were using public services at such high rates that California's coffers were going dry. The state was thus increasingly unable to take care of its citizens and legal residents: "The people of California have suffered for too long from the impact of illegal immigration, specifically in the areas of crime and from the costs of health, education and welfare for illegal aliens. The time has come to stop rewarding illegal aliens for breaking our laws. With California's budget deficits spiraling out of control, the taxpayers of this state must conserve their scarce financial resources for the benefit of citizens and legal immigrants" (Citizens for Legal Immigration n.d.).

Those who supported Proposition 187 hoped that the denial of public benefits would reduce, if not altogether stop, the flow of undocumented immigrants, as well as compel those illegally inside the state to go back to their countries of origin: "Many of the hundreds of thousands of illegals who arrive every year will be discouraged from coming. Many of the more than two million illegals already here will be encouraged to leave" (Citizens for Legal Immigration n.d.). The state would thus be relieved of a significant burden on its monies, paving the way for a healthier and more affluent California: "Prop 187 will save taxpayers billions of dollars. . . . California's public services (health, education, and welfare) won't be depleted by funding illegals. With more money available for citizens and legal residents, the quality of services will improve" (Citizens for Legal Immigration n.d.). The proposition's goal, in short, was to solve California's social, political, and economic problems. The key was getting rid of the state's main problem: the illegal immigrant.

In addition to constructing illegal immigrants as cultural and economic burdens, racialized nativist discourses have also linked immigrants to a host of other social problems. For example, the Federation for American Immigration Reform, one of the most important and powerful immigrant reform groups in the country, has associated illegal immigrants with such problems as population growth ("immigration is directly responsible for over sixty percent of population growth in America, and three quarters of all Americans feel that overpopulation is a serious threat to their children and grandchildren in the next twenty-five year"), urban sprawl ("an estimated 1774 acres are 'developed' every week due to immigrant population growth, and the additional public infrastructure costs for immigrant population growth come to $1.37

billion a year"), unemployment ("an estimated 1,888,000 American workers are displaced from their jobs every year by immigration"), wage depression ("because too much immigration keeps wages low, wage increases in low-immigration cities have been 48 percent higher than in high-immigration cities"), inefficiency ("poor English skills among foreign-born residents cost more that $175 billion a year in lost productivity, wages, tax revenues and unemployment compensation"), housing ("the share of overcrowded housing is seven times higher in high immigration cities [at 22 percent] than in low immigration cities [at 3 percent]"), crime ("one fourth of the federal prison population is foreign-born, and the INS must deport over 30,000 criminal aliens every year"), and energy ("half of the increase in US energy since 1970 has been due to immigration, and, on average, an immigrant's use of energy more than doubles after arriving in the United States") (Federation for American Immigration Reform 2000, 7–8). Thus, from the perspective of the Federation for American Immigration Reform, immigrants represented a general, not just an economic or cultural, threat to the welfare of the nation.

Racialized nativist discourses have in general constructed undocumented immigrants as enemies who threaten the overall well-being of the body politic.[10] They have figured immigrants as hostile foreign bodies, as dangerous beings who only bring malaise to the nation. Since the name of the game is to preserve the health or well-being of the population, such negative construction of immigrants makes it imperative to control their presence in the social body: the nation can only be healed if the body of the immigrant is expunged. Thus, it is on behalf of the population that the attempts to exclude the immigrant from the nation are justified. The idea of "the population" functions as a mechanism for distinguishing those bodily interests that can be represented in the polity from those which cannot, from those that need to be eliminated in order to foster the well-being of the nation. The care and governing of the population thus becomes one with the fight against the enemy. This is the logic of biopolitics. With regard to immigration, the biopolitical division is also very much a racialized division. Not just any immigrant, but the "illegal"—and principally Mexican—immigrant is constructed as the enemy; it is therefore the illegal immigrant who must be controlled in the name of the common good.

The story does not end here. Nativists have not only constructed illegal immigrants as enemies and attempted to expel or exclude them from the body politic in the name of preserving the welfare of the population, but they have also created a climate so intensely anti-immigrant that it has spawned a number of immigration-control policies (or proposals) that have increased (or would have increased) the risk of death for immigrants. In other words, the extremity of the racialized anti-immigrant climate has led to the development of policy initiatives that implicitly judge the lives of immigrants to be unworthy, or at least not as worthy as the lives of U.S. citizens. This biopolitical rationality is most evident in two policy arenas: the control and management of the U.S.-Mexico border and the regulation of the reproductive capacity of immigrant women.

Deadly Crossings

"They keep coming," a voice inflects as the television ad commences with black-and-white footage of about a dozen putatively undocumented immigrants running between cars at the U.S.-Mexico border in San Ysidro. The words "Border Crossing, Interstate 5, San Diego County" are inscribed on the lower left-hand corner of the screen. "Two-million illegal immigrants in California," the voice continues. "The federal government won't stop them at the border, yet requires us to pay billions to take care of them."

"While Congressman Huffington voted against new border guards," another ad begins, "Dianne Feinstein led the fight to stop illegal immigration." An image of undocumented immigrants flowing over the border appears on the screen while Senator Feinstein's voice explains that 3,000 undocumented immigrants attempt to cross the border on many nights. She adds that despite being a senator for only a short time, she has already worked diligently to tighten the border with more agents, fencing, lighting, and other equipment. The ad ends with Feinstein addressing the camera: "I'm Dianne Feinstein, and I've just begun to fight for California."

What is interesting about these two 1994 campaign advertisements—one by former governor Pete Wilson, then running in the Republican gubernatorial primary, the other by Democratic senator Diane Feinstein, then running for re-election against Republican congressman Mike Huffington—is their striking similarity. Political figures from both the right and the left not only constructed undocumented immigration as a problem but also chose to dramatize the issue by focusing on immigrants illegally crossing the U.S.-Mexico border. This convergence simply reflected the notions, widely held in mid-1990s California, that the state had an illegal-immigration problem and that this was primarily because the border was out of control, under perpetual assault by seemingly endless waves of illegal aliens. Indeed, as Néstor Rodríguez points out, "In the late twentieth century, social construction of the border has reached intense levels as various actors (for example, politicians, government personnel, restrictionist groups, appointed commissions, academic researchers, and media agencies) create 'knowledge' of an everyday life 'reality' that the US southern border is out of control, that immigration is overwhelming US institutions (especially public ones), that present levels of immigration threaten the established social order and underlying US core values and identity, and so on" (1997, 225).

Thus, it seems that many of the ills that afflict the United States can be traced to the porosity of the U.S.-Mexico border. It is the permeability of this border that has made it possible, in the minds of many, for undocumented immigrants to invade the United States and threaten the welfare and security of the nation. In order to survive, then, that nation has to do a better job of controlling its borders. Its borders must be controlled. It is imperative. "They" must be stopped from coming.

One important outcome of singling out the permeability of the U.S.-Mexico border as a major source of the undocumented immigration "problem" has been the implementation of a policy of intensified border policing. In 1994, the Immigration and Naturalization Service (INS), under the direction of Commissioner Doris Meissner (and more broadly of Attorney General Janet Reno and the Bill Clinton administration), began implementing an ambitious plan to strengthen control of the Southwest border and thus to reduce the flow of illicit immigration from Mexico into the United States. As articulated in the *Border Patrol Strategic Plan: 1994 and Beyond, National Strategy*, this comprehensive border-control scheme was based on a strategy of "prevention through deterrence" (U.S. Border Patrol 1994). The objective was to increase fencing, lighting, personnel, and surveillance equipment along the main gates of illegal entry—such as San Diego, California, and El Paso, Texas—in order to raise the probability of apprehension to such a high level that unauthorized aliens would be deterred from crossing the border. Such localized practices of governmental intervention, it was argued, would disrupt traditional illegal crossing patterns, forcing migrants to consider passage through more arduous, remote locations. Potential border crossers would thus either be dissuaded from ever attempting to cross or fail repeatedly and give up due to sheer frustration and/or exhausted resources (Andreas 1998; Andreas 2000). The INS's utopian vision aimed for nothing less than a sweeping "restoration" of the integrity and safety of the Southwest border.

In California the INS's strategic plan manifested itself in the particularly intense policing of a stretch of border in western San Diego County that runs from the Pacific Ocean to the Otay Mesa port of entry (Cornelius 2001).[11] This stretch has historically been the main illegal-entry point into California. East of this area, the terrain is mountainous and rugged, making it a more difficult, dangerous, and less-desirable crossing point. The intensified enforcement of the western San Diego County border, dubbed Operation Gatekeeper, began on 1 October 1994.[12] The operation's goal was in essence to blockade the border, thereby either discouraging would-be illegal immigrants altogether or pushing them east of the San Diego–Tijuana zone into rural hills and forests where enforcement was deemed easier (Rotella 1994). This blockade entailed a number of tactics, primarily an amassing of agents along the border. Using horses, bicycles, sedans, all-terrain vehicles, military helicopters, and small, high-speed boats, agents of the U.S. Border Patrol were deployed along fields, canyons, riverbanks, and beaches throughout the San Diego–border area. The number of agents increased from 980 in fiscal year 1993 to 2,215 in fiscal year 2000 (U.S. General Accounting Office 2001, 31).[13] These agents have employed a host of technologies: light towers, sensors, mobile night-vision scopes, remote video-surveillance systems, and a ten-foot-high metal fence that covers the fourteen westernmost miles of the border. Operation Gatekeeper amounts to a quasi-military operation that combines fencing, lights, manpower, and high technology at the California-Mexico border in order to dissuade illegal immigrants from crossing into the United States and to make it easier to capture those who do attempt illicit entry.

Operation Gatekeeper has now been in effect for more than twelve years, with mixed results. On the one hand, the number of people attempting to cross the border at San Diego has dramatically decreased, as can be gleaned from the number of people arrested for unlawful entry in the San Diego area; during fiscal year 2004, for instance, arrests totaled about 138,608 (U.S. Department of Homeland Security 2005, 156), a remarkable change from the 524,231 arrests recorded during Gatekeeper's first year (U.S. Immigration and Naturalization Service 2002, 212). "Operation Gatekeeper," notes Senator Feinstein, "has really been an unprecedented success. What it tells me is it's a myth that the border can't be enforced. It can be enforced" (Ellingwood 1999b, A3). However, many indicators suggest that enhanced border enforcement has not had much impact in reducing the overall number of unauthorized boundary crossings. During fiscal year 2004, for instance, arrests of undocumented immigrants across the entire Southwest border totaled 1,139,282 (U.S. Department of Homeland Security 2005, 156)—only marginally less than the 1,212,886 arrests recorded for fiscal year 1993 (U.S. Immigration and Naturalization Service 2002, 212), prior to the commencement of Operation Gatekeeper. Despite all the resources poured into boundary enforcement, not much of a dent has been made in the number of apprehensions: the total is basically the same today as it was in 1993.

The reason behind the steady overall number of illicit border incursions is relatively simple: as the Border Patrol closed urban routes to illicit traffic, would-be immigrants instead sought to cross through more-remote and less-policed mountain and desert locations (Andreas 2000; U.S. General Accounting Office 2001; Nevins 2002). In California, for example, the fortification of San Diego County pushed immigrant traffic into Imperial County, a stretch of desert in eastern California and western Arizona. Thus, rather than stopping the flow of unauthorized immigrants, the strategy of prevention through deterrence merely displaced it. INS apprehension statistics provide evidence of this displacement, clearly demonstrating that as the number of arrests plummeted in San Diego in the late 1990s, they concomitantly increased along other parts of the U.S.-Mexico border. The most dramatic upsurge was registered in the El Centro, California, area: the number of arrests rose from 30,058 in fiscal year 1993 to 238,126 in fiscal year 2000 (U.S. General Accounting Office 2001, 31)—an increase of 692 percent. The number of arrests in Yuma, Arizona, rose from 23,548 in fiscal year 1993 to 108,747 in fiscal year 2000; during the same years, in Tucson, Arizona, it rose from 92,639 to 616,346 (ibid.). While Border Patrol operations may have successfully stemmed the flow of illegal immigration into specific areas like San Diego County, overall its efforts have proven ineffective. And any success has come with a rather high price: the lives of migrants.

In some ways, the U.S.-Mexico border has always been a place of danger for those trying to cross it illegally (Eschbach et al. 1999). Immigrants have had to traverse the Rio Grande and other fast-moving waterways under the cover of darkness, travel in sealed and inadequately ventilated freight compartments of trains or trucks, trek through the desert terrain of the Southwest, and climb fences and other steel barriers erected by the U.S. government to secure the border. Given such dangers, clandestine border crossings have sometimes had tragic consequences. Over the years, many immigrants—it's hard to say exactly how many—have lost their lives trying to reach the United States. Some have drowned in swollen rivers, swept away by force of the current. Others have suffocated, the air in their poorly ventilated train compartments having run out. Still others have died of dehydration or hypothermia as they attempted to cross the rugged deserts of the Southwest. Today, crossing the border is even more perilous due to the shifting of undocumented immigrant traffic away from urban areas to less-policed, remote locations (Cornelius 2001; Eschbach et al. 1999; Nevins 2002). The deserts and mountains through which most undocumented immigrants currently enter the United States are less-than-ideal crossing points. Immigrants attempting to cross through these areas are likely to be ill-prepared for the rigors of a walking journey that may last several days. Some immigrants may carry insufficient supplies of food or water; others may not bring the clothing appropriate for the notoriously extreme (both hot and cold) temperatures of this rugged terrain. As a consequence, immigrants who dare to cross the border do so at great risk. According to the California Rural Legal Assistance Foundation (2004), the peril is so great that, since Operation Gatekeeper began, on average more than 100 immigrants have died each year trying to enter California without documents. By contrast, only twenty-three such deaths were recorded in 1994, prior to the full implementation of Gatekeeper (Cornelius 2001, 669). Taking the Southwest border as a whole, the number of migrants who have died trying to cross has averaged more than 300 per year since 1997 (California Rural Legal Assistance Foundation 2004). Enhanced boundary policing appears to have made illegal border crossing more perilous. In fact, as the traffic of illicit bodies has moved from urban to rural locations, the risk of death has increased to such a degree that the border has in effect become an exhibit of death.[14]

The fact that large numbers of border crossers are dying has not escaped the notice of the Border Patrol, which appears to be concerned about this development. In 1998, for example, it launched an operation designed to curtail the number of border-related injuries and deaths (U.S. General Accounting Office 2001, 24–28). This operation, called the Border Safety Initiative, focuses on educating would-be undocumented immigrants about the dangers of crossing the border and on search-and-rescue. However, while the Border Patrol may have noticed that immigrants are dying and taken some steps to remedy the situation, it has not acknowledged that its operations brought about the problem in the first place. Indeed, the agency has failed to take any responsibility for the rise in migrant deaths. As one Border Patrol officer put it: "Death on the border is unfortunate, but it's nothing new. It's not caused by the Border Patrol. It's not caused by Gatekeeper" (Ellingwood 1999a, A28). Contending that it is simply doing its duty of safeguarding the nation's border by closing off busy urban crossing points, the Border Patrol argues that if immigrants consequently choose to cross through rural terrains, the responsibility for any unfortunate incidents lies with the immigrants themselves and with the smugglers who guide them. The reality is, however, that as long as urban crossing points remain closed and immigrants are forced to seek passage through risky mountain and desert locations, the death toll will continue to climb. So, while the Border Patrol may not strictly speaking be liable for the fatalities at the border, it does bear responsibility insofar as these deaths are an effect of strict border policing. Immigrants are dying, and they are dying as a consequence of a stringent policy that propels them to cross the border through dangerous terrain.

What is the biopolitical significance of these issues? For one, the general logic of border control is a biopolitical one. Certain bodies—immigrant bodies—have been discursively constructed as dangerous to the body politic and must therefore be eliminated or excluded. The same discourses trace many of the ills that plague the United States to the permeability of the U.S.-Mexico border, which purportedly allows illegal immigrants to overrun the United States, endanger the welfare and security of the nation, and threaten the existence of the basic social, cultural, and political institutions of the body politic. If the nation is to survive and prosper, the logic goes, its borders must be controlled. This is precisely what the Border Patrol has attempted to do, through regulatory strategies such as Operation Gatekeeper, and insofar as it aims to control the border in order to ensure the welfare of the social body, it is operating according to the rationality of biopolitics. Foucault suggests that the concern of modern forms of government is to produce a healthy and productive citizenry, with a general commitment to foster the health of particular bodies in order to nurture the well-being of the composite body of the population. In the case at hand, the Border Patrol, as a state institution, plays a role in cultivating the life of the population by controlling borders and regulating the flow of people into the national body. This allows the state to exclude those foreign bodies deemed dangerous to the welfare of the population and to preserve the nation's resources for those members seen as properly belonging to the body politic. In short, the entrance of illegal bodies into the body politic is managed and regulated for the greater good of all. It is in defense of the population that borders are controlled.

Through the control of the border, the state creates a wedge between the normal and the pathological, distinguishing those bodies that can be represented in the polity from those that cannot, from those against whom society must be defended. But the biopolitical implications of the policing of the border do not end here. Not only does the state construct illegal immigrants as undesirable and prevent them from entering the United States, it also implicitly judges them to be expendable, suggesting that their lives are not quite worthy of being lived. The current policing of the border, insofar as it pushes immigrants to cross through dangerous territory, increases the risk of death for immigrants. The officials of the U.S. Border Patrol know this, yet the policing of the border continues unabated, which suggests that the immigrant deaths are acceptable to the state in its quest to enforce its borders. This does not mean that the Border Patrol wants immigrants to die; it simply signifies that, in order to protect its population, the Border Patrol, and the federal government more generally, is willing to tolerate a few casualties. The biopolitical implication is that the state is making a decision on the value and nonvalue of life, distinguishing between those lives that deserve to be lived and those that can be disallowed to the point of death. The lives that deserved to be lived are those of the citizens who make up the population—the lives the federal government aims to foster. Those that can be disallowed to the point of death are those of the immigrants who attempt to cross the border illegally—the lives from which the body politic must be defended. The value of an immigrant's life is therefore not quite the same as that of a citizen's and can be disallowed to the point of death in order to nurture the life of the population. This is the rationality of biopolitics: it does away with life in the name of life itself.

Denying Care

The second policy arena in which the rationality of biopolitics is at work involves the attempts during the 1990s to deny undocumented immigrant women, particularly Mexicans, access to prenatal care. Since 1986, undocumented women in California have been eligible to receive government-financed checkups, nutritional supplements, fetal monitoring, and other prenatal aid.[15] The rationale for providing such care seems to be pragmatic in nature: "Prenatal care saves money by reducing the number of sickly infants who, if born in the United States, are citizens anyway" ("Cutoff of Prenatal Care" 1997, A28). All the same, critics contend that providing such assistance is unwise, for it acts as a magnet for illicit immigration (McDonnell 1998, A24). The scenario they paint is one in which "poor immigrant women are drawn to the US to give birth in publicly financed county hospitals, allowing their children to be born as US citizens and subsequent recipients of taxpayer-supported medical care, public assistance, and education. Immigrants and their children constitute a growing underclass, draining education and medical resources in the United States" (Hondagneu-Sotelo 1995, 173). Moreover, critics argue, it is not really fair for illegal immigrants to receive free prenatal care since most citizens of California are not eligible for such benefit (McDonnell 1997b, A29).

The most vociferous of these critics has been the former governor of California Pete Wilson. While in office, he took it on himself to block undocumented women from having access to prenatal care. The governor first tried to end prenatal care for undocumented immigrants in 1994, right after California voters overwhelmingly adopted Proposition 187. One of the main aims of the ballot measure was the elimination of nonemergency medical care for those in the country illegally. From the perspective of the governor, this meant, among other things, barring undocumented women from access to prenatal care. However, a federal court blocked the execution of most of the proposition, so the governor was unable to implement his plan. This failure did not seem to discourage him. A couple of years later, he again moved to end prenatal care for illegal immigrants, this time finding justification for his plan in Congress's 1996 revision of U.S. welfare law. His revised plan incorporated many issues that had been enunciated in Proposition 187, one of them being that states were generally prohibited from providing nonemergency aid to illegal immigrants. For Governor Wilson this again included denying women access to prenatal care—and again his move was blocked. In March 1998, a Los Angeles superior-court judge issued an injunction preventing Governor Wilson from denying prenatal care to undocumented women (McDonnell 1998, A24). The rationale for this injunction: while Congress did prohibit states from providing nonemergency aid to undocumented immigrants, it also guaranteed that poor immigrants, of whatever status, could retain access to publicly financed diagnosis and care of transferable diseases. Congress reasoned that to bar immigrants from such aid would compromise the public health. For the court, the treatment and diagnosis of communicable diseases in pregnant women could not be disassociated from prenatal care.

While Governor Wilson was never able to carry out his plan and more recent governors (Gray Davis, Arnold Schwarzenegger) do not seem to oppose prenatal care for immigrant women, the fact that prenatal care was ever at issue is highly significant in and of itself. Biopolitically speaking, it suggests that reproduction ceases to be a "fact of Nature" and becomes instead a social-technical object, a manageable social practice (Horn 1994, 66). Thus, in order to ensure the welfare of the social body, the body of the immigrant woman is turned into an object of ongoing surveillance and management. This biopolitical imperative takes two forms. On the one hand, biopolitical logic suggests that in order to foster the welfare of the population, illegal immigrants need to be provided with prenatal care, for such care helps prevent the spread of communicable diseases; it also saves money in the long run by curtailing the number of unhealthy infants born in the United States, infants who would likely need and be entitled to long-term, government-funded care. Either way, the population as a whole benefits from providing immigrants access to prenatal care. Therefore, it is in the name of the greater good of all that such access is provided. This logic underpinned the decision of the Los Angeles superior court, as well as the viewpoint of various government officials who supported prenatal care for undocumented women.

On the other hand, biopolitical logic paradoxically suggests that in order to nurture the well-being of the population, undocumented women must be denied access to prenatal care, which serves as a magnet that draws more immigrants, who represent a threat to the welfare of the social body, into the United States. Denial of prenatal care to this population should discourage others from crossing the border and thus make it possible to foster the well-being of those who properly belong in the United States. The explicit aim of efforts to deny undocumented women access to prenatal care is thus to discourage immigrants from coming illegally to the United States. One could argue, moreover, that with respect to those illegal immigrants already living in California, such efforts function as attempts to govern the reproduction of an undesirable population.[16] Since undocumented immigrants are deemed, at least in some circles, to pose an uncontrollable threat to the nation's economic, cultural, and political health, any law or policy that would bar them from using reproductive-health services can be seen as an effort to discourage them from reproducing and thus to control their numbers, which sends a "powerful message about who is worthy to add their children to the future community of citizens" (Dorothy E. Roberts 1997b, 205). Such "population" policies thus demonstrate how certain elements of the body politic seek to regulate the reproductive capacity of unworthy segments of the general population in defense of the interests of the nation-state. These policies seem to be formulated and exist in direct relation to any group's perceived value within the polity (Collins 1999). They are designed to foster the welfare of the nation through the elimination or exclusion of those bodies deemed dangerous.

Efforts to discourage or prevent the propagation of unworthy segments of the population is hardly a new phenomenon in the United States. The regulation of the immigrant woman's body is only the latest in a long string of policies aimed at promoting the health of the population through the elimination of the unfit. During the first half of the twentieth century, for example, the eugenics movement proffered a theory stipulating that intelligence and other character traits were genetically conditioned and thus inherited (Dorothy E. Roberts 1997b, 212–14). This theory drove a campaign to redress U.S. social problems by guarding against biological degeneracy. Eugenicists thus promoted policies such as compulsory sterilization to prohibit people "likely" to produce defective offspring.[17] Eugenicist thinking was so influential that by 1917 sixteen states had enacted involuntary-sterilization laws aimed at those considered burdens on society: habitual criminals, the mentally retarded, epileptics, and various categories of the insane (Porter 1999, 170). And the influence of eugenics did not stop there. It extended even to the U.S. Supreme Court. In a 1927 decision, *Buck v. Bell*, the court upheld the constitutionality of a Virginia involuntary-sterilization law. Reflecting the majority opinion, Oliver Wendell Holmes expressed the eugenicist tenor of this decision: "It would be strange if it could not call upon those who already sap the strength of the state for these lesser sacrifices, often not felt to be such by those concerned, in order to prevent our being swamped by incompetence. It is better for all the world, if instead of waiting for their imbecility, society can prevent those who are manifestly unfit from continuing their kind. The principle that sustains compulsory vaccination is broad enough to cover cutting the Fallopian tubes. ... Three generations of imbeciles is enough" (quoted in Collins 1999, 272). The basic view of eugenicists was that social problems were technical problems amenable to biological solutions; the control of reproduction was thus crucial to their project.[18] It was only through regulating the propagation of the unfit that the future prosperity and security of the population could be ensured. As such, the eugenicist project can be seen as a precursor to contemporary efforts to control the reproduction of immigrants. In both cases the objective is the same: to control the reproduction of those deemed a burden to society. And they are both manifestations of a politics aimed at fostering the well-being of the population.

From a biopolitical perspective, U.S. efforts to deny undocumented women access to prenatal care are really attempts to govern the proper form of species reproduction. The fight against the enemy takes place on the terrain of the immigrant woman's body, the aim being to eliminate the enemy through controlling its capacity to reproduce. The rationality of biopolitics thus takes the form of a social-technical intervention designed to transform the procreative practices of undocumented immigrants, managing and regulating them for the greater good of all. In addition, some lives are implicitly judged worthy, while others are not. Had Governor Wilson's plan gone into effect and undocumented women been denied access to prenatal care, it would have led, most medical experts warned, to an increase in infant mortality, birth abnormalities, and illness (McDonnell 1997a, A49). For example, Dr. Brian D. Johnston, speaking as president of the Los Angeles County Medical Association, noted that "cutting prenatal care for pregnant women will cause unwarranted suffering, avoidable birth complications, sicker, smaller babies and needless disability" (McDonnell 1996, A3). Similarly, Dr. Jack Lewin, speaking as executive vice president of the group, stated that the denial of prenatal care to undocumented women "will cause an epidemic of low-birth-weight babies and expectant mothers presenting late to emergency rooms" (A3). According to medical authorities, then, prenatal care is crucially important to the well-being of a pregnant woman and her child, and a healthy society must include the provision of such care irrespective of a woman's legal status.[19] Despite the suggestions of medical experts, however, Governor Wilson maintained that limited state funds should go to legal residents and not to illegal immigrants (McDonnell 1997b, A3). Denying such care would have been tantamount to exposing the immigrant child and mother to death, or at least to multiplying their risk of death. Governor Wilson thus established a fundamental division between those who must live (or whose lives must be fostered) and those who must die (or whose lives can be disallowed to the point of death). This division pivots around the legal-illegal axis, suggesting that illegal lives are expendable, that the lives of undocumented immigrant women and their children are not worth living. Such is the rationality of biopolitics. It sets up a confrontation between life and death, giving credence to the idea that the elimination of the enemy—that is, of the undocumented immigrant—will make the body politic stronger and more vigorous. The sovereign right to kill thus appears here "as an excess of 'biopower' that does away with life in the name of securing it" (Stoler 1995, 84).

Conclusion

It is in the space between life and death that one must locate present-day rejection of the immigrant. The logic of anti-immigrant politics is such that it aims to fortify the welfare of the population through the elimination of those influences deemed harmful to the well-being of the nation. The exclusion of the immigrant and the control of the immigrant woman's reproduction are thus judged as necessary to ensure the survival of the social body. If this is the logic of anti-immigrant politics, then one is dealing with nothing other than biopower. This concept describes a technology of power whose main object is to foster the welfare of the population. As such, the function of biopower is to regulate the species body and its reproduction, its highest function being to invest life through and through. However, as Jennifer Terry points out, "under the guise of health and welfare, the administrative state turns politics into biopolitics, where decisions and choices are constructed in terms of preserving life and determining benevolent destruction" (1989, 33). Under the logic of biopower, it is thus possible to simultaneously protect life and authorize a holocaust. The correlate of the power to safeguard an individual's lasting existence is the power to expose a whole population to death. While the repudiation of the immigrant in the United States may not be tantamount to a holocaust, the logic in both cases is the same: it is that of biopower, which posits that to protect life one must disallow it to the point of death.

Notes

1 I want to make two things clear. First, not all immigrants have been necessarily constructed as problems. Certain categories of immigrants, notably undocumented immigrants and Mexicans, have received a disproportionate share of anti-immigrant sentiment. Others, such as high-skilled Indian immigrants, have received relatively little attention. Second, not everyone constructs immigrants as problems. Numerous sectors of the population, including foundations, immigrant-rights groups, business

leaders, governmental agencies, politicians, and laypeople more generally, have actively argued that the presence of immigrants actually benefits the United States. My totalizing here is intended to emphasize that the general climate in the United States, particularly in California, has been distinctly anti-immigrant during the past couple of decades. While the highest level of anti-immigrant sentiment occurred in the early to mid-1990s, it is still very much alive today.

2 Biopower actually has two poles, or forms. One form, which Foucault calls a biopolitics of the population or simply biopolitics, is concerned with the species body, "the body imbued with the mechanics of life and serving as the basis of the biological processes: propagation, births and mortality, the level of health, life expectancy and longevity, with all the conditions that can cause these to vary" (1978, 139). This form will be the primary focus of the essay. The second form, which Foucault calls an anatomo-politics of the human body, or discipline, implies the management of the species body in its depths and details. Here biopower centers not on the species body per se but on the individual bodies that compose it. Indeed, the target of discipline is not the collective mass but the individual human body: the body taken as an object to be manipulated. The goal of discipline is to produce human beings whose bodies are at once useful and docile. It is to optimize the life of the body, to augment its capabilities, extort its forces, and increase its utility and docility. For more on this pole, see Foucault 1979.

3 The following reading of Foucault is influenced by the work of Giorgio Agamben (1998) and Ann Laura Stoler (1995).

4 Foucault (1991a) views this fight against the enemy as a form of racism. For him, however, as Diane Nelson notes, "racism is not just the assignment of hierarchical value to a range of phenotypic expressions such as hair, skin color, and nose shape. . . . Foucault sees racism instead as a grid of intelligibility, a grammar that is not necessarily about any particular group of people but about a more generalized division within a body politic. He connects racism to a pervasive sense of threat from internal enemies whose identities vacillate. Racism, understood as the constant war against these threats to the health and happiness of this body politic, promises a common good—it is not merely a negative or repressive discourse" (1999, 94).

5 This goal was perhaps most clearly articulated in a booklet of national-socialist ideology published by Ottmar von Vershuer, one of the most authoritative German specialists in matters of health and eugenics: "'The new State knows no other task than the fulfillment of the conditions necessary for the preservation of the people.' These words of the Führer mean that every political act of the National Socialist state serves the life of the people. . . . We know today that the life of the people is only secured if the racial traits and hereditary health of the body of the people [*Volkskörper*] are preserved" (quoted in Agamben 1998, 147).

6 Jews were typically characterized as a diseased race, as a cancer in the body of the German Volk. One physician, for example, described Jews in the following terms: "There is a resemblance between Jews and tubercle bacilli: nearly everyone harbors tubercle bacilli, and nearly every people of the earth harbors the Jews; furthermore, an infection can only be cured with difficulty" (quoted in Proctor 1995, 173). What the Nazis did then, according to Zygmunt Bauman, was "split human life into worthy

and unworthy: the first to be lovingly cultivated and given *Lebensraum*, the other to be 'distanced,' or—if the distancing proved unfeasible—exterminated" (1989, 67–68). It was thus in the name of the preservation of life that Nazi Germany was able to massacre millions of Jews.

7   In 1970 the foreign-born accounted for 8.8 percent of the population of California, while in 2000 the statewide total was 26.2 percent. As for the Latino population, the numbers went from 8 percent to 32.4 percent (Cleeland 1997; U.S. Bureau of the Census 2005). These demographic transformations have a lot to do with the changing nature of the U.S. economy. As industrial production has moved oversees, to take advantage of wage differentials, the traditional U.S. manufacturing base has deteriorated and been partly replaced by a downgraded manufacturing sector, one characterized by an increasing supply of poorly paid, semiskilled or unskilled production jobs. The economy has also become more service oriented. Financial and other specialized service firms have replaced manufacturing as the leading economic sectors. This new core economic base of highly specialized services has tended to polarize labor demand into high-skill and low-skill categories. The upshot is that these changes in the economy, particularly the creation of low-skill jobs, have created the conditions for the absorption of vast numbers of workers. For a longer exposition on these economic transformations, see Calavita 1996.

8   The suit was based on Article IV, Section 4, of the U.S. Constitution: "The United States shall guarantee to every State in this Union a Republican Form of Government, and shall protect each of them against Invasion" (Quoted in Weintraub 1994, A3).

9   Although the measure was overwhelmingly approved (59 percent to 41 percent) by the voters of California, it never went into effect. Its main provisions were declared unconstitutional.

10 See also Chavez 2001; Coutin and Chock 1995; Hing 2004; Ono and Sloop 2002; Schneider 1998; Takacs 1999.

11 On 1 March 2003 the INS, the federal agency traditionally responsible for enforcing the nation's immigration laws, was officially abolished and its duties—including border management—transferred to various agencies within the newly created Department of Homeland Security. As part of this realignment, the U.S. Border Patrol, the entity historically in charge of policing the border between ports of entry, was placed under Customs and Border Protection, a new agency within Department of Homeland Security responsible for overall border security.

12 Operation Gatekeeper actually covers the sixty-six westernmost miles of the U.S.-Mexico border (U.S. General Accounting Office 2001). But the more heavily policed stretch runs from the Pacific Ocean to the Otay Mesa port of entry.

13 The fiscal year runs from 1 October through 30 September. The staffing numbers are for the entire San Diego Border Patrol sector, which covers the sixty-six westernmost miles of the U.S.-Mexico border.

14 I thank Julie Dowling for helping me come up with the phrase "exhibit of death."

15 For a more thorough legislative history, see California Primary Care Association 1999.

16 For a more general treatment of population policies aimed at poor women and women of color, see Patricia Hill Collins 1999.
17 Eugenicists also lobbied for restrictions on the immigration of inferior races (e.g., Jews, Italians) as a means of protecting the nation from genetic contamination (Dorothy E. Roberts 1997b, 212–13).
18 In *The History of Sexuality* Foucault notes that as the practice of modern government came to center on population as its object, reproduction, as well as sexual conduct more generally, became an important target of management and intervention. It was important for the state to administer the reproduction of individuals, for this could affect the health and future prosperity, eugenics, and security of the population.
19 Many studies have shown that inadequate prenatal care is linked to health risks such as low birthweight, premature delivery, birth defects, and HIV infection (Schwartz 1997, 697–703).

THE TOPOGRAPHY OF VIOLENCE

PART 2

Manufacturing Sexual Subjects:
"Harassment," Desire, and Discipline
on a Maquiladora Shopfloor

LESLIE SALZINGER

✸ On first entrance, the shopfloor is eerily familiar: the nubile women workers of managerial dreams and feminist ethnography, theory, and nightmare are brought to life in its confines. Rows of them, darkened lashes lowered to computer boards, lids fluttering intermittently at hovering supervisors who monitor finger speed and manicure, concentration and hair style, in a single glance. Apparent embodiments of availability—cheap labor, willing flirtation—these young women have become the paradigmatic workers for a transnational political economy in which a highly sexualized form of femininity has become a standard "factor of production."[1]

In this context, allegations of "sexual harassment" repeatedly surface among critics and journalists, sitting uneasily amid reports of job loss in the First World and exploitative wages and male unemployment in the Third. However, few have stopped to investigate the relationship between the sexualization and the cheapening of production or its role in the transformation of working-women into "nimble fingers." Within this analytic vacuum, the language of sexual harassment serves to obscure more than it illuminates, as it focuses attention on isolated, aberrant, generally dyadic interactions, rather than on social and organizational processes.

Although I spent eighteen months doing participant observation in Mexico's border export-processing (*maquila*) industry, it was during the months I spent in Panoptimex, the plant described above, that I first began having difficulty responding to journalistic questions about sexual harassment.[2] In Panoptimex, sexuality is an integral part of the fabric of production, an essential aspect of the process through which labor is transformed into labor power and women into the "docile and dexterous" workers of transnational repute. Within this context, there is nothing out of the ordinary about sexuality on the shopfloor. On the contrary, it is fundamental to efficient labor control and hence to production itself. Therefore, only by removing the lens of "sexual harassment," with its focus on individual perpetrators and unwilling victims, does it become possible to see the role of sexuality on the shopfloor—that is, to discern the systematic role of desire in constituting productive workers.

The journalists' repeated inquiries had some basis, of course. Sexual harassment as conventionally understood—as "unwanted sex-related behavior at work that is appraised by the recipient as offensive, exceeding her resources, or threatening" (Fitzgerald, Swan, and Fischer 1997, 15)—is certainly a problem in the maquila industry, as it is in a wide variety of industries and cultural contexts (Gruber, Smith, and Kauppinen-Toropainen 1996). However, their questions envisioned psychologically or morally troubled individuals, impelled by obstreperous libidos and secretly targeting unwilling individual victims. In this framework, the organization is obscured by the image of the "offender" and the ongoing constitution of consent is similarly hidden by the image of the "victim." While such a lens does reveal important workplace problems, in focusing attention on the isolated, closeted dyad it impedes investigation of more social and systemic manifestations of shop-floor sexuality.

The academic literature on sexual harassment is built on many of the same underlying assumptions (Stockdale 1996b; Welsh 1999; Williams, Guiffre, and Dellinger 1999). Because the field is dominated by lawyers and psychologists, individuals (as both targets and perpetrators) rather than organizations become units of analysis. This tendency is often accentuated methodologically, as most psychotherapists, whatever their disciplinary origin, recruit a cross-section of the population to survey or participate in experiments, rather than interviewing or observing people located within a single workplace.[3] This leads to a set of questions about the statistical likelihood of particular sorts of people harassing or being harassed, specific individuals' tendency to label these interactions as "harassment," and predicted resiliency of targets in the face of harassment. Even in studies where organizational structure is an explicit issue (Gruber 1998; Hulin, Fitzgerald, and Drasgow 1996), workplaces themselves are treated as individual units within a set and sorted by particular characteristics, rather than investigated as productive wholes.

Just as the emphasis on individual perpetrators distracts researchers from analyzing the role of sexuality in the workplace as a whole, so the emphasis on individual victims obscures the more subtle role of sexuality in the constitution of shop-floor consent.[4] Thus, investigators tend to focus on the impact of shop-floor sexualization on those explicitly targeted, at the expense of analyzing its meaning for workers overall. Similarly, they highlight blatant coercion, and in so doing neglect situations in which women workers are successfully interpellated as sexual objects and so respond affirmatively, even enthusiastically, to be addressed as such (Althusser 1971).[5]

In recent decades the term sexual harassment has served an important intellectual and political function, drawing attention to the sexual coercion of women at work. However, precisely because of its capacity to name the problem, it has effectively come to stand in for all problematic workplace sexuality. As a result, its essentially psychological rather than social perspective increasingly constrains broader analysis of the role of sexuality in the workplace. "Sexual harassment" implies a process that is an intrusion in the workplace, rather than an integral part of production. That is, it highlights isolated, hidden, individual interactions at the expense of systemic, visible, and structural processes. In addition, by focusing on dyadic interactions, it leads to questions about individual choices and the allocation of blame, rather than about the way in which a given workplace evokes particular sexual subjectivities in managers and workers alike. In this way, the notion of sexual harassment impedes investigation of other manifestations of sexual exploitation at work.

Panoptimex

Panoptimex, a highly successful television manufacturer, is a subsidiary of Electroworld, an enormous electronics transnational.[6] Since moving into its new building several years ago, the plant has been remarkably successful. Its production quantities and quality levels rival those produced by the same corporation at far higher cost in the United States. Recently, another TV assembler in the area, in the Mexican border city of Juárez, was so impressed by the plant's results (and look) that it bought the building blueprints for its own second plant.

Panoptimex's success is directly, if unintentionally, related to the extreme sexual objectification of the plant's workforce. Visually oriented managers have created a structure of labor control in which everything is designed to produce the right look. In the process, they have designed a machine that evokes and focuses the male gaze in the service of production (Berger 1972; Mulvey 1975). The building is a panopticon, an architecture designed to control through visibility, a visibility that is ultimately as much abotut fostering self-consciousness as it is about the more mundane operations of supervision. The logic which designed it is also at work in populating and managing it. Thus, a generation of managers accustomed to electronics factories full of young women have taken care to fill their own factory accordingly.

Labor control operates within this visually oriented context. The enactment of managerial practices based on men obsessively watching young women creates a sexually charged atmosphere, one in which flirtation and sexual competition become the currency through which shop-floor power relations are struggled over and fixed. In this framework, women are constituted as desirable objects, and male managers as desiring subjects. Male workers become not-men, with no standing in the game. Far from impeding production, aggressive, often coveted, supervisorial sexual attention is the element through which labor control operates. In Panoptimex one finds a workplace in which sexuality is integral to production, not an intrusion on it. Rather than impairing efficiency through myriad isolated and closeted encounters, sexuality is made a highly visible and central element in the labor-control process. Televisions are produced not through the excision of distracting sexuality, but through the ongoing, systemic incitement of desire in production.

Over-seers

The structure of production on any given shopfloor is initially imagined and established by management. In the maquila industry, where capital faces a disorganized workforce and a captive state apparatus, the situation is particularly acute. While founding decisions do not ensure managerial control, they do set the context within which struggles over control will take place. Thus, with regard to the role of gender in production, one must first analyze the frameworks within which managerial "common sense" is established and the strategies that emerge from this cluster of understandings.

At Panoptimex this common sense is remarkable for its consistent bias toward visual signs and symbols of success or failure. Management's visually skewed attention is the product of a cluster of forces, both institutional and discursive. Standard maquila accounting practices, the erosion of profit margins in the production of low-end televisions and the high internal mobility of top Electroworld managers combine to undermine a focus on costs and profits for their own sake and to encourage a focus on impressing headquarters instead. At the same time, these institutional predilections are solidified and underlined by the more general, visual rhetoric of TV production, in which "the picture" is the frame within which everything is understood and evaluated.

This attitude has distinct consequences when it is turned from managers' bosses to their subordinates. Once focused "down," both literally and metaphorically, this visual attention is transformed into the gaze of sexual objectification. The focus on the "look" of the factory, combined with a long tradition of women workers in electronics, leads to a rigid form of job-gendering, one in which filling the lines with young women becomes a goal in itself. Together, these institutional routines and attentional habits lead to a highly sexualized pattern of hiring and labor control—a pattern that ultimately proves both pleasurable and titillating (if also disturbing) for the young women on the shopfloor and, in part because of this, proves remarkably effective in shopfloor control.

Projecting Up

Production at Panoptimex occurs in a highly symbolic system, one in which appearances are as much the currency as dollars. To a certain extent, this is an issue throughout the industry. Most maquilas are far from any point of sale, and their accounting systems are organized to "make their budget" rather than to make a profit.[7] As a result, local managers find themselves more subject to the managers at corporate headquarters than to external competition, and they direct their energy accordingly. However, at Panoptimex, the tendency to make headquarter approval the primary goal of work on a daily as well as long-term basis is particularly accentuated. For example, late in my sojourn in the factory Electroworld was forced by international creditors to cut its workforce by 10 percent across the board, and Panoptimex responded with a major effort—of bookkeeping. No one was fired. No money was saved. But 10 percent of salaries were moved to the "miscellaneous" category of the budget. Looking credible was enough: there was no countervailing price or profit pressure direct enough to undermine this entirely symbolic solution.

Two sets of institutional forces—intense price competition in the international television industry and Electroworld's career trajectories—frame Panoptimex's operations and evoke such responses. Television production's low profit margin is a rarely discussed backdrop against which daily decisions are made on the shopfloor. "TVs are not a business," the manager of Electrofeed, a local Electroworld parts-maker, told me early on. "If you had to face stockholders with only a TV business...." He shook his head. The profit margin on the low-end televisions produced by Panoptimex are so slim, according to the plant manager Carlos, that making the budget frequently means literally selling below cost. So, why produce televisions at all? Because, he explained, it's worth it to Electroworld to keep its name in the marketplace in general. Once that's accomplished, profit can be made elsewhere—in VCRs, for instance. Thus, Panoptimex managers are not alone in treating costs symbolically; the overall corporate decision to continue television production is predicated on the calculation that it is worth it even under conditions in which it may not turn a profit on its own.

The sense among Panoptimex managers that appearances are paramount and that the relevant audience is headquarters is further encouraged by Electroworld's corporation-wide managerial placement policies. Electroworld is a U.S. subsidiary of an even larger European corporation. Panoptimex managers report to bosses in the United States, but their personal career trajectories move throughout the corporation as a whole. Top managers around the world are brought in for several-year periods and then moved on to keep them from being overly attached to—and hence losing their "objectivity" about—the factory they're running. As one of them matter-of-factly explained to me, "The truth is I'd get less emotional about fighting for this place than for my little radio plant in England." This external staffing policy has obvious implications for the perspective of those brought in from the outside, including the Panoptimex manager Carlos. Carlos, a Brazilian on a three-year contract, made it clear that his sights were set far above Panoptimex; he spent the better part of a first interview discussing details of the corporate structure and explaining where he'd like to be and when. These were no idle daydreams. His attention was firmly fixed on those who had the power to move him where he'd like to be.

These institutional patterns—a market in which profits cannot be the primary criteria for success; a structure of career opportunities in which top managers are not deeply tied to "their" factories; and a set of accounting practices which formalize local managers' absolute reliance on headquarters—together encourage a highly symbolic attitude toward production. Televisions still must be produced, if possible without huge cost overruns and with reasonable quality. However, top management attempts all this with an eye focused neither on "the consumer" nor on "the competition," but on the boss.

Seeing Is Believing

Such institutional patterns encourage a focus on appearances, but they do not ensure it. The institutional structures that influence Panoptimex are far more common among Juárez maquilas than is the plant's overwhelming focus on the look of things. What makes these structures so significant at Panoptimex is that they create an appearance-directed context within which the visual rhetoric available in television production can, and does, frame managerial perspectives on the shopfloor. In listening to Panoptimex managers, the sight-related criteria through which success and failure are assessed is striking and pervasive. Ultimately, this visual rhetoric is both symptomatic, and constitutive, of the habit of watching as a practice of control.

The general visual focus held throughout the factory emerged almost obsessively in Carlos's conversation, most clearly as the centerpiece of his triumphal autobiography. With a practiced gesture, he would pull from a top desk drawer photos of a factory he had run in Singapore. "It was all shit, just shit, girls working with garbage all around. Dark, ugly, I change all that. We paint, we make it nice." He slammed down the before-and-after pictures for emphasis, expostulating on the importance of color scheme and pointing out details of the shift. The color scheme was of particular importance, he pointed out, and his first act in Juárez was to paint Panoptimex in identical tones. His commentary on daily management practices revealed the same visual emphasis: he discussed at great length his capacity to see production from his office window, describing calls down to floor supervisors to check on problems and remind them he was watching. And with regard to the importance of politic ignorance, he covered an eye with his hand and commented, "I have to keep my eyes closed here all the time."

This visual idiom of control is most clearly embodied in the physical structure of the shopfloor. Clean, light, spacious, and orderly, the production area is the very image of a well-run factory. Top managers are highly aware of and invested in this fact, and they often boast about the factory's attractiveness. The shopfloor is not only easy on the eye, however; it is organized for visibility, a fish bowl in which everything is marked. Yellow tape lines the walkways; red arrows point at test sites; green, yellow, and red lights glow above the machines. On the walls hang large, shiny white graphs documenting quality levels in red, yellow, green, and black. Just above every worker's head is a chart that indicates, say, one defect, or three defects, or perfect days. Workers' bodies, too, are marked: yellow tunics for new workers; light blue tunics for women workers; dark blue smocks for male workers and mechanics; orange tunics for (female) "special" workers; red tunics for (female) group chiefs; ties for supervisors. Everything is signaled.

Ringing the top of the production floor is a wall of windows, a manager behind every one. They sit in the semiprivacy of the reflected glare, watching at will. From on high, they keep track of the flow of production, calling down to supervisors to ask about slowdowns, which are easily visible from above as accumulations of televisions in one part of the line, as gaps farther along, or as a mound of sets in the center of a line, with technicians clustered nearby. It is from the glassed-in balcony that managers show the factory to visitors, boasting about the plant's large capital investment and unique labor process. In the past, men with cameras sat behind the glass walls and watched for stealing, and it's common knowledge on the shopfloor that there are still cameras embedded in the ceiling for this purpose—even the walls have eyes.

Hiring for Looks

Panoptimex managers' focus on the look of things is expressed particularly clearly in the plant's gendered hiring practices. In the five years since Electroworld began producing entire televisions, including the two years since that process was moved into this showcase factory—years in which there was a dramatic "shortage" of young female labor in Juárez—Panoptimex has almost never had less than 70 percent women on the line, and rarely less than 75 percent.[8] The average age on the shopfloor continues to be under twenty, and the managers have yet to place a man in the chassis-building section.

When queried about their absolute commitment to hiring women for most line jobs, Panoptimex managers tend to point out that electronics—certainly Electroworld—*always* hires women, whatever country they're in. When I asked about the decision to hire women even when they're much harder to find than men, Panoptimex's last manager (prior to Carlos) commented matter-of-factly that "electronics traditionally used female types." Other upper-level managers had similar narratives.[9] Supervisors request not only the number of workers they need for their line but the gender of each position as well. The personnel department puts a great deal of daily planning and energy into hiring the "right" gender for the jobs available. The plant's head of personnel details criteria for most line jobs, which begin with being female and young, and continue with slimness, thin hands, and short nails. The criteria also include not being pregnant, using birth control, and being childless or (if absolutely necessary) having credible childcare arrangements. The most basic of these requirements is being female, closely followed by having a particular, sexualized body type. As a result, on hiring days guards admit all the female applicants who come to the maquila gates, but only a previously specified number of men. The few men hired for the line's "heavy" jobs are not subject to the bodily strictures required of their female counterparts; in place of those strictures are a substantially more demanding set of social requirements. Unlike their female co-workers, men must be vouched for by the union or someone else already known in the plant, and they must present a certificate of high-school graduation.

While these criteria and practices were not unheard of among other Juárez maquilas, what set Panoptimex apart was the lengths to which its managers went to ensure a female workforce even during the shortage of young women workers in the late 1980s, even as their colleagues in other maquilas began hiring men, albeit reluctantly. Panoptimex managers decided to recruit workers from a village with an "agrarian economy" an hour out of the city. In an extended "public relations" campaign involving all levels of the personnel department as well as top managers from other departments, Panoptimex first courted the mayor, then treated the whole village to a picnic with mariachis, then knocked on all 150 doors in the village with pictures of the plant, and finally agreed to pay transportation for all young women willing to come to work in the factory. Four years later, these young women still work the lines, and Panoptimex is still paying for their transport.

Panoptimex's relentlessly visual managerial framework is expressed not only in how managers deal with their superiors but also in their hiring and labor-control practices. As a result, they hire assembly-line workers who are overwhelmingly female and young—the age to be beautiful and to be invested in that beauty—and then monitor them through obsessive observation. The essence of the Panoptimex hiring criteria was succinctly expressed by a woman supervisor in another Electroworld plant: "In Panoptimex they don't look for workers, they look for models—short skirts, heels, beauties." To my eye, Panoptimex workers are no more beautiful than young women in other maquilas, but they *are* hired as "models," that is, to look the way managers expect workers to look. Sexual objectification is part and parcel of the hiring process.

In the Fishbowl

Panoptimex's managerial focus on control through vigilance is expressed throughout the factory in a hierarchy of sight. While top managers sit behind windows above the shopfloor, supervisors walk the lines below. As supervisors tour the shopfloor, workers sit before them. In front of workers, however, there is only their work and their individualized quality charts, with co-workers glimpsed from the corners of their eyes. Shop-floor control is orchestrated through a set of embedded panopticons: managers watch supervisors and workers, supervisors watch (most) workers, workers watch themselves and, when they can, each other.

At the same time, one could also describe men watching men watching women (and ignoring a few emasculated men). Or, one might more accurately include both these social realities: a panopticon in which male managers watch male supervisors who watch women workers and ignore a few male workers. The hierarchy of sight is as defined by gender as it is by the relations of production, with predictable sexual effects.

Managers' attentional practices and the physical space they have spawned have constituted a highly visual system of labor control, which differentially affects women workers—the central objects of supervisorial attention—and male workers—the objects of aggressive disregard. Although it can be described with no reference to sexuality, the tremendous interpellatory power of the plant's system of labor control comes from its organization of desire. Even the most cursory tour of the shopfloor reveals an intensely sexualized atmosphere, and conversations with workers only add to this impression. These subjectivities in turn have repercussions for the level of managerial control on the shopfloor, accounting both for the shopfloor's intense atmosphere of titillation and control, and for its highly successful production record.

Super-vising

Unlike Electroworld's other maquilas in Juárez, Panoptimex produces a final product. From the beginning to the end of its long, looping lines, hundreds of tiny components are combined with monitors and cabinets to emerge as televisions, ready for sale. Production takes place in five lines—each one a perfect replica of the next. One hundred and twenty workers make up each line. Backs to their supervisors, eyes to their work, they repeat the same gestures a thousand times during the nine-and-a-half-hour day.

The first part of the line assembles the television's innards. This is "chassis," the plant's most "critical" operation, wherein several hundred miniature electronic parts are inserted into prepunctured boards. The work is done by forty seated young women, each of whom inserts six to eight tiny, color-coded parts during every thirty-second "cycle." From there, the chassis is tested before moving on to the end of the line where ten young men, standing, attach it to monitors and cabinets. Turning the corner into "final," the now recognizable television reenters the women's domain, where the electrical system is assembled, wires soldered and twisted—the facsimile made real. On to the "tunnel," where young women peer at the screen, seeking straight lines, ninety-degree angles, and clear pinks and greens. When the television is ready for use, it moves back into male territory, at the line's end, where it is packed, boxed, and marked with one of a half-dozen brand names, finally rising to the ceiling in a glass tube and vanishing from sight. Soon it will reemerge in warehouses on the other side of the border, last stop before the large chains that bring it to consumers throughout the United States.

As in almost all maquilas, the workers who produce these televisions are paid poorly, even in local terms. Most workers took home roughly forty dollars weekly during the period I studied the plant.[10] While this is not a negligible sum, it is well below what is required to live independently in Juárez, and even this amount is contingent on perfect attendance. Missing a single day of work costs a third of the weekly paycheck. Seniority doesn't change this, as promotion is extremely rare. As a result, three-quarters of the workforce is replaced over the course of a year. Not surprisingly, therefore, most workers are teenagers and live with family. Given this pay structure, labor control cannot depend too heavily on financial incentives or hopes of promotion. This is where the tremendous scrutiny under which workers operate in the plant and the sexual self-consciousness that emerges from that scrutiny become fundamental.

Lines are "operator controlled." The chassis comes to a halt in front of the worker, and she inserts her components and pushes a button to send it on. There is no piece rate, no moving assembly line, to hurry her along. But she hurries anyway. In this fishbowl, with managers peering from their offices above, no worker is willing to be seen with the line clogged behind her, an empty space ahead of her. And if she does slow momentarily, the supervisor materializes. "Ah, here's the problem. What's wrong, my dear?" He circles behind seated workers, monitoring "his girls" as he is monitored from above.

There are layers upon layers of supervision. Above the shopfloor hover those known from below as "the Americans"—top managers who, for all their varied origins, are marked by the U.S. headquarters to which they report. Their presence is often noted by workers and supervisors seeking to explain the difference between Electroworld plants. A Mexican assistant personnel manager commented, "[At Panoptimex] there are visitors all the time, and the windows all around. . . . All the time you know they're watching you." And they do not only watch from afar. In the late afternoons Carlos and his chief of production descend to observe more closely. Hands clasped behind backs, they stroll the plant floor, stopping to berate a supervisor about a candy wrapper lying on the floor or to chat with workers on the line.

Below the production manager are the supervisors. Two to each line, they are all Mexicans, all men, most in their early thirties, and all but one with some technical or managerial training.[11] Both watching and being watched, they are particularly sensitive to, and reflective of, the prevailing visual idiom in the plant. After I had spent several months in the plant, one supervisor told me of rumors pervasive among them that my car, a fifteen-year-old Ford with a smashed-up front, had an incredible motor camouflaged beneath the battered exterior. This visual expression of distrust, the assumption that something is hidden from the eye, expresses both their vulnerable position in the plan hierarchy and their immersion in a world of visual signs and symbols. True to this focus, they spend virtually all day standing just behind workers' shoulders—watching. They alternately compliment efficiency and deride mistakes, decide who can still work when they arrive late and who can't, initiate and bar conversations, commandeer and offer forbidden candies, lecture and cajole whenever quality or speed falter. Their attentions are not evenly distributed, however. Although they are responsible for their entire half of the line, supervisors in chassis can generally be found in the section where components are inserted by hand, and supervisors in final can be found in the testing tunnel. That is, they hang out where the girls are.

The sense of being watched comes not only from being looked at in the moment but also through the managerial production of signs and symbols that are then available for surveillance. The chart above each worker's head, for example, is fully visible to her at all times, as well as to anyone walking by. Group leaders fill them out each day. Gold stars signify perfection. Green dots signify errors. Red dots signify trouble. The resulting sense of exposure has consequences for workers' senses of self and self-worth. A woman whose chart was full of green and red dots commented, "I feel ashamed. It's all just competition. You look at the girl next to you and you want to do better than she does even though it shouldn't matter." At the end of each day, announcements echo over the shopfloor as each line finishes its daily quota of a thousand televisions. In lines that are far from reaching their quota, the group leader begins circulating anxiously an hour before the shift's end, urging workers to "get a move on" or theirs will be the only line that doesn't make it. The line always picks up speed at this point. When I asked a young woman generally notable for her jaundiced attitude what was going on, she shrugged: "When they start congratulating the other lines for having finished and we haven't, you feel bad. Competition makes you work harder."

Labor control in Panoptimex is achieved through practices—primarily but not exclusively visual—that speak directly to workers' senses of self. Whatever their center of attention in any single situation, managers' ultimate goal in the factory is to see that televisions get built to their bosses' satisfaction. They achieve this somewhat indirectly, however, by focusing on who workers are, rather than on the work they do. In this process, worker subjectivities are directly addressed, and their success or failure as workers is easily conflated with their success or failure as human beings. The merging of workers' work and personal identities gives management tremendous leverage on the shopfloor.

But that is not the whole story. The managers' psychological leverage is achieved by addressing neither a concrete "worker" identity nor a more abstract "human" identity. The set of subjectivities addressed on the Panoptimex shopfloor are highly heterosexualized, and the narrative of shop-floor quiescence begins to make sense only when one investigates the substance of the subjectivities that are constituted and spoken to in the panopticon. Therefore, I will retell the story above with the "empty places" filled (Burawoy 1979, 150), investigating the impact not of bosses watching workers, but of male bosses watching young female workers, of the male gaze in the service of managerial control. It is thus that the depth of shop-floor control becomes comprehensible.

Ogling and Dis-regarding

The visually defined practices that typify labor control at Panoptimex are imbued with sexual energies and gendered meanings when they are practiced in this girl-filled, guy-dotted space. Inside the panopticon managers and supervisors are situated as voyeurs, while women workers are at the center of attention. Monitoring becomes the gaze of sexual objectification as soon as it locks on the women. Male workers, on the other hand, are at the periphery, beneath notice. Neither watching nor watched, they are as emasculated as their female co-workers are objectified. Thus, the plant's visually defined practices frame a highly sexualized set of meanings in and for production.

Supervisorial subjectivity reflects and embodies this symbolic framework. As the plant's official watchers in this gendered space, the supervisors, as much as their charges, are located in a sexual relationship. This is expressed in their initial self-presentations, as well as in their routinized daily behaviors. The supervisors are generally married with children, yet they openly flout their marriages on the shopfloor, and their children make appearances only in joking references to their manhood. They are required to wear ties, and whether a booted, blue-jeaned "cowboy" or a "serious professional," each stamps his line with an idiosyncratic version of this symbol of masculine predominance.

Beneath the gaze of these monitors, female and male workers are incorporated into production in distinctive ways. They are given different identification numbers, different uniforms, different jobs and are subject to different modes of supervision. Women do "detail" work such as inserting components and checking quality; men do "heavy" work such as assembling the cabinet and packing the finished product. On top of this base, other differences arise. Women sit, men stand. The center of the line is a female domain; its ends are male. Chassis, with a one to fifteen ratio of group leaders to workers, is all women. Final, with a one to twenty-seven ratio, is almost half men. Within final, the group leader does all communication with the men, which leaves the supervisor free to spend all his time with the women in his line. The cumulative, symbolic, and practical effects of these differences are overwhelming. Women are centralized—watched, constrained, pinned down. Men are de-centered—ignored and relatively free to move.

The differences between men and women—and (also therefore) the meanings of femininity and masculinity in the plant—are marked as much by ongoing managerial behavior as by managers' initial setup in the structure of production. Every afternoon, Carlos walked the lines, all masculine and proprietary expansiveness, and "joked" with women workers; he ignored those who would be "men" on the line. Among the women, too, he only recognized some. As he walked, he stopped and talked to an ever-changing favored few. These conversations were flirtatious and titillating, full of teasing on both sides, with mild, blushing self-revelations on the part of workers, and pseudo-paternal supportiveness on his part. He did not stop at speaking, either. It was well known in the plant that he had a mistress on the lines, as did the chief of production. Thus, every conversation was tinged by ambiguity and the flavor of forbidden sexuality.

The plant manager was not alone in this. His example echoed down through the ranks and in any case followed a plant tradition that predated his tenure. Nonhourly workers, from low-level engineers on up, prowled the lines in search of entertainment of all sorts. In this context, supervisors took full advantage of their superior access. One of the workers favored by Carlos's attentions commented pitilessly on her co-workers. She reported that the supervisor on her line propositioned everyone and that some made the mistake of going out with him in the hopes that it would lead to promotions. Not she, however, to whom it was obvious that he was very "hard" about all that. Another supervisor had gotten a worker pregnant and was currently dating another, both on his line. As the due date drew near, personnel staff teased him flirtatiously, threatening to tell his wife or throw him a baby shower. He strutted complacently. The norm was encapsulated by workers' approving comments about one of his (also married) colleagues, who all agreed was different from the others. "Why, as far as I know," said one woman, "he's only gone out steadily with one girl on his line, none of this using all the operators [workers]."

Supervisors not only use their position in production for sexual access but also use a highly sexualized discourse around workers as a means of labor control. It is striking to watch them wandering their lines, monitoring efficiency and legs simultaneously, their gazes focused sometimes on fingers at work, sometimes on the nail polish that adorns them. Often supervisors will stop by a favorite operator, chatting, checking quality, flirting. Their approval marks a "good worker" and "desirable woman" in a single gesture. Each supervisor has a few workers he hangs around with, laughing and gossiping throughout the day. It is not lost on their co-workers that these favorites eventually emerge elsewhere, in slightly higher paid positions on the line and, among those with the self-confidence to enter, in the plant's beauty contest. Through each day, managers and supervisors frame women workers as sexual beings and sexual objects. In this process, women workers become vulnerable to personal, as well as work-based, evaluations.

Women workers are not the only ones controlled through heterosexual discourses. Sexuality is also the arena in which managers and supervisors struggle for predominance, both in individual cases and in the larger symbolic context. The shopfloor is rife with supervisory and managerial complaints regarding how the other group's sexuality undermines shop-floor discipline. One supervisor complained that Carlos's tendency to talk to some workers and not others undermined "motivation" on the line. Another told of being forced by the production manager to allow a worker in on a day she arrived late. "Okay," he reported having agreed resentfully, "but then I'm not the supervisor any more." There were stories of a line where the production manager's mistress threw her weight around, making the other girls cry, yet remaining exempt from sanction. And the European Organization and Efficiency (O&E) manager for Juárez commented, "In the Mexican environment . . . you can imagine what are the other things a young girl can offer to a supervisor. . . . We've tried to crack down, but within the limits of the culture. . . . Macho is strong here." In these incidents, supervisors and managers jostle for control of the shopfloor in order to legitimate and affirm their masculinity, since this panopticon is about sexual mastery (or in the case of the European manager, about mastering sexuality), and they jostle for control of women workers in order to legitimate and affirm their shop-floor power. In the process, a configuration of production and labor-control processes are established that are as much about gender and sexuality as they are about efficiency and manufacturing televisions.

Struggles over and through the mantle of masculinity also mark relations between management and male workers, although it's an unequal battle from the outset. Top managers casually belittle men who work on the line. Dave, the Juárez personnel manager, offhandedly exempted male line workers from the category of "men" in explaining why they are excluded from his general policy to pay men more than women: "From a macho standpoint, a guy wouldn't take an operator's job." Supervisors are less offhand, but equally scathing in their assertions. A supervisor who found a young man behind schedule one afternoon was withering: "Just like I said, you have to keep an eye on these guys. He thinks he's some kind of Latin Lover." His target, a shy young man new to Juárez, looked at his shoes.

Managerial claims remain far more potent than those of male workers, in large part because they are reasserted in the structure of daily life in the factory. Like their female co-workers, male workers are disciplined within an essentially visual framework. However, rather than being placed at the center of an immobilizing optic, male workers are relegated to its periphery—actively ignored. Men are physically segregated, standing at the line's ends. The plant manager does not even slow down as he passes them during his daily perambulations, and the supervisor is conspicuous in his absence.

Emasculation does undercut male workers' capacity to resist, but as a mode of control, disregard also has its dangers for management. Men on the line are subject to little direct supervision. They move with relative freedom, trading positions among themselves and covering for each other during extra bathroom runs, joking and laughing, catcalling women as they pass by. Nonetheless, male workers' relatively autonomous physical location, while it does permit some degree of mobility and the enactment of a few masculine rituals, also provides a powerful tool for managerial control. Supervisors can always move male workers out of male territory, and occasionally they do just that. When men on the line get too cocky, the supervisor materializes and brings it to a halt. He might place the loudest of them in soldering, in conspicuous discomfort among the "girls," while the others make uneasy jokes about how boring it is "over there." Ultimately, the supervisor has the last word in masculinity. Male workers can challenge his behavior, but he can reclassify them as women. In such moments, he retains control precisely through this capacity to throw into question young male workers' localized gender and sexual identities.

Productivity at Panoptimex is born of the routinized sexual objectification of women workers by their male superiors. The plant's architecture and labor process incite and channel supervisorial and worker desire. In this context, supervisors become voyeurs, and women workers become productive objects of the male gaze. Labor control is established within this relationship, as young women workers are under constant watch and evaluation, both as sexual and as productive subjects, and the few young men workers are ignored, also in both capacities. Thus, just as young women become subject through their admission to a category dependent on managerial approval, young men—neither watchers nor objects of desire—become subject through their inability to claim any category through which to act. Sexuality is neither hidden nor extraneous to production in this context. On the contrary, it is powerful precisely because of its very visibility. In this process, it emerges as central to worker compliance and managerial control and thus as an intrinsic aspect of the process of production itself.

Making "Models," Making "Drifters"

In Panoptimex's labor-control practices, workers are hailed as gendered and sexual beings, and as gendered and sexual beings of particular kinds. Workers' response to this address is not preordained. Insofar as they emerge from this process as productive subjects, it is due to their capacity and willingness to answer to this ascription and to come to recognize themselves in these discourses. Thus, workers' factory-level experiences of themselves as (or as not) sexual subjects or objects, encapsulate the process through which sexualization operates through targets' desire, rather than "against their will," even as it effectively objectifies and disempowers them.

Any glance at the Panoptimex shopfloor encounters a sea of stockinged legs and high heels, rows of meticulously curled bangs and brightly manicured hands, women painting their lips on every line. It is difficult to be a woman on the Panoptimex shopfloor without feeling self-conscious. The light, the windows, the eyes, the comments—each and all are persistently, glaringly evident. This gaze affects women at all levels in the plant. As the weeks went by, I found myself buying lipstick and agonizing over my outfit in the cold darkness of a predawn winter's morning. Despite my best efforts, women in the plant were quick with more elaborate suggestions: it wasn't that I wasn't *feminine*, they would suggest diplomatically, but with a bit of makeup.... One young woman, explaining how much such things mattered, mentioned that she had missed work the day before because she slept too late—too late, that is, to do her hair and makeup and still make the bus. To enter the plant as a woman is to be immersed in objectification—to be seen, to watch, and so to watch and see yourself.[12]

A young woman on the line told her own story of transformation. When she started work, she used no makeup and wore only calf-length dresses. Soon her co-workers began telling her she looked bad, that she should "fix herself up." Thus encouraged, she decided to be less shy. Now, mini-skirted and made-up, she reported she finally felt self-confident in the plant. As she spoke, her best friend surveyed her physique with an affectionately proprietary air, remarking, "They say one's appearance reveals a lot." Later, they both appeared at the Electroworld beauty contest, an affair both badly organized and poorly attended, except for the fifty contestants, many from Panoptimex, who infused the occasion with a deep symbolic seriousness. The stories traded over cookies and shared lipsticks revolved around the lack of courage shown by those who "chickened out" at the last minute and the value of participating, whether or not one won, as an act of bravery and an assertion of self-worth. There were also extensive discussions about those left behind, about the importance of representing those on one's line who lacked the necessary bravery to be present themselves. To claim one's own desirability became an act of courage, independence, loyalty, and solidarity all at once.

The ultimate arbiters of desirability, of course, are supervisors and managers. Workers gossip constantly about who is or is not chosen. On every line, they can point out those Carlos speaks to and those the supervisor favors—women only too happy to acknowledge their special status. For those so anointed, the experience is one of personal power. "If you've got it, flaunt it!" a woman named Estela commented gleefully, her purple-lined eyes moving from her black lace bodysuit to the supervisor hovering nearby. This power is often used more instrumentally as well. On my first day in the plant, a young woman—known as one of the "young and pretty ones" favored by managerial notice—was stopped by guards for lateness. She slipped upstairs and convinced Carlos to intercede for her and was allowed to work after all. The personnel office was incensed, and the lines sizzled with gossip.

Gossip is the plant pastime and weapon of choice, as well as its most cited cruelty. "Did you see him talking to her?" The lines bristle with eyes. Quick side-glances register a new style, make note of wrinkles that betray ironing undone. "Oof, look how she's dressed!" With barely a second thought, women workers can produce five terms for "giving her the once over," words that shade in meaning from "gossip about" to "cut down" to "censure." The issue of favoritism is a constant source of conflict, and everyone is always watching. A frequent target of sexual rumors, Estela was torn about whether to be hurt or proud of her notoriety. The first time I met her she boasted, "The other girls don't like me, I get on their nerves." Turning to a co-worker, she asked, "Isn't that true?" The other girl nodded calmly. In this bounded space, femininity is defined and anointed by male supervisors and managers. Women workers have little to offer each other in comparison to the pleasures of that achievement and the perils of its loss.

If the young women in the Panoptimex plant have little to offer each other, the young men have even less. One unfortunate young man said he came here intentionally for all the women. "I thought I'd find a girl friend. I thought it would be fun." "And was it?" I asked. He paused. "No one paid any attention to me," he responded finally, a bit embarrassed, laughing and downcast. His experience brings specific scenes to mind: women on the line discussing the gendering of production, mocking men's "thick fingers" and lack of attention to detail, giggling helplessly at the notion of a male group leader. I hear again a comment made by one of the women who returned to the factory after having quit: "It's a good atmosphere here. In the street they [men] mess with us, but here, we mess with them a little. We make fun of them and they get embarrassed."

In the face of such commentary, men on the line struggle to affirm a legitimate masculinity in production. Like their female counterparts, they also look to supervisors to affirm their gendered location. Unlike their female counterparts, however, both what they want and how they attempt to get it require confrontation rather than intimacies. Eschewing indirect appeals for legitimation, they make constant, carefully ritualized demands that the supervisor acknowledge their masculinity, both on the shopfloor and off. In sotto voce rebellions in the plant, they impugn their supervisors' manhood and imply his fear of theirs. "If he has a problem, he should come tell us himself, not send Mari (the group leader) down. He's just afraid it could come to blows," complained a worker named Juan, in a characteristic (and characteristically hushed) critique. A group in final excitedly told me what had happened after I left their line's Christmas party. The supervisor showed up late and they asked him, "So what's the story here, do we talk to you like the supervisor or like a man?" Like a man, he responded. "So we gave it to him, almost insulting his mother!" they reported with relish.

Despite such performances, the plant denies male workers' masculinity in its very architecture, and supervisors have no reason to undercut this. On the contrary, male workers' desperate desire for respect becomes a potent tool of control. When supervisors tire of the constant challenges and move male workers into female territory, the effect is dramatic. Once snatched from their domain and relegated to the "womanly task" of soldering, even eye-stinging black smoke amid broken ventilators evokes no complaints.

In Panoptimex to be male is to have the right to look, to be a super-visor, as it were. Gender and production relations are discursively linked. Standing, facing the line, training his eyes on work, the male line-worker does not count as a man. In the plant's central game he is neither subject nor object. As a result, he has no location from which to act—neither in his relation to the women in the plant, nor in relation to factory managers. Just as his female co-worker becomes a productive subject through her response to managerial discourse, so does he. However, in her case the process has its pleasures. In his case it is the lure of fixing things, the recurrent desire to remake an untenable, local gender identity, that ties him into factory life.

Within the panopticon, workers are incorporated into production through the pleasures and pains of sexual objectification, and it is only through their willing participation in these processes that they become effective. The framework embedded in the language of sexual harassment directs one's attention to situations in which subordinates object to managerial overtures, at least internally. However, in Panoptimex all workers are interpellated into production as sexual beings, and in responding to this address, they become participants in the process through which they are controlled. It is this participation which makes labor control in Panoptimex so effective and so troubling. "Sexual harassment," recognizable and offensive, would not incorporate workers into their own subjugation, would not increase productivity, and would not affect those unattended to. However, the routinized operations of sexual objectification in Panoptimex accomplish all those goals, addressing workers as sexual and productive subjects simultaneously, and in so doing increasing supervisorial control and production quality in a single move.

Making Sexual Subjects

Panoptimex is a highly monitored space, yet rather than weighing down production through cumbersome checks and antagonisms, supervisorial vigilance is woven into the very fabric of the relationship between supervisors and workers, enhancing control and productivity simultaneously. Sexual objectification is central, as it is within this process that the male supervisorial gaze evokes productive subjects, thus integrating sexual subjectivities directly into the structure of production. Rather than interfering with production, sexualized surveillance creates workers both willing and able to produce.[13]

This suggests a fundamentally different image of the role of sexuality in production than that which is generally highlighted by the term "sexual harassment," yet it is, if anything, more consequential and problematic. Sexuality in the workplace is indeed sometimes extraneous, isolated, and hidden. However, as at Panoptimex, it can also be intrinsic to production, social, and highly visible—part of the basic infrastructure through which the factory operates. Much of the discussion of sexual harassment assumes that it is an impediment to production, and researchers tend to analyze its corrosive effects on productivity via increases in turnover, absenteeism, and lowered morale (Hanisch 1996; Knapp and Gustis 1996). These studies conclusively demonstrate the destructive impact of individual, aberrant, and stigmatized acts of sexual harassment on individual productivity. However, when the labor process itself is sexualized, as is the case in Panoptimex, sexuality and desire can themselves become productive forces, more than compensating for the random inefficiencies they introduce into the production process by their outsized capacity to constitute productive subjects. For those disturbed by forced sexual contact, the managerial capacity to harness workers' most intimate sense of self in the service of production might give pause.

By the same token, in scores of workplaces, malicious or troubled perpetrators harass individual, unwilling victims. In Panoptimex, however, flirtation is a social relation that defines and frames the interactions of supervisors and workers overall. In this context, the sexualization of work becomes significant for everyone on the shopfloor, whether or not they are personally involved in sexual game playing. Recognizing this more generalized process in turn suggests that an exclusive focus on worker refusal and supervisorial culpability in identifying problematic sexual contact misses much that matters. The most effective forms of labor control are interpellatory structures in which productive subjectivities are evoked within daily shop-floor interaction. Panoptimex's mode of shop-floor control is of this kind, and its content is highly sexualized. Workers are addressed and incorporated into production only (although not exclusively) within this framework. Indeed, it is the very demography and architecture of the plant which incites desire in its occupants—supervisors and workers alike. Insofar as one looks to the psyches of the particular individuals involved to explain this excess of shop-floor sexuality, one misses its primary structural catalyst. Factories produce widgets, but they also produce people. In Panoptimex this production process is a sexual one. Neither the supervisorial voyeur nor the seductive factory girl are personality types: they are Panoptimex products.

This recognition returns one to where one began, to the production of the "docile and dexterous" workers who are a staple of transnational production. Both managers and academic analysts tend to discuss this as a hiring issue. But the central story of Panoptimex's success is not one of effective hiring, but of the effective interpellation of those hired. Both job choice and hiring in the industry is remarkably casual, and young women workers who end up elsewhere show little of the sexualized docility evident at Panoptimex.[14] In fact, Panoptimex workers are striking precisely for their uncanny resemblance to the sexual objects and productive subjects implicitly promised in advertising brochures by maquila promoters. The process through which they have been so constituted is a sexual one, and its power suggests how essential it is that one develop a language that makes it visible. "Sexual harassment" is indeed an important concept, but one should not let it obscure sexuality's other shop-floor incarnations. Insofar as sexual objectification is a significant mode of shop-floor control, it requires further attention and analysis.

Notes

1 Benería and Roldán 1987; Elson and Pearson 1986; Fernández-Kelly 1983a; Fuentes and Ehrenreich 1983; Iglesias Prieto 1987; Kamel 1990; Sklair 1993; Standing 1989.

2 All factory, corporation, and personal names used here are fictitious. *Maquiladoras*—

or *maquilas*, as they're popularly known—are export-processing factories located in Mexico, generally along the country's northern border, which assemble parts produced in the United States for sale on the U.S. market. The highest concentration of maquila workers is in Ciudad Juárez, where I did my research.

3 Christine Williams (1997) and Jeff Hearn and Wendy Parkin (1995) make similar points. The overrepresentation of survey methods is evident in Margaret Stockdale's collection (1996a), in which every essay based on empirical data uses either survey or experimental methods.

4 For defining analyses of the production of shopfloor consent in general see Burawoy 1979; Burawoy 1985.

5 The definition of sexual harassment as unwanted is so ingrained in the academic literature that the 1999 *Annual Review of Sociology* commissioned two separate reviews, one focused on coercive sexual contact and the other on "positive and autonomous expressions of workers' sexual desire" (Williams, Guiffre, and Dellinger 1999, 73).

The troubling and intimate relationship between sexuality and power was first explored in depth by feminists in the 1980s (Snitow, Stansell, and Thompson 1983; Vance 1984) and by Michel Foucault (1980). Wendy Hollway and Tony Jefferson (1996) raised these issues explicitly in the context of sexual harassment, but the discussion is focused on psychological rather than structural processes.

A few ethnographic researchers studying service industries (Guiffre and Williams 1994; Loe 1996; Rogers and Henson 1997) have looked at the productive function and ambivalent worker experience of workplace sexuality. However, these studies don't explore the ways in which sexual interaction between superiors and subordinates can become an intrinsic element in labor control even in an industry in which femininity is unrelated to the product sold. Kevin Yelvington (1996) discusses sexuality at work in factory production, but he focuses on sexuality as a site of resistance rather than managerial control. Christine Williams (1997) also calls for such studies.

6 The research on which this article is based is part of a larger study of four Juárez maquilas done over eighteen months in the early 1990s (see Salzinger 2003). I spent three of those months in Panoptimex. During that time, I spent every weekday wandering the shopfloor, sitting in the personnel department or in meetings, or interviewing managers. I later interviewed ten workers I knew well at my home.

7 Panoptimex managers propose a budget to their U.S. superiors. Once accepted, their task is to spend no more than projected to assemble the promised quantity of goods. Spending more is a failure, but spending less is also penalized, as the following year's budget is cut accordingly.

8 The shortage of female labor is a reflection of how many young women are willing to work for below-subsistence maquila wages, not of how many young women workers are available in total.

9 The current plant manager, Carlos, is a notable and not terribly credible exception to this pattern. Having decided that as an American woman I would be an advocate of "gender-blindness," he eschewed any consciousness of gender in conversation with me, repeating that nothing mattered but the will to work. After one of our interviews, he was so concerned to prove this that he began badgering the (extremely irritated)

Juárez personnel manager to hire a blind man. When I mentioned Carlos's stance with regard to gender in the workplace, the Panoptimex personnel manager expressed skepticism, an unsurprising response given that Carlos's clear and not exactly disinterested preference for young women was an ongoing subject of office gossip.

10 Wages have since fallen further. Base pay is supplemented by a variety of coupons (e.g., for lunch and transportation) and yearly bonuses. Even with such additions, however, pay remains low. Some workers supplement their income by illicitly selling candy, jewelry, makeup, and other items on the shopfloor. This is difficult in chassis because of the high level of supervision, but relatively easy elsewhere. Management doesn't interfere unless it becomes too blatant. As a wage subsidy, it has its advantages for them, too.

11 There is one female supervisor, but she is on second shift. I have focused my analysis on first shift because, once managers leave their windowed offices in the evening, the panopticon is replaced by distinct modes of control.

12 Critiques of women's objectification have long been a staple of feminist theory (MacKinnon 1982; Mulvey 1975). Feminist analysis of its troubling pleasures have been less developed; two authors who do discuss this are Lynn Chancer (1998) and Valerie Steele (1985).

13 Here sexuality functions as one of Foucault's "disciplines" (1979).

14 See Salzinger 1997 for a comparison of varied labor-control strategies and their outcomes in distinctive shopfloor femininities and masculinities in the maquila industry.

The Dialectics of Still Life: Murder, Women, and Maquiladoras

MELISSA W. WRIGHT

Ambiguity is the pictorial image of dialectics, the law of dialectics seen at a standstill. This standstill is utopia and the dialectical image therefore a dream image. Such an image is presented by the pure commodity: as fetish. Such an image are the arcades, which are both house and stars. Such an image is the prostitute, who is saleswoman and wares in one.
—Walter Benjamin, *Reflections*

❋ During 1994–99 almost two hundred women were found murdered and dumped along the desert fringes of the Mexican industrial city of Ciudad Juárez.[1] On 21 March 1999 another young woman was found half-buried in the desert and bearing signs of rape and torture. Most of the women ranged in age from their teens to their thirties, and many worked in the export-processing *maquila* factories that have been operating in Mexico for three decades.[2] With international and national attention occasionally turning toward these brutal murders, a number of stories emerged to explain the troubling phenomenon.

The image of the Mexican woman formed within these narratives accords with Walter Benjamin's notion of a dialectical image, one whose apparent stillness obscures the tensions that actually hold it in suspension—a caesura forged by clashing forces.[3] The Mexican woman depicted in the murder narratives can be seen as a life stilled by the discord of value pitted against waste. A focus on the narrative image of this woman, rather than on the lives of the murder victims, reveals the intimate connection binding these stilled lives to the reproduction of value in the maquiladoras located in Ciudad Juárez. Through a comparison of a maquila narrative that categorically disavows responsibility for the violence with a maquila narrative that explains the mundane problem of labor turnover, the Mexican woman freezes as a subject, immobilized by the tensions linking the two tales.

In the tale of turnover told by maquila administrators, the Mexican woman assumes the form of variable capital whose worth fluctuates from a status of value to one of waste. Variable capital refers to the labor power—what the worker provides in exchange for wages—that produces a value in excess to itself (see Harvey 1982). The excess coalesces into surplus value. Marx says that labor power is a form of variable capital since it is worth less than the value of what it produces. In the turnover story the value of the Mexican woman's labor power declines over time even as her labor provides value to the firm. Furthermore, this deterioration produces its own kind of value as she furnishes a necessary flow of temporary labor. Her labor power is subsequently worth less than the value of her labor in a number of ways, given that her labor is valuable also for its inevitable absence from the labor process. Although the maquila spokespeople deny any similarity between the women described in the tale of turnover and those described in the stories absolving the maquilas of any responsibility in their murders, the notion of the dialectical image nevertheless points to the connections.

Turnover refers to the coming and going of workers into and out of jobs, and it often comes up during interviews in relation to the problem of worker unreliability. Industry analysts and administrators cite turnover as an impediment to a complete transformation of the maquila sector from a low-skilled and labor-intensive industry to one with more sophisticated procedures staffed by highly skilled workers (see Villalobos, Beruvides, and Hutchinson 1997). Workers who turn over, that is, do not demonstrate job loyalty, are not good prospects for the training necessary for creating a skill base. This form of variable capital is therefore the temporary kind. However, the turnover problem has not completely inhibited the development of a higher technological base in the maquilas since some workers are not of the turnover variety. Training programs, combined with an emphasis on inculcating loyalty among workers, have created a two-tiered system within maquila firms for distinguishing between "untrainable" and "trainable" workers. Gender is a critical marker for differentiating between these worker types.

Walter Benjamin (1969a) provides a good point of departure for this feminist interrogation into one of Karl Marx's staple concerns: the dehumanizing process behind forming variable capital, which, Marx writes, "converts the worker into a crippled monstrosity" (1977, 481). Through the image of dialectical stillness, Benjamin helps explain how this process involves not only the creation of value at the worker's expense but also a value that is valorized only insofar as it is counterposed to what it is not: waste. The kinship between discourse and materiality is key. In the maquilas, managers depict women as untrainable laborers; Mexican women thus represent workers of declining value since their intrinsic value never appreciates into skill but instead dissipates over time. Their value is used up, not enhanced. Consequently, the Mexican woman personifies waste in the making, as the materials of her body gain shape through the discourses that explain how she is untrainable, unskillable, and always a temporary worker.[4]

Meanwhile, her antithesis—the masculine subject—emerges as the emblem of that other kind of variable capital whose value appreciates over time. He is the trainable and potentially skilled employee who will support the high-tech transformation of the maquila sector into the twenty-first century. He maintains his value as he changes and develops in a variety of ways. She, however, is stuck in the endless loop of her decline. Her life is stilled as her departure from the workplace represents the corporate death that results logically from her demise, since at some point the accumulation of the waste within her will offset the value of her labor. And after she leaves one factory, she typically enters another and begins anew the debilitating journey of labor turnover.

In her wasting, therefore, the Mexican woman represents a value to capital in and of herself in at least two respects. First, she establishes the standard for recognizing the production of value in people and in things: value appreciates in what is not her. Second, she incorporates flexibility into the labor supply through her turnover. To use Judith Butler's formulation, this process reveals how discourses of the subject are not confined to the nonmaterial realm or easily shunted off as the "merely cultural." Rather, the managerial discourses of noninvolvement in the serial murders of young female employees is indeed linked to the materialization of turnover as a culturally driven and waste-ridden phenomenon attached to Mexican femininity. The link is the value that the wasting of the Mexican woman—through both her literal and her corporate deaths—represents for those invested in the discourse of her as a cultural victim immune to any intervention.

The Murder Stories

Circulating through the media and by word of mouth—as onlookers try to determine if the murder victims were prostitutes, dutiful daughters, dedicated mothers, women leading "double lives," or responsible workers—is the question: "Was she a good girl?" The question points to the matter of her value as one assesses if she is really worthy of concern.

When news of these murders first captured public attention in 1995, Francisco Barrio, then governor of the State of Chihuahua, raised this question when he advised parents to know where their daughters were at all times, especially at night, the implication being that "good girls" don't go out at night. It followed that since most of the victims disappeared in the dark, they probably weren't good girls. The local police regularly introduce this issue when bereaved parties seek official assistance in locating their daughters, sisters, mothers, cousins, and family friends. The police frequently explain how common it is for women to lead double lives and ask the grieving and frightened family and friends to consider this possibility (Limas Hernández 1998). By day, she might appear the dutiful daughter, wife, mother, sister, and laborer, but by night she reveals her inner prostitute, slut, and barmaid. In other words, she might not be worth the worry.

Related to the narrative of excessive female heterosexuality is the plot of the "foreign serial killer" woven by the special prosecutor. In this tale, one hears of how these murders are far too brutal for a Mexican hand and resemble events more common to the country's northern neighbor: the suave foreigner appeals to a young woman's yen for sexual adventure, lures her into his car, then murders her after having sex. On this theory, an Egyptian with U.S.-resident status working in the maquiladora industry was arrested in 1996. But since then another hundred bodies have surfaced.

The foreign-serial-killer version ties into the long-standing Mexican tradition of casting Ciudad Juárez as a city whose cultural values have been contaminated by greedy and liberal forces emanating from the United States (Tabuenca Córdoba 1995–1996). Such was the narrative woven by a Spanish criminologist, José Parra Molina, contracted by Mexican officials in 1998 to examine the crimes. He surmised that Ciudad Juárez was experiencing a "social shock" due to an erosion of its "traditional values" resulting from contact with a "liberal" American society. Consequently, he concluded, you now "see in the maquiladora exits . . . the women workers seeking adventure without paying attention to the danger" (Orquiz 1998, 3C).[5] The logic internal to this narrative implied that exposure to the United States had eroded traditional Mexican values to such a degree that young women were offering themselves, through their impudent behavior, to their murderers. Molina, among others, suggested that those women and girls could also have been walking into traps set by an international organ-harvesting ring that killed the victims for their organs, which were sold on the U.S. market. The problem, according to this story, is a cultural one. In such a cultural climate, such murders are bound to happen, and thus a cultural shift is required to "sanitize" the environment in which women along the border live and work. The cultural decline is found within the girls themselves. As Molina asked in reference to the discovery of a girl's body, "What was a thirteen-year-old girl doing out at night anyway?"

Evidence of her presence outside her home at night does not suggest her economic need or acknowledge a city full of nighttime commuters. Rather, it points toward a cultural decline within which her death, a form of absence, can be logically anticipated. Indeed, her absence ameliorates, to some degree, the cultural decline represented by her presence in the night since it takes her off the street for good. Her death is explained as a cultural corrective against the decimation of traditional values. As Molina said, these girls out at night are "like putting a caramel in the door of an elementary school" (ibid.). When somebody gobbles them up, like children with candy, at least the source of the tawdry temptation is destroyed.

This rendition can be characterized as a "death by culture" narrative, which points to forces internal to a cultural system that are driving the deviant behavior. Death by culture is Uma Narayan's characterization (1997) of the global discourses for explaining women's death in the Third World as somehow embedded in tradition, internally driven, and resulting from the distortion of "traditional" cultural values. The preceding murder narratives recreate the possibility that these women and girls are not only victims of a culture out of whack but are also emblems of the loss of values. They represent culture value in decline and therefore may not be valuable enough in death to warrant much concern. When one finds girls and women out on the streets at night, seeking adventure, dancing in clubs, and free from parental vigilance, one finds evidence of diminished value in their wasted innocence, their wasted loyalty, and their wasted virginity. The logical conclusion is, therefore, not to seek the perpetrators of the crime as much as to restore the cultural values whose erosion these women and girls represent.

A number of *Juarense* activists and local women's groups have countered these murder narratives with a version of the victims as hardworking and poor members of the community who deserve more public attention than they are receiving. Through editorial writing and public appearances, they warn that a "climate of violence against women" pervades the city. They identify male jealousy of wives' and girlfriends' economic independence and sexual and social liberty as motivating factors behind the crimes, as well as behind police reluctance to treat the murders seriously. And they have met with the Association of Maquiladoras (AMAC), the principal maquiladora trade association in Juárez, to ask for assistance in curbing the violence. During one meeting, the director of AMAC explained that he saw no relation between the industry and the murders. Therefore, even though thousands of workers have to cross unlit, unpatrolled, and remote stretches of desert as they make their way to the buses that stop only on main thoroughfares, and even though many victims disappear while on such commutes, there is nothing that the industry can do to stop the violence. Rather, the industry's stance is that neither funding for security personnel, nor outlays for improved streetlighting, nor in-house self-defense workshops, nor changes to production schedules will help.

This position has not changed noticeably even in light of more obvious connections linking maquiladora industrial activity with the murders. For instance, in March 1999, when the driver of a maquiladora bus raped, beat, and left to die in the desert a thirteen-year-old girl who worked in a U.S.-owned maquiladora—she miraculously recovered and named her attacker—activists implored the maquiladoras to acknowledge some connection between the murders and the city's industrial activity. Esther Chavez Cano, the director of the city's new rape crisis center, said, "This case is absolutely horrible. The maquilas should have as much trust in the bus drivers as they have in the managers. This is an example of how terrible things are in this city" (Stack and Valdez 1999). The maquiladoras have yet to respond to this indictment, and their position appears to be much the same as it was when Roberto Urrea, the spokesperson for AMAC, was interviewed in January 1999 by ABC. He cited female sexuality and nighttime behavior as the principal issues, asking "Where were these young ladies when they were seen last? Were they drinking? Were they partying? Were they on a dark street? Or were they in front of their plant when they went home?"[6] The silent corollary to these questions is the understanding that "men will be men," especially macho men, and if a woman is out drinking or partying or dancing on Juárez Avenida, then she should be prepared for the risks.

Urrea invokes a death-by-culture narrative to absolve the maquiladora industry of any implication in the violence. The maquila narrative depicts the murdered women as cultural victims of machismo combined with Third World female sexual drives and rural migrant naïveté. This narrative gains purchase with the city's long-standing reputation as a cultural wasteland, where American contamination and loose women have led to moral decay (Sklair 1993; Tabuenca Córdoba 1995–1996). And in such a cultural milieu, the murder of women cannot be avoided. Their deaths are only symptoms of a wasting process that began before the violent snuffing-out of their lives. The sorting through of the victims' lives illustrates the deep, cultural roots of waste, for as one scrutinizes the victims' sexual habits and sifts through the skeletal and clothing remains, one is supposed to wonder, "What was *she* doing there anyway?" What sort of culture devours its own?

Similarities link the death-by-culture narrative with descriptions of labor turnover. In the latter, the Mexican woman also plays a leading role, in this case as the perpetrator of extreme turnover as well as the reason why some measure of turnover is necessary for profit. She emerges in this story as a dialectic image built of both waste and value. Her odd configuration has roots in the cultural construction of female sexuality, motherhood, and a fleeting work ethic. It also has roots in the physiognomy of the Mexican female form—in her nimble fingers and sharp eyes that eventually, and always eventually, stiffen and lose their focus. The manager of any maquila faces the challenge of having to monitor this wasting process, which, again, according to the turnover narrative, is a culturally driven cycle whose deleterious effects on women's working lives are inevitable. The maquila industry is helpless to divert this culturally driven, corporate death.

Turnover and Corporate Death

To understand how in the maquiladora context the story of turnover produces a female Mexican subject around a continuum of declining value, one must examine it in relation to the value-enhancing process of training. While turnover refers to the coming and going of workers, training refers to the cultivation of worker longevity and firm loyalty. Both processes unfold through the materialization of their corresponding subjects: a temporary, unskilled labor force and trained, loyal employees, respectively. Trained workers are those whose intrinsic value has matured and developed into a more valuable substance, whereas temporary workers do not develop or transform over time: they simply leave when their value is spent.

Seeing turnover and training in this light adds another dimension to Marx's analysis of variable capital. The value of labor power varies not only because it produces value, as Marx suggests: labor power varies also because it produces waste. The laborer who is worth less than her labor is, in the story of turnover, eventually worthless even as she creates value. The trained subject, by contrast, is one whose intrinsic value increases over time and matures into a more valuable form of labor power, one that is skilled. As one American manager of a U.S. automobile manufacturer in Mexico put it, "Our goal is to take someone who just walked in the door and turn this person into a different kind of worker. Someone whose basic abilities have matured into something special."[7] Skilled labor power does not vary from the value that it produces to the extreme degree that unskilled labor does. Of course, there is some variation; otherwise, profit would not be produced. At issue is not a precise calculation of the dollar amount of profit that skilled labor creates but instead a sense that the more valuable the labor that goes into the production process, the more valuable the commodities emerging from it. In 1996, the German general manager of a hi-fi sound-systems manufacturer explained the situation to me this way: "To make quality goods, you need quality workers.... We still need some unskilled workers. Some of this work is still just assembly. But now we've got products that require people who are willing to learn something new."

Marx begins his analysis of capital with the commodity precisely to demonstrate that the things of capital cannot be understood without seeing their intimate relationship to the people who make them. He, too, was extremely concerned with subjectivity even though he overdetermined the parameters for considering what sorts of subjects mattered in his analysis. The notion of skill as a negotiated quality of value assigned to labor power takes its cues from feminist analyses of the valorization of workers and work, and the formation of skill categories. Feminist scholars have demonstrated that one must consider how perceptions of the subject inform perceptions of the value promised by the subject's labor power and how skill is key for the differential valorization of the labor force (McDowell 1997; Cockburn 1985; Elson and Pearson 1981). This feminist contribution does not replace a Marxian analysis, but rather reveals how poststructuralist theorizations of subjectivity are not necessarily at odds with a Marxian critique of capital (see Joseph 1998). Critical for Marx is an exploration of how value materializes as it does in capital, as one continually makes abstract connections linking human energies with inanimate objects. Marx made this point clearly, but he failed to recognize how the many forms of labor abstraction that are categorized variably as degrees of skill complicate the relationship, linking the value perceived in laborers to the value perceived to be embodied in the commodities that make.

Events over the last decade reveal how maquiladora boosters and managers recognize the tight connection between perceptions of worker quality and recognition of the sorts of products workers can make. There are now about 3,100 maquiladora facilities in Mexico, with a total employment of more than one million workers. Almost one-fourth of these workers are employed in maquiladoras located in Ciudad Juárez, and approximately 60 percent of these employees are women. Since the late 1980s, efforts to "skill up" the maquiladora labor force in the maquila industry have coincided with a concerted push by city developers and industry spokespeople to stress the labor market's ability to accommodate the global focus on product quality over quantity (Jorge V. Carillo 1990). Industry proponents, mindful of heightened competition for foreign direct investment by Asian countries that guarantee even lower minimum-wage rates for an immense labor supply, have emphasized that the city offers not only vast amounts of unskilled labor but also a sizable labor force that is trainable in just-in-time organizational systems, computer technologies, and even research and design capabilities. "Our workers can do anything here with some training, make the best products in the world," the director of a Juárez development firm asserted in 1994. Rarely is the claim made that this labor force *already* exists in the city. Instead, emphasis rests on the *potential* transformation of the existing labor market into one that will someday be brimming with skilled workers. In 1994 the administrator at one of the largest and most prestigious maquiladora development consultant firms explained the potential this way: "We know that if Juárez is going to prosper into the future, we have to adapt. And we already are. You don't find sweatshops opening here like before. Now we have high-technology companies, and they are looking for workers who can be trained. We are having more of these workers now, and they will help this city grow in the right direction." One highly lauded example of this sort of growth is the General Motors Delphi Center, which opened its doors in 1995. In a 1997 *Twin Plant News Staff Report* article, "Brain School," the director of Chihuahua's Economic Development Office exclaimed, "The Delphi center will revolutionize industrial production in our area." His view was seconded by a maquila manager who explained, "Without a doubt the most significant change has been the high technology manufacturing.... It just proves how the Mexican worker has been able to assimilate the ways of American business" (39).

Sorting subjects into trainable and untrainable groups is a first step toward upgrading that minority of the maquila labor force that will eventually assimilate to the demands of a dynamic global economy. Discerning between the trainable and the untrainable—the "quitters" and the "continuers" (Lucker and Alvarez 1985)—requires an evaluation of employees early in their careers in order to put them on the right track. The Brazilian manager of a factory that manufactures automobile radios explained, "We can tell within one week if the operator is training material. It's obvious from the beginning." The principal marker of the untrainable subject is femininity. As feminist histories of industrialization note, the notion of women's untrainability has a genealogy that reaches far beyond the maquila industry (Fernández-Kelly 1983a). The specificities of this untrainable condition vary depending on how the relations of gender unfold within the matrices of other hierarchical relations found within the workplace: the family, heterosexuality, race, and age, to name but a few. In the maquilas, the discourse of female untrainability plays out through explanations that describe what women do well as "natural" (e.g., dexterity) and that explain the cultural constitution of Mexican femininity as adverse to training. "Most of the girls aren't interested in training. They aren't ambitious," the manager of the automobile-radio factory told me in 1996. "I have tried to get these women interested in training," the American manager of an automobile firm explained in 1996, "but they don't want it. They get nervous if they think they will have to be someone else's boss. It's a cultural thing down here. And if they're not ambitious, we can't train them."

This culturally ingrained lack of ambition, nervousness with regard to responsibility, and flagging job loyalty create the profile of an employee whose untrainable position cannot be shifted through training. In 1994, when I asked the human-resource manager of a television manufacturer how he could recognize those workers who were involved in in-house training programs, he said, "Well, most of the workers in the chassis assembly [all are women] aren't taking training. They're not as interested. Most of our trained workers come from the technical and materials handling areas [which are completely staffed by men]." The gendering of work positions in this particular firm, as in many others, also reveals a gendering of trainability and the skilling-up of the maquila labor force. There are no statistics calculating the percentage of women participating in the multitude of training programs offered throughout the city in addition to in-house training opportunities. However, my interviews with the managers of seven "high-tech" maquilas and with instructors who offer maquila training programs indicated that women represented fewer than 5 percent of those enrolled in any type of skills training. The rate of female promotion into positions defined as skilled in three high-tech firms was less than that.

As a result, Mexican women are said to be principal contributors to turnover because untrainable workers are those who demonstrate the lowest degree of longevity on the job. "If you have a plant full of these girls," the Mexican general manager of a sewing operation explained, "then you're gonna have high turnover. And you can't train workers in that kind of environment." While the trade-journal literature rarely mentions gender as a variable in a maquiladora-related phenomena, managers are quick to mention sex difference as a key component of their "turnover problem." The Brazilian plant manager of a television manufacturer elaborated on this connection: "We have about 70 percent females here. That means high turnover. Sometimes 20 percent a month. Now the guys also sometimes leave but if they get into a technical position ... [they] usually stay longer. Our turnover is high because we have so many girls." The American human-resources manager of this same firm said, "You can't train workers if they won't stay around. That's the problem with these girls. You can't train them. They don't understand the meaning of job loyalty." The tautology described in this turnover narrative revolves around the following syllogism: that women are not trainable; that trained workers remain with the same firm longer than untrained ones; and, therefore, that women do not have any corporate loyalty.

Minimized, if not completely missing, from this narrative, as well as from the many articles dedicated to the turnover problem in the industry literature, is a consideration of how the pigeonholing of women into the lowest-waged and most dead-end of jobs throughout the maquilas contributes to their high turnover rate.[8] Instead, within the maquila narrative of female unreliability one hears how a woman's intrinsically untrainable condition cannot be altered through training. There is no remedy for her situation, at least none that the maquila industry can concoct. Even though trade-journal articles that make the connection between training and enhanced worker loyalty abound, these lessons do not apply to her. Meanwhile, Mexican men who are relative newcomers to the industry are climbing the ranks into skilled and higher-salaried positions, while Mexican women remain where they have been for over three decades: in the positions of least skill, least pay, and least authority. In fact, recent press attention to the skilling-up of the maquila labor force and renovation of the industry reveals the masculine image of the new maquila training and trainable subject (Wright 1998). Things are changing in the maquilas, one learns, not because women are changing but because Mexican men are. They have added a masculine and trainable dimension to the formerly unskilled, feminine labor force. As the American human-resources manager of a television manufacturer put it, "The men are more involved in the new technologies here. They are changing the industry." The women, meanwhile, with their status as untrainable employees, represent what does not change about the maquilas.

However, the untrainable Mexican woman is not completely worthless to the firm, for if she were, she would not continue to be the most sought-after employee in the maquiladora industry. Local radio stations frequently air advertisements promising good jobs, the best benefits, and a fun social atmosphere for young women seeking employment. Some maquilas contract agencies to recruit women throughout the city's scattered neighborhoods and migrant squatter settlements. These agencies generally seek female employees and are often expected to recruit a hundred women for a particular firm in a single day. As an employee of one such agency explained in an interview with a local newspaper in July 1998, "The agency offers jobs to both sexes, masculine and feminine, but for the moment, they are looking only for women to work in the second shift" (Guzmán 1998, 5).

Women are so explicitly desired for a number of reasons. Discourses that detail a blend of natural qualities combined with cultural proclivities establish the Mexican woman as one of the most sought-after industrial employees in the Western Hemisphere. For one thing, as throughout industrial history, Mexican women are still coveted for what are constructed to be the feminine qualities of dexterity, attention to detail, and patience with tedious work (Elson and Pearson 1989). They are, therefore, felt to be perfectly suited for the repetitious tasks of minutiae that still constitute much of contemporary manufacturing and information processing. Adding to the attractiveness of their supposedly innate abilities is the widespread perception that they have a cultural predisposition to docility and submissiveness to patriarchal figures. These discourses outline a figure who is not only aptly designed for assembly, sewing, and data entry but is also, unlike her northern counterparts, thankful for the work, unlikely to cause trouble, and easily cowed by male figures should thoughts of unionization cross her mind. Discourses of this sort explain, in part, why since the passage of NAFTA maquilas have set up operations at an unprecedented pace and have continued to employ more women than men across the industry, even as they emphasize trainability.

Another property underlying the Mexican woman's popularity among maquiladora executives is the inevitability of her turnover. Her lack of corporate loyalty is, in the proper proportion, a valuable commodity since her tendency to move into and out of factory complexes reinforces her position as the temporary worker in a corporate climate that responds to a fickle global market. As a 1998 *Wall Street Journal* article about the General Motors Delphi operation noted, "Delphi says it relies on rapid turnover in border plants to allow it to cut employment in lean times and add workers in boom times" (Simison and White 1998, 13). Part of what is so valuable about the Mexican woman is the promise that she will not stick around for the long haul. Her absence represents for the firm that value that flexibility affords it in a flexible market economy.

Turnover itself is therefore not necessarily a waste but the by-product of a process during which human beings turn into industrial waste. The trick facing maquila managers is to maintain it at the proper levels. Excessive turnover means that women are leaving at too high a rate for the firm to extract the value from their dexterous, attention-oriented, patient, and docile labor. An insufficient degree of turnover, however, represents another form of waste: an excessive productive capacity. Articles appear regularly in the principal industry journal, *Twin Plant News*, offering advice on how to manage the "very real problem" of *high* turnover (see Beruvides, Villalobos, and Hutchinson 1997; Villalobos, Beruvides, and Hutchinson 1997). A turnover rate that is too high means that unskilled workers are leaving before they have exhausted their value to the firm. The desired rate of turnover most often quoted to me was 7 percent, which required that most of the new workers remain at least one year. "If we could get these girls to stay here two years," the human-resources manager of the automobile-radio factory said in 1994, "then I would be happy. ... [A]fter that they always move on and try something new." The problem, therefore, is not that the women leave, but instead has to do with the timing of their departure in relation to the rate at which their value as workers declines with respect to the value of their turnover.

This task of monitoring the correct turnover rate requires a measurement of the amount of value residing in the labor of the Mexican woman who labors in unskilled work. Such measures are necessary in order to balance the value of her productive capacity as an active laborer with the value of her turnover. How does the value of her presence measure against the value of her absence? This is the question that maquila managers constantly pose, and they rely on a cadre of supervisors and engineering assistants to figure it out. These lower-level managers track the march of repetitious tasks through the bodies of the female laborers who occupy the majority of such jobs through the industry. They watch for signs of slower work rates resulting from stiff fingers, repetitive stress disorders, headaches, or boredom (Wright 2001). They note declining work performance in order to justify dismissals that deny eligibility for severance pay. As the Brazilian manager of a television manufacturer told me, "This is not the kind of work you can do for years at a time. It wears you out. We don't want the girls here after they're tired of the work." In this, as in many other maquilas, an elaborate system of surveillance focuses on the work performed primarily by women workers on the assembly line (Salzinger 1997). Furthermore, according to my informants, any worker who reveals an interest in expressing grievances or organizing worker committees is routinely subject to harassment if not immediate dismissal. The Mexican human-resources manager of an outboard-motor company said, "We have a policy not to allow workers to organize. It's like that in all the factories.... These lawyers [the ones involved in union activities] are lying to the workers and trying to trick them. We try to protect them from this." Workers with feisty attitudes are thus less valuable to the firm. If a Mexican woman loses her docility, one of her values has been spent.

Another method for monitoring the depletion of value in the bodies of women workers involves the surveillance of the reproductive cycles. Women seeking employment in a maquiladora commonly have to undergo pregnancy tests during the initial application process (U.S. Department of Labor 1998; Castañon 1998). However, scrutiny of their reproductive cycles does not end there, a common practice being to continuously monitor their cycles once they begin work. Reports vary depending on the age of the employee and the particular factory, but a number of women have described to me (during interviews conducted in 1992–99) and to others how on a monthly basis they are forced to demonstrate to the company doctor or nurse that they are menstruating. In several facilities women have been pressured to show their soiled sanitary napkins. "They even make the señoras do it," one woman explained. "They treat us like trash." The pregnancy test is hardly fail-safe, and a number of women explained how they got around it. One woman, who worked for a television manufacturer, said, "I was pregnant, so I sprinkled liver's blood on the napkin. They never knew. But when I started to show, my supervisor got really mean." She was then moved into an area where she was required to stand on her feet all day and lift heavy boxes. "I left because I was afraid for the baby." Although illegal, harassment of pregnant women is common, which demonstrates that noticeably pregnant women are ripe for turnover. "This is not a place for pregnant women," one supervisor in a machine shop told me. "They take too many restroom breaks, and then they're gone for a month. It slows us down." With the identification of the pregnant woman as a problem for the work process, her value as a worker plummets while her removal—her turnover—appreciates.

These procedures revolve around a dialectic determination of the female subject as one continuously suspended in the ambiguity separating value from waste. She is a subject always in need of sorting because eventually the value of her presence on the production floor will be spent while the value of her absence will have appreciated. Such sorting must occur in order to maximize the extraction of her value before declaring her to be overcome with waste. This inevitability, according to the death-by-culture logic, is driven by a traditional Mexican culture whose intrinsic values are in conflict as women spend more time outside the home. The many characteristics—lack of ambition, overactive wombs, flagging job loyalty—that managers attribute to the Mexican woman in order to explain high turnover represent cultural traits that are designed to check her independence. She might be subverting some cultural traditions by working outside the home, but to ensure that she not go too far afield, her culture inculcates her with a disposition that makes her impossible to train, to promote, or to encourage as a long-term employee. The maquilas are helpless to divert the forces of a culture that, in effect, devours its own, as women's careers are subsumed to such ineluctable traditional pressures.

Her disposability therefore represents her value to the firm, since her labor power eventually, as it is a cultural inevitability, will not be worth even the cost of her own social reproduction, which is the cost of her return to the workplace. And she, the individual who comes to life as this depleting subject, experiences a corporate death when her waste overrides her balance, because "the laborer receives . . . the value of labour power, and that is that" (Harvey 1982, 43). Turnover is thus the turning over of women from being those who offer value through their labor power to being those who offer value through the absence of their labor. And as women repeat their experiences on this continuum during several-month stints in different maquilas, as they move from one maquiladora to the next in a career built of minimum-wage and dead-end jobs, their own lives are stilled. They experience a stilling of their corporate lives, their work futures, and their opportunities inside and outside of the workplace that might emerge were they to receive training and promotions into jobs with higher pay and more prestige.

All the managers I talked with agreed that the turnover rate could not be diminished by corporate measurers such as higher salaries and benefits. The American human-resources manager of the television manufacturer responded, "These girls aren't here for a career. If we raise the wages, that would have a negative effect on the economy and wouldn't produce any results. Turnover comes with the territory down here." The American general manager of the motorboat manufacturer said, "Turnover is a serious issue here, especially in the electronic work that the female operators do. But that's how they are. They're young and looking for experiences. You just have to get used to it down here.... I don't think wages would make any difference." The Mexican general manager of the television manufacturer replied, "Wages aren't the answer to everything, you know. Most of these girls are from other places in Mexico. They don't have much experience with American attitudes about work. And that's why we have problems with turnover." The German general manager of the electronic assembly plant explained, "We always try to cut down on turnover, but we don't expect to get rid of it. That wouldn't be realistic. Not in Juárez."

Within such comments lurks the death-by-culture narrative, which vindicates the maquila industry of any responsibility in the multiple corporate deaths experienced by most of their female workers. By spinning tales full of vague referents to the obstinate turnover condition of Mexican women, the managers are explaining how turnover is part and parcel of a cultural system immune to maquiladora meddling. The specificities of that culture are not the issue: it is instead the exculpation of the maquila industry from any responsibility in guiding a turnover process that serves their purposes in some critical ways. Consequently, according to the death-by-culture narrative, maquila preventative measures would be fruitless or even a further waste; competitive wages, training programs for women workers, day care, flexible work schedules, attention to repetitive-stress disorders, a compassionate stance toward maternity would not make one whit of difference. These Mexican girls and women are going to turn over, as they always do, because of who they are. Turnover is part of their cultural constitution. And as the women come and go, one after another, day after day, the managers exclaim their impotence against the wasting of women workers. These women, they maintain, are victims of their culture. Their eventual corporate deaths are evidence of death by culture.

Death by Culture

In March 1999 a research psychiatrist from Texan Technical University who specializes in serial murders commented to the *El Paso Times* that the Juárez murderers "tend to 'discard' their victims once they get what they want from them" (Stack and Valdez 1999, 1A). Such a vision of the Mexican woman as inevitably disposable is common to both the murder and turnover narratives. At the heart of these seemingly disparate story lines is the crafting of the Mexican woman as a figure whose value can be extracted, whether it be in the form of her virtue, her organs, or her efficiency on the production floor. And once "they"—her murderers or her supervisors—"get what they want from" her, she is discarded.

The vision of her disposability, the likelihood that this condition could exist in a human being, is what is so valuable to those who extract what they want from her. When she casts the shadow of the consummate disposable laborer whose labor power is not even worth the expense of its own social reproduction, she is a utopian image. In this particular manifestation the Mexican woman symbolizes a culturally victimized variation of labor who guarantees her replacement—after being worn down by repetitive-stress syndrome, migraines, or harassment over pregnancies—with fresh recruits who are, perhaps, leaving another place of employment for one of the same reasons. That the same women are turning over as they move from one place to another does not disrupt the utopian image of their constant decline as part of their continuum toward disposability. To the contrary, their value circulates through their continual flow from one factory to the next, since as a woman leaves one place of work, perhaps having been dismissed for missing a menstrual period, then enters another once her menstrual flow resumes, she again represents value. Her fluctuation between value and waste is part of her appeal for her employer.

This image of the female worker as the subject formed in the flux between waste and value provides her contours as a variation of capital. With such a constitution, she can be nothing other than a temporary worker, one whose intrinsic value does not mature, grow, and increase over time. And therefore, as a group, Mexican women represent the permanent labor force of the temporarily employed. The individual instances of this subject come and go as women deemed wasteful to a firm's project are replaced by new recruits. A woman's cultural constitution is internally driven and immune to any diversionary attempts by the industry to put Mexican women on a different path. Instead, she will repeat the pattern like women before her and perpetuate the problem of turnover so valuable to the maquilas.

Such a utopian image of the Mexican woman as a figure permanently and ineluctably headed toward decline, always promising that her labor power will be worth less than the cost of her own social reproduction, evokes Benjamin's elaboration of the fetish. Benjamin renovates Marx's analogy of the fetish as phantasmagoria to refer not only to the social relations of representation that are sustained in the commodity. According to Susan Buck-Morss, Benjamin's concern with "urban phantasmagoria was not so much the commodity-in-the-market as the commodity-on-display" (1989, 82). Benjamin's point is that the mechanics of representation are as critical to the creation of value as the actual exchange of use values in the marketplace.

The fetish of the Mexican woman as waste in the making offers evidence for Benjamin's view of the fetish as an entity "on display." As a figure of waste, she represents the possibility of a human existence that is perhaps really worthless, and this representation is valuable in and of itself. If one really can see and believe in her wasted condition, then she opens up a number of valuable possibilities for numerous people. For the managers of the maquiladora industry, her worthlessness means they can count on the temporary labor force necessary to remain competitive in a global system of flexible production. The murder victims—many of them former maquila employees abducted on their commutes between home and work—also represents value for the industry, as cultural victims. Through descriptions of Mexican cultural violence, jealous machismo, and female sexuality, maquiladora exculpation finds its backing. No degree of investment in public infrastructure to improve transportation routes, finance lighting on streets, boost public security, or hold seminars in the workplace will make any difference. Others, too, can benefit from the widespread and believable representation of the Mexican woman as waste in the making. The perpetrators of serial murders, domestic violence, and random violence against women can count on a lack of public outrage and official insouciance with regard to their capture. And the city and state officials in Chihuahua who are concerned about their political careers under the public scrutiny of their effectiveness in curbing crime can defer responsibility.

The stories of this wasting and wasted figure must always be told since, to adapt Butler's calculation, the naming of her as waste is also "the repeated inculcation of the norm" (1993, 8). The repetitive telling of the wasting woman in the turnover and murder stories is requisite because of her ambiguity: the waste is never stable or complete. The possibility of her value—of fingers still flexible or of a murdered young woman who was cherished by many—lurks in the background, and so the sorting continues as one searches for evidence of the wasted value. Her dialectic constitution is suspended through the pitting of the two antithetical conditions that she invariably embodies. One finds this dialectic condition through the questions that ask: Is she worthy of our concern? Are her fingers nimble or stiff, her attitude pliant or angry, her habits chaste or wild? Through the posing of such questions, her ambiguity is sorted as if it were always present for the sorting. Meanwhile, she hangs in the balance.

Notes

I would like to thank Rosalba Robles, Miranda Joseph, Esther Chavez Cano, Sarah Hill, Felicity Callard, Erica Schoenberger, David Harvey, David Kazanjian, Michael Denning, Alys Weinbaum, Brent Edwards, Neil Smith, Carol A. Breckenridge, the anonymous reviewers at *Public Culture*, and the participants at the University of Chicago Center for Gender Studies workshop for their comments on earlier versions of this essay, although any inconsistencies or lapses are mine alone. Research for this project was partially funded by the National Science Foundation.

1. The number of murders varies, depending on the source, from about one hundred forty to more than two hundred. Local activists in Ciudad Juárez have voiced a suspicion that not all of the murders were brought to public light, and for this reason I am persuaded that the larger number represents a more accurate assessment of the scope of the problem. My material for this essay derives from interviews and research conducted over a several-year period of ethnographic fieldwork in Ciudad Juárez, Chihuahua.
2. The word *maquila* is a shortened form of *maquiladora*, which refers to the export-processing factories located in Mexico.
3. Much of my discussion of Benjamin's theory of dialectics draws on Susan Buck-Morss's (1989) account.
4. My discussion of the woman as waste in the making is informed by the conceptualization of waste as a continual negotiation elaborated by Sarah Hill (1998).
5. All translations are provided by the author.
6. Roberto Urrea, president of AMAC, interview by John Quinones, 20/20, ABC, 20 January 1999.
7. I conducted this and other interviews that I draw on throughout the text during a several-year period of ethnographic research (1992–99) within specific maquiladoras located in Ciudad Juárez. I specify the nationality of the managers in this text in order to demonstrate how a cultural explanation is widespread throughout the industry among managers of many nationalities. With the exception of one human-resources manager, all of the interviews used here were with men. I also use the problematic referent of

American as it is used by my informants and commonly along the U.S.-Mexico border to identify residents and citizens of the United States who do not identify themselves as Mexican.
8 For more on the industry literature, see Beruvides, Villalobos, and Hutchinson 1997; Villalobos, Beruvides, and Hutchinson 1997.

Rape as a Weapon of War: Militarized
Rape at the U.S.-Mexico Border

SYLVANNA M. FALCÓN

✵ The U.S.-Mexico border is a contentious region where militarization violently reinforces the territory of the United States. Daily, attacks against border crossers occur in the form of brutal beatings, assaults (including rape), and harassment by state and federal officials as well as by regional vigilantes. Like all militarized endeavors, the state is ultimately accountable for this violence. Rape as a tactic against women is considered a weapon of war by the international community because of its rampant use in every military conflict. And, as discussed in this essay, rape is routinely and systematically used by the state in its militarization efforts at the U.S.-Mexico border.

How rape has been one of the outcomes of militarization along the border is revealed through analysis of rape cases involving Immigration and Naturalization Service (INS) officials or Border Patrol agents documented by nongovernmental organizations, government communities, and U.S. newspapers.[1] Each of the women in the case studies took some form of action against the INS. Some even used an advocate to move their cases forward through an investigation. Though these cases do not involve U.S. armed forces directly, it is clear that military culture heavily influence the Border Patrol.

The vast majority of rapes involve women victims and survivors, whether at the border or throughout the world, although data indicate that some men have reported being raped at the border (Amnesty International 1998). Motivations for raping women in a war-torn country may differ from those for rapes committed along the U.S.-Mexico border, but the outcome remains the same: the systematic degradation of women.

The interconnections between militarism, hyper-masculinity, colonialism, and patriarchy contribute to violence against women. Susan Brownmiller (1993) likened female bodies to territory in the context of mass war rape in the former Yugoslavia. "Rape of a doubly dehumanized object—as woman, as enemy—carries its own terrible logic. In one act of aggression, the collective spirit of women *and* of the nation is broken, leaving a reminder long after the troops depart" (1993, 37). Beverly Allen extends this analogy to the imperialist practice of colonization (1996, 159). In the case of rapes at the U.S.-Mexico border, migrant women's bodies denote an "alien" or threatening presence subject to colonial domination by U.S. officials. Their bodies represent a country over which the United States has maintained long-term colonial rule resulting in a symbolic connection between women's bodies and territory (see the Inda and Wright essays in this volume).

The militarization of the U.S.-Mexico border involves two key processes: first, the introduction and integration of military units in the border region (primarily motivated by the War on Drugs and national security concerns); and second, the modification of the Border Patrol to resemble the armed forces via its equipment, structure, and tactics. At one time, domestic duties were not part of the U.S. military's mandate. In 1982 the National Defense Authorization Act nullified a hundred-year statute that prohibited cooperation between the army and civilian law enforcement and changed the role of the military in domestic affairs.[2] This act encouraged an alliance between civilian law enforcement and the military. Subsequent DOD authorization acts advanced and expanded this cooperation. Ideological and institutional shifts have also had a role in border militarization. Transferring the INS from the Department of Labor to the Department of Justice in 1940 (Dunn 1996) altered the classification of immigration as an issue of labor to one of national security. And more recently, by moving the INS to the Department of Homeland Security (the INS is now U.S. Citizenship and Immigration Services), the link between immigration and national security issues has intensified.

The sociologist Timothy Dunn draws on low-intensity-conflict (LIC) military doctrine to contextualize the militarization of the U.S.-Mexico border. Constructed by the U.S. military-security establishment to target Third World uprisings and revolutions, particularly in Central America, LIC doctrine advocates "unconventional, multifaceted, and relatively subtle forms of militarization" and emphasizes "controlling targeted civilian populations" (1996, 21). It is characterized by "(1) an emphasis on the internal defense of a nation, (2) an emphasis on controlling targeted civilian populations rather than territory, and (3) the assumption by the military of police-like and other unconventional, typically nonmilitary roles, along with the adoption by the police of military characteristics" (21).

According to Dunn, LIC doctrine is still evolving. Although applying LIC doctrine to the U.S.-Mexico border therefore has limitations, testimony at the 1996 hearing on Operation Gatekeeper indicated that Dunn's usage of LIC doctrine in the border region could be appropriate. Gus de la Viña, chief of the U.S. Border Patrol and a thirty-year INS employee, stated, "In February 1994, Attorney General Reno and INS Commissioner Doris Meissner announced a multi-year border enforcement strategy that committed this Nation to a new course of border control to combat illegal immigration. This was a practical and realistic strategy development by law enforcement professionals in the Border Patrol, utilizing the advice of outside entities such as the Department of Defense Center for Low-Intensity Conflict" (U.S. House 1996, 65).

The execution of LIC doctrine can create a climate conducive to rape. When LIC doctrine is applied to controlling people and threats to national security, militarized rape, with its associations to power, control, and national security, can result (Enloe 2000). Cynthia Enloe (111) explores three conditions under which rape has been militarized.

1. "Recreational rape" as the alleged outcome of not supplying male soldiers with "adequately accessible" militarized prostitution;
2. "National security rape" as an instrument for bolstering a nervous state; and
3. "Systematic mass rape" as an instrument of open warfare.

She contends that certain conditions allow militarized rapes to emerge, and four of these are in place on the U.S.-Mexico border.

1. A regime is preoccupied with "national security";
2. A majority of civilians believe that security is best understood as a military problem;
3. National security policy making is left to a largely masculinized policy elite; and
4. The police and military security apparatuses are male-dominated (Enloe 2000, 124).

That these conditions exist along the U.S.-Mexico border is apparent in a number of ways. First, the institution of LIC doctrine and other U.S. government policies suggest these conditions are present in the region. Second, in the 1990s the definition of national security expanded to include "domestic political concerns and perceived threats to culture, social stability, environmental degradation, and population growth" (Jonas 1996, 72). During this time, immigrants and refugees became top national-security issues (72). Third, in the aftermath of 9/11 a complete shutdown of the U.S.-Mexico border occurred in the name of national security, contributing to the classification of the border as an area for national security. Fourth, a masculinized elite has always constructed military operations for this country's engagement. Fifth, security, and national security in particular, has always been understood as a military operation or endeavor: ensuring security is about exerting control. At the U.S.-Mexico border, security is about controlling labor migration, border crossers, and women—that is, it's about letting migrants and borderland residents know the United States is in control. Security also involves protecting certain interests—political interests, business interests, elite interests—and certain people, such as Arizona ranchers who have picked up arms to protect their property, residents in San Diego who have organized anti-immigrant campaigns, people involved in English-only initiatives, and people who are fearful of the diminishing power of the white population. The State is not concerned with the security of migrants who experience the consequences of a militarized border region and whose human rights are repeatedly violated.

According to Enloe, occurrences of rape are systematic if they fall into a pattern which would suggest that they have not been left to chance: "They have been the subject of prior planning. Systematic rapes are *administered* rapes" (2000, 134). In the cases discussed here, the planning involved is palpable. They were not random acts of violence against women, but rather violent crimes that involved detailed planning in order to try and avoid being caught. The men who raped these women knew who to target and how to capitalize on their institutionally supported power over these undocumented women. Each man followed his own scripted pattern in attacking these women. The patterns became clear during court testimonials by victims and survivors. One Mexican immigrant woman told Arnoldo Garcia of the National Network for Immigrant and Refugee Rights in Oakland, California, that women heading north started using birth-control pills because they anticipated possible sexual assaults (Martínez 1998, 58), which suggests that border rapes are not random or isolated.

Certain practices distinguish militarized border rape from other forms of militarized rape. Many women report that being raped was the price they had to pay to cross the border without being apprehended or deported, or to have their confiscated documents returned to them. For example, according to Human Rights Watch, "An INS inspector stationed in San Ysidro [California] was indicted on November 4, 1994, and accused of pressuring at least seven female border-crossers to have sex with him in exchange for returning confiscated documents" (1995a, 3). The power of legal papers and the threat of deportation place women in a vulnerable position, which can be exploited by border-enforcement agents and thus lead to incidents of rape. The use of documentation and deportation to control women distinguishes militarized border rape from militarized rape.

Historically, migrants who ventured across the border were predominately male. But patterns of migration have altered over the years, and women are crossing the border alone in greater numbers (Ruiz and Tiano 1987, 9). "Violent rape or the demand for sex as the price of safe passage to *el norte* is an old custom" that happens on both sides of the border (Martínez 1998, 58). Has rape changed due to militarization? The absence of comparative data makes it impossible to assess whether the frequency of rape has increased since the militarization of the border. However, since the "pre-militarization" of the border, new factors have emerged that could affect the incidence of rape, including an increase in the number of border-enforcement agents, the construction of a racialized enemy, and a shift in the goals of enforcement work.[3]

In the early 1900s the border was less guarded (Takaki 1993, 312). The institution of a war zone in the border region over the last few decades reflects a shift in work objectives. Beyond targeting undocumented border crossers, Border Patrol agents are now concerned with deploying drug interdiction efforts in collaboration with military units (Dunn 1996). Moreover, the "us versus them" philosophy espoused by border-enforcement agents affects people from Mexico and Latin America, and Chicanos and Latinos from the United States in a potentially explosive and violent manner, which jeopardizes human rights. Moreover, this ideology contributes to the construction of a racialized enemy—a social construction that is associated with women's bodies, which symbolize a nation (and its future). In this hostile environment, the militarized border facilitates violence and the raping of women.

In 1997 the Office of the Inspector General's (OIG) semiannual report to Congress included rape investigations. One case involved an official at the San Ysidro, California, crossing point: "An INS special cases officer, who used his position to extort sexual favors and sexually abuse female aliens while employed at a California Port of Entry, was sentenced to nine years incarceration and three years probation" (U.S. Department of Justice 1997b, 7). However, insufficient evidence often hindered criminal prosecution: "Investigations of alleged civil rights violations often result in evidence that misconduct occurred, but the evidence may not support criminal prosecution. INS terminated six employees in such cases during this reporting period. Compared to earlier reporting periods, this is a significant increase in the number and gravity of administrative actions taken by INS in civil rights-related cases" (U.S. Department of Justice 1997b, 7). The OIG report was important because it classified rape as a civil-rights violation and acknowledged institutional awareness of border rapes.

Since militarization ideology is embedded with issues of hypermasculinity, patriarchy, and threats to national security, the gendered effects of militarization at the U.S.-Mexico border on women should be assessed. Legally proving a rape occurred is extremely difficult in court, usually because of problems with criminal evidence and witnesses.[4] As a government prosecutor commented after successfully convicting two Border Patrol officials of rape in Texas in 1982, "It is really difficult to win civil rights cases against law enforcement officers. They have a lot of power" (United Press International 1982).

Rape Cases at the U.S.-Mexico Border

Border-crossing women who have been sexually violated and who decide to prosecute not only confront an individual but also challenge the State and an institutional system of power and social control. Proceeding with an investigation is particularly difficult for women since INS officials (typically male), who are arguably invested in the organization, tend to interrogate them over the alleged incidents. The following rape cases occurred between 1989 and 1996.

Juanita Gómez

Juanita Gómez and her female cousin crossed through the hole in the border fence between Nogales, Sonora, and Nogales, Arizona, on 3 September 1993.[5] They were on their way to meet two male friends at a nearby McDonald's to go shopping. Larry Selders, a Border Patrol agent, stopped all four of them but detained only Gómez and her cousin in his Border Patrol vehicle. According to both women, Selders took advantage of the fact they did not have papers, informing them that he would not take them to the Border Patrol station for processing and deportation to Mexico if they would have sex with him. Both women refused. He eventually asked Gómez's cousin to exit his vehicle. After driving off with Gómez, Selders allegedly raped her.

Gómez and her cousin found each other at the Mexican Consulate in Nogales, Arizona. The Mexican Consulate immediately contacted the Nogales Police Department and Border Patrol to inform them of the situation. One of the Nogales detectives did not believe either of the women's statements, inquiring whether the women were prostitutes and threatening them with jail time if they failed to pass a lie-detector test. However, Gómez and her cousin identified Selders in a photo lineup. Police incompetence led to the loss of important evidence regarding the rape: Selders was picked up for questioning more than three hours after Gómez reported the rape to the police, by which time he had already changed his clothes. In addition, the police seized the wrong Border Patrol vehicle and realized the error only a week and a half later.

Selders eventually entered a no-contest plea on a reduced charge on 25 July 1994. The county attorney decided to reduce the original charge of "rape and kidnapping" to "attempted transporting of persons for immoral purposes . . . while married." As the lowest class of felony available, this charge upset many immigrant-rights advocates (*Arizona Republic* 1994). Selders attempted to get immunity from prosecution on federal charges, but because investigators found Gómez's story to be credible, he was unable to negotiate that aspect into his plea-bargaining with the U.S. attorney for Arizona. Selders received a one-year prison sentence on 7 October 1994, with eligibility for parole after six months. He served only six months of the sentence and resigned from the Border Patrol in August 1994 (Human Rights Watch 1995a, 12–13).

In April 1995 a federal grand jury in Tucson, Arizona, indicted Selders in connection with the rape of Gómez (*Phoenix Gazette*, 6 April 1995). He faced one count of civil-rights violations, two counts of bribery, and two counts of harboring undocumented people by driving them through Nogales. He pleaded guilty in federal court to violating Gómez's civil rights. He received a fourteen-month sentence in the federal trial, but received credit for time served (Associated Press State and Local Wire 1999).

On 13 October 1999 Gómez received a $753,045 award for the rape (Associated Press State and Local Wire 1999). Her attorney argued the rape could have been prevented had Selders been held accountable for previous acts of violence against women. Three other women had testified at Gómez's trial that Selders had attacked them (Associated Press State and Local Wire 1999; Human Rights Watch 1995a, 13). The women had been afraid to pursue charges and the statute of limitations in their cases had expired by the time of Gómez's trial. Since Selders was a government employee at the time of the incident, the U.S. government paid the monetary award to Gómez.

Women from Van Nuys, California
In May 1990 a Van Nuys, California, district attorney's office charged INS officer James Riley with "forcible rape with the use of a firearm, kidnapping and rape under the color of authority" (*Los Angeles Times*, 16 May 1990). Prosecutors claimed that on 11 April 1990 Riley had raped a woman at gunpoint in his home. He allegedly conducted an unauthorized "one-man raid at gunpoint on a Van Nuys bar" (Connelly and Klein Lerner 1990, B3). During this "raid,"

authorities claimed, he abducted and reportedly raped a twenty-four-year-old woman from the bar, having told her she was under arrest for lacking legal documents to be in the United States. After the alleged rape, he released the woman.

Jailed without bail on 12 May 1990, Riley entered a plea of not guilty to the charges. At the time of his arrest, Riley "was already facing eight felony charges stemming from incidents involving four other women" (Connelly and Klein Lerner 1990, B3). He pleaded not guilty to these charges as well, which included "three counts of rape, three counts of kidnapping and one count each of false imprisonment and assault" (B3). One month later the *Los Angeles Times* reported that three more women had filed nine additional charges against Riley, bringing the total to seventeen charges against him (Connelly and Klein Lerner 1990, B3). According to the women, he had approached them in the San Fernando Valley area and threatened to deport them unless they had sex with him. The crimes had occurred in August and November 1989 and January 1990. The Los Angeles County district attorney's office filed numerous charges against Riley and accused him of "using his position as a federal agent to commit the crimes." Deputy District Attorney Andrew J. McMullen stated that all "the victims were young illegal immigrants who lived in the Van Nuys (Los Angeles) area." Riley followed a pattern in his attacks against women: he "approached the women, identified himself as an INS officer, and forced them to go with him." Authorities suspected women were raped either in his apartment or in his INS car (B3).

Riley was an employee of the INS Employee Sanctions Unit, a unit that does not patrol for undocumented people. Created because of a provision in the 1986 Immigration Reform and Control Act, the unit bars employers from "hiring, recruiting, or referring for a fee aliens known to be unauthorized to work in the United States." In the end, Riley was found guilty of false imprisonment and acquitted on several other counts involving kidnapping and rape (Connelly 1992, B1). Riley's lawyer planned an appeal for the conviction. The guilty conviction carried a sentence of up to three years. Riley already had served twenty-two months in prison by the time of the verdict (B1).

Gloria

Charles Vinson, an eight-year agent at the time of his arrest for alleged rape in December 1995, was immediately placed on leave from the Border Patrol. By March 1996, he was suspended without pay (Anne-Marie O'Connor 1996, A3). The INS eventually fired him. During the investigation into Vinson's alleged rape of Gloria, an undocumented El Salvadorian woman who had crossed the border, the San Diego police and OIG officials discovered "other allegations of misconduct with immigrant women." They realized that "six years before his arrest, Vinson had been removed from a horse patrol after fellow Border Patrol agents complained that he was conducting aggressive and improper searches of women" (A3).

Gloria had been trying to reunite with her husband and son, who were already in the United States. The INS provided them with "temporary legal status pending the court proceedings against Vinson" (Repard and Sanchez 1995, B1). Gloria gave investigators specific details about the incident, describing the Border Patrol uniform and the physical appearance of the agent. She also selected his picture from photos presented to her. According to San Diego Police Captain Tom Hall, Gloria was alone when she was assaulted in a secluded canyon covered by brush. Vinson was apparently without his partner at the time of the alleged assault, his shift having just ended. Hall stated that after Vinson left, Gloria "went a short distance to the road and flagged down a Border Patrol unit" (B3). The unit that picked her up notified their supervisor about the incident.

In November 1996 Vinson pled guilty to raping Gloria and received a ten-year sentence. He was mandated to undergo lifetime AIDS testing and required to register as a convicted sex offender for life (U.S. Department of Justice 1997b, 11). Vinson could have served up to twenty-five years in prison, but negotiations with the San Diego deputy district attorney reduced the sentence. Vinson, charged originally with four counts of sexual assault, pled guilty to a single charge of "oral copulation under color of authority while armed with a firearm" (U.S. Department of Justice 1997b; also see Anne-Marie O'Connor 1996).

Edilma, Maria, and Rosa
Luis Esteves had a violent past with women, having allegedly beaten his first wife, raped his second wife, and threatened to rape his second wife's ten-year-old daughter (Human Rights Watch 1993, 7; McDonnell and Rotella 1993). These three incidents of sexual misconduct surfaced against Esteves when he was a Border Patrol agent.

EDILMA CADILLA On 6 October 1989, Edilma Cadilla, a U.S. citizen, was driving her car on the highway in Imperial County, California, and was stopped at a checkpoint in the area. During this routine stop, Esteves questioned her, but allowed her to continue driving. Further down the road, however, he pulled her over, asked her more questions, and then talked about himself, eventually getting her phone number. Cadilla believed these questions were official.

Cadilla's boyfriend called Esteves's supervisor in El Centro to report the suspicious stop. The supervisor told the boyfriend to notify the office if Esteves attempted to call Cadilla. Three days later, on 9 October, Esteves called Cadilla and allegedly requested a date with her for the weekend. When she turned him down, "Esteves told her that was 'too bad' because he wanted to take her out dancing, get drunk, and have her 'sexually abuse his body.' She told him she had a boyfriend and he then asked if she could fix him up with one of her friends" (Human Rights Watch 1993, 8).[6]

After Cadilla reported the phone call to Esteves's supervisor, the Border Patrol relocated Esteves to the Calexico, California, border-crossing point. Esteves received no disciplinary action for his inappropriate behavior toward Cadilla (Human Rights Watch 1993, 8; McDonnell and Rotella 1993) and remained an employee with the Border Patrol. His new position enabled him to continue having contact with women.

MARIA On 16 December 1989, Esteves had problems in Calexico. He stopped Maria, a young woman from the area, and asked to see her immigration papers. While on duty, he asked for her phone number and for a date later that evening. She initially agreed to the date, but called him later to say she could not go out with him. Esteves looked for her at her workplace and then pursued her at a shopping center. Maria agreed to the date on the condition they first stop at her house to get her mother's approval. He agreed to the request, but indicated he wished to first stop at his place to change out of his Border Patrol uniform. According to the court records, "Esteves told her he wanted her to 'be with him.' At this point, Maria describes him 'changing' his attitude and he became angry. He told her she had to have sex with him. He told her to take a shower. Esteves positioned a gun on each side of the bed on two nightstands" (Human Rights Watch 1993, 8).[7]

Fearful for her life, Maria complied with Esteves's sexual orders. According to Maria's testimony at the trial, Esteves allegedly "force[d] an object into her vagina, placed his hands into various parts of her body, orally copulated her and forced her to have intercourse with him" (Human Rights Watch 1993, 9). She testified that none of these sexual acts were consensual. She escaped from his apartment when he left the room after the alleged rape. Maria got help from people passing in a car. The police were immediately notified, and Esteves was subsequently arrested. Maria did not show up to the preliminary hearing in court, so the charges against Esteves were dropped and he resumed active duty as an agent.

ROSA The third incident, which occurred in June 1991, involved Rosa, a minor. At the time, Rosa was talking to family members at the U.S.-Mexico border fence, she and her mother being on the U.S. side, their family members on the Mexico side. Esteves approached them for documentation. When Esteves learned from Rosa's mother that Rosa had an upcoming deportation hearing, he informed them he could be of assistance to Rosa in that hearing.

Esteves reportedly took Rosa out a few times after meeting her at the border. On 28 June 1991, he picked up Rosa around 10:45 p.m. and bought her alcoholic drinks before taking her to the vacant apartment of a co-worker. At this time, Esteves allegedly instructed her to take off her clothes. Rosa stated in her testimony that Esteves "ordered her to masturbate." At first she refused, but complied when "he placed his hand on his gun." She testified that throughout the encounter, Esteves "repeatedly slapped her and at one point, he punched her. Rosa contends that Esteves then sodomized her. At one point he told her, 'I know what I'm doing. And I am capable of everything and if I want I can rape your mother.' According to Rosa's testimony, Esteves then told her that he wanted to sell Rosa to his friends. Finally, he told her that he wanted to have sex with her and another woman" (Human Rights Watch 1993, 9).[8]

The police arrested Esteves again in July 1991 and prosecuted him for the alleged rapes of Maria and Rosa. He was acquitted for Rosa's rape, but convicted for Maria's rape; Rosa's testimony apparently played a role in securing that conviction. In July 1992 Esteves received a twenty-four-year prison sentence for the felony rape charge. However, he was released on 22 December 1994.[9]

Luz López and Norma Contreras

Luz López and Norma Contreras filed an INS complaint against an El Paso Border Patrol agent who allegedly sexually assaulted them. The assault occurred on 7 March 1996 (Amnesty International 1998). The agent arrested them near the Rio Grande River and detained them in his vehicle. López and Contreras, both from Guatemala, were both twenty-three years old at the time of the assault. According to the complaint the women filed, the agent "lifted up Contreras' dress, pushed her legs open, pulled aside her underwear and stuck his fingers in her vagina. The other woman, López, was told to undo the buttons on her jumpsuit and the agent put his hands inside her top and felt her breasts. The two women said they stared at each other, paralyzed by terror" (24).

López later said, "We feared the worse. We didn't know where he was going to take us. Just the sight of him with a badge and a gun was enough to intimidate anyone." The agent briefly left the women in the car. He spoke to another agent, who was alone in a different vehicle nearby. Both men returned to the car. At this time, "in full view of the second agent, the arresting agent allegedly assaulted both women again." The women were then taken to the Border Patrol office. At the office, the same agent allegedly committed a third sexual assault "in a detention cell and in a bathroom." After torturing them for several hours, "the agent gave the women one dollar each and released them" into the United States (Amnesty International 1998, 25).

Following the ordeal, López and Contreras filed a formal complaint against both agents. The women stayed in El Paso in order to cooperate with the investigation. They recounted the alleged attacks to male OIG investigators, identified the agents from photographs, and received rape counseling. The OIG began an investigation, but did not pursue the complaint. The OIG investigators "reportedly accused (López and Contreras) of lying and threatened to prosecute them" (Amnesty International 1998, 25). The women then filed a lawsuit against the Border Patrol. Both women were severely traumatized by the ordeal, and Contreras attempted to commit suicide later that same year (Amnesty International 1998). The lawsuit is still pending.

Review of Cases

The preceding case studies demonstrate the systematic nature of militarized border rape, including prior planning and agents' use of the authority associated with their position to threaten women with deportation if they did not comply with the agents' sexual demands. These hierarchical expressions of power over women cannot be readily dismissed as "isolated" or "individual" cases. Rather, they are part of an overall strategy to maintain a border system ideologically committed to "national security," a system in which power is wielded materially by systematic violence against women. Since the border system is a hegemonic tool, militarized border rapes are demonstrations of this power and control. For Selders to have been alone with Gómez during the reported attack was not necessarily unusual. The power differential between a U.S. official representing a powerful nation and an undocumented woman is huge, with accountability difficult and often impossible to secure.

Riley intentionally misled women into believing he had the authority to question and repeatedly demand sex from them. Although the actual number of rapes committed by Riley is unknown, the sheer number of women accusing Riley of sexual assault suggests he recurrently abused and manipulated his power and position as an INS employee in order to violate women's human rights. However, though the allegations against him revealed a similar pattern of behavior among the attacks, he was found guilty on a relatively minor charge. Even though these rapes did not occur at the border per se, Riley's case indicates that women's security is continually threatened.

Vinson and Esteves were removed from border-enforcement work, but this occurred only after several women had been raped or sexually assaulted. Despite the fact that Vinson's colleagues were uncomfortable with his treatment of women during his early days with the Border Patrol and even issued a complaint against him, six years passed before the OIG investigation uncovered the initial complaints against Vinson. The rape of Gloria could have been prevented had previous indicators of misconduct been appropriately investigated. The Border Patrol quickly repaired negative publicity about the trial by calling the case "isolated." The *San Diego Union-Tribune* reported, "Border Patrol spokeswoman Ann Summers said she was shocked when she heard that an agent had been accused of raping an undocumented immigrant in the field. More than 300 agents patrol a busy 5-mile stretch of the border west of the San Ysidro Port of Entry. Activists over the years have accused the immigration service of tolerating abusive agents. Federal authorities say they investigate every formal complaint, but few are ever presented to a grand jury or result in an indictment because of insufficient evidence—usually lack of witnesses or the absence of visible injuries" (Repard and Sanchez 1995).

Given Esteves's violent history with his spouses, the Border Patrol might never have hired him had a thorough background check been conducted. That he was hired with an existing record of violence suggests questionable INS hiring practices. Furthermore, Esteves exhibited signs of problematic behavior toward women early in his career as an agent, and the failure of the INS to investigate these allegations allowed him to commit multiple acts of violence against women.

This case illustrates the systemic nature of militarized border rape because the officer reportedly raped López and Contreras in different locations as part of an overall campaign against women whose lack of legal documentation rendered them unprotected targets. Both women were eventually released into the United States, with forced sex allegedly having been the price of entry. Ultimately, these rapes can be considered a form of state violence against women and egregious violations of women's human rights.

Human-rights literature indicates that attempting or committing suicide after a rape can occur during an insensitive investigation. A United Nations report on the former Yugoslavia states, "Health care providers are concerned about the effects on women of repeatedly recounting their experiences without adequate psychological and social support systems in place. The danger of subjecting women to additional emotional hardship in the course of interviews is a real one. There have been reports of women attempting suicide after being interviewed by the media and well-meaning delegations" (United Nations Economic and Social Council 1993a, 5). Perhaps the insensitivity displayed by the OIG investigators was a factor in López's suicide attempt.

Factors Associated with Militarized Border Rape

Factors contributing to the prevalence of militarized border rape include the INS complaints process, abuse of power, ineffective hiring protocols, the minimizing of civil-rights standards, and a culture of militarization.

The INS complaint process is ineffective, inadequate, and cumbersome, leading to the failure to properly investigate the vast majority of allegations of human-rights abuses. The INS reports that since 1989 "only one registered complaint for every 17,000 arrests" has occurred, implying abuses along the border are minimal (Human Rights Watch 1995a, 21). Human Rights Watch, Amnesty International, the INS's Citizens' Advisory Panel, and the United States Commission on Civil Rights's state advisory committees for Arizona, California, New Mexico, and Texas all concluded that no effective or useful mechanisms existed to enable victims of human-rights violations to file formal complaints against border-enforcement agents (Human Rights Watch 1995a, 21; Amnesty International 1998; U.S. Immigration and Naturalization Service 1997; State Advisory Committees 1997). According to the Citizens' Advisory Panel, "In 1996, 99% of the complaints received by the Justice Department's Civil Rights Division were not prosecuted. Furthermore, most cases investigated by the Federal Bureau of Investigations do not result in criminal charges or presentation to a grand jury" (U.S. Immigration and Naturalization Service 1997, 6). The nonexistence of a standard complaints form and appeals process is systematic and exemplifies the structural shortcomings that allow the INS to minimize the gravity of the situation at the border. Moreover, the lack of standardized process and the lack of the option to report incidents to duty supervisors of the local Border Patrol offices probably lead to underreporting of abuses. The existing format presents overwhelming obstacles to getting complaints properly investigated.[10] In addition, increases in the number of border-enforcement agents are never met with proportionate increases of investigative staff (Amnesty International 1998).

Border enforcement agents have wide discretionary power while on the job. The Border Patrol's regional offices hire agents for a particular area. Given that border-enforcement agents have wide discretion in how they perform their jobs and that it is impossible to micromanage their work, there exists the potential to abuse the power that accompanies the job. Such broad, unaccountable discretionary power can therefore contribute to human-rights violations in the region.

Ineffective and misguided hiring process leads to the employment of questionable staff. Since 1996, when federal immigration policy increased the presence of agents at the border, the INS has hired individuals at an unprecedented rate. The rapid growth in personnel has led to concerns about the quality of the individuals being hired. A 1992 study by the inspector general of the Department of Justice found that the INS "is often indifferent when it comes to screening its employees and training them, much of their work is unsupervised, and administrative discipline is sometimes haphazard.... [N]ot only is [the INS] not managing its employees well, but it also, by this neglect, is fostering a climate in which corruption can occur" (State Advisory Committees 1997, 10; see also U.S. House 1993, 2). A 1993 *Los Angeles Times* investigation of the Border Patrol also uncovered questionable hiring practices: "The Border Patrol hires agents with dubious pasts, including criminal records and checkered careers with police agencies and the military. Pressures to rush agents to the international line exacerbate a flawed screening process" (U.S. House 1993, 24; see also McDonnell and Rotella 1993).

Another concern in the INS hiring process is the recruitment of former military officers.[11] Military agents are not routinely trained in civil- and human-rights standards, which is problematic for upholding the status of human rights. More important, a high concentration of former military agents in the Border Patrol tends to make the border-enforcement region more analogous to a war zone.

The failure to enforce and abide by law-enforcement standards places human rights in jeopardy. Since civil rights are a component of human rights and law enforcement standards incorporate civil rights, the failure to enforce basic law-enforcement standards, including human safety concerns, ultimately risks human rights. Mismanagement and the lack of a proportionate increase in investigative staff exacerbate the problem. When investigative units are understaffed and there is insufficient supervision, agents can violate basic civil-rights standards. Most funding for border enforcement goes into hiring agents and securing the border, not into hiring an internal staff that regulates, investigates, evaluates, and supervises agents to ensure that civil-rights standards are met.

Mixing different types of training for military forces and law-enforcement agents can create conflicts. Military officers receive training in how to "see the enemy" and swiftly react to that enemy. Law-enforcement agents (including those of the Border Patrol) receive training on issues of due process and civil rights.[12] Army Lieutenant General Thomas Kelly, director of operations for the Joint Chiefs of Staff, discussed the difficulties arising from the cultural differences between the military and law-enforcement agencies, commenting that police officers often think in terms of going to court, but the military does not (Dunn 1996, 122; see also U.S. House 1989, 8).

The "code of silence" found in law-enforcement and military cultures prevents agents from reporting on each other. This cultural norm sustains human-rights violations because agents fail to report one another regarding incidents of wrongdoing. The code of silence is integral to the militarized border system because it maintains the system's legitimacy. The code is difficult to penetrate, and if an individual breaks it, negative consequences can result.

The level of militarization produces warlike characteristics that make rape and other human rights violations an inevitable consequence of border militarization efforts. Several aspects of LIC doctrine apply to the militarization efforts at the U.S.-Mexico border (Dunn 1996, 31), and such conflict ultimately facilitates the violation of human rights. United Nations monitors have documented the systematic rape of women during war and have categorized rape as a war crime, a weapon of war, and a form of torture. Warlike conditions at the border reinforce a climate that sustains the systematic rape and degradation of women. Agent impunity and the absence of accountability contribute to a border climate in which rape occurs with little consequence.

Advancing Human Rights for Women

Discourse on human rights has largely neglected the needs of the world's women (Binion 1995). Since the United Nations attempt to make human rights "non-gendered," most human-rights conventions lack components specific to women's issues. The purpose of human rights is to ensure the dignity of all people, but when gender is not integrated into official human-rights documents, "people" tends to be translated as "men."[13] Feminist activism started to change this shortcoming in the early 1990s. After the 1993 Vienna World Conference on Human Rights, women's rights as human rights, and human rights as women's rights, became a standard that resonated throughout the world. The Vienna Conference situated women's human rights at the center of the discourse and struggle worldwide.

The Statute of the International Criminal Tribunal for the Former Yugoslavia of May 1993 identified rape as a crime against humanity. This statute took an important step toward recognizing that armed conflict affects women differently than men, but it did not take the issue far enough. That is, the statute characterized rape in a limiting manner by considering it only within the context of ethnic cleansing, rather than as serving "purposes which are central to the enterprise of war-making" (Philipose 1996, 52).

Mallika Dutt contends that human-rights frameworks and instruments can compel the United States to be answerable for its human-rights violations against women. According to Dutt, "Using human rights as a framework allows groups to hold the U.S. government accountable for its acts of commission and omission with regard to the violation of the human rights of women" (1994, 6–7). The United States polices the human-rights records of other countries, but minimizes its own violations. Dutt criticizes Americans' mainstream belief that the United States is an exemplary model for other countries to emulate.

Human-rights discourse concerning the U.S.-Mexico border challenges border-enforcement strategies, institutional power, and U.S. hegemony. The pervasiveness of human-rights abuses, including militarized border rape, calls into question the legitimacy of border-enforcement efforts in an international context. "Rights talk," Robert W. Connell argues, "can provide a language of resistance to a system of inequality. It provides, specifically, a counter-hegemonic language through which the self-justifications of the rich and powerful can be discredited, and the system's legitimacy contested" (1995b, 26).

A human-rights framework can effectively allow advocates to move beyond an issue-based approach to consider multiple circumstances in women's migration (e.g., fleeing domestic violence or lives of abject poverty). Positioning militarized border rape within a human-rights context enables advocates and activists to consider women's migration and freedom of movement as human rights. A more holistic approach to addressing militarized border rape thus becomes possible. Advocates of women's and immigrants' rights and of decolonization can form cross-border partnerships around different issues that advance women's human rights in the border region and strive to end violence against women at the border.

Conclusion

"Allegations of sexual misconduct with immigrant women surface periodically in California and other border states, though full prosecutions and convictions are rare" (O'Connor 1996, A3). Officials who commit sexual assault often are not held accountable. Rape is difficult to prove under many circumstances, so attorneys reduce charges in order to secure a conviction. Because of their undocumented and "illegal" status in immigration law, women form a highly vulnerable group. The criminalization attached to crossing the border without appropriate U.S. government documents facilitates a disregard for human rights. Limited resources accessible to women unfamiliar with U.S. laws and the English language compound the problem.

Rape is generally underreported, but statistics on border rape are nonexistent. According to Special Rapporteur Mazowiecki, "Rape is among the most underreported crimes in peacetime throughout the world. Because of the stigma attached to rape, shame and secrecy often silence the victims. Rape continues to be underreported during wartime" (U.N. Economic and Social Council 1993b, 67). Though this report addressed the specific situation in the former Yugoslavia, many of its arguments were relevant to all forms of rape. "Many women will not talk about their experience of rape for fear of reprisals," the report continued. "Some were reluctant to tell the experts the names of the perpetrators because of fear for their own and their family's safety" (67). Human Rights Watch (1995a, 21) has documented similar responses while collecting information on abuse cases at the U.S.-Mexico border.

In *Rape Warfare* Beverly Allen describes the situation of women during the wars in Bosnia-Herzegovina and Croatia. Some aspects of her analysis are applicable to the U.S.-Mexico border: "The atrocities these women had suffered or witnessed were clearly the result of a combination of social causes: murderous misogyny coupled with rabid nationalism, all released by the specter of limitless power of one human over another, where the one with the power bears absolutely no responsibility, no accountability, for his actions" (Allen 1996, xii). Border-enforcement agents exercise power with a high degree of discretion and independence in carrying out their official duties. As Allen observes, rape occurs when fear and insecurity are joined with power and immunity from prosecution in a sexist social system. All rape is related in that "it derives from a system of dominance and subjugation that allows, and in fact often encourages, precisely the violent crime of rape as a way of maintaining that system" (Allen 1996, 39).

Susan Brownmiller likens female bodies to territory in the context of mass war rape in the former Yugoslavia: "Rape of a doubly dehumanized object—as woman, as enemy—carries its own terrible logic. In one act of aggression, the collective spirit of women *and* of the nation is broken, leaving a reminder long after the troops depart" (1993, 7). Allen (1996, 159) extends this analogy to the imperialist practice of colonization. In this logic, a form of colonization occurs at the border in the symbolic connection between women's bodies and territory. Migrant women's bodies represent a country over which the United States has maintained long-term colonial rule. Thus, women's bodies denote an "alien" or threatening presence subject to colonial domination by U.S. officials.

The involvement of the United States in "wars of aggression" has its counterpart in the tolerance of aggression by immigration authorities along the U.S.-Mexico border (Allen 1996, 105). Rape and sexual assault are rationalized in wartime due to the construction of the (racialized) enemy, and incidents of rape exemplify the systematic abuse of women along the U.S.-

Mexico border. Human-rights violations result when massive deployments of border-enforcement agents, untrained in human-rights discourses and shielded by codes of silence, manifest their power over women by violating them sexually.

Gendered violence against women goes beyond militarized border rape. In Ciudad Juárez the mass murder of women, mostly *maquiladora* workers (U.S. Department of State 2000), parallel the rapes of women crossing the border.[14] The feminization (or emasculinization) of maquila work (Devon G. Peña 1997; Salzinger 1997) is analogous to the hypermasculinization (due to militarism) of border-enforcement work. Both systems—the maquiladora industry and border control—exert social control over women's bodies. These forms of gendered violence and oppression are palpable in the U.S.-Mexico border region and are in need of further study.

Women migrate for several reasons: to reunite with family members, to seek economic opportunities via employment, to flee domestic violence, or to escape political strife and instability in their homelands (Chavez 1998, ix).[15] Human-rights treaties seek to ensure basic security and protection for women who decide to migrate. Therefore, women have the human right to be free from the threat and occurrence of sexual violence in the border region. However, the reality clearly indicates otherwise. Women's human rights have been jeopardized because the U.S.-Mexico border reinforces an environment that condones militarized border rape. It is essential to question the construction and legitimacy of the militarized border system and to integrate that system into the larger discourse of human rights the United States has committed to upholding.

Notes

The author would like to thank Denise Segura, Patricia Zavella, José Palafox, and Cynthia Bejarano, as well as acknowledge her family and Matthew Lehman.

1. For this essay, I selected a few cases which were representative of other cases of abuse. Due to space limitations and underreporting, I can provide only a glimpse of human rights violations regarding violence against women. The small number of cases discussed here does suggest important directions for future research. My intent is to exemplify the violation of women's human rights via cases of militarized border rape.
2. The National Defense Authorization Act of 1982 (Public Law 97-86), in *United States Statutes at Large Containing the Laws and Concurrent Resolutions of the 97th Congress of the United States of America* (Washington: U.S. Government Printing Office, 1982).
3. Some Chicano historians, such as David Montejano, argue that the U.S.-Mexico border has always been "militarized" (see Palafox 2000, 68n2).

4   Rape convictions in the United States are extremely low (see Mackinnon 1991).
5   Human Rights Watch (1995a) acquired the information in this account through interviews with the victim, her lawyer, the OIG, and press reports.
6   See also *People v. Luis S.Esteves*, case no. 14855 (Imperial County, California, 1992), 40.
7   Ibid., 2–3.
8   Ibid., 37.
9   See Human Rights Watch (1995a). *Luis S. Esteves, Plaintiff/Appellant, v. County of Imperial, Mary Ann Carter-Birkman, and Irma Partida, Defendant/Appellees*, no. 97–55481, no. CV-95–03956-JNK (submitted 6 November 1998 to the U.S. Court of Appeals for the Ninth Circuit).
10 On 29 September 1993 the House Subcommittee on International Law, Immigration, and Refugees held a hearing on the House of Representatives Bill 2119. This bill wanted to establish an independent review commission to investigate complaints of civil-rights abuses in the border region (U.S. House 1993). As of 7 October 1994, the bill was stalled in committee (LexisNexis 1995). Establishing an independent review commission to investigate border violence continues to be an important goal for immigrant-rights groups.
11 San Diego's INS is among the most successful in hiring military officers. In March 1999 the San Diego Border Patrol launched an aggressive recruitment campaign geared toward military officers: the Southern California All-Military Recruiting Events. During these events, teams of recruiting agents visited five to ten military bases to talk about the Border Patrol as a possible career. Following this intensive recruitment effort, the INS stated, "With the advent of new initiatives such as the 'all-military' campaign in the San Diego sector, we hope to see an even greater number of applicants from this key group in the coming year" (U.S. Immigration and Naturalization Service 1999, 11).
12 Evidence indicates law enforcement does a poor job of abiding by civil rights standards, especially for poor people and people of color. Recent cases suggest law enforcement resembles the military in its practice (i.e., shooting of unarmed Amadou Diallo over 40 times by police in New York City on 4 February 1999). Therefore, the overlap of human rights violations by civilian police forces and border enforcement agents exists because police forces are acting militaristically.
13 The Convention on the Elimination of All Forms of Discrimination against Women attempts to acknowledge the discrimination specific to women, but racial issues are noticeably lacking in it. Because racial discrimination is not mentioned, many U.S. women of color and Third World women have protested this exclusion in their activism.
14 Lourdes Portillo has directed a poignant documentary about the missing women of Ciudad Juárez entitled "Senorita Extraviada." Refer to her Web site (http://www.lourdesportillo.com) to obtain further information on this international crisis. See the September/October 2002 issue of *Frontiers* for an article by Cynthia Bejarano on the missing women of Ciudad Juárez.

15 The overwhelming theme of migration literature is that people migrate for labor. Migrating women, however, may primarily be escaping domestic violence, but once they arrive in the United States, they must search for employment. It is important to not reduce women's narratives to the search for work when the motivation may actually be to escape domestic violence.

"Nunca he dejado de tener terror":
Sexual Violence in the Lives of Mexican
Immigrant Women

GLORIA GONZÁLEZ-LÓPEZ

✳ This essay examines the testimonies of eight Mexican immigrant women who have experienced sexual violence in their lives.[1] Sexual violence includes the use of force, aggression, or intimidation performed sexually against a woman's will including, but not limited to, incest, acquaintance rape, date rape, sexual assault by an unknown individual, and marital rape or sexual coercion within marriage.[2] I argue that Mexican immigrant women's testimonies of sexual violence reflect the multiple connections between gender relations, migration experiences, and injustice against women.

Interdisciplinary and activist scholarship has documented the voices of immigrant women for whom violence in Mexico has been an important reason for migrating to the United States (Guzmán and Zeledón 1994). Paradoxically, however, women who use migration as a door to escape oppression may also encounter violence in the United States; for them, return migration becomes a strategy to deal with the abuse (Argüelles and Rivero 1993). In the midst of these transnational labyrinths, some Mexican immigrant women have been forced into sexual slavery to pay off their smuggling fees to their "coyotes" (Skerry and Rockwell 1998).[3] Thus, violence mediates some Mexicanas' migration journeys while reiterating the relevance of gender in immigration scholarship. Immigrant Mexicanas' narratives reflect how and why women are uniquely vulnerable because of poverty and narrow patriarchal notions of honor, wherein women have no right to resist intrusions on their bodies. The eight case studies expose how and why sexual victimization reinforces the gender and sexual inequalities that shape women's pre- and postmigration experiences. They also illuminate the context for women's contestation, resistance, and personal-empowerment experiences.

Immigrant Mexicanas and Sexual Violence

Recent immigration studies have argued that gender relations are crucial for understanding the immigration and settlement experiences of women and men (Hondagneu-Sotelo 1994; Woo Morales 1997). In general, research on Mexican immigrants' sex lives tend to focus on men's experiences or the spread of HIV/AIDS in transnational communities in both countries.[4] An examination of Mexican immigrant women's narratives of sexual violence, however, reveals how gender and migration begin to unfold the social dynamics that shape Mexicanas' vulnerability to sexual assault in both countries. Some of these include economic vulnerability, cultural and sexual silences, patriarchy, state-sanctioned violence with a cultural cast (*el rapto* or *el robo*, literally meaning "kidnapping" or "stealing" of a woman), and rape. As heterosexual women cope with the emotional ordeal caused by sexual trauma, they deploy mechanisms to either accommodate (keeping silence about abuse to parents and husbands, enduring coercive marriage) or resist (migrating to the United States, promoting gender equality as they educate their children in the United States) these social dynamics.

Methods

Drawn from a larger study of forty women, the eight case studies that follow involve women who experienced sexual violence. Of these eight, five experienced violence in Mexico only, one experienced it in the United States only, and two experienced it in both regions. Most of the offenders were well known to the women who experienced one or more forms of violence.

Study participants included heterosexual women living in the Los Angeles area and from a variety of educational, socioeconomic, and marital-status backgrounds. I recruited them at four community-based agencies and three elementary schools located in inner-city Latino immigrant barrios. All of the study participants identified themselves as heterosexual during the interview. As a native speaker, I conducted all of the interviews in Spanish. I use pseudonyms in order to assure study women's confidentiality.

The high proportion of exposure to violence among the overall sample of forty informants ($N = 12$) resembled the experiences of other women in the United States. At her highest exposure to risk, a woman living in urban areas

Table. Study Participants: Survivors of Sexual Violence

	Age at time of interview	Years living in the U.S.	Offender's relationship with study participant (Location of assault[a])
Study Participants from Jalisco			
1. Candelaria	36	11	Neighbor (MX), Brother (MX)
2. Nora	33	9	Boyfriend (L.A.)
3. Tomasita	30	9	Uncle (MX)
4. Victoria	34	14	Unknown (MX), Husband (L.A.)
Study Participants from Mexico City			
5. Belén	43	9	Father, Cousins, Boyfriend (all MX)
6. Fernanda	31	8	Uncle (MX), Unknown (L.A.)
7. Irasema	39	9	Boyfriend and Husband (MX)
8. Trinidad	40	10	College professor (MX)

[a]MX: Mexico, L.A.: Los Angeles.

encounters a one-in-three probability of being sexually victimized.[5] What was particularly stunning about the experiences of the Mexicanas, however, was the high proportion of women who were sexually violated by close family members, relatives, or friends and the various forms this violence took.

None of the research sites (i.e., agencies and schools) offered violence-prevention or treatment programs. I made contact with the study participants for the first time while they visited these social service agencies in order to request medical services, or as they came by to their children's schools to pick up report cards or to address other school-related issues. The snowball technique offered me the opportunity to identify future informants, but always within the same contexts. I did not ask any of the forty women if they had ever been abused or forced to have sexual relations; the women offered their testimonies voluntarily during our interviews.[6] Of twelve women who reported events of sexual violence, eight women shared similar or parallel patterns of sexual violence; in order to offer consistent examinations, only those eight are discussed in-depth in this essay.[7]

Overall study participants were women who migrated to the United States at the age of twenty years old or older. At time of interview, they were between the ages of twenty-five and forty-five, the average age being thirty-five. Half of the sample were women born and raised in the State of Jalisco; the other half were women born and raised in Mexico City. With the exception of two Jalisco informants who had lived in the United States for twenty and twenty-five years, respectively, all participants had lived permanently in the United States for between five and fifteen years. Women from Jalisco had lived longer as permanent residents of the United States (average = 11.68 years) than the Mexico City group (average = 8.85 years). On migration, women were more likely to be either married (16) or single (15) than divorced (5) or in a cohabitation relationship (4). Women had an average of three children, most of whom were being raised in the United States. Four women had children living in Mexico. The children of these women were more likely to be young adults or adolescents being cared for by the study participants' parents.

The lowest level of formal education for both groups was *educación primaria*, which is equivalent to completion of sixth grade; the highest level was a *licenciatura*, equivalent to a bachelor's degree. However, women from Jalisco were more likely to have a lower level of formal education (average = 7.1 years) than their Mexico City counterparts (average = 10.15 years). Accordingly, Jalisco women were less likely to have paid employment (9 out of 20) and more likely to be full-time homemakers (11 out of 20) when compared to the Mexico City informants. Most women from Mexico City reported to have paid jobs (15 out of 20); only a few of them reported they were full-time homemakers (5 out of 20). Overall, participants identified themselves with a wide variety of occupations: domestic work and childcare; factory and sweatshop jobs; clerical, secretarial, and tax services; sales and public relations; apartment management; and medical services and community education.

Jalisco and Mexico City represent two of the main regions of origin for Mexican immigrant women who enter the United States through Tijuana (Woo Morales 1995). Socioeconomic differences between the two regions offer contrasting social scenarios that influence female sexuality in distinctive ways. Mexico City is the capital and the largest city of the nation. Jalisco encompasses the city of Guadalajara (the second largest city in Mexico and the capitol of state), but also includes pre- and semi-industrialized rural areas including small villages and pueblos. Jalisco is also the birthplace of tequila, mariachi music, and a *charro* culture, all dominant folklore images central to the creation of national, masculinist identities.

While this study does not attempt to generalize to the experiences of other heterosexual Mexicana survivors of sexual violence, the following narratives of rape illustrate how and why gender and migration become mutually interconnected processes as women cope with the social and cultural prescriptions that promote injustice and sexual violence against Mexicanas. Their testimonies reveal how and why women's experiences of sexual violence both reflect and shape the ways in which gender and migration are lived by women on both sides of the border.

Mexicanas' Gendered Constructions of Sexual Violence

Both gender and violence intertwine with women's pre- and postmigration experiences. From the women's testimonies emerged evidence of two sets of gendered dynamics within family contexts surrounding women's narratives of sexual violence: family honor anchored in notions of female purity and motherhood; and fear of the repercussions associated with contesting male violence. Critically evaluating the historical conditions that have led to women's vulnerability to sexual violence, the women incorporated their critiques into alternative ways of approaching their own daughters' sexual education.

Family Honor, Female Purity, and Motherhood

In Mexico a young and single woman's sexual body is controlled by the family. An expression of patriarchal morality, a sophisticated ethic of family respect or *respeto a la familia* links female sexuality to family honor and respect. Some families attempt to repair the moral damage to family honor caused by premarital pregnancy by forcing their daughters to marry. Rapes of virgin women might therefore unfold painfully complex consequences, especially when pregnancy follows the act of violence. In extreme cases, daughters must marry their rapists. This gendered prescription has its origins in Mexican colonial society, which linked female sexuality with a woman's moral virtue (i.e., virginity), socioeconomic status, and family honor (Espín 1986; Twinam 1989; Tostado Gutiérrez 1991; Ramos Lira, Koss, and Russo 1999).[8]

In addition, a woman's exposure to sexual violence by an older male within the family context (father, brother, uncle, cousin) becomes a personal secret; *vergüenza* (shame) and family conflict must be avoided by women while they keep their pain in silence. Although "sexual silence" might not be exclusive to Mexican families (Alonso and Koreck 1993; Díaz Olvarrieta and Sotelo 1996), it functions as a protection from a fear of family rejection and shame in the lives of Mexican women exposed to sexual assault (Ramos Lira, Koss, and Russo 1999; Low and Organista 2000).

As they attempted to resolve their own experiences of sexual abuse, women in my study who mothered children in the United States explored ways in which they could protect their daughters from a similar fate. Many of them sought to accomplish this by making use of educational material received from *pláticas*, or workshops, on parenting skills, which they attended at community-based clinics and schools. All of them passionately objected to coercive marriage as a solution should their daughters become pregnant out of wedlock. They condemned family secrecy and tolerance around issues of intrafamily rape. All reflected on the damage done to their personal lives by such practices of social adjustment.

Fear of Repercussions

The second set of dynamics is connected to women's socially learned fear that premarital sex will lead to exacerbated gender inequality in marriage. Several of my informants used *macho, machismo,* and *machista* in order to describe sexist beliefs and practices in their stories, a sentiment exemplified by a comment made by many women: "Los esposos te lo echan en cara cuando no eres virgen" (Husbands throw it in your face when you are not a virgin). Women who were nonvirgins at marriage due to sexual violence (e.g., incest, rape) often reported that their husbands blamed them. Fearing rejection by a future husband for not being a virgin at marriage, a raped woman might either feel convinced to accept the coercive marriage imposed by her parents or to arrange a marriage herself without her parents' knowledge about the event of violence. In rural Mexico, rape of virgin women may therefore have extreme effects. For example, for some rural women, a "damaged" hymen represents diminished opportunities of marriage and, therefore, of survival (González-López 2005). Since the late 1960s, Guadalupe Irma Solís, a physician from northern Mexico, has been conducting hymen reconstruction of women who have lost their virginity because of rape. In a personal interview, Solís reported that fear of rejection by and/or conflict with a romantic partner (and potential husband) is one of the reasons why rural mothers began to take their young teenage daughters to receive this medical intervention.[9]

Sexual Violence in Mexico: Women from Jalisco

Tomasita migrated from a small town in Jalisco to Los Angeles when she was twenty-one. Now thirty, she is a full-time housewife educating four daughters and one son in Los Angeles. Although she struggled to remember if she was five or six when her uncle sexually molested and raped her, she articulated her recollection of the event precisely: "At first, he just wanted to touch my legs, and to do this and that. But at that moment, I did not react. I was so innocent because I was little. I do not remember at what age that happened, but I was little. . . . I remember that I fell asleep and I woke up, I woke up screaming because he had put his hand down there and I remember a very intense pain, and I think that man took away my virginity."

Tomasita said she was brave enough to tell her mother about it when she became a teenager. Her mother expressed concern for her, but asked Tomasita not to tell her father in order to avoid conflict or to prevent a family tragedy (e.g., her father killing her uncle). Tomasita associated her early experiences of abuse with the intense hatred she currently feels toward rapists, a chronic migraine problem, and some of the sexual difficulties she experienced early in her marriage, including marital rape. She reported not feeling worthy of wearing a white dress when she got married. She said, "Ya no hay la illusion" (There is no illusion/dream anymore). Then, she added, "Me casé por la iglesia por la presión de la familia" (I married by the church because of family's pressure).

Other women from Jalisco also shared their experiences of sexual abuse while growing up in their small towns. Victoria, now thirty-four, was violently raped when she was sixteen. Crying, she vividly recalled the day when a man in his forties pushed her inside his car and drove her to his home. She said she had seen him only once before, from a distance. She sobbed while recalling the sexual, physical, and emotional abuse to which she was exposed while living in terror, locked up, for about a month before she was able to escape. "When he ... when he took me up there, all the way to the top of the hill, it was dark because there's just mountains, right? And I felt like ... I do not know. I felt like dying, I do not know. But I did not want him to touch me; I did not want him to touch me! I was terrified! I was so scared! But then, after all this happened, I felt like throwing up, I was so enraged. But then, after everything happened, all that I wanted was to get away from there."

Victoria said her family was understanding and supportive; they made a police report, and the offender (a married man) was sent to prison for eight years. After he was released, however, she left for Los Angeles to live with her relatives out of fear of retaliation. "¡Vete! ¡Vete!" (Go! Go!), she paraphrased her parents' words of encouragement, recalling the day when the three of them talked about her migrating to the United States. She had gotten pregnant as a consequence of being raped; her child stayed in Mexico and has been raised by her parents.

Victoria was kidnapped and raped in the late 1970s while living in her small town in Jalisco. Her story is not an isolated or unique case. Fiona Wilson (1990) offers anthropological examinations of el rapto or el robo ("kidnapping" or "stealing" a woman) and *la violación* (rape) as recurring forms of sexual violence against Mexican women living in rural areas located in the western region of Mexico. According to Wilson, these forms of sexual brutality were prevalent in this particular geographical area in the 1950s and 1960s (78–80); families and husbands were especially protective of their daughters and wives. Wilson argues that education and women's increased participation in paid labor have been responsible for a decrease in the incidence of these types of sexual crimes.[10]

Beyond this expression of gender inequality, the concept of el robo has more nuanced and sophisticated meanings in Mexican society. My larger study including twenty Mexican immigrant men revealed that some young women and men decide to run away in order to get around family disapproval. With some exceptions, couples that elope eventually establish a formal relationship. Their parents have no choice but to accept a legal marriage. For other young couples, running away may help them avoid the financial expenses of an official wedding (see González-López 2005). Ana Amuchástegui (2001) and Jennifer Hirsch (2003) have reported similar findings in their sexuality research with Mexican populations.

A thirty-six-year-old housewife from a small town in Jalisco, Candelaria was sexually abused by her brother when she was ten. The abuse stopped after she consistently threatened to tell their parents about it. Shortly after, one of her uncles attempted to sexually assault her at night while she was sleeping. She did not tell anyone about it, but she successfully used a strategy of becoming *grosera* (rude) to him to keep him at a distance. After that, she was never harassed by any of her family members. However, in her early teens, a fifty-year-old neighbor she identified as "un amigo de la familia" (a family friend) sexually harassed her, raped her on multiple occasions, and eventually got her pregnant in spite of the sexual impotence problem he experienced at times. "I was seventeen or eighteen . . . and he never had . . . he hit himself against the wall because he wanted to have sex but he could not do it and I always told him to leave me alone, I told him, '¡Déjeme en paz porque yo quiero rehacer mi vida!'" (Leave me alone because I want to start all over with my life!) She spoke this last in a high-pitched voice. Explaining how the situation had become unbearable for her, she asserted, "He was one of the reasons why I came to the United States." After he got her pregnant, she had an abortion and left for the United States as a way to escape the abuse of many years.

Candelaria explained to me how the neighbor had helped her family with many money loans when they were in need. She described an obligation she felt toward this man: letting him touch her body was a sense of responsibility she experienced toward the financial status of her family. Candelaria's story illustrates the vulnerabilities of women living in socioeconomic marginality. "In rural sectors of Mexico, a tradition of violence against the vulnerable has existed for centuries, first at the hands of the *conquistadores* and later at the hand of the landowners" (Díaz Olavarrieta and Sotelo 1996, 1938). Thus, single women who live in poverty like Candelaria are also sexually disenfranchised and vulnerable on behalf of their families' survival, economic welfare, and safety. Candelaria's excruciating experience became her secret. Like Tomasita, she feared a family tragedy (i.e., her father would kill the rapist). To this day, she has told none of her family members nor her husband with whom she now lives in Los Angeles.

Tomasita, Victoria, and Candelaria have many things in common. They were born and raised in small towns in Jalisco; they were in their early or mid-thirties when the interview was conducted; they were full-time housewives in Los Angeles; and all of them had their first sexual experience through some type of sexual violence. Even though they had experienced first intercourse against their will, these women's husbands reproached them at some point in their marital lives for having not been virgins at the time of marriage. Shame, guilt, or their husbands' refusal to listen kept them from revealing the truth about their rapes to their partners. Thus, silence about the abuse and lack of virtue at marriage caused marital conflicts in the lives of all three women.

How do these women's stories of sexual abuse and marital life relate to their current lives and experiences in the United States? Via motherhood, these women recall their own experiences of sexual abuse as they educate their daughters in the new country. As these women explore the sex education they would like to offer their daughters in the United States, their past sexual histories begin to shape their current perceptions of female heterosexuality. For instance, since exploring issues with regard to sexuality, virginity, and their daughters' sex education triggered their own recollections of the impact of sexual abuse on their own sex lives, they expressed discomfort and concern as they began to anticipate sexism in their daughters' futures. For instance, Tomasita said, "What if they end up with a machista man like it happened to me? 'Well, you were not even a virgin. God knows who was the first man, or how many touched you.'" Such comments reflect a mother's concern about the potential conflict a daughter may encounter in the future for not being virgin at marriage. Thus, as a way to protect their daughters from potential emotional abuse and sexism, Tomasita, Victoria, and Candelaria advocated the value of preserving premarital virginity.

The testimonies offered by this trio of mothers resonate with the accounts of other Mexican parents educating adolescent girls in different Southwest regions of the United States. Research with families from New Mexico and Texas observed that young Mexican American girls who "secretly date older boys" prompted family reactions. Some of these parents perceived older men's interest in "a young virgin to ultimately marry" to be part of sexism and gender inequality (Barkley and Salazar-Mosher 1995, 262).

Thus, as a Mexicana educates a daughter in the United States, her perception of premarital virginity is shaped by the gender inequalities she has experienced as a woman, including the experiences unfolding due to the intra-

and extrafamilial sexual abuse she might have lived in Mexico. On the other hand, the U.S. social and economic contexts and everyday life experiences in their immigrant communities may offer Mexicanas alternative avenues to promote a more egalitarian sex education for both genders, to contest the reproduction of sexual abuse against girls and women, and to protect Mexican American children from potential sexual abuse. Women like Tomasita, Victoria, and Candelaria may become survivors of sexual abuse who transform their painful past experiences into passion they can use to actively develop a more egalitarian immigrant community.

"¡A las mujeres no se les toca ni con el pétalo de una rosa!" (You do not touch women, not even with a rose petal!), exclaimed Tomasita, explaining that she used this expression to teach her only son to practice "el respeto a la mujer" (respect for women) with his four sisters, classmates, and neighbors. As Tomasita, Victoria, and Candelaria described how they were educating their children with regard to sex education, they reflected on the fear and violence they had experienced in their lives. They used motherhood to contest patriarchal ownership of the female body as they coped with their still-painful past. As they actively participated in the socialization of their children, they became keenly aware of the reproduction of sexism across generations. As Tomasita critically stated, "Because some parents teach their little boys to be machistas from the very beginning."

Tomasita, Victoria, and Candelaria had not received specialized professional attention at the time of our interviews. However, they reported an intense desire and endless efforts to promote gender sensitivity as they provided sex education to a new generation of Mexican American children. Tomasita and Victoria said they have attended and benefited from parenting classes offered to them by a school and a hospital, respectively. Both said they have openly asked their daughters to tell them about any type of sexual contact they may have experienced, as well as to discuss other sexuality-related topics. Tomasita also reported that the parenting workshops helped her to talk openly to her children about the best ways to protect themselves from sexual abuse. Victoria said she constantly practiced "role playing" in her mind as she explored in silence the best ways to talk more comfortably to her children about sexuality. Candelaria's only daughter is still an infant, but Candelaria reported that her children's school counselor helped her to develop skills for talking openly to her older children about sexuality and related issues. Like Tomasita, she actively taught her three sons to protect and respect her daughter. And like Victoria, she was already thinking about how she would teach her daughter to protect herself from potential sexual abuse.

Tomasita, Victoria, and Candelaria described their pueblos with heartfelt nostalgia. However, all described the unfortunate economic limitations they found in Mexico, reporting having found in their immigrant communities more information and resources addressing how to educate their children in many areas, including sexuality and child abuse.

Women from Mexico City

Irasema was thirty-nine at the time of our interview; she had migrated to Los Angeles when she was thirty. Unlike the vast majority of the study participants, she described herself as a former daddy's girl who "had no need to work," having been an upper-middle-class woman in her native Mexico City. Tears dissolved Irasema's well-done makeup as she switched from describing her privileged family background to disclosing the pain she had experienced as a teenager. Irasema had her first sexual experience at the age of nineteen, after an episode of deep confusion and anxiety. While she was riding with her boyfriend in his car, he took an unknown detour, then drove to a hotel, where he raped her. She described her emotional experience after being raped: "Oh my God! I felt so dirty; I did not even want to see my parents. I felt as if they were going to point the finger at me, like they were going to guess what had happened to me. But you know, I got home all relaxed with all my makeup on pretending as if nothing had happened to me. I felt so dirty and guilty. I used to share my bedroom with one of my sisters and I did not even want her to touch me or get close to me. And I cried and cried because I asked myself why?"

After a deep sigh, Irasema added, "I do not know, but it feels ugly, very ugly." She then reported that when the assault took place, she did not have any information about reproduction. Later on, she realized she had become pregnant and underwent failed attempts at abortion. Irasema tried to hide her pregnancy for as long as she could, but about the fourth or fifth month it became impossible. Her pregnancy disturbed family stability: pregnancy out of wedlock brought into question the family's morality and therefore family respect. She was coerced by her father to get married.

> Yes, because I was forced to do it ... because *me casaron a la fuerza* [they forced me to get married]. My father said, "We're not going to leave it like this." And he grabbed me and let's go! Boom! He took me to the house of my husband and I do not know how many things they said ... that he had to repair the damage. And then ... you wear white in front of society, in order for you to be okay with them. But then after a few months you give birth to your baby. The week after I got married I was

already wearing dresses for pregnant women because I already was five months pregnant.

Irasema's marriage became an ordeal. Even though she did not perceive it as marital rape, she said she felt like a rag doll while lying face up in bed, looking at the ceiling, and praying so her husband would fall asleep or get tired of forcing her to have sex. Irasema at some point left her husband and became a single mother of their two young children. She had a job in Mexico, but after migrating to the United States with her children, she was able to establish a modest, stable life working as a seamstress. Irasema's face glowed as she talked about her current marital relationship with a Latino immigrant man she had met at work. She described her relationship as the healthy and peaceful one she had always wanted to have since she was very young.

Irasema's story is not an isolated case. Other women in this study who had gotten pregnant out of wedlock for reasons other than rape also reported being coerced by their families to get married.[11] Some of them, however, experienced rape later in their lives. Trinidad, now forty, was similarly raised in an upper-middle-class family in Mexico City. She attended college and completed a bachelor's degree, but as she made plans to pursue a professional career, she was forced by her family to get married. At seventeen, she dated a young man she was not planning to marry, but experienced intercourse for the first time with him. She used the expression "Me comí el pastel antes del recreo" (I ate the cake before recess) to explain that she was aware she was not supposed to have sex before marriage. Then she elaborated: "She [her mother] sent me to get married. I pleaded with her. I cried, I begged. I did not want her to force me to get married. She said, 'No, no, she has to get married. After she gets married, she can get divorced if she wants to.' And yes, later on I got divorced because I knew it was not going to work."

Like Irasema, Trinidad gave birth after failed attempts to have an abortion, and her marriage did not last. However, she continued to attend college. While working on a school project, she requested the mentorship of one of her professors. On different occasions, he invited her to discuss her school projects at his home, and she always felt relaxed and safe. However, one time, the unexpected happened. As she recalled, "Suddenly, he got on top of me, like crazy, and I saw in his eyes like the devil, and the truth is that if you resist at that moment, he may even kill you. The truth is that I never knew if it was rape or not because I opened my legs; that is the truth, but I was so scared."

During our interview, Trinidad reported she had not been seriously affected by this experience. She explained, for example, that she had been able to have a healthy sex life and a stable relationship in her second marriage.

She also reported attending a support group in Los Angeles, which helped her to overcome some emotional difficulties. However, like other women in this study, Trinidad accepted responsibility for her own sexual victimization and pointed to what she shouldn't have done. As Trinidad said, "Hasta cierto punto yo tuve la responsabilidad" (To some extent, I was responsible). Being at the house of a single man was not safe for a woman, she recalled as one of the many warnings her mother had long given her: "Vas y te metes a la casa de un soltero, así que, ¿qué te estás esperando?" (You go to a single man's house, so then, what are you expecting?)

The Migration Experience

In discussing the experience of sexual assault, Trinidad and Irasema, like their counterparts from small towns in Jalisco, came to reflect on the sex education they were offering to the daughters they were raising in the United States. Describing themselves as caring and understanding mothers, they said they became passionate foes of coercive marriage and pro-choice advocates of women's rights to have an abortion. Irasema, for example, said she would immediately consider abortion in case her only, young adult daughter went through her same ordeal. Because abortion is legal in the United States, she would consider it as an alternative to cope with an unexpected pregnancy due to rape. Both Trinidad and Irasema were critical of a legal system that fails to protect rape survivors in Mexico. Even though abortion is permitted under Mexican federal law in cases of rape, local regulations in each state and a complex bureaucracy transform a woman's right into a shameful ordeal, especially when the Catholic Church and conservative right-wing groups interfere with a woman's decision to interrupt a pregnancy (Poniatowska 2000).

Both mothers reflected on the sex education they would like to offer to their daughters. Unlike their counterparts from Jalisco, who survived rape and were blamed by their current partners for not being virgins at marriage, neither Irasema nor Trinidad expected her daughter to preserve premarital virginity. However, like the rural women, their attitudes reflected a maternal desire to contest gender oppression via socialization of her children. Their expectations were also a consequence of their Mexico City background. Urban social contexts expose women to multiple possibilities for education, paid employment, and women's organizations—all of them are social circumstances that may enable women to challenge gender inequalities (Figueroa Perea 1997).[12]

Belén, a third participant from Mexico City, was educated in a working-class family and migrated to Los Angeles in her early thirties. At the time of our interview, Belén was forty-three and still had memories of the pain and confusion she had experienced when she was nine years old: her father had forced her to have intercourse, an ordeal that had continued until she was an adolescent, but Belén had never talked to her mother about it for fear of hurting her feelings. However, she had attempted many times to convince her mother to leave her alcoholic father after witnessing the episodes of physical and emotional violence that took place in the home. Her father's explosions of rage had reaffirmed Belén's decision to accept the sexual abuse she was experiencing while keeping her pain in silence.

Many incest survivors are exposed to sexual abuse later in their lives (Los Angeles Commission on Assaults Against Women 1999), and Belén was no exception. Belén was sexually abused in her early teens by male cousins on both sides of her family. Belén's sexual encounters with her cousins might be perceived as socially acceptable by those who believe in *la sabiduría*, or the wisdom of popular sayings in Mexican culture: the Mexican adage "A la prima se le arrima" (You can get physically/sexually close to your female cousin) is a reflection of the sexual objectification Mexican women might be exposed to within the family context.

In my research work, I define incestuous sexual relationships as the sexual experiences between an individual and her or his immediate relatives, including siblings, parents, nieces, nephews, grandparents, cousins, aunts, and uncles, but these relationships may also include those who are not genetically related and/or who are members of the extended family, such as stepparents, the partners of biological aunts and uncles, sisters-in-law and brothers-in-law, and romantic partners of other blood-line relatives. During a presentation I offered at a sexuality conference in Mexico City in 1998, I was questioned by a male Mexican about my definition of incest. According to him, a self-identified sex educator and physician, uncles and cousins should not be included in the definition. While passionately arguing that sex between a woman and her male cousin should not be considered incestuous, he used the saying "A la prima se le arrima," emphasizing that it was not unusual for Mexican males to experience sexual initiation with their female cousins. The comments made by this professional illustrate the frightening ways in which Mexican society condones, perpetuates, and reproduces the gender inequalities that confiscate the female body while exposing women like Belén to sexual violence.

As a young adult, Belén was also a victim of date rape. "I wanted to get married, I said to myself, 'Nobody would ever love me,'" she said, explaining her decision to maintain a relationship with the boyfriend who date raped her and with whom she has lived in a physically and emotionally abusive marital relationship. Belén's personal decision to marry the man who raped her was due to the profound fear of rejection she developed as part of post-incest trauma. "Not being a virgin means to be devalued and worthless as a woman," she said, describing the message she learned as a young teenager listening to her girlfriends in their conversations about virginity, premarital sex, and men. Fear of being rejected by a potential husband made Belén marry the boyfriend who had raped her. Even her husband had expressed disappointment and anger at the fact that she was not a virgin when he raped her. The expression often used by the women in this study—"Husbands throw it in your face when you are not a virgin"—became real for Belén after she decided to marry: "Well ... when my husband raped me, he believed that I was a señorita [virgin], but later on he realized that I was not and he got very angry. Later on he asked me, 'Why were you not a virgin?!'"

To this day, fear has kept Belén from telling her husband she was raped by her father and cousins. Even though she has endured an unstable and at times abusive relationship, she still lives with her husband as a full-time housewife and has not had a paid job outside the home since she migrated nine years ago. She has, however, worked as an active community volunteer in her immigrant barrio in Los Angeles. During our interview, Belén reported she had just begun attending therapy sessions at a clinic not far from her house. Beyond exploring the abuse, she hopes that therapy can help her explore ways to develop a healthy marital relationship and a nurturing family life.

Fernanda, thirty-one, was raised in a working-class family. She and her sister were sexually assaulted by one of their uncles when they were thirteen and fourteen, respectively. At the time, they were on a family Christmas visit to the small hometown of her mother's family in the southeast region of the country. Fernanda recalled enjoying Christmas Eve. But later that night, when she and her sister were walking down a street, they were attacked by her uncle and three of his friends. She described how she and her sister defended themselves, kicking and scratching the men's faces, even as their clothes were ripped off. Fernanda was able to get her uncle's gun and used it to threaten them: "They pushed us. And they hit me, because I did not let them unbutton my pants, and they hit me, and some type of grass leaves scratched my face and my body, and I got some kind of skin rash. It scratched my face and my arms and as I resisted, I got one of these men's gun. Everything happened very quickly."

Fernanda remembered only bits and pieces of the rest of the episode, then being with her sister in a hospital, recovering from the painful bruises and cuts they had all over their bodies while trying to answer their mother's endless list of questions about the painful event. Fernanda's mother requested a doctor to examine for evidence of forced vaginal penetration. The result was negative. A police report was never filed, not only because of the doctor's findings but also, as Fernanda explained, "por vergüenza de nosotros, por vergüenza para ellos, y porque eran parte de la familia" (because it would be shameful for my immediate family, because it would be shameful for the extended family, and because the perpetrator was part of the family). Her words exemplify the perception that families may legitimately control women's sexualized bodies and be silent about intrafamily sexual violence as part of an ethic of family respect and loyalty.

Fernanda sadly recalled her return to Mexico City from her mother's hometown. She talked with her boyfriend about her painful experience, then never heard from him again, because, she explained, "he believed that I had been deflowered." Like Belén, Fernanda also learned a fear of being rejected by men after losing their virginity due to incest or rape.

At the age of eighteen, Fernanda established a relationship with a boyfriend. She agreed to have sex for the first time, but the experience resulted in an unwanted pregnancy. As happened with Irasema and Trinidad, Fernanda's parents forced her to marry when they learned about her pregnancy. Her marriage was difficult and short-lived; she soon separated from her husband and kept the custody of their child. At the age of twenty-three, she migrated to Los Angeles, where she currently cohabitates with an immigrant Latino. Both live with Fernanda's child from her first marriage and an infant born from their relationship.

For a Mexican immigrant woman, being a rape survivor before migrating to the United States has unfolding consequences as she establishes her life and becomes a mother within the socioeconomic contexts of the immigrant community. When rape becomes a part of the immigration experience, additional gender dynamics get unmasked.

Sexual Violence in the United States

None of the forty women reported being raped during their actual immigration journeys to the United States, that is, being raped by an immigrating man, a coyote (immigrant smuggler), or an immigration officer. However, two of the women experienced sexual violence after they had established a permanent life in Los Angeles.

Nora, thirty-three, was exposed to sexual violence by a boyfriend she had met in Los Angeles—also a Mexican immigrant. Nora had grown up in a stable middle-class family and recalled having been a happy adolescent and young adult who had had the opportunity to attend college and to receive a bachelor's degree in Mexico. She migrated alone from an urban area in Jalisco to Los Angeles when she was twenty-four. After four years of a financially stable and satisfying life in Los Angeles, Nora experienced intercourse for the first time while being raped, and impregnated, by a Mexican immigrant man she had previously dated.

During our interview, she experienced immense emotional pain and anxiety while discussing the topic of virginity and the sex education of children. When asked if she wanted her daughter to preserve her virginity until marriage, Nora replied, "Oh! . . . Well, to tell you the truth I do not even know. . . . I spent such a long time taking care of myself [not having sex], for such a long time, and now I say, what for? if you finally end up being. . . . Now the truth is that I do not know what to think about it. I do not even know if I want my daughter to do the same or to explain, well, to her the way things are, you know, sexuality, your sex life, because I do not even know if it is worth preserving your virginity or if it is better to give yourself to a man when you are in love, I do not know!" She began to cry. Nora's loss of virginity through rape created the possibility for her daughter to be educated such that she could claim and possess her sexuality.

At the time of the interview, Nora was cohabitating with a Mexican immigrant man who had been supportive and caring after he had learned about her rape experience. He has never complained about her not being a virgin. Thus, Nora said that in spite of her painful experience, she now considers herself very fortunate.

The social consequences of rape in the United States were different for Nora than they would have been had she been raped in Mexico. Although she experienced emotional trauma after being raped, geographical distance from her family and a sense of anonymity in a foreign country protected her from potential family confrontations and conflict, and feelings of shame, guilt, and moral prosecution. An ethic of respeto a la familia, however, survived the test of immigration, distance, and time. When asked if her family knew about the rape experience, she replied, "No, nobody knows." Asked about the rationale behind her decision not to tell her family, she said, "Well, I do not know, shame perhaps, I do not want to shame them."

Physical and geographical distance, personal isolation, and a sense of anonymity helped Nora to avoid some of the negative social consequences she might have encountered had she been raped in Mexico. However, the everyday life experiences of immigrant women living in an urban context often expose them to socioeconomic segregation, demanding work schedules, lack of transportation, unsafe neighborhoods, and unprotected work areas—all of which combine to create dangerous social spaces. Thus, many Mexican immigrant women are vulnerable and easy targets for sexual violence.

Fernanda, after finishing her recollection of the events that unfolded after she was sexually assaulted at the age of thirteen in her mother's hometown, reported that she had recently been experiencing painful flashbacks of that event; a post-immigration experience of sexual assault had caused her to relive the episodes of sexual violence in Mexico. A man used a bicycle to block her way as she walked down a dark alley leading to the sweatshop where she still works, a modest shop very close to downtown Los Angeles. With graphic language, Fernanda explained that the man masturbated in front of her, then sexually attacked her. As she tried to run away, she experienced an intense state of panic: "I was on la Washington and . . . and it was early and dark, because it was wintertime. That is the place where I still work. It was kind of an experience . . . ! [Her voice became high pitched.] Because for the second time it was happening to me, all over again. And what I say is that if you already had an experience like that, you do not become a coward at that moment. But then you feel so scared . . . then you feel all this terror. Then, when you think about it, *Ay Dios mio!*"

Neither Nora nor Fernanda filed a police report. They said that the police would not have believed them because they were "too old," as they put it. Furthermore, they were simply too overwhelmed by the emotional trauma. As Fernanda discussed both pre- and postmigration experiences of sexual assault, she stated, "Nunca he dejado de tener terror" (I have never stopped being in terror).

Final Considerations

These women's narratives illustrate the complex relationships between traditional notions of gender and contemporary experiences of migration. The stories of sexual violence told by these women unmask the mechanisms of power and control connecting sexuality, gender, and class relations that begin to unfold these women's pre- and post-migration experiences. That these women endured incest, kidnapping, rape, and coercive sex as a family obligation reveals how gender inequality is exacerbated by poverty in rural Mexico, although urban women do experience similar vulnerabilities. The objectification of women within family contexts via sexual abuse of girls and young women by male relatives, date and acquaintance rape, and the forced marriage of young pregnant women to maintain family honor (even in cases of rape) confiscates a woman's control over her body within these patriarchal families.

Sexual violence is the major and immediate reason prompting migration for some of these women. However, migration may help Mexicanas to cope with sexual violence only temporarily, for gender equality is not a social guarantee after they enter the United States. Migration automatically translates not into lifestyle improvement, but into a collection of new socioeconomic and sociopolitical scenarios that surround family, couple relationships, and the rest of the immigrant world, which Mexicanas decipher as immigrant women. On the one hand, socioeconomic segregation, language limitations, citizenship status, and dangerous inner-city life make Mexicanas vulnerable to sexual violence. On the other, geographical distance, a sense of isolation, and anonymity may offer some strategies for coping with shame and other consequences that may accompany being raped in the United States.

For all women, migration and everyday life experiences in the new country lead them to revisit their personal histories of gender inequality. Regardless of their places of origin, immigrant women survivors of violence find through motherhood potential avenues to reflecting and coping with pain, as they explore ways to protect their children from a similar fate. As mothers, they eagerly promote egalitarian gender relationships in the sex education they provide to a new generation of women and men in the United States.

Thus, after women migrate to and establish a permanent life in the United States, new economic and legal structures, along with a dynamic and reportedly resourceful immigrant community, may offer them unexplored ways to contest ideologies that promote tolerance of violence. Under the Violence Against Women Act (VAWA), signed into law in 1994, an undocumented woman living in an abusive relationship with a U.S. citizen or permanent resident may be eligible for legal-resident status under a "self-petition" provision. Under VAWA, she may also be eligible to suspend deportation and receive her residency.[13] Furthermore, according to Ana Santamaría, a Latina professional working at the Los Angeles Commission on Assaults Against Women (LACAAW)—the oldest rape crisis intervention and treatment agency in Los Angeles—the agency's program for Latinas attends an average of 2,500 telephone calls per year with Spanish-speaking women survivors of violence, many of whom are from Mexico.[14]

After I completed the forty interviews, I myself joined LACAAW as a volunteer therapist. At this agency, I witnessed with deep joy how Mexican immigrant women survivors of sexual violence may heal their wounds via therapy, sometimes becoming passionate and empowered activists and volunteers who organize, educate, and counsel other Mexicana and Latina survivors living in the Spanish-speaking immigrant community. In this way, Mexicanas interact with agencies and schools where they learn to protect a new generation of girls and boys and to prevent them from reproducing the same patterns of abuse they, themselves, have actively struggled to overcome.

An examination of the male actor in the heterosexual equation of sexual violence is beyond the scope of this essay. It is unquestionable that patterns of sexual violence against women cannot be challenged without a profound examination of the masculine identities and social forces that are oppressive to men, as well as a careful exploration of misogynous and nonmisogynous expressions of masculinities via parenthood, education, activism, and research (see, e.g., Connell 1995a; Kimmel and Messner 2001; Gutmann 1996). Exemplary activist organizations invested in this common effort include the National Latino Alliance for the Elimination of Domestic Violence; the *círculos de hombres* (men's circles) in Orange County, Los Angeles, San Francisco, Albuquerque, San Antonio, and elsewhere (Mena 2000a); and the Collective of Men for Egalitarian Relations in Mexico City.[15]

Gender inequality resembles a puzzle scattered on both sides of the border, with migration serving as the social dynamic that connects women to a holistic critique of hitherto fragmented histories of violence and objectification. Sexual violence is one of the pieces that may remain hidden for some women, but it becomes increasingly salient for those who try to accommodate it into their personal lives. In the midst of this transnational process, both women and men are gradually becoming more aware of how the dynamics of violence against women are produced and reproduced. May the testimonies presented in this essay enhance understanding of Mexican women's lives and offer some avenues for social justice and change on both sides of the border.

Notes

I want to express my gratitude to the forty women who trusted me with their personal lives and sexual stories. I am profoundly grateful to the Social Science Research Council for the generous dissertation fellowship I received through its Sexuality Research Fellowship Program. I want to thank my friend Patricia Emerson for helping with the editing of the manuscript.

1 I conduct my examinations based on in-depth interviews conducted with self-identified heterosexual Mexican immigrant women living in the city of Los Angeles. I collected this data during the 1997–1998 academic year.

2 Being not a sex act per se, but an act of violence that is enacted sexually, rape has been redefined and reconceptualized for quite some time (Ramos Lira, Koss, and Russo 1999), with both women and men identified as potential victims. Feminist academics and activists examining sexual violence, however, have consistently referred to statistics to indicate that women are disproportionately affected when compared to men (see Brownmiller 1975; Rich 1977; Griffin 1979; Paglia 1992; Lagarde 1997; Lamas 1998).

3 In addition, numerous examinations of sexual violence and Mexican immigrant women have been conducted in the behavioral and mental-health sciences. And,

human-rights and policy-making academics and activists have invested intense efforts in addressing the complexities of legal and political concerns, and violence in Latino immigrant communities.

For examinations on how citizenship status may increase women's vulnerability to systematic domestic and sexual abuse within the marital relationship, see Anderson 1993. For a social and political perspective on domestic violence in immigrant communities, see Perilla 1999.

4 For research that focuses on Mexican immigrant men's sex lives, see, for example, Carrier 1995; Bronfman and López Moreno 1996; Cantú 1999. For research that focuses on the spread of HIV/AIDS in transnational communities see, for example, Magis-Rodríguez et al. 1995; Mishra, Conner, and Magaña 1996; Salgado de Snyder et al. 1996; Salgado de Snyder et al. 2000; Mena 2000b.

5 North American women living in urban areas have a higher risk of being raped than women living in rural areas; living in the city exposes women to a probability of being raped as high as one in three, and from a one-in-five to a one-in-eight chance of being sexually attacked in her lifetime (Gordon and Riger 1989, 36–37). Some California legislators advocating for women's rights have similarly reported, "A young woman today faces a one in three chance of being a victim of rape in her lifetime" (Wildman 1997). Official statistics are less alarming but are based on police reports and do not include many cases, which are overwhelmingly underreported. "The FBI estimates that only 37% of all rapes are reported to the police" (Florida Council Against Sexual Violence 2002). "The true rate of rape in the United States is at least twice the official rate and may be as much as twenty times as high" (Gordon and Riger 1989, 32–33). Between 1980 and 1999, reported cases of forcible rape represented a rate of 33 per 100,000 people in the United States (U.S. Bureau of the Census 2001b). The vast majority of these cases were women.

6 As the study participants disclosed their pain, I offered them the choice to have the tape recorder turned off and the interviews stopped. This intervention became necessary when the women's emotions became intense and their tears would not allow them to continue talking. At such moments, I made use of my previous training as a therapist to make a brief clinical intervention, which generally consisted of two or three sentences that expressed my caring. While such exchanges reportedly made the informants feel safe and comfortable, my self-identification as a *consejera* may represent a bias during the data-collection phase. While my professional identity and clinical training facilitated the collection of a wide range of information, these interventions could have led the women to perceive the interview as a potential opportunity for healing and/or future therapy sessions with me. But when I explained to the women both the research nature of my interviews and my genuine interest in listening to their pain after our official interviews if necessary, the interviews were in all cases completed successfully. At the end of each interview, I offered each woman a list of professionals who specialized in the treatment of sexual violence against women.

7 Elsewhere, I examine the equally important testimonies of the additional four women who experienced sexual violence in their lives (see González-López 2000, 2005).

8 Oliva M. Espín, Ann Twinam, and Marcela Tostado Gutiérrez examine the links

between Latina women's sexuality, family respect, and socioeconomic status. Espín observes, "The honor of Latin families is strongly tied to the sexual purity of women" (1986, 277). Twinam (1989) offers an analysis of the historical and elitist roots of a link between a woman's virginity, family honor and respect, socioeconomic status, and decency in colonial Latin America. As Twinam states, "Illegitimate women not only found their pool of potential marriage partners restricted, but their illegitimacy could adversely affect the occupational choices of their sons and the marriage potential of their daughters. Absence of honor could thus limit the social mobility of both sexes, as well as the future of succeeding generations" (124). And Tostado Gutiérrez illustrates the experiences of Mexican women in colonial society with regard to virginity and its social exchange value: "The law recognized for the woman, the importance of the preservation of her sexual virtue, a condition upon which her possibilities to get married, to maintain family honor and social status depended" (1991, 200; my translation).

9 Guadalupe Irma Solís, interview by author, 3 January 1998, Ciudad Valles, San Luis Potosí, Mexico, tape recording. In our interview, Dr. Solís explained her rationale for starting to conduct himenoplastía: rural mothers requested her services while feeling deeply afflicted by both the trauma of their daughters having been raped and the fear that their daughters were at risk of not getting married due to a lack of an intact hymen. Althoug Dr. Solís has noticed a decrease in her number of appointments by women requesting himenoplastía, women still request this type of medical intervention. A gradually increasing urbanization of rural Mexico and thus of higher education and employment opportunities for women might be responsible for this change.

10 See Fiona Wilson's 1990 *De la casa al taller: Mujeres, trabajo y clase social en la industria textil y del vestido, Santiago Tangamandapio, Zamora, Michoacán: El Colegio de Michoacán*, published in English as "Sweaters: A History of Gender, Class, and Workshop-based Industry in a Town in Rural Mexico."

11 In a sex research project I conducted with Mexican men, I learned that men also—either they themselves or their brothers or friends—are exposed to coercive marriage by their family after their girlfriends got pregnant (González-López 2005). This mandate comes at times only from the pregnant woman's family, but at other times, it comes from both partners' family. Based on these men's narratives, this dynamic of family respect seems to be consistent across all socioeconomic strata. Coercive marriage under these circumstances has also been identified by scholar Ana Amuchástegui (1994) in her sexuality research with youth living in Mexico.

12 Elsewhere, I introduce the concept of *machismos regionales* (regional patriarchies) to illustrate how different expressions of sexism in rural and urban Mexico shape gender inequalities and might therefore exacerbate violence against women (González-López 2000). I have revisited these concepts and realized that the term *machismo* as a theoretical category has contributed to the reproduction of stereotypes identified in Latina/o studies and Latin American studies. Thus, I use the term *regional patriarchies*, but I no longer use *machismos regionales* as its counterpart. The more intense expressions of gender inequalities appear in small provincial locations or pueblos. I refer

to these as *rural patriarchies*. Disguised or de-emphasized sexism, more common in metropolises such as Mexico City, is identified as *urban patriarchies*. For example, young heterosexual men from Mexico City are more likely than rural men to perceive their female counterparts as more equal in their sexual encounters and heterosexual experiences than are rural men (Amuchástegui 1994).

13 For more information on VAWA laws and information for immigrant women, see WomensLaw.org, 21 July 2006, http://www.womenslaw.org/immigrantsVAWA.htm.
14 Ana Santamaría, personal communication, 31 July 2001, Los Angeles, California. See also Arredondo 2001. In 2001, LACAAW celebrated its thirtieth anniversary.
15 For more information on the National Latino Alliance for the Elimination of Domestic Violence, see Alianza, 21 July 2006, http://www.dvalianza.org.

FLEXIBLE ACCUMULATION AND RESISTANCE

PART 3

Changing Constructions of
Sexuality and Risk: Migrant Mexican
Women Farmworkers in California
XÓCHITL CASTAÑEDA AND
PATRICIA ZAVELLA

✳ María García, twenty-six years old, had lived in California for only two years, yet she knew that how she displayed her body had significant consequences. When she went seeking work, she avoided a nearby farm because her kin informed her that the supervisor had a couch in the back of the shed and women were forced to have sex in exchange for a job. Eventually she found a job as a farmworker, but the work was hard on her body and she developed several health problems. Furthermore, women were subject to sexual harassment while working in the strawberry fields. María explained, "We work almost all the time bent over with our 'rumps' in the face of whoever comes from behind, which is usually a man." Male workers occasionally would touch women's genitalia or buttocks, or make lewd comments about their bodies. According to focus groups with Mexican women, male workers outnumbered women workers by about twenty to one and there was little workplace monitoring.[1] Outside work María entered into a sexual relationship with a farmworker. She had heard that male farmworkers often spend time with sex workers and that she might be at risk for sexually transmitted infections (STIs), yet she was unable to request that he use condoms to protect her since she perceived he would regard her as violating notions of decency, which we explain below. Because she was undocumented, María did not seek medical care until a neighbor informed her about a local farmworker clinic, where she joined a women's group.[2]

María's experiences illustrate contradictions about power, women's bodies, and gendered sexuality in predominantly Mexicano communities in rural California. After Mexican women migrate, they are enmeshed in processes of racialized, gendered sexuality that constitute a political economy of risk (Rapp 2000). That is, migrant women face risks related to changing constructions of gender and sexuality that are contingent on Mexicans' placement within the local economy and that are shaped by political and social forces. The social body (Scheper-Hughes 1994; Martin 1995) of Mexicana migrant farmworkers is molded by local expressions of transnational processes that shape this context.

Our interpretation builds on the framework established by feminist scholars who argue that social reproduction—to which sexuality is central—should be seen as local expressions of transnational inequalities (Ginsburg and Rapp 1995b; Moore 1988; Martin 1995). In this framework individuals imagine and enact cultural logics and social formations through varied mechanisms: personal struggle, generational mobility, participation in social movements, or contestation of powerful religious and political ideologies or of the state. Situated within this framework, migrant Mexican women construct complex local knowledges and practices regarding sexuality and the body, reflecting their lived experience in a regional political economy that is choreographed by multiple, intertwined forces: globalization sets in motion capital, technology, popular culture, and sexually transmitted infections, which cross national borders toward the south and push workers into the migrant stream within Mexico and toward the north.[3] Catholic-based patriarchal ideologies and practices in Mexico and the United States create ambiguous notions regarding women's bodies and constrain their views of pleasure (Zavella 1997a).

When Mexican women migrate to the United States, they are racialized in multiple ways that overlap with gender, class, and social forces. That is, there are historically and geographically specific meanings or practices that construct particular groups as racially inferior (Omi and Winant 1994). Racialization can be seen in the concentration of Mexican migrants, predominantly immigrant co-workers, in "brown-collar jobs" (Catanzarite 2000; Ibarra in this volume), along with farmworkers at the bottom of the labor market (Villarejo et al. 2000). Mexican women farmworkers labor in California agribusiness that is dependent on transnational migration, with more than 90 percent of the labor force being from Mexico (Villarejo et al. 2000; Immigration and Naturalization Service 1998). Sixty-three percent of adult farmworkers are legally authorized to work in the United States.[4] Seventy percent of farmworkers receive annual salaries between $7,500 and $10,000, placing them well below the federal poverty level (Villarejo et al. 2000).[5] In addition, some employers of agricultural businesses or labor contractors do not report the workers' salaries.[6] Consequently, many farmworkers who become injured or reach retirement age cannot obtain Social Security benefits (Medicaid) or

Medicare, a predicament that can further endanger their health (Office of Minority Health Resource Center 1988).

Although they live and work in one of the richest nations, migrant farmworkers in the United States have a Third World health status (Dever 1991). Farmworkers have some of this nation's most severe social problems and are at greater risk for infectious diseases and chronic health conditions than the general population due to poverty, malnutrition, exposure to pesticides, and hazardous working conditions. Farmworkers' life expectancy is estimated to be only forty-nine years. Some health concerns are clearly attributable to the occupational hazards of farm work and include toxic chemical injuries, dermatitis, respiratory problems, dehydration, heat stroke, and urinary-tract infections. Others stem from social isolation, stress, and poor living conditions, and include depression, diabetes, and tuberculosis (Environmental Work Group 1987). Seventy percent of farmworkers lack health insurance (Villarejo et al. 2000). Women farmworkers also face high rates of reproductive problems and an infant mortality rate that is 25 percent higher than the national average. This constellation of poverty and poor health conditions is crucial for situating migrant women's racialized, gendered sexuality.

A major hazard for migrant women is that their male partners may be involved in risky sexual behaviors, such as having unprotected sexual relations with women and men, including commercial sex workers who work at or near the camps, mainly during the peak of the harvest season, thus increasing the possibility of acquiring an STI.[7] The number of potential clients at the camps—where there is a high proportion of single men who are lonely, carry cash, endure peer pressure, and have few alternatives for amusement—is highly attractive for the sex workers and their pimps (Organista et al. 1996). For male farmworkers, vulnerability to HIV or other illnesses sometimes pales in comparison to their experiences of crossing the border, especially those who are undocumented.[8] Married men are unlikely to carry condoms, which could jeopardize their credibility as faithful spouses (Organista et al. 1996). Furthermore, the mobility of the farmworker population means that there is a positive relationship between migrant status and the increase in HIV and AIDS in Mexico as well (Castañeda, Brindis, and Castañeda 2001).

In this binational context, the epidemic has been concentrated mainly among men. Of those diagnosed with AIDS in Mexico, 86 percent are men who have sex with men, and there is a ratio of six men for every woman diagnosed with AIDS. When the analysis is based on sexual transmission alone (rather than through injection-drug use or other means), the proportion is even higher—90.3 percent men, 9.7 percent women—but the rates of heterosexual transmission for women are expected to increase (Magis-Rodríguez,

Bravo, and Rivera 2001).[9] In 1996 the number of AIDS-related deaths for men in Mexico was 20 per 100,000, while the number for women was 2.5 per 100,000. By 1998, however, the rate for men had begun to decline, while the rate for women continued to increase (ibid.).[10] In California the pattern is similar. Among those of Mexican origin, 69 percent of AIDS cases are men between twenty and forty years of age who have sex with men; of these, 32 percent were born in the United States and 68 percent were born in Mexico (California Department of Health Services 2000a). Between 1988 and 1997, there was a steady increase in the percentage of AIDS cases among women between the ages of thirteen and forty-five in California, with Latinas moving from 3.3 percent to 11 percent of all cases (California Department of Health Services 2000b). Women of Mexican origin have disproportionately higher rates of HIV.[11] Research shows that Latinas have a particular epidemiology for contracting HIV: 46 percent of AIDS cases among Latinas are due to heterosexual contact with men (Centers for Disease Control and Prevention 1994), and women often are unaware of their risk status.[12] Despite the increased numbers of women contracting HIV in Mexico and the United States, there has been little research on the social context that places migrant women at risk.

For Mexican women in the United States there are many barriers to accessing healthcare, including low incomes, low rates of medical insurance, language use (either predominantly Spanish or indigenous language use), and lack of transportation. Furthermore, condom use is often seen as socially inappropriate (Richwald, Schneider-Muñoz, and Valdez 1989; Romero and Argüelles 1993; Center for AIDS Prevention Studies 2001a). Similar to other Catholics, Latinos are unlikely to use condoms because the church considers them an "unnatural" form of contraception. One study indicated that 78 percent of the Latino respondents had never used a condom (Ryan et al. 1988), while another study noted that 75 percent of Mexican female migrant workers reported not carrying condoms (Balls, Organista, and Soloff 1998).[13] Condom use is often associated with extramarital sex or prostitution, which, one study notes, "makes the Spanish word for condom a vulgar term to both male and female Mexicans. In [one] study, women expressed feelings of shame and embarrassment about their partners' use of a condom" (Ryan et al. 1988, 1).

In addition to these economic and social barriers, Mexican women may not seek healthcare because of politics. Leo Chavez (1997, 2001) argues that Mexican migrants, women in particular, were key in the debates on whether immigrants drained state coffers, a belief that led to the passage of Proposition 187 in 1994 and public anti-immigrant discourse. Jonathan Xavier Inda (2002) further argues that regulating access to prenatal care limits Mexican women's reproduction (including HIV testing) and carries the implicit message that the lives of the undocumented are expendable. Even though Proposition 187 was overturned in the courts, many migrant Mexican women are uninformed about the rights to which they are entitled, particularly regarding access to healthcare. However, in the United States the immigrant, labor, Chicana/o, feminist, and gay and lesbian social movements have created countervailing discourses on race, citizenship, sexuality, and Mexicanas' rights as racialized women. Thus, on migration, Mexicanas must negotiate gender and sexuality within a highly contested social and political context shaped by transnational forces.

The availability of long-term jobs in agriculture has enabled many migrants to establish homes in California, and increasingly migrants are settling permanently. These processes have fueled the "Mexicanization" of rural California, where migrant farmworkers have become the majority population and have changed the character of social life in these communities (Palerm 1991). Rural communities in California have become places of concentrated and persistent poverty, dual societies with a few Anglos who make up the land owners, professionals, and white-collar workers, and Mexicans who work in the fields, factories, and service sector (ibid.; Griffith et al. 1995). However, predominantly Mexican communities are also vibrant social places where cultural expressions often resemble those in Mexico. One study of Mexican farmworkers found that a significant portion (13 percent) had "binational families," that is, they maintained occupied homes on both sides of the U.S.-Mexico border. These families provide an anchor for recent migrants and those who return seasonally, and often continue to return, to their communities in Mexico (Palerm 1991).[14] Thus, Mexican farmworkers maintain key relationships in two social worlds: the predominantly Mexicano farmworker communities in California and the communities in Mexico from which they migrated.

Whether residing in Mexico or in poor Mexican communities in the United States, Mexican women are marginalized as gendered subjects and live in "divided social worlds" that require frequent negotiation. In their research with commercial sex workers in Mexico City, Xóchitl Castañeda and her colleagues (1996) suggest that when women remove their "social masks"—that is, provocative work costumes and heavy makeup designed to entice customers—they mark a social transformation from secret worker-warriors who must negotiate everything from violence to STIs to "normal women." Thus, sex workers experience estrangement as they move between the violent worlds of work and varied family contexts. In a similar fashion, migrant farmworkers survive the dangers of crossing the border, struggle within socially violent work sites, and negotiate changes in their daily lives. Simultaneously, they are linked to kin and other social relationships in Mexico and are reminded that they should conform to "traditional" Mexican gendered expectations regarding sexuality and social relations in general.

One way in which subjects imagine and negotiate these complex changes is through the perspective of "peripheral vision" (Zavella 2000). Whether they reside in Mexico or the United States, migrants imagine their own situations and family lives in terms of how they compare with *en el otro lado* (on the other side of the border). Peripheral vision originates in the power imbalance between Mexico and the United States, and Mexicans on both sides of the border experience social dislocation. Peripheral vision is a perspective that includes the frequent reminders that one's situation is unstable in comparison to others en el otro lado. That is, peoples' daily lives are contingent on the vagaries of the U.S. and Mexican economies, which informs how they respond to globalization, including whether to migrate.

Ethnographic research reveals how material circumstances of migration and sociocultural constructions related to sexual behavior and the body place Mexican women migrants at risk for sexual harassment and acquiring STIS. Hegemonic discourses—based in gendered political inequalities—are inscribed or "mapped" on the bodies of Mexican women farmworkers in California, who must then develop survival mechanisms. We argue that it is precisely in women's transgressions of boundaries that they construct moments of "remapping" whereby they contest those discourses and create their own poetics of desire despite others' attempts to control their sexuality. These women delineate clear notions of the body rife with gendered conflict and construct practices and meanings that situate them as subjects in relation to communities of origin *and* settlement.

Methodology

Our analysis is based on exploratory research that used ethnographic methods, including focus groups, individual life histories, and participant observation. Between 1998 and 1999, we organized seven focus groups with a total of sixty-eight women of Mexican origin. We also conducted individual life histories with twelve women, all mestizas born in Mexico.[15] The participant observation was done in communities where farmworkers live and work: we observed at the clinics and social-service agencies where we conducted the focus-group discussions; we frequented businesses and public places with a farmworker clientele or presence (such as parks, the flea market, plazas, and the county fair); we toured farms, distribution warehouses, and canneries; and we attended public protests by the United Farm Workers and Madres por la Paz (Mothers for Peace), an organization devoted to antigang violence that organizes annual Mothers' Day events.

The focus groups were formed with the help of staff at community-based health clinics or organizations that work with migrant farmworkers and their families, and participants were given a modest stipend. The focus groups were based on a dialogic process designed to elicit women's views on the themes of changing expectations regarding gender, sexuality, and Mexican women's vulnerability to STIs in the United States.[16] We asked the women to honor confidentiality and to allow each woman to take a turn speaking. After we had explained the purpose of the focus group and the participants had agreed to the ground rules, we screened a film about women's vulnerability to HIV in Mexico, which served as a springboard for discussion of these issues for migrant Mexican women in their own communities.

We used *La Vida Sigue* (Life goes on), a thirty-minute Spanish-language film directed by María Del Carmen De Lara and produced by the National Council for the Control and Prevention of AIDS (CONASIDA) in Mexico in 2000.[17] The film is designed to educate heterosexual women about HIV risk in relation to men who migrate to the United States. Set in a small town in Mexico, the film uses a telenovela (soap opera) format that is familiar to women in both Mexico and the United States. The film is a dramatic narrative about a married woman whose husband dies from a mysterious illness after his return from working in the United States. A physician approaches her and informs her that she is HIV-positive and that she has contracted the illness from her spouse. The film then focuses on how she pieces together how her husband could have contracted HIV. There is an interesting character—a Mexican woman who has spent time in the United States and seems savvy—who explains the temptations that men face. Interspersed are the protagonist's flashbacks to conversations wherein her spouse denied any infidelities, as well as scenes of Mexican men consorting with *tranvestis* (transgender subjects) in bars—all of which contextualize the complexities of risk for Mexican men who migrate to the United States. The protagonist experiences rejection and homophobia by local members of the community who believe that her husband must have been gay if he contracted AIDS, and she must educate her children about the disease. A sensitive widower strikes up a friendship with her, and the film ends with indications that they may establish an intimate relationship. He is prepared to use condoms as well as defend the protagonist against local prejudice and be kind to her children.

In the discussions that took place after the film, we sought women's observations about the changing expectations and practices in the communities in which they lived, but did not ask about individual at-risk behavior. The discussion was audiotaped and transcribed. During follow-up, in-depth interviews—conducted by the authors in Spanish or English, usually in women's homes, occasionally at the clinics or agencies—with individuals who volunteered, we explored concepts raised during the focus groups and discussed their life histories, including sexual practices. Select quotations from focus groups and interviews illustrate general processes that we found. (All names are pseudonyms.)

Silences y Mujeres Decentes

All of the women we interviewed had low incomes and, like other farmworkers, few benefits. They ranged in age from sixteen to fifty-six. They had migrated from the classic sending states of west central Mexico (Michoacán, Jalisco, and Guanajuato) or southern Mexico (Oaxaca) and were from both rural communities and urban centers. Their length of residence in the United States varied from two months to over thirty years. Most of these women had not completed an elementary education, although three had degrees from Mexican universities and eventually moved to other occupations. Many of the migrants from rural areas had little labor-market experience nor did they know how to drive prior to migration. If they did have work experience, it had often occurred near their homes in gender-segregated workplaces where they had little direct exposure to male workers. The women reported that they migrated to the United States for varied reasons: escaping poverty, labor displacement, seeking refuge from abusive male kin or lovers, accompanying their families, looking for adventure, or bettering their lives. Most had multiple reasons for migration. All had migrated as adolescents or adults and thus had been socialized in Mexico. The women lived in predominantly Mexican communities in north-central California's agricultural regions: the Pájaro Valley in Santa Cruz County, the Salinas Valley in Monterey County, and the San Joaquin Valley in Fresno County. According to one survey, farmworker households are large (6.8 members on average), with 2.6 workers per household, and 65 percent have seasonal or temporary farm jobs (Santa Cruz County Farmworker Housing Committee 1993). According to focus groups, some farmworker households contain up to thirty-five men, who rotate schedules for sleeping, showering, and eating.

The women we worked with were for the most part reared within a repressive cultural framework that is not unique, but is particular to Mexican culture. Centered in Catholicism, which instructs them to repress carnal pleasures unless it occurs within church-sanctified marriage, women are pressured to construe their yearnings in heterosexual, conventional terms. While the virgin–whore cultural discourse has been eroded by a number of social forces, its salience is evident in how these women subscribe to notions of silence about sexuality, the importance of virginity prior to marriage, and guarding their reputations as *mujeres decentes* (good women).[18] As an attempt to control their behavior, women were told that there was a whole array of signs that their bodies would display if they were to engage in transgressions and that mothers or other kin would be able to "read" those signs. As Irene explained, "When they lose their virginity, women walk different—with their legs separated—and in their faces and their eyes you can tell that they know more [*saben más*], that they have been used by a man [*han tenido uso de hombre*]." According to this discourse, even after marriage women are supposed to dress and move their bodies in ways that do not appear too provocative. Under such patriarchal constraints, the body is regarded as a map: its transgressions can be read by others, and it becomes a source of betrayal if women do not control how they move or display themselves in public. Simultaneously, women's bodies are viewed as uncontrollable, subject to the whims of passion or provoking male reactions. Therefore, women's bodies should be policed and their reputations guarded.[19]

In the focus groups and interviews, women provided many examples of how their lives were circumscribed to protect them from dishonor or serious social risks. Some women from rural areas were not allowed to walk alone in public for fear of gossip or sexual assault. The journey *al norte* (to the north) was itself fraught with literal and symbolic danger for women who traveled without male protection; rumor held that the women who come by themselves to the United States usually have sex with the smugglers. However, the women in our study were neither passive recipients of normative strictures nor uniformly "decent" all the time, but contested patriarchal notions about their conduct and their bodies.

Sexualization of the Racialized Body in the Fields

After moving to agricultural communities, these women experienced an array of changes in gender relations and expectations, and faced possibilities they had only imagined prior to migration. For those women who worked in the strawberry fields racialized sexualization took on specific forms. During the peak of the harvest season of the late 1990s, the labor force was predominantly male. Furthermore, the male farmworker population was internally heterogeneous. It included those older men who originally worked as braceros (1942–1964), those who were younger and had come with more recent waves of migrants who settled permanently, and those who sojourned annually, returning to Mexico after the harvest season. The sojourners included those who left behind wives, lovers, and families in Mexico, as well as those who were single and looking for a partner to take back to Mexico or with whom to settle in California. Unlike in Mexico, where they experienced highly gender-segregated worksites, in California women farmworkers were placed in close proximity with men who had varied motivations for establishing intimate relationships. Becoming farmworkers created risks for women, for they were outside the norms that protected women and had to learn to defend themselves.

In this context, how women presented themselves in public was subject to close scrutiny. Women's worksites in the fields became sexualized social gauntlets. Any expression of availability, signified by wearing makeup or "provocative" clothing, was noticed by male co-workers and became the basis on which the women were invited on dates, propositioned for sexual encounters, or sexually harassed on the job. Women learned that wearing cosmetics or colognes in the fields provoked unwanted responses. In this regard, María noted, "I can't even wear mascara or they will bother me, want to touch me, and start something." Women's bodies were inscribed by social structures, "marked with instructions on how to be *mujer* . . . working class, Chicana" (Anzaldúa 1990, xv)—that is, Mexican women in the United States.

Masking the Body

Women farmworkers protected themselves from men's advances or abuse by utilizing a variety of strategies, including covering their bodies. Because the women had to wear clothing to protect themselves from the weather and pesticides, normal work regalia included heavy shirts, baggy pants, sturdy shoes, gloves, hats (often attached to scarves covering their necks), and kerchiefs over their mouths—so they appeared cloistered while working, with only their eyes visible. In addition, despite the heat, women had to wear shirts tied around their waists to cover their buttocks and genitalia from male scrutiny, commentary, or touching when they bent over to work. María explained, "Well, the number of women in the fields is much smaller than that of the men; we can't always be in a crew of only women. It's important to protect ourselves from them [the men] and from what the other women can think. If one walks around showing off her body, then the gossip will get around that we're not there to pick strawberries but to find men."

Removing the layers of clothing was time-consuming, and, given their short lunch breaks, women often retained most of their attire during breaks:

"Many times we don't even uncover ourselves to eat." Women farmworkers also had to inform newcomers about fields to avoid because the men were particularly disrespectful or about the farm where, according to rumors, jobs were exchanged for sex. Certain areas of town were dangerous for women alone, particularly close to bars or other sites where men congregated. In addition to protective clothing related to their jobs, then, women appeared at work with few parts of their bodies exposed and helped one another to protect themselves. We did not hear of instances in which women complained to their supervisors or confronted sexual harassers directly, an omission that indicated a sense of relative disempowerment. After all, the consequences of complaining could be severe: they could be fired or even accused of instigating trouble.

Working in such conditions was not always pleasant and women felt as if they were participating in an alien environment, similar to women who work in "clean rooms" in high-tech firms (Lamphere et al. 1993). Irene said, "Sometimes when we are outside the fields, we don't recognize ourselves, we don't know who is working in the crew because there are so many layers of clothing and everything is covered up. It's by voice and the eyes that we can recognize one another. We are covered up [*enmascaradas*]." Such cloistering challenged women's abilities to bond with fellow women, apart from their close workmates. As Margarita explained, "This happened to me: when I went to pick up my daughter at school, I hear someone's voice and then 'the light bulb goes on' and I say to myself, 'I think that Juana was working with me today.'" Irene expressed her unhappiness regarding her work conditions: "At first it is difficult; later you get used to it. It's as if you are not yourself."

After the workday, within working-class communities one would see tired women workers driving, walking home, or shopping in their work clothes, with only the face coverings removed—so the women were still marked as farmworkers. Occasionally, one could see them removing their "uniforms" while in transit, in preparation for their private lives. On removing their sartorial barriers to the elements and harassment, they were transformed from farmworkers and sexual objects to women situated within varied social settings. Furthermore, when the women were not working in the fields, they freely wore makeup, nail polish, colognes, and clothing that emphasized their femininity. Indeed, manicured hands were markers that one did not perform manual labor.

In the context of heavy male-to-female ratios and unregulated worksites, women farmworkers faced a dislocation similar to the sex workers that Xóchitl Castañeda and her colleagues (1996) studied in Mexico City. At their worksites, farmworker women felt alienated and estranged, wrapped in

Enmascarada: a female farmworker in work regalia.

many layers of clothing that functioned as a protective barrier to the hostile environment—including work and weather conditions, as well as male harassment and women's gossip. Like the "johns" who sought sex workers, male farmworkers lived in decontextualized social environments where the sanctions for inappropriate behavior were inadequate or missing if their kin were in Mexico. In this transnational context, the productive body as well as the sexualized body of migrant women farmworkers was mapped by the physical and social consequences of being Mexican women.

Women Remap the Body

While they may accept the necessities of cloistering their bodies at work, women also contest or "remap" the social body in relation to traditional discourses about marriage and the family. For single women there is a wealth of potential lovers or marriage partners, and women find that traditional customs, such as use of chaperones or expectations to marry as a virgin, are challenged by the changes in their lives after migration. In contrast to the constraints they experienced in Mexico, women have more freedom of movement in the United States. Even older women and women with children, who would not necessarily think of themselves as good marriage prospects, find that the high male-to-female ratios work in their favor. For example, after migrating to California, Alicia, a single mother with five children, was abandoned by her spouse. She considered herself to be not particularly attractive since she was overweight and middle-aged. She enrolled in a local community clinic's literacy and an English as a Second Language program. Over the course of many months, between stints of farm work, she worked on her human capital, joining a women's support group whose activities included aerobics classes and discussing personal problems. During a focus group, she told her story and disclosed her newfound attractiveness in the farmworker community with great aplomb: "Look at me, I'm getting old, I'm fat, and I have five kids. And already I've had two marriage proposals! One man promised to support me and be a father to my kids. But I decided it's better not to [accept his proposal]. You can't trust men. It's better if I work to support them myself." Alicia's new sense of independence as a single mother who occasionally dates meant that her desire for stability for her children would be achieved through her own efforts rather than through marriage.

With the availability of so many potential sexual partners in a context of less social control than they may have experienced in Mexico, women seeking adventure learned to negotiate choices they did not have previously, from how they dressed in public to where they walked on the streets to new recreation possibilities. Perhaps the most disapproving and elaborate comments concerned the attire of young Mexican women, which was considered "scandalous": "They walk around wearing mini skirts or short shorts, showing off everything!" The women were well aware of the fine line between dressing attractively and dressing too provocatively, which would subject them to harassment in public. For example, women advised others to avoid the streets where sex workers congregated so as not to face propositions from drunken men who could not tell "working girls" from other women.

Some women, however, intentionally sought circumstances wherein the boundaries of social control were more fluid. On weekend nights the local bars and dance halls became sites of aggressive encounters with men, where women were sexual objects in a different social context. If they came with partners, they or their partners did not appreciate the competition and fights would break out when competitors became too aggressive. However, women who came without partners often desired the attention and were in fact at the nightclubs precisely to find adventure and pleasure. Through their provocative dress and makeup, flirting, or dancing, some women found romance at the dance halls. Margarita had sparkles in her eyes as she said, "I can go to the night club and pick and choose my partners. The men line up and I choose: 'You, you, and you.' I go for the tall cowboys." Even married women frequented the dances as sites of pleasure. Marisela, a married, middle-aged woman, confided, "I can dance all night long. It's *so* much fun! And then I go home by myself." It was unclear if her spouse knew about these outings or what his reaction might be; however, Marisela was not the only attached woman who frequented nightclubs, and some of them did not stop at dancing.

Regardless of whether they frequented nightclubs or not, women who were happily married found that they had to take care of their bodies and make time for sexual relations with their spouses. In large farmworker households, this could be quite a challenge. For example, Carmen, her spouse, and young son lived in a household with twenty male farmworkers, and the family slept in a corner of a room cordoned off with a rope and blanket. She considered herself "unnatural" since her innate sex drive (*la naturaleza*) was stronger than her husband's and was "like a man's." (During the focus group when she said this, there was general agreement that men have stronger sex drives than women.) Thus, she repeatedly had to negotiate securing privacy from her apartment mates and child so the couple could have sexual intercourse. Other women, married to men who traveled regularly for their jobs (e.g., produce truckers) and living in nuclear households, made it a point to schedule time for privacy from the children so they could have sex. Dora explained, "My husband is gone all week. And he meets lots of women while making his deliveries. I want to make sure that he *wants* to come home. So I take care of myself and we spend time together apart from the kids. . . . I never had to think about this in Mexico."

When the women migrated and settled in California, they encountered different expectations about the body. They often felt vulnerable in competition with white women. Alicia elaborated on her sense of needing to work at being attractive to her spouse: "Sometimes over there [in Mexico] you don't take care of yourself. You let yourself get fat. Here there are many ways to take care of married women and there are many places that help you lose weight. It's as if the men are attracted to something different [here], as if they make a few comparisons."

Alicia's comments are not in fact supported by clinical research, which shows that obesity actually *increases* after migrants settle in the United States. Furthermore, Mexican farmworker women who are permanent residents and have lived in California the longest run the greatest risk of becoming obese (Villarejo et al. 2000).[20] Alicia's feelings of vulnerability about comparisons to white women reflect gendered racialization processes in California, where body types like hers are not valued by the dominant society. Georgina, too, expressed a sense of bewilderment over the different expectations in the United States: "In Mexico when you are socialized in a conservative way [*educado en una manera recatada*], well, you don't go out much to the dances. You get married and you live your nice life, married with only your husband and that is what you believe. Later when you come here [United States], you expect more, but you live in poverty and you worry about what others think about you."

In the new social context, and with such high proportions of men to women in the fields, the constraints imposed by kin or others could be transgressed. There were many opportunities for establishing sexual encounters, as Susana explained: "We all work in pairs and many times in the furrow right behind me there is a man. The crews are not always only women; it depends on where there is work." Thus, women got to know a great number of men and could establish personal relationships if they wished. The high demand for women's sexual favors was highly desirable for some women, like Susana: "Well, it is difficult to resist so many temptations [*tantas tentaciones*]. I have had various young men offer me, as the song says, 'the moon, the heavens, and the stars' if I will spend some time with them. They are very lonely and have strong urges [*el instinto alto*]."

Women may also experience relative empowerment by working outside the household and earning money that provides resources and autonomy for pursuing their own interests. Women unaccustomed to such explicit attention by men may find the possibilities enticing, especially in the context of anonymity. Gloria explained: "Our best people [*nuestra mejor raza*] are working in the fields. There are young men who are handsome and very strong [*guapos y fuertotes*], and sometimes are very solicitous and they promise love. Sometimes it is difficult to resist. And since many of them come from the small towns of Mexico, well, one thinks that there won't be a problem; they can't have 'those' problems, such as AIDS. In addition, they are so alone; they don't know anyone here."

The women felt sorry for men who were alone or without family members; because they were often lonely themselves, they thus empathized with the changes in the men's lives. Elaborating on the opportunities for privacy for sexual encounters that had not been available to her in Mexico, Esperanza said, "Here in the U.S. things are easier. There are motels, everyone has a car, and since one works, well, you can escape and no one will notice. For that reason you have to take care of yourself, not show that you have been 'in something,' even your facial expression [*hasta de la expresión de la cara*], or else you will get stuck." Getting stuck, or caught (with multiple meanings), had significant consequences. With little experience in negotiating such possibilities, some women had unprotected sex and placed themselves at considerable risk for losing their reputations as well as for contracting STIs.

The new social context in which these women remapped their bodies was often less restrictive than in Mexico. Modernity and its artifacts (work outside the home, their own income, credit cards, cars, motels, telephones, nightclubs, etc.) enabled some women to subvert patriarchal mechanisms of control and to pursue their own notions of pleasure (Guendelman 1987). However, there were limitations to their empowerment, and despite pushing the boundaries, women often accepted some notions of being mujeres decentes, continuing to experience anxieties generated by the traditional embodied norms and values en el otro lado. The expression of their sexual desires was often checked by the fear of being betrayed by signs inscribed on the body, the sanctions for which could be severe. In this sense, these women turned peripheral vision on themselves and their deportment. They faced a series of new opportunities for sexual encounters or relationships and reconstructed how they conducted their bodies as they negotiated whether they were available for sexual relations or not. Similar possibilities would have faced them had they migrated from rural to urban sites in Mexico; however, these women saw change as products of migration to the United States, where Mexicano communities provided a context highly different from Mexico and where their racialized, sexualized bodies stood out.

Transgressing Borders: Purity and Risk

Women discussed the risks of unprotected sex openly during the focus groups. They were well aware of the potentially deadly consequences of their partners' behavior but also knew that requesting their partners to use condoms was unthinkable since, within patriarchal discourse, the woman would be to blame for being indecent, for transgressing notions of honor. Irene said, "For me, it would be worse if my boyfriend thinks badly of me, that I am not 'clean.' I would rather not confront him." Margarita was starker: "It's male privilege [*el machismo*] to think that 'it won't happen to me and it won't happen to you because I'll take care of you.' But in reality it can happen to anyone." During one focus group, a woman shared that she used condoms under the guise of contraception, even though the Catholic Church prohibited it. She advised other women to use condoms in this manner so as to protect themselves from STIs, since contraception was more socially acceptable to men: "Just tell him [her spouse] that you want to space your kids. And the pill is bad for you." Condom use for contraception would not jeopardize a woman's image of "purity" because there was no corresponding assumption that she might be having sex with multiple partners. In contrast, using condoms for prevention of HIV was threatening because of prevention's association with the possibility of multiple partners—that is, sex for pleasure rather than for procreation.

Mindful that the United States provided complex new freedoms and dangers to be negotiated, Marisela stated, "Here the struggle is different than the struggle we face in Mexico [aquí la batalla es diferente que la en México]." Gloria was clear about the risks of her newfound independence, as well as the oscillation in her thinking: "What I do here I cannot do over there, and the risks that I face if I am discovered are not the same [she sighed]." Anonymity and less social control enabled women to have more room to maneuver, even though social surveillance was still present through transnational social networks. Regardless of whether they remembered Mexico with nostalgia, felt relief at having left, or experienced anxiety about what those en el otro lado would think, they compared their current lives to their previous lives. Despite the women's newfound sense of independence, heterosexual relations in the United States were often fraught with dangers for migrant Mexican women.

Conclusion

The social inequalities in which migrant Mexican farmworkers live are inscribed on their bodies, as is evident in poor health indicators, and constitute a political economy of risk wherein women face particular dangers. Despite the enormous and valuable fruits of their labor, women migrant farmworkers frequently are marginalized by society and are racialized and sexualized in the communities where they live and work. Clearly, there is a critical need for higher wages, health insurance, and better monitoring of working conditions that create such problems. The lack of enforcement of existing laws preventing sexual harassment constitutes an important barrier for women farmworkers, pushing them into situations in which they are discriminated against as racialized women and forced to work in hostile environments. Effective programs for HIV prevention among Mexican farmworkers must address the context of their lives as well as the interpersonal and sociocultural factors that put them at risk for the acquisition of sexually transmitted infections. As Jeffrey Kelly and his colleagues stated, "HIV behavioral research can only stop HIV infection when results of the research can be used to make applied programs better" (2000).

Apart from the changes in social policy and practice that would help women who work as farmworkers, migrant Mexican women themselves are social actors. They develop strategies to protect themselves, covering their sexualized bodies while working in predominantly male environments and displaying them while socializing, and to negotiate gendered expectations about sexuality, occasionally transgressing notions of being mujeres decentes. They are mindful that California's agricultural regions are like "little Méxicos"—social worlds that are predominantly Mexicano and, simultaneously, profoundly different from Mexico. In the process, they construct complex identities that are shaped by powerful repressive discourses and express their own notions of desire. Reflecting on the patterns of gendered sexuality our research uncoverd, we find the metaphors of mapping and remapping useful to characterize how women are objectified, and how they construct and contest hegemonic discourses respectively. Women see the different perceptions and behaviors related to gender and sexuality as originating in new circumstances brought on by transnational migration. In this unstable and contested social climate, these women migrants construct new subjectivities regarding their worksites, their social lives, and their bodies.

Notes

Thanks to the Transborder Consortium for Research and Action on Gender and Reproductive Health at the Mexico-U.S. Border (comprising the Southwest Institute for Research on Women, the University of Arizona, Colegio de la Frontera Norte, Tijuana, and el Colegio de Sonora) that funded this research. Thanks to Allison Davenport, Shéla Young, and Francisca Olaíz who worked as research assistants on this project. Aída Hurtado, Norma Klahn, Olga Nájera Ramírez, Kurt Organista, Caridad Souza, Mary Weismantel, and five anonymous reviewers gave us helpful suggestions for revisions.

1 Sexual harassment is a common problem for women farmworkers. The federal Equal Employment Opportunity Commission settled a sexual harassment lawsuit in 1999 against Tanimura and Antle, the nation's largest lettuce grower, yet enforcement of the existing law is lax (Rodebaugh 1999; Ann Aurelia López 2002).
2 For research on farmworkers in general, see Griffith et al. 1995. For the little research on farmworker women, see de la Torre 1993 and Buss 1993.
3 Only 15 percent of all Mexican migrants (2.1 million of 13.9 million total migrants) actually leave Mexico and move to the United States (Santos Preciado 2001).
4 There are about 8 million undocumented residents in the United States (U.S. Bureau of the Census 2001a); 72 percent of the undocumented residents are of Latino origin (U.S. Department of Justice 1997a); and about 40 percent of undocumented Latinos live in California. Mexicans are the largest undocumented population in the United States, composing 55 percent of the total undocumented population (U.S. Department of Justice 1997a).
5 A survey of California farmworkers indicated that 42 percent lived in dwellings shared by two or more households, 20 percent of those dwellings had no telephone service,

and 68 percent of the respondents had no assets in the United States (Villarejo et al. 2000).

6   California Assembly Bill 2862, passed in 2001, increased civil and criminal penalties for growers and farm-labor contractors for failure to pay wages to farmworkers (interview with I. Hernandez, chief of staff for California assemblywoman Gloria Romero, cited in Ann Aurelia López 2002, 290).

7   In Mexico and the United States there is little stigma for men to have sex with men if the initiator is the *activo* (penetrator) (Almaguer 1991).

8   Many migrant men do not have enough knowledge about HIV and STIs and do not believe these concern them, since AIDS is seen as a gay or white problem (Center for AIDS Prevention Studies 2001b). Unsafe sexual behavior occurs for complex and multifaceted reasons, including a sense of invulnerability, the perception that unsafe sex is more pleasurable than safer sex, depression or sadness, conflicting allegiances with sexual identity, and use of alcohol or other drugs (Kegeles et al. 1999). Furthermore, Latina/o adolescents are twice as likely as white adolescents to have misconceptions about the causal transmission of AIDS and prevention, and hence may be at greater risk of HIV infection. Among adult Latinas/os, those of Mexican origin—particularly the elderly and those with fewer than twelve years of schooling—are more likely to have less knowledge about HIV and AIDS (DiClemente, Boyer, and Morales 1988; Dawson and Hardy 1989; Center for AIDS Prevention Studies 2001b).

9   Among the twenty-five- to thirty-four-year-old age group, AIDS represents the fourth main cause of death for men and the seventh for women (Magis-Rodríguez, Bravo, and Rivera 2001).

10 Carlos Magis-Rodríguez, Enrique Bravo, and Pilar Rivera (2001) chart the cases of mortality for people between twenty-five and thirty-four years of age. For men, the cases of mortality increased steadily beginning in 1988, peaking at 20 per 100,000 people in 1996, then dropping to 17 in 1998. For women in the same age group, the data was recorded beginning in 1989 and showed a steady increase, reaching 2.5 per 100,000 in 1996, then dropping slightly, then increasing to 2.75 per 100,000 in 1998 (Magis-Rodríguez, Bravo, and Rivera 2001, 7).

11 According to the Centers for Disease Control and Prevention (1994), by 1994 Latinos accounted for 17 percent of total AIDS cases while composing only 9 percent of the U.S. population. Also see Russell 1993; Ickovics and Rodin 1992; and Mishra, Conner, and Magaña 1997.

12 In California about 70 percent of Latinas/os are of Mexican origin. For further discussion of Latinas at risk for AIDS, see Amaro 1988a; Argüelles and Rivero 1988; Romero and Argüelles 1993; Mays and Cochran 1988; Nyamathi and Vasquez 1989; Selik, Castro, and Pappaioanou 1989; and Singer et al. 1990.

13 Many Spanish-speaking (or indigenous) Latinos have trouble reading instructions on condom use. One-third of Latinos between the ages of fifteen and forty-five report that they are illiterate in English, and almost 40 percent report they are illiterate in Spanish.

14 Remittances, the third-largest source of revenue for the Mexican economy, help to

maintain households in sending communities in Mexico (Consejo Nacional de Población 2000).

15 We had a male researcher conduct focus groups with men, and Patricia Zavella conducted interviews with seven male Mexican farmworkers regarding the working conditions and production process in the fields. Those focus groups and interviews inform our discussion here, but we focus on the women and quote only from focus groups or interviews with women.

16 For a discussion of focus-group methodology, see Morgan 1993.

17 Recently renamed the Centro Nacional para Prevención y Control del SIDA (National Center for the Prevention and Control of AIDS).

18 For a full discussion and critique of this cultural master script, see Zavella 1997a.

19 For a full discussion of this analysis along with ethnographic support, see Zavella 2003.

20 Among women ages twenty to twenty-nine, 12 percent of undocumented women and 45 percent of documented women are likely to be obese, having a body-mass index of thirty points or greater (Villarejo et al. 2000).

Space, Gender, and Work:
Home-Based Workers in Mexico

FARANAK MIRAFTAB

✳ Spatial and social dynamics initiated through the process of urbanization and industrialization have turned the city of Guadalajara into one of the most important centers of home-based production in Mexico today. Small-scale industries began to proliferate on Guadalajara's urban landscape in the 1930s, when a large rural population moved to the city to escape the violence of the Cristiada wars. These wars were between the federal state, with its agenda of implementing postrevolutionary land reforms, and the Catholic Church, which was the center of resistance against land reforms. To evade reform measures, landholders converted their wealth into urban investments, buying properties and financing small and medium-sized manufacturing workshops that produced consumer goods (Vásquez 1989).

Contrary to the assumption of modernization theorists, the influx of outside capital and the introduction of modern and large-scale industry during the 1960s did not replace small firms (Arias 1985). Instead, large manufacturers took advantage of the personalized work relations in small family workshops, which had their roots in a rural rather than an industrial tradition, and subcontracted part of their production to these workshops. Today, it is estimated that 20 to 40 percent of manufacturers in Guadalajara are involved in subcontracting (Vega and Kruijt 1988). Sending out production work to be performed by workers in their homes allows large firms to maximize profits. It cuts the costs that would be incurred if manufacturers provided infrastructure such as workspace, electricity, and water and transfers these costs to workers living in already congested and substandard homes (Benería and Roldán 1987). Fragmenting and informalizing the production process further allows firms to avoid paying regulatory fees and taxes as well as worker's fringe benefits. A large supply of cheap labor also encourages subcontracting. Married women who are constrained to remain at home because of child-rearing obligations are eager to take in home-based work (Bryan R. Roberts 1989).

In the context of Mexico's economic crisis since the early 1980s, women have played a crucial role in alleviating economic pressures on poor households (Chant 1991; Benería and Feldman 1992; de la Rocha 1986). Mexican low-income families have been able to survive the economic shocks by drawing on the combined contributions of family members, with women being essential to the survival strategies of poor households during the time of crisis. Women have increasingly taken on low-paid income-generating activities in addition to their unpaid homemaking and child-rearing efforts and have performed the magical work of stretching scarce family resources (Moser 1988; de la Rocha 1986). Home-based work has been one strategy that has made it easier for women to combine their multiple roles and responsibilities.

Home-based production operates outside the regulatory framework of the state and is therefore illegal.[1] Subcontractors avoid paying taxes and regulatory fees related to their labor force (such as social security fees), and homeworkers avoid paying fees for obtaining and renewing licenses to carry out production within the home. Therefore, home-based work is often performed as a semi-illegal activity that all involved try to keep out of sight. The clandestine nature of home-based work affects spatial arrangements in individual homes and urban zones.

The integration of informal production into the homes of low-income families alters established social and spatial patterns. Because it is a remunerated rather than a subsistence activity, home-based production has significant implications for gender roles in the family and in society at large. Furthermore, the spatial juxtaposition of productive and reproductive activities affects the organization of homes and families. At play are the gendered divisions of home-based work, the influence of patriarchal gender images and identities, and the spatial modifications that occur in homes accommodating economic activities. The relationship between gendered divisions of labor and spatial patterns and the role of space not only express but also influence social relations of gender.

Methodology

The sites of my study are Guadalajara—Mexico's second largest city, with four million inhabitants—and Zapotlanejo, a small town with thirty-five thousand inhabitants, located thirty-five kilometers south of Guadalajara. In Guadalajara, home-based producers make a range of consumer goods including clothing, food, wood products, crafts, and leather products such as shoes, bags, and belts. Home-based workers in Zapotlanejo produce clothing almost exclusively. The completion of the Zapotlanejo-Guadalajara highway contributed to Zapotlanejo's conversion from being a pueblo, where women have traditionally produced embroidered goods, to being an economic annex of Guadalajara, with a variety of home-based clothing manufacturers. Residents and businesses in Guadalajara have literally adopted Zapotlanejo as the city's clothing production center.

I carried out the first phase of this research in Guadalajara during the summer of 1992, gaining a broad view of the range of home-based activities and their spatial requirements. I conducted open-ended interviews with individuals and families involved in home-based work, sketched their homes, and drew maps of spatial modifications made to accommodate production activities. During this phase of research, I was a participant-observer and lived with a homeworking family in one of the major urban zones of informal home-based production in Guadalajara. Because of the technically illegal nature of home-based work, this arrangement was essential in gaining the workers' trust and establishing contact with other homeworkers in the neighborhood.

The second phase of research was conducted during the fall of 1992 in Zapotlanejo. The objective of this phase was to examine how male and female homeworkers treat and use domestic space differently for production purposes and how home-based work affects gender roles within the home. I focused on twelve cases of male and female homeworkers who were involved in one- or multiperson *maquila* work or who had established entrepreneurial home-based workshops.

Types of Home-Based Work and Gender Division of Labor

A snapshot picture of home-based activities in Guadalajara indicates that women (mostly mothers) are more likely to be involved in subcontracted maquila work and men are more likely to be microentrepreneurs running multiperson family workshops. Maquila workers subcontract with a manufacturer or a middleman; they perform only part of the production process and are paid based on the number of pieces produced. The tools of production may belong either to the maquila worker or to the work supplier. For example, in the clothing industry the sewing machine used in the home could be owned either by the manufacturer, who loans it to the worker, or by the maquiladora herself.

Because informal production in the home is often illegal, multiperson home-based units recruit workers primarily among close relatives or trusted neighbors. Therefore, these units are referred to as family workshops, or *talleres familiars*.[2] In a family workshop either the household head provides the machines or the workers bring their own machinery to the taller. Some workshops operate as microentrepreneurial units selling directly to stores, and others subcontract with larger firms. In microentrepreneurial units homeworkers perform and control the whole production process. If more than one homeworker is involved in the process, the head of the workshop (who is often the household head) will seek clients and contracts. Such microentrepreneurial units have a greater opportunity for growth than subcontracting units in which the homeworkers are involved in only part of the production process and receive orders from larger manufacturers. For example, in one subcontracting family workshop, the husband daily picked up about one thousand pairs of socks from a manufacturer to be dyed and packed.[3] He was in charge of dying and drying the socks, using his own equipment, and his wife and daughters were responsible for packaging the finished product for distribution to retail stores. However, the family had no equipment or knowledge to produce socks and therefore had little potential for becoming an independent microentrepreneurial unit.

Home-based work may start out as one-person maquila operation and develop into a multiperson taller or even a home-based microenterprise. In the clothing sector, women who start out as maquiladoras often initiate home-based workshops. If conditions are right, they may expand their activities to include additional family members and perhaps even start selling directly to retail stores. Both women and men participate in family workshops, but usually a male family member represents the work team to the business world when the workshop becomes an entrepreneurial unit. He deals with the business agents and takes charge of work contacts outside the home-based unit.

The expansion of a family workshop and its transition to being an entrepreneurial unit does not necessarily marginalize women, but it does make gender roles more specific within the work team. Men take charge of external relations, and women take charge of relations within the workshop. This division of labor is related to social images that associate men with the public and women with the domestic domain, and a workshop benefits if it conforms to these images. For example, a female homeworker played the key role in managing a shoe-producing family workshop in Guadalajara but used her husband as a "front" to secure new contracts. They had started by working as subcontractors and later managed to develop their workshop into an entrepreneurial unit. Because the husband was deaf and could not speak, he was unable to handle relations with dealers and retailers, so the wife took care of bargaining with retail stores. But she gave her husband's name as the person in charge of production, and when she received business calls, she pretended she was only taking messages for her husband. She believed that using the husband's name helped them get new customers and contracts. It was not her husband's activity but rather his masculine image that served as a connection between the workshop and the public sphere of business.

Although such a masculine image may attract business contracts, the feminine image of a female homeworker plays an important role in the work relations within the taller. Fiona Wilson, in her study of cloth-producing home-based workshops in Santiago, Mexico, introduces the notion of a "domestic model of labor relations" to describe the dynamics of work relations within these units (1991). She stresses that the performance of work within a domestic space and the presence of a motherly figure create an environment of trust for families who send their young daughters to work in the workshops. The use of home as a place of production, she argues, conveys a personalized model of work relations that makes employment in these units preferable to work in large factories for many homeworkers.

Gender Identities and the Use of Time and Space within the Home

Male and female homeworkers take on different identities in the production activities they perform within the home. Female producers most often perceive themselves as housewives and their homework as merely helping their husbands; male producers perceive themselves as breadwinners and their homework as no different from working outside the home. The different ways in which women and men treat their time, space, and earnings influence the way in which female and male homeworkers perceive the value of their productive activities.

For female homeworkers, the spatial juxtaposition of paid labor and unpaid domestic work has a double effect. On the one hand, the incorporation of income generation into the domestic space undoubtedly makes it easier to juggle productive and reproductive responsibilities. On the other hand, the spatial juxtaposition and the temporal intermingling of different responsibilities obscures the work performed for pay and may diminish the perceived importance of women's contribution to the family budget. The mixed use of time and space by female homeworkers may create a disadvantageous situation whereby the women's economic role within the family is rendered invisible.[4] Despite her constant participation in family work (paid and unpaid), the wife is often perceived as being no more than a helper because she "takes time off from work" to do the domestic work.

The way women insert their earnings into the family budget also differs from men. Numerous studies have shown that women contribute a greater share of their income (often all of it) to the household budget, whereas men tend to use their income for personal expenses (Blumberg 1991, 97–127; Benería and Roldán 1987). Women often spend whatever they earn directly on family needs—in the words of one seamstress, "to buy whatever needs to be bought on a daily basis." Therefore, because of the instability of their homework earnings, it becomes more difficult to keep clear accounts of their contribution to the family budget.

Among male homeworkers, the use of time, space, and money is more compartmentalized. The gender division of domestic work does not radically change when men work at home. Therefore, the time men spend on paid work continues to be perceived as distinct in the same way that their jobs outside the home are perceived as distinct. In addition, men dispose of their earnings in a more compartmentalized way, for example, giving a certain daily or weekly allowance to their wives for household expenses. Therefore, a man's contribution to the family budget is often well-defined and well-known. Whether the man earns a fixed salary or has a more flexible income, whether he works inside or outside the home, does not affect these distinctions. One thing does change: it becomes more difficult for men who work at home to hold back information about their earnings because the number of pieces produced, and thus their total earnings, becomes open knowledge.

Spatial Typology of Homes Used as Places of Work

Home-based work requires a certain minimum of urban services, mainly reliable electricity and access to transportation. Therefore, home-based production is less likely to occur in the peripheral settlements of Guadalajara that lack these services. Home-based work is also rare among poor families in the *vecindades* of the city center, even though services are available and quite a bit of crafts production did take place there during the 1950s and 1960s. A major reason for this rarity is that home-based work is only semilegal. Residents in the vecindades live in multitenant buildings where they share common entrances, central patios, and sanitary services. They lack the privacy and security required to conduct semiclandestine home-based work. The rapid growth of the city during the past three decades has weakened networks of trust. As a result, home ownership and security of tenure have become important in assuring contractors that the workers will not disappear with the put-out material or the equipment lent to them. Accessibility of market centers, access to urban services, a certain degree of spatial control (privacy), and home tenure are key conditions that make homework more feasible for low-income families.[5]

In areas where infrastructure and social conditions permit the integration of production processes into individual homes, dwellings may undergo various types of modification. Modifications differ depending on the type of production, its spatial requirements, and the number and gender of persons involved in the activity. The most important difference is between homes made up of one worker and those that include more than one.

Spatial Modifications in One-Person Units
When one person's maquila work is spatially incorporated into the home, households modify the existing space in one of two ways: either they put space to multiple use, or they set aside space for paid work only. In the first case, families may reorganize furniture to accommodate living and working activities simultaneously, or they may organize their time so that the same space can be used for different purposes at different times of the day. For example, an existing family room or bedroom may be used as a workspace during the day and as living space during the evening or night. If sufficient space is available, maquila households may convert living space into a designated workspace. Because individually performed maquila work requires relatively little space and because it is sporadic and insecure, households rarely construct additional rooms for maquila work.

My case studies indicate different types of modifications in the use of existing space depending on the gender of a maquila worker. Women often reorganize living space to accommodate a mixed use of space for domestic and production tasks. Men more commonly create a specialization of existing space, separating production and living arrangements. For example, in most cases women located their sewing machines in the living room or in a large kitchen in order to be able to both work and supervise their children. Figure 1 shows how a female homeworker locates her machine between the kitchen and living room so that she can accomplish several tasks simultaneously. In this case, the female homeworker has a young female helper who irons the pieces she has completed sewing. As the plan of the house and map of activities show, this female homeworker was able to combine cooking with keeping an eye on her children, entertaining visitors, watching television, and supervising her helper.

Men, by contrast, usually appropriate a certain space for production and tend to spatially separate their work from other activity areas. Figure 2 depicts two cases in which the male homeworkers set up their sewing machines in areas separate from the living and cooking areas, even when that arrangement placed their work activities in a congested, narrow entrance corridor or a semioutdoor terrace. Among male homeworkers there is little concern with combining production and domestic responsibilities, nor does the presence of men radically change the gender division of work within the home.

Spatial Modifications in Multiperson Units

The spatial impact of home-based work is different when it involves several workers. Two considerations are paramount: first, it is much more difficult to hide home-based production that involves several people; second, more machines and workers need more space.

In order to conceal production from the public, homeworkers establish their workplaces on the back sides of their houses. A person—say, an inspector—walking along the streets of homeworking neighborhoods can identify homes used for production only with difficulty. But the concern with secrecy varies in different locations based on the extent of the work taking place in the home and on the cost of potential modifications. In some cases—especially in Zapotlanejo, where I observed a more relaxed attitude toward inspectors—homeworkers found it cheaper to pay an occasional bribe than to make spatial modifications to hide their activity.

In order to accommodate home-based production workshops, families often make incremental additions to their houses that ultimately lead to a segregation of work and living spaces. Among workshops that expand, it is possible to distinguish phases of spatial organization (see figure 3). When these families first start out, they often incorporate work into living spaces, a phase that may be referred to as the "congestion phase." As working hands and machines invade living space, one can observe a deterioration of the spatial well-being of family members. As soon as financial resources become available, however, a specialization of activity zones begins, and homeworking families may construct an additional room or cover part of the back yard. This "expansion phase" starts with horizontal separation and commonly leads to vertical segregation of activity zones. Working and living spaces separate onto different floors as the workshop or the living area moves upstairs. Homeworkers in Guadalajara and Zapotlanejo like such vertical arrangements because they provide more separation between work and rest. If they can afford to do so, they favor going even one step further: buying the house of the lot next door and having their houses and workshops separate but adjacent. This arrangement allows them to eliminate from the living space the dirt and odor of the work environment and its hazards for small children. Women in particular

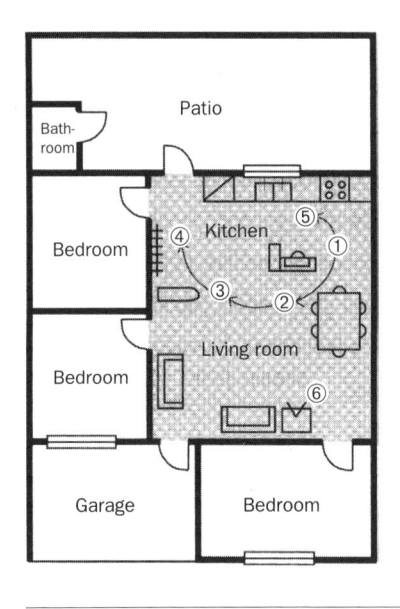

① Work space of a female homeworker.

② Dining table appropriated for work during the working hours for cleaning the sewn pieces.

③ Ironing and press board for the use of an employee to iron the finished pieces.

④ Hanging rack for completed jobs to be picked up by the middle man.

⑤ Cooking area.

⑥ Television watched while working.

1. A female homeworker's mixed use of space for clothing production in Zapotlanejo.

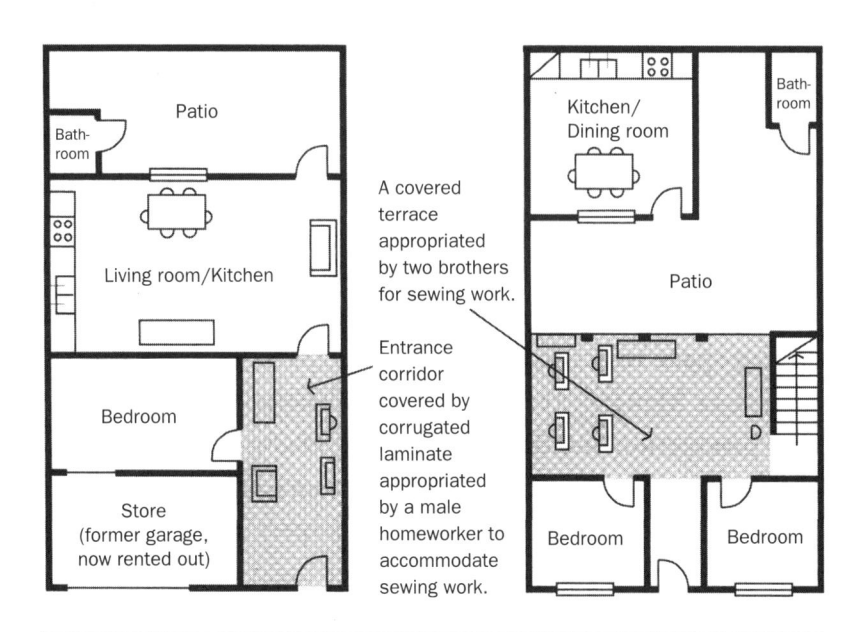

A covered terrace appropriated by two brothers for sewing work.

Entrance corridor covered by corrugated laminate appropriated by a male homeworker to accommodate sewing work.

2. A male homeworker's specialized use of space for clothing production in Zapotlanejo.

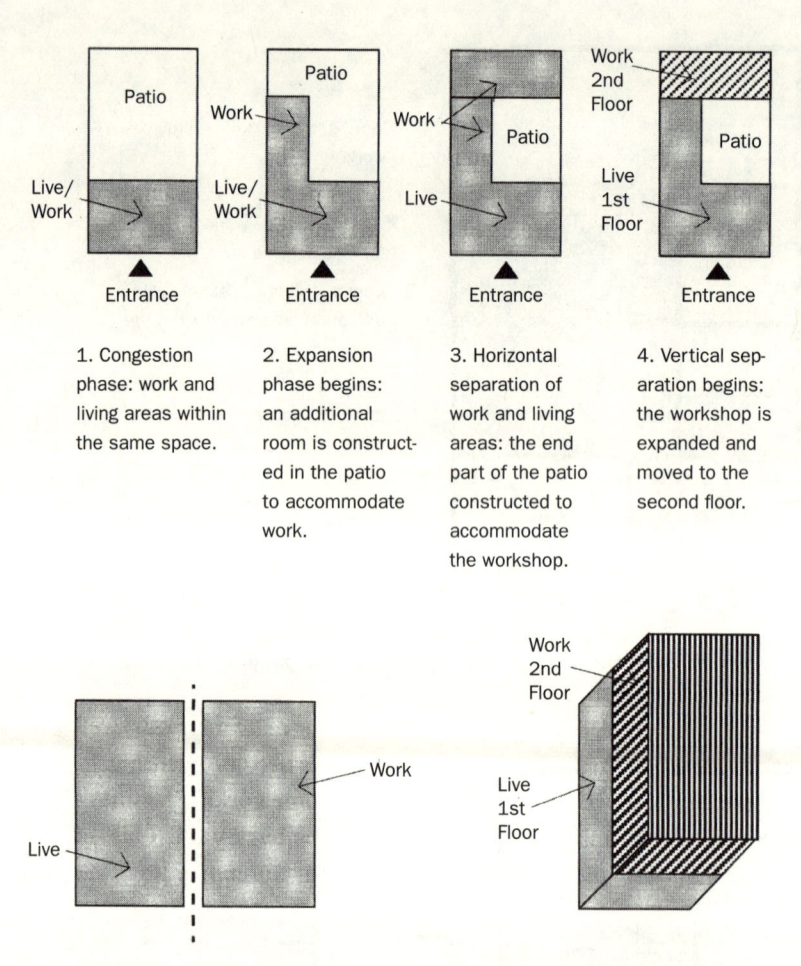

1. Congestion phase: work and living areas within the same space.

2. Expansion phase begins: an additional room is constructed in the patio to accommodate work.

3. Horizontal separation of work and living areas: the end part of the patio constructed to accommodate the workshop.

4. Vertical separation begins: the workshop is expanded and moved to the second floor.

Prosperous home-based workshops may separate work and living areas completely by construction of an additional floor or by purchase of two adjacent properties.

3. Stages in the spatial evolution of homes used for production.

preferred to separate living areas and workspace because other arrangements generated a much heavier cleaning load.

How does the gender division of labor in the home influence patterns of spatial modification in one- and multiperson units? Can differences in spatial modification be explained by the fact that women do most of the one-person maquila work, while men tend to run family workshops? It could be argued that internalized patriarchal values cause women maquiladoras to devalue the legitimacy of their spatial needs and that therefore one-person maquila

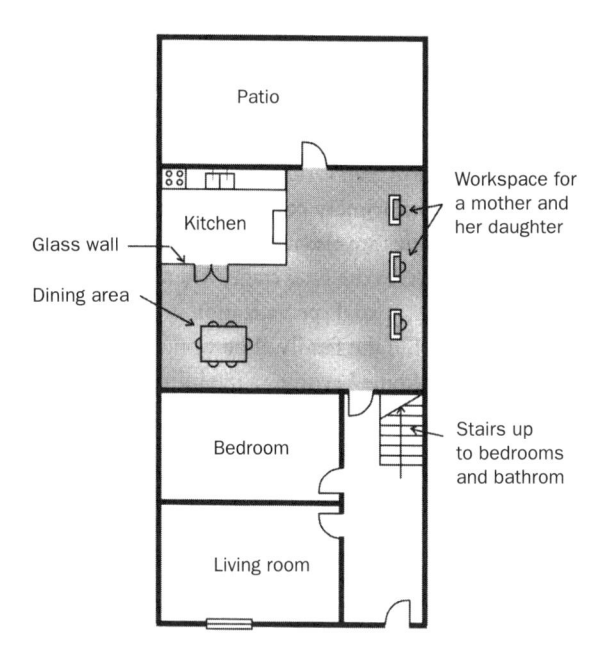

4. A female homeworker's home design for clothing production in Zapotlanejo.

units make fewer spatial modifications.[6] Women's paid work at home often appears to be an extension of their domestic work, with its contribution to family income not acknowledged. As a result, women themselves are often not convinced of their need for work-related construction and thus are less likely to consider adding space or appropriating existing space.

There may be some truth to this argument. More important than perception and ideology, however, may be the practical considerations of combining domestic and productive roles. For example, one woman who ran a home-based workshop constructed an additional room in her courtyard and moved her five sewing machines and workers from her living room to the new addition. However, it was not practical for her to move back and forth between the workshop and the kitchen and living room where her children spent most of their time. Soon she moved her own machine back to the living room, away from the newly constructed workshop. Although this homeworker perceived the legitimacy of her spatial needs and invested in new workspace for herself and her workers, the gendered division of work within the home led her finally to adopt spatial modifications that integrated living and workspace. In another case where the home was designed by the female homeworker, the workspace was set in the same area as the kitchen (see figure 4). The homeworker came up with the idea of a glass wall between the work and cooking areas to cut out the grease and odors while facilitating her combined efforts of sewing and cooking.

When both the male and female heads of the family had at first participated in home-based work, the evolution of workshops from conditions of mixed use and congestion to specialized and separate activity zones often corresponded to changes in the division of responsibilities. Through interviews with those working in older home-based workshops, I reconstructed the gender division of work with the family throughout the life of the workshop and was able to map various physical stages in the spatial modification of such homes. In the primary congestion phase, when use of space is mixed, women's responsibilities are also mixed, including both productive and domestic activities. However, in the final stage, when the work is completely separated from living spaces, spatial specialization is accompanied by a clear gender division of labor within the family. The woman often no longer takes part in production, and the home becomes a feminine realm of reproductive responsibilities. One older owner of a home-based workshop told me that since they had moved the workshop to the house next door, his wife no longer worked on the machines. It could be argued that this situation represented the rise to a new level of economic prosperity. But the owner disagreed: "We were doing well for some time before moving the workshop out. It took some time because we were waiting for the house next door to become available to move the workshop there. But it is hard to be at home and watch others working. Had we kept the workshop in the house she would have continued to work on one of the machines. But now it is better; she can attend the house and sometimes come to the workshop and help me by choosing the style or the cloths."

The separation of workshop and home may entail the demise of the wife's direct economic role but not of her symbolic role within the workshop. Additional workers (who are predominantly female) are often recruited from the pool of the female partner's personal relationships. Thus, even in the cases where she no longer works in the workshop, her on-and-off presence and feminine image associated with the taller are important resources for managing work relations.

The Double Face of Homework for Women

Does the use of the home as a workplace provide increased wealth and well-being to low-income families, and in particular to women with childcare responsibilities? Or does the invasion of production lead to an exploitation of family members and a deterioration of their living conditions? The viewpoints implied in these questions are too restrictive, for the use of domestic space for production embodies possibilities both of exploitation and of economic gain.

Maria Mies's study of lacemakers in India (1982) and Lourdes Benería's and Martha Roldán's work on women subcontractors in Mexico City (1987) explore in depth the exploitative aspects of home-based work, including unpaid domestic work, underpaid homework, and the unpaid labor of children. These scholars argue that processes of subcontracting atomize the labor force and minimize awareness among workers of their own power. This fragmentation reduces the possibility of organization, the chances of collective action, and thus the bargaining power of workers vis-à-vis their employers. Home-based work serves the interests of the manufacturers by cutting down production costs and allowing them to tap into the home leads to exploitation of homeworkers and to a deterioration of living conditions for them and their families.

But home-based work may also bring domestic and public spheres together and provide an opportunity to generate income and increase wealth. Western feminists have written much on the notion that spatial organization, both of cities and homes, establishes the "ground rules of gender."[7] They have argued that contemporary cities express and reinforce patriarchal assumptions that assign women to the domestic sphere of unpaid caregiving and men to the public sphere of paid economic activities (Hayden 1981; Little, Peake, and Richardson 1988; Wekerle, Peterson, and Morley 1980). The separation of suburban homes from central workplaces has further isolated women with children from economic opportunities. In general, the spatial separation of public and domestic spheres, of production and reproduction, is seen as resting on the duality of male and female, enhancing patriarchal notions of gender.[8]

When this argument is applied to informal home-based work, the integration of paid work in domestic space might be seen as an appropriate means of bridging the separation between male and female. It is a strategy for women (especially mothers of young children) to bring the paid activities of the public world into their homes. It may turn women's confinement into economic opportunity. One might even argue that the use of the home as a workplace could create a situation that reduces the duality between the two spheres and thus between women and men.

According to my case studies, however, the presence of men at home did not radically increase their participation in domestic chores. Within a culture of machismo, male homeworkers often feared they might become *mandelones* (soft men) and be despised by their peers. Therefore, they preferred their wives to remain at home, in charge of domestic matters, while they attended to paid work. Female homeworkers in all cases continued to play the key role in tasks such as cleaning, cooking, and taking care of children. But in Zapotlanejo, where people were aware of the value of women's work, there was a relatively higher degree of male participation in domestic chores among homeworking families. Female homeworkers often mentioned that in busy periods, when there was great pressure to complete subcontracting work, their husbands did help them with cleaning and cooking.

According to the female homeworkers, the idea of wives working did not initially appeal to husbands. But eventually the men became supportive simply because the family could not survive on one income, and the work of the female homeworker improved the family's economic situation. This realization even convinced them to participate in domestic work at times. One of the women interviewed in Zapotlanejo described how this played out in her household.

> My husband has changed a lot. He used to do nothing around the home, absolutely nothing. He also used to drink a lot; this was while often our children and I went hungry. We didn't have a home; we were living in a ruined shack loaned to us by a relative, which we couldn't afford even to rent. Since I started working things have changed a lot. We bought this lot and built this house mainly with the money I have earned. You know what the love for a home does. Because I wanted to buy a home, I sometimes got up at three or four o'clock in the morning and started the machine to save money to have a home. Well, he watched me working so hard. I told him, "I will not work if you are going to drink it up." He knows that; I will not work. Thank God, somehow he changed. He doesn't drink anymore; he also helps me every day with sweeping, feeding the kids, and even doing the laundry every Sunday. He sees I cannot move away from the machine. I have to have the work ready for the next day; otherwise I'll lose my contractor. It is hard. There are many women who want to do the work I am doing, so I know, and he knows it too, that I'd better keep my contractors happy. Sometimes for days I cannot step out of the house and for hours can't step away from the machine. He sees that; he is not blind. He comes home and sees I am still left with another fifty pairs to finish up, so he helps me. He goes to the kitchen and puts something together.

One female homeworker's husband, who held a sporadic job in the informal sector (buying and selling used bottles and barrels), mentioned that in busy periods, when there was a lot of maquila work for his wife, he would cook and do whatever needed to be done around the house. He said, "Life is tough these days, with my work we can't always make it. I sometimes sell a lot and sometimes nothing. So every piece she sews is a few more little pennies [*unos centavitos mas*]. I cannot sew, so I get into the kitchen and put something together. This way she doesn't have to get away from the machine. When there is work we have to take advantage of it, right? So I help her and she helps me to get ahead."

Conclusion

The social and spatial relations within households that have incorporated income-generating activities express the patriarchal relations in society at large. However, the spatial organization of activities is not only a passive expression of existing gender roles and relations but may also reinforce or weaken these relations. The spatial juxtaposition of domestic and public spheres, of the realms of reproduction and production, to a certain degree facilitates the participation of men and women in each others' worlds and may encourage a limited step toward the moderation of engendered divisions of labor.[9] For example, when men work at home for pay, their wives are more likely to know how much their husbands earn. Gaining such knowledge, formerly the province of men alone, eliminates an important means of male control. Although women's income earnings usually result in a double shift for women (Hochschild with Machung 1989), the extreme work pressure on women can also become a motivation for men's participation in housework, especially when men are present at the site of women's double burden. The fact that they literally observe the load of piecework to be completed, along with the unwashed dishes, has led some men to help with domestic tasks and softened engendered division of work within the family.

Just as the household embodies both support and conflict, so does home-based work embody conditions of both exploitation and opportunity. It provides the practical advantage of making it easier for women to juggle their various roles and responsibilities. At the same time, it creates the disadvantage of obscuring the perceived amount of time and energy women invest in increasing the wealth and well-being of the family. These two aspects of home-based work do not necessarily negate each other. There is no question that home-based work involves exploitation (or self-exploitation). Workers and their families are excluded from fringe benefits; they have to put up with greater job insecurity; they have to work in environments that are hazardous and poorly equipped for work; and they have to live in environments that have been invaded by work and thus made increasingly stressful. However, home-based work also provides the possibility for earning an income for many women who could not do so otherwise, a benefit that cannot be ignored.

The integration of paid work in domestic space is an appropriate strategy for turning the home, which in urban societies has served as a site of confinement for women (especially mothers of young children), into a site of economic opportunity. My case studies in Zapotlanejo indicate that the use of the home as a workplace significantly increases the wealth and well-being of many women. It allows them to sidestep personal and structural constraints that might prevent them from earning an income. Home-based microenterprises often open a way out of poverty.

Notes

1 This outside status is what defines home-based work as an informal economic activity. See Castells and Portes 1989, 12.
2 Family workshops may involve as many as fifteen family members living and working together. In one case, I found an extended family of seventeen persons housed within an area of 7 by 25 meters, with ten adults and two children (aged twelve and fourteen) producing women's leather bags. In addition, four daughters-in-law, who were also living in the house, contributed to their labor on a sporadic basis when needed. Of course, the size of the production unit is not an indication of its success; it could rather be an indication of a struggle to survive by pooling the labor of as many family members as possible, including young children, in order to sell products below market prices.
3 In some cases the manufacturer delivers and picks up piecework.
4 However, my findings show that perceptions about the economic contributions of women are different in Zapotlanejo than in Guadalajara. In Zapotlanejo both women and men were more aware of the importance of women's sewing work at home, not only to their families' budgets but also to the economic life of the whole town. This awareness can be understood by considering economic developments in Zapotlanejo during the past few years. In less than a decade, and predominantly as the result of women's home-based work in the clothing industry, this small rural center has experienced an economic boom and a rapid growth in its population. Economic prosperity came at a critical point when income from agriculture was steadily decreasing and men saw few options but to migrate to the United States. In conversations, the residents of Zapotlanejo often mentioned that their town was now economically prosperous thanks to women's work. In this context, the use of the home as a workplace has not hidden women's economic contribution to the family: it has instead provided conditions of increased economic power for women and for the town as a whole, and with that has come a recognition of women's economic role.
5 The astonishing degree of home-based clothing production in Zapotlanejo is due to

multiple factors and must be understood as part of a larger trend that embraces a series of small towns in the Altos de Jalisco.

6. Amartya Sen (1990) presents an excellent analysis, arguing that women's perception of the value of their work defines their sense of entitlement and thus their sense of the legitimacy of their needs. Men's and women's perceptions about their contributions to household welfare affect how they bargain for their own welfare in the household.
7. This term is taken from Ardener 1982.
8. Michelle Rosaldo and Louise Lamphere (1974) argue that relations of gender cannot be changed unless men and women actively participate in each others' spheres and that in societies where men and women are more separated the inequalities are greater.
9. Here I am talking about moderation and not a qualitative transformation of gender roles. The social construct of gender roles and relations is far more complex, and its moderation would require the transformation of patriarchal relations at many levels within the society, in economic as well as social and cultural terms.

Mexican Immigrant Women and the New Domestic Labor

MARÍA DE LA LUZ IBARRA

✳ In every society housework reflects the universal human need for material and emotional sustenance. As such, its general content is predictable, but the elaboration—who does the work, for whom, and how—is historically and culturally specific. In the post–World War II United States, the gendered division of labor was one in which women were responsible for housework. Elite white women fulfilled their obligations by hiring domestics, but larger numbers of middle-class women—like working-class women before and after the war—did their own cleaning, took care of their own children, and often looked after the elderly.

Today, economic restructuring has shifted this pattern and produced what might be called a new domestic labor. While women continue to be primarily responsible for social-reproductive labor, restructuring has pushed more of it into the market and led to changes among employers and employees and in the configuration of domestic work. Employers include not only the wealthy but also members of the middle and even working classes, and they are more racially and ethnically diverse than in the past. Employees, likewise, are a heterogeneous group that includes immigrant women with diverse racial, ethnic, class, and educational backgrounds. These employees are asked to perform a wider range of work, which consists of a variety of housecleaning and elder- and childcare jobs, some unique to the contemporary period. In addition, the new domestic labor is polarized in terms of wages, working conditions, and potential for personal fulfillment. As Christine Stansell noted for women caught in the tide of the early industrial revolution, the development of a postindustrial economy and its attendant restructuring of housework has "created a new configuration of suffering and possibility" for the women who undertake these labors (1987, iv).

Anthropologists interested in the effects of postindustrial restructuring on workplaces offer important insights for the study of the new domestic labor. Informed by political economy and concerned with power relations, these scholars have identified the appearance of anachronistic conditions in U.S. workplaces in the last thirty years, including decreased worker-safety precautions (Stull, Broadway, and Erickson 1992), the expansion of informality and subcontracting (Mines and Avina 1992), and increasing levels of part-time employment and worker turnover (Newman 1998). Paying attention to the structure of production and to the labor process, some scholars argue that the revival of old forms of accumulation signals a new phase in the development of global capital. As Alejandro Portes, Manuel Castells, and Lauren Benton note, "An old form in a new setting is, in fact, new since all social relationships can only be defined in their specific historical context" (1989, 13).

Responding to an earlier literature in which the role of agency had been ignored, anthropologists of labor have also theorized the interactive relationship between individuals and work structures (Scott 1985). Feminist scholars detail the historically specific conditions constraining women's experiences and also link these conditions to the ways in which women respond to and create cultural representations of their experiences (Di Leonardo 1984; Kondo 1990). Chicana feminists, moreover, address how "social location" is critical for understanding both similarity and difference between women of the same racial, ethnic group, thereby expanding understanding of the socially constructed and materially rooted basis of gender (Nájera-Ramírez 1999; Zavella 1987, 1991a).

Scholars who focus on household work have also identified structural changes in that occupation within the last thirty years and have investigated the ways in which worker agency is responsible for some of these changes. Mary Romero (1992), for example, undertakes the important task of documenting the resistance strategies of Chicana domestic workers in Denver, Colorado, and the consequent transformation of housecleaning there. However, she does not discuss the differences among Chicanas who perform the work or the contemporary economic conditions that both give rise to a demand for cleaners and help shape the contemporary structure of housework. Likewise, Shellee Colen (1995) writes about the precarious legal position of a growing number of West Indian women who provide live-in childcare in New York. Until recently, "undocumented" nannies or those "working for the green card" were not a prominent feature in U.S. society.[1] Colen provides a global context within which to understand the demand for immigrant childcare providers and why women "choose" to do this work, but she gives less attention to the work itself—to the daily practices that constitute a fundamental part of women's lives.

To gain a better appreciation of the diverse constraints faced by household workers and the parameters within which they exercise the agency that Romero and Colen reveal, a more detailed examination of the global and local interstices that shape domestic labor markets, of the labor process, and of women's social location is necessary. As a means of addressing the transformation of household work and gaining a better understanding of the pitfalls and possibilities of the new domestic labor, this essay focuses on Mexican immigrant women—Mexicanas—employed as household workers in the Southern California city of Santa Barbara.[2] It contextualizes Mexicana workers within a global system and notes the impact of global and U.S. labor markets on the employment of immigrant women. In particular, it describes the economic restructuring, demographic change, and Mexican migration in Santa Barbara, and, by means of the life histories of two workers, illustrates how these factors are inseparably related to the new domestic work and the changing roles of American and Mexican women in the late twentieth century.

International Migration, Restructuring, and Social Reproduction

The migration of Mexicanas to Santa Barbara is only one example of a global phenomenon. Since the 1970s, millions of people have left their homes in Africa, Latin America, Eastern Europe, and Asia, many in search of work in postindustrial regions of economic growth such as the United States, Western Europe, and Japan (Zlotnik 1995). Migrations from the Third World to the First are not haphazard occurrences, but rather form part of the logic of capitalist development (Amin 1974; Sassen 1988). Recent internationalization of the economy has exacerbated this flow and significantly affected its character: half of all migrants are women, many of whom labor as domestics (Enloe 1990; United Nations Population Fund 1993).

Mexicans have a long history of labor migration to the United States, one that spans more than a hundred years (Gamio 1930). The recent period of immigration, however, is unprecedented in scale and scope. Since 1965, more than seven million Mexicans have moved to the United States, 45 percent to California (David G. Gutiérrez 1998). The bulk of these seven million migrants left Mexico in the 1980s and 1990s. During this time, the Mexican government, in the midst of a severe economic crisis, opened up the country to increased foreign investment, including the development of export-processing zones, and instituted structural-adjustment programs to satisfy the demands of international bankers. Mexican citizens of all social classes saw their wages, social services, and opportunities for formal-sector jobs decrease and were consequently forced to rethink their strategies for survival (González de la Rocha 1994). Many chose to take advantage of social networks and of expanding labor markets which targeted immigrants for employment in the United States (Sassen 1988). Most immigrants derive from central-western Mexican states, which have traditionally sent migrants to the United States, as well as from new sending areas in central and southern Mexico such as Estado de Mexico, Oaxaca, and the Federal District. The immigrant profile is currently much more diverse than it was in the past and includes professionals and persons with high levels of formal education (Cornelius 1992). Furthermore, unlike in the post–World War II period, many of the new Mexican immigrants are women, many of whom labor as domestics (Ruiz 1987).

In the United States, policies implemented at national and international levels, as well as demographic changes, help mold social-reproductive experiences in households and contribute to a growing demand for Mexicana and other immigrant domestic workers. First, the restructuring of the U.S. economy and its attendant wealth polarization help explain demand (Bluestone and Harrison 1986). Ruth Milkman, Ellen Reese, and Benita Roth convincingly argue that "a crucial determinant of the extent of employment in paid domestic labor in a given location is the degree of economic inequality there" (1998, 486). Thus, in many cities new professional and managerial jobs expand the ranks of the wealthy who demand a broad range of personal services to subsidize high-income lifestyles and declining amounts of discretionary time (Sassen 1988). Second, the restructuring of the economy has led to an unprecedented feminization of the waged labor force (Frobel, Heinrichs, and Kreye 1981). Many women seek employment out of a personal desire for fulfillment, but others do so to try to maintain or raise "comparatively modest standards of living" (Fernández-Kelly and Sassen 1995, 117). More women than ever before form part of dual-earner households and are employed over longer periods of their lifetimes than in the past. This results in a labor shortfall in many homes where men's participation in household work has not kept pace with women's employment (England and Farkas 1986). By 1995, 64 percent of married mothers with preschool children were employed, compared with 30 percent in 1970 (U.S. Bureau of the Census, cited in Hofferth 1999). Lastly, the changing demography of the United States contributes to an increased demand for household workers. Because increasing numbers of people survive to be at least sixty-five years of age, the elderly constitute a higher proportion of the population than at any other time in history (Hayes-Bautista, Schink, and Chapa 1988). As in all postindustrial societies, aging citizens are likely to live independently or with an elderly spouse, but they frequently require special assistance in a variety of areas including physical care and companionship (Ibarra 1998).

In this context, Mexicanas, like other women impacted by global and national policies in the Third World, migrate north and undertake domestic employment in U.S. households. This pattern is glaringly apparent in Southern California. Since 1980, both the absolute number and the percentage of immigrant women employed in households has grown in the three largest metropolitan areas of Southern California (Milkman, Reese, and Roth 1998). As Milkman, Reese, and Roth observe, this growth is particularly notable given that domestic service—which at the turn of the century represented the most common occupation of women in the United States—had by 1960 declined so dramatically in economic importance that some were predicting its demise (483). Today, instead of an elimination of the occupation, a new domestic labor is flourishing.

The Contours of the New Domestic Labor

The literature on U.S. domestic employment is not extensive. By the late 1970s only two books addressed the history of the occupation (Katzman 1978; Salmon 1897), and it was only after 1980 that the bulk of academic studies were published.[3] A small number of these studies address the post-1970 period, during which time the U.S. economy underwent restructuring, and most focus on immigrant and other minority women who fulfill the demand for cleaning services in middle-class and upper-class households.[4] The rest focus on childcare providers in elite, white households.[5]

A review of the historical literature shows that from the advent of industrialization, U.S. employers of domestics have been wealthy and middle-class white women, while domestics have predominantly been women from socially marginalized or oppressed groups.[6] Domestic employment has for the most part been unregulated, undervalued, and stigmatized as the labor of inferiors. Not surprisingly, women have left the occupation as soon as other work becomes available. These workers are then replaced by more vulnerable groups (Sanjek and Colen 1990).

In addition to changes in personnel, the structure of work has also changed over time and reflects transformations in class relations, the advent of new home technologies and home design, and the availability of commoditized services, such as laundry, and products, such as prepackaged food (Dudden 1983). Changes to the structure of work have resulted from employee agency as well. Housecleaners, for example, have consistently attempted to create better working conditions, the most dramatic of which has been the delimiting of hours. In the 1920s black domestic workers in northeastern cities pushed for live-out work; by 1945 live-in workers represented only a small proportion of those employed (Palmer 1989). Domestics also, albeit unsuccessfully, struggled for unionization and successfully organized for Social Security benefits in the 1950s and for inclusion under minimum-wage laws in the 1970s (Martin and Segrave 1985).

Another important area of struggle involves employers' demands for "emotional labor," the taken-for-granted effort of managing "feeling to create a public observable facial and bodily display" that produces the proper state of mind in others (Hochschild 1983, 3). The physical mechanisms include spoken word, tone of voice, and other "efforts that are expressed through behavior" (Steinberg and Figart 1999, 10). Historical and contemporary literature provides examples of the demand for such labors (Clark-Lewis 1994). In Boston during the 1980s, for example, Judith Rollins found white employers preferred to hire African American women because the employers were able to extract "rituals" of linguistic and spatial deference from them and to practice "maternalism" toward them (1985, 155). An employee's linguistic deference included addressing the employer by her last name while the employer addressed the worker by her first name. Spatial deference included not touching the employer and staying out of her way. The employer's maternalistic behavior included viewing the worker as a child and demanding to meet the worker's friends. Rollins considered these rituals atavistic, observing, "The typical employer extracts *more than labor*" (1985, 155; emphasis added). Arlie Hochschild (1990) contends that this layer of work is emotional labor and represents a fundamental part of the new service economy.

Mary Romero also sees emotional labor as a fundamental aspect of the domestic-labor process, an aspect that is problematic for many workers. Consequently, live-out housecleaners have undertaken a "structural transformation" of the occupation in order to eliminate emotional labor. Romero argues that in the 1980s Chicanas in Denver, Colorado, "professionalized" by specifying hours, tasks, and wages for specific labor services so that undesirable emotional labors would not be included. Professional workers included independent "job workers" and those who subcontracted. The types of emotional labors they abolished included listening to employer's problems, performing "mothering" duties such as cooking, and undertaking "personal" tasks such as picking clothes up off the floor. While addressing the importance of agency in eliminating emotional labors and therefore promoting change in the informal housecleaning sector, Romero does not develop the economic context within which to situate the contemporary demand for housecleaners. She also does not address immigrant workers, women whose social position is distinct from the native-born Chicanas she studies.

Other scholars who focus on housecleaners situate the growing supply of and demand for domestic workers within a restructuring global economy and focus on immigrant Latinas within the occupation. In so doing, both Pierrette Hondagneu-Sotelo, whose research is based in Redwood City, California (1994), and Leslie Salzinger, whose research is based in San Francisco, California (1991), discuss demand among a more diverse group of employers. These employers include not only the wealthy but also the elderly and other people living on fixed incomes. Hondagneu-Sotelo and Salzinger also find that the housecleaning labor market is segmented and that some workers have undertaken a professionalization of the occupation similar to that found among Chicanas in Denver. Neither scholar, however, addresses the broader dimensions of the labor market at the local level or the differences between women who perform the work.

In addition to the literature on domestic cleaning, a growing number of contemporary studies also focus on immigrant women who undertake childcare. Immigrant childcare providers labor for the predictable upper-class households like those targeted in the "nannygate" scandal of the early 1990s, as well as for middle-class households and even for working-class households.[7] Childcare providers are hired to maintain the physical well-being of children and—just as important—to provide entertainment, learning, and emotional support.

Shellee Colen's research among West Indian women in New York demonstrates that unlike previous groups of domestic workers, women from the West Indies are often highly educated former nurses, police officers, and teachers. Their human capital, however, has little impact on their present situation. In part this is a result of their legal status in the United States: they are not permanent residents or citizens, but rather temporary laborers "working for the green card." West Indian childcare providers, Colen argues, form part of the bottom tier in a system of "stratified reproduction" whereby "some categories of people are empowered to nurture and reproduce, while others are disempowered" (1995, 78). Other research mirrors Colen's findings that unlike professional housecleaners, informal-sector childcare workers often live in residence, receive low wages, have unclear job descriptions, and work long hours. Workers consequently have limited time to spend with their families or create families of their own (Nathan 1991; Richardson and Torres 1999; Wrigley 1995). Others have to live apart from their children as "transnational" mothers (Hondagneu-Sotelo and Avila 1997). Less addressed in scholarly literature is what women actually do when they are working, what daily practices constitute the labor process.

The domestic-labor literature focusing on the contemporary period has sketched the outline of a new domestic labor, wherein a broader spectrum of employers hire a more diverse group of employees to undertake a wider range of jobs, some in which emotional labor is central. In sketching this outline from many places and many perspectives over the last twenty-five years, these studies have not brought the macro- and microperspectives together in a single place; that is, they have not investigated the effects of restructuring on the contours of the local labor market, the social location of the women who do it, and the everyday practices that constitute work. Because domestic work is not a homogeneous, static enterprise, one must better understand the parameters of "choice" in particular places in order to better understand the context within which agency is exercised.

Household Work in a Polarized, Aging City

Santa Barbara is located ninety miles north of Los Angeles, and two hundred and forty miles from the U.S.-Mexico border. It is an immaculately groomed city with palm-lined drives, exclusive boutiques, jazz festivals, and resident Hollywood movie stars. It is also part of the territory ceded to the United States by Mexico and as such has a long history of a Mexican presence. This presence, however, as in many other Southern California communities, has recently undergone dramatic changes.

Between 1980 and 1990 the Mexican-origin population in Santa Barbara grew from 16,000 to over 26,000 people, representing 33 percent of the population in a city with 87,000 people (U.S. Bureau of the Census 1990). In general, the earnings of these workers were low: Mexican-origin families earned less than half of the median family income in the city, and 20 percent lived below the poverty line (Barber 1994). Low wages and high rents in the city led individuals and families to subdivide houses and even rooms, or to live in unorthodox shelters such as garages and tool sheds in order to keep living expenses down.

As in the rest of California, the growing number of Mexican immigrants in Santa Barbara has inspired a contradictory welcome. On the one hand, employers are anxious to hire immigrants. On the other hand, Mexicans have been denounced as drains on public coffers. This was particularly apparent in the period preceding the passage of Proposition 187, designed to create a state-run system for verifying the legal status of all persons seeking public benefits in California. One worker showed me the following stanza from a poem she received from an employer who objected to her participation in anti–Proposition 187 marches. This stanza illustrates the centrality of gender in these attacks.

> We have hobby, it's called "breeding,"
> Welfare pay for baby feeding
> Kids need dentist? Wife need pills?
> We get free, we got no bills.

The contradictory welcome is further illustrated by Border Patrol raids in the city following Santa Barbara's nannygate scandal. In 1994 the city was the site of media attention as the then senatorial candidate and local resident Michael Huffington was accused of having employed an undocumented Latina childcare provider. In this context the patrol agent in charge of the region, lamenting the lack of funds, said that by late 1994 the U.S. Border Patrol "[had] only made about six trips into Montecito [where] we know the numbers [of undocumented immigrants] are high" (Burns 1994, A3). For Mexicanas, however, each of these incursions was a threat and a reminder that they are criminalized outsiders.

It is within this political context that the supply of household workers thrives in Santa Barbara. A drive through the city's Mexican neighborhoods in the early morning reveals a steady number of women headed to bus stops on their way to their employers' homes. Later in the day, in different neighborhoods throughout the city, Mexicanas can also be seen pushing strollers or walking alongside elderly wards. Because much of this labor is unregulated, however, there are no reliable statistics documenting the number of domestics in the city. The census, for example, reports that there were 342 household workers in the city in 1980 and that this number had grown to 644 by 1990. Anyone who lives in the city knows that these numbers are low, and their principal usefulness, therefore, is simply to show a growth trend. According to the census data, the number of domestics in Santa Barbara grew at a rate 5.5 times that of the general population.

As in other parts of the nation, changes to the structure of the economy and within households help explain the demand for domestic workers. Between 1970 and 1997, the city's economy underwent two principal economic transformations. First, there was a rise in the amount of pension and property income flowing into the city. While in 1970 pension and property income represented almost one-third of the economic base, by 1980 pension and property income represented more than one-half of the economic base (Economic Research Associates 1981, 77). This change reflects a growth in the number of retirees settling in the city, an increase also evident in the local age demographics. By the early 1990s the percentage of people who were at least sixty-five years old had grown to represent 20 percent of the population, as compared to 13 percent nationally. Today, people over the age of sixty-five and those between the ages of forty-five and sixty-four represent the fastest growing age groups in Santa Barbara (Schniepp 1997, 47).

As Santa Barbara's aging, white elite grew in the 1990s, they contributed to the skyrocketing cost of single-family homes in the city and surrounding areas. By 1998 the average home price topped $400,000, with modest homes in the barrios often fetching as much as $350,000. Prohibitive house prices combined with a second important change to the economy—the substantive deindustrialization of the region due to military downsizing in the early 1990s—to push younger and middle-income households out of the city (Schniepp 1997). Such households that remain frequently require or choose to have two wage earners, even when they have young children. Fully 62 percent of the employed female labor force in Santa Barbara have children under the age of three (U.S. Bureau of the Census 1990). Thus, the demand for domestic labor in Santa Barbara reflects the broader range of economic and demographic processes at work in the United States, as well as the particular circumstances of a retirement paradise less than a two-hour drive from the global city of Los Angeles.

Methodology

Over a period of eighteen months between 1994 and 1996, I undertook anthropological fieldwork among Mexican immigrant women employed as domestic workers in Santa Barbara's informal sector. As in most cities, in Santa Barbara there is no centralized public work or meeting place for the informal-sector household workers who were the focus of my study. Moreover, as workers are dispersed and hidden from view in private homes, getting access to them is difficult. Even more difficult is getting access to women who are undocumented and who fear being deported. Thus, I turned to social-service agencies, friends, and the workers themselves to help me contact household employees. The Mexicanas interviewed form part of a nonprobabilistic, snowball sample of fifty women.

I undertook initial semistructured and structured interviews in order to assess the range of household work in the city, as well as the range in Mexicanas' backgrounds. From these interviews, I created a database comprised of workers' states and cities of origin, reasons for migration, periods of residence in the United States, education, and most recent domestic employments. Thereafter, I conducted short-term interviews with forty women and long-term, key-informant interviews with ten women.

Mexicanas and the Structure of Work

Focused short-term and long-term life-history interviews among fifty Mexicana household workers revealed that, like other recent Mexican immigrants throughout Southern California, they are highly diverse (see table). The age of Mexicanas I interviewed ranged from twenty-two to sixty-two years of age. Some women were married with children, some were widows, and some were single, with and without children. As a group, they also reflected the range of occupational and educational backgrounds found among new Mexican immigrants throughout Southern California. Prior to arriving in the United States, these women labored in rural markets, private homes, multinational factories, restaurants, department stores, bars, hospitals, and elementary and secondary schools. Eighteen of the women had not worked for wages at all, but had instead engaged in farming tasks, running the household, and/or raising their children. Others attended school and lived with their parents. Their educational backgrounds, too, ranged from no formal education at all to high-school or university diplomas. The women in the sample also reflected the growing diversity in states of origin; while many still arrived from traditional sending states, almost a third hailed from central and southern Mexico.

Household work in the city's informal sector is highly varied. Based on descriptions offered by the Mexicanas I interviewed, I have categorized household workers into two general groups: housecleaners and human-care providers. Within these two categories I distinguish between a total of seven analytical types which are useful for comparison. Within the housecleaning category are the ubiquitous live-in and live-out housecleaners, as well as labor contractors, employees for labor contractors, and live-in caretakers for absentee homeowners; the latter three types of housecleaner are unique to the contemporary period. Within the human-care category are elder-, child-, and/or convalescent-care providers, which include both live-in and live-out workers; human care—with the exception of childcare—as the sole responsibility of an immigrant household worker is also unique to this period (Sutherland 1981).

The following case studies of two Mexicana workers form part of this larger research project. Although both women derive from rural communities in Jalisco, Mexico, the differences between the two women become clear as they describe their migration histories, their recruitment into household work, and their present employment and its labor process. These case studies

Table. Profile of Women in Sample

Pseudonym	State of Origin	Years in U.S.	Years in school	Age	Married	Children
Hilda Puerto	Mexico City	3	9	33	No	4
Angelita Perez	Oaxaca	8	6	56	Yes	2
Guadalupe Nora	Jalisco	10	7	31	Yes	4
Gloria Salinas	Jalisco	6	12	21	No	0
Ludivina Rodríguez	Zacatecas	8	6	44	Yes	3
Renata González	Guanajuato	7	6	36	Yes	2
Viviana Solís	Michoacán	8	6	35	D	2
Anabel Ledesma	Chihuahua	5	9	28	No	0
Erlinda Gómez	Oaxaca	3	10	29	No	2
Sonia Terrazas	Guerrero	2	6	29	Yes	1
Mercedes Guzmán	Jalisco	1	6	32	Yes	3
Ivonne Pérez	Jalisco	2	6	27	Yes	1
Sara Ledesma	Jalisco	2	9	29	No	1
Eva Sánchez	Durango	1	14	29	No	0
Rosario González	Aguascalientes	1.5	3	27	Yes	2
Xóchitl Amera	Oaxaca	2.5	0	29	No	0
Sol González	Michoacán	2	9	24	Yes	1
Tania Domínguez	Zacatecas	3	9	33	No	2
Sara Ibarra	Oaxaca	4	6	28	Yes	0
Lucia Sierra	Mexico City	4	11	32	No	0
Margarita Pérez	Jalisco	5	14	36	No	1
Consuelo Archuleta	Jalisco	5	0	59	W	5
Perla Contreras	Michoacán	2	12	31	Yes	0
Chelo Quintanilla	Durango	4	0	55	D	3
Linda López	Sinaloa	0.25	3	21	Yes	0
Luz Ortiz	Jalisco	3	0	54	W	2
Esperanza Luna	Oaxaca	3	9	27	No	0
Yesenia Cruz	Mexico City	2	17	26	No	0
Veronica Valdez	Mexico City	3	9	27	No	0
Antonia Osuna	Mexico City	2.25	6	27	No	0
Cristina Salinas	Durango	6	12	31	No	2
Maria Vera	Mexico City	2	17	28	No	0
Dora Prado	Mexico City	0.5	17	22	No	0
Sara Pérez	Jalisco	2	12	26	No	0
Beatriz Redondo	Jalisco	2	6	34	No	2
Rosa Serena	Puebla	5	0	27	No	0
Trini Castañeda	Jalisco	5	0	40	Yes	4
Cecilia Piñon	Guerrero	6	0	36	No	3

Table. *Continued*

Pseudonym	State of Origin	Years in U.S.	Years in school	Age	Married	Children
Alejandra Curiel	Aguascalientes	4	6	30	Yes	0
Leticia Fierro	Durango	4	6	31	Yes	2
Doris Sánchez	Michoacán	3	5	22	Yes	2
Mrs. Cordero	San Luis Potosí	10.00	5	56	Yes	3
Graciela Pineda	Mexico City	4	9	38	Yes	3
Verónica Osuna	Durango	5	6	29	No	2
Laura García	Mexico City	4	9	30	Yes	3
Ana Sandoval	Jalico	4	6	24	No	0
Melissa Tamayo	Sinaloa	5	6	29	Yes	1
Laura Figueroa	Michoacán	3.75	12	39	No	2
Gloria Romero	Chihuahua	10	0	62	W	5
Santa Herrera	Mexico City	4	6	26	No	1

help illustrate the broad contours of the labor market in the city and the "pain and possibility" inherent in the new domestic labor.

Guadalupe Nora: Labor Contractor

Migration, Recruitment, and Work

Guadalupe Nora is a stout woman with light skin and dark eyes. She is thirty-two years old, has a seventh-grade education, four children, and was born and raised in the rural community of Zocotlán, Jalisco. She left Mexico in 1985, at the age of twenty-two, primarily because her ex-husband was physically abusive. In Mexico, moreover, her employment options were limited, and the money she could earn was insufficient for maintaining herself and her then three small children. Following the advice of a friend, Nora migrated to Santa Barbara, where her mother had lived and labored since 1965. Nora said, "It was a moment of decision to say yes. I didn't think about it, because when I did, I didn't want to leave. And so, I didn't think about the possible consequences, nor did I think about what I would find in this country. What changes, what atmosphere, or what people—overall the language. But I said to myself, I'm going, I'm going to be with my mother, and I went."

In October 1985 Nora, two of her cousins, and her children—who were eight, three, and one—took a bus from Zocotlán to Tijuana, Baja California, and after two attempts and several days of waiting, crossed the international border into San Diego with the paid assistance of a coyote, or human smuggler. Nora and her family were transported to Los Angeles, then to Santa Barbara. On arriving, Ms. Nora briefly worked picking strawberries in the northern half of the county, but found the job too arduous and low paying. Through a friend of her mother's, she got a job at a janitorial company, where she "learned the [cleaning] business." She obtained her first "real," independent house-cleaning job when she agreed to help a female co-worker clean a house after they punched out. Several months later the co-worker made plans to leave for Mexico and "offered" Nora the house. Through referrals, Nora was able to build up her list of private clients and to leave the janitorial job after a year.

Nora considers herself to have been "lucky" during this period because she was able to afford childcare at an in-home day-care center; she says the center took "pity" on her and only charged her twenty dollars a week. It was a "difficult" year of working all the time, saving money to buy a car, and putting down a deposit on an apartment. She said, "My mother wanted to help, but I told her it was not her responsibility. It was I who had a responsibility to my children, and with my own hands, I worked to care for them."

By her third year in Santa Barbara, Nora had settled in an apartment and bought a used car. For three more years, she cleaned houses by herself and acquired a reputation as a good worker. As Nora acquired the ability to support herself and her children without the help of a husband, kinswomen began to see her as successful and ask for her assistance to migrate. Thus, in 1991 Nora began to hire her relatives as "helpers" and to obtain more cleaning jobs. Today she manages her own business and lives with her common-law husband and four children in a two-bedroom apartment.

Present Employment and Its Labor Process
Nora works Monday through Saturday, and she carefully coordinates her monthly schedule. The number of houses she cleans varies by the day and by the week and consequently, so does the number of workers required. When two houses need cleaning, she brings one helper, and when she is responsible for three or four houses, she brings two helpers.

She trains all of her workers and transports them to the houses to be cleaned. She assigns them rooms and specified periods of time in which to clean them, while she also does some of the labor. Nora pays her helpers $9 an hour, and according to the six-month work schedule I compiled with her help, they average approximately $1,200 per month. Most of Nora's work is "basic" cleaning, which does not include washing windows, dusting blinds, washing, or ironing. The price for a basic cleaning is $65 for a three-bedroom, two-bathroom house. After paying her helpers, Nora earns $2,400 a month.

In regard to the daily labor process she once commented, "Sometimes it gets boring, all routines are boring, but then we joke around to get through the day." The work relationship with kin is not without its problems, however, due to the "position of authority" she has to assume, which bring up issues like helpers who resent being told what to do or who want higher wages, an equal partnership, or a medical loan. Now, when she hires a new family member, she tells her from the outset that "within work we have to forget kinship, or we'll have problems."

In spite of these difficulties, Nora prefers to hire family members because non-kin have "taken" houses from her by underbidding her price or offering more services. One year, for example, one of her helpers decided to temporarily return to Mexico and give birth there, where she would have more support from family and where her husband's U.S. earnings would stretch further. During her helper's absence, Nora hired a non-kin replacement. When this employee quit her job a few months later, three of Nora's clients also told her they no longer needed her services. It was later discovered that the ex-employee had "taken" these houses by charging one-third less.[8]

Another stressful aspect of Nora's job is to get clients to respect the verbal agreement. Some clients initially agree to the price, thinking that later "they can add" more work tasks—a practice so common that Nora and her daughter created a flyer listing prices for extra services such as washing and ironing. Interestingly, she lists "conversation" as a service, which she added as a result of the fact that her older, "retired" employers often wanted to talk. No one hired her for this job during my six months of fieldwork with her, but when questioned about it, she said that it had cut down on interruptions.

During the six-month period in which I monitored Nora's weekly schedules, she was employed an average of seven hours a day during the first and the third weeks of the month, although some days she worked up to eleven hours. Work was often concentrated between 8 A.M. and 4 P.M. with little time for breaks. She worked a total of fifty hours during these weeks, not including the time spent on planning. On the second and fourth weeks of the month, her schedule was more relaxed, averaging six hours per day, with long breaks. On these weeks she worked a total of thirty-nine hours, not including work planning. When I met her in June 1995, she had twenty regular "houses," as she referred to her employers; six months later, she had added two new weekly clients. Because both she and her husband shared the household expenses, the bulk of the money she made was deposited into a savings account, destined for a down payment on a house. In regard to her employers, she said, "I have worked with people who have a lot of money, and they don't look at me as if I was a nobody, as if I was a service. They don't look at me like a person who does not belong here—they treat me like a person. If I did this same job in Mexico, the women would abuse me. This job that I do here—although it is not humiliating or dishonest in Mexico—is a job where people think they are above you. Here I have not personally seen that, although I have heard of people who are despots. To those people I would say, 'People come here because they have to and most of them work, so don't look at women as a service, but as human beings.'"

Mrs. Consuelo Archuleta: Elder-Care Provider

Migration, Recruitment, and Work
Consuelo Archuleta is a small woman with light-colored skin and hazel eyes. She is fifty-nine years old, has little formal education, and was born and raised in the village of Mazamitla, Jalisco. She is a widow with five adult children, three of whom live in the United States. Archuleta migrated to Santa Barbara in 1990 and began working as a live-in, elder-care provider in 1992. This is not, however, Archuleta's first time in the United States. As a younger woman she had for a period of ten years—between 1958 and 1968—traveled regularly to the United States to visit her husband, a contracted laborer under the Bracero Program for guest workers.[9] In 1969 she settled with her husband in Oxnard, an agricultural town forty miles south of Santa Barbara. In 1975 her husband died of a heart attack, and Archuleta, thinking it too difficult to raise her two youngest children on her own, returned to her family in Mexico, leaving three adult sons behind. Fifteen years later, in 1990, one of these adult sons asked her to come live with him and his wife in Oxnard. Archuleta agreed, knowing that he and his wife needed help with their child.

Archuleta took a plane from Guadalajara, Jalisco, to Los Angeles, entering the United States with her permanent residency card. For the next year, she took care of her four-year-old granddaughter in Oxnard. The following year, Archuleta worked at a fast-food restaurant; a co-worker told her about a live-in job caretaking for Mrs. Sara, an eighty-year-old Mexican American woman in Santa Barbara. In March 1992 Archuleta called one of the elderly woman's daughters, who spoke some Spanish, and they set up a time to meet at Mrs. Sara's government-subsidized apartment. The daughters told her they wanted someone to live in and be available Monday through Saturday. Mrs. Archuleta took the job for $700 per month plus food.

Present Employment and Its Labor Process
Describing the first two-and-a-half years of employment, Archuleta said that the work was "easy." As long as Mrs. Sara was relatively healthy, the routine

was the same from day to day. Archuleta's assessment that it was easy work, however, was the result of both her experience and her comparison with present working conditions. In fact the job required considerable skill, effort, and responsibility. To begin with, she had to establish a routine, to plan ahead and coordinate the day's movements so that the hours flowed smoothly and her ward was comfortable. Each day was more or less the same, because of Archuleta's intentional, crafted efforts.

Beginning her workday at 9 A.M., Archuleta gave Mrs. Sara her prescription medicine and breakfast, then assisted her to the bathroom to be changed, bathed, and dressed. At the very beginning, however, Mrs. Sara did not want Archuleta to touch her. Recognizing that this would make the morning more stressful, Archuleta verbally soothed her ward, consciously helping her manage the idea of stranger touching her. As Archuleta said, "Poor old woman, she would get very embarrassed. Then when she got embarrassed she would try to hide herself and it would make the job more difficult on me. So I decided that she had to be comfortable. I told her, 'I have done this all of my life, so this is not the first time I change somebody's diapers. Before I came here I took care of my own mother, who was very much like you.'" Putting herself in the position of daughter, she said, helped "normalize" the experience for Mrs. Sara. After being bathed, Mrs. Sara liked to sit in the sun next to the living-room window, and Archuleta kept her company while knitting, talking, or watching television.

At noon, Archuleta prepared the midday meal, then fed Mrs. Sara, gave her another medication, and took her for a short walk. After the walk, Archuleta asked Mrs. Sara if she would like to take a nap. If she did, Archuleta settled her in bed, then picked up around the house and had lunch. When Mrs. Sara woke up, they both watched television while Archuleta undertook chores like laundry or ironing. At 5:30 P.M., she prepared dinner, then fed her employer. In the evening, Archuleta sat with Mrs. Sara, sometimes massaging her legs, talking, and watching soap operas on the television until Mrs. Sara was ready to go to sleep, usually around 9 P.M. Archuleta then changed Mrs. Sara's clothing, took her to the bathroom, washed her teeth, and put her to bed.

In her third year of employment Archuleta no longer felt the job to be easy. As a consequence of deteriorating health, Mrs. Sara had trouble sleeping peacefully and demanded more attention. Archuleta came to feel not only physically tired but also lonely, and sad on behalf of her ward. To cope, she and several other elder-care providers—all Mexicanas—met regularly in a public area in the apartment complex, until other residents complained about noise. Archuleta recalled, "Because we speak Spanish, some of the Americans complained about the noise. They said they could hear us talking through the windows. Well, this caused me a lot of shame. At my age, I don't have the need for people to scold me."

After that incident, Archuleta stopped meeting with other workers in the yard, her principal source of outside company being her son and his family who visited on Sundays—Archuleta's day off. Mrs. Sara's daughters, however, often neglected to visit on Sundays. During the six months in which I interviewed Archuleta, her employers were absent a total of thirteen Sundays, more than half of all the Sundays for which I was present.

When asked how she felt about her job, Archuleta said she had forged a strong relationship with and felt responsible for her ward. Because taking care of elderly people was respected in her Mexican community, and because she understood how important it would be to be cared for at the end of life, Archuleta felt she had a job with value. She compared this work to the fast-food restaurant, saying that there "everything was about moving quickly," and here "everything is about patience." She recognized that she was uniquely skilled, not only because of her past experience but also because she had gained the trust of her ward. She once said, "What I do is not just anything."

The job also meant future independence for her. She wanted to live in Mexico without having to rely on her children, as she understood how financially difficult it was to raise a family. Thus, every month she saved most of her earnings. Reflecting on different problematic aspects of the job, she said, "I am not complaining, you understand. For a woman my age it is difficult to find job that has some dignity. I think that this job gives me dignity because no one is looking down at me. What does sadden me, though, is that the only person who can know what I do, does not understand anymore."

Conclusion

Global economic restructuring is linked not only to the international migration of people from south to north but also to the reshaping of social reproduction. As the organization of production has changed, so has the organization of social reproduction. In First World countries more and different types of housework can be bought on the market, including the privatized labor of immigrant women. The contours of the domestic-labor market, however, are not everywhere the same. The domestic-labor market is also uniquely shaped by economic structures and history at the local level. In Santa Barbara increasing wealth polarization, the aging of the population, and the feminization of the waged labor force have created a demand for domestic workers among a broader class of employers at different stages of the life-cycle. These employers hire a diverse group of Mexicanas to undertake a multiplicity of domestic work forms—some unique to the contemporary period. These multiple forms are part of a "new" domestic labor.

The new domestic labor is characterized by co-evolving opportunities for pain and promise. As the life histories of Guadalupe Nora and Consuelo Archuleta demonstrate, employment is polarized with housecleaners on one end and human-care workers on the other. Within human care, elder care, and adult-convalescent care are new areas of employment for immigrant women. The labor process and skills required from workers in each of the two categories are qualitatively distinct, as are the material rewards. The wages made by Nora, a labor contractor, are the highest found among fifty workers in this study. Archuleta, an elder-care provider who is the actual and proximate person responsible for her ward seven days a week, twenty-four hours a day, earns the lowest wages. This is due in part to the fact that emotional and physical labors, which are a fundamental aspect of human care, are devalued as unskilled, easy, and "natural."

Mexicanas' choice of jobs within this polarized labor market depends in great part on their social location. Women with access to broader social networks in the city and who are in earlier stages of the life-cycle, often find other work as soon as possible or stay out of human care altogether. Many Mexicanas who undertake human care do so because they have few other employment options. Human-care work, and particularly elder care, leaves its mark on the body and mind: there is both the psychic pain which accompanies feelings of compassion as well as physical afflictions which arise from lifting and holding adult wards. Nonetheless, in contrast to the generalized devaluation of emotional and physical labors manifest in the wider society, some Mexicanas speak about finding dignity and meaning in this work. While more research among human-care providers, especially elder-care workers, is necessary, life histories suggest that in the region's evolving culture of care, Mexicanas are at the center.

Notes

1 In describing immigrants who are in the United States without legal documentation, immigration scholars often use the term *undocumented*, rather than the term *illegal*, in order to avoid negative characterization of individuals.

2 Among the many ethnic labels used to describe persons of Mexican origin in the United States, none is unanimously regarded as the "most correct" (see de la Torre and Pesquera 1993). The terms *Mexicana* and *Mexicano* herein refers to female and male

immigrants from Mexico; *Chicana* and *Chicano* refer to women and men of Mexican descent residing in the United States; *Latina* refers to women of Latin American descent.

3 These include Biola (1992), Childress (1986), Clarke-Lewis (1994), Colen and Sanjek (1990), Coley (1981), Cott (1992), Dill (1994a), Dudden (1983), Jones (1985), Martin and Segrave (1985), Palmer (1984, 1989), Sólorzano-Torres (1987), Sutherland (1981), Tucker (1994), and Van Raaphorst (1988). Because I am arguing that there is a new domestic labor in the United States, here I focus only on the U.S. waged domestic labor literature. There is an extensive literature for Mexico, and Latin America in general, as well as a growing literature for Africa and Asia that I do not address here (see, for example, Arizpe 1994; Chaney and Castro 1989; Cock 1980; Constable 1997). Moreover, while the references I have cited represent the bulk of the U.S. academic literature focusing on household work, not all is represented here. Some other important sources which I have not cited are historical studies which, while not focusing exclusively on domestic workers, do note the presence of Mexicana household workers (see, for example, Deutsch 1987; Sanchez 1985; Gónzalez 1985; García 1981).

4 For studies that focus on immigrant and other minority women who fulfill the demand for cleaning services in middle-class households, see Chang 1994; Mary Romero 1992; Ruiz 1987; Salzinger 1991; Sólorzano-Torres 1988. For those that focus on the same phenomenon in upper-class households, see Hondagneu-Sotelo 1994; Nakano-Glenn 1986; Repak 1995; Rollins 1985.

5 For studies that focus on child-care providers in elite, white households, see Colen 1986, 1989, 1995; Wrigley 1995.

6 In California, Chinese and Japanese men also labored as domestics from the 1860s through 1910. Japanese men continued to labor as gardeners until 1930 (Cheng and Bonacich 1984).

7 For studies that examine immigrant work in childcare for upper-class households, see Brown 1994; Colen 1989; Repak 1995; Wrigley 1995. For studies that examine such work in middle-class households, see Mattingly 1997; Nathan 1991; Wrigley 1995. For studies that examine such work in working-class households, see Hondagneu-Sotelo and Avila 1997; Zlolniski 1998.

8 Interviews with other domestics suggest that this practice is commonplace and that in response some labor contractors regularly rotate their workers and prefer to hire monolingual Spanish speakers.

9 The Bracero Program was a formal agreement between the United States and Mexico wherein Mexico agreed to send temporary, legal agricultural workers to the United States. The program spanned the period 1942–1964.

"¡Aquí estamos y no nos vamos!"
Justice for Janitors in Los Angeles
and New Citizenship Claims
CYNTHIA CRANFORD

※ Employer-driven and state-supported strategies to gain flexibility through contract, temporary, and informal employment relationships has led to a growth in precarious jobs with low-pay, few benefits, little job security, and poor work conditions. This restructuring marks a break with the postwar compromise between labor and capital—the business unionism that exchanged a "family wage" and job security for loyalty and labor peace. It loudly announces the need to move beyond regulations of collective bargaining and strategies of collective action that came out of that compromise if labor and its allies are to challenge the current hegemony of flexibility. Restructuring has also made clear the problematic, narrow focus of business unionism on white, citizen, male industrial workers. This is nowhere more clear than in global cities, such as Los Angeles, which are characterized by a polarized economy with immigrant women, and some men, holding the most precarious jobs. Some unions have turned to new organizing strategies, replacing their view of immigrants and women as unorganizable with the hope that they will fuel a new labor movement.

The Justice for Janitors (JJ) campaign of the Service Employee's International Union (SEIU) local 1877 in Los Angeles County has been billed as the success story of "community unionism" and cast as a "mini-movement" that is revitalizing labor (Banks 1991; Lerner 1991).[1] In a seven-year period (1988–1995), JJ organized over 8,000 workers to bring roughly 80 percent of Los Angeles janitors under a master contract (Waldinger et al. 1998). Los Angeles janitors work for cleaning companies who in turn compete for short-term contracts with building owners. The janitors are immigrant women and men from Mexico, El Salvador, and Guatemala, and many are (or have been) undocumented with no legal right to live or work in the United States. Over half of janitors are women, many single, breadwinning mothers (Cranford 1998). The mix of economic restructuring and immigration calls for organizing in the neighborhoods and in the streets—which indeed has been fueled by the janitors. A message of social justice resonates with nonunion Latina/o immigrants, whose American dreams contrast sharply with their place in the city. Throughout the 1990s, as an antifamily politics of citizenship arose in response to immigrant settlement, that message mobilized union members to organize the unorganized. The Year 2000 campaign marked the movement of women members into union leadership alongside men. Various public actions surrounded this campaign, including janitors' entitlement claims, for themselves and for their children, based on the value of their work to the city—claims that have the potential to upset the gendered and racialized hegemony of flexibility that operates in the contemporary city.

The Hegemony of Flexibility and Oppositional Politics

Urban scholars, particularly those theorizing from Los Angeles, envision a new urban politics with immigrant workers at the center contesting their racialized place in the global city (Mike Davis 1987; Keil 1998; Sassen 1998). Although much urban theorizing has kept the public/private split intact, processes of gendering intersect with those of racialization to shape immigrant workers' place in the contemporary city (McDowell 1991; Sassen 1998; Elizabeth Wilson 1995, 209).

The term *flexibility* refers to flexible production (just-in-time, contract, temporary, triangular employment relationships), neoliberal state policies (privatization, structural adjustment), and a common-sense understanding of both flexible production and neoliberalism as inevitable and as progress (Bourdieu 1999; Harvey 1989). As such, employer flexibility marks the current state of hegemony. Processes of racialization and gendering are central to the maintenance of flexibility (Laclau and Mouffe 1985). The growth of part-time, temporary, and low-paid jobs—jobs traditionally held by women—has led to a gendering of the urban labor market that is downgrading the work of some men as well as women (Vosko 2000). The intersection of this gendering with racialization is clear in the most precarious "servicing" work, which is done primarily by immigrant women and some men (Glenn 1992). Saskia Sassen (1998) theorizes how this gendered and racialized downgrading is produced within the "service complex regime" that dominates global cities. The overvalorization of the corporate work of finance, marketing, design, and the like is made possible through a devalorization of servicing work of cleaning buildings, hotels, and homes, of preparing and serving food, and of assembling specialty goods for new urban professionals. Furthermore, overvalorized corporate work is done by white, citizen, professional men and some women, and devalorized servicing work is done by Latina/o and Asian immigrant women and some men. These power relations are also gendered through the ideological erasure of the value of this paid reproductive work to the global economy (Sassen 1998). The Los Angeles janitorial industry embodies this gendered and racialized flexibility. The owners of commercial real estate are primarily white. They produce the (over)valorization of the corporate sector by outsourcing cleaning work to companies who compete for short-term contracts. Cleaning companies remain competitive by hiring Latina/o immigrants, many of whom are undocumented (Cranford 1998). They pay these workers low wages with no benefits, violate worker protection laws, and wage strong campaigns against unions (Fisk, Mitchell, and Erickson 2000).

The reemergence of citizenship as a central axis of inequality also reflects intersecting processes of racialization and feminization in the contemporary city. The overvalorization of the corporate sector is bolstered by its ability to evade the social-reproduction costs of workers and their children. While employers gain flexibility through the use of contract, "undocumented," and other noncitizen labor, as states become facilitators of a privatized flexible market for employers, fewer legal citizens enjoy state-supported social welfare (Glenn 2000). These two reconstructions of citizenship come together in the recent California politics of immigration. Public concern in the 1980s focused on "illegals" taking the jobs of "natives," which prompted the 1986 Immigration Reform and Control Act (IRCA), which included fines for employers who hired the undocumented. In the 1990s California politicians and community groups, alarmed by the increasing settlement of nonwhite immigrants, organized to curtail supports for their social welfare through the populist proposition system; the movement reached its peak with California's Proposition 187, which sought to deny education, healthcare, and other social services to the U.S.-born children of undocumented immigrants. In 1998 Californians voted to end bilingual education through Proposition 227, coupling anxieties about English as the official language with an effort to evade the costs of educating immigrant children. This political discourse was both racist and misogynist, focusing on Latinas' bodies and racist notions of population control (Hondagneu-Sotelo 1995). For example, in his campaign for governor, Pete Wilson drew heavily on television images of women carrying children illegally across the U.S.-Mexico border. While the demand for immigrant women's labor increased with the growth of service economy, these images reproduced the idea of immigrant women as economic burdens. This antifamily politics feminized Latino men alongside women, obscuring the contradictions that arise from a society and economy dependent on devalued labor.

By constructing immigrant women and men as both cheap labor and economic burdens, urban economic and state restructuring makes space for the emergence of a new oppositional politics. Sassen theorizes urban "contested spaces" as outgrowths of the polarized "service complex regime" (Sassen 1996; Sassen 1998). The informalization that has accompanied subcontracting, (immigrant) network job recruitment, and limits to state-sponsored social welfare brings social relations from the community and the household into the city. This makes what one thinks of and experiences as *corporate* space actually *contested* space. Sassen's formulation is explicitly feminist and antiracist as she conceptualizes a site (the global city) and a mechanism (place-based claims) for the valorization of servicing work: "If place, that is, a certain type of place, is central in the global economy, we can posit a transnational economic and political opening in the formation of new claims and hence in the constitution of entitlements, notably rights to place, and more radically, in the constitution of 'citizenship'" (1998, xx).

One can theorize the emerging new unionism, as well as other movements calling for entitlements tied to place, as making space for a less-exclusive city. One can further suggest that challenging the hegemony of flexibility in the city will only follow from an oppositional politics aimed at unequal relations of gender and citizenship as well as class.

The oppositional politics of J4J is articulated through an immigrant familism that constructs immigrant rights "for the family" as synonymous with workers' rights. This unionism is also practiced as a family affair, which places immigrant women, children, and entire families (including single mother and extended) at the center. These interrelated aspects of J4J's public protests bring potential for disrupting the gendered and racialized processes bolstering the hegemony of flexibility.

Putting the Movement Back into Labor:
The Impetus for Community Unionism

It is now widely accepted that the necessary overhaul of labor law to protect the rights of primarily immigrant and women workers in the most precarious jobs will only follow a social movement.[2] As Richard Bensinger, director of the AFL-CIO Organizing Institute, commented, "At some point we in the labor movement have to contend with the fact that unions are virtually outlawed in this country and someday there's going to have to be a complete overhaul of labor law in this country. But that change—and change in legislation in general—follow the creation of a movement" (quoted in Labor Research Review 1991, 88). The Wagner model regulating collective bargaining, based on the experience of male industrial workers, limits the economic power and freedom-of-association rights of those working under temporary, contract, and other triangular employment relationships (Bronfenbrenner et al. 1998; Cobble 1994). A primary structural problem with the Wagner model is the definition of "bargaining unit," which is based on a single worksite and a single employer. The Wagner model also limits union-organizing strategies necessary to pressure the agent with economic power in triangular employment relationships. The law defines the client of a "direct employer" as a "neutral secondary employer" and prohibits "coercive" action, like picketing, against the latter and does not require the latter to bargain in good faith with workers. However, many "secondary employers" are not at all neutral; witness the power the garment retailer has over competing sewing contractors (Bonacich 2000). The law also gives employers great leeway to oppose unionization by allowing "technical refusals to bargain" and appeals of labor-board decisions all the way to the federal courts (Fisk, Mitchell, and Erickson 2000). Employers have developed an industry of lawyers to pursue their appeals and of management consultants to prevent unionization. Hindering workers from forming a union is an illegal unfair labor practice; unfair-labor-practice charges against employers increased in the 1980s and 1990s (Freeman 1985; Compa 2000). U.S. unions won less than half of union elections in 1990. Furthermore, due to persistent employer appeals, even when a majority of workers voted for the union only one-third resulted in collective-bargaining agreements (Crump 1991, 33).

Several unions have begun to organize outside the Wagner model. Some have turned to noncontract organizing in an effort to make contact with workers and move toward union representation, including the community-based workers' centers and associations of garment and domestic workers (Bonacich 2000; Hondagneu-Sotelo and Riegos 1997). The SEIU, Hotel Employees and Restaurant Employees Union, and other unions continue to seek a union contract by pressuring both direct and secondary employers to remain "neutral" during organizing drives and to accept the union if a majority of workers signs cards in favor. They then seek to link the direct employer to the secondary employer through public pressure brought by a social movement. This pressure requires active participation of both the unorganized and union members and a broad mobilization of community support. Organizing outside the law is expensive and time consuming, which dissuades many unions

(Sherman and Voss 2000). Nevertheless, the probability of winning and signing a contract is increased when unions build a broad movement around the organizing (Bronfenbrenner et al. 1998). In short, the current debate within the United States is not whether labor should organize despite the law, but how.

Organizing Justice for Janitors in Los Angeles

The traditional (Wagner) model of collective bargaining makes extending freedom-of-association rights to janitors very difficult. If the (generally not more than fifteen) workers at one building voted for the union, the cleaning company would pass on the higher costs to the building owner, who would not be required to bargain in good faith but could instead contract with a less-expensive, nonunion company. To organize in this situation, J4J must take wages out of competition by organizing nonunion companies in an entire market. This strategy is also meant to ensure a first contract through the demonstration of union power through collective action. While in other regions J4J organized entire cities, it could not do so in a sprawling metropolis like Los Angeles. It was necessary to split the metropolis into "mini-cities" of concentrated commercial real estate, such as Century City. Beginning in 1988, the movement moved from mini-city to mini-city, pressuring cleaning contractors to accept the union based on the card-check method and pressing building owners to use union contractors through mass public action (Waldinger et al. 1998). One could not attend a J4J action or meeting without hearing the maxim "It's in the streets where we win." By protesting in the streets, janitors sought to put pressure on the building owners to take responsibility for their work conditions. Their ability to do so rested on the simultaneous use of three strategies: legal action, direct action, and symbolic action.

Two forms of legal action are central to the corporate campaigns of J4J. First, J4J files suits against nonunion cleaning companies for violating labor standards, such as wage and hour and occupational-health-and-safety regulations, and for sexual harassment and other discrimination. These suits can cost the cleaning contractors thousands of dollars, pressuring the larger companies to negotiate and driving the smaller ones out of business. Second, J4J files unfair-labor-practice suits with the National Labor Relations Board for employer interference with workers' rights to organize. Many janitors told me how employers' illegal acts led them to initially reject the union. One Mexicana, Concepción, described the worker surveillance that occurred: "When the people from the union would come, the supervisors would always stay and listen. So many people, when they had something to say, they didn't say it, because the supervisors were listening. And then they would grab the workers afterward."

Workers also described how anti-union campaigns drew on workers' precarious citizenship status, a practice not uncommon in other industries (Compa 2000). When IRCA was passed, bringing employer sanctions for hiring undocumented workers, Enrique, a young Mexicano, was working for a nonunion company. His supervisor called the workers into her office and placed all their Social Security cards in two piles: a pile for fake cards and a pile for real ones. She told them that it was illegal for them to be working but agreed to allow them to "get new cards" and come back to work. Despite the fear produced through anti-union campaigns, many of the people in J4J actions were undocumented. Their fear was overcome through a long process of building relationships in the community, which created a "culture of solidarity" (see Fantasia 1988). Of particular importance was connecting union members to nonunion workers to ensure that unionism began before official representation and continued well after it. As a result, many "anti-union" workers became active union members and helped to organize the unorganized in order to win better contracts for themselves (Cranford 2001).

One journalist noted the importance of legal action by calling it J4J's "hard currency" (Gardetta 1993, 19). However, the currency of legal action requires linking it to the building owner. While unfair-labor-practice suits allow the union to picket the cleaning company, they cannot target the building owner because such "dangerous speech" directed at a "neutral secondary employer" is outlawed. Connecting violations of labor standards and collective-bargaining law to the building owner requires combining legal action with direct action. J4J relies on a Supreme Court decision in the DeBartolo case[3] that found that free-speech rights override the National Labor Relations Act as long as the union uses "non-coercive" tactics. While the act defines picketing as "coercive," leafleting or holding rallies in public space are protected by freedom of speech (Fisk, Mitchell, and Erickson 2000). J4J actors not only occupy the public spaces of the city—the streets, intersections, and sidewalks—but also transgress onto the private property that increasingly dominates the global city. Theoretically, these escalating tactics bring servicing work into the "corporate spaces of power," opening up the hegemony of flexibility to contestation (Sassen 1998). In the language of the janitors, taking to the streets (*saliendo a las calles*) produces enough racket (*bulla*) or enough disorder (*escándalo*) to pressure building owners to take some responsibility. Reflecting on the invisibility of the work that janitors do, a longtime Salvadoran worker-activist, Lupe, spoke of the necessity of direct action, regardless of the dangers involved: "If we do not go public, who is going to know us? It's necessary that we take the struggle into the streets, and what happens happens. Without risk, there is no action, nor recognition."

In order to build support and assert moral pressure, J4J combines legal and direct action with a set of tactics akin to what Bourdieu (1999) calls "symbolic action." Symbolic action is a set of discursive "acts of resistance" meant to disrupt taken-for-granted ideas such as flexibility. Central to the concept of symbolic action is the necessity of bringing the social into the solely economic arguments of neoliberalism. The janitors' symbolic action presents unionism as an issue of social justice "for the family" using the media, flyers, street theater, and other symbolism. In public statements, primarily through the press, women janitors link wage earning to mothering, thus making visible the costs of the social reproduction of workers and their children. For example, Elena, a Mexicana janitor, emphasized the moral currency of immigrant familism: "It's necessary that we're publicly against the building owners because it is our manner of communication. In addition, it's good when the building owners, the contractors, and the press see the children at the marches."

Similarly, Eliseo Medina, the Mexicano vice-president of the SEIU, also drew on immigrant familism to mobilize janitors during a rally, saying, "Brothers and sisters, most of us came to this country for a better future for our families and for our children. And no owner or contractor is going to take this dream away from us." In short, immigrant familism is not merely a framing strategy used to garner sympathy and support, although it works to do so. It is part of an oppositional politics shaped by the antifamily politics of citizenship that janitors experience daily at work and in urban public spaces.

Symbolic action used jointly with legal and direct action can effectively target the building owner. Speeches made in public spaces or to the press, text on flyers, street theater, or other symbolism is more likely to be interpreted by the courts as free speech rather than threatening speech. For example, each year around Thanksgiving J4J holds an action featuring someone dressed up like a giant turkey, who gives a building owner and its cleaning contractor the Turkey of the Year award. One year the event included a sit-in Thanksgiving dinner. Flyers and speeches often refer to pending investigations or citations of labor-law violations, effectively linking legal action against the cleaning company to the building owner. The employers might appeal an unfair-labor-practice claim, yet through symbolic action the moral currency of the claim remains.

Combining direct action and symbolic action able to target the building owners, with legal action against the cleaning contractor, J4J actors link the poor working conditions of nonunion janitors, the cleaning contractor that oversees them, and the building owner that ultimately manufactures them. While the effect of this action might wane if employers successfully challenge J4J tactics in court (Fisk, Mitchell, and Erickson 2000), the movement is significant because it can upset the hegemony of flexibility.

The Year 2000 Campaign: Protect, Advance, and Grow "For the Family"

The potential for J4J to contest the gendered and racialized underpinnings of the flexible city could be seen clearly in the Year 2000 campaign. From the beginning of J4J organizing, the grassroots work was accomplished as a "family affair" that placed women, children, and entire families at the center. However, not until the Year 2000 campaign did women move in significant number into leadership positions alongside men. The promotion of staff with feminist politics to top positions ensured that both women and men janitors would sit on the newly formed committees that strategized, implemented, and spoke for the Year 2000 campaign. Women's leadership alongside men bolstered the janitors' entitlement claims to healthcare and living wages for the family.

The campaign sought to increase the power of the union through growth from new organizing in order to protect union buildings from going nonunion and to advance wages and benefits for union janitors in the new contract. The central focus on healthcare was shaped by a set of compromises in the previous (1995–2000) union contract. The 1995–2000 contract brought newly organized suburban janitors under the same contract with longtime union members in the urban core on the condition that the former would initially accept lower wages and fewer benefits. Over the life of the contract, janitors in the suburbs, where there was higher nonunion competition, would receive benefits and significant wage increases each year so that by the end of the contract janitors across the metropolis would be closer to parity. This set of compromises would result in what janitors called the *golpe* (blow) in January 2000, when suburban janitors would receive 40-cent-per-hour raises, and family health insurance (costing roughly $2 per hour per janitor), only three months before the expiration of the union contract. When cleaning contractors passed on these costs to building owners, the incentive for the building owner to switch to a nonunion cleaning company would be very high. If buildings were to go nonunion, the power of unionized janitors at the bargaining table would be reduced.

In order to pressure building owners to make sure that the janitors who cleaned their building had family health insurance and living wages, the

Table. Union Leadership Positions by Gender (1999)

Position	Women	Men	Women (%)
Executive Board[a]	5	6	45
Shop Stewards[a]	124	168	42
Committees:			
Year 2000	10	11	48
Organizing	14	17	45
Negotiating[a]	10	14	42
Leadership	4	7	36
Political	3	7	30

[a]Elected positions.

campaign began with organizing drives focused on building owners most likely to feel the "blow." Until organizing significant enough to exert economic pressure occurred, and due to the lack of legal responsibility under collective-bargaining law, the union would focus public attention on the building owner's moral responsibility not only to the janitors but also to the city. The janitors exerted moral pressure in part through the "Principles for a Responsible Commercial Real Estate Industry." The principles began with a list of "considerations" that stated, among other things, that over 5,000 janitors should receive family health insurance and living wages (by January 2000), which would bring thousands of dollars to the poorest neighborhoods and mitigate the healthcare crisis; that these benefits to the city could easily be lost because building owners were not required to maintain contracts with the union cleaning companies who provided them; that due to low vacancy rates that allowed building owners to demand high rents from tenants, ensuring benefits for janitors would only cost owners a penny for each rental dollar. Drawing on these propositions, the janitors called for three commitments from "owners of responsible buildings": (1) to ensure that janitors received family health insurance paid for by the cleaning company; (2) to provide the necessary funds to pay janitors wages above the poverty level; (3) to use union cleaning companies who could ensure that janitors were protected from violations of labor standards and thus treated with dignity and respect.

Within the racialized and gendered politics of immigration, this message not only challenged the flexible employment relationship but also contested its racialized and gendered underpinnings by constructing the servicing work of immigrant janitors as valuable to the city. In the janitors' message, the building owner was the "public charge" gaining profit by forcing janitors to depend on (poor quality) public health and other services.

"¡Aqui estamos y no nos vamos!"
(We're here and we are not leaving!)

An ethnographic look at the public protests surrounding the organizing drives illustrates how janitors upset the hegemony of the flexible city and its racialized and gendered underpinnings. This occurs at three, related levels. First, at the level of a given building, janitors transform corporate spaces into contested spaces by transgressing onto private property using the complex of direct, symbolic, and legal action. At the second level, janitors occupy the public spaces of a given mini-city, which, together with the first action, challenges the city as a site solely for flexible production. Furthermore, the presence of women and children in such actions contests the representation of the city as exclusively Euro-masculine and corporate by bringing the work of social reproduction into the city and explicitly linking it to production. However, in order to pressure the building owner into taking some responsibility for the workers and their children, janitors must engage in a third level of action: they must mobilize a broad base of community and political allies by constructing unionism as an issue of social justice.

A series of actions surrounding one of the buildings targeted for organizing illustrate how these three levels of action allow janitors to also target the building owner. The building had recently canceled its contract with a union cleaning company, throwing the union janitors out of work, then contracted with a nonunion company that brought in new workers. At the time, union janitors were about to receive full family health insurance. The protestors heightened their ability to provoke a response from the building owner by a creative use of the design and location of the building. The building was located in a suburban neighborhood across a narrow street from apartments. Like most central business districts, the neighborhood was primarily middle class and Euro-American, contrasting sharply with the Latina/o immigrant protesters and their Spanish chants. In addition to place, time marked the corporate culture of the city, so in their public protests janitors emerged from the invisible nightshift and inserted themselves into the perceptions of the building's tenants and customers on their lunch hour, thus transforming corporate space into contested space.

The janitors' practices of protest were exemplified in an action taken by fifty workers (twenty-nine of whom were women), seven children, and several union staffers. Collecting our picket signs, which declared "Unfair Labor Practice" against the cleaning company, we began with a simple line on the thin public sidewalk. In less than five minutes, however, we walked closer to the glass-door entrance. As we passed by the doorways, janitors whistled, hit their palms against the picket signs, and shook their seed-filled coke cans. A few times a male worker opened the door for tenants to go in, and longtime union member Berta Barros, alongside others, added a louder intonation to her chanting, projecting Spanish into the corporate lobby. After about twenty minutes, we moved to the public spaces surrounding the building. As the stoplight turned green for the oncoming traffic, union members Bernice and Oscar and union staffers stood between the traffic and the rest of us to keep the cars at bay. When I remarked to Cecelia, a nonunion worker, about the closeness of the apartment buildings, she explained that after the last action, residents complained to the building owner.

Repeated occupation of the public spaces surrounding this building and transgression into the private space closest to the entrance during several demonstrations elicited a response from the building owner. During another protest, he stormed in and out of the building several times, walked across the street to talk to the police, and made several calls on a cell phone. During the subsequent rally on the "private" planters, the lead organizer referred to the building owner's frantic appearance and told the janitors that the owner was upset to see so many Latinos in front of his building during the daytime, when the tenants were present. "We need to give him a clear message that 'we are here and we are not leaving!'" (¡aqui estamos y no nos vamos!). It is significant that the organizer used this popular immigrant-rights slogan. Declared during both protests that called for an amnesty for undocumented workers in the 1980s and protests against Proposition 187 in the 1990s, this maxim laid claim to a space that one was denied a right to inhabit. Using this slogan was therefore a powerful way to focus the struggle on the racialized power relations that structured the building-services industry. Conceptually, it constituted an entitlement claim to the city and its resources by undocumented immigrant women, men, and children. These claims were based not on a legal form of citizenship but on the value of the janitors' work to the city.

The construction of the labor dispute as an issue of social justice and immigrant rights was strengthened through speeches from janitors and community supporters at this and subsequent rallies. For example, a woman janitor spoke about how she was laid off when the building owner contracted with the nonunion company and professed that she was "fighting so that all workers have benefits and good wages." A second woman, a longtime union activist, articulated the crux of the campaign message when she challenged janitors to "continue on in the streets" in order to organize the nonunion competition and thus win a better union contract. And a male member of the organizing committee gave a specific report about how he had visited the (now nonunion) workers in the building to encourage them to organize. Finally a Euro-American man from the neighborhood committed the support of his community group. The mobilization of political and community support, and the additional pressure on the building owner this brought, was most visible during the strike.

"Que limpien los ricos. ¡Estamos en huegla!"
(Let the rich clean. We're on strike!)

The Year 2000 campaign culminated in a three-week, citywide strike prompted by a breakdown in negotiations for a new union contract. Spanish-language newspapers printed the common saying during the strike: "Que limpien los ricos. ¡Estamos en huegla!" Because employers can permanently replace economic strikers under U.S. labor law, most strikes throughout the 1980s and 1990s required a significant mobilization of community and political support (Breecher and Costello 1990). The pressure of a social movement during this strike was even more important due to the triangular employment relationship.

The union asked for full family health insurance and yearly $1 per-hour raises for janitors across the metropolis. The contractors offered a first-year fifty-cent raise to janitors in the highly unionized urban core but wanted to freeze the wages of janitors in the less-unionized suburban areas. The contractors argued that since the janitors in the suburban areas had received family health insurance and a forty-cent raise, additional wage increases would cause building owners to contract with one of the many nonunion competitors. Furthermore, the Building Owners and Managers' Association argued that they had no part in the negotiations between janitors and cleaning contractors. In the words of a Salvadoran member of the Year 2000 committee, Magdalena, "The rich old men [were] very tough." Through extensive popular education, passed down from committee leaders to shop stewards to janitors in the buildings, janitors understood the power of the building owner; indeed, many had created a racket for building owners with nonunion accounts in the public protests. Winning a new contract required continuing this movement during the contract fight.

In public action janitors and their supporters constructed the strike as a deserving claim to some of the city's enormous wealth. The day after the initial walk-out, over 3,000 janitors and supporters marched in the streets of downtown, occupied the business district, and held a brief sit-in at a busy intersection. Short-lived occupations of intersections and blockades of freeway entrances and exits were combined with drawn-out acts of civil disobedience that led to arrests. Making the racialized inequality of wealth clearly visible, 400 mainly Latino janitors, their children, and supporters in their bright red "on-strike" T-shirts briefly sat down in an intersection in the shopping district of the wealthiest mini-city, Beverly Hills. Janitors led an all day "pilgrimage" from the immigrant neighborhoods of central Los Angeles to the wealthy west side of the city.

The janitors' months of mobilizing work meant that other unions, religious leaders, local politicians, and community supporters would join them in the streets. The Los Angeles Federation of Labor urged other unions to join picket lines, and the Teamsters refused to deliver packages or pick up trash from striking buildings. Moral pressure and the focus on social justice were bolstered by the support of religious clergy and laity. In a clear effort to draw on the moral currency of religion, janitors ended their procession with a Catholic Mass wherein Cardinal Mahoney called on building owners to become involved in negotiations. In a second, Palm Sunday Mass, Bishop Zavala blessed the "implements of work and labor," that is, the broom and the mop that appear on most J4J shirts and picket signs (Cleeland and Rabin 2000). This symbolic action was a powerful way to value the work of the janitors. During Passover, Rabbi Jacobs compared the janitors' struggle to the Jews' exodus from Egypt and led them in a Seder meal in front of the headquarters of a large firm that owns buildings across the city. The janitors recited their own ten "plagues," including unsafe working conditions, anti-immigrant sentiment, poor housing, lack of healthcare, and poverty wages (Haynes 2000). The support of local politicians was strong throughout the strike, a reflection of the grassroots political organizing, for pro-immigrant politicians and against the anti-immigrant initiatives, of this union local. The city council passed a resolution urging building owners to intervene and prevent a strike. As janitors marched to county offices, blocking the downtown exits of a major freeway on the way, the county supervisors also passed a resolution in support. Several politicians participated in an act of civil disobedience in which more than forty people participated. The state assembly representative Cedillo constructed the demonstration in the following way for the press: "This is a massive demonstration for social justice for all men and women workers in the city" (Linares 2000).

Through this alliance of labor, religious, and political support, janitors were able to focus attention on the building owners and pressure them to take some part in negotiations. By the third week of the strike, Cardinal Mahoney, key county and city politicians, and Mayor Riorden organized a meeting with some building owners, prompting them to call the contractors back to the table.

Toward New Citizenship Claims

The broader significance of the alliance of labor with religious leaders and politicians during the strike was widely recognized. As a journalist said of the rally that concluded the strike, "With a county supervisor holding a mop, a state assemblyman holding a broom and a prominent downtown building owner donning a strike cap, the scene was a reminder of how much the political and economic landscape has changed in recent years" (Cleeland 2000). It was part of an emerging coalition of immigrant workers, union leaders, and progressive members of the Democratic Party in California. Through this alliance, public acts of protest and the building of political support for organizing and contract campaigns were combined with grassroots organizing for pro-labor and pro-immigrant candidates and issues. And through this alliance, janitors called for entitlement to the benefits of the city tied to residency as immigrant workers and the value of their work to the city.

Drawing on the events during the strike, politicians highlighted the significance of the janitors' political action, as immigrants, in and for the city. At the rally celebrating the end of the strike, Antonio Villaraigosa, former speaker of the California State Assembly, linked the janitors' political action more concretely to the polarized global city: "The immigrants have clearly shown that they are determined to look for justice, and that the wealth is shared" (Támara 2000, A1). A city council representative for the San Fernando Valley, Alex Padilla, highlighted the "lesson" janitors had taught the rest of the city through their strike: "The janitors have given us a lesson in political and economic education on how to struggle for equality in this country" (Támara 2000, A6). Both of these politicians, and several others, were elected through the grassroots precinct walking of janitors, hotel, and restaurant workers (of HERE local 11) and other Latina/o union members.

Throughout U.S. history, it has been residents without full benefits of citizenship, and often immigrants within unions, who have brought lessons on social, economic, and political equality to the broader citizenry (Glenn 2000). Like immigrants of previous generations, Latina/o immigrants today teach that the fulfillment of "American dreams" requires struggle. While leftists—among both academics and activists—have largely written off the progressive potential of the Democratic Party (Breecher and Costello 1996), as happened during the Congress of Industrial Organizations' organizing efforts in the late 1930 and early 1940s, the struggle involves linking unionism to electoral politics. Mexicana union activist Delia articulated the context of this contemporary struggle well during a union meeting mobilizing her fellow janitors to help gain political support for the Year 2000 campaign: "The building owners all the way to the politicians know that we are contributing to the country. But they treat us as if we're robbing it. If we want to be a human being equal to all, we have to participate in this country. We all make up the country. So we all have to give our opinions."

One key difference between today and earlier eras, however, is the fact that many of these workers are undocumented. Women, alongside men, are engaging in political practice not as legal residents but as workers. As Bernice, a Salvadoran member of the union's political organizing committee, stated, "Even though we cannot vote, we can collaborate with others to help our community." Salvadoreña Magdalena also stressed that unions must connect their members who cannot vote to "the group of elected leaders who make the decisions." Through this connection, Magdalena imagined a more inclusive citizenship that would be tied to residency: "We say we are against the propositions that are bad for the community. All of us are in this country and working to produce it. We also have the right to give our opinion. Not only as a member of the union but as a person that is in this country, because we are part of the community. It shouldn't matter if one is a citizen or not in terms of the rights one has in this country. Or if one is undocumented one still should have one's rights."

Many women drew their citizenship claims from their new gendered responsibilities as immigrant breadwinning mothers. Dora, a Nicaraguan union member, spoke at length about how she became politically motivated by a combination of factors: that immigrants lack a political voice, that there is much racism, and that she is the main economic provider for her children. As she said, "There is much racism, maybe because one isn't a citizen with all her/his vote.... But, we say, we are in a free country, and with a free union, and we have the opportunity to express ourselves. I see that here the union is a great thing; it is helping the immigrants.... Even though I'm not a citizen, even though I still don't have my residency, I will fight for the same rights as a citizen.... I want to see if I can achieve something better for my children. I have children and that's why I've joined the union."

Similarly, Maria, a single mother of three, focused on her need to fight for her rights in order to fulfill her breadwinning responsibilities, which had spurred her migration from León Guanajuato: "We immigrants come here to work, nothing else. It's time they respect our work, because we are workers and we work well.... One thinks that because she is an immigrant she doesn't have any rights in this country. But I realized that this wasn't so. I realized that I had to fight for my rights."

One can think of the public protests, mobilization of political support, and grassroots political organizing as new practices of citizenship in response to the racialized and gendered polarization of wealth in the global city and to attempts to evade the social-reproduction costs of immigrant workers through the series of anti-immigrant initiatives in the 1990s. Through these new practices of citizenship, janitors and other immigrant union members are claiming new "rights to place" for themselves and their children as resident workers at the urban level.

Implications and Concluding Thoughts

Through picket lines and demonstrations, bodied by union members and nonunion janitors, and through widespread community and political support, Los Angeles janitors pressured the building owners to take some responsibility for the social welfare of their workers and their workers' children. The janitors realized some organizing gains when a key real-estate investment trust that owned several buildings switched to a union contractor. In addition, due to the ability of the janitors and their allies to make the strike an issue of social justice for the city, building owners played some role in contract negotiations. The new contract was a significant step toward bringing a living wage and a better standard of living to janitors across the city: all janitors received family health insurance in a new contract, and by 2003 the wage gap between urban and suburban janitors was much smaller, with a minimum wage of $9.70 per hour for urban janitors and $8.05 for suburban workers.

The community unionism of Justice for Janitors opened up to contestation the gendered and racialized hegemony of flexibility operating in the contemporary city. It took significant steps toward directing responsibility for the terms of employment to those who had the economic power to determine them. Transgressing into private spaces and occupying public ones, women and children, alongside men, became political actors contesting the representation of the city as exclusively Euro-masculine and corporate. Through the mobilization of political and community support, janitors broadened their entitlement claims for the family into an issue of social justice for the city at large. In doing so, they were able to emphasize the worth of their service work in the city, convince key politicians of its value, and claim some of that value in a new union contract. Within a politics of citizenship that represented Latina/o immigrant women, children, and men as economic burdens, making visible the benefits building owners received from janitors' labor, then claiming social welfare benefits as tied to the value of their work in the city, upset relations of gender where they intersected with relations of citizenship and class. Janitors and their allies offered a solution to the fiscal crisis of the state that presented building owners, rather than immigrant families, as the dependents: it was the owners who were perpetuating the healthcare crisis, income inequality and hostile race relations in the city. In this way, the political activism of the janitors moved the community toward a more inclusive citizenship that could have implications for other immigrant, or nonimmigrant, workers as well. Drawing on their interrelated political practices of unionism and grassroots involvement in electoral politics, immigrant janitors pushed the community to envision a citizenship based on residency, political participation, and work, at the level of the urban.

Nevertheless, certain structural factors complicate this optimistic account. First, protecting these gains requires continual movement, which might be difficult to sustain. After the 1995 contract fight, the lack of attention and funds for servicing the membership resulted in organized resistance to new organizing, led by the relatively privileged janitors in the urban core; this internal politics ultimately led the international to put the local into trusteeship. The events examined herein are signs of a move toward a more democratic mass movement. They are the result of the entrance of more women into leadership alongside men, extensive training and education for shop stewards, and strong efforts to link members and non-union janitors (Cranford 2001). However, whether the janitors' local avoids the age-old problem of bureaucratization remains to be seen. Second, despite the entrance of women into leadership, the janitors' local has not sufficiently addressed "women's issues," which is unlike many women-dominated locals but similar to locals representing low-wage immigrant women and men. Organizing as a family affair works well in the mass demonstrations where children are valued actors, but if women's leadership is to be supported and sustained, the union must address formal childcare in the local and in bargaining. These difficulties are not insurmountable. J4J and other islands of community unionism are creating the movement necessary to propel reform of state and union regulations and practices. Only with such structural change can labor and their allies ensure collective-bargaining rights for immigrant women and men in precarious jobs and thus posit an alternative to racialized and gendered flexibility in the contemporary city.

Notes

Thanks to Rob Wilton for intellectually stimulating discussions, which helped me to develop these ideas. Thanks also to Pierrette Hondagneu-Sotelo for helpful comments on previous drafts.

1 This research is based on ethnographic fieldwork from September 1997 to April 2000. Data are drawn from in-depth interviews and participant observation. I conducted thirty-five in-depth interviews with women janitors through the snowball sampling method. I interviewed six key union staffwomen. I also engaged in numerous informal conversations with both women and men janitors and staff. These informal conversations as well as my observations were recorded in field notes. I participated in training sessions, strategy meetings, demonstrations, organizing drives, and social events. I also worked as a janitor for two months.
2 This section, "Putting the Movement Back into Labor," builds upon Cranford 2004.
3 See Edward J. DeBartolo Corp. v. NLRB, 463 U.S. 147 (1983).

FAMILY FORMATIONS AND TRANSNATIONAL SOCIAL NETWORKS

PART 4

Transborder Families and Gendered
Trajectories of Migration and Work

NORMA OJEDA DE LA PEÑA

✳ The U.S.-Mexico border is a site where internal and international migration processes converge. Despite the border's significance, there is little research on the effects of migration on the social reproduction in the region. Nevertheless, migration and transmigration strongly influence the formation and reproduction of transborder families in Tijuana, Baja California. Transmigration refers to two simultaneous processes: internal and international migration, as well as their convergence into a unique crossing zone where significant numbers of migrants help shape the local, social, and demographic environment. Reliable research is difficult, however, given the nonsystematic formulations of what has been identified as transmigration vis-à-vis the ever-changing conditions and characteristics of the border population. In addition to the lack of reliable information, there is inadequate theorizing on the social consequences of migration and, in particular, of transmigration in this region of the country.[1]

Transmigration is closely linked to other population movements across the U.S.-Mexico border. Migratory histories indicate passages of U.S.-born residents to Mexico as well as Mexican citizens to the United States. Moreover, international migrants often move internally to each respective country's border area. Transmigration also takes place between the native border populations that, without necessarily changing their residence, maintain close contact with the other country through a wide variety of practices. The daily character of these population movements permits one to consider transmigration as a characteristic sui generis of the sociodemographic dynamics of the border region. Daily transmigration includes commuters who reside in one country but frequently travel to the neighboring country to work. Other transborder activities include education, tourism, shopping, entertainment, and other diverse services. Perhaps one of the most important reasons for transmigration is to visit family and friends who live "on the other side."

Daily contact between the populations of both countries has facilitated the development of unique social formations, one of the most significant being the transborder family, wherein members of conjugal, nuclear, or extended families reside in cities on both sides of the border. Transborder families are also caught up in the larger phenomenon of international migration, in that they join the migrant stream toward the United States yet also participate in daily activities to maintain familial relationships on either side of the border.

Because of the social, economic, and demographic heterogeneity of the border, the intensity of these relationships varies between different border cities, but in Tijuana and San Diego, the connection between transmigration and international migration is fundamental to understanding the processes of formation and reproduction of transborder families.[2]

Methodology

To assess the effects of migration and transborder employment on the social reproduction of the border population—and, specifically, their importance in the formation of transborder families and how they are initially constructed—I utilize a life-course analysis of conjugal couples who resided in Tijuana at the time of their interviews. That is, I undertake a retrospective study of women's and men's experiences from their first migration to the conclusion of the study.

Examining the process of formation and reproduction of transborder families is a complicated enterprise. As a means of accessing the complexity of their domestic lives, I employ a method that reconstructs the creation and maintenance of the transborder families among my sample. To reveal the nature of such families, I examine the relationship between the migratory and work trajectories of men and women, specifically with regard to the timing of migration and work on changing economic opportunities and how families reshape to accommodate their needs.

My analysis is based on thirty-eight life histories drawn from twenty-three transborder families that I interviewed in 1991 in Tijuana.[3] I selected these couples after reviewing the frequency and variety of their transborder relationships and determining that their families had the highest levels of characteristics associated with transborderization, including study and/or work in the United States, frequent visits with relatives living nearby in the United States, having children born in the United States, and living or having lived in the United States. As is also typical of transborder families, the majority of the couples had formed a conjugal union for at least ten years, independent of their legal condition or stability.

Strictly speaking, the definition of the transborder status of families should be based on the respective characteristics of all of its members. For the purposes of the present study and in light of the methodological complexity that the joint analysis of the histories of all the family members implies, only the couples that formed conjugal unions were chosen for analysis in the study. Consistent with my findings in an earlier study (Ojeda de la Peña 1990), the work status of the male head of household ultimately determined whether or not the family unit was a transborder family.

As a case study, these findings cannot be generalized to all families living in the U.S.-Mexico border region. However, as part of a larger longitudinal examination on migration, work, and family, this research provides a nuanced portrait of processes that influenced couples to form transborder families in relation to their respective trajectories of migration and work. Quotations from interviews with two subjects—a married man and woman—illustrate the thinking among transborder families.

Life Course and Transborder Families

The life-course perspective has been assessed as an appropriate analytical tool for the study of individuals and families over time, be it within the limits of a single generation or across the historical context defined by successive generations (Elder 1985). From this point of view, the family is not a static social agent; rather, it comprises a dynamic unit that changes over the life course of its members. The family is thus a unit of mutually contingent life trajectories and individuals who adapt over time (Hareven 1977).

Using the life-course framework, the family as a unit of analysis facilitates a focus on individuals. Due to the constant shift of a family's composition and structure over time, a life-course study is useful in demonstrating important structural and behavioral changes. Using the individual as the unit of analysis does not necessarily mean an interest in the individual per se but rather in how the individual's distinct trajectories contribute to an understanding of family dynamics. Modifications in family structure can often occur as individuals respond to and redirect economic need according to social priorities. A life-course analysis highlights the synchronization of individual life trajectories in the formation of the family unit and the changes that it experiences over time. Thus, it is analytically advantageous to consider interactive events in the processes of family transition derived from distinct trajectories of the life course of individuals—of work, migration, education, and so on—with the life trajectory of the entire family unit. This focus accomplishes a historical study of families and of the changes that take place in family transitions according to reflexive accounts of individual life trajectories.

In this study, the focus on the life course allows the analytic flexibility necessary to examine the role of conjugal couple members in determining the transborder condition of the family units. This perspective illuminates the relationship between the formation of transborder families and the migratory and labor trajectories of the men and women in these families.

Typology of Transborder Homes

Transborder families hold an important place in the family structure of the northern Mexico border because they are historically linked to the origins of the boundary between Mexico and the United States (Piñera Ramirez 1985). Likewise, this type of family is the expression of a more contemporary phenomenon that is reproduced by means of various social practices that ensure the reproduction of some families in the face of the unequal social and economic characteristics in the area (Anderson and De la Rosa 1990). Furthermore, transborder families are sustained by the international migratory tradition of Mexicans to the United States, which spans several generations and includes extensive family networks between both countries (Alvarez 1987). Transborder families of northern Mexico are family units that are transformed daily in the geographic-social space of the border, where two societies with significant economic and social differences are in distinct stages of demographic transition. In light of the demographic flux in this area, a systematic definition of transborder families is elusive.

One exception was a study that provided an integrated analysis of key variables, including the birthplace of different family members, residence, family relations, and work in the United States (Ojeda de la Peña 1990). In this study three categories of transborder homes were identified: (1) families with at least one member living in the United States; (2) families with at least one child born in the United States but currently residing in Tijuana; and (3) families with one member whose economic activity crossed the border. These are non–mutually exclusive categories. A single family may have characteristics that pertain to more than one category, as in the following cases based on interviews. Describing her family's transborder circumstances, a woman whose spouse commutes to their home in Tijuana said, "My husband and my son live in Los Angeles. He also lives here. He brings money to us every weekend. He arrives to Tijuana on Friday and goes back to Los Angeles Sunday night. He has been a U.S. resident for more than fifteen years. I was born in the U.S. as well as my son. However, I have lived in Tijuana all my life. I crossed to San Diego to have my son born in the other side because [of] the Mexican economy. It is for his future, you know."

In another instance, a married man originally from the United States who now resides in Tijuana with his spouse, explained, "I worked in the other side for periods of six or seven months during almost seventeen years. The last time was in 1980. Actually, I live in Tijuana and work in the construction in San Diego. I also like to work in Los Angeles sometimes. I was born in National City but I prefer to live in Tijuana. I married my wife fifteen years ago. She is Mexican."

These qualitative descriptions illustrate a variety of situations through which families acquire transborder characteristics, as well as the mechanisms that reproduce these conditions. In general, transborder families are closely associated with changes in the socioeconomic environment, in the life course of the individuals, and in the family's life cycle. Each configuration is unique; therefore, each family represents an example of different ways to respond to the challenges of economic change within a global context.

In spite of the uniqueness of each case, the transborderization of homes has been found to coincide frequently with important changes in the labor-related migratory trajectories of its members, in particular, male heads of household. Therefore, international migration, associated both with economic activity and other key life-course events such as marriage or the birth of children, plays an important role in the initial transborder character of these homes. Successive temporary migrations to the United States for economic reasons helps shape the form of other related activities, including employment, education, resource exchanges between people living on the other side of the border, and assistance to relatives to secure jobs in the United States. Finally, the same study found that the physical location of transborderized homes has been shifting. Some transborder families develop in nonborder areas but moved northward largely in response to economic development in this region. For some of these families the border area is a crossing place to the United States. For others it becomes a permanent residence, with some members moving to the United States but contributing to the economic well-being of families in Mexico. In almost every case permanent residence coincided with the maturation of the family across its life cycle.[4]

Trajectories of Migration and Work in Transborder Families

I begin my analysis by examining the interaction between the timing of individuals' and couples' migration, labor status, and family trajectories that initiated the transborder condition of the families. At the time of the interviews, men in conjugal unions (regardless of legal status) headed fifteen of the twenty-three families, and women without partners headed eight. The majority of these homes had been established for at least ten years. Overall, the results indicate that the transborder formation was based on a process of key transitions in the family's life cycle corresponding to changes in the individual and joint life trajectories of the couple or single mother. Frequently, important changes in the family life cycle coincide with shifts in the migratory or labor trajectories of at least one of the members of the family unit. These interrelated changes initiate the transborder nature of the families that continue, to a lesser degree, in later stages of their social reproduction.

In a previous stage of this research (Ojeda de la Peña 1992), I found that men's and women's migration in search of work often separated families and initiated their transborder status. The nature of this relationship, however, is distinct for men and women. The consideration of gender differences is important because they help delineate the presence of certain "traditional" patterns in the way families are formed and reproduced throughout their life cycle.

In every case men and women had experienced migration at least once, but it had taken place at different stages of their life cycle and in different ways. Some changes in residence occurred at very early ages. About half of the women migrated for the first time as girls—before the age of twelve—usually in the company of their parents or other relatives; the rest of the women migrated during their productive and reproductive years. Almost three-quarters of the men, however, migrated for the first time beginning at age fifteen.

There were other gender differences regarding respondents' first migratory experiences. On their first migration, almost half of the women left their state of origin while a somewhat smaller number moved to a different municipality within their native state. Very few women moved to the United States on their first migration. For men, too, interstate migration was the most frequent initial migratory experience. In contrast to the women, the number of men who made an initial intrastate migration was less than for those who migrated to the United States. Thus, men's first migration experience was much more likely to have the United States as the final destination. Despite these gender differences, in the majority of cases for both sexes, first migration to the United States did not occur until their second or subsequent migration.

There were other critical differences between the sexes with respect to employment. Work was an important experience for women despite the tendency to underreport their work because of the traditional conceptualization that work, per se, is a male domain. This situation is clearly reflected in the contrasting empirical information about the active participation of men and women in the economy. Regarding the age at which women first entered the workforce, the majority reported earning wages at thirteen years of age, while the rest entered the labor force at the age of eighteen. In contrast, the majority of the men secured jobs before seventeen years of age, with a high proportion earning wages before the age of thirteen.

There were also a number of gender differences regarding the location of their first job. Because most of the women had migrated at a young age, their job histories began away from their place of birth either in a different part of the state or the nation. In contrast, the majority of men indicated that they worked for the first time in the same state where they were born, and among these, a notable number first worked in the municipality of their birth. Unlike the women, the men migrated at a later point in their work histories.

Migration and Work in the United States

The population in Tijuana includes a significant proportion of migrants. Likewise, in all of the interviewees' homes, I found that the breadwinner, male or female, had been born in a place other than Tijuana, which means that practically all the family units studied were formed by migrants.

Previous studies identified gender differences in the experiences of men and women undergoing family separation, which were confirmed in relation to their migration and work in the United States. As figure 1 illustrates, the majority of men and women first migrated to the United States before entering into marriage or a domestic partnership, or before having had a child. Thus, first contact with the other side of the border via migration took place before the formation of their families.

Research indicates that Mexico-U.S. migration fundamentally consists of Mexican workers who, be they legal or undocumented migrants, head to the United States in search of employment (Bustamante 1989; Cornelius 1989). Another characteristic of Mexico-U.S. migrations is that they have traditionally been temporary, lasting weeks, months, or even years, but do not necessarily lead to a permanent separation of migrants from their communities. However, the temporary nature of migration has recently been changing, since permanent migration and settlement has been more frequent since the 1980s (Bustamante 1991). Also important is the transborder movement

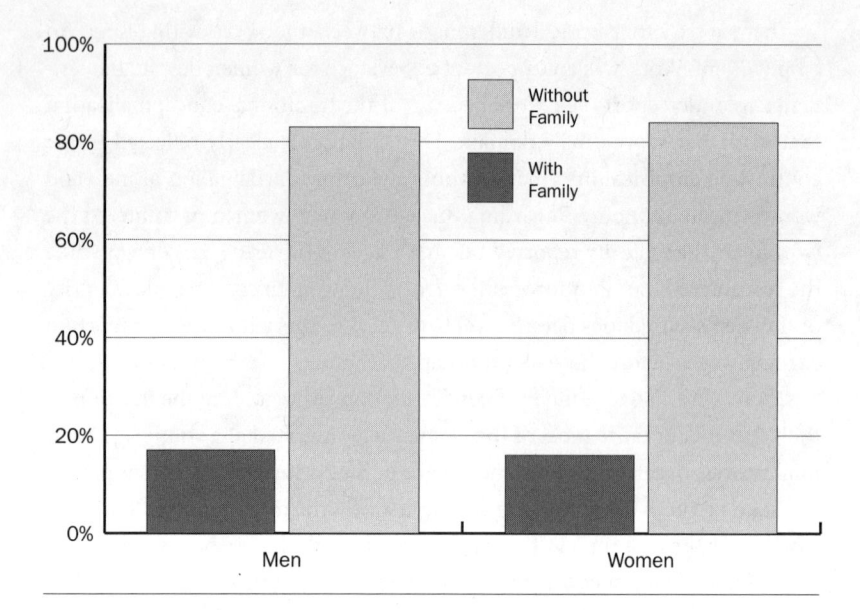

1. First Migration to the United States by Men and Women Regardless of Parental Status. Source: "Life Histories of Transborder Homes in Tijuana Project" (Tijuana: Department of Population Studies, El Colegio de la Frontera Norte, 1991).

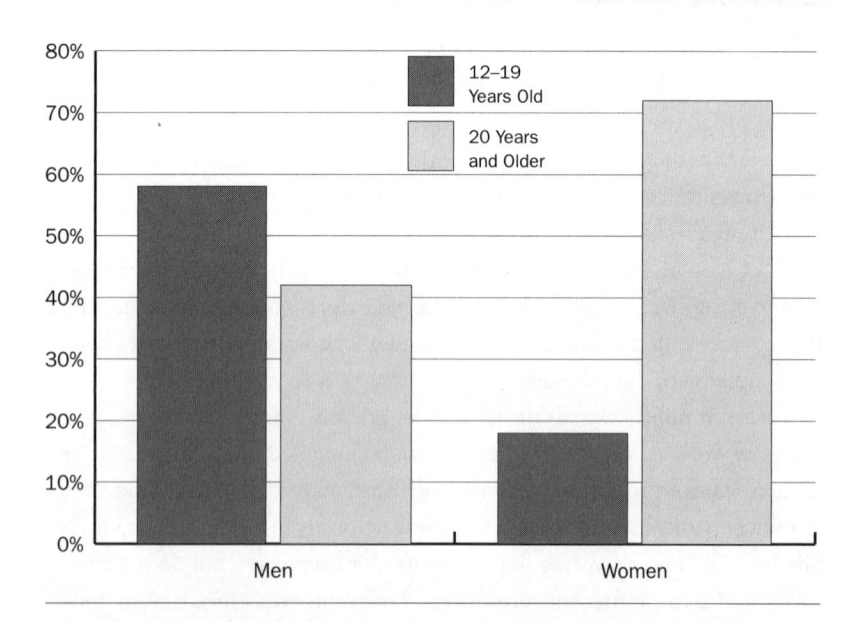

2. Age of Acquiring First Job in the United States in the Labor History of Men and Women with Transborder Homes. Source: "Life Histories of Transborder Homes in Tijuana Project" (Tijuana: Department of Population Studies, El Colegio de la Frontera Norte, 1991).

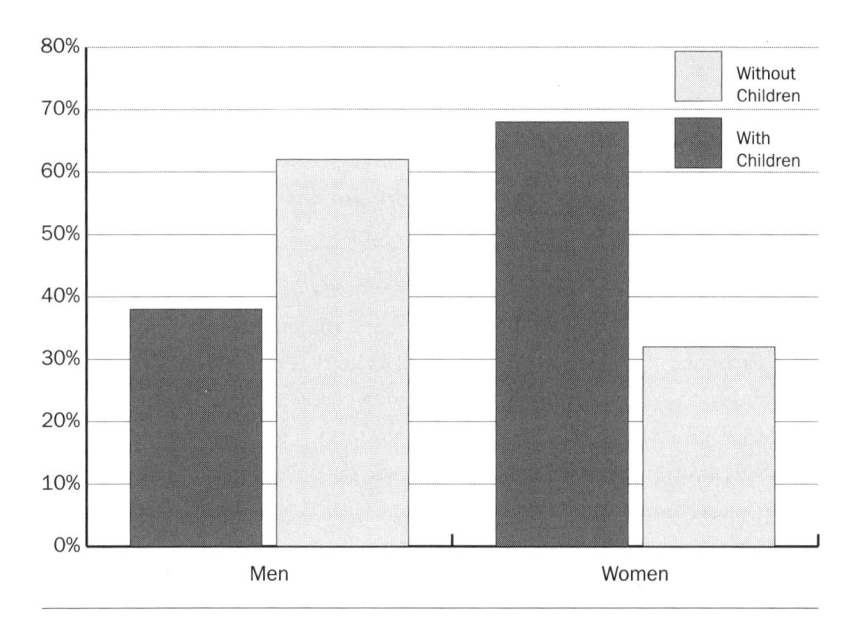

3. First Job in the United States in the Labor History of Men and Women with Transborder Homes, According to Their Parental Status at the Time. Source: "Life Histories of Transborder Homes in Tijuana Project" (Tijuana: Department of Population Studies, El Colegio de la Frontera Norte, 1991).

of commuters who live on the Mexican side of the border and work in the United States at places relatively close to the border.

The formation of transborder families is based on both phenomena: migration and work in the United States. The course of an individual's work history is characterized by temporary migrations for work in the United States and transborder work. However, a life-course analysis of the economic participation of men and women according to age and the formation of nuclear families shows important differences in their first work contacts in the United States. In general, men's economic participation in the United States began at ages younger than that of women.

Figure 2 illustrates that most of the women acquired their first job in the United States at the age of twenty, whereas more than half of the men got their first job at a younger age. On the other hand, more women than men secured their first job in the Untied States after they had married or were living in a domestic partnership and/or had at least one child. In contrast, a similar proportion of men obtained their first jobs in the United States while unmarried and childless (see figure 3).[5]

Data on the work of married or partnered men and women and single mothers show significant gender differences in the work and international migration of Mexicans. These differences are critical to the formation and reproduction of transborder families in Northern Mexico.

The Joint Experience of Couples in the Formation and Reproduction of Transborder Family Units

An analysis of the life histories of both members of a couple indicates that among changes in residence and work, marriage and the birth of children were particularly important. Figure 4 illustrates that migration between municipalities coincided most often with family changes related to the birth of children. The birth of children was also important for interstate migration, marriage, and/or the formation of a domestic partnership.

Changes in residence from Mexico to the United States corresponded with a number of family modifications, among which marriage and/or the formation of a domestic partnership predominated, while the birth of children, divorce, and other family events played a less significant role. In the case of return migrations from the United States to Mexico, the birth of children was very important, as was marriage. Respondents explained that the birth of a child was a primary reason for return migration, given the higher economic cost of raising and caring for children in the United States versus Mexico.

The impact of children extended to job changes among the respondents. Job changes within Mexico mainly coincided with the formation of the couple and the birth of children and, to a lesser degree, with other events like divorce or conjugal separation (see figure 5).

Crossing the border in search of employment was associated with a greater variety of family forms. Respondents' movement from jobs in Mexico to the United States coincided principally with marriage and, to a lesser degree, with the birth of children. Divorce, conjugal separation, economic crisis, or other family crises, such as the death of a close relative, also influenced respondents' decisions to migrate to the United States in search of employment. In contrast, the birth of children highly influenced job changes from the United States to Mexico, which confirms the relationship between international return migrations and the birth of children. As figure 5 illustrates, divorce also precipitated job changes from the United States to Mexico.

Based on the presence of small children or the marital status of all family members, I identified four life-cycle stages in the formation of transborder families: (1) the formation of the conjugal unit; (2) the birth of children; (3) the departure and/or marriage of children; and (4) the dissolution of the conjugal unit. The majority of the families established their first contact with

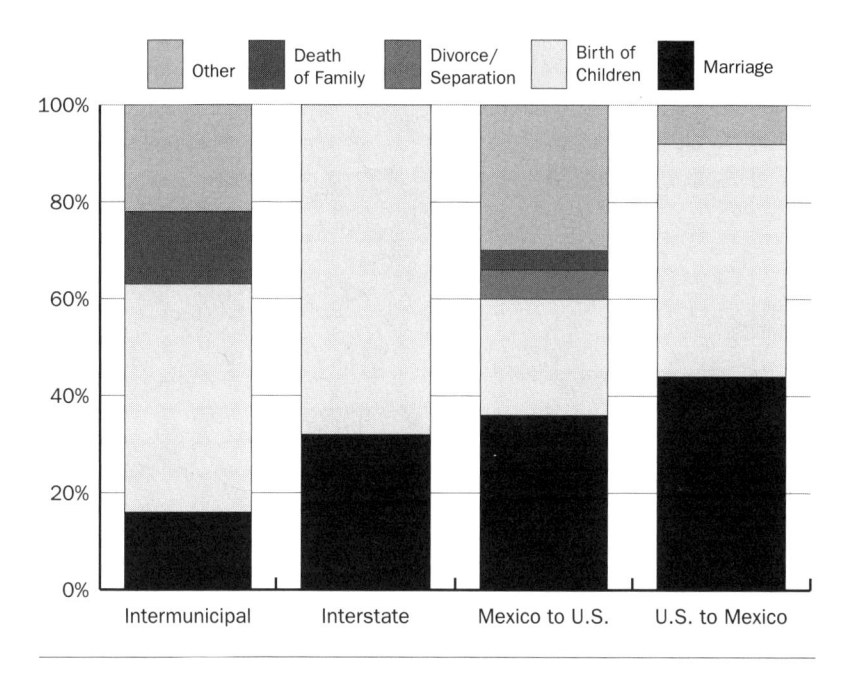

4. Migratory Movements and Family Changes that Occurred in the Same Year, According to the Couple's Experience with Transborder Homes. Source: "Life Histories of Transborder Homes in Tijuana Project" (Tijuana: Department of Population Studies, El Colegio de la Frontera Norte, 1991).

the United States within the first five years of their relationship, which also typically included the birth of their first child. In contrast, few transborder families established their first contact with the United States in more advanced stages of their life cycle.

In general, the couples in this study maintained a traditional division of labor. That is, men instigated and maintained the transborder relationship, although there were several cases in which the couple shared these responsibilities. Women rarely instigated and maintained this relationship except in the homes headed by women. Neither case contradicted traditional gender roles in internal family organization. In transborder families, one would expect to find more flexibility in the division of labor in light of their mobility across a set of social spaces characterized by changes in gender inequality. Inasmuch as the majority of families had been together for ten years, the data suggests continuity in a traditional family organization despite changes in residence and in work by both members of the couples.

Although migration and work were not the sole determinants for defining transborder families at the northern border, they nonetheless exercised strong

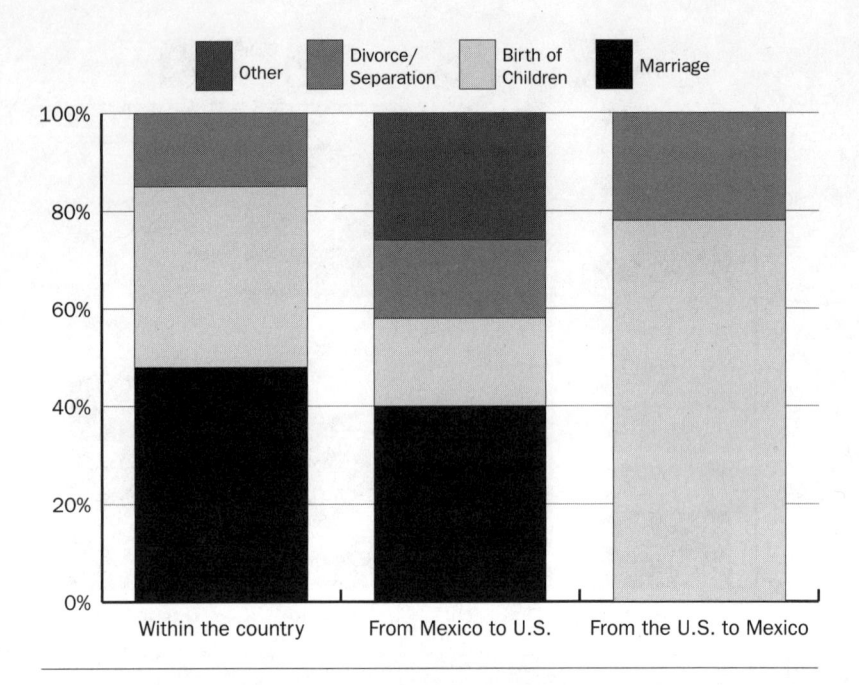

5. Workplace and Family Changes Occurring in the Same Year, According to the Experience of Couples with Transborder Homes. Source: "Life Histories of Transborder Homes in Tijuana Project" (Tijuana: Department of Population Studies, El Colegio de la Frontera Norte, 1991).

influence on their formation. For this reason it is critical to extend the analytic lens beyond the individual level to incorporate the lived experiences of families within the context of a transborder family formation process along the U.S.-Mexico border. Despite the emergence of transborder family units that integrate individual life trajectories, gender differences will not necessarily disappear within the family and society at large. On the contrary, an analysis of the respective life trajectories of men and women in this dynamic clarifies the sexual division of family roles. That is, women focus their activities on the family environment, enabling them to maintain and reproduce the transborder character of the household.

Sociodemographic study of transborder family dynamics must not substitute one level of analysis for another, but rather should utilize the individual and the couple as complementary units of analysis. My approach, wherein the family is the unit of analysis, is part of a theoretical and methodological shift in population studies.

Conclusion

The relatively small number of cases in this study sets limits on generalizing the findings for "transborder families" in Tijuana. Nevertheless, the qualitative value of the information advances knowledge of the sociodemographic characteristics of emerging family relationships in northern Mexico.

The experiences of the interviewed men and women, as individuals and as couples, illustrate frequent temporal coincidences of vital family events and changes in the trajectories of work and migratory life, all of which are critical in the transborderization of family units. This highlights the importance of considering family processes vis-à-vis other demographic phenomena.

The life histories of the couples reveal gender differences within the labor and migratory processes as they move from Mexico to the United States. This situation in turn translates into differences in the relationship of work and migration with key family events that precipitate the transborderization of families. These differences are mitigated if one considers the joint experiences of the couples; they persist, however, when one examines the gender of the person in charge of establishing and maintaining contact with the other side of the border through migration and work.

This study expands understanding of family arrangements at the northern border of Mexico. A number of questions remain regarding the qualitative and quantitative characteristics of transborder families in this economic, social, and politically strategic part of the country. It is critical to obtain regional information through traditional sources, including the census and demographic surveys. Without an integrated analysis that includes both qualitative and quantitative approaches, awareness of emerging social processes related to globalization will remain limited.

Notes

Rebecca Gamez, Denise Segura, and Patricia Zavella translated this article from Spanish.

1 Studies on the topic of international migration are an exception; of note are the important contributions of Jorge Bustamante (1989) and Wayne Cornelius (1989). Likewise, interesting advances have taken place in the theoretical elaboration of transmigration (Acuña 1988; Alegría 1989; Herzog 1991).
2 The current economic and urban characteristics of these twin cities are unique because of the economic dynamism of the State of California and the economic dependence of Tijuana on the United States in general and California in particular. The concept of "twin cities" describes the close-neighboring communication networks and the eco-

nomic, social and cultural links between both cities on the U.S.-Mexico border. Other cities in similar conditions are Laredo–Nuevo Laredo and Ciudad Juárez–El Paso.

3   These couples were chosen from an initial sample of 232 homes that participated in the pilot phase of the Bi-National Demographic Survey on the Mexico-United States Border, which took place in October 1988 in the Tijuana municipality. As part of this study, a similar questionnaire was administered to 150 homes of Hispanic origin living in southern San Diego County, California, to measure the frequency and variety of transborder relationships among populations on both sides of the border.

4   It is not exclusive of transborder families to have family and other relationships with people who live in the United States. The frequency of Mexican migration to the United States allows numerous families and homes from other parts of Mexico to also have such relationships. Nevertheless, the concept of transborder people can only be applied in the cases in which those relationships take place on a daily manner and in a space of border continuity. Both attributes imply some very particular social aspects in the daily family dynamic.

5   In a study of couples this discrepancy is explained in part by cases wherein single mothers have worked on the other side of the border and part by cases wherein members of the couples had been previously divorced or separated.

Women, Migration, and Household Survival
Strategies: Mixtec Women in Tijuana

LAURA VELASCO ORTIZ

✳ Since approximately the 1970s, the city of Tijuana, in the state of Baja California, has been a major urban center of northern Mexico that attracts the greatest number of Mixtec migrants from the Oaxacan region.[1] Oaxaca and Tijuana are thus linked through the migration process of the Mixtecs: one as place of origin and the other as destination. Migration has been one of the most influential social processes in the development of urban centers on the northern border of Mexico. Its impact on demographic growth and on labor markets of the border cities has been the focus of numerous studies. Meanwhile, migration from the point of view of migrants has received less scholarly attention. This essay contributes to the study of women's migration from the Mixtec region of Oaxaca, arguing that the migration of these indigenous women to Tijuana is a household survival strategy.

My research is based on a 1981 survey of 1,528 subjects in the High Mixtec region of Oaxaca and a 1989 survey of 121 households in the *colonia* Obrera of Tijuana. I also conducted six in-depth interviews of selected Mixtec women in households surveyed in this colonia in the same year.[2] The first survey is representative of six of seven districts in the High and Low Mixtec regions and thus effectively documents women's participation in the regional migration in the early 1980s and offers reliable data about the phenomenon in the place of origin. However, the temporality of these sources of data—there is almost a decade between them—limits the development of a synchronic description of migration in these two regions.

Research on Women's Migration

In the early 1970s research on migrant women typically occurred within so-called larger global explanations of female migration in Latin America (Elton 1978; Orlansky and Dubrovsky 1976; Todaro and Thadani 1979). Thus, the increasing numbers of women in rural-to-urban migratory flows during the 1940s was interpreted as a historic stage of migration and was associated with women's entrance into job markets. The determinants and consequences of women's migration therefore paralleled those of men. This research compared differences in the migratory behavior of men and women according to their age, marital status, number of children, destination, duration of stay, geographic distance, and employment in their place of destination.

In the late 1960s and early 1970s research on women and migration was conducted within the context of a growing urban problematic (Crummett 1986). Research increasingly focused on migrants, especially women, because of their impact on the occupational structure of large cities, in particular, urban services. In this context, the migration of women signified, above all, a transfer of labor from the rural to the urban labor market.

A historical-structural perspective on migration that developed during the 1970s (Paul Singer 1974; García, Muñoz, and Oliveira 1982) analyzed relationships between structural forces and regional dynamics (e.g., attraction and displacement of male and female migrants). This perspective highlighted the importance of analytic bridges that related individual behavior with global processes of macroeconomic change. In this research the home was considered a key linkage between individuals and larger social processes (Crummett 1986). The home was also a space where the sexual division of labor was expressed with greatest clarity. Dora Orlansky and Silvia Dubrosky (1976) argued that the situation of migrant women could best be understood within a theory inclusive of the sexual division of labor.

Seen from the context of the home (household), the significance of migration in general, and that of women in particular, acquires a different meaning. Displacement and attraction occur within the context of unequal social relations vis-à-vis a woman's location within her household (Singer 1974). In this perspective, migration is one survival strategy among many, and the nuances of choice can be fruitfully assessed in a microlevel analysis (Torrado 1981).[3] These strategies are not generated in a vacuum but occur within the predominant structure of opportunity. At each phase of family life (household formation, procreation, etc.), men and women seek resources for subsistence (ibid., 10). In the case of women's migration, the life cycle of the household is fundamental for the development of survival strategies.

Migration within the Mixtec Region

Since ancient times the Mixtec region of Oaxaca has been an area of high emigration. Even as of the 1980s, three out of every ten Mixtecs left the region, four worked temporarily in other parts of the country, and three remained in the area (Gobierno Constitucional del Estado de Oaxaca n.d.). According to a survey of migrants conducted in this region, 38 percent of those interviewed had migrated at least once in their lives (Javiedes 1981).

In order to understand the type of migration that the region generates, as well as the reasons for it, it is important to keep in mind both cultural and economic characteristics. The ethnic composition of the Mixtec population shapes any process that takes place in the region. The Mixtec is a historically indigenous zone, and until 1980 the Mixtecs were the second largest ethnolinguistic group, after the Zapotecs, in the State of Oaxaca, and the fourth in size at the national level (Valdez and Menéndez 1987, 39).[4] Regarding economic factors, the poverty in the region has been related to the persistence of a structure of small-farm production favoring the seasonal cultivation of corn and beans with an extremely low proportion of irrigation (1 percent). A large portion of arable land used in agricultural, forestry, or cattle activity is eroding rapidly. According to El Programa de Desarrollo de las Mixtecas (Mixtec Development Program), 30 percent of the land in this region cannot sustain human, vegetable, or animal life.[5]

The possibility of employment in the region rests basically in agriculture; given the absence of other sources of employment, the labor force exceeds available jobs. This results in lower salaries (in seasonal areas 90 percent of the population has an income below the subsistence level), unemployment in the place of origin, and the need to seek employment outside the region. A high seasonal migration has existed since the early twentieth century. The primary destinations have been Veracruz, Chiapas, Morelos, Mexico City, Sinaloa, Sonora, Baja California, and the United States (Gobierno Constitucional del Estado de Oaxaca n.d.). Between the towns of origin and places of destination a cycle is generated by the departure of the labor force from one and remittances sent from the other. According to interviews conducted in banks and telegraph offices, remittances surpassed more than two billion pesos per year, a sum comparable to the value of all agricultural and livestock production in Mexico (Gobierno Constitucional del Estado de Oaxaca n.d.).

Two important migratory flows leave the region. One is direct, with an urban destination, mainly Mexico City, where men tend to work in services and masonry and women in domestic service. The second is circular and occurs in stages, with rural destinations that sometimes include temporary residence in cities along the migratory route, which include Tijuana and Nogales. Veracruz and Morelos are principal destinations for harvesting sugar cane; Obregón, Sonora, for picking cotton; Culiacán, Sinaloa, for tomato picking; and Baja California and the United States, for the horticultural fields. While this flow is predominantly seasonal, it has not precluded settlement in peripheral colonias of Tijuana since the early 1960s and on the outskirts of agricultural fields of San Quintín in Baja California more recently.

The seasonal migratory flow reached its peak by the 1960s, when the agricultural economy of the northwestern part of the country (Sinaloa, Sonora, and Baja California) entered a period of growth and subordination to international capital. The technology and investment of U.S. agribusiness, corporations, and banks converged in the modern and mechanized cultivation of safflower, chickpeas, beans, rice, and corn. Intensive agriculture was transformed into an employment option for Mixtec migrants, especially in the case of fresh vegetables for export (Besserer 1988). This classification of migratory routes is not a rigid definition of migration possibilities but describes trends of migratory behavior, since individual migrants often combine these routes.

The Migration of Women from the Mixtec Region

Similar to other rural regions of Latin America, the Mixtec region in the early 1980s experienced less migration by women than by men, with women representing only 32 percent of the regional migration.[6] Mixtec women migrated to the cities in a greater proportion than the men, which confirmed the findings in other studies on the urban direction of women's migration (Oliveira 1984; Orlansky and Dubrovsky, 1976).

In the city Mixtec migrants entered gender-segregated labor markets. Nearly half (49 percent) of women migrants worked in domestic service in the place of their destination. Of the total of migrant women, 44 percent were headed for Mexico City, 12 percent to Veracruz, 3 percent to Morelos, 10 percent to Sinaloa, and nearly 3 percent to Baja California. These places constitute destination points of a staged cyclical migration process (Guidi 1988; Besserer 1988; Kearney and Stuart 1981). Almost 17 percent of the women migrated either to the agricultural markets of the northwestern part of the country or to the United States.

Characteristics of Mixtec Migrant Women

An analysis of who decides to migrate reveals considerable selectivity, that is, "the level at which men and women of distinct ages, and that occupy different positions in the occupational structure, experience the impact of structural and socio-economic determinants, or are able to overcome obstacles to migration" (Urzúa 1979, 224).

Age is an important factor in the decision to migrate. Confirming research on other women migrants, Mixtec women who had migrated by 1981 had first departed at a younger age (eighteen years old) than the men (nineteen years old) (Arizpe 1979; Young 1978; Elton 1978). Thirty-eight percent of the migrant women completed their initial departure between six and fifteen years of age, compared to 27 percent of the men. Thirty percent of the women departed from the region for the first time between ages sixteen and twenty, in contrast to 41 percent of the men.

Regarding marital status, 66 percent of the female migrants were single when they departed for the first time, and 29 percent were married or partnered. The educational level of the migrants was not much different than that of the nonmigrants: the average number of years completed were 4.09 and 4.08, respectively. Only 39 percent of the Mixtec women completed six years of school, and almost 23 percent did not have access to any education.[7]

Ethnicity creates important differences among migrants. Language is an extremely important indicator of ethnic membership. Mixtec is the primary language of the indigenous people in the low area of Oaxaca, and Mixtec migrants' and nonmigrants' Spanish-language proficiency varies. Over half of the women (57 percent) who had migrated at some time and 68 percent of the women who had never migrated spoke only Spanish. Migrant women indicated higher levels of Spanish-Mixtec bilingualism than nonmigrant women (41 percent and 28 percent, respectively). Mixtec monolingualism was greater among women who had never left the community (4 percent) than among those who had migrated at least once.[8]

Reasons for Leaving

In addition to exploring the actual causes of migration, it is important to analyze Mixtec women's motivations to migrate insofar as they reflect the cultural standards through which they interpret their needs and provide an understanding of their optimistic ethnic imaginaries (Nuttin 1982). This analysis begins with the hypothesis that a discrepancy exists between the level of life that Mixtec women have prior to migration and the one that they seek as an ethnic group.

Mixtec women's objectives are critical in their decisions to migrate, which I investigated in my survey. In the interviews, women prioritized distinct objectives linked to their emigration: finding work which could generate resources to help with the money, harvest, children's schooling, the family, as well as learning survival skills, respect, and knowing other places. Men placed money first, followed by work and harvest. These results, which signify women's concern with domestic labor and men's breadwinner responsibilities, contradict other studies, which find family and the education of children are women's principal motivations for migration (Elton 1978).

Why do women prioritize work over money, in contrast to the men? And why is the group of objective-goals the same for both sexes when their migratory behavior differs? The answers to these questions require an analysis of migratory behavior in the context of household dynamic in the place of origin.

Women and Household Organization in the Place of Origin

The Mixtec region is characterized by persistent poverty and dependence on subsistence agriculture. The households in the region maintain a sexual division of labor, wherein men work in agriculture, commerce, and construction, and women are responsible for domestic reproduction, the production of crafts, and limited informal commerce.

Analysis of the division of household labor by sex and age points to a critical context for the decision to migrate. Adult women work at home, cultivate family land plots, and enter into commerce, while young girls take care of toddlers, wash clothes, sweep, and weave hats and sleeping mats. As young women lose their "functionality" in the new economy of the regional market, they becomes candidates to migrate. Women who stay in the community of origin assure the economic continuity and social reproduction of the household during periods of migration by other members, men and women (Crummett 1986, 221).

Adolescence is a period without many job opportunities, especially since the penetration of manufacturing into the regional market, which has weakened demand for artisan work and agriculture by girls and young women (Young 1978; Elton 1978). Before migrating, Mixtec girls usually abandon their schooling and take up work like grinding *nixtamal*, making tortillas, carting water, caring for younger children, and when they are older, weaving sleeping mats. Research indicates that young, single women from large households leave for Mexico City in search of domestic work, forming part of a direct migratory flow (Facultad de psicología 1981).

The coordination between the individual behavior of women and the needs of their households does not necessarily indicate harmony and equality within the family. On the contrary, conflict and inequality were present, at times in a dramatic way, in the lives of the interviewed women. For example, the memory of the indigenous ritual of "surrendering a young woman to her husband" as a family strategy of "unburdening" themselves of females by transferring them to another man provoked tears from the women interviewed. Beatings by alcoholic husbands and the flight of the women and their children to northwestern Mexico as a form of survival speak to an oppression that disputes an idealized portrait of indigenous life in which strategies are developed in harmony and solidarity.

Women who left for Veracruz, Morelos, Sinaloa, and Baja California formed part of a staged migratory flow that involved a number of migrations with their husbands or other relatives (e.g., traveling from agricultural field to agricultural field and crossing to the United States with difficulty).[9] This does not, however, suggest that there were no single women traveling alone. However, even if this were so, the migratory route requires the recruitment of relatives or neighbors to facilitate arrival and provide knowledge of the route of the region's agricultural cycle. Migrating women generally belong to families in formation or with very small children and often seek their families' guidance to receive help in caring for children during some of their absences.

This reconstruction of migratory routes is based on information gleaned from interviews about the women's initial departures, and as such it gives a somewhat static image of the migratory phenomenon. On the other hand, the interviews conducted in Tijuana indicated that the northwestern agricultural route did not preclude Mexico City from being the first destination. Some of the women interviewed began with domestic work there, but as their life cycle advanced, they headed for the northern part of the country with frequent returns to the Mixtec region.

Beyond the Place of Origin: The Road to Tijuana

To follow the route of the migratory flow directed to the northern border of Mexico, especially the route that the women followed until their arrival and settlement in Tijuana, I did a retrospective analysis of the in-depth interviews of the Mixtec women and used the results of the sample survey of the Mixtec households residing in the same border city. Both sources of data are from 1989.

The conditions under which migration occurred toward the northern part of the country and the United States has been associated with the demand of day laborers for the agricultural harvests of the region—first, with the Bracero Program, between 1942 and 1964, and later, in the early 1970s, with the expansion of tomato cultivation in Sinaloa and cotton cultivation in Sonora. In the 1970s the growth of agriculture on the Ensenada coast attracted a significant number of Mixtecs. By the end of that decade, a new migratory cycle to the United States was generated and included California, Oregon, Washington, Arizona, and, occasionally, Idaho and Utah, with a return in the winter to northwestern Mexico (Besserer 1988, 41–42). These three markets allowed the Mixtecs to complete an annual migratory cycle and to support themselves, along with their families, outside the town for years.

The Departure

The departure of the women from their communities was related to their contact with migrants. Notwithstanding that the interviewed women were at different stages of their life cycles, all migrated when they were very young, between thirteen and seventeen years of age. Migration appeared in their lives through a relative or countryman (*paisano*), as happened in the case of Señora Natalia: "At fifteen years old I met a seventeen-year-old boy; he was a migrant . . . he would come and go from the fields in Sinaloa. I was his girlfriend for a year and I got married when I turned seventeen. . . . He left for the United States, returned and told me that then, yes, we were going together, and we left for San Quintín to work by the day."

At times, as in this case, migration was associated with marriage or engagement and was tied primarily to the migratory route that the male partner had established. In other cases, migration appeared before engagement or marriage and was linked more to the strategies that the family adopted to send young women under certain secure conditions. As the interviewee Paz described, "Well, it was more difficult for me, because I was little, so my mom would have me make tortillas, some five or six kilos, because we were about eight in the family, and it was for lunch, breakfast, and dinner and well, it was a lot. Until the time came when I told myself, 'No, I'm not going to stay here anymore,' and I came to Mexico [City]. . . . That time they sent me with an aunt . . . she took charge of situating me in a house."

Juana's situation was different. She migrated at the age of fourteen with her father and brother, and is now nineteen years old; Juana and her brother are the oldest of ten siblings, eight of whom stayed behind with their mother.

Juana's family had a long migratory tradition to the north, her father having migrated to the agricultural fields of Sinaloa since Juana was very young.

These cases reflect the different "precipitating conditions" under which migration occurred (Arizpe 1979).[10] The manner in which migration is managed, be it a "global" or "conjunctural" strategy, depends on the form of organization and the situation of each household. In a global domestic strategy, female migration is part of the collective response to every day life. In a conjunctural strategy, a woman migrates because of an unplanned situation, like domestic violence, a family death, or to resolve a specific personal problem (e.g., rejoin her boyfriend). Juana's migration was integrated into an established family tradition. Guadalupe, on the other hand, migrated alone to Mexico City because of some family problems and later returned to her hometown to care for her widowed brother's children—a conjunctural strategy.

This heterogeneity of situations in which the first migration occurred for Mixtec women had two features in common: first, migration occurred between the ages of thirteen and seventeen years of age; second, the family continued to exert control over the women after they migrated. As single women, they remained under the control of their brothers or parents. As married women, they were supervised by the husband and, in his absence, the mother-in-law or her family. This supervision affected the conditions under which the women left, stayed, or returned. Finally, the migratory route that the women "chose" was conditioned by the information provided by the migrant agent.

On the Road

"Once you migrate, life changes; you either find a boyfriend, or you get married or you have a child; you're no longer the same person that left town," commented the interviewee Paz.

The differences in the ages of the interviewees and the migratory route they followed suggest that a change occurred in the migratory pattern of the region. For example, Guadalupe and Ofelia, who were more than forty-five years old, migrated for the first time to Mexico City and Veracruz, respectively; they later returned to their home community, where they lived for some time and had children, after which they again migrated, this time to the agricultural fields of the north. Ofelia described her journey: "From there [Mexico City] I returned home, when I saw that my mother was sick and there was no longer anyone to care for my [widowed] brother's children, since my other sister had married and had gone to another town. I stayed there seven years taking care of them, until I got married with another man. I spent three years with him and had three children, but he left for Culiacán, found another woman and never returned. I left the children with my mother and I went to Culiacán, too. There I met another man.... I started living with him in Culiacán; then we left for Obregón."

The younger interviewees were nineteen and twenty-four years old. The first of these, Juana, traveled directly to Tijuana: "To travel to Tijuana we traveled from town to town, in a bus. My father played the saxophone, and my brother and I would collect money from the good people who had the will to help. After two or three months we arrived in Tijuana." Natalia was twenty-four years old; she had gotten married in her hometown, waited for her husband to return to the United States, and migrated with him to San Quintín, Baja California. Both Juana and Natalia were among the younger migrants that left the region, which coincided with direct Mixtec migration patterns toward different places in the northern part of the country (Besserer 1988).

Women developed a migrant lifestyle with departures and returns that varied depending on a multiplicity of factors including distance, the stage of their life cycle, and procreation. Marriage, widowhood, or separation, however, did not detain migration. All of the women interviewed had some of their children in their community of origin during one of the first returns.

Natalia and her husband lived approximately six months in San Quintín and returned to San Miguel Tlacotepec, where their first child was born. They stayed for one year, during which time they were able to survive on what they had earned during their migration to San Quintín. From San Miguel Tlacotepec they went to Mexico City, and Natalia returned again to the hometown for the birth of their second and third children. The interviews revealed the importance women placed on returning home for childbirth for practical and affective support for themselves and their newborns. This does not mean that women inevitably returned to their hometowns to give birth to each of their children, but that they maximized any opportunity to time their returns to coincide with labor.

There were two exceptions to such behavior: Juana, who in Tijuana became the girlfriend of a transmigrant to the United States, married him, and bore their two children in that city; and Paz, who got married to a man from Guadalajara, Jalisco, and followed his migratory route. Of Paz's nine children, six were born in Guadalajara and three in Tijuana; her husband's family became for Paz the family group of reference and support, since she lived with them during the long periods of her husband's migration to the United States, before she moved to Tijuana. Paz's case demonstrates migratory behavior marked by union with a man who is not from the Mixtec region.

Women's employment varied over the course of their migratory history depending on their residence, whether in domestic work, agricultural day labor, or commerce. Regardless of the type of work, women usually worked alongside members of their family or community networks. On the migratory route, the place of origin appeared frequently in the in-depth interviews as a notion of "home." Women made multiple return trips to care for their families and their land. Often the woman stayed home for a period while the husband migrated. But there was an "agreement" about this pattern: the departure of the man did not mean female inactivity.

In view of the life cycle of the household, the migration of women was integrally bound to family interests, economic possibilities, and norms, be it their family of origin or of procreation. Notably, each woman interviewed in Tijuana, without exception—single, married, or separated—migrated with a member of her nuclear family and with a shared strategy of survival in the place of destination.

Arrival in Tijuana

Tijuana has been a key destination point for the Mixtecs in the migratory route to the northern region of the country and to the United States. These Mixtec settlements permitted the migratory flow to revitalize itself, constructing a safeguard for the wives and children of the workers who moved through the agricultural corridor of northwestern Mexico and the southern United States.

The first settlement in Tijuana was established in the early 1970s, a period that coincided with a peak in agricultural production in Sinaloa, Sonora, and Baja California. The Mixtec settlements resulted from migration that began in Veracruz, then moved to Cuautla, later to Culiacán, and continued to the United States. Similar to other international migrants, many Mixtecs stayed in Tijuana before crossing the border and continued establishing irregular settlement zones in the city (Yáñez 1985, 42). Over time, this circular migratory pattern changed and came to include direct migration patterns between Oaxaca and Tijuana.

As a border city, Tijuana is strategically located next to the United States and has a diverse economy with a large and expanding service sector and *maquiladora* industries. Living in Tijuana makes migrating to or working in the United States possible.

Household Organization and Survival Strategies in Tijuana

The terrain where the Mixtec families have established themselves in the colonia Obrera in Tijuana is very similar to their region of origin: hills, houses on the slopes, and small roads. An element unique to the poor colonias of Tijuana has been added to the terrain: tires used as support for the slopes, as stairs, as back support for fences, as flowerpots, and so on. A large proportion of the inhabitants of this colonia came from the Low Mixtec region, where 43 percent of the total population spoke Mixtec. The district of Silacayoapán stood out as the principal point of departure (86 percent) for the families in the colonia Obrera; few migrated from Huajuapan de León (9 percent) and even fewer from Juxtlahuaca (3 percent).

Reasons for differences in the migratory direction across the Mixtec region have not been well examined. Nonetheless, diverse sources indicate that the towns belonging to the districts of Silacayoapán, Huajuapan de León, and Juxtlahuaca have been the primary sources of Mixtecs for this migratory flow. Although there is no supporting information, I suggest two factors that may determine this action: first, the economic conditions reflected in occupational alternatives; second, the risky direction that the first migrants took, which created a family and community social network that established a tradition to migrate in a northwesterly direction. Subsequent migrants used these networks, which were then incorporated into a cultural dynamic that maximized strategies for ethnic reproduction. These processes have been crucial because they provide a dynamic vision of the organization of the household being transformed over time.[11]

The networks of family solidarity that women constructed during their lives in the communities of origin and in the course of their lives as migrants were reflected in the arrangements made between households. Migrants developed three types of survival strategy: family organization, shared housing, and the collective organization of spending and consumption. Each one of these strategies covered different group needs. The conservation of family organizational norms, for example, maintained social reproduction of the ethnic group inasmuch as it avoided the disarticulation of the indigenous group.

Shared housing enhanced survival by integrating family, community, or friends within a shared physical space, thereby saving money and maximizing resources. The collective organization of spending and consumption built on the division of labor by age and sex. Significantly, all the interviewed women arrived with family members that had already settled in a Tijuana colonia;

only Paz traveled with her children from Guadalajara to the city without any contract.

There were two important characteristics of the households that settled in Tijuana. First, the majority of them owned a plot of land when they built their houses and had been there for more than four years. Second, for the Mixtecs, Tijuana served as a strategic point for geographic mobility and facilitated access to other regional labor markets (Sinaloa, Sonora, the Valley of San Quintín, Baja California, and the United States). These settlement patterns were important factors in the development of a permanent Mixtec presence in the city. Almost half of the households had a member working in the United States (44 percent), and a large number of relatives that were not part of their households resided in the United States.

The Role of Women in Household Survival Strategies in Tijuana

Migrant women often reproduced their subordinated role in the places of destination. However, new occupations allowed them to gain leverage in developing strategies for family survival, which further allowed them to see themselves as important social actors. Women took charge of family decisions that generated survival strategies given the temporary or permanent absence of the husband. This opened up new spaces for action in everyday life and allowed women to earn some autonomy in a wide range of social processes (Oliveira 1988, 39).

In both the place of origin and place of destination, women acted as heads of household in terms of being responsible for the care of the children and for supporting them while awaiting the absent husband's remittance. Ofelia described her role.

> I got married again there in the town, and my husband, well, he didn't have a job, he left for the fields of Culiacán; he would come and go. I had two children with him.... While he was on his way to come see us, I worked in the corn *maquila*. They would give me five liters of corn for my children. It was like that until he left for good ... he found another woman in Culiacán. And then it was better that I go to Culiacán, too. There I got together with another man; he would go between Culiacán and Obregón, back and forth. I didn't make any money there. I took care of twenty day laborers, I would feed them; I made them *pozole*, tamales; I sold candy. Meanwhile, he would drink and go out with other women. He wouldn't turn over any money to me.

Paz worked in each of the five places where she had resided. Now in Tijuana, where she considered staying, her situation remained unchanged: "Right now my problem is that he's not at home and then he doesn't send money.... During all this time I've been working outside the house, helping out in other things, and I still have to ask for loans from the store, and so we go on just with financial troubles."

Thirty-eight percent of the mothers of families obtained jobs. Street vending and domestic service were popular, since both could be combined with caring for children and the home. Maquiladora activity also constituted an important job opportunity in the city, but very few young Mixtec women worked in this subsector. According to Maria Patricia Fernández-Kelly (1983b, 160), female maquila workers have an educational level higher than the national average, and they come from urban areas. The educational requirement may therefore have limited Mixtec women's employment in this industry.

Street Vending

Women's market activities have historically been of great economic, political, and social importance not only in the Mixtec region but also throughout the state of Oaxaca. The complicated market system that has existed in the region has worked for centuries and has been part of indigenous culture. At a young age, Mixtec women receive cultural training for commerce, especially women from San Jerónimo, in the municipality of Silacayoapán. With 76 percent of the women who work outside the home in Tijuana doing so as street vendors, Tijuana society has become informed of the presence of the Mixtecs in large part by the work of female indigenous vendors on Avenida Revolución.

The tourist boom in Tijuana, particularly from the United States, facilitated the growth of vending and other commodification of cultural activities and products. For the Mixtec women, street vending involved all members of the household organized within a strict division of labor to make various products (e.g., bracelets), buy crafts from producers, transport merchandise, and sell. Typical work hours responded to the flow of American tourists, the busiest times being Friday afternoons and weekends. During the week, it was common for Mixtec women to go out selling for a few hours, but during the days and hours of heavy tourism, work time lengthened for women and all of their family members.

Systematic observation allowed confirmation that the maximum number of female vendors could be found on Sunday mornings on Avenida Revolución and the pedestrian bridge leading to the international checkpoint, the main mode of transit for tourists. I observed fifty-seven adult women,

21 percent of whom carried babies on their backs. The younger street vendors were notably more numerous (83); of these, 59 percent were girls and 41 percent were boys. Adult women and children vendors participated in joint production, acquisition, and selling of products and, in turn, the distribution of generated income. In this organizational process, adult women played an important role, above all in the prioritizing of household needs.

Street vending seemed to occupy women and children exclusively. The Mixtecs have established a presence in the Tijuana street-vending enterprise by an effective use of labor organization; following the initial incursion of their merchandise on the streets, women secured street-vending permits with defined place assignments. Despite their acknowledgment as legitimate street vendors, however, Mixtec women have been beaten and dislocated on several occasions, which forces their return to the streets with their merchandise. Ofelia described her response: "They've told me, 'Indian, go to your place.' But I say, we are all Indian because we are Mexican. I am a Mexican woman, so I have a right to work since I'm not robbing anyone." She continued, "Look, not all of us have permits and there are a lot of us, well, we also want something for our daughters . . . that's why, well, what else can we do but make a little space for them and their share among ourselves; but they've already told us that if we do that, well, they're going to take the permits away from us."

Confronted by a border situation of high competition among street vendors, particularly crafts vendors, Mixtec women responded with strength in numbers, constantly incorporating new *compañeras*. Community and family links helped reinforce their labor organizing, a space for action in which they achieved a degree of autonomy.

Domestic Service

Fewer women worked in domestic service (11 percent) than in street vending and at times they combined domestic service with selling on the weekends. In general, domestic service was practiced by going in and out of employers' houses or by doing work in their own homes (e.g., washing and ironing clothes). Domestic service offered flexible hours and workdays, which combined well with caring for children and women's own household chores, as Paz described.

> Imagine, I thought about working in this factory here, but then I begin to think: if someday I don't go to work, or if I get there late, they probably wouldn't let me in. Or the day I don't feel well they'll send me to the hospital, and the hospital won't pay me. No, it's better, I say "I'll work at

home," at least I'll have food. And if someday I don't feel well, I'll send word and when I come back I'll have my job. Working in a factory I can earn 75,000 or 90,000 pesos a week, and it's a pain, because they go in at seven in the morning, even if it's raining, even through the mud, you have to get there. On the other hand, at home, if I have to go to my son's festival, well, all I have to do is say so and I have permission, because you see how important it is to go see your children dance, it makes them feel real important.[12]

Paz's commentary demonstrates the type of economic calculations that women performed, wherein they included the costs of consumption for their family, work conditions, and the value that they assigned to caring for their children.

It is important to point out the social context in which domestic service occurred in Tijuana. While the middle class solicited domestic service, the border situation with the United States made the demand for service in Tijuana compete with the demand and salaries offered on "the other side." Paz, for example, earned 600 new pesos a month by working six days a week, eight hours a day, in different houses in Tijuana; those who worked on the "other side" could earn $100 per week—approximately twice what Paz earned.[13]

If it is true that domestic work on the United States border has higher relocation costs than on the Mexican side, such as different "cultural" criteria that define housecleaning, salaries offered on the other side work as a contrasting factor present in the daily life of the border population.

Sustaining Migrant Networks

It is critical to analyze migrants' social relations, which situate their households with other groups, individuals, and the larger social context (Oliveira and Salles 1989, 19). In addition, examining the Mixtecs' "network of relations" allows a wider level of analysis that reveals a social and geographic space based on kinship and community links. Prior research has discussed the importance of these networks for the social reproduction of Mixtec migrants, in particular for those who go to the United States (Henning and Paulsdorff 1985).

Because Tijuana is a strategic point for the mobility of Mixtec migrants, households settled in this city act as host stations for paisanos. In addition to performing regular domestic work, women offered assistance to relatives or compatriots from the Mixtec region or from the United States. The women interviewed stated that they had arrived in Tijuana with a family member and little by little become established on their own, which made their adaptation easier. Once established on the border with the United States, they become hosts for migrants who come and go, share information, and send news with great speed across the networks. The women's function as hosts is situated in the economic and cultural terrain whose social action allows for the collective reproduction of a migratory chain for the indigenous group. This process generates cohesion and reinforces ethnic identity. In light of the life conditions of the women, this work constitutes a "duty added" to domestic work, especially for those women whose husbands work in the United States for long periods and who find themselves alone in charge of their households.

Some Final Considerations

The participation of women in the two major migratory flows from the Mixtec region—urban and rural—depends on age and marital status, as well as the stage of the life cycle of each household of reference. Differences in women's migration varied by the number of family members involved in migratory flows and by the extent to which a migratory tradition developed in the home. The presence of a migratory tradition, in turn, was an important motivation in the migratory behavior of women.

A series of "stops" in intermediary points, the number of which depends on the age of the migrant, has emerged between the towns from which these women left and the city of Tijuana. Older women, in general, passed through several places before arriving in Tijuana. Younger women tended to migrate directly from their hometowns to Tijuana, which suggests that the migratory pattern is probably in the process of transformation.

Women's incorporation into remunerated work is a survival strategy that 38 percent of the households practice. The income obtained in this work is a weighty contribution to the domestic economy, above all for single women or for those whose husbands spend long periods in the United States, since the total income generated by their labor acquires greater relevance.

Women's economic contributions to family survival complement their participation in the maintenance of migrant networks, which makes possible the high mobility of Mixtecs moving to northwestern Mexico and the United States. Tijuana is an important crossing point to the United States, and in this context families already settled in Tijuana offer boarding and support to those who come and go to the other side. In almost half of the households, the father of the family works on the other side, sometimes making the round trip daily or with long absences. Thus, it is the wife who acts as the principal person responsible for the home and for the attention given to compatriots, and sustaining the migrant network adds to their domestic labor. Moreover, women's socially necessary labor diminishes the migrants' relocation costs and provides affective support as well. The implications of these multiple domestic responsibilities have not been studied. Nevertheless, because "attention to migrants" transcends the domestic sphere, it can also be evaluated by its significance for ethnic reproduction. The importance of women's work in the integration of migrants will undoubtedly grow as the pressure to migrate increases across the region and nation.

Notes

This article was translated and edited by Rebecca Gámez, Denise Segura, and Patricia Zavella. It is important to note that it was written at the beginning of the 1990s and published as "Migración Femenina y Estrategias de Sobrevivencia de la Unidad Doméstica: Un Caso de Estudio de Mujeres Mixtecas en Tijuana," in *Mujeres, Migración y Maquila en la Frontera Norte*, ed. Soledad Gonzalez Montes, Olivia Ruiz, Laura Velasco, and Ofelia Woo (Mexico City: El Colegio de la Frontera Norte, 1995), 37–63.

1. The Mixtec region extends over three states of the Mexican Republic: Oaxaca, Puebla, and Guerrero. The Mixtec region of Oaxaca is divided into three areas by ecological criteria: high, low, and coastal.
2. The women interviewed in-depth constitute a subgroup of adult married women and heads of household surveyed in the Obrera colonia. The only selection criterion was age: two were between fifteen and twenty-five years of age, two were between sixteen and forty, and two were between forty-one and sixty-five years of age. All were married, had between three and ten children, and lived with their husbands, although in two cases the men worked in the United States for long periods of time and in another two cases they crossed daily to work in that country.
3. I utilize the classic concept that Joaquín Duque and Ernesto Pastrana (1973) developed with respect to poor populations, as I believe that it maintains the appropriate connotation with reference to the ethnic group studied. However, I agree with the critique developed by Susana Torrado (1981) regarding the limitations of the use of "subsistence or survival" with respect to certain social sectors and the proposal of the concept of "family life strategies."
4. This situation was the same until 2000.
5. For a complete review of the Mixtec situation through the 1980s see Gobierno Constitucional del Estado de Oaxaca n.d. and the proceedings report of La Comisión de Asuntos Indígenas por la Mixteca Oaxaqueña presented at the regular public session on 28 November 1983, by Heladio Ramírez, the senator at that time.
6. This section is primarily based on the results of the survey conducted in 1981 in the seven districts of High and Low Mixtec Oaxaca. The aforementioned results were reported in Laura Velasco, "Los motivos de la mujer migrante," Tesis de licenciatura, UNAM, 1985.
7. The interviewed women ranged between fifteen and sixty-four years of age, which

can elevate the level of education, since girls of six to fourteen years of age are not represented.
8. Since the data with which I developed this section was conducted in the place of origin, it cannot be determined if bilingualism facilitated the departure of the women or if they developed greater bilingualism in the migration process.
9. This tendency has changed since the 1980s. There is an increasingly large number of settler families in Tijuana, Ensenada, and more recently in the agricultural Valley of San Quintín.
10. Lourdes Arizpe (1979) differentiates between causal and precipitating conditions of migration: the first one operates on the structural level, the second one on the family level.
11. In relation to the persistence of certain towns and states of the Mexican Republic as places of constant origin of international migrants, Víctor Zúñiga (1992) emphasizes the importance of migratory traditions and their reproduction through family socialization.
12. These amounts are in old pesos; after 1989, three zeros were eliminated from the currency. For example, in 1988 the exchange rate was 2,281 pesos per U.S. dollar, and after 1989 it was 3.15 pesos per U.S. dollar.
13. The newspapers offered employment for a live-in maid at $100 dollars per week, which equaled approximately 1,200 new pesos per month (*Ultimas Noticias* 1989, 10a).

Single-Parent Families: Choice or Constraint?
The Formation of Female-Headed Households
in Mexican Shanty Towns

SYLVIA CHANT

✳ In almost all urban areas throughout Latin America and other parts of the Third World, nuclear households headed by males appear to be the predominant family structure in low-income urban communities. However, in Latin America and the Caribbean, there are also significant numbers of households headed by women. The proportions of female-headed households vary from one place to another, but a common denominator among studies which have attempted to account for the existence of the mother-child household has been the explanation that it is the result of male instigation. Furthermore, the family which the man "leaves behind" is often thought to be worse off socially and economically in his absence, be it temporary or permanent.

Material collected in a survey of 244 low-income owner households in three irregular settlements in Querétaro, Mexico, shows first how female-headed households survive in comparison with male-headed households, and second clarifies the various reasons for the formation of single-parent units, indicating that they often result from female initiative.[1] In this essay the terms *household* or *family* will refer exclusively to the co-residential domestic unit, and the term *matrifocal* will indicate a household with female leadership where the husband-father is absent permanently and plays no role in the household economy.

In three irregular settlements in Querétaro, a sample of owner households was randomly selected for interview.[2] Owner households were selected in order to examine the role of the family in housing improvement, which was less applicable to renters. This may suggest that the study deals with a relatively privileged group of low-income households. Within Querétaro, however, the rental submarket was far smaller than in other cities because of an abundance of land and the tolerance of squatting by the authorities during the 1970s. Two-thirds of the poor—defined by the urban-development plan as those households surviving on less than two minimum wages (52 per cent of the total urban population)—lived in peripheral barrios. Within the study communities, the figures of rented accommodation are low: only 4 percent of the population rent in Bolaños, 7 percent in Los Andadores, and 2 percent in Las Américas. Therefore, one may assume that the sample is fairly representative of the lowest income groups in the city.

Within the total sample of 244 households, there were 167 male-headed nuclear families and twenty-two female-headed, single-parent units. Male household heads averaged thirty-two years of age, and female heads averaged forty. The average size of a nuclear family was 6.2 people and of a single-parent family was 5.4 people.

Wage of the Household Head

One of the principal reasons offered for the disadvantageous position of single-parent households compared to nuclear families is the fact that women in Mexico on the whole earn less than men.

While the head of household's wage may be the principal source of income for the family, it is not the only indicator of economic well-being. Contributions from other household members are also important. In nuclear households, there are an average of 1.2 workers, and the earnings of women and children make a negligible contribution to the total budget in comparison to the male head. But in single-parent families, which have an average of 1.6 workers, the head's contribution may represent a lower proportion of the total income, but the children provide up to one-third of the weekly household budget. The Querétaro data indicate that in terms of per-capita income, female-headed families are only marginally less well off than nuclear families.

Spending Patterns within Households

"Secondary poverty" is a term used to describe the situation of women and children in low-income families where the man withholds part of his wage for personal expenditure. The unequal allocation of economic resources means that women and children are often underfed or undernourished. In the subsample of in-depth interviews carried out with twenty-two nuclear families, just over half (twelve) of the heads retained as much as 50 percent of the wage for their personal use. Female heads, on the other hand, seem to contribute all their wages to family welfare. Many female heads emphasized that they were better off financially once their husbands had died or deserted, because they could then plan their budgets more efficiently for the week ahead. Many women who lived with volatile husbands stressed that they could not budget effectively because of the variable amount that their husbands gave them for "housekeeping" each week.

Household Management

There were important differences in the organization of domestic labor between the two types of family. A strict sexual division of labor in nuclear families dictated that a woman's place was in the home, and 69 percent of female spouses in those structures were full-time housewives, whereas in single-parent structures over 80 percent of the women had paid employment. This had major implications for the running of households.

In 55 percent of the nuclear families, especially those with young children, women carried out the housework single-handedly. When they were aided, help was solicited from daughters and not sons. The key issue, however, is the presence of a full-time houseworker, especially given that in irregular settlements deficient housing and help with housework pose major obstacles to comfort and hygiene. Women in single-parent families, on the other hand, have to take on the role of both wage-earner and housewife, which may mean that the housework doesn't get done as efficiently. This problem is often solved in two ways: first, in all but two of the twenty-two cases of single-parent families, household work is shared by the children; and second, women who are employed effectively work a "double day"—they begin on the housework when they return home from their jobs. In the single-parent units, notably, both boy and girl children actively share the task of running the household, which means that the time invested per houseworker in domestic labor in such units is roughly only half that invested by full-time housewives in nuclear families.[3] The fact that boys participate as well as girls contains important implications for the socialization of children.

The Socialization of Children in Male-Headed and Female-Headed Families

Authority patterns in the families are important, because socialization (i.e., the process by which the children's characters are developed and molded in accordance with dominant social and cultural values) has its origins in the family. It is not entirely clear how parental behavior affects children's attitudes. On the one hand, it is suggested that boys become confused about their psychological identity in households where the father is absent, an insecurity that leads to an exaggerated need to demonstrate masculinity. On the other hand, it is more commonly believed that because Latin American fathers withhold affection, their sons develop inferiority complexes, accompanied by frustration and anxiety, which results in the perpetuations of machismo.

The question of whether children's behavior is largely imitative or develops in reaction to their parents' attitudes is difficult to answer, given the limitations of the present study: longitudinal studies of the effect of family structure on subsequent generations were not carried out. However, two important features emerge from the fieldwork. The first is that husbands who were understanding and responsible toward their spouses frequently said that they had seen their own fathers treat their mothers badly and that when their fathers had finally left home they had sworn not to treat their own wives and children in a similar fashion. Second, in female-headed families there tended to be less discrimination against female children, and girls were given opportunities equal to those of boys. In fact, female family heads stressed the need for girls to have education in case they should be deserted by their future husbands. There was no apparent pathological behavior in children of female-headed families; they seemed, on the contrary, to be mature and responsible, probably as a result of early participation in household welfare. Children of such families also tended to consider their mothers to be capable, as demonstrated by their role as the family's overall provider and mainspring.

The Formation of Single-Parent Families

The reasons behind the formation of single-parent units were explored in detail in the semistructured interviews. While there were only eleven such families in the study, the subsample of households was selected with the aim of highlighting different sorts of responses and thus the variety of reasons behind the formation of these units. Most women (five) had been deserted by their husbands and were on average eight years older than their counterparts in nuclear families. Abandonment was most likely to occur when the woman was approaching middle age. In three of these cases of desertion the man had left in order to establish a home with another woman; in the other two cases the man had left "in search of work" and had never returned. Two female heads in the subsample were widows. In the remaining four cases the women themselves had taken the initiative, leaving their husbands when they could no longer cope with situations of violence, infidelity, or lack of financial commitment; in these cases the women had had to move out of their husbands' homes and find alternative accommodations for themselves and their children.

In cases of desertion one might suppose that, in accordance with the dominant view in the literature, the men are frustrated at their inability to provide adequately for the family and thus feel they cannot enjoy a position of respect. However, it is more likely that frustration on the part of the male leads him into behavior that elicits disapproval from his wife, and a two-way process develops. In an effort to assert his masculinity, the man may abuse his position and assert himself through beating his wife or withholding the wage packet. Such behavior causes his wife to upbraid and undermine him (Fromm 1959; Goode 1963). In this way, the female may also contribute to "breakdown."

Nonviability of the nuclear family, as reflected in widespread divorce, separation, and desertion, is perhaps the logical outcome of a situation where men and women are divided in their activities, interests, and priorities, with women in a position of subservience. Female dependence and domesticity may actually be antithetical to the development of strong emotional bonds (Arizpe 1982; Hutter 1981). The data from Querétaro show that the split is precipitated by female initiative in as many as one-third of the cases—a significant minority, given that it is difficult for the female partner to initiate a separation for a number of reasons. Not only is it unlikely for women to earn enough money to support their families, especially when the children are young, but also there are social stigmas attached to being a single parent in Mexico. The Roman Catholic Church, with its ideology of the suffering mother, is rigid in its view of the sanctity of marriage; women who complain about their husbands' behavior to the local priest and ask for advice are more than likely to be told, "It's your cross and you have to bear it." Single parents are viewed suspiciously by both men and women. To be a single woman may be conceived by others as an indication of weakness.

Generally, marriage is felt by women to be so binding that nuclear families may continue for many years in unhappy domestic situations, as did several households in the study. However, some women are prepared to take the initiative and to risk discrimination and a period of financial adjustment and hardship in order to avoid conflictive and insecure domestic situations.

The Extension of Female-Headed Units

The survey data indicate that a significant number of single-parent households result from choice and achieve a high degree of economic security and stability within a relatively short period of time. Among the total sample of households and their extended families were two reasons that led to the extension of female-headed families.

First, when households are young, women may find it difficult to cope with a full-time job in addition to housework and childcare. In order to provide greater economic security and to enable greater flexibility, female-headed units often incorporate relatives to help them manage survival. Extension of the family unit is more prevalent among households headed by women than households headed by men—one-third of the female-headed units in the survey contained additional relatives, as opposed to only one-fifth of the households headed by males.

Second, single-parent units often become extended at a later stage of the life cycle, when the children are grown up and getting married. In order not to forgo the economic support of sons and daughters, female heads may invite their prospective in-laws to come and live with them in their homes.

Conclusion

In this discussion of the differences between the economic and social welfare of female-headed and male-headed families in low-income communities in Querétaro, two important factors have emerged. First, in terms of economic welfare, household management, and authority patterns, the male-headed nuclear unit displays certain characteristics less desirable than those of female-headed households. Second, single-parent structures are often the outcome of a deliberate and positive choice by low-income women. However, as Olivia Harris points out, there is a "cruel paradox" in that while the overall increase in the proportion of female-headed households in Latin America may be interpreted as an indication "that women are beginning to free themselves from the more repressive and restricting aspects of *machista* culture," their potential freedom is put in a stranglehold by virtue of the fact that they are often found "among the poorest strata where life is most precarious" (Harris 1982, 6). Despite this, the data from Querétaro show that the formation of a female-headed unit, whether through male or female initiative, often results in family life becoming more secure and stable in a variety of ways. Sexual discrimination in the labor market often means that women earn low wages, but these earnings are boosted by economic cooperation from their children. Difficulties in carrying out the two full-time roles of worker and housewife are smoothed out by the help of both male and female children in the home. An absence of violence and of the abuse of authority within the family not only results in greater psychological security but may also be conducive to both a reduction of machismo and of hostility between men and women. The fact that female-headed units often seek to incorporate kin is indicative, however, of the difficulties that single mothers face in a society which discriminates against women; nevertheless, the study shows that female-headed units contain several positive elements in the struggle for survival. Furthermore, single-parent families which exist without the safety net of a state-welfare system may well improve the viability of single-parent households in other important respects.

Certainly, the heavy dependence of mothers on sons and daughters may be interpreted as imposing an obstacle to their children's education; however, the fact that female-headed units tend to form at a stage in the life cycle when many children from all kinds of families in the communities work part-time to further their studies may lessen the threat to the "normal" development of the child's potential.

Despite major structural constraints on the economic and social potential of female-headed families, single-parent units often fare better than male-headed nuclear households under the conditions described in this essay. However, it is possible that single-parent families may not function so well in other situations. The majority of the poor in Querétaro have access to home ownership, which gives greater scope for flexibility and security than renting. Future research should consider the position of families in rental accommodation in order to establish how effectively male- and female-headed families manage survival in other low-income tenure categories.

Notes

This essay is based on fieldwork carried out in Mexico between June 1982 and June 1983. The work was funded by the Social Science Research Council of Great Britain (now the Economic and Social Research Council) in connection with a research project entitled "Public Intervention, Housing and Land Use in Latin American Cities," directed by Alan Gilbert and Peter Ward at University College London. The project was sponsored by the Overseas Development Administration.

1 Irregular settlement may be used to describe three main kinds of low-income neighbourhoods in Mexico.

—*Squatter settlements*. These are formed by invasion on either public or private land and legal title is, at least initially, nonexistent.
—*Ejidal urban settlement*. An *ejido* is an area of land handed over by the state to a specific agricultural community. This land may not be sold or in any other way alienated. Despite that, many ejidal communities sell off lots illegally. Legal title

does not pass into the hands of the settlers until a presidential decree makes expropriation possible.
—*Low-income subdivisions*. These arise as the result of land being sold to low-income families without services. The subdivision is irregular in the sense that it offends planning regulations.

The study settlements in Querétaro comprised Bolaffos, an ejidal settlement in the northeast of the city which had originated in 1970; Los Andadores, a fraudulent subdivision in the south of the city dating from 1976; and Las Américas, an ejidal urban settlement in the northwest of the city which began in the late 1970s.

2 The samples in each settlement were 30 percent representative of a complete listing of all co-residential owner families.

3 Domestic labor in irregular settlements is time-consuming and arduous because housing is of poor quality and there are few basic services such as piped water, electricity, and paved roads. Housework needs to be done very thoroughly in order to combat potential health risks arising from such problems as unpurified tanker water, an absence of trash collection, and unhygienic improvised lavatory facilities. Domestic labor is often carried out single-handedly by female spouses in nuclear families, who frequently work an eleven-hour day on household chores alone. When the work is carried out by one person, she runs the risk of fatigue or injury, because much of the work is heavy. Other family members are also at risk of cross-infection arising from the mixing of culinary, lavatory, and cleaning duties in quick succession. Sharing chores in single-parent families helps to reduce health risks to individual workers by reducing their expenditure of time and energy, and it also minimizes threats to hygiene.

Working at Motherhood: Chicana and Mexican Immigrant Mothers and Employment

DENISE A. SEGURA

✳ In North American society, women are expected to bear and assume primary responsibility for raising their children. This socially constructed form of motherhood encourages women to stay at home during their children's early or formative years and asserts that activities that take married mothers out of the home (e.g., paid employment) are less important or "secondary" to their domestic duties (Wearing 1984; Berg 1986; Folbre 1984).[1] Motherhood as a social construction rests on the ideological position that women's biological abilities to bear and suckle children are "natural" and therefore fundamental to women's "fulfillment." This position, however, fails to appreciate that motherhood is a culturally formed structure whose meanings can vary and are subject to change.

Despite the ideological impetus to mother at home, over half of all women with children work for wages (Grossman 1982; Hayghe 1984; U.S. Bureau of the Census 1990).[2] The growing incongruence between social ideology and individual behaviors has prompted some researchers to suggest that traditional gender-role expectations are changing (e.g., greater acceptance of women working outside the home).[3] The extensive literature on the ambivalence and guilt employed mothers often feel when they work outside the home, however, indicates that changes in expectations are neither absolute nor uncontested.

Some analysts argue that the ambivalence felt by many employed mothers stems from their discomfort in deviating from a socially constructed idealized mother, who stays home to care for her family (Hochschild with Machung 1989; Gerson 1985; Berg 1986).[4] This image of motherhood, popularized in the media, schoolbooks, and public policy, implies that the family and the economy constitute two separate spheres, private and public. Vicki Ruiz and Ellen DuBois (1994) argue, however, that the notion of a private-public dichotomy rests largely on the experiences of white, leisured women and lacks immediate relevance to less-privileged women (e.g., immigrant women, women of color), who have historically been important economic actors both inside and outside the home.[5] The view that the relationship between motherhood and employment varies by class, race, and/or culture raises several important questions. Do the ideology of motherhood and the ambivalence of employed mothers depicted within American sociology and feminist scholarship pertain to women of Mexican descent in the United States? Among these women, what is the relation between the ideological constructions of motherhood and employment? Is motherhood mutually exclusive from employment among Mexican-heritage women from different social locations?

In this essay I explore these questions using qualitative data gathered from thirty women of Mexican descent in the United States—both native-born Chicanas (including two Mexico-born women raised since preschool years in the United States) and resident immigrant Mexicanas.[6] Notions of motherhood for Chicanas and Mexicanas are embedded in different ideological constructs operating within two systems of patriarchy. Contrary to the expectations of acculturation models, Mexicanas frame motherhood in ways that foster a more consistent labor market presence than do Chicanas. I argue that this distinction—typically bypassed in the sociological literature on motherhood, women and work, or Chicana/o studies—is rooted in their dissimilar social locations, that is, the "social spaces" they engage within the social structure created by the intersection of class, race, gender, and culture (Zavella 1991b, 75).

Mexicanas, raised in a world where economic and household work often merged, do not dichotomize social life into public and privates spheres, but appear to view employment as one workable domain of motherhood. Hence, the more recent the time of emigration, the less ambivalence Mexicanas express regarding employment. Chicanas, on the other hand, raised in a society that celebrates the expressive functions of the family and obscures its productive economic functions, express higher adherence to the ideology of stay-at-home motherhood and correspondingly more ambivalence toward full-time employment—even when they work.

The differences between Mexicanas and Chicanas challenge current research on Mexican-origin women that treats them as a single analytic category (e.g., Hispanic), as well as research on contemporary views of motherhood that fails to appreciate diversity among women. Examination of the intersection of motherhood and employment among Mexican immigrant women also reinforces emerging research that focuses on women's own economic and social motivations to emigrate to the United States (rather than at the behest of husbands and/or fathers) (see Solorzano-Torres 1987; Baca and Dexter 1985; Guendelman and Perez-Itriago 1987).

Theoretical Concerns

The theoretical concerns that inform this research on Chicana and Mexicana employment integrate feminist analyses of the hegemonic power of patriarchy over work and motherhood with a critique of rational choice models and other models that overemphasize modernity and acculturation. In much of the literature on women and work, familial roles tend to be portrayed as important constraints on both women's labor-market entry and mobility. Differences among women related to immigrant status, however, challenge this view.

Within rational-choice models, motherhood represents a prominent social force behind women's job decisions. Gary S. Becker (1975, 1981, 1985) and Polachek (1975, 1981a, 1981b), for example, argue that women's "preferences" to mother are maximized in jobs that exact fewer penalties for interrupted employment, such as part-time, seasonal, or clerical work.[7] According to this view, women's pursuit of their rational self-interest reinforces their occupational segregation within low-paying jobs (e.g., clerical work) and underrepresentation in higher-paying, male-dominated jobs that typically require significant employer investments (e.g., specialized training). Employers may be reluctant to invest in or train women workers, who, they perceive, may leave a job at any time for familial reasons.[8] This perspective views motherhood as a major impediment to employment and mobility, but it fails to consider that the organization of production has developed in ways that make motherhood an impediment. Many feminist scholars view this particular development as consistent with the hegemonic power of patriarchy.

Unlike rational-choice models, feminist scholarship directs attention away from individual preferences to consider how patriarchy (male domination, female subordination) shapes the organization of production, resulting in the economic, political, and social subordination of women to men (Kuhn 1978; Hartmann 1976, 1981; Barrett 1980). While many economists fail to consider the power-ideological constructs such as "family" and "motherhood" in shaping behavior among women, employers, and the organization of production itself, many feminist scholars focus on these power dynamics.

Within feminist analysis, motherhood as an ideology obscures and legitimizes women's social subordination because it conceals particular interests within the rubric of a universal prerogative (reproduction). The social construction of motherhood serves the interest of capital by providing essential childbearing, childcare, and housework at a minimal cost to the state, and it sustains women as a potential reservoir of labor power, or a "reserve army of labor" (Benería and Roldán 1987; Benería and Sen 1986; Dorothy Smith 1987). The strength of the ideology of motherhood is such that women continue to try to reconcile the "competing urgencies" of motherhood and employment despite the lack of supportive structures at work or within the family.[9]

Because employers view women as mothers (or future mothers), they encounter discrimination in job entry and advancement (Kanter 1977).[10] Because women are viewed as mothers, they also work a "second shift" at home (Hochschild and Machung 1989). The conflict between market work and family work has caused considerable ambivalence within women. Berg, for example, notes that one of the dominant themes in analyzing women and work is the "guilt" of employed mothers based on "espousing something different" from their own mothers (Berg 1986, 42).

The notion of conflict, or guilt, that Berg describes rests on several suppositions: that motherhood is a unilaterally oppressive state; that employed mothers feel guilt; and that today's employed mothers do not have working mothers (which partially explains their guilt feelings). Inasmuch as large numbers of working-class, immigrant, and racial-ethnic women have long traditions of working in the formal and informal economic sectors, such assumptions are suspect.

Research on women of Mexican descent and employment indicates their labor force participation is lower than that of other women when they have young children (Hayghe 1984; U.S. Bureau of the Census 1991; U.S. Bureau of the Census 1987).[11] Moreover, Chicanas and Mexicanas are occupationally segregated in the lowest paying of female-dominated jobs (Dill, Cannon, and Vanneman 1987; Malveaux and Wallace 1987; Ruiz 1988). Explanations for their unique employment situation range from analyses of labor-market structures and employer discrimination (Barrera 1979; Almaguer 1975; Segura 1984) to deficient individual characteristics (e.g., education, job skills) (Tienda and Guhleman 1985) and cultural differences (Kranau, Green, and Valencia-Weber 1982; Mirande and Enriquez 1979).

Analyses of Chicana and Mexicana employment that utilize a cultural framework typically explain the women's lower labor force participation, higher fertility, lower levels of education, and higher levels of unemployment as part of an ethnic or cultural tradition (Kranau, Green, and Valencia-Weber 1982). That is, Chicano and Mexican culture emphasizes a strong allegiance to an idealized form of motherhood and a patriarchal ideology that frowns on working wives and mothers and does not encourage girls to pursue higher education or employment options. These attitudes are supposed to vary by generation, with immigrant women (from Mexico) holding the most conservative attitudes (Ortiz and Cooney 1984).

There are two major flaws in the research of Chicana and Mexicana employment, however. First, inconsistency in distinguishing between native-born and resident immigrant women characterizes much of this literature. Second, overreliance on linear acculturation persists. Both procedures imply either that Chicanas and Mexicanas are very similar or that they lie on a sort of cultural continuum, with Mexican immigrants at one end holding more conservative behaviors and attitudes grounded in traditional (often rural) Mexican culture, and U.S.-born Chicanos holding an amalgamation of cultural traditions from Mexico and the United States (Keefe and Padilla 1987; Richard H. Mendoza 1984). In terms of motherhood and employment, therefore, Mexicans should have more "traditional" ideas about motherhood than U.S.-born Chicanas. Since the traditional ideology of motherhood typically refers to women staying home to "mother" children rather than going outside the home to work, Mexicanas theoretically should not be as willing to work as Chicanas or North American women in general, unless there is severe economic need. This formulation, while logical, reflects an underlying emphasis on modernity—or the view that traditional Mexican culture lags behind North American culture in developing behaviors and attitudes conducive to participating fully in modern society (Zinn 1979, 1980, 1982). Inasmuch as conventional North American culture, in developing views of motherhood, typically idealizes exiting the labor market to care for children, embracing this prototype may be more conducive to maintaining patriarchal privilege (female economic subordination to men) than facilitating economic progress generally. In this sense, conceptualizations of motherhood that affirm its economic character may be more accommodating to women's market participation in the United States.

Methods and Sample

This essay is based on in-depth interviews with thirty Mexican origin women—thirteen Chicanas and seventeen Mexicanas—who had participated in the 1978–1979 or 1980–1981 cohorts of an adult-education and employment-training program in the greater San Francisco Bay area.[12] All thirty respondents had been involved in a conjugal relationship (either legal marriage or informal cohabitation with a male partner) at some point in their lives before I interviewed them in 1985; all had at least one child under eighteen years of age. At the time of their interviews, six Chicanas and fourteen Mexicanas were married; seven Chicanas and three Mexicanas were single parents.

On average, the married Chicanas had 1.2 children at home, and the Mexicanas had 3.5 children. Both Chicana and Mexicana single mothers averaged 1.6 children. The children of the Chicanas tend to be preschool age or in elementary school. The children of the Mexicanas exhibit a greater age range (from infant to late adolescence), reflecting earlier marriages and slightly older average age.

With respect to other relevant characteristics, all but two Mexicanas and five Chicanas had either a high-school diploma or its equivalent. The average age was 27.4 years for the Chicanas; and thirty-three years for the Mexicanas.[13] On leaving the employment-training program, all the women secured employment. At the time of their interviews, about half of the Chicanas ($N = 7$); and three-fourths of the Mexicanas were employed ($N = 12$). Only two out of the seven (28 percent) employed Chicanas worked full-time (thirty-five or more hours per week), whereas nine out of the twelve (75 percent) employed Mexicanas worked full-time. Most of the Chicanas found clerical or service jobs (e.g., teacher assistants); most of the Mexicanas labored in operative jobs or in the service sector (e.g., hotel maids), with a small minority employed as clerical workers.

I gathered in-depth life and work histories from the women to ascertain what factors motivated them to enter, exit, and stay employed in their specific occupations; whether familial roles or ideology influenced their employment consistency; and whether other barriers limited their job attachment and mobility. My examination of the relationship between motherhood and employment forms part of a larger study of labor-market stratification and occupational mobility among Chicana and Mexican immigrant women (Segura 1986).

Motherhood and Employment

Nearly all of the respondents, both Chicana and Mexicana, employed and nonemployed, speak of motherhood as their most important social role. They differ sharply in their employment behaviors and views regarding the relationship between motherhood and market work. The women studied fall into four major groups.

The first group consists of five involuntary nonemployed mothers who are not employed but care full-time for their children. All of these women want to be employed at least part time but either cannot secure the job they want and/or feel pressured to be at home mothering full time. The second group consists of six voluntary nonemployed mothers who are not employed but remain out of the labor force by choice. They feel committed to staying at home to care for preschool- and/or elementary-school-aged children. The third group, ambivalent employed mothers, includes eleven employed women who have either preschool- or elementary-school-aged children. Although women in this group believe that employment interferes with motherhood and feel guilty when they work outside the home, they are employed at least part-time. The fourth group, nonambivalent employed mothers, includes eight employed women, all Mexicanas. What distinguishes these women from the ambivalent employed mothers is their view that employment and motherhood are compatible social dynamics irrespective of the age of their children. Some of these women believe employment could be problematic, however, if a family member could not care for their children or be at home for the children when they arrived from school.

Chicanas tend to fall in the second and third groups, whereas Mexicanas predominate in the first and fourth groups. Three reasons emerged as critical in explaining this difference: (1) the economic situations of their families; (2) labor market structure (four-fifths of the nonemployed Mexicanas were involuntarily unemployed); and (3) women's conceptualizations of motherhood, in particular, their expressed need to mother. The age of the women and the number of children did not fall into any discernible pattern, so I did not engage them in depth within my analysis.

Voluntary Nonemployed Mothers

The voluntary nonemployed mothers include three married Chicanas, one single-parent Mexicana, and one single-parent Chicana. All but one woman exited the labor market involuntarily (for reasons such as layoffs or disability). All five women remain out of the labor force by choice. For all, the expressed need to mother appears to be strong—overriding all other concerns. They view motherhood as mutually exclusive with employment. Lydia, a married Chicana with a small toddler, articulates her perspective.

> Right now, since we've had the baby, I feel, well, he [her husband] feels the same way, that I want to spend this time with her and watch her grow up. See, because when I was small my grandmother raised me so I felt this *loss* when my grandmother died. And I've never gotten that *real love*, that mother love from my mother. We have a friendship, but we don't have that "motherly love." I want my daughter to know that I'm here, especially at her age, it's very important for them to know that when they

cry that mama's there. Even if it's not a painful cry, it's still important for them to know that mommy's there. She's my number one—she's all my attention ... so working-wise, it's up to [her husband] right now.

Susana, a Chicana single parent with a five-year-old child, said, "I'm the type of person that has always wanted to have a family. I think it was more like I didn't have a mother and a father and the kids all together in the same household all happy. I didn't have that. And that's what I want more than anything! I want to be different from my mother, who has worked hard and is successful in her job. I don't want to be successful in the same way."

Lydia, Susana, and the other voluntarily unemployed Chicanas adamantly assert that motherhood requires staying home with their children. Susana said, "A good mother is there for her children all the time when they are little and when they come home from school." All the Chicanas in this category believe that motherhood means staying home with children—even if it means going on welfare. This finding is similar to other accounts of working-class women.[14]

The sense, shared among this group of women, that motherhood and employment are irreconcilable, especially when children are of preschool age, is related to their social locations. A small minority of the Chicanas were raised by nonemployed mothers ($N = 3$), and they feel they should stay at home with their children as long as it's economically feasible. Most of the Chicanas, however, resemble Lydia and Susana, who were raised by employed mothers. Although these women recognize that their mothers worked out of economic need, they believe they did not receive sufficient love and care from their mothers. Throughout their interviews, this group of Chicanas expressed hostility and resentment against their employed mothers for having left them with other caretakers. These feelings contribute to their decisions to stay at home with their children and/or their sense of guilt when they are employed. Their hostility and guilt defies psychoanalytic theories that speculate that the cycle of gender construction locking women into exclusive mothering roles can be broken if the primary caretaker (the mother) undertakes more diverse roles.[15] Rather, Chicanas appear to value current conceptualizations of motherhood that prioritize the expressive work of the mother as distinct from her economic activities.

This group of Chicanas seems to be pursuing the social construction of motherhood that is idealized within their community, their churches, and society at large (Ramírez and Castañeda 1974; Peck and Diaz-Guerrero 1967; Escobat and Randolph 1982). Among Chicanos and Mexicanos the image of *la madre* as self-sacrificing and holy is a powerful standard against which women often compare themselves (Mirande and Enriquez 1979; Melville 1980a; Anzaldua 1987; Linda C. Fox 1983). The Chicana informants also seem to accept the notions that women's primary duty is to provide for the emotional welfare of the children and that economic activities which take them outside the home are secondary. Women's desire to enact the socially constructed motherhood ideal was further strengthened by their conviction that many of their current problems (e.g., low levels of education, feelings of inadequacy, single parenthood) are related to growing up in families that did not conform to the stay-at-home mother/father-as-provider configuration. Their evaluation of the close relationship between motherhood and the economic or emotional well-being of offspring parallels popular emphasis on the primacy of individual efforts and the family environment to emotional vigor and achievement (Parsons and Bales 1955; Bradley and Caldwell 1984; Parcel and Menaghan 1990; Caspi and Elder 1988).

Informants in this group speak to a complex dimension of mothering and gender construction in the Chicano and Mexicano communities. These women reject their employed mothers' organization of family life. As children, most had been cared for by other family members, and they now feel closer to their grandmothers or other female relatives than to their own biological mothers. This causes them considerable pain—pain they want to spare their own children. Many, like Susana, do not want to be successful in the tradition of their own employed mothers. Insofar as success means leaving their children with other caretakers, it contradicts their conceptualization of motherhood. Rather, they frame success in more affective terms: having children who are happy and doing well in school. This does not suggest that Chicanas disagree with the notion that having a good job or a lucrative career denotes success. They simply feel that successful careers could and should be deferred until their children are older (for instance, in the upper grades of elementary school) and doing well academically and emotionally.

Only one married Mexicana, Belen, articulated views similar to those of the Chicanas. Belen left the labor market in 1979 to give birth and care for her newborn child. It is important to note that she has a gainfully employed husband who does not believe mothers should work outside the home. Belen, who has two children and was expecting a third when I interviewed her, said, "I wanted to work or go back to school after having my first son, but my husband didn't want me to. He said, 'No one can take care of your child the way you can.' He did not want me to work. And I did not feel right having someone else care for my son. So I decided to wait until my children were older."

Belen's words underscore an important dynamic that affects both Mexicana and Chicana conceptualizations of motherhood: spousal employment and private patriarchy. Specifically, husbands working in full-time, year-round jobs with earnings greater than those of their wives tend to pressure women to mother full time. Women who succumb to this pressure become economically dependent on their husbands and reaffirm male authority in the organization of the family. These particular women tend to consider motherhood and employment in similar ways, which suggests that the form the social construction of motherhood takes involves women's economic relationship to men as well as length of time in the United States.

Involuntary Nonemployed Mothers

Four Mexicanas and one Chicana were involuntarily nonemployed. They had been laid off from their jobs or were on temporary disability leave. Three women (two Mexicanas, one Chicana) were seeking employment; the other two were in the last stages of pregnancy but intended to look for a job as soon as possible after their child's birth. All five women reported feeling "good" about being home with their children, but wanted to rejoin the labor force as soon as possible. Ideologically these women viewed motherhood and employment as reconcilable social dynamics. As Isabel, an unemployed production worker, married with eight children, said, "I believe that women always work more. We who are mothers work to maintain the family by working outside, but also inside the house caring for the children."

Isabel voiced a sentiment held by all of the informants—that women work hard at motherhood. Since emigrating to the United States about a decade before, Isabel had been employed nearly continuously, with only short leaves for childbearing. Isabel and nearly all of the Mexicanas describe growing up in environments where women, men, and children were important economic actors. In this regard they are similar to the nonambivalent employed mothers—all of whom are also Mexicanas. They tend not to dichotomize social life in the same way as the voluntary nonemployed Chicanas and ambivalent employed informants. Although all of the Chicanas believe that staying home best fulfills their mother roles, slightly fewer than half actually stay out of the labor market to care for their young children. The rest of the Chicanas are employed and struggling to reconcile motherhood with employment.

Ambivalent Employed Mothers

Ambivalent employed mothers express guilt about working and assert they would not work if they did not have to for economic reasons. Seven of these women are Chicanas; four are Mexicanas.

To alleviate their guilt and help meet their families' economic goals, most of the Chicanas work in part-time jobs, an option that permits them to be home when their children arrive from school. Despite this, they continue to feel guilty and unhappy about working. As Jenny, a married Chicana with two children, ages two and four, who is employed part-time, said, "Sure, I feel guilty. I *should* be with them [her children] while they're little. He [her husband] really feels that I should be with my kids all the time. And it's true."

Despite their guilt, most of the women in this group remain employed because their jobs offer them the means to provide for family economic betterment—a goal that transcends staying home with their children. However, women's utilization of economic rationales for working sometimes served as a smoke screen for individualistic desires to "do something outside the home" and to establish a degree of autonomy. Several women, for example, stated that they enjoyed having their "own money." When asked to elaborate, they typically retreated to a familistic stance. That is, much of *her* money is used *for the family* (childcare, family presents, clothing). When money is used *for the woman* (makeup, going out with the girls), it is often justified as necessary for her emotional well-being, which in turn helps her to be a good wife and mother.

The Mexicanas mothers who are employed express their ambivalence somewhat differently from the Chicanas. One Mexicana works full-time; the other three are employed part-time. Angela, a Mexicana married with one child and employed full-time as a seamstress, told me with glistening eyes, "Always I have had to work. I had to leave my son with the baby-sitter since he was six months old. It was difficult. Each babysitter has their own way of caring for children which isn't like yours. I know the babysitter wouldn't give him the food I left. He always had on dirty diapers and was starving when I would pick him up. But there wasn't any other recourse. I had to work. I would just clean him and feed him when I got home."

Angela's guilt stemmed from her inability to find good, affordable childcare. Unlike most of the Mexicanas, who had extensive family networks, Angela and her husband had few relatives to rely on in the United States. Unlike the Chicana informants, Angela did not want to exit the labor market to care for her child. Her desire is reinforced by economic need; her husband is irregularly employed.[16] For the other three Mexicanas in this group, guilt as an employed mother appears to have developed with stable spousal employment. That is, the idea of feeling guilty about full-time employment emerged *after* husbands became employed in secure, well-paying jobs and "reminded" them of the importance of stay-at-home, full-time motherhood. Lourdes, married with eight children and working as a part-time hotel maid, said, "I was offered a job at a factory, working from eleven at night to seven in the morning. But I had a baby and so I wasn't able to work. I would have liked to take the job because it paid $8.25 an hour. I couldn't though, because of my baby. And my husband didn't want me to work at night. He said, 'If we both work at night, who will take care of the children?' So I didn't take the job."

To thwart potential guilt over full-time employment and to ease marital tension (had she taken the job, she would have earned more money than her husband), Lourdes declined the high-paying job. When her child turned two, she opted to work part time as a hotel maid. Lourdes and the other Mexicanas who were employed part time, told me that they would work full time if their husbands supported their preferences. Mexicanas' ambivalence, then, is related to unease about their children's childcare situations, as well as to anger at being held accountable to a narrow construction of motherhood enforced by their husbands.

All of the ambivalent employed mothers report worrying about their children while at work. While this does not necessarily impair their job performance, it adds another psychological or emotional burden on their shoulders. This burden affects their ability to work full time (overtime is especially problematic) or to seek the means (especially schooling) to advance in their jobs.

Women seem particularly troubled when they have to work on weekends, which robs them of precious family time. As Elena, a Chicana single parent with two children, ages nine and three, who works part time as a hotel maid, said, "Yes, I work on weekends. And my kids, you know how kids are—they don't like it. And it's hard. But I hope to find a job soon where the schedule is fixed and I won't have to work on weekends—because that time should be for my kids."

There is a clear sense among the women I interviewed that a boundary should exist between family time and market time. When this boundary collapses, women experience both internal conflict (within the woman herself) and external conflict (among family members). They regard with disfavor and unhappiness jobs that overlap with family time. When economic reasons compel women to work during what they view as family time, they usually try to find as quickly as possible a different job, one that allows them to better meet their mother roles.

Interestingly, the Chicanas appear less flexible in reconciling the boundaries of family time and market time than the Mexicanas. That is, Chicanas overwhelmingly "choose" part-time employment to limit the amount of spillover time from employment on motherhood and family activities. Mexicanas, on the other hand, overwhelmingly work full time ($N = 9$) and attempt to do both familial caretaking and market work as completely as possible.

Nonambivalent Employed Mothers

This category consists of Mexicana immigrants, both married and single-parent (six and two women, respectively). Mexicanas in this group do not describe motherhood as a need requiring a separate sphere for optimal realization. Rather, they refer to motherhood as one function of womanhood compatible with employment insofar as employment allows them to provide for their family's economic subsistence or betterment. As Pilar, a married Mexicana with four children, employed full time as a line supervisor in a factory, said, "I work to help my children. That's what a mother should do." This group of Mexicanas does not express guilt over leaving their children in the care of others so much as regret over the limited amount of time they could spend with them. As Norma, a Mexicana full-time clerical worker, who is married with two children, ages three and five, said,

> I don't feel guilty for leaving my children because if I didn't work they might not have the things they have now.... Perhaps if I had to stay at home I would feel guilty and frustrated. I'm not the type that can stay home twenty-four hours a day. I don't think that would help my children any because I would feel pressured at being cooped up [*encerrada*] at home. And that way I wouldn't have the same desire to play with my daughters. But now, with the time we have together, we do things that we want to, like run in the park, because there's so little time.

All of the Mexicanas in this group articulate views similar to Norma's. Their greater comfort with the demands of market and family work emanates from their social locations. All of the Mexicanas come from poor or working-class families, where motherhood embraced both economic and affective features. Their activities were not viewed as equal to those of men, however, and ideologically women saw themselves as helping the family rather than providing for it.

Few Mexicanas reported that their mothers were wage laborers ($N = 3$), but instead described a range of economic activities they remembered women doing "for the family."[17] Mexicanas from rural villages ($N = 7$) recounted how their mothers had worked on the land and made assorted products or food to sell in local marketplaces. Mexicanas from urban areas ($N = 5$) also discussed how their mothers had been economically active. Whether rural or urban, Mexicanas averred that their mothers had taught them to "help" the family as soon as possible. As Norma said, "My mother said, 'It's one thing for a woman to lie around the house but it's a different thing for the work that needs to be done.' As the saying goes, 'work is never done; the work does you in' [el trabajo acaba con uno; uno nunca acaba con el trabajo].''

Lourdes and two other Mexicanas cleaned houses with their mothers after school. Other mothers sold clothes to neighbors, cooked and sold food, or did assorted services for pay (e.g., giving penicillin shots to neighbors). The Mexicanas do not view these activities as separate or less important than the emotional nurturing of children and family. Rather, they appreciate both the economic and the expressive as important facets of motherhood.

Although the Mexicanas had been raised in worlds where women were important economic actors, this did not signify gender equality. On the contrary, male privilege, or patriarchy, characterizes the organization of the family, the economy, and the polity in both rural and urban Mexican society (Fernandez-Kelly 1983c; Guendelman and Perez-Itriago 1987; Baca and Dexter 1985). The Mexicanas indicated that men wielded greater authority in the family, the community, and the state than women. The Mexicanas also tended to uphold male privilege in the family by viewing both domestic work and women's employment as less important than the work done by men. As Adela, a married Mexicana with four children, said, "Men are much stronger and do much more difficult work than women." Mexicanas also tended to defer to husbands as the heads of the family—a position they deemed both "natural" and "holy."[18]

Working at Motherhood

The differences presented here between the Chicanas and Mexicanas regarding motherhood and employment stem from their distinct social locations. Raised in rural or working-class families in Mexico, the Mexicanas described childhoods where they and their mothers actively contributed to the economic subsistence of their families by planting crops, harvesting, selling homemade goods, and cleaning houses. Their situations resonate with what some researchers term a family economy, where all family members work at productive tasks differentiated mainly by age and sex (Rothstein 1983; Cowan 1987; Tilly and Scott 1978). In this type of structure, there is less distinction between economic life and domestic life. Motherhood in this context is both economic and expressive, embracing both employment as well as childbearing.

The family economy that Mexicanas experienced differs from the family organization that characterizes most of the Chicanas' childhoods. The Chicanas come from a world that idealizes a male wage earner as the main economic provider, with women seen primarily as consumers and only secondarily as economic actors (Bernard 1974, 1981; Hood 1986). Women in this context are mothers first, wage earners second. Families that challenge this structure are often discredited or perceived as dysfunctional and the source of many social problems (Walker and Best 1991; Doherty and Needle 1991; Clark and Ramsey 1990). The ambivalence Chicanas recurrently voice stems from their belief in what Rosabeth Moss Kanter (1977) calls "the myth of separate worlds." They seek to realize the popular notion or stereotype that family is a separate structure—a haven in a heartless world. Their attachment to this ideal is underscored by a harsh critique of their own employed mothers and themselves when they work full-time. Motherhood framed within this context appears irreconcilable with employment.

There are other facets to the differences between Chicanas and Mexicanas. The Mexicanas, as immigrant women, came to the United States with a vision of improving the life chances of their families and themselves. This finding intersects with research on selective immigration, that is, that Mexican immigrants tend to possess higher levels of education than the national average in Mexico, as well as a wide range of behavioral characteristics (e.g., higher achievement orientation) conducive to success in the United States (Chavez and Buriel 1986; Buriel 1984; Chavez 1985).

The Mexicanas emigrated hoping to work—hence their high attachment to employment, even in physically demanding, often demeaning jobs. Mexican and Chicano husbands support their wives' desires to work so long as this employment does not challenge the patriarchal structure of the family. In other words, so long as the Mexicanas (1) articulate high attachment to both motherhood and family caretaker roles, (2) frame their employment in terms of family economic goals, and (3) do not ask men to do equal amounts of housework or childcare, they encounter little resistance from husbands or other male family members.

When Mexican and Chicano husbands secure good jobs, however, they begin pressuring wives to quit working or to work only part time. In this way, Mexican and Chicano men actively pursue continuity of their superordinate position within the family. This suggests that the way in which motherhood is conceptualized in both the Mexican and Chicano communities, particularly with respect to employment, is wedded to male privilege, or patriarchy. Ironically, Mexicanas' sense of employment's continuity with motherhood enhances their job attachment but does not challenge a patriarchal family structure or ethos.

Similarly, Chicanas' preference for an idealized form of motherhood does not challenge male privilege in their community. Their desire to stay at home to mother exercised a particularly strong influence on the employment behavior of single-parent Chicanas and women with husbands employed in relatively good jobs. This preference reflects an adherence both to an idealized, middle-class lifestyle that glorifies women's domestic roles, as well as to maintenance of a patriarchal family order. Chicanas feel they should stay at home to provide their children with the mothering they believe children should have—mothering that many of them had not experienced. Chicanas also feel compelled by husbands and the larger community to maintain the status of men as good providers. Men earning wages adequate to provide for their families' needs usually urged their wives to leave the labor market. While the concept of the good provider continues to be highly valued in U.S. society, it also serves as a rationale that upholds male privilege ideologically and materially, and reinforces the myth of separate spheres that emanates from the organization of the family and the economy.

Conclusion

By illustrating how Chicanas and Mexicanas differ in their conceptualizations and organization of the motherhood and employment nexus, this essay demonstrates how motherhood is a culturally formed structure with various meanings and subtexts. The vitality of these differences among a group who share a common historical origin and many cultural attributes underscores the need for frameworks that analyze diversity among all groups of women. Most essential to such an undertaking is a critique of the privileging of the separate spheres concept in analyses of women and work.

This essay provides additional coherence to recent contentions that the private-public dichotomy lacks immediate relevance to less-privileged women (e.g., Chicanas and Mexican immigrant women). In the process of illustrating how Chicanas and Mexicanas organized the interplay between motherhood and employment, it became clear that a more useful way of understanding this intersection might be to problematize motherhood itself. Considering motherhood from the vantage point of women's diverse social locations revealed considerable heterogeneity in how one might speak of it. For example, motherhood has an economic component for both groups of women, but it is most strongly expressed by Mexicana immigrants. The flavor of the expressive, however, flows easily across both groups of women, and for the Mexicanas embraces the economic. What this suggests is that the dichotomy of the separate spheres lacks relevance to Chicanas and Mexicanas, as well as to other women whose social origins make economic work necessary for survival.

This leads one to consider the relative place and function of the ideology of motherhood prevalent in U.S. society. Motherhood constructed to privilege the woman who stays at home serves myriad functions. It pushes women to dichotomize their lives rather than develop a sense of fluidity across roles, responsibilities, and preferences. Idealized, stay-at-home motherhood eludes most American women with children, but as an ideology it tells them what "should be," rendering them failures as women when they enter the labor market. Hence the feelings of ambivalence that for the most part characterized employed mother's lives—except among those who had not yet internalized these standards. The present research provided examples of such women, along with the understanding that other women from different social locations may demonstrate distinct ways of organizing the motherhood-employment nexus as well.

Feminist analyses of women and work emphasize the role of patriarchy in maintaining male privilege and domination economically and ideologically. But male privilege is not experienced equally by all men and that patriarchy itself can be expressed in different ways. Notions of motherhood among Mexicanas and Chicanas are embedded in different ideological constructs operating within two systems of patriarchy. For Mexicanas, patriarchy takes the form of a corporate family model, with all members contributing to the common good. For Chicanas, the patriarchal structure centers more closely around a public-private dichotomy that idealizes men as economic providers and women primarily as caretakers-consumers.

The finding that women from more traditional backgrounds (such as rural Mexico) are likely to approach full-time employment with less ambivalence than more "American" women (such as the Chicanas) rebuts linear acculturation models that assume a negative relationship between ideologies (such as motherhood) constructed within traditional Mexican society and employment. It also complements findings on the negative relationship between greater length of time in the United States and high aspirations among Mexicans (Buriel 1984).[19] This suggests that employment problems are related less to traditional cultural configurations than to labor-market structure and employment policies. Understanding the intersections between employment policy, social ideology, and private need is a necessary step toward expanding possibilities for women in U.S. society.

Notes

This essay is a revised version of "Ambivalence or Continuity? Motherhood and Employment among Chicanas and Mexican Immigrant Women," *Aztlán* 20, nos. 1–2 (1991): 119–50. I would like to thank Maxine Baca Zinn, Evelyn Nakano Glenn, Arlie Hochschild, Beatriz Pesquera, and Vicki Ruiz for their constructive feedback and criticism of earlier drafts of this essay. A special thanks goes to Jon Cruz for his assistance in titling this essay. Any remaining errors or inconsistencies are my own responsibility. This research was supported in part by a 1986–1987 University of California President's Postdoctoral Fellowship.

1 The view that mothers should not work outside the home typically pertains to married women. Current state-welfare policies (e.g., Aid to Families with Dependent Children, workfare) indicate that single, unmarried mothers belong in the labor force, not at home caring for their children full-time. See Gerstel and Gross 1987; Zinn and Sarri 1984; Folbre 1991.

2 In June 1990 over half (53.1 percent) of women between the ages of eighteen and forty-four who had had a child in the last year were in the labor force. This proportion varied by race: 54.9 percent of white women, 46.9 percent of black women, and 44.4 percent of Latinas were in the labor force (U.S. Bureau of the Census 1991, 5).

3 Simon and Landis (1989) report that a 1986 Gallup poll indicates that support for married women to work outside the home is considerably greater than in 1938: 76 percent of women and 78 percent of men approve (270). In 1938, only 25 percent of women and 19 percent of men approved. The 1985 Roper poll finds the American public adhering to the view that a husband's career supersedes that of his wife: 72 percent of women and 62 percent of men agree that a wife should quit her job and relocate if her husband is offered a good job in another city (Simon and Landis 1989, 272). In the reverse situation, 80 percent of women and 22 percent of men believe a husband should quit his job and relocate with his wife (272). Simon and Landis conclude, "The Women's Movement has not radicalized the American woman: she is still prepared to put marriage and children ahead of her career and to allow her husband's status to determine the family's position in society" (269).

4 The concept of separate spheres is approached in a variety of ways and often critiqued (Barrett 1980; Glazer 1984). Eli Zaretsky (1976) contends that distinct family and market spheres arose with the development of industrial capitalism: "Men and women came to see the family as separate from the economy, and personal life as a separate sphere of life divorced from the larger economy" (78). This stance is substantially different from that of early radical feminist approaches, including that of Shulamith Firestone (1970), who argued that the separation antedates history. Other scholars assert that the relations of production and reproduction are intertwined and virtually inseparable (Hartmann 1976).

5 Jane C. Hood (1986) argues that the "ideal" of the stay-at-home mother and male provider has historically been an unrealistic standard for families outside the middle and upper classes. She points out that early surveys of urban workers indicate that between 40 and 50 percent of all families supplemented their income with the earnings of wives and children.

6 Native-born status is not an essential requirement for the ethnic label *Chicana/o*. There are numerous identifiers used by people of Mexican descent, including: *Chicana/o, Mexican, Mexican American, Mexicana/o, Latina/o,* and *Hispanic*. People of Mexican descent often use two or three of the above labels, depending on the social situation (e.g., *Mexican American* in the family, *Chicana/o* at school) (John A. Garcia

1981; Keefe and Padilla 1987). My designation of study informants as either *Chicana* or *Mexicana* represents an analytic separation that facilitates demonstrating the heterogeneity among this group.

7. Gary S. Becker's classic treatise, *Human Capital*, uses the following example borrowed from George Stigler (1961): "Women spend less time in the labor force than men and, therefore, have less incentive to invest in market skills; tourists spend little time in any one area and have less incentive than residents of the area to invest in knowledge of specific consumption activities" (Becker 1975, 74).

8. Some institutional economists argue that statistical discrimination is a critical labor-market dynamic that often impedes women and minorities (Arrow 1987; Phelps 1980). This perspective suggests that prospective employers often lack detailed information about individual applicants and therefore utilize statistical averages and normative views of the relevant group(s) to which the applicant belongs in their hiring decisions (e.g., college-educated men tend to be successful and committed employees; all women are potential mothers; women tend to exit the labor force for childbearing).

   William T. Bielby and James N. Baron (1987) pose an important critique to the underlying rationale of statistical discrimination, arguing that utilizing perceptions of group differences between the sexes is "neither as rational nor as efficient as the economists believe" (216). That is, utilizing stereotypical notions of men's work and women's work is often costly to employers and is therefore irrational. This suggests that sex segregation is imbedded in organizational policies which reflect and reinforce "belief systems that are also rather inert" (221–22).

9. The phrase "competing urgencies" was coined by Arlie R. Hochschild and quoted in Rubin 1983.

10. Bielby and Baron (1987) note, "employers expect certain behaviors from women (e.g., high turnover) and therefore assign them to routine tasks and dead-end jobs. Women respond by exhibiting the very behavior employers expect, thereby reinforcing the stereotype" (221).

11. In June 1986 (the year closest to the year I interviewed the respondents), nationally 49.8 percent of all women with newborn children were in the labor force. Women demonstrated differences in this behavior: 49.7 percent of white women, 51.1 percent of black women, and 40.6 percent of Latinas with newborn children were in the labor force (U.S. Bureau of the Census 1987, 5).

12. For additional information on the methods and sample selection, see Segura 1986.

13. The ages of the Chicanas range from 23 to 42 years. The Mexicanas reported ages from 24 to 45. The age profile indicates that most of the women were in peak childbearing years.

14. See, for example, Wearing 1984.

15. See, for example, Chodorow 1979.

16. For a full discussion of the interplay between the economic goals and economic status of the respondents and their employment decisions, see Segura 1989b.

17. Two of the Mexicanas reported that their mothers had died while they were toddlers, and the women were therefore unable to discuss the economic roles of their mothers.

18 Research indicates religious involvement plays an important role in gender beliefs (Baker, Epstein, and Forth 1981; Peek and Brown 1980). Of particular interest for the present study is that involvement in fundamentalist Christian churches is positively related to adherence to traditional gender-role ideology (Wilcox and Cook 1989; Wilcox 1987). Half of the Mexicanas (and all but two Chicanas) adhered to the Roman Catholic religion; half belonged to various fundamentalist Christian churches (e.g., Assembly of God). Two Chicanas belonged to other Protestant denominations. The women who belonged to the Assembly of God tended to both work full time in the labor market and voice the strongest convictions of male authority in the family. During their interviews many of the women brought out the Bible and showed me the biblical passages that authorized husbands to "rule" the family. Catholic women also voiced traditional beliefs regarding family structure but did not invoke God.

19 In their analysis of differences in educational goals among Mexican-Americans, Raymond Buriel, Silverio Caldaza, and Richard Vasquez (1982) found that "third generation Mexican Americans felt less capable of fulfilling their educational objectives" (50). Similar findings were reported by Francois Nielsen and Roberto M. Fernandez (1981): "We find that students whose families have been in the U.S. longer have *lower* aspirations than recent immigrants" (76).

In their analysis of Hispanic employment, Frank D. Bean, C. Gray Swicegood, and Allan G. King (1985) reported an unexpected finding: English-proficient Mexican women exhibit a greater "constraining influence of fertility" on their employment vis-à-vis Spanish-speaking women (241). They speculate that more acculturated Mexican women may have "a greater desire for children of higher quality" and therefore "be more likely to devote time to the informal socialization and education of young children" (241). They wonder "why this should hold true for English-speaking but not Spanish-speaking women" (241).

"I'm Here, but I'm There": The Meanings
of Latina Transnational Motherhood
PIERRETTE HONDAGNEU-SOTELO
AND ERNESTINE AVILA

✳ While mothering is generally understood as practice that involves the preservation, nurturance, and training of children for adult life (Ruddick 1989), there are many contemporary variants distinguished by race, class, and culture (Collins 1994; Dill 1988, 1994b; Glenn 1994). Latina immigrant women who work and reside in the United States while their children remain in their countries of origin constitute one variation in the organizational arrangements, meanings, and priorities of motherhood—an arrangement we call "transnational motherhood." The meanings of motherhood are rearranged to accommodate such spatial and temporal separations. In the United States there is a long legacy of Caribbean women and African American women from the South leaving their children "back home" to seek work in the North. Since the early 1980s, thousands of Central American women, and increasing numbers of Mexican women, have migrated to the United States in search of jobs, many of them leaving their children behind with grandmothers, with other female kin, with the children's fathers, and sometimes with paid caregivers. In some cases the separation of time and distance are substantial; ten years may elapse before women are reunited with their children. In this essay we confine our analysis to Latina transnational mothers currently employed in Los Angeles in paid domestic work, one of the most gendered and racialized occupations, and examine how their meanings of motherhood shift in relation to the structures of late-twentieth-century global capitalism.[1]

Motherhood is not biologically predetermined but historically and socially constructed. Many factors set the stage for transnational motherhood. These factors include labor demand for Latina immigrant women in the United

States, particularly in paid domestic work; civil war, national economic crises, and particular development strategies, along with tenuous and scarce job opportunities for women and men in Mexico and Central America; and the subsequent increase in the numbers of female-headed households (although many transnational mothers are married). Of more interest than the macro-determinants of transnational motherhood, however, is the forging of new arrangements and meanings of motherhood.

Central American and Mexican women who leave their young children "back home" and come to the United States in search of employment are in the process of actively, if not voluntarily, building alternative constructions of motherhood. Transnational motherhood contradicts both dominant U.S., white, middle-class models of motherhood and most Latina ideological notions of motherhood. On the cusp of the millennium, transnational mothers and their families are blazing new terrain, spanning national borders, and improvising strategies for mothering. It is a brave odyssey, but one with deep costs.

Immigration: Gendering Transnational Perspectives

In pursuing this project, we draw from and engage in dialogue with literature on immigration and transnational frameworks, on family and motherhood, and on women's work, place, and space. The last decade has witnessed the emergence of transnational perspectives of migration. Arising primarily from postcolonial, postmodern-inspired anthropology and explicitly challenging the linear, bipolar model of "old country" and "new world," of "sojourner" and "settler" that is typical of assimilationist models and other well-established immigration paradigms, transnationalist proponents argue that the international circulation of people, goods, and ideas creates new transnational cultures, identities, and community spheres (Basch, Glick Schiller, and Szanton Blanc 1994; Kearney 1995a; Rouse 1991). Accordingly, these fluid entities become semiautonomous spheres in their own right, transcending national borders. The new emergent cultures and hybrid ways of life resemble neither those in the place of origin nor the place of destination.

Although these insights are useful, the transnational perspective entails three questionable assumptions. First, transnationalism emphasizes circulation and the indeterminance of settlement, but while significant segments of foreign-born Latinos regularly return to their countries for annual fiestas or to visit family members, most Latino immigrants are here to stay, regardless of their initial migration intentions. The majority of Latina/o immigrant workers in California are not working in industries with seasonal labor demand—agriculture employs only a small fraction of Mexicans for example—but in urban-based jobs requiring stability of employment.[2] A glance at cities, suburbs, and rural areas around California testifies to the demographic transformation, as new Latina/o communities have emerged in neighborhoods that were previously African American or white. While some of the Latina/o residents in these diaspora communities are involved in transnational political organizations and hometown associations, many more are involved in activities and organizations firmly rooted in the United States, with local Catholic parishes or storefront evangelical churches, parent-teacher associations and schools, and workplace associations. Transnationalism's emphasis on ephemeral circuits understates the permanency of Latina/o settlement.

The celebratory nature of the transnational perspective also merits caution. In some of the writings, it is almost as if resistance is suggested merely through movement across borders and by the formation of circuits which enhance the possibility of survival in places full of uncertainty. In these renditions, the power of the nation-state is often underestimated, and the costs—financial, social, and emotional—to the individuals involved in transnational perspective migration may be overlooked.

A final objection to the transnational perspective is with its assumption of genderless transnational migrants. In recent years, literature on women and migration has flourished (Pedraza 1991; Tienda and Booth 1991), but many studies that do look at women in migration—especially those informed by demography—examine gender as a variable rather than as a construct that organizes social life. With the exception of Sarah J. Mahler's recent work (1996), transnationalism, like assimilationist models that it counters, ignores gender altogether. Examining transnational motherhood, defined not as physical circuits of migration but as the circuits of affection, caring, and financial support that transcend national borders, provides an opportunity to gender views of transnationalism and immigration.

Rethinking Motherhood

Feminist scholarship has long challenged monolithic notions of family and motherhood that relegate women to the domestic arena of private-public dichotomies and that rely on the ideological conflation of family, woman, reproduction, and nurturance (Collier and Yanagisako 1987, 36).[3] Rethinking the family prompts the rethinking of motherhood (Glenn 1994; Thorne and Yalom 1992), allowing one to see that the glorification and exaltation of isolationist, privatized mothering is historically and culturally specific.

The "cult of domesticity" is a cultural variant of motherhood, one made possible by the industrial revolution, by breadwinner husbands who have access to employers who pay a "family wage," and by particular configurations of global and national socioeconomic and racial inequalities. Working-class women of color in the United States have rarely had access to the economic security that permits a biological mother to be the only one exclusively involved with mothering during the children's early years (Collins, 1994; Dill 1988, 1994b; Glenn 1994). As Evelyn Makano Glenn puts it, "Mothering is not just gendered, but also racialized" and differentiated by class (1994, 7). Both historically and in the contemporary period, women lacking the resources that allow for exclusive, full-time, round-the-clock mothering rely on various arrangements to care for children. Sharing mothering responsibilities with female kin and friends as "other mothers" (Collins 1991), by "kin-scription" (Stack and Burton 1994), or by hiring childcare workers (Uttal 1996) are widely used alternatives.

Women of color have always worked. Yet, many working women—including Latinas—hold the cultural prescription of solo mothering in the home as an ideal. This ideal is disseminated through cultural institutions of industrialization and urbanization, as well as from pre-industrial, rural peasant arrangements that allow for women to work while tending to their children. It is not only white, middle-class ideology but also strong Latina/o traditions, cultural practices, and ideals—Catholicism, the Virgin Madonna figure—that cast employment as oppositional to mothering. Cultural symbols that model maternal femininity, such as the Virgen de Guadalupe, and negative femininity, such as La Llorona and La Malinche, serve to control Mexican and Chicana women's conduct by prescribing idealized visions of motherhood.[4]

Culture, however, does not deterministically dictate what people do.[5] Many Latina women must work for pay, and many Latinas innovate income-earning strategies that allow them to simultaneously earn money and care for their children. They sew garments on industrial sewing machines at home (Fernandez-Kelly and García 1990) and incorporate their children into informal vending to friends and neighbors, at swap meets, or on the sidewalks (Chinchilla and Hamilton 1996). They may perform agricultural work alongside their children or engage in seasonal work (Zavella 1987). They may clean houses when their children are at school or, alternatively, incorporate their daughters into paid housecleaning (Romero 1992, 1997). Engagement in "invisible employment" allows for urgently needed income and the maintenance of the ideal of privatized mothering. The middle-class model of mothering is predicated on mother-child isolation in the home, while women of color have often worked with their children in close proximity (Collins 1994). In both cases, however, mothers are with their children. The long distances of time and space that separate transnational mothers from their children contrast sharply to both mother-child isolation in the home or mother-child integration in the workplace.

Transnational Mothers' Work, Place, and Space

Feminist geographers have focused on how gendered orientations to space influence the way people organize their daily work lives. While sociologists have tended to explain occupational segregation as rooted either in family or individual characteristics (human-capital theory) or in the workplace (labor-market segmentation), feminist geographers observe that women tend to take jobs close to home so that they can fulfill child-rearing and domestic duties (Hanson and Pratt 1995; Massey 1994). Transnational mothers, on the other hand, congregate in paid domestic work, an occupation that is relentlessly segregated not only by gender but also by race, class, and nationality/citizenship. To perform child-rearing and domestic duties for others, they radically break with deeply gendered spatial and temporal boundaries of family and work.

Performing domestic work for pay, especially in a live-in job, is often incompatible with providing primary care for one's own family and home (Glenn 1986; Rollins 1985; Mary Romero 1992, 1997).[6] Transnational mothering, however, is neither exclusive to live-in domestic workers nor to single mothers. Many women continue with transnational mothering after they move into live-out paid domestic work or into their jobs. Women with income-earning husbands may also become transnational mothers.[7] The women we interviewed did not necessarily divert their mothering to the children and homes of their employers but instead reformulated their own mothering to accommodate spatial and temporal gulfs.

Like other immigrant workers, most transnational mothers came to the United States with the intention to stay for a finite period of time. But as time passed and economic need remained, prolonged stays evolved. Marxist-informed theory maintains that the separation of work life and family life constitutes the separation of labor-maintenance costs from the labor reproduction costs (Burawoy 1976; Glenn 1986). According to this framework, Latina transnational mothers work to maintain themselves in the United States and to support their children—and reproduce the next generation of workers—in Mexico or Central America. One precursor to these arrangements was the mid-twentieth-century Bracero Program, which in effect legislatively mandated Mexican "absentee fathers" who came to work as contracted agricultural laborers in the United States. Other precursors, going back further in history, include the eighteenth and nineteenth centuries' coercive systems of labor, whereby African American slaves and Chinese sojourner laborers were denied the right to form residentially intact families (Dill 1988, 1994b).

Transnational mothering is different from some of these other arrangements in that now women with young children are recruited for U.S. jobs that pay far less than a family wage. When men come north and leave their families in Mexico—as they did during the Bracero Program and as many continue to do today—they are fulfilling familial obligations defined as breadwinning for the family. When women do so, they are embarking not only on an immigration journey but on a more radical gender-transformative odyssey. They are initiating separations of space and time from their communities of origin, homes, children, and—sometimes—husbands. In doing so, they must cope with stigma, guilt, and criticism from others. Furthermore, these women work primarily not in production of agricultural products or manufacturing but in reproductive labor, paid domestic work, and/or vending. Performing paid reproductive work for pay—especially caring for other people's children—is not always compatible with taking daily care of one's own family. All of this raises questions about the meanings and variations of motherhood in the late twentieth century.

Methodology

Materials for this article draw from a larger study of paid domestic work in Los Angeles County and from interviews conducted in adjacent Riverside County. The materials include in-depth interviews, a survey, and ethnographic fieldwork. We had not initially anticipated studying women who live and work apart from their children but serendipitously stumbled on this theme in the course of our research.

For this essay, we draw primarily on tape-recorded and fully transcribed interviews with twenty-six women who work as housecleaners and as live-out or live-in nanny-housekeepers. Of these twenty-six women, eight lived apart from their children to accommodate their migration and work arrangements, but other respondents also spoke poignantly about their views and experiences with mothering, and we draw on these materials as well. We also draw, to a lesser extent, on in-depth, fully transcribed interviews with domestic agency personnel. All of the interview respondents were located through informal snowball sampling. The domestic workers interviewed are all from Mexico, El Salvador, and Guatemala, but they are diverse in terms of demographic characteristics (such as education, civil status, and children), immigration (length of time in the United States, access to legal papers), and other job-related characteristics (English-language skills, driver's license, CPR training).

While the interviews provide close-up information about women's experiences and views of mothering, a survey administered to 153 paid domestic workers in Los Angeles provides some indicator of how widespread these transnational arrangements are among paid domestic workers. Because no one knows the total universe of paid domestic workers—many of whom lack legal papers and work in the informal sector where census data are not reliable—we drew a nonrandom sample in three types of sites located in or near affluent areas spanning from the west side of Los Angeles to the Hollywood area. We solicited respondents at evening English-as-a-second-language classes, at public parks where nannies and housekeepers congregate with children they care for in the midmorning hours, and at bus kiosks on Mondays and Tuesdays during the early morning hours when many domestic workers, including live-in workers, are traveling to their places of employment. While we refrained from conducting the survey in places where only certain types of domestic workers might be found (the employment agencies, or organizations of domestic workers), going to the bus stops, public parks, and English-as-a-second-language classes means that we undersampled domestic workers with access to private cars, driver's licenses, and good English skills. In short, we undersampled women who are earning at the higher end of the occupation.

The study also draws on ethnographic field research conducted in public parks, buses, private homes, a domestic workers' association, and the waiting room of a domestic-employment agency. A tape-recorded group discussion with about fifteen women—including several whose children remained in their countries of origin—in the employment-agency waiting room also informs the study. Nearly all of the in-depth interviews, structured survey interviews, and fieldwork were conducted in Spanish. The climate of fear produced by California voters' passage of anti-immigrant legislation in November 1994 perhaps dissuaded some potential respondents from participating in the study, but more important in shaping the interviews is the deeply felt pain expressed by the respondents. The interview transcripts include tearful segments in which the women recounted the daily indignities of their jobs and the raw pain provoked by the forced separation from their young children.

Transnational Motherhood and Paid Domestic Work

Just how widespread are transnational motherhood arrangements in paid domestic work? Of the 153 domestic workers surveyed, 75 percent had children. Contrary to the images of Latina immigrant women as breeder with large families—a dominant image used in the campaign to pass California's Proposition 187—about half (47 percent) of these women have only one or two children. More significant for our purposes is this finding: 40 percent of the women with children had left at least one of their children "back home" in their country of origin.

Transnational motherhood arrangements are not exclusive to paid domestic work, but there are particular features about how domestic work is organized that encourage temporal and spatial separations of a mother-employee and her children. Historically and in the contemporary period, paid domestic workers have had to limit or forfeit primary care of their families and homes to earn income by providing primary care to the families and homes of employers, who are privileged by race and class (Glenn 1986; Rollins 1985; Mary Romero 1992). Paid domestic work is organized in various ways, and there is a clear relationship between the type of job arrangement women have and the likelihood of experiencing transnational family arrangements with their children. To understand the permutations, it is necessary to explain how the employment is organized. Although there are variations within categories, we find it useful to employ a tripartite taxonomy of paid-domestic-work arrangements, including live-in and live-out nanny-housekeeper jobs and weekly housecleaning jobs.

Weekly housecleaners clean different houses on different days according to what Mary Romero (1992) calls modernized "job work" arrangements. These contractual-like employee-employer relations often resemble those between customer and vendor, and they allow employees a degree of autonomy and scheduling flexibility. Weekly employees are generally paid a flat fee, and they work shorter hours and earn considerably higher hourly rates than do live-in or live-out domestic workers. By contrast, live-in domestic workers work and live in isolation from their own families and communities, sometimes in arrangements with feudal remnants (Glenn 1986). There are often no hourly parameters to their jobs, and as our survey results show, most live-in workers in Los Angeles earn below minimum wage. Live-out domestic workers also usually labor as combination nanny-housekeepers, generally working for one household, but contrary to live-ins, they enter daily and return to their own home in the evening. Because of this, live-out workers better resemble industrial wage workers (Glenn 1986).

Live-in jobs are the least compatible with conventional mothering responsibilities. Only about half (16 out of 30) of live-ins surveyed have children, while 83 percent (53 out of 64) of live-outs and 77 percent (45 out of 59) of housecleaners do (see table). Furthermore, 82 percent of live-ins with children have at least one of their children in their country of origin. It is very difficult to work a live-in job when your children are in the United States. Employers who hire live-in workers do so because they generally want employees for jobs

Table. Domestic Workers: Wages, Hours Worked, and Children's Country of Residence

	Live-ins (N = 30)	Live-outs (N = 64)	Housecleaners (N = 59)
Mean hourly wage	$3.79	$5.90	$9.40
Mean hours worked per week	64	35	23
Domestic workers with children	(N = 16)	(N = 53)	(N = 45)
All children in the United States (%)	18	58	76
At least one child "back home" (%)	82	42	24

that may require round-the-clock service. As one owner of a domestic employment agency put it, "They [employers] want a live-in to have somebody at their beck and call. They want the hours that are most difficult for them covered, which is like six-thirty in the morning till eight when the kids go to school, and four to seven when the kids are home, and it's homework, bath, and dinner."

According to our survey, live-ins work an average of sixty-four hours per week. The best live-in worker, from an employer's perspective, is one without daily family obligations of her own. The workweek may consist of six very long workdays, which may span from dawn to midnight and include overnight responsibilities with sleepless or sick children, making it virtually impossible for live-in workers to sustain daily contact with their own families. Although some employers do allow for their employees' children to live in as well (Mary Romero 1996), this is rare. When it does occur, it is often fraught with special problems. In fact, minimal family and mothering obligations are an informal job-placement criterion for live-in workers. Many of the agencies specializing in the placement of live-in nanny-housekeepers will not even refer a woman who has children in Los Angeles to interviews for live-in jobs. As one agency owner explained, "As a policy here, we will not knowingly place a nanny in a live-in job if she has young kids here." A job seeker in an employment-agency waiting room acknowledged that she understood this job criterion more broadly: "You can't have a family, you can't have anyone [if you want a live-in job]."

The subminimum pay and the long hours for live-in workers also make it very difficult for these workers to have their children in the United States. Some live-in workers who have children in the same city as their place of employment hire their own nanny-housekeeper—often a much younger, female relative—to provide daily care for their children. Most live-ins, however, cannot afford this alternative; 93 percent of the live-ins surveyed earned less than the minimum wage (then $4.25 per hour). Once their children are in the same city, however, most women try to leave live-in work to live with their children.

At the other end of the spectrum are the housecleaners that we surveyed, who earn substantially higher wages than live-ins (averaging $9.46 per hour as opposed to $3.79) and who work fewer hours per week than live-ins (twenty-three as opposed to sixty-four). We suspect that many housecleaners in Los Angeles make even higher earnings and work more hours per week, because we know that the survey undersampled women who drive their own cars to work and who speak English. The survey suggests that housecleaners appear to be the least likely to experience transnational spatial and temporal separations from their children.

Financial resources and job terms enhance housecleaners' abilities to bring their children to the United States. Weekly housecleaning is not a bottom-of-the-barrel job, but rather an achievement. Breaking into housecleaning work is difficult because an employee needs to locate and secure several different employers. For this reason, relatively well-established women with more years of experience in the United States, who speak some English, who have a car, and who have job references predominate in weekly housecleaning. Women who are better established in the United States are also more likely to have their children here. The terms of weekly housecleaning employment—particularly the relatively fewer hours worked per week, scheduling flexibility, and relatively higher wages—allow them to live with, and care for, their children. It is therefore not surprising that 76 percent of housecleaners who are mothers have their children in the United States.

Compared with live-ins and weekly cleaners, live-out nanny-housekeepers are at an intermediate level with respect to the likelihood of transnational motherhood. Forty-two percent of the live-out nanny-housekeepers who are mothers report having at least one of their children in their country of origin. Live-out domestic workers, according to the survey, earn $5.90 per hour and work an average workweek of thirty-five hours. Their lower earnings, more regimented schedules, and longer workweeks than housecleaners, but higher earnings, shorter hours, and more scheduling flexibility than live-ins explain their intermediate incidence of transnational motherhood.

The Meanings of Transnational Motherhood

How do women transform the meaning of motherhood to fit immigration and employment? Being a transnational mother means more than being the mother to children raised in another country. It means forsaking deeply felt beliefs that biological mothers should raise their own children and replacing that belief with new definitions of motherhood. The ideal of biological mothers raising their own children is widely held but is also widely broken at both ends of the class spectrum. Wealthy elites have always relied on others—nannies, governesses, and boarding schools—to raise their children (Wrigley 1995), while poor, urban families often rely on kin and "other mothers" (Collins 1991).

In Latin America, in large, peasant families, the eldest daughters are often in charge of the daily care of the younger children, and in situations of extreme poverty, children as young as five or six may be loaned or hired out to well-to-do families as "child-servants," sometimes called *criadas* (Gill 1994).[8] A middle-aged Mexican woman that we interviewed, now a weekly housecleaner, homeowner, and mother of five children, recalled her own experience as a child-servant in Mexico: "I started working in a house when I was eight ... they hardly let me eat any food.... It was terrible, but I had to work to help my mother with the rent." This recollection of her childhood experiences points out how contemporary notions of motherhood are historically and socially circumscribed and also correspond to the meanings assigned to childhood (Zelizer 1994).

The expectation that the child help financially support her mother required daily spatial and temporal separations of mother and child. There are, in fact, many transgressions of the mother-child symbiosis in practice—large families where older daughters care for younger siblings, child-servants who at an early age leave their mothers, children raised by paid nannies and other caregivers, and mothers who leave young children to seek employment—but these are fluid enough to sustain ideological adherence to the prescription that children should be raised exclusively by biological mothers. Long-term physical and temporal separation disrupts this notion. Transnational mothering radically rearranges mother-child interactions and requires a concomitant radical reshaping of the meanings and definitions of appropriate mothering.

Transnational mothers distinguish their version of motherhood from estrangements, child abandonment, or disowning. A youthful Salvadoran woman at the domestic-employment waiting room reported that she had not seen her two eldest boys, now fourteen and fifteen years old and under the care of her own mother in El Salvador, since they were toddlers. Yet, she made it clear that this was different from putting a child up for adoption, a practice that she viewed negatively, as a form of child abandonment. Although she had been physically separated from her boys for more than a decade, she maintained her mothering ties and financial obligations to them by regularly sending home money. The exchange of letters, photos, and phone calls also helped to sustain the connection. Her physical absence did not signify emotional absence from her children. Another woman who remains intimately involved in the lives of her two daughters, now seventeen and twenty-one years old in El Salvador, succinctly summed up this stance when she said, "I'm here, but I'm there." Over the phone, and through letters, she regularly reminds her daughters to take their vitamins, to never go to bed or to school on an empty stomach, and to use protection against pregnancy and sexually transmitted diseases if they engage in sexual relations with their boyfriends.

Transnational mothers fully understand and explain the conditions that prompt their situations. In particular, many Central American women recognize that the gendered employment demand in Los Angeles has produced transnational motherhood arrangements. These new mothering arrangements, they acknowledge, take shape despite strong beliefs that biological mothers should care for their own children. Emelia, a forty-nine-year-old woman who left her five children in Guatemala nine years ago to join her husband in Los Angeles, explained this changing relationship between family arrangements, migration, and job demand: "One supposes that the mother must care for the children. A mother cannot so easily throw her children aside. So, in all families, the decision is that the man comes [to the U.S.] first. But now, since the man cannot find work here so easily, the woman comes first. Recently, women have been coming and the men staying."

A steady demand for live-in housekeepers means that Central American women may arrive in Los Angeles on a Friday and begin working Monday at a live-in job that provides at least some minimal accommodations. Meanwhile, her male counterpart may spend weeks or months before securing even casual day-laborer jobs. While Emelia, formerly a homemaker who earned income in Guatemala by baking cakes and pastries in her home, expressed pain and sadness at not being with her children as they grew, she was also proud of her accomplishments. "My children," she stated, "recognize what I have been able to do for them."

Most transnational mothers, like many other immigrant workers, come to the United States with intentions to stay for a finite period of time, that is, until they can pay off bills or raise money for investment in a house, their children's education, or a small business. Some of these women return to their countries of origin, but many stay. As time passes, and as their stays grow longer, some of the women eventually bring some or all of their children. Other women who stay at their U.S. jobs are adamant that they do not wish for their children to traverse the multiple hazards of adolescence in U.S. cities or to repeat the job experiences they themselves have had in the United States. At the waiting room at the domestic-employment agency, a Salvadoran woman whose children had been raised on earnings predicated on her separation from them put it this way: "I've been here nineteen years, I've got my legal papers and everything. But I'd have to be crazy to bring my children here. All of them have studied for a career, so why would I bring them here? To bus tables and earn minimum wage? So they won't have enough money for bus fare or food?"

Who Is Taking Care of the Nanny's Children?

Transnational Central American and Mexican mothers may rely on various people to care for their children's daily, round-the-clock needs, but they prefer a close relative. The "other mothers" on which Latinas rely include their own mothers, *comadres* (co-godmothers) and other female kin, the children's fathers, and paid caregivers. Reliance on grandmothers and comadres for shared mothering is well established in Latina culture and signifies a more collectivist, shared approach to mothering in contrast to a more individualistic, Anglo-American approach (Griswold del Castillo 1984; Segura and Pierce 1993). Perhaps this cultural legacy facilitates the emergence of transnational motherhood.

Transnational mothers express a strong preference for their own biological mothers to serve as the primary caregivers. Here, the violation of the cultural preference for the biological mother is rehabilitated by reliance on the biological grandmother or by reliance on the ceremonially bound comadres. Clemencia, for example, left her three young children behind in Mexico, each with his or her respective *madrina*, or godmother.

Emelia left her five children, then ranging in ages from six to sixteen, under the care of her mother and sister in Guatemala. As she spoke of the hardships faced by transnational mothers, she counted herself among the fortunate ones who did not need to leave the children alone with paid caregivers: "One's mother is the only one who can really and truly care for your children. No one else can.... Women who aren't able to leave their children with their mother or with someone very special, they'll wire money to Guatemala and the people [caregivers] don't feed the children well. They don't buy the children clothes the mother would want. They take the money and the children suffer a lot."

Both Central American and Mexican women stated preferences for grandmothers as the ideal caregivers in situations that mandated the absence of the children's biological mother. While such preferences may seem to have grown out of strategic availability, they in fact assumed cultural mandates. Velia, a Mexicana who hailed from the border town of Mexicali, improvised an employment strategy whereby she annually sent her three elementary-school-age children to her mother in Mexicali for the summer vacation months. This allowed Velia, a single mother, to intensify her housecleaning jobs and save money on day care. But she also insisted, "If my children were with the woman next door [who babysits], I'd worry if they were eating well, or about men [coming to harass the girls]. Having them with my mother allows me to work in peace." Another woman specified more narrowly, insisting that only maternal grandmothers could provide adequate caring. In a conversation in a park, a Salvadoran woman offered that a biological mother's mother was the one best suited to truly love and care for a child in the biological mother's absence; according to her, not even the paternal grandmother could be trusted to provide proper nurturance and care. Another Salvadoran woman, Maria, left her two daughters, then fourteen and seventeen years old, at their paternal grandmother's home, but before departing for the United States, she trained her daughters to become self-sufficient in cooking, marketing, and budgeting money. Although she believed the paternal grandmother loved the girls, she did not trust the paternal grandmother to cook or administer the money that she would send her daughters.

Another variation in the preference for a biological relative as a caregiver was captured by the arrangement of Patricia, a thirty-year-old Mexicana who came to the United States as a child and was working as a live-in, caring for an infant in one of Southern California's affluent coastal residential areas. Her arrangement was different: her daughters were all born, raised, and residing in the United States, but she lived apart from them during weekdays because of her live-in job. Her three daughters—one-and-a-half, six, and eleven years old—stayed at their apartment near downtown Los Angeles under the care of their father and a paid nanny-housekeeper, Patricia's teenage cousin. Although her paid caregiver was not an especially close relative, Patricia rationalized the arrangement by emphasizing that her husband, the father of the girls and therefore a biological relative, was with them during the week. "Whenever I've worked like this, I've always had a person in charge of them also working as a live-in. She sleeps here the five days, but when my husband arrives he takes responsibility for them. . . . When my husband arrives [from work] she [the cousin and paid caregiver] goes to English class and he takes charge of the girls." Another woman, who did not have children of her own but who had worked as a nanny for her aunt, stated, "As Hispanas, we don't believe in bringing someone else to care for our children." Again, the biological ties help sanction the shared child-care arrangement.

New family fissures emerge for the transnational mother as she negotiates various aspects of the arrangement with her children, and with the other mother who provides daily care and supervision for the children. Any impulse to romanticize transnational motherhood is tempered by the sadness with which the women relate their experiences and by the problems they sometimes encounter with their children and caregivers. A primary worry among transnational mothers is that their children are being neglected or abused in their absence. While there is a long legacy of child-servants being mistreated and physically beaten in Latin America, transnational mothers also worry that their own paid caregivers will harm or neglect their children. They worry that their children may not receive proper nourishment, schooling and educational support, and moral guidance. They remain unsure as to whether their children are receiving the full financial support they send home. In some cases, their concerns are intensified by the eldest child of a nearby relative who is able to monitor and report the caregiver's transgression to the transnational mother.

Transnational mothers engage in emotional work and financial compensation to maintain a smoothly functioning relationship with the children's daily caregiver. Their efforts are not always successful, and when problems arise, they may return to visit if they can afford to do so. Carolina, after not seeing her four children for seven years, abruptly quit her nanny job and returned to Guatemala in the spring of 1996 because she was concerned about an adolescent daughter's rebelliousness and about her mother-in-law's failing health. Carolina's husband remained in Los Angeles, and she was expected to return. Emelia, whose children were cared for by her mother and sister, with the assistance of paid caregivers, regularly responded to her sister's reminders to send gifts, clothing, and small amounts of money to the paid caregivers. "If they are taking care of my children," she explained, "then I have to show my gratitude."

Some of these actions are instrumental. Transnational mothers know that they may increase the likelihood of their children receiving adequate care if they appropriately remunerate the caregivers and treat them with the consideration their work requires. In fact, they often express astonishment that their own Anglo employers fail to recognize this in relation to the nanny-housekeeper work that they perform. Some of the expression of gratitude and gifts sent to caregivers appear to be genuinely disinterested and enhanced by the transnational mothers' empathy arising out of their own similar job circumstances. A Honduran woman, a former biology teacher who had left her four sons with a paid caregiver, maintained that the treatment of nannies and housekeepers was much better in Honduras than in the United States, in part, because of different approaches to mothering: "We're very different back here.... We treat them [domestic workers] with a lot of affection and respect, and when they are taking care of our kids, even more so. The Americana, she is very egotistical. When the nanny loves her children, she gets jealous. Not us. We are appreciative when someone loves our children and bathes, dresses, and feeds them as though they were their own."

These comments are clearly informed by the respondent's prior class status, as well as by her simultaneous position as the employer of a paid nanny-housekeeper in Honduras and as a temporarily unemployed nanny-housekeeper in the United States. (She had been fired from her nanny-housekeeper job for not showing up on Memorial Day, which she erroneously believed was a work holiday.) Still, her comments underline the importance of showing appreciation and gratitude to the caregiver, in part, for the sake of the children's well-being.

Transnational mothers also worry about whether their children will get into trouble during adolescence or if they will transfer their allegiance and affection to the "other mother." In general, transnational mothers, like African American mothers who leave their children in the South to work up North (Stack and Burton 1994), believe that the person who cares for the children has the right to discipline. But when adolescent youths are paired with elderly grandmothers or ineffective disciplinary figures, the mothers may need to intervene. Preadolescent and adolescent children who show signs of rebelliousness may be brought north because they are deemed unmanageable by their grandmothers or paid caregivers. Alternatively, teens who are in California may be sent back in hope that it will straighten them out, a practice that has resulted in the migration of Los Angeles-based delinquent youth gangs to Mexican and Central American towns. Another danger is that the child who has grown up without the transnational mother's presence may no longer respond to her authority. One woman at the domestic-employment agency, who had recently brought her adolescent son to join her in California, reported that she had seen him at a bus stop, headed for the beach. When she demanded to know where he was going, he said something to the effect of "And who are you to tell me what to do?" After a verbal confrontation at the bus kiosk, she handed him ten dollars, perhaps hoping that money would be a way to show caring and to advance a claim to parental authority.

Motherhood and Breadwinning

Milk, shoes, and schooling—these are the currency of transnational motherhood. Providing for children's sustenance, protecting their current well-being, and preparing them for the future are widely shared concerns of motherhood. Central American and Mexican women involved in transnational mothering attempt to ensure the present and future well-being of their children through U.S. wage earnings, which requires long-term physical separation from their children.

For these women, the meanings of motherhood do not appear to be in a liminal stage. That is, they do not appear to be making a linear progression from a way of motherhood that involves daily, face-to-face caregiving toward one that is defined primarily through breadwinning. Rather than replacing caregiving with breadwinning definitions of motherhood, they appear to be expanding their definitions of motherhood to encompass breadwinning that may require long-term physical separations. For these women, a core belief is that they can best fulfill traditional caregiving responsibilities through income-earning in the United States while their children remain back home.

Transnational mothers continue to state that caregiving is a defining feature of their mothering experiences. They wish to provide their children with better nutrition, clothing, and schooling, and most of them are able to purchase such items with dollars earned in the United States. They recognize, however, that their transnational relationships incur painful costs. In addition to worrying about negative effects on their children, transnational mothers also experience the absence of domestic family life as a deeply personal loss. Those who primarily identified as homemakers before coming to the United States identified the loss of the daily contact with family as a sacrifice ventured to financially support the children. As Emelia, who had previously earned some income by baking pastries and doing catering from her home in Guatemala, reflected, "The money [earned in the United States] is worth five times more in Guatemala. My oldest daughter was then sixteen, and my youngest was six [when I left]. Ay, it's terrible, terrible, but that's what happens to most women [transnational mothers] who are here. You sacrifice your family life [for labor migration]." Carolina also used the word *sacrifice* when discussing her family arrangement, claiming that her children "tell me that they appreciate us [parents], and the sacrifice that their papa and mama make for them. That is what they say."

The daily indignities of paid domestic work—low pay, subtle humiliations, inadequate food, invisibility (Glenn 1986; Rollins 1985; Mary Romero 1992)—mean that transnational mothers are not only stretching their U.S.-earned dollars further by sending the money back home but are also, by leaving the children behind, protecting them from the discrimination they might encounter in the United States. Gladys, who had four of her five children in El Salvador, acknowledged that her U.S. dollars went farther in El Salvador. Although she missed seeing those four children grow up, she felt that she had spared them the indignities to which she had exposed her youngest daughter, whom she brought to the United States at the age of four in 1988. Although her live-in employer had allowed the four-year-old to join the family residence, Gladys tearfully recalled how that employer had initially quarantined her daughter, insisting on seeing vaccination papers before allowing the girl to play with the employer's children. "I had to battle, really struggle," she recalled, "just to get enough food for her." For Gladys, being together with her youngest daughter in the employer's home entailed new emotional costs.

Patricia, the mother who was apart from her children only during the weekdays when she lived in with her employer, put forth an elastic definition of motherhood, one that included both meeting financial obligations and spending time with the children. Although her job involved different scheduling than most employed mothers, she held a view similar to those held by many working mothers: "It's something you have to do, because you can't just stay seated at home, because the bills accumulate and you have to find a way. . . . I applied at many different places for work, like hospitals, as a receptionist—due to the experience I've had with computers working in shipping and receiving, things like that, but they never called me. . . . One person can't pay all the bills." Patricia also believed that motherhood involves making an effort to spend time with the children. According to this criterion, she explained, most employers were deficient, while she was compliant. During the middle of the week, she explained, "I invent something, some excuse for her [the employer] to let me come home, even if I have to bring the [employer's] baby here with me . . . just to spend time with my kids."

Transnational mothers echoed these sentiments. Maria Elena, for example, whose thirteen-year-old son resided with his father in Mexico after she lost a custody battle, insisted that motherhood did not consist of only breadwinning: "You can't give love through money." According to Maria Elena, motherhood required an emotional presence and communication with a child. Like other transnational mothers, she explained how she maintained this connection despite the long-term geographic distance: "I came here, but we're not apart. We talk [by telephone]. . . . I know [through telephone conversations] when my son is fine. I can tell when he is sad by the way he speaks." Like employed mothers everywhere, she insisted on a definition of motherhood that emphasized quality rather than quantity of time spent with the child: "I don't think that a good mother is one who is with her children at all times.... It's the quality of time spent with the child." She spoke these words tearfully, reflecting the trauma of losing a custody battle to her ex-husband. Gladys also stated that being a mother involved both breadwinning and providing direction and guidance: "It's not just feeding them, or buying clothes for them. It's also educating them, preparing them to make good choices so they'll have a better future."

Transnational mothers seek to mesh caregiving and guidance with breadwinning. While breadwinning may require long-term and long-distance separations from their children, they attempt to sustain family connections by showing emotional ties through letters, phone calls, and remittances. If at all financially and logistically possible, they travel home to visit their children. They maintain their mothering responsibilities not only by earning money for their children's livelihood but also by communicating and advising across national borders and across the boundaries that separate their children's place of residence from their own places of employment and residence.

Bonding with the Employers' Kids and Critiques of "Americana" Mothers

Some nanny-housekeepers develop very strong ties of affection with the children they care for during long workweeks. It is not unusual for nanny-housekeepers to be alone with these children during the workweek, with no one else with whom to talk or interact. The nannies, however, develop close emotional ties selectively, with some children, but not with others. For nanny-housekeepers who are transnational mothers, the loving daily caregiving that they cannot express for their own children is sometimes transferred to their employers' children. Carolina, a Guatemalan woman with four children between the ages of ten and fourteen back home, maintained that she tried to treat the employers' children with the same affection that she had for her own children "because if you do not feel affection for children, you are not able to care for them well." When interviewed, however, she was caring for two-year-old triplets for whom she expressed very little affection—but she recalled very longingly her fond feelings for a child at her previous job, a child who vividly reminded her of her daughter, who was about the same age: "When I saw that the young girl was lacking in affection, I began to get close to her and I saw that she appreciated that I would touch her, give her a kiss on the cheek. ... And then I felt consoled, too, because I had someone to give love to. But I would imagine that she was my daughter, ah? And then I would give pure love to her, and that brought her closer to me." Another nanny-housekeeper recalled a little girl for whom she had developed strong bonds of affection, laughingly imitating how the preschooler, who could not pronounce the "f" sound, would say, "You hurt my peelings, but I don't want to pight."

Other nanny-housekeepers reflected that painful experiences with abrupt job terminations had taught them not to transfer mother love to the children of their employers. Some of these women reported that they now remained very measured and guarded in their emotional closeness with the employers' children, so that they could protect themselves when that relationship might be abruptly severed.

> I love these children, but now I stop myself from becoming too close. Before, when my own children weren't here [in the United States], I gave all my love to the children I cared for. That was my recompensation [for not being with my children]. When the job ended, I hurt so much. I can't let that happen again.
>
> I love them, but not like they were my own children because they are not! They aren't my kids! Because if I get to love them, and then I go, then I'm going to suffer like I did last time. I don't want that.

Not all nanny-housekeepers bond tightly with the employers' children, but most of them are critical of what they perceive as the employers' neglectful parenting and mothering. Typically, they blame biological mothers (their employers) for substandard parenting. Carolina recalled advising the mother of the little girl who reminded her of her own child that the girl needed to receive more affection from her mother, whom Carolina perceived as self-absorbed with physical-fitness regimes. Carolina had also advised other employers on disciplining their children. Patricia, too, spoke adamantly on this topic, and she recalled with satisfaction that when she had advised her current employer to spend more than fifteen minutes a day with the baby, the employer had been reduced to tears. As a comparison to her employer's mothering, Patricia cited her own perseverance in going out of her way to visit her children during the week: "If you really love your kids, you look for the time, you make time to spend with your kids. . . . I work all week and for some reason I make excuses for her [employer] to let me come [home] . . . just to spend time with my kids."

Her rhetoric of comparative mothering is also inspired by the critique that many nanny-housekeepers have of female employers who may be out of the labor force but who employ nannies and hence do not spend time with their children: "I love my kids, they don't. It's just like, excuse the word, shitting kids. . . . What they prefer is to go to the salon, get their nails done, you know, go shopping, things like that. Even if they're home all day, they don't want to spend time with the kids because they're paying somebody to do that for them." Curiously, she spoke as though her female employer were a wealthy woman of leisure, but in fact both her current and past female employers were wealthy business executives who worked long hours. Perhaps at this distance on the class spectrum, all class and racially privileged mothers look alike. "I work my butt off to get what I have," she observed, "and they don't have to work that much."

In some ways, transnational mothers who work as nanny-housekeepers cling to a more sentimentalized view of the employers' children than of their own. This strategy allows them to critique their employers, especially homemakers of privilege who are occupied neither with employment nor with daily caregiving for their children. The Latina nannies appear to endorse motherhood as a full-time vocation in contexts of sufficient financial resources, but in contexts of financial hardship such as their own, they advocate more elastic definitions of motherhood, including forms that may include long spatial and temporal separations of mother and children.

As observers of late-twentieth-century U.S. families noted (Skolnick 1991; Stacey 1996), no single normative family arrangement predominates in the modern era. As among the white middle class, no one type of mothering unequivocally prevails among Latina immigrant women. In fact, the exigencies of contemporary immigration seem to multiply the variety of mothering arrangements. Through our research with Latina immigrant women who worked as nannies, housekeepers, and housecleaners, we have encountered a broad range of mothering arrangements. Some Latinas migrate to the United States without their children to establish employment, and after achieving some stability, they may send for their children; or they may work for a while to save money, and then return to their countries of origin. Other Latinas migrate and may postpone having children until they are financially established. Still others arrive with their children and search for employment that allows them to live together with their children. And some Latinas may have sufficient financial support—from their husbands or kin—to stay home full-time with their children.

In the absence of a universal or at least widely shared mothering arrangement, there is tremendous uncertainty about what constitutes good mothering, and transnational mothers must work hard to defend their choices. Some Latina nannies who have their children with them in the United States condemn transnational mothers as "bad women." One interview respondent, who was able to take her young daughter to work with her, claimed that she could never leave her daughter. For this woman, transnational mothers were not only bad mothers but also could not be trusted to adequately care for other people's children. As she said of an acquaintance, "This woman left her children [in Honduras].... She was taking care [of other people's children], and I said, 'Lord, who are they leaving their children with if she did that with her own children!'"

Given the uncertainty of what constitutes good mothering, and to defend their integrity as mothers when others may criticize them, transnational mothers construct new scales for gauging the quality of mothering. By favorably comparing themselves with the negative models of mothering that they see in others—especially those that they are able to closely scrutinize in their employers' homes—transnational mothers create new definitions of good-mothering standards. At the same time, selectively developing motherlike ties with other people's children allows them to enjoy affectionate, face-to-face interactions that they cannot experience on a daily basis with their own children.

Transnational Motherhood

In California, with few exceptions, paid domestic work has become a Latina immigrant women's job. One observer has referred to these Latinas as "the new employable mothers" (Chang 1994, 151), but taking on these wage-labor duties often requires Latina workers to expand the frontiers of motherhood by leaving their own children for several years. While today there is a greater openness to accepting a plurality of mothering arrangements—single mothers, employed mothers, stay-at-home mothers, lesbian mothers, surrogate mothers, to name a few—even feminist discussions generally assume that mothers, by definition, will reside with their children.

Transnational mothering situations disrupt the notion of family in one place and break distinctively with what some commentators have referred to as the "epoxy glue" view of motherhood (Blum and Deussen 1996; Scheper-Hughes 1992). Latina transnational mothers are improvising new mothering arrangements that are borne out of women's financial struggles, played out in a new global arena, to provide the best future for themselves and their children. Like many other women of color and employed mothers, transnational mothers rely on an expanded and sometimes fluid number of family members and paid caregivers. Their caring circuits, however, span stretches of geography and time that are much wider than typical joint-custody or other-mother arrangements that are more closely bound, both spatially and temporally.

The transnational perspective in immigration studies is useful in conceptualizing how relationships across borders are important. Yet an examination of transnational motherhood suggests that transnationalism is a contradictory process of the late twentieth century. It is an achievement, but one accompanied by numerous costs and attained in a context of extremely scarce options. The alienation and anxiety of mothering organized by long temporal and spatial distances should give pause to the celebratory impulses of transnational perspectives of immigration. The experiences of these mothers resonate with current major political issues. For example, transnational mothering resembles precisely what immigration restrictionists have advocated through California's Proposition 187 (Hondagneu-Sotelo 1995).[9] While proponents of Proposition 187 have never questioned California's reliance on low-waged Latino immigrant workers, this restrictionist policy calls for fully dehumanized immigrant workers, not workers with families and family needs (such as education and health services for children). In this respect, transnational mothering's externalization of the cost of labor reproduction to Mexico and Central America is a dream come true for the proponents of Proposition 187.

Contemporary transnational motherhood continues a long historical legacy of people of color being incorporated into the United States through coercive systems of labor that do not recognize family rights. As Bonnie Thornton Dill (1988), Evelyn Nakano Glenn (1986), and others have pointed out, slavery and contract-labor systems were organized to maximize economic productivity and offered few supports to sustain family life. The job characteristics of paid domestic work, especially live-in work, virtually impose transnational motherhood for many Mexican and Central American women who have children of their own.

The ties of transnational motherhood suggest simultaneously the relative permeability of borders, as witnessed by the maintenance of family ties and the new meanings of motherhood, and the impermeability of nation-state borders. Ironically, just at the moment when free-trade proponents and pundits celebrate globalization and transnationalism, and when "borderlands" and "border crossings" have become the metaphors of preference for describing a mind-boggling range of conditions, nation-state borders prove to be very real obstacles for many Mexican and Central American women who work in the United States and who wish to be with their children. While demanding the right for women workers to live with their children may provoke critiques of sentimentality, essentialism, and the glorification of motherhood, enabling women workers to choose their own motherhood arrangements would be the beginning of truly just family and work policies, policies that address not only inequalities of gender but also inequalities of race, class, and citizenship status.

Notes

1 No one knows the precise figures on the prevalence of transnational motherhood, just as no one knows the myriad consequences for both mothers and their children. However, one indicator hints at both the complex outcomes and the frequencies of these arrangements: teachers and social workers in Los Angeles are becoming increasingly concerned about some of the deleterious effects of these mother-child separations and reunions. Many Central American women who made their way to Los Angeles in the early 1980s, fleeing civil wars and economic upheaval, pioneered transnational mothering, and some of them are now financially able to bring the children whom they left behind. These children, now in their early teen years, are confronting the triple trauma of entering adolescence, which has its own psychological upheavals; entering a new society, often in an inner-city environment that requires learning to navigate a new language, place, and culture; and entering families that do not look like the ones they knew before their mothers' departure, families with new siblings born in the United States and new stepfathers or mothers' boyfriends.

2 Even among Mexican farmworkers, researchers have found a large and growing segment who settle permanently with their families in rural California (Palerm 1994).

3 Acknowledgment of the varieties of family and mothering has been fueled in part by research on the growing numbers of female-headed families, involving families of all races and socioeconomic levels—including Latina families in the United States and elsewhere (Zinn 1989; Fernández-Kelly and García 1990)—and in part by recognition that biological ties do not necessarily constitute family (Weston 1991).

4 La Virgen de Guadalupe, the indigenous virgin who appeared in 1531 to a young Indian boy and for whom a major basilica was built, provides the exemplary maternal model, *la mujer abnegada* (the self-effacing woman), who sacrifices all for her children and religious faith. La Malinche, the Aztec woman who served Cortes as a translator, a diplomat, and a mistress, and La Llorona (the weeping one), a legendary solitary, ghost-like figure reputed either to have been violently murdered by a jealous husband or to have herself murdered her children by drowning them, are the negative and despised models of femininity. Both are failed women because they have failed at motherhood. La Malinche is stigmatized as a traitor and a whore who collaborated with the Spanish conquerors, and La Llorona is the archetypal evil woman condemned to eternally suffer and weep for violating her role as a wife and a mother (Soto 1986).

5 A study comparing Mexicanas and Chicanas found that the latter are more favorably disposed to homemaker ideals than are Mexican-born women. This difference is explained by Chicanas' greater exposure to U.S. ideology that promotes opposition to mothering and employment and by Mexicanas' integration of household and economy in Mexico (Segura essay in this volume). While this dynamic may be partially responsible for this pattern, Mexicanas may also have higher rates of labor-force participation because they are also a self-selected group of Latinas; by and large, they come to the United States to work.

6 See Mary Romero 1997 for a study focusing on the perspective of domestic workers'

children. Although most respondents in this particular study were children of dayworkers, and none appear to have been children of transnational mothers, they still recall significant costs stemming from their mothers' occupation.

7 This seems to be more common among Central American women than Mexican women. Central American women may be more likely than Mexican women to have their children in their country of origin, even if their husbands are living with them in the United States, because of the multiple dangers and costs associated with undocumented travel from Central America to the United States. The civil wars of the 1980s, continuing violence and economic uncertainty, greater difficulties and costs associated with crossing multiple national borders, and stronger cultural legacies of socially sanctioned consensual unions may also contribute to this pattern for Central Americans.

8 According to interviews conducted with domestic workers in La Paz, Bolivia, in the late 1980s, 41 percent got their first job between the ages of eleven and fifteen, and one-third got their first job between the ages of six and ten. Some parents received half of the child-servant's salary (Gill 1994, 64). Similar arrangements prevailed in preindustrial, rural areas of the United States and Europe.

9 In November 1994, California voters passed Proposition 187, which legislates the denial of public-school education, healthcare, and other public benefits to undocumented immigrants and their children. Although currently held up in the courts, the facility with which Proposition 187 passed in the California ballots rejuvenated anti-immigrant politics at a national level. It opened the doors to new legislative measures in 1997 to deny public assistance to legal immigrants.

＃ TRANSCULTURATION AND IDENTITY IN DAILY LIFE

PART 5

Reproduction of Gender Relations in the Mexican Migrant Community of New Rochelle, New York

VICTORIA MALKIN

✳ Carla lives in a small wooden house, part of a small row of houses that face the housing developments in New Rochelle, a suburban city eighteen miles outside of New York City. Carla's house is a fifteen-minute walk from Union Street, the main street that runs through the city's expanding Mexican neighborhood. I first contacted Carla with a message from her sister, Consuelo, who lives in Buenavista, Michoacán, in western Mexico. I had spoken to Carla on the phone several times before finally managing to find a time when I could meet her between her part-time job at the local McDonald's and my time spent teaching English or volunteering at the Catholic community center, the only community center that specifically caters to the Mexican community. Carla opened the door into a dark wooden hall, at the end of which I glimpsed a sprinkling of fairy lights that circled a Virgin Mary. We walked past it into the kitchen, where her youngest son had just arrived home from school. During this visit, people walked in and out of the front door but never appeared. It was only later that I learned they were going upstairs to visit her husband, from whom Carla is nominally separated. By the end of my fieldwork she had managed to divorce him and buy him out of the house in the hope that he would stop influencing the children against her.

In Mexico Consuelo had told me little about Carla's life; in fact, she knew very little, except that Carla owned her own house in New York and that she still didn't help Consuelo as much as needed. Consuelo was on her own, having left her husband some seventeen years before, and now survived on the earnings from a small restaurant she ran out of her front room. Consuelo's oldest son had left for New York some months before, and she hoped he would have better luck in New York than in Los Angeles where he might be at risk of joining the methadone-gang rings (see Malkin 2001). Neither sister, however, had much idea what he was up to, and as Consuelo waited for news in her small restaurant, she would watch her youngest son after he came home from school and remind him that he couldn't leave her or there would be no one left.

Carla told me that she envied their other sister who was in Mexico City and thought about returning.

> Maybe I'll go to Mexico with the youngest, he's still all right and I can get him ahead.... I could go back to the town or whatever. [The children] will have a place here and they won't be in the street. And if I go maybe they'll appreciate me more.... My sister, the one in Mexico City, she's divorced too, and even so her children aren't so indifferent. They invite her out to lunch sometimes; it's like, "Mama, don't you want to come eat?" They keep her company. And my children have never taken me out anywhere. My husband he never took me anywhere. Not now, like you see couples who go out every week to eat.

Carla's story emerged during a series of my visits and phone calls. She arrived in 1967 with the help of her uncle, Don Eduardo, the founder of the Mexican community in New Rochelle. She was twenty-eight-years old, single, and at the mercy of a wealthy employer for whom she worked as a housekeeper until her uncle helped her find another job in the local nursing home. She soon became pregnant—"Yo fracasé" (I failed)—and married a migrant from Michoacán. She had six children, three of whom remain at home. Her two daughters left home with their boyfriends in their late teens. Her youngest child is twelve. Eventually, Carla managed to buy her own house by selling supper in her house and renting rooms to young men arriving from her hometown. Materialistically, Carla achieved more than she could have imagined when she arrived in the United States; she managed to turn her life around, like many Mexican women I met in the United States. And yet she still feels her status in the United States to be ambiguous, especially relative to a life of respect and value in Mexico as she imagines it. As women negotiate their new roles as migrants, they often encounter such ambiguities, which redefine normative ideas of what a woman is or should do. These new roles and practices challenge the symbolic construction of gender and what it means to be a respectable person within the migrant community in New Rochelle.

Mexican women in New Rochelle have been arriving in large numbers since the 1980s. Economic changes in Mexico increased emigration, and women and children started to arrive in greater numbers as a result of the amnesty in 1986, which led to the passage of the Immigration Reform and Control Act. The community is a newly settled one relative to many of the older, settled communities that are present on the West Coast and elsewhere. Female migrants in New Rochelle are arriving in uncharted territory: no substantial cohort of women preceded them to help their passage. While migration between Mexico and New Rochelle dates back to the late 1950s, it was until recently primarily a male circular migration, and the community is only just beginning to be integrated into the fabric of social relations in New Rochelle. The recent increase in the number of migrants, in particular of young couples with children, has correspondingly increased the visibility of the Mexican community, which is no longer considered just a source of labor for various employment niches in suburban Westchester and a quiet motor for the economy; it is now perceived to be a community unto itself that interacts with and affects the city as a whole.

Mexican women in New Rochelle, like Carla, may engage in a variety of practices that are new to them. Some are employed for the first time. Others are forced to negotiate the bureaucratic mazes of schools, hospitals, and Medicaid applications, interactions in which men, who appeared as early-morning shadows looking for work or late-night drinkers looking for consolation, were less likely to engage. Others go to suburban shopping malls. Mothers walk their children to and from school, navigating roads with no sidewalks and SUVs with no manners. Through all this, multiple voices emerge (women as mothers, women as income earners, women as migrants), but here I explore how these individual experiences of change contribute to a new self-definition for the women or to a redefinition of gender relations as seen from the migrants' worldview.

This essay is the result of my observations and interviews during fieldwork in New Rochelle and in two different towns in western Mexico.[1] My work focused on women and families within the transnational circuits that connected the two Mexican towns to New Rochelle, although these were just nodes in a complex web of movements that spanned rural and urban Mexico and fanned out throughout the United States. These expansive networks were legitimized and maintained through family ideologies. Husbands, sisters, brothers, cousins, and parents were all part of a network that women used to facilitate their migration. Through the presentation of some of these women's voices and stories, albeit it in an edited version, I show these women to be social actors who are consciously engaged in their own identity construction and who have, in all senses, been active agents in their fate. These women negotiate a minefield of contradictory practice and seek to determine their actions in ways that allow them to maintain viable social identities that contribute to a coherent sense of self. Their stories, however, are not free-floating fictions: they are realized in the particular geography and history that have organized the migration networks and social relationships that women navigate both for their practical survival and for their social identities. This essay is therefore grounded in the idea that these women's experiences must be understood within their local spaces and that conversations about gender and social change cannot be analyzed in a purely discursive framework that remains ungrounded from the local realities of everyday life.

In spite of the odds, and through what was often a series of serendipitous encounters coupled which sheer tenacity and will, women found jobs or began entrepreneurial ventures, raised children (often alone), sent money home to others in Mexico, and negotiated marriages through changing circumstances and values, either remaining with their husbands or seeing the marriage fall apart. It is through the women's subjective understanding of their particular experiences and how they choose to represent themselves within these new experiences that one can begin to appreciate the complexity of the process.

Mexican Migration in New Rochelle

Mexican migration to New Rochelle dates back to the late 1950s and is traced to Don Eduardo, the original migrant who arrived and then began to bring his extended family. Currently, although there are small numbers of Colombians, Peruvians, and Central Americans, Mexicans are the largest migrant group in the city as a result of Don Eduardo's early networks.[2] Initially, migrant flows were dominated by men, single or married, who engaged in circular migration. Many worked in country clubs throughout Westchester County or entered the landscaping businesses that were dominated by Italians whose children were entering other professions. These jobs were most often seasonal and frequently also came with accommodation. Other early migrants also found stable jobs with steady contracts, often in the small-scale manufacturing industries. In contrast, migrants today enter a more competitive and unstable job market, encountering the same economic restructuring that has taken place throughout the East Coast. The small factories have all but disappeared, and stable employment is hard to come by. Most migrants find temporary employment: gardening, country-club work, and construction. Day laborers line up on Union Avenue, where many Mexicans live, and wait for work, and animosity toward those who are prepared to undercut wage levels is growing.

Female employment has also been affected by the city's economic restructuring. Only five of the twenty-three presently employed women worked in factories. In contrast, of the twenty-two unemployed women, sixteen had

Table. Employment of Mexican Women in New Rochelle

	Currently employed	Currently unemployed after previous employment	Never employed
Manufacturing	5	16	NA
Cleaning/childcare	12	4	NA
Other	6	2	NA
Total	23	22	31

Source: Surveys taken outside the food pantry or the community center; interviews by the author.
Note: $N = 76$.

previously been employed by factories. Long-term migrant women were likely to have been employed at some time in the small-scale manufacturing industries. Most notable, however, is that thirty-one women (almost 50 percent) had never been employed. Nevertheless, ethnographic observation shows that many women who said they were unemployed were engaged in income-earning activities. They frequently sold from home, looked after relatives' children, had sporadic cleaning work, and made lunch for male relatives. Paradoxically, female migration to New Rochelle increased as manufacturing jobs were declining. Employment has moved toward the domestic sector—cleaning and childcare—and most women now search for employment in this sector, which, they claim, has higher wages and more flexibility, although job security and conditions vary. Employment in general, and domestic work in particular, is difficult to find for recently arrived migrants. Like men, women suffer from lack of English, lack of transport to nearby towns, and lack of information. Unlike men, who at the very least can wait on Union Avenue hoping for work as day laborers, women have no congregation point where they can look for work.

A twenty-eight-minute train ride to Manhattan represents far more than physical distance. In New Rochelle the concepts of diversity, multilingualism, and immigration, with all their implications, are only just being tackled. At the time of my fieldwork, there was just one community group that exclusively focused on helping Spanish-speaking migrants, and that had only just opened. This was a Catholic charity that employed one Mexican woman who was directly responsible for immigrants. She was swamped with work and concentrated primarily on helping people with green-card and Medicaid applications, on organizing a food pantry with the Ursuline nuns, and on running English-as-a-second-language classes. The church had only had a full-time Spanish-speaking priest for years, and no notable civic groups existed to negotiate local quality-of-life issues that were a growing source of contention between the older residents (mostly old Italians, many of whom also rented their houses to Mexicans) and the newer arrivals. Some hometown associations existed but these were controlled by specific local groups and maintained local ideologies. Furthermore, the community had no political representation in city hall; there was not one Hispanic, let alone Mexican, on the school board; no Mexican had yet been employed by the city; and no teacher, even the bilingual ones, were of Mexican origin (most being Puerto Rican). Unlike California, New Rochelle offered few Spanish-speaking translation services in its public institutions; schools had only recently begun to offer translation, but this was limited and the social workers were swamped. City hall had no Spanish speaker in the clerk's office, there was no Spanish speaker at the library, and the hospital had only recently employed a Spanish speaker under pressure from the local priest. Few mechanisms existed for migrants to obtain information and help outside of their immediate social networks, which were crucial to most migrants' daily life in this suburban city.

Migrants in New Rochelle experience a degree of structural exclusion that may be different than in larger metropolitan areas where social-service agencies and community groups may be available for those who can find them. Aside from linguistic, geographic, and political isolation, the community itself remains divided—a reality that is less-often documented in Mexican migrant communities, but which becomes all the more real when immigrants remain isolated from other sources of social interaction and social identity. These complex fissures, based on class, migrant status, and access to resources, exacerbate the isolation of many migrants, in particular women.

The structural cleavages based on class and time in the United States are further intensified by the origins of the migration. Don Eduardo came from the rural *municipio* of Quitupan, Jalisco, in western Mexico. He arrived in the United States to work as a housekeeper for a former mayor of New Rochelle, whom he had met while working in Mexico City. After his employer's death, Don Eduardo continued to work for his widow. Through the advantageous connections that his employment provided, Don Eduardo enabled the migration of his relatives and friends, and his notoriety allowed him to find work for many recently arrived migrants. To this day, a visit to his house might still be interrupted by a phone call or visit from someone looking for help. Many migrants claim a distant-kin relation to him and cite him as the first person to have helped them on their arrival. The influence that Don Eduardo wielded cannot be underestimated: he mediated problems with city hall, found jobs, knew major employers, helped with housing, and was active at many other levels. During many of the emerging problems between the community and larger institutions (such as schools, city hall, and the fire department), he is still frequently consulted. Well-known throughout the city, he is considered responsible for the "Mexican Connection." He has been written about in the local press as well as in the *New York Times*. His activities and mediations are in many ways comparable to that of a *cacique* (a type of a power broker), but without the personal enrichment that usually attends this role. He himself sees his activities as fitting in with Christian ideals of charity.

These original networks have now extended to encompass different points of origin in Mexico, both urban and rural, and from areas that have long histories of migration to those that have only just started. Although younger community leaders are emerging, they neither challenge Don Eduardo nor possess his contacts and status. The new community leaders, some from the original migrant community and others who are urban professionals in New Rochelle, act primarily as community spokespeople, without facilitating access to employment and resources as Don Eduardo did. The community's isolation accentuates the fact that a connection to Don Eduardo was and is advantageous, something which exacerbates divisions already present within the community. Migrants who arrived some time ago and had connections to Don Eduardo have had better access to the social networks which have enabled their social mobility. Not only did they arrive at a time when employment conditions were more favorable but they also benefited from Don Eduardo's influence. This is made clear in various ways. For example, of the small number of Mexican-owned shops established in the neighborhood, nearly all belong to people from Quitupan, Don Eduardo's municipio, which does not go unnoticed by the rest of the community and in fact causes much gossip and *envidia* (jealousy). It is also used to explain some of the fights that take place within the community. As Alejandra, a twenty-nine-year-old undocumented migrant from Cotija who has been in New Rochelle for four years, commented,

> It's that people love a fight, it's that many are like the *machistas mexicanos*, they have their pistols and *puro rancho*, and then a lot of them have little or no education.... Near Cotija [a small town near Quitupan] there is a rancho that they call Las Lagunillas, and they say that many years ago it used to rule Cotija, and then they had to give [Cotija] up because it was in Michoacán. [Las Lagunillas is across the border in Quitupan, Jalisco.] But they are always fighting, who knows why.... And you see that here, they speak badly about one another. For example, you see that there on Union Avenue almost all the businesses are owned by people from Quitupan, and how good they are getting ahead, but I realized that

whenever someone started a business from somewhere else, like from Cotija, they don't want it. Almost like they don't want them to get ahead, that's what you hear around here.

Cotija is a small town near Quitupan. Although separated by the border between Jalisco and Michoacán, the towns are connected through kinship, business, and history, and have an intertwined and contentious political relationship. Alejandra uses local Mexican history to represent the current tensions in New Rochelle. The local rivalries, now faded into local lore in Mexico, emerge in a new context to represent the fact that individuals from Quitupan were more likely to receive help on their arrival due to their close connection to Don Eduardo. Such networks are now a factor in the social differentiation that is taking place in the United States. Limited opportunities in an increasingly competitive job market mean that social networks are even more important to a migrant's social mobility. Serendipity is less and less part of the migrant myth, and roads are rarely paved with gold.

Class tensions are also expressed through a gendered discourse. As Alejandra suggests, those who wait on Union Avenue and cause problems can be likened to people from the ranchos in Mexico: undisciplined and rowdy. In Mexico people often discuss the ranchos in images of status and modernity, implying that those still in the ranchos (real or metaphorical) are stuck in a lower class (see Malkin 1998). Alejandra criticizes the disorder on Union Avenue in the same way—as being from the rancho. Both women and men, although mostly women, have begun to complain about Union Avenue and the *bolas de mustaches*. Women often lament the constant harassment and *groserías* and *la falta del respeto*, all experiences women strive to avoid. Norma, a twenty-nine-year old single mother and documented migrant from Nayarit who has lived in New Rochelle for six years, said,

> Well I don't go out. I know some do but I don't. . . . I didn't go out in Mexico either. In Mexico I lived with my grandmothers and I was at home, I didn't work there. Sometimes in the afternoon I went to classes they gave in the church. . . . Sometimes I go out with my son because he needs to more, I take him to the park but I don't want him to go out here too much. . . . Having a child here is difficult but he wants to go out more. . . . I never went anywhere [in New Rochelle], only to church. . . . For the first time in five years I went to the city with him and his father to take him to the park and it was pretty, but I wouldn't go alone. . . . With my son I go out more because you have more courage [*valor*] with the child. Alone, no. And the lack of respect, you know how they all hang out in

crowds and talk to you and say stuff you don't want.... I know there are women who go out alone or with friends but not me.

These visible changes—the increasing numbers of day laborers waiting for work, the unemployed, the young men who spend the day in the cafés downtown and on Union Avenue, the rumors of prostitutes, the drinks and drugs in local bars Mexicans are known to frequent, the large crowds of Mexicans during the summer soccer games that the city complains about—are all part of a social identity that many individuals in the community strive to resist.

Furthermore, some migrants arrive in New Rochelle from other areas in the United States, most often California. They come to New Rochelle thinking it will be *mas tranquilo* (calmer) and hoping to find a place where they can avoid the social problems they have experienced, or heard about, through friends and family in other places. While New Rochelle is still a suburban city, the new arrivals and increasing poverty levels have generated a perceived and real increase in social problems. But many of the social problems being discussed at city hall and in the media, and often blamed on the Mexicans, are problems that existed in this corner of town long before their arrival and that are the product of urban blight that started in the 1970s when many of the Italians started to move out. Nevertheless, the social constructions of this "problem" filter down and influence the ability of men and women to feel they occupy a moral and respectable role as migrants and a respectable position within the city, something that many of the women arrived with the hope of achieving, especially as they had been threatened at home with the *chisme* (gossip) that often accused them of migrating for their own, immoral, desires (see Malkin 2004). Women are, perhaps, even more acutely aware of this position, as they interact with hospitals, welfare agencies, and schools. Some of the women I interviewed told stories about being accused of freeloading and of being a waste of resources by clerks who were tired of having to manage budget cuts while facing an increasing workload. Migrants are obliged to contest what it means to be Mexican as they resist this social identity, and as a result, many women and men maintain a discursive distance from Mexicans as a group, resentful that their own respect is in jeopardy. Aida, a twenty-four-year-old who had arrived from Jiquilpan three years before and was waiting for her papers, said,

> When I got here, I almost hardly went out. Yes I know my way around, I know all the buses.... I want to learn how to drive and speak English. ... I also came to improve myself a bit. You have to go out. If I stay here, I have to go out. Now I find things out, I'm not going to sit here with my

arms crossed.... Really often they marginalize us Mexicans. They think we're really lazy [*relajos*], drunks, but we're not all the same, like we're not like the Colombians, the Guatemalans. There are problems everywhere. When we were looking for an apartment people would say to us, "We don't want Mexicans," because you know how sometimes the Mexicans all live together.... I said that we just want the apartment for myself and my husband, that we're not like them. They think we're all the same.

I met Aida and Alejandra in my English class. Both had migrated to join their husbands and were attempting to maintain a respectable position for themselves within the migrant community on which they remained dependent while striving to avoid being labeled by other city residents as a rowdy Mexican or other Latino. They were immediately aware not only of the internal divisions of the community but also of the potentially negative social location that Mexicans can occupy within the social and racial hierarchy. The search for both social mobility and respectability motivated many people to migrate—for *el respeto* either at home or in the United States—and resulted in community divisions, as some migrants divorced themselves from any potential or discursive association with the muchachos who waited on streetcorners. Some migrants deliberately looked for housing away from the core Mexican neighborhood or sought alternative churches, which further divided and isolated the community.

For young and newly married women, this quest for respect is particularly important as they fight the gossip that inevitably is provoked by their migration. The women quoted above are actively involved in maintaining a respectable position for themselves, and most of their complaints focus on the difficulty that their migrant status presents for this aspiration (see Rouse 1992). The desire for social mobility and to not be cast in a negative role, both within the Mexican community and within American society, promotes further divisions between women from different places as they struggle to create status and respect within their community and in New Rochelle. Migrants who have arrived from a more urban, middle-class background are also aware of class differences and can highlight them. Ana, a thirty-five-year-old documented migrant from Mexico City who has been in New Rochelle for ten years, saw herself as different:

> I want to get ahead. I want to study. My husband loves the way I am because he appreciates my knowledge [*cultura*] and my way of being. ... Those are rural women. No one is ever happy here, they complain about everything.... I complain, but I appreciate things too. At home the government just screwed us; here they help us.... They help with the

kids, with food stamps.... I'm a citizen, my daughter is too, she is born here, and my husband.... Rural women don't like it here, they complain about being locked up at home, they don't want to learn English ... but my husband likes me the way I am and he likes that I am from Mexico City and that I am knowledgeable.... Almost none of the women from Michaela like it here.... And then they let their husbands come and leave them behind. I'm not letting my husband leave me alone; why get married? And a lot of them drink ... upstairs they drink, the guys come and go, that's why we want to get out from this apartment. They won't speak to us anymore.

This commentary is particularly vitriolic and is also related to a particular family situation: Ana's husband is from a small town in Michoacán, and she is surrounded by various members of his family with whom she does not get along. Nevertheless, its exaggerated response perhaps highlights the strength and impact of the divisions that can exist. While women often forge new friendships and overcome some of the community divisions, the divisions are worth highlighting as they have not been documented extensively in migrant communities.[3] Furthermore, these divisions have hindered political organization and community building. All these women struggle with the fact that as migrants they not only have to manage the gendered definitions of what it is to be a moral person worthy of respect within the community, but they also have to strive to ensure that the very idea of "Mexican" is not turned into a social marker that itself implies a lack of morality.

Networks, Gender, and Agency

Migration rarely occurs without the use of networks even in larger cities, and migrants, especially women, rarely arrive as autonomous agents (Delauney 1995; Donato 1993). In New Rochelle, of the seventy-six women I surveyed, twenty-one had arrived as single women, but all came with the help of their kin, most often parents or siblings. The rest arrived with their husbands or joined them later. While many of the women may have migrated for individual reasons, all had to manipulate their roles within the family and use their kinship networks to obtain these ends. These kinship networks were constructed and maintained by family ideologies that provided different possibilities for different family members, and women negotiated their movements within these social relationships for their own ends but still within the roles that kept the networks going. For example, women frequently migrated to New Rochelle with the help of older siblings, but may have been expected to help with childcare and fulfill a domestic role. Older women may arrive to look after grandchildren. Young wives may arrive wishing to join their husbands. All these movements take place within a framework of respectability that constructs women in specific ways, most frequently through relational roles within a family. Women frequently negotiate this in order to migrate and avoid chisme, which could criticize their migration without regard to these roles.

On arrival, social relationships continue to be constructed around kinship relationships. The family is one of the main ideological constructions through which migrants understand their migration (Rouse 1989), and the family unit (in the extended sense) remains the primary organizing structure of most migrants' lives (Alvarez 1987; Lomnitz 1977; Tapia 1995; Vélez-Ibañez 1988).[4] Within the family, women not only have a symbolic importance, but it is these kinship relationships that are most often used for the construction of personhood (Goodson-Lawes 1993; Joanne Martin 1990; Napolitano 1995) and which are intrinsic to the creation of a social identity that continues to be relational as opposed to individual (Napolitano 1995; Rouse 1989, 1995a).

In New Rochelle, for most women social networks are organized and consolidated through their kinship relationships. Women still rarely do things alone and frequently look for kinship members to accompany them as they go shopping, join English classes, attend church, or catch the bus to White Plains to look for bargains. Kinship groups frequently dominate apartment buildings, and small businesses most often employ extended families. Women remain dependent on alternative social networks to negotiate and challenge gender relations (Hondagneu-Sotelo 1994) and employment situations (M. O'Connor 1990). In New Rochelle alternative social networks that could enable women to forge new friendships or, more important, a support system are rare. While women do make friends and interact with other women, their employment situations are most often isolated and sporadic. Many earn money through an extension of their domestic roles: making sandwiches for other workers, babysitting, selling Tupperware to friends—not unlike money-earning schemes that many of them ran in Mexico. Cleavages within the community have further blocked the formation of new social networks. For example, many Quitupan migrants attend the local church, but other migrants, resenting the dominance of the Quitupan network, have chosen churches outside the community. Given the increasing divisions among the community, it is neither easy for women to find and gain access to alternative social networks for support nor clear when and how such networks will be created over time, or if they will emerge among coethnics, as opposed to elsewhere.

The crucial role that kinship relationships play has a considerable impact not only on women's practical options but also on female agency, given that women's personhood and social identities are still constructed through these networks. However hard they try, regardless of their desire to resist their situations, some of the poorest and most vulnerable women are particularly limited by their social networks. Sara was a migrant I first met at the community center; she had come to ask for help with a school form. In the middle, talking about her husband who drank and her job situation, she burst into tears. Sara had been in New Rochelle for eight years; her husband had been there for fifteen. During his first seven years in the United States, he had rarely sent her money. Desperate, she arranged to cross the border into Texas with the help of her brother-in-law.

> He saw how poor I was, and I said I'm going, and they saw me with the earth and nothing else if I stayed.... I didn't tell the man [her husband], but I came here and he came to pick me up. I didn't come for that, if he wanted to follow me he could. I came here to get ahead and he couldn't say anything because he didn't know I was coming. [Her husband had been told by his family that she was in Texas.] ... It's that they [her in-laws] are very Catholic, and they didn't want me on the street alone. They supported me because he is the father of my children and they didn't like to think of him alone on the street.... So I came and he calmed down a bit. He helps with the rent but with his vice [*vicio*] it depends. All the drunks here in the street. Yes, they work here, but on the weekends or the days it rains. Then at home they don't even work. At least here they work.

Sara managed to get the papers for herself and her children, who then came to the United States.

> It took two years, and they [the children] were with my mother-in-law, and I was here suffering, with so much anxiety [*nervios*] about them I had to take pills for the depression.... I never went; I couldn't do it, because there are people like that, who don't care. I fought for them.... I was here, and sometimes I started to think, and I asked God, "oh God, I would be so happy if they came to this country," and I would imagine like a spaceship that would appear in the sky that came flying with my kids who would come out ... and it was almost like that, they arrived in the plane and came out like I asked God.

When I met Sara, she had been laid off from her job in the kitchen where she had been working. She now did a bit of babysitting for her *comadre*. Her eldest daughter had gone to Texas with a boyfriend, and her two other daughters had stopped school for the time being, having found work over Christmas in one of the few remaining factories in the city, which assembled small crystal ornaments. Her eldest son had moved to California to look for work, after feeling too discouraged at the high school and dropping out. He sent her money from California. Sara was resting.

> I am looking for work; but at the moment I am resting.... In the club I had to work a lot, cutting vegetables, potatoes and everything. Now I am at home. First, I take the boy to school even if it's cold. Yes there are women who take children to school, but I can't pay. They charge ten dollars, and now without work how can I pay? Then I come home and do the housework and everything else. Then I make lunch for the girls and at twelve o'clock I take it to them ... and come home and do what I can of the housework. The house is always dirty.... Then I come to school to pick up the boy and that's how the day goes; but I am used to it.... When I worked in the club, I came and went walking.... I never have been—oh, I can't, God forgive me—I do what I can. People would say, "You didn't really come walking?" Well yes, I don't have a car and what could I do?

Sara's autonomy in a female-headed household in Mexico did not compensate for her dependence on kinship networks. Her in-laws helped her reunite with her husband, which had not been the primary goal of her migration, but they determined what they felt was the best way to help her, her husband, and the children. Their support was garnered through concepts of respectability and a united family: her husband, reunited with his family, became more respectable as he could claim a family and not be seen as an abandoned alcoholic. Sara, in the meantime, received some (limited) financial help from him. She negotiated between competing discourses: one in which she rejected her husband and contested his role as a worthy father due to his lack of support and help (see Stern 1995), and another that constructed the respectability of a nuclear household and its patriarchal roles. It was the latter vision that was sanctioned by her in-laws. In Mexico her in-laws helped her because she was an abandoned wife; once Sara joined her husband, however, they could retire from such responsibility. Her poverty and insecure employment also made it unlikely that she could separate from her husband, unless her children could help her financially—a situation also common in Mexico, where older mothers may rely on their elder children for support, both emotional and financial, in order to obtain more autonomy from their husbands (Goodson-Lawes 1993). Sara's main pride was her children, her primary hope was that they could do better than her, and her biggest wish was that her youngest son (eight years old) finish school and learn English.

Although many women had more fortunate or positive experiences, Sara's story demonstrates the interaction of gender, networks, and poverty. Most women remain bound to kinship networks that constrain or enable them in various ways. Younger women who migrate with their husbands often arrive at the decision jointly, both husband and wife wishing to avoid separation and to reject older models wherein women remained behind in Mexico. At the same time, the actual experience of the women often depends on the networks that surround them. New Rochelle has as yet offered little possibility for change for those women who wish to completely challenge their situations. Not all women are bound into social relationships that are necessarily detrimental, of course. But while variety and heterogeneity are visible in these relationships, this cannot automatically be attributed to the migration experience. Heterogeneity is present throughout Mexico and documented in many communities, both migrant and nonmigrant.[5] And, as feminist theorists have cautioned, there is no one monolithic gender identity in any community, even in those labeled "traditional." In fact, for many women, personal agency in the suburban environment of New Rochelle may be more constrained than in Mexico. In Mexico several women transgressed their roles in complex ways, using the protection of the church, their status as mothers, or other tactics. In Mexico, moreover, they did not have to struggle to legitimize their status as a migrant, nor did they suffer linguistic and personal isolation in the same way. In New Rochelle female immigrants had language problems, some were undocumented, there was little access to public transport, jobs were dependent on social networks, and the community remained divided and full of chisme (gossip), just as in many small towns in Mexico. Finally, women had to remain respectable within a community wherein their very presence signaled their desire to be different from those who had left.

Migrant Women and Social Change

The situations that women encounter as migrants are rich and varied. Although it would be foolish to assume that this is not part of a process of change, caution is nevertheless advisable before assuming that the variety of new practices and experiences are causing women to redefine their selves and their identity. It is not enough to assume that practical strategies lead to a transformation of self or identity, nor to assume that changing roles leads to changing status within the household (see Brettel and Berjeois 1992).[6] Discourses around gender and women mean that changing roles—for example, the integration of women into the production process—can often be reinterpreted such that women's exploitation and marginalization is further exacerbated. Gender interacts with class, race, and nation building in ways that do not allow one to predict similar outcomes for what appear to be similar processes (Kopinak 1995; Ong 1991; Tiano 1986). It is too often assumed that the incorporation of migrant women into a paid labor force is part of an emancipation process. For many women, incorporation into the labor force is a source of pride when it supports other routes to respectability. Hortensia, who has been in the United States for twenty-two years, immigrated with her husband eight days after they married, refusing to remain behind. "I got married to be with him, so I am happy because I am with him." They first migrated to California, then returned to Jiquilpan, Mexico (a town near Quitupan), for four years, "so that the children learnt Spanish well." They then moved to New Rochelle. When I spoke to her, she and her husband had recently bought their own house in an area removed from the core Mexican neighborhood. Her children all lived at home and had not caused any major problems. Her husband worked as a butcher. In California she had been too busy looking after the four children to work, and her husband had not encouraged her to work. However, seven years prior to our meeting, her eldest son had helped her look for work without her husband's approval and she had found her first job in a dry-cleaning factory; there she remained for seven years, finally quitting because she didn't like her boss. She then worked in a kitchen in a club which closed a few months later. She had made friends through this work, one of whom was Sara, also from Jiquilpan. In contrast to Sara, Hortensia was enthusiastic about her family's achievements as well as her past job and her new friends.

> I had this friend Juanito [a co-worker], his name was Jean but that's Juan in Spanish. . . . Then also an Italian used to come by a lot, he was a baker and he said, "Hortensia if you learn English then I'll give you a job." But I never learned. . . . Juanito went to Philadelphia and he calls and we talk when we can, and he says, "Always I phone you . . . ." But I do like to work. I worked sometimes twenty hours a day. . . . They would phone and say, "Work all day," and I went. Sara said, "Why do you kill yourself like that?" But I like it. I tell you, maybe [Sara] just doesn't want to get ahead or what . . . but me, even though I grew up really poor, now we have a house.

Later in our conversation, which took place in her living room on a new sofa set covered in plastic for protection, Hortensia enthused about how far they had come.

> I had a dream that was the *quinceaños* [fifteenth birthday] of my daughter, and we did it all, and we spent ten thousand dollars, and none of that godparents this and godparents that. We did it all on our own—and in

Mexico. I told my family here if they want to come they have to come to Mexico, and a lot came. The second dream was the house—that now we've bought with credit. And now the dream is to have a business here. That's what I dream.... I ask God a lot that he helps us, and now that I'm studying, to help me learn English.[7]

Hortensia was increasingly separating from the community back in Jiquilpan. She complained about Union Avenue and disliked going there. She emphasized that she preferred to remain inside and have nothing to do with her neighbours. Her two best friends at work were not Mexicans. Meanwhile, she criticized Sara, claiming that Sara's "failure" was self-inflicted and that she didn't seem to want to get ahead. They were friends nevertheless, and Hortensia would occasionally invite Sara over. However, while Sara told stories about feeling snubbed and unsupported by various people in the community, Hortensia was proud to be able to give her daughters their quinceaños without the help of godparents. This autonomy not only represents a new social class but also avoids a *compadrazgo* relationship that would create reciprocal obligations.

Hortensia negotiated her role with her husband to enable her to work, using her son and in some sense her status as a mother to gain independence from her husband, a practice familiar in Mexico with older women. She was learning English and had thus far succeeded in her ambitions for her children and engaged in the practices seen as part of social change. But she separated herself from the Mexican community, stressing her friendships with non-Mexicans and condemning those who did not seem to get ahead. Hortensia and her family exemplified the type of migrant that many other migrants complained about: their gold, their cars, the North going to their heads, and so on. Not only were they successful, but they seemed to be "turning their back" on the social obligations of *la familia*. However, as Larissa Adler Lomnitz (1977) showed, separation from kin-based networks and their obligations may be what helped such migrants get ahead. Although Hortensia may represent change and a new construction of herself which includes friendships outside of the community, satisfaction from work, and a sense of identity that emerges from relationships other than familial, what contribution she therefore makes to the Mexican community at large is less clear, as she separates herself from it, rejects arrangements of reciprocity, and is criticized by others.

As many women do when they imagine their return to Mexico, Carla wondered about a return to a place where she could perhaps generate more respect. Carla had already returned to Mexico once before, with her children, and it had not helped reunite her marriage, as she had imagined. Her circumstances had worsened after she returned, with her husband taking over the house and other women living there. Her brother was also murdered in Mexico.

> Since my brother died and all the problems I don't go out anywhere. And I was one of the happiest, but now I don't want to.... I went to Mexico for five months and when I got back [the kids] didn't even want a mother. Everything started to fall apart in high school.... I got back and the house was a disaster. There was a leak here, people living everywhere.... They told me that there had been black women who came in and out.... [My husband] says [the children] never saw anything. But I asked them and they said yes.

Carla finally decided to initiate her divorce. Except for her youngest, Carla's children were going their own way—one had left with her boyfriend, another was living with her boyfriend in New Rochelle, and Carla felt she had lost control of her two eldest sons—and she no longer saw the marriage as worth preserving. "I never had a husband. Since I got married I took responsibility for everything.... It's like being on a boat: you have to be rowing so it stays straight, and I was always rowing. I always led the boat.... And then when everything sunk I said I won't row anymore.... We've gone downward since then." Several months after I had completed my fieldwork, as I was on my way to London to finish writing, Carla phoned and told me she had taken over a small store and was going to sell toys and party items. "I can only ask God it will work."

Hortensia and Carla point to the different fates of migrant women. Both women are long-term migrants who have renegotiated their marriages. They have negotiated new roles in a complicated system, but neither position challenges the dominant gender hierarchies within the community as a whole. Both women are struggling for a sense of respect, and both women discuss this respect as being generated within their kinship networks and in terms of their status as mothers and wives. They continue to have a primary identity that is relational and to see themselves within these webs of relationships. But for Carla, a social identity that would generate the same respect and status she has strived for as a migrant seems farther and farther away in the United States. Other women who had known Carla throughout her travails commented on how she loved to go out dancing, which in their context subtly undermined her success by questioning her attempt to enjoy life despite a failed marriage. Both Carla and Hortensia were assigned dubious status within the community: Hortensia as being above her station, Carla as being just a little too *alegre* (gay) and refusing to suffer in a way that is expected of abandoned women. Should Carla and Hortensia help form new networks, they will be networks wherein women will always be aware that their membership is a possible sign of transgression and thus may defeat their quest for new status. Finally, both women's real or imagined separation from the larger community suggests that a redefinition of "woman" may not be obtained if these experiences are sectioned off from the community at large. If those women whose greatest experiences of new practices or new subjectivities are separated from the community or are rejected by it, then it is less likely their new strategies can contribute to reorganizing the dominant expression of gender within the community—thus allowing the status quo to remain the same and forcing women to look elsewhere for something new.

Conclusion

The different experiences and opinions expressed by some of the women in New Rochelle regarding their lives and surroundings provide insight into how women may be experiencing these changes. Women attempt to incorporate the new practices and changes within a framework of respect and the search for a moral identity that could guarantee this. The complexity of female migrants' lives in a suburban environment is exacerbated by a community which itself remains divided and provides individuals with few other resources to help them. Women negotiate and construct their gender identity within migrant networks, which most often remain bound to ideologies that continue to construct women within their familial roles. Migrant women still consider their primary identity to be derived from these social relationships, and migration has not as yet changed many of their ideas about what a moral person is. While women will often play with these roles and use them against each other—for example, single mothers who gain status as mothers (Melhuus 1992)—most women use the same negotiations that they used in Mexico to resist and renegotiate their roles. When their practices fail to gain them the respect to which they aspire, they experience significant anxiety, as happened with Carla. Practices defined as empowering or emancipating from one point of view are not necessarily so when they conflict with ideas about what a moral person represents and about how status and respect are generated. Empowerment, as a concept, is constructed from an individual's own ideas about what women and men can, should, and do do, and it runs the risk of being predicated on a Western feminist model—a model criticized by many given that "woman" itself can no longer be assumed to represent a monolithic category (Di Leonardo 1991). The road to empowerment can take many turns according to who defines the road. Roles or practices that one may assume provide a possibility for empowerment may not do so when they conflict with women's representation of themselves as moral people who deserve respect. One must understand how women use their own value systems to gain status within their communities and serve as boundaries against other communities.[8]

Although many women are certainly engaged in new practices and experiences, women experienced profound isolation—even those who had managed to obtain many of their goals. The women I interviewed took pride in their migration primarily through a family context; although this did not preclude their desire for change within these contexts, their primary goal was constructed around these relationships, and should these aims not be achieved, the women were unwilling to take on more individualistic identities in order to understand their experiences. Women and men continued to discuss themselves through the gender ideologies that they had experienced in Mexico, gender ideologies that were contradictory and ambiguous. Added to this was their desire, once in the United States, to remain in a social location separate from other minorities; this desire also led them to emphasize family values and the united familia, as opposed to what happened to los Americanos. Roger Rouse (1989, 1992) discussed Mexican men who stress their avoidance of *la calle* (the street) and its associated danger, criminality, and lawlessness. The creation of a Mexican identity that escaped these stereotypes was coupled with an emphasis on la familia and its role in separating migrants from la calle and the delinquent behavior associated with it. This discursive use of la familia had implications for women, who remained at the symbolic center of the family unit and thus became key to defining what was different and better about Mexicans in their roles as minorities and migrants in the United States. This normative role may have given pride to those women who could fulfill it, but women who could not suffered the double problem of having to challenge both predominant gender identities and roles, and an ethnic identity constructed around ideas of la familia and its presupposed unity.

It takes more than a new practice to engender a new social identity and social change. Scholars largely continue to imagine a line that moves from "traditional" to "modern" and to interpret any contradictions observed between discourse and practice as representative of a transitory period, after which new gender roles and identities will emerge at the modern end of the spectrum. But such contradictions are not necessarily part of an overall change that will refashion new gender identities that tread a linear progression toward the production of more-or-less acculturated or assimilated persons, with the Western feminist model as the reference point (Pessar 1995).[9] Contradictions and conflict are part of many gender ideologies and identities, even in the most traditional societies. Multiple gender ideologies often coexist and permit flexibility and negotiation to occur in practice, as can be observed in most communities.[10] Similar ambiguities are applicable to Mexico; recent historical studies show that gender roles have never gone uncontested (Boyer 1989; Fowler-Salamini and Vaughan 1984; Mallon 1984; Stern 1995) and that contradiction and negotiation have been a core element of a family ideology that proposes both individual choice and free will through the church, alongside the familial duty and obligation necessary to continue family wealth and generate status (Gutiérrez 1989). In Mexico adherence to hegemonic gender ideologies is both frequently impossible in reality, and also a point of conflict in many communities, even those not experiencing large-scale social change (Melhuus 1992, 1996, 1997; Stern 1995; Wade 1994). Conflicts and struggles form part of the process of the construction of any gendered identity; ambiguity within gender discourses allows for a flexibility that may be necessary in the process of the construction of the gendered subject. Contradiction cannot therefore be assumed to be the result of change and disruption but may be part of the multiple subject positions that are present in most social relationships.

Notes

Fieldwork for this research was funded by the Royal Anthropological Society, Great Britain, and the Secretaria de Relaciones Exteriores, Mexico. I also thank the Colegio de Michoacán for their support during my research and John Gledhill for his thoughtful comments.

1 Fieldwork for this project took place over eighteen months in Mexico and New Rochelle, from 1995 to 1997. I used a combination of open-ended interviews and participant observation in both places. In New Rochelle I surveyed seventy-six women outside of a food pantry and in the community center where I volunteered and taught English. The longer and more ongoing relationships on which this essay is based were developed from contacts I had in Mexico before I arrived in New Rochelle and with women in my English classes or through the community center. My informants and relationships were thus based on snowball samples, and while not statistically representative, my work aimed to capture particularities and singularities in order to counteract some of the theoretical arguments about migrants, in particular migrant women (see Abu-Lughod 1991). I also interviewed local leaders, politicians, land owners, business owners, and other important community members in Mexico and New Rochelle. In Mexico I joined a bible group. I also got to know other kinship members, both men and women, at many social events. During most interviews (unless otherwise noted), I wrote as the women talked, something at which I became very adept; I took this approach because the most relaxed and informative conversations often took place in impromptu meetings, after class, over coffee, and over meals. All the women knew, however, that I was working as a researcher working on a thesis.

2 The numbers of Mexicans in New Rochelle (total population 67,000) is hard to estimate. Hispanics are the fastest-growing group in Westchester County and New Rochelle. The 1990 Census shows New Rochelle to be 10.8 percent (7,247) Hispanic; of these, 2,570 were of Mexican origin. School figures show the student body to be almost 20 percent Hispanic, and most of these children are of Mexican origin. This number is increasing annually. Many migrants, in particular women and children, have arrived since the last census, both as a result of legalization after the Immigration Reform and Control Act and as a result of worsening economic conditions in Mexico. Undercounting in the census is also very likely, as migrants are aware that they live in overcrowded conditions and could be penalized for this.

3 See Mahler 1995, however, for a good discussion of inter-ethnic divisions and Villar 1994 for an analysis of the divisions within a Mexican business community.

4 I use the term *family* as an ideological construct, rather than in reference to a reproductive or productive unit, thus allowing for the idea that the members themselves define who they see and don't see as family. This idea extends Rayna Rapp's argument (1982) that family is what recruits individuals into households.

5 Numerous studies on gender in Mexico exist. Those on urban women or gender include Del Castillo 1993; Chant 1991; Fernández-Kelly 1983a; Levine and Correa 1993; Finkler 1994; Gutmann 1996. For studies on rural women, see Fowler-Salamini and Vaughan 1984; González Montes and Salles 1995; Villareal 1996. All these studies demonstrate the variety and heterogeneity in gender roles and identities, with change occurring due to industrialization, migration, education, urbanization, and shifting labor practices.

6 The growing literature on migrant women includes Buijs 1993; Chant 1992; Gabaccia 1992; Simon and Brettel 1986; 1976 issues of *Anthropology Quarterly*; and *International Migration Review*'s 1987 issue number 4. For case studies, also see, among others, Mills 1997; Grasmuck and Pessar 1991; Radcliffe 1986; Wolf 1992. For studies on Mexican women (I do not include Chicana studies), see Delay and Simon 1987; Fernández-Kelly and Garcia 1990; Goodson-Lawes 1993; Hondagneu-Sotelo 1994; Hondagneu-Sotelo and Messner 1994; Melville 1980b, 1988; M. O'Connor 1990; Solorzano-Torres 1987; Sullivan 1987; Vega et al. 1990.

7 The quinceaños is a celebration for girls turning fifteen. It can be very elaborate as it signifies the transition from child to woman (Napolitano 1995).

8 For example, Sikh women in East London manipulate the dowry to gain more autonomy, while still retaining a strong ethnic identity through its use (Bhachu 1993). And Bedouin women use a veil and take pride in a modesty that they associate with their social identity as Bedouin women (Abu-Lughod 1996).

9 For example, Patricia Pessar (1995), amplifying her previous fieldwork, admits leaving out half the ethnographic story when describing Dominican women's understanding of their wage work in New York. She reassesses her interpretation and criticizes the feminist project that sees work as emancipation, for she finds that most women continue to define their work within a family context and also derive a greater sense of achievement and fulfillment in upholding a united family and achieving the immigrant dream of social mobility than in challenging the gender ideology that holds

the family together, even if they object to the patriarchal construction of the family. Pessar also notes the problem inherent in assuming that contradictions in discourse and practices are necessarily a sign of linear change: "For poor men and women the issue is not so much the pressure of the sexual division of labor, or the persistence of patriarchal ideologies but the difficulties in upholding either" (Maria Patricia Fernández-Kelly, quoted in Pessar 1995, 44). "The struggle working class women face is neither simple nor necessarily unilineal from patriarchy to parity.... I have learned that an approach to our ethnographic subjects which acknowledges and respects their multiple and sometimes contradictory identities and subjectivities gives us greater license and cause to explore the 'inconsistencies' and 'ambivalences' in their words and actions" (Pessar 1995, 44).

10 See, for example, Reeves Sanday and Gallagher Goodenough 1990, especially the essays by Lila Abu-Lughod, Rena Lederman, and Anna Miegs.

"En el norte la mujer manda": Gender, Generation, and Geography in a Mexican Transnational Community

JENNIFER S. HIRSCH

✳ Women and men in rural western Mexico and their relatives in Atlanta discuss differences between life in the United States and Mexico in terms of gender, saying, "En el norte la mujer manda" (In the North, women give the orders). Young Mexican women on both sides of the *frontera* (border), however, call attention to the role of history rather than migration in the transformation of gender, claiming that they are not as easily pushed around as their mothers. Although older women in this community were hardly powerless in their time, in the space of a generation men and women have begun to express a different, companionate ideal for marriage—an ideal with significant implications for the politics and emotional terrain of marriage. Younger women (and some of their husbands) on both sides of the frontera articulate a vision of intimate partnership influenced both by romantic love and by the increasing economic and social possibility of leaving a violent or even just unsatisfying marriage. But, as expressed by the saying "En el norte, la mujer manda," young Mexican women have greater opportunities for realizing these companionate ideals in the United States. There are two trajectories of change in gender: generational and geographical. Each story would be incomplete on its own, but interwoven the stories form the complex recent history of gender in this transnational community.

Beyond presenting an ethnographically grounded description of migration and historical changes in marriage, this essay also makes two substantive points about transnationalism. First, theorists of transnationalism have presented a valuable critique of simplistic ideas about assimilation by pointing to the ways in which strong social ties, frequent travel, and constant communication facilitate the construction and maintenance of cross-border social identities (see, for example, Glick Schiller et al. 1992). In doing so, however, they tend to underemphasize the real constraints in social contexts between sending and receiving communities. There are differences in women's lives on both sides of the border—differences that exist in spite of shared ideas about sexuality, gender, and marriage. Second, transnational communities are located in time as well as in space, and so to understand the gender regime (Connell 1987) of a transnational community one must talk not just about migration-related change but also about history, in particular the history of the sending community. Important cultural changes accompany migration, but these changes can only be understood in the broader historical context of how the sending communities themselves are changing.

Although migration scholars have made great strides over the past two decades in including women in migration research (Cornelius 1991; Goodson-Lawes 1993; Grassmuck and Pessar 1991) and even some significant progress in exploring how gender shapes and is in turn shaped by migration (Foner 1997, 1998; Hondagneu-Sotelo 1994; Pedraza 1991; Pessar 1998), it is time to reorient the question of whether migration empowers women and to move away from the relentless search for one or two universal causes for this empowerment. The emphasis on women's relative empowerment through migration has become a set of theoretical blinders, focusing attention excessively on the question of women's resources and bargaining power, making male gender invisible and obscuring the fact that what changes with migration may not just be the bargaining itself but what couples bargain for—that is, their marital goals.[1]

Methodology

This essay presents the results from an ethnographic study with two generations of Mexican women. The sample is composed of twenty-six women, ages fifteen to fifty, all from the same sending community in western Mexico; half lived in Atlanta, whereas the other thirteen (their sisters and sisters-in-law) remained in or returned to the sending community. Most of these women's mothers were interviewed as well. The primary method was life-history interviews, consisting of six interviews with each participant on the following topics: childhood and family life; social networks and stories of U.S.-Mexico migration; gender and household division of labor; menstruation, reproduction, and fertility management; health, reproductive health, sexually transmitted diseases, and infidelity; and courtship and sexuality. Interviews were also conducted with nine of the life-history informants' husbands.

The interviews took place during fifteen months of participant observation in Atlanta and in the sending community of western Mexico. The substantive focus on gender and sexuality dictated working with a relatively small sample of women in order to develop the necessary rapport. At the same time, the goal was to produce results that would be generalizable to the experiences of Mexican women in transnational communities. A method of systematic ethnographic sampling that built on existing social networks was employed, as I discuss in greater detail elsewhere (Hirsch 1998b; Hirsch and Nathanson 1997). This method entailed several months of preliminary research in the migrant receiving community (Atlanta), both to select the sending community and the research participants in Atlanta and to understand how their specific experiences might compare to those of the larger Mexican migrant population. The sending communities were Degollado, a town of approximately 15,000 in Jalisco, and El Fuerte, a small *ranchito* outside of Degollado. In Atlanta some informants lived in Chamblee, an urban neighborhood of small apartment complexes with good public transportation and a heavy concentration of Mexican and Vietnamese immigrants, whereas others lived in trailer parks on the outskirts of the city.

Once I had interviewed the first group of life-history informants in Atlanta, I traveled to Degollado. As with others who move between locations of this transnational community, my arrival was no secret; those I was hoping to interview were expecting me, looking forward not just to meeting *la gringa* who had been visiting their sisters in Atlanta but to receiving the letters, photos, and small gifts that their sisters had given me to carry. These *encargos* put my introduction to the families in Mexico in a familiar context—that of any member of their transnational community who, as a routine part of the frequent back-and-forth travel, aids in the construction and reservation of social ties across borders. In the course of the six trips I made between Atlanta and Degollado, I carried *huaraches*, wedding videos, yarn, baby clothes, jewelry, cash, herbal remedies, birth-control pills, letters, and photographs for the families of the women I was interviewing. As a U.S. citizen, my border crossings were quite different from those of my informants, many of whom were more likely to cross with a coyote (human smuggler) than in an air-conditioned jet. Nevertheless, my deliberate insertion into these migrant social networks, and the use of these networks to build a research sample, helped identify informants and build rapport.

Flexibility was another key aspect of the research design. My interest in generational changes in marriage grew in response to being told repeatedly that "ya no somos tan dejados como las de antes" (we are no longer as easily pushed around as the women of the past). As the months passed, I saw that in spite of having neatly constructed two similar groups of women, the women themselves would not sit still to be compared: during the course of my fieldwork, several of those interviewed in Atlanta either moved permanently back to Mexico or else spent months at a stretch living there, whereas some of the women I interviewed in the Mexican field sites have since journeyed north. Women's physical mobility makes it hard to compare those who go to those who stay—perhaps one of the reasons why studies of transnational communities have focused more on cultural continuity than on changes. The analysis of differences between the communities focused of necessity much more on differences in social and economic context (and, thus, in women's opportunities) than on a strict comparison of women in Atlanta and Degollado.

Key Findings

From Respeto to Confianza

A generational change is evident in the shift from the older women's focus on *respeto* to the younger women's discussion of *confianza*. The change goes beyond ideals: young couples were more likely to make decisions jointly, to regard a spouse as a companion, to share the tasks of social reproduction, and to value sexual intimacy as a source of emotional closeness. Doña Elena, now sixty-two and a widow, still remembers vividly how more than forty years ago her grandmother instructed her in the art of a successful marriage: "Just be quiet—don't answer back, and don't talk to him this way or that way.... You need to serve them with love." To have a good marriage, Doña Elena said, she tried to "have his food ready for him, his clothes all nicely ironed, and all mended like we used to do, and ... take care of him as best I could." He, in turn, should "provide all that one needs, food and clothes, and not run around misbehaving." At the core of this marital bargain is the idea of separate spheres (with women in the house and men in the street) and respect for one's spouse. Women of this generation evaluate their marriages against a gold standard of gendered respect, rather than in terms of intimacy or sentiment. (Some were also quite fond of their spouses: Doña Elena started to cry while telling me how much she missed Miguel.) Doña Elena credits her marital success to her husband's gentle character—she notes that he never hit her—and to her own ability to get what she wanted "por las buenas" (through his good side). This meant keeping conflict underground and carefully managing her speech to stay within the bounds of respect. Doña Elena was lucky to marry a kind man, but other women were less so. Any inability to get along, to *saberse llevar*, cast shame on the woman's natal family; women knew their parents would not take them back once they married. "Mi'ija," they would say, "es tu cruz" (My daughter, it's your cross to bear).

I ended my interviews with the older women with a question that I hoped would tell me what their marriages were really like. "Señora," I would say, "some people tell me that in Mexico the man has to be the boss at home, but it seems to me that you all are not so *dejados* [easily pushed around], that you let the man think that he is in charge but that you know how to get your way. Is this true?" Those women whose husbands had histories of being violent or otherwise obtrusive said to me that this was not true, that they really did have to obey. Other women, though, would smile conspiratorially in response. As long are you are respectful, they would tell me, you can do what you want.

In contrast to their mothers' emphasis on respect, younger women talk more about confianza. *Confianza* implies trust, particularly trust that one's secrets will be kept. It denotes a relationship among social equals, in contrast to respect, which describes a hierarchy appropriately acknowledged. *Confianza* also suggests the ability to admit to sexual knowledge: women said that they did not ask their mothers about menstruation because they had a lot of respect for them and not enough confianza, and it is a mark of that same confianza to tell a sexual joke among married women. Young women said that they waited until they had confianza with their boyfriends before giving in to their requests for a kiss, and they talk about the importance of having confianza with their husbands. These women have imbued the word with new meaning, combining previously separate concepts of privacy, sexual behavior, and the freedom to be oneself into an idea of a special, shared, sexual intimacy. The younger women did not downplay the importance of respeto—many of them, for example, talked about courtship as a time of testing how respectful a young man might be as a husband—but they have also redefined respect, using it to claim new areas of power in marriage, such as expecting the basic respect of being able to voice an opinion; for their mothers, in contrast, direct disagreement with one's husband was hardly an indication of respect on anyone's part. Although space does not permit a discussion of heterogeneity among younger women's marriages, it should be noted that not all the younger women achieved the new ideal of confianza combined with respeto—but they all believed that it was the ideal.

In marriages of confianza among the younger generation, both men and women were more likely than their parents to say that they made decisions together. In response to the question "Quien manda en su casa?" (Who gives the orders in your house?), both husbands and wives (separately) told me that both give orders or that neither one does. The meaning of women's speech has been redefined: whereas for their mothers, to voice disagreement with their husbands would have been *resongona* (sassy), some of the young women took pride in the fact that they did not always automatically do what the man said. Unlike their fathers, the younger men did not automatically interpret a woman's disagreement as an attack on their authority and thus their manhood. As one young woman in Atlanta said, "Tengo opiniones" (I have opinions). Her mother, doubtless, also had her own opinions, but she had to be much more careful about how she shared them with her husband.

A second feature of marriages of confianza is heterosociality, expressed as the erosion of the gendered boundaries of space between the house and the street (Gutmann 1996; Rouse 1991). In the context of explaining what it meant to share *el mando* (the power), men and women frequently mentioned spending time together. Whether it involves staying at home together or going to the plaza or the mall as a family, heterosociality stands in strong contrast to the idea that men belong in the street and women in the house and that choosing to be in the house somehow lessens a man's masculinity just as too much time in the street imperils a woman's moral character. The notion that men and women can be companions lessens the social distance implied by respeto.

A third feature of the younger generation's marriages is the slipping of gendered task boundaries. Despite the myriad ways in which the younger generation's mothers helped their fathers, income was perceived to be generated by the men. In the past, women had worked, but the labors of social reproduction were defined into invisibility by being *quehacer* (that which must be done). "El hombre tiene que mantener la casa" (The man has to support his house), the older generation said. Both in Degollado and Atlanta, men are still publicly evaluated by their ability to provide, and women are still judged by the tidiness of their daughters' braids and the spotlessness of their floors, but there has been a generational movement toward *ayudando* (helping) with the other person's job. Although helping does not change the gendered primary responsibility for certain tasks, offering to help—or accepting an offer of help—no longer casts feminine virtue and masculine power in doubt. Behind closed doors, some men sweep, cook meals, clear the table, and wash dishes. Women's helping is even more widespread: almost half of the women interviewed in Mexico and most of those in Atlanta were involved in some kind of income-generating activity.

In other ways too, the younger men and women were striving to create families different from the ones in which they had been raised. They continue to say, as did their mothers, that "los hijos son la felicidad de la casa" (children are the happiness of a home), but none of them aspired to have as much of that happiness as their mothers had. The average parity of life-history informants' mothers is above nine, whereas the life-history informants (admittedly much earlier in their reproductive careers) have an average of three children each, and many want more. This striking fertility decline reflects, among other things, the transformation of sexuality's role in the work of making a family.[2] Young couples want smaller families so that they have the time and energy to focus on each other; the affective relationship that is at the core of the family seems to have shifted from that of the mother and her children to that of the husband and wife. Whereas for their mothers, children—the sooner after marriage the better—were the bond that built a family (*tener familia* means to have a child), for the younger women and men sexual intimacy has become in and of itself constitutive of family ties. Sexual closeness has taken on a new, productive (as opposed to reproductive) aspect.

For older women, sexual intimacy within marriage held a husband's attention (and his resources) and served to generate children; a woman's sexual pleasure was certainly a bonus, but hardly a requirement. For younger women, the mutual pleasure and emotional sharing are in and of themselves a goal. For example, many of the older women—even those who seem to have shared a pleasurable intimacy with their partners—employ the word *usar* (to use) to describe vaginal intercourse; they might say, for example, "cuando el me usa" (when he uses me) to describe sexual relations. *Usar* describes the utilization of an inanimate object; it is the word one might employ to talk about an iron or a plow. Younger women, in contrast, talk about making love (*hacer el amor*), being together (*estar juntos*), or having relations (*tener relaciones*).

Together, these qualities—an emphasis on a new kind of confianza in addition to respect, more room for explicit disagreement, a growing heterosociality, increased helping, new meanings for marital sexuality—combine to form a new marital ideal. Both women and men self-consciously see this ideal as modern: women, whether in Mexico or the United States, told me repeatedly that they were not as easily pushed around as their mothers, and many men strove to convince me that they were not macho like their fathers. A thorough discussion of how these ideological changes are the product of deliberate choices men and women make in response to changing social conditions—an explanation, in other words, that integrates both structure and agency—is beyond the scope of this essay (but see Hirsch 1998a), so I will instead note some of the macrolevel changes and strategic advantages that have facilitated this trend. In addition to the influence of migration (both on the migrants themselves and, via return migration, on the sending communities), factors worthy of mention include increasing neolocal residence, access to mass media through satellite dishes, rising rates of female education, three decades of government-sponsored family-planning programs and sex education, and even the Catholic church's efforts to co-opt this new discourse of sexuality (see Hirsch 1998b).

What benefits do women and men think they will derive from being modern? Some men say that living as bachelors in the United States has taken away the shame of grabbing a broom or heating a tortilla—but it did not do so for their fathers, and some of the men who help their wives have spent little or no time in el norte. Men's helping women can only be understood together with the ground that men have ceded in decision making and with the fracturing of the sharply gendered distinction between the house and the street as part of a larger redefinition of masculinity. These men are not just helping with the housework: they are helping with the work of making a family. What men stand to gain is *cariño* (tenderness). The benefits to men of a marriage of confianza are emotional; they gain access to an intimacy that their fathers sacrificed as part of the cost of being *respetados* (respected). Some men in the sending community see this new masculinity as a strategy for social mobility; the fact that Mexican telenovelas and advertisements portray modern, successful men with cellular phones who speak softly to their wives, rather than machos with mustaches and guns who shout at them, does not escape notice among men and women in Degollado.

For male migrants, there are additional advantages to this alternative masculinity. The aggressive postures of the stereotypical macho are exactly the behaviors most likely to catch the attention of the *migra* (Immigration and Naturalization Service) or the local police. Furthermore, many Mexicans in Atlanta work for gringo bosses who care more about whether they are suspected of being *maricones* (a deprecatory term for homosexuals) because they refuse to go drinking with their buddies. More subtly, Mexican men in Atlanta see the pervasive image of the leisure-time togetherness of the gringo nuclear family at the mall, in television commercials, in public parks, and in church. Ultimately, men's embrace of this alternative masculinity seems due to a combination of influences: their family histories, their ages, and the situational factors that make it advantageous. It is a strategy for social mobility and self-protection, but it also feels really good.

The companionate marriage has many benefits for women—pleasure in the possibility of closeness, a path to power, marital security—and women press their husbands as far as they can toward this model. Women who felt that they had significant input in matters pertaining to their families (whether economic or social) told me proudly that "I have opinions" (i.e., opinions that count). Companionate marriage gives women a moral language with which to define the limits of acceptable behavior. Women believe that strong emotional ties guarantee not just a better marriage but one that is more likely to endure; therefore, maintaining affective bonds is part of the work women do to strengthen their marriages. Finally, some women use this new marital ideal as a justification for migration and for working outside the home. Young women make marital togetherness an explicit negotiation point during courtship, telling their boyfriends that if they plan to go north, they should save or borrow to pay the coyote for both of them because "no me voy a casar para estar solo" (I am not getting married to be alone). Companionate ideology lends weight to women's desire to participate in the previously largely male adventure of migration.

Although women may see a promise of power in these new ideas about confianza, companionate marriage as an ideology has more to say about the emotional intimacy couples can achieve through talking than it does about who gets the last word. Furthermore, these ideas about marriage emphasize the extent to which it is a bond of desire rather than of obligation—which may put women in a difficult position when, as is so often the case, desire falters. Several women mentioned that the negative aspect of knowing that they could support themselves is that their husbands know too, that is, that seeing their wives work and earn money could diminish men's feeling of obligation to take care of them. In the United States the transformation of marriage into a relationship that is ideologically (though not actually) a purely affectionate (as opposed to both affectionate and economic) relationship has lessened women's claim on men's resources after a marriage breaks up (see Giddens 1992 on the "pure relationship"). It is easy to see how the ongoing incorporation of this ideology, which privileges the emotional work of a relationship over men's economic role, could lessen men's feelings of obligation to their families. Furthermore, companionate marriages can be very isolating for women, especially for migrants, as the ideal encourages women to invest time and energy primarily in the marital relationship, rather than in a wider social network of female friends and relatives.

En el Norte la Mujer Manda: Migration-Related Differences in Gender

A constant refrain in both Atlanta and Mexico was that "en el norte la mujer manda" (in the North, women are in charge). When Doña Elena criticized Maria and her other daughters in Atlanta for answering back to their husbands, she said that Maria explained to her, "No, mom, here the woman is the boss, it's not like back in Mexico where the men are the boss. . . . No, here they don't hit you. . . . Here, the men are the ones who stand to lose" (No mama, aquí uno manda, no es como allá en México que los hombres mandan allá.... No, aquí no me friegan.... Aquí los hombres le llevan de perder). Comments such as this direct attention to differences between various locations of the same transnational community. In terms of shared culture, the intensity of physical movement, and social and economic links, Degollado and El Fuerte are typical of the kinds of transnational communities others have discussed (e.g., Glick Schiller, Basch, and Blanc-Szanton 1992). When people in Mexico asked for me, for example, how long I had been "here" doing my research, they expected an answer dated from my first entry into the community in Atlanta and including all the time I had been talking with their relative in either place. "Here with us" encompasses the expanded social space of their transnational community. There are, however, important differences between geographic locations of a transnational community, many of which are cast in terms of the social organization of gender. Three key areas of difference distinguish the sending and receiving communities: privacy and the social organization of public space, domestic violence, and economic opportunities for women. When combined, these factors make the women in Atlanta less socially and economically dependent on men, thus revealing some of the meanings underlying the assertion that "en el norte la mujer manda."

Gender does not mark the house-street division in the United States quite as strongly as it does in Mexico. In the United States the danger of being picked up by the migra while in the street raises the costs of certain types of flamboyant behavior. As Roger Rouse (1991) points out, Mexican men do not "own" the street; they are well aware they are just visiting. Women's widespread participation in the formal labor market in Atlanta further neutralizes the street's gendered aspects; going to and from work gives women as much justification to be outside as men have. Women use the ideology of family progress—"salir adelante como familia" (making it as a family)—to justify other previously masculine privileges such as driving and owning a car. In Degollado and El Fuerte, only women from the wealthiest families drive at all, and very few women own cars. For migrant women, mobility is power. The Mexican women I know in Atlanta who do drive never tire of the thrill of the freedom of being able to go wherever they want without having to ask, of their new mastery of the street.

Furthermore, the audience in the street is not the same as in small-town Mexico. The sense of shared vigilance of all public behavior (characteristic perhaps of any small town) is lost in the urban United States. A feeling of freedom accompanies the realization that "aquí nadie te conoce" (here, no one knows you). In the field sites in Mexico women put on stockings and hairspray to walk two blocks to the market to buy tortillas. In Atlanta they relax this resolute management of their appearance, dressing more for comfort than to express social status. Older women whose husbands never would have let them wear slacks, let alone jeans, go out in sweatpants (without asking permission). On returning to Mexico after having lived with her older sister, one unmarried woman left behind all the Bermuda shorts she had bought in Atlanta; she knew without asking that her father would never let her wear them in the rancho.

Women in Atlanta still dress up to go out at night with their husbands, but on a day-to-day basis they feel almost invisible and thus freed from some of the performative demands of gender and class. Although they delight in the relatively low prices and wide selection in U.S. stores, they stockpile their sartorial treasures to wear for the first time on visits back to Mexico. This invisibility is expressed in other ways as well. In Mexico women sweep outside their front doors first thing in the morning and sometimes again in the afternoon, but never in all my visits to Atlanta (some quite early in the morning) did I see anyone sweeping outside her door. Women hint at how privacy expands the range of the possible, joking about how easy it would be to take a lover—all one would need to do would be to hop on the bus, or into the car, and go meet him. In Degollado to be seen riding in a car with an unknown man would at best require some serious explaining and at worst be grounds for divorce; amid Atlanta's urban anonymity it would in all likelihood pass completely unnoticed. Staff at family-planning clinics—or even abortion providers—are not inevitably the *comadre* of one's mother's cousin or some other relative. More than likely, they do not even speak Spanish, which complicates service delivery but certainly increases the sense of privacy. The lack of an audience that monitors gendered behavior as an indicator of prestige greatly increases the possibilities for experimentation (and transgression).

One example of the greater privacy in Atlanta is in how the Catholic Church loosens its hold on women's reproductive behavior. Couples who marry in Degollado and El Fuerte are routinely (although not always) asked if they will accept "todos los hijos que Dios les manda" (all the children God sends them). Women and their husbands are scolded in confession—the priests ask them directly—for using anything but periodic abstinence as a method of contraception. The women and men who do use a method forgo Communion altogether—which also means forgoing any *compadrazgo* (godparent relationship) that would be formalized at a Mass—or else confess their sin once a year, do penance, take Communion, and then resume using contraception. The authority of the confessional is absolute; lying in confession is a mortal sin, perhaps even worse than the initial sin of nonprocreative sex. In Atlanta, in contrast, some priests ask about contraception and some do not, and women cannily choose their confessors. Furthermore, some women—especially those who do not drive and live far from public transportation—sidestep the question altogether by no longer attending Mass. Others drift toward other Christian sects such as the Southern Baptists or Jehovah's Witnesses.

Men say that one reason Mexican women have more power in the North is that a man cannot hit his wife without the government interfering. In contrast to Mexico, where police are reluctant to intervene in cases of men's violence toward their wives or of parents' toward their children, Mexicans, whether or not they live in the United States, know that in the United States help is literally a phone call away. Consider the difference between Maria in Atlanta and Josefina in Degollado, both of whom had been slapped by their husbands. Josefina admitted it to me, saying that the reason that Pedro could always get the last word ("la mujer con el hombre nunca va a poder") was that he could always beat her up ("me puede chingar"). Maria, meanwhile, spoke with great bravado to her mother about how men could not hit women in the United States, about how men were the ones who stood to lose if it came to violence. It is, of course, a myth that men's violence against women does not exist in the United States, just as it is untrue that there are not social controls against men's violence in Mexico. But domestic violence does take on new meaning in the United States, and the U.S. legal system—combined with the legal vulnerability of many Mexicans who live in fear of deportation—gives women important leverage. Eva and Pancho, for example, fought constantly during the time I was getting to know her, but she said she could usually get him to calm down by threatening to "call her lawyer." Whether she really had a lawyer or (more likely) a domestic-violence counselor, the function of having a lawyer was clear: both she and Pedro knew that if things got bad enough she could get a restraining order and throw him out of the house.

Some women do call the police, but their reasons for not involving the authorities are as significant as the possibility that they might. Juan, who has been working in the United States since before he turned twenty, is now in his early thirties and a U.S. citizen. He and Mercedes have one son, born in Atlanta. He spoke of Mercedes's right to have her own opinions, even to correct him, and of wanting to create a family bonded by warmth and physical affection rather than by the respectful reserve his parents showed each other. The most important way a man respects his wife, he said, was in not forcing her to have sex against her will; intimacy should always be mutual and voluntary. Yet Juan reserved the right to slap his wife "to get her to calm down" and to remind her that he was ultimately the boss. He suggested that "getting along well" and having a "happy and harmonious home" depended on her accepting that there was only one pair of pants in their home and that they belong to him. Their interactions around violence—his slapping her, her refraining from calling the police—are messages not just about gender hierarchy per se but also about the gendered nature of Mexican identity for immigrants to the United States. He is not just showing her her place: he is making sure that it is the same place that she occupied in Mexico. By not dialing 911, she allows him to continue to believe that he really does have the last word, that although they are in the United States, she has not forgotten what she learned as a girl about how to get along *por las buenas* (by being nice). Under these conditions, direct resistance resonates with meaning: just because a woman lives in a country in which the police will respond to her call does not make it easier to pick up the phone. This may explain at least in part why a woman like Maria, who has been in the United States for ten years, drives her own car, speaks English, and earns more than her husband, does not call the police when he hits her. By enduring the violence, she allows him to reassert his power. She pays for her mobility and economic success with bruises.

The other reason Mexican women have more power in the United States than in Mexico, men say, is that they work. El mando, the power to give the orders, is conceptualized at some level as an economically earned right: men should have the last word because they have the ultimate responsibility of supporting their families. Women's labor-force participation in the United States is perceived to somehow encroach on men's sole right to el mando, but this is hardly just a case of female employment translating directly into domestic power. Leaving aside the fact that social reproduction is work as well, albeit unpaid and undervalued, women also work in Mexico. Three of the thirteen life-history informants in Mexico had their own businesses, and another five occasionally sold cheese, needlework, goats, or chickens or did housework. Older women were economically active as well. One of the older women was available to be interviewed only on Wednesday afternoons because in addition to running a small grocery store she managed her son's restaurant (he lived in the United States), which was open every night except on Wednesdays. Another ran a workshop out of her home, sewing piecework for a factory in a large town nearby. And though they were hardly the norm, I met a number of older women who had accompanied their husbands north at least once to try their hands at factory or fieldwork.

The difference, then, is not that women work in the United States and do not work in Mexico; rather, it is that women's labor in the United States brings them much closer to economic independence than do their sisters' efforts south of the border. In Atlanta it is eminently possible for a woman to support her children by earning just above the minimum wage, especially if she has only a few children or if they are U.S. citizens (and hence qualify for Medicaid) or if she has her own family nearby to help. In Degollado and El Fuerte few jobs available to women of limited education pay even half the weekly minimum wage (about 300 pesos, or not quite $40, at the time of my fieldwork). A housekeeper who works from eight in the morning until three in the afternoon, for example, earns seventy pesos a week; by taking in washing and ironing, it might be possible to earn another seventy. One hundred and forty pesos a week would not feed a family of four (by Mexican standards, a small family) even the barest meals of beans, tortillas, and chiles, much less provide for housing, clothes, shoes, schoolbooks, and the occasional medical emergency.

The net effect of all these differences—violence, women's work, increased privacy—is that women do not need men in the same way in Atlanta as they do in the sending communities. Economically speaking, they can take care of themselves in a pinch. Socially, a single mother can be *respetada* (respected) in a way that would be difficult in Mexico without a man. This is not just an abstract set of differences in the social construction of gender. Several years ago, Maria's husband began staying out all night drinking. In the morning, he would refuse to drive her to work. He stopped giving her any of his paycheck, and she suspected he was running around with other women. She threatened to buy her own car and learn to drive, but he just laughed—so she took her savings, called a friend, and bought a car. Once she could drive, she threw him out. She told him she did not need his nonsense—"mejor sola que mal acompañada" (better to be alone than in bad company)—and that he should not come home until he could be a more responsible husband and a better father to his two children. Several weeks later, he was back, asking for forgiveness. They still have occasional difficulties, but for the most part they live well together.

Maria had certain advantages that not all migrants have—that is, there is not one story to be told about women's migration from Mexico to the United States but rather many stories. As discussed elsewhere (Hirsch 1998a), whether these stories have happy or sad endings depends in part on a number of factors (legal status, kin networks, the moment in the family cycle at which migration takes places, women's and men's personalities) that make women more or less able to take advantage of the social and economic opportunities offered by life in the United States.

Implications for Future Research

On a methodological note, the life-history method—combined with patient participant observation, hours spent knitting and watching telenovelas, and repeated visits—proved to be extremely useful for sexuality research with Mexican women. Once Mexican women had confianza with me, they were quite willing to talk about sex in a variety of ways, ranging from sharing the ribald jokes told among married women to answering questions (in the final life-history interview) about the nature of desire, sexual positions, pleasure, and communication. The repeated visits and relationship building that were already necessary as part of researching their life histories were also crucial in promoting confianza. A second methodological point is that the findings here underline the importance of flexibility in research strategy (and, by implication, with regard to the research questions themselves). I only turned my attention to generational change after being told repeatedly and by many women that their lives and marriages were different from their mothers'—that "ya no somos como las de antes." Those embarking on migration studies may want to remember that migrants can offer much more than just grist for an academic's mill: if one listens carefully, one can find in their words important directions about the theoretical and methodological approaches that best suit the problem at hand.

Furthermore, rather than looking at the sending community as the cultural and social control group in order to foreground the changes that accompany migration, one should explore how the sending communities themselves are changing. Without acknowledging historical processes in the sending communities, one implies a comparison between life in the traditional developing world with that in the modern developed world—an error that scholars have specifically sought to avoid by adopting the transnational perspective, with its emphasis on the intensity of connection between sending and receiving communities. After all, the sending communities are a moving target, as subject to historical change as the receiving communities. In addition, as Nancy Foner (1997) has pointed out, "traditional" migrant culture is not a fixed body of norms but rather a category that is deliberately manipulated by migrants as they forge new cultures, drawing both on the old and the new. The main point—and this is both a theoretical and a methodological recommendation—is that studies of gender that neglect historical transformations in the sending communities miss key cultural developments without which migration-related changes cannot be fully understood. Even if one's research designs are cross-sectional, one's theoretical and methodological approaches can be longitudinal.

This study also speaks to theoretical concerns about migration and cultural changes. At first glance, the emphasis on intimacy, choice, and cooperation that runs throughout younger women's and men's descriptions of their marriages might seem to be directly influenced by North American ideals of companionate marriage (see Giddens 1992; Simmons 1979). The comparative perspective employed in this essay, however, highlights how the cultural changes in the study community are a result both of transnational linkages and of social processes within Mexico. Women in both the U.S. and Mexican field sites shared similar ideals for marriages of confianza; the key difference was that women in the United States seemed to have more leverage to negotiate toward that ideal—or, perhaps, that men were more willing to adopt the new paradigm away from the watchful eyes of their fathers and uncles in Mexico. The generational paradigm shift from marriages of respeto to marriages of confianza—that is, the trend toward companionate marriage—has interesting parallels in Africa, Europe, and North America (see, for example, Gillis, Tilly, and Levine 1992; Inhorn 1996; Simmons 1979; D. Smith n.d.), parallels that suggest the value of exploring links between widespread processes such as industrialization and technological change and ideologies of the nuclear family. It is not that Mexicans are adopting some universally homogeneous ideal of family relations, but rather that they are actively transforming a globally available ideology into a specifically Mexican companionate marriage.

This study suggests a route to disaggregating the ideological and material components of cultural change that would also hold true for areas of interest other than gender; that is, comparative, historically grounded research in migrant sending communities could lay a solid foundation for sorting out which aspects of cultural change in migrants are actually a product of migration and which are the result of changes in the sending community. Of course, changes in the sending community cannot be separated from migration-related changes: one of the key historical processes in these sending communities is their increasing integration into international migrant circuits. A comparison of the gender culture of towns and ranchos such as Degollado and El Fuerte to other towns and ranchos less intensely tied to migration might disentangle the influence of migration and return migrants from those of more specifically Mexican historical changes—if it were possible to find any such towns.

The time has come to move away from bargaining as the metaphor guiding the scholarly approach to gender and migration. Although the idea of bargaining and negotiation has been useful for how it highlights the constrained agency of migrants (see Pessar 1998), the ethnographic evidence presented in this essay suggest that the focus on the causes of women's empowerment has limited understanding of gender and migration in a number of ways. First, the debate about the relative importance of wage labor versus the broader cultural and legal differences of life in the United States in giving women more power misses the interrelatedness of these factors (see Gibson 1988; Hondagneu-Sotelo 1994): Maria would not have thrown her husband out if she could not have supported herself, but she would never have worked as a waitress in Mexico, because the contact with unknown men that such a job entails would have risked her, and her family's, honor.

Second, whether women can take advantage of these economic, cultural, and legal opportunities depends on a number of other factors such as legal status, kin networks, and labor-force experience. There is not, and never will be, just one answer to the question of how migration affects gender. A simplistic focus on how migration affects gender takes one back two decades in gender theory, to the idea of "woman" as a unified category. As Patricia Pessar argued (1998), gender may not even be the defining axis of women's lives; scholars need to look at race and class as well.

Although this essay focuses on ideals and practices within marriage, there are certainly other relationships that are relevant to broader issues of how migration affects the social construction of gender. As Katherine Donato (1993) and Pierrette Hondagneu-Sotelo (1994) point out, not all women who migrate do so with their husbands; some move north under the moral protection of other male relatives such as fathers or brothers, whereas other women (in particular, those who become pregnant outside of marriage) migrate to distance themselves deliberately from their male kin. Further research should go both beyond a narrow emphasis on women's resources within marriage and beyond looking at gender as if it only structured relationships between married couples. In addition, one should not assume that migration to the United States is always beneficial to women. There are important ways that migration can limit some women's power; rather than being able to walk next door to her mother's house, for example, a Mexican woman seeking social support may have to struggle with language difficulties and public transportation—if in fact she is lucky enough to have her own kin nearby. Again and again, women who do not work told me, "Me siento como en la cárcel" (I feel as if I were in jail); other researchers have encountered similar experiences (see Pessar 1995, 45).

Most important, the question of why migration empowers women, or even of which women are empowered, makes other aspects of changes in gender invisible. As Micaela di Leonardo argued (1991), gender is relational; that is, it is not possible to understand gender without interviewing both women and men. Men's preferences are perhaps the most important constraint on the kinds of marriages that Mexican women in this community can negotiate. Without attention to how masculinity is changing, it is impossible to make sense of the new marriages of confianza. Looking at the issue of gender and migration by focusing on women's changing resources takes male gender as the invisible, immutable, reference category; it assumes that men continue to want what they wanted in Mexico and that what they wanted in Mexico has not changed. Although some, such as Rouse (1991) and Pessar (1995), have looked at how male migrants' resources (especially their social power as men) change, not enough attention has been paid to the ways in which the goals themselves may be changing. Foner notes that the Jamaican women she interviewed were influenced by "American values extolling the ideal of marital fidelity and 'family togetherness'" (1997, 967). The Mexican couples in this study are influenced both by those "American values" and by new, Mexican ideals about marital intimacy and togetherness. Some Mexican men, although they may not long to pack their children's lunches or clean the toilets, do yearn for a different kind of family life, and they are remaking their families to achieve that goal. As Juan said in talking about his parents' marriage, "I've never seen them kiss, or even hug." He said he wants to do both, to act "closer [mas unido] so that the children really know you love each other, that you feel both tenderness and respect [que conozcan que uno se quiere y que tiene uno cariño que hay respeto]." Ethnography can remind scholars to listen to the voices of their research subjects; in this essay those voices say that although Mexican migrants may be poor and struggling and sometimes undocumented, they deserve the basic humanity of being understood to make decisions not just out of strategy and advantage, but out of love and longing as well.

Notes

1 Throughout this essay, references to younger women mean the younger life history of informants—generally speaking, those younger than thirty-five—whereas references to older women include the opinion and experiences of the older life-history informants and the mothers of the life-history informants.
2 A number of other factors have contributed to this sharp fertility decline. Although the subject can hardly be discussed adequately here, factors worthy of mention include social changes such as rising rates of education among both men and women and a concurrently rising age at first marriage; economic transformations such as women's increased labor-force participation and the increased availability of nonagricultural jobs for which a secondary education is desirable, if not necessary; and political factors such as the Mexican government's concerted effort, since the 1970s, to slow population growth through national family-planning campaigns.

Unruly Passions: Poetics, Performance, and Gender in the Ranchera Song
OLGA NÁJERA-RAMÍREZ

I am convinced that a fruitful study of the *canción ranchera* would be one that interprets the cruel, fickle woman, so bitterly denounced in many of these songs, and alcohol, so ready at hand, as symbols that scapegoat for social and economic oppression.
—Manuel Peña, *The Texas-Mexican Conjunto*

Since the mid-nineteenth century a country's music has become a political ideology by stressing national characteristics, appearing as a representative of a nation, and everywhere confirming the national principle.... Yet music, more than any other artistic medium, expresses the national principle's antinomies as well.
—Theodor W. Adorno, *Introduction to the Sociology of Music*

❋ The Mexican ranchera is an expressive musical form intimately associated with Mexican cultural identity on both sides of the U.S.-Mexico border. With regard to the ways in which Mexican culture is perceived, constructed, and represented, the ranchera functions as a critical site for exploring issues of *lo mexicano* or Mexicanness. While the ranchera has occasionally been taken up as a topic of serious scholarly inquiry, detailed analyses of it are limited.[1] Moreover, most of these studies have failed to adequately theorize, and in some cases have even failed to acknowledge, women's participation as performers, composers, and consumers of the ranchera.[2] With reference to recent scholarship on melodrama and performance studies, one can argue that the ranchera embodies a poetics that resists facile and essentialist interpretations. It may be considered a form of melodrama—a discursive space characterized by the intensity of emotion in which issues of profound social concern may be addressed. Furthermore, women have employed the ranchera as a site through which they may make feminist interventions. Although my ethnographic research is preliminary, based on formal interviews with Lydia Mendoza and a working-class woman, some participant observation, and numerous informal conversations, it demonstrates that the ranchera is a rich site for feminist investigation.[3]

La Ranchera as a Form of Melodrama

The ranchera is a type of Mexican popular music characterized by theme (lyrical content), performance style, and to some extent, musical structure. In general the themes revolve around fervent sentiments toward particular people and specific places (town, state, region or country). Punctuated with *gritos* (soulful cries of emotion), the ranchera is characterized by the intense expression of emotions, and, in this respect, may be favorably compared to the blues and country-western music.[4] Although the musical structure of the ranchera is not rigid, scholars generally agree that, particularly in commercially recorded versions, it is strophic, often including an instrumental introduction, a verse, a refrain, and an instrumental interlude (Mendoza 1988). The number and structure of the verses varies from song to song.

The term *canción ranchera* (country song) first emerged in the early twentieth century during the postrevolutionary period, when Mexico experienced a surge in urban migration. Evoking a rural sensibility, the ranchera expressed a nostalgia for a provincial lifestyle and projected a romanticized idyllic vision of the past.[5] As cultural critic Carlos Monsiváis observes, "El estruendo y la melodía implorante y la letra sacrificial bosquejan una actitud distante de lo 'urbano' y lo 'contemporáneo.' En su adjetivo, la canción ranchera elije el estilo y la calidad de las emociones al alcance de su auditorio y opta por aquellas inscritas en la idea de 'rancho,' de epoca anterior a lo industrial y lo tecnológico" (The cries and imploring melody and the sacrificial lyrics delineate an attitude distant from the "urban" and the "contemporary." As an adjective, the ranchera song chooses a style and quality of emotions appropriate for its audience and opts for those inscribed in the idea of the "ranch" of the era before the industrial and the technological) (1994b [1977], 90).

Considered an ideal expression of lo mexicano by romantic nationalists of the 1930s, the ranchera attained widespread popularity through radio and film, especially the *comedia ranchera* (western comedy).[6] According to ethnomusicologist Manuel Peña, "People respond, instinctively, to a ranchero sound, whether it be interpreted for them by a *conjunto*, an *orquesta* or a *mariachi*. And inevitably, by virtue of its symbolic association, it gives rise to vaguely articulated feelings of *mexicanismo*—momentary recreations of a simpler and romanticized folk heritage, tempered nonetheless by the realization that it is an ineffable existence, lost forever like the elusive lover of most ranchera song lyrics" (1985, 11). Particularly important in Peña's commentary is his suggestion that the nostalgic longing for another time or place becomes expressed metaphorically as the longing for an elusive lover. His insight anticipates my own argument that the ranchera has to be understood in poetic, rather than literal, terms. Peña's observation that the canción ranchera evokes a sentimental response among its (Mexican) audiences on both sides of the border is also noteworthy.

While other scholars also associate passionate sentimentalism with the ranchera song, few have considered it a distinctive stylistic attribute of the song form. Instead, in the most extreme cases, sentimentality and emotion are read as uniquely Mexican cultural attributes. Claes Geijerstam, for example, claims, "The performance of the ranchera songs exhibits an inimitable sentimentality, even tearfulness, which seems to be characteristically Mexican" (1976, 125). Injecting a class and gendered dimension, Mark Fogelquist goes even further, stating that "the underlying sense of desperation of the lower-class Mexican male, the fatalism, and the view that *la vida no vale nada* (life is worth nothing) and of course large quantities of alcohol, give rise to the total rejection of reason and the indulgence of passion" (1975, 60).

Without espousing Fogelquist's negative stereotypes of the lower-class Mexican male as desperate, fatalistic, and alcoholic, William Gradante also attributes the popular appeal of the ranchera to the fact that the experiences embodied within the text resonate with those of the everyday working-class individual. "The brevity, simplicity and straightforwardness of the poetic structure of the *canción ranchera* served as the most appropriate vehicle for the expression of the sentiments of the lower classes without pretense or unnecessary elaboration" (1983, 112).

In addition to assuming that indulgence in passion is uniquely Mexican, such readings assume that the ranchera, like the people to whom it speaks, is simple, unsophisticated, and therefore transparent in meaning.[7] However, as Américo Paredes skillfully demonstrated years ago, the failure to recognize the artistic dimension of Greater Mexican expressive behavior has resulted in gross interpretative inaccuracies by scholars who "proceed as if language had only one level of meaning or as if informants were incapable of any kind of language use but that of minimum communication" (1977, 8). Paredes's work on proverbs is particularly instructive, for he clearly illustrates that the brevity and apparent simplicity of an expressive form are not accurate indicators of the sophistication of the speaker or meaning of the message. Consequently,

Paredes warns, "If explanations can be so far off the mark with proverbs—which seem to be all 'message'—this is even truer of the more complex forms of folklore, such as legends, *corridos*, customs, or beliefs. We must know the situation in which this folklore is performed; and we must know the language and the people well" (1982, 11). Paredes provides a compelling argument for attending to both the poetics and the performative dimensions of an expressive form. That is, rather than assume that the expression of passion in the lyrics and/or in the performance is a "naive expression of a simple people" (Stewart 1993, 221), one must recognize emotional excess as a deliberate aesthetic quality of the ranchera.[8]

The emphasis on the "emotional excess" of the ranchera points to its affinity with melodramatic forms. Indeed, melodramatic forms are by definition a rollercoaster of emotion. As film theorist Marcia Landy observes, "Seduction, betrayal, abandonment, extortion, murder, suicide, revenge, jealousy, incurable illness, obsession, and compulsion—these are part of the familiar terrain of melodrama" (1991, 14). Significantly, as in the case of the ranchera, the emotional excess in melodrama previously provided scholars with sufficient grounds on which to regard melodrama as vulgar and insignificant. In recent years, however, cultural critics from a number of theoretical perspectives—feminism, psychoanalysis, Marxism, and semiotics—have reevaluated melodrama as an aesthetic practice with its own set of strategies of communication. These critics now affirm that melodrama offers far more important insights into culture than had been previously considered (Brooks 1976; Landy 1991; Linda Williams 1991; Gledhill 1987).

Not only is emotional excess expressed in its narrative content (i.e., the lyrics), but the performance of melodrama calls for a style intended to induce emotional responses from the audience as well (Landy 1991, 15). The emotions exhibited—and, one may assume, induced—in the performance style of the ranchera include sadness, despair, contempt, love, and pride. Typically, the ranchera performance style includes not only a vocal display of emotions but also *ademanes* (facial, hand, and body gestures) and even tears. Such displays of emotion render the performance one in which the singer, in the words of many ranchera performers, "vive lo que canta" (lives what s/he sings). In contrast to claims that rancheras transparently express what the singers (and their audiences) live, the ranchera singers claim they live what they sing *as* they perform, thus emphasizing the fact that it is a performance. For instance, in an interview I conducted with Lydia Mendoza, she explained to me, "Yo vivo lo que canto. Cuando estoy cantando siento como si estuviera viviendo aquellos sentimientos" (I live what I sing. When I am singing, I feel as if I were living those sentiments).[9] According to Mendoza, and judging by the audience's reactions to her live performances, her ability to sing as if she were experiencing the narrative is precisely what makes her music touch others. Similarly, nine-year-old singing sensation Tatiana Bolaños—who belts out ranchera songs with the emotion and sentimentalism of some of the greatest ranchera singers—clearly illustrates that the ability to exhibit a range of emotions is a performance style that can (and should) be acquired and manipulated by an accomplished ranchera singer.

How well ranchera singers render a performance is a subject of great attention. The singer's ability to engage the audience depends on her or his ability to invoke a broad range of emotions, rather than to limit the performance to one emotion. Singers who merely sob through an entire song lose the emotional tension that a skilled ranchera performer manages and prompt such criticism as "es muy llorona" (she's just a whiner).

In addition to an emphasis on sensibility and emotion, other characteristics of melodrama include the "dichotomizing of the world, its Manicheanism, and its inflation of personal conflicts and its internalization of external social conflicts" (Landy 1991, 16). The latter point has been especially evident in the recent research on Mexican melodramatic films by scholars who cogently assert that melodramatic films serve as fictional spaces in which issues of Mexican identity and social change are explored and represented (Monsiváis 1992; Ana M. López 1991b; Podalsky 1993). In particular, Laura Podalsky (1993) and Ana M. López (1991b) persuasively argue for a more nuanced reading of Mexican melodramas that acknowledges their contestative potential even as they reinforce the dominant ideology. For instance, Podalsky claims that "melodrama is formally and practically linked with the specific trajectory of Mexican national identity and the significance of the Revolution for the nation-building project." Yet, she argues, "the ability of melodrama to incorporate contradictory messages about the nation made it a viable formula for political as well as cinematic texts" (1993, 63). Similarly, López concludes that "to dismiss melodrama as a simple 'tool of domination' is to ignore the complex intersections of strategies of representation and particular social relations of difference" (1991b, 47). These insights on Mexican film are particularly noteworthy because the Mexican movie industry serves as a critical site for the dissemination and popularization of the ranchera song.[10]

Understood as a form of melodrama, rancheras may productively be approached as a discursive space in which topics of emotional weight may be addressed in culturally appropriate ways. That is, rancheras may be considered culturally sanctioned sites in which the ideas and values of a community are not merely displayed but, more important, transmitted, produced, reproduced, and contested. Far from being transparent expressions of a simple people, rancheras are complex forms rife with contradictions. Moreover, rancheras, like other melodramatic forms, are "inextricable from social conflict, revealing, obliquely or directly, class, gender, and generational conflicts" (Landy 1991, 18). Because the ranchera relies heavily on the use of metaphor, the meanings are much more open-ended and situationally sensitive than scholars have heretofore suggested. Songs about abandonment, loss, and desire, for example, take on new meanings when examined within the context of the increased globalization that has intensified domestic as well as transnational migrations within Greater Mexico. Such displacements often rupture families (at least temporarily, sometimes permanently), threaten partnerships, and complicate preexisting notions of national identity. The nostalgia, longing, and despair that Mexicanos experience in all aspects of their life, not just their love lives, is given expression through the ranchera.

CRUZ DE OLVIDO	THE BURDEN OF FORGETTING
Con el atardecer me iré de ti	At sunset I will leave you
me iré sin ti	I will leave without you
me alejaré de ti	I will distance myself from you
con un dolor dentro de mi	With a pain deep within me
Te juro corazón	I swear to you, sweetheart
que no es falta de amor	It's not for lack of love
pero es mejor asi	But it's better this way
un día comprenderás	One day you'll understand
que lo hice por tu bien	That I did it for your own good
que todo fue por ti	That everything was for you

Clearly, the song speaks about the emotional turmoil experienced by a person who must leave a loved one. Although the composer Juan Zaizar most likely wrote this song about an adult love relationship, the text is sufficiently fluid to apply to various situations. Engaged listeners can read the song according to their own experiences, filling in specific details regarding exactly why the departure has to occur and the nature of the relationship between the subject and the object. Considering the long history of labor migration within Greater Mexico, which has caused the fragmentation of families, I argue that for many listeners such songs may apply as much to parent-child separations as they do to separations experienced by two lovers.[11]

The notion of multiple, and even contested, meanings within melodrama also lays the groundwork for exploring issues of gender.

> The figure of woman, which has served so long as a powerful and ambivalent patriarchal symbol, is also a generator of female discourses drawn

from the social realities of women's lives—discourses which negotiate a space within and sometimes resist patriarchal domination. In order to command the recognition of its female audiences, melodrama must draw on such discourses. Thus in twentieth-century melodrama the dual role of woman as symbol for a whole culture and as representative of a historical, gendered point of view produces a struggle between male and female voices: the symbol cannot be owned but is contested. (Gledhill 1987, 37)

Similarly, as López argues, Mexican melodrama "always addresses questions of individual (gendered) identity within patriarchal culture" (1991b, 33). Extending their insights into my analysis of the ranchera, I now turn to examine the question of how one might consider women's participation in the performance, production, and consumption of the ranchera as a feminist intervention. By participating actively in what was predominantly a male genre, women have been able to employ the ranchera for their own purposes, sometimes highlighting their subordination, sometimes talking back to that subordination, but always calling attention to their concerns, desires, experiences, and needs. Through the manipulation of text, costume, and performance style, women use the ranchera to challenge, transgress, and even ameliorate gender constraints prevalent in Mexican society.

Engendering Performances

The lyrics of the ranchera provide an opportunity for women to make important interventions. In a short but provocative study, the Mexican anthropologist Marta Lamas provides a feminist interpretation of ranchera lyrics, noting the use of metaphor as a strategy for objectifying women and for discussing sexual themes that would otherwise be considered taboo. For example, women are often spoken of as flowers to be cared for, plucked, or stolen by their lovers, while their fathers, brothers, or husbands are the protective gardeners.

ROSA DE CASTILLA	ROSE OF THE CASTLE
que buena te estas poniendo	You are getting so ripe
para cortarte en una fresca	That I can cut you on a fresh
mañana	morning

ROSITA AMARILLA	YELLOW ROSE
Ah que aroma de esa flor	Oh what an aroma that flower has
de esa rosita amarilla	That yellow rose
el trabajo que me dió	The trouble it caused me

para verle la semilla	To see her seed
pero no se me escapo	But she didn't escape me
le corte hasta la ramilla	I even cut her limbs

Lamas's attention to the use of metaphor is instructive, for even this limited treatment of the poetic dimension challenges Gradantes's claim and Fogelquist's assumption that the ranchera is simple and straightforward. Together with Paredes's observations, Lamas's insights call attention to the need for taking fuller account of the poetic and performative dimensions of a ranchera. Consider, for example, what happens to the traditional ranchera text when a woman performs it: the poetics of the ranchera are reconfigured from a male to either a female or a gender-neutral point of view. The same text may assume a very different meaning when the subjective "I" is a woman and the "you" is a man. Sexist double standards are blatantly revealed when a woman sings a "male song" such as "Ni en defensa propia" (Not Even in My Own Defense). In this song the male protagonist decides to leave his girlfriend when he discovers that she is not a virgin; when the lyrics are sung by a woman, however, the protagonist may be interpreted as a female. That a woman would leave her male partner simply because he is not a virgin seems absurd within Mexican cultural conventions. The changes produced by transposing the gender roles in this case are monumental because they powerfully expose male privilege. Furthermore, by making very small but critical changes, women (and for that matter, men) can decenter the male perspective embedded in the narrative. For example, in the song "Tu solo tu," women singers such as Selena have changed the opening line from "Mira como ando mujer" (Look at the state I'm in, woman) to "Mira como ando mi amor" (Look at the state I'm in, my love).[12] Such changes open the text to a wider range of possible meanings.

A famous potpourri performed by José Alfredo Jimenez and Alicia Juarez entitled "Las coplas" (The Couplets, or The Verses) illustrates how performers can manipulate the meaning of the ranchera text. "Las coplas" consists of a series of excerpts from various well-known rancheras. By singing the verses in a call-and-response fashion, the two singers create an intertextual dialogue between the rancheras and between a man and a woman. Accordingly, the "I" and "you" shift depending on who is singing. Further, each singer takes the liberty of changing certain words to alter the meaning even more profoundly.[13] The performance thus becomes a sort of contest in which the singers try to outdo the other by engaging a range of sentiments, including desperation, control, pride, self-pity, submission, and reconciliation. In "Las coplas" José Alfredo Jimenez initiates the dialogue by singing the following excerpt of "No me amenaces":

> *No me amenaces, no me amenaces*
> *cuando estés decidida a buscar otra vida*
> *pos, agarra tu rumbo y vete*
> *Pero no me amenaces, no me amenaces*
> *ya estas grandecita, ya entiendes la vida*
> *y ya sabes lo que haces*
> *porque estás que te vas y te vas*
>
> *y te vas y te vas y te vas, y no te has ido*
> *y yo estoy esperando tu amor, esperando tu amor, esperando tu amor*
> *o esperando tu olvido*

> Don't threaten me, don't threaten me
> when you decide to search for another life
> well hit the road and go, but
> don't threaten me, don't threaten me
> you're grown, you understand life
> and you know what you're doing.
> Because you say that you're leaving,
> leaving, leaving, but you haven't gone
> and I'm waiting for your love, waiting for your love, waiting for your
> love or waiting to be forgotten.

[Alicia Juarez responds with excerpts of "Cuando vivas conmigo"]

> *De tus ojos esta brotando llanto*
> *a tus años estás enamorado*
> *traes el pelo completamente blanco*
> *ya no vas a sacar juventud de tu pasado*
> *¿qué me vas a enseñar a querer si tu nunca has querido?*
> *Díme ¿qué es lo que voy a aprender*
> *cuando viva contigo?*

> From your eyes a cry is erupting.
> At your age, you're in love.
> Your hair is completely white.
> You can't get youth from your past.
> What are you going to teach me about love if you've never loved?
> Tell me what am I going to learn
> when I live with you?

[Jiminez responds with excerpts of "La media vuelta"]

> *Te vas porque yo quiero que te vayas*
> *a la hora que yo quiero te detengo*
> *yo se que mi cariño te hace falta*
> *porque quieras o no yo soy tu dueño*
> *yo quiero que te vayas por el mundo*

> You're leaving because I want you to.
> I can keep you any time I want to.
> I know that you need my love
> because like it or not I own you.
> I want you to travel around the world.

y quiero que conozcas mucha gente	I want you to meet lots of people.
yo quiero que te besen otros labios	I want other lips to kiss you
para que me compares hoy como siempre	So you can compare me as always.

[Juarez sings excerpts of "Me equivoque contigo"]

Me equivoqué contigo	I made a mistake with you
como si no supiera	as if I didn't know
que las mas grandes penas	that my biggest regrets in life
las debo a mis amores	are due to my loves.
pero que triste realidad me has ofrecido	But what a sad reality you offer me.
que decepción tan grande	What a big deception
haberte conocido	it's been knowing you.
yo no se Dios porque	I don't know why God
te puso en mi camino	put you in my path.

[Jiminez sings excerpts of "La mano de Dios"]

Porque solamente la mano de Dios	Because only God's hand
podrá separarnos	can separate us.
nuestro amor es mas grande	Our love is much bigger
que todas las cosas del mundo	than anything in the world.
yo se bien que nacimos los dos	I know well that we were born
para siempre adorarnos	to always adore each other.
nuestro amor es lo mismo	Our love is like the sea,
que el mar cristalino y profundo	crystal clear and deep.

[Juarez sings excerpts of "Amanecí entre tus brazos"]

Amanecí otra vez entre tus brazos	I woke up again in your arms
y desperté llorando de alegria	and I woke up crying of joy.
me cobijé la cara con tus manos	I covered my face with your hands
para seguirte amando todavía	to continue loving you still.
te despertaste tu casi dormido	You awoke almost asleep
y me querías decir no se que cosa	and you wanted to say something
pero callé tu boca con mis besos	but I hushed your mouth with my kisses

UNRULY PASSIONS 465

y así pasaron muchas muchas horas	and we spent many hours that way.

[Together, Jiminez and Juarez sing excerpts of "Si nos dejan"]

Si nos dejan nos vamos	If they let us, we're going to love
a querer toda la vida	each other all life long.
si nos dejan nos vamos	If they let us, we're going to live
a vivir a un mundo nuevo	in a brand new world.
yo creo podemos ver el nuevo	I think we can see a new world
amanecer de un nuevo día	a new sunrise of a new day.
yo pienso que tu y yo podemos	I think that you and I can
ser felices todavía	still be happy.

The shifting of subjects in the performance of the ranchera clearly underscores the fact that the text cannot be adequately interpreted outside of its socially situated use. Singers may manipulate the meaning of the texts in subtle yet powerful ways. Simply by participating as performers of the ranchera, that is, by virtue of singing in their "female" voice, women recontextualize a text even when they do not change a single word.[14] As Richard Bauman and Charles Briggs argue, "To decontextualize and recontextualize a text is an act of control" (1990, 76). Each performance presents women with the opportunity to take control of the text to convey her own, subversive, message.

In recent years women have pushed further to expand the scope of the ranchera by composing and performing songs that speak more openly about premarital sex, talk back to sexist tenets, and project women as taking a more reflective and active stance in selecting and shaping a relationship. Lamas mentions two specific examples of ranchera songs composed and performed by women: "La leona" (The Lioness), in which the protagonist defiantly asserts her right to seek a relationship on her own terms, claiming that "que sea feo pero sincero" (it doesn't matter if he's ugly as long as he's sincere); and "La arrepentida" (The Repented One), in which the protagonist refuses marriage altogether (1978, 27). More recently there are "Es demasiado tarde" (It's Too Late) and "Tu lo decidiste" (You Made the Decision), composed and sung by Ana Gabriel; both feature a protagonist who refuses to take back her lover after their breakup.

ES DEMASIADO TARDE	IT'S TOO LATE
Tu quisiste estar allá	You wanted to be there
dijiste que quizá ese era tu destino	You said that perhaps that was your destiny
después que todo te falló	after everything failed you

hoy quieres regresar	Now you want to return
y ser felíz conmigo	and be happy with me
Pero tu no piensas que mi amor	But you don't think that my love
por siempre me olvido	has forgotten me forever
y exiges mi cariño	and you demand my affection
de veras lo siento no podré	I am truly sorry that I can't
volverme a enamorar	fall in love with you again
de ti ya no es lo mismo	it's just not the same anymore
(coro)	(chorus)
solo espero que entiendas que un amor	I just hope that you understand that love
se debe de cuidar y no jugar con nadie	should be cared for and never played with
porque yo te daba mi querer	because I gave you my love and though I
y aun si merecer no te dolió dejarme	didn't deserve it, it didn't hurt you to leave me
ahora vuelves buscando mi calor	Now you return, looking for my warmth
diciendo que jamás lograste olvidarme	telling me you never managed to forget me
pero yo te aclaro de una vez	but I want to be perfectly clear
lo debes entender es demasiado tarde	you should understand that it's too late
Yo no te guardo rencor	I don't resent you
pero tampoco amor	but I don't love you either
de ti ya nada queda	there's nothing left of you (for me)
no niego fue mucho mi dolor	I don't deny that it was very painful
pero eso ya pasó	but that's over now
mejor ya nunca vuelvas	it's best that you never return
(se repite el coro)	(repeat chorus)
Porque tu quisiste estar allá	Because you wanted to be there

Such songs are powerful because they do not assume a heterosexual relationship and because they portray women with agency staunchly refusing to become victims. As such, they broaden notions of womanhood.

The implicit and explicit gendering of a text is only one example of how paralinguistic communication can be accomplished in a ranchera performance. Just as important as the texts are the dynamics of performance—the singing style, costuming, gestures and other theatrical devices—as well as the sites of performance.[15] Together these elements provide the ranchera singer the means by which she can express that which is otherwise unspeakable.

The singing style constitutes a particularly important aspect of performance. In general, the ranchera singing style encompasses a whole range of emotions which includes "feminine" qualities such as tenderness, softness, and sweetness and "masculine" qualities of assertiveness, toughness, and bravado. Yet, while men who sang softly or tenderly in their performances were read as romantic rather than feminine, women who evinced masculine qualities in their singing were regarded as vulgar and therefore not appropriate—at least until the appearance of Lucha Reyes, a famous ranchera singer in the early part of the twentieth century who popularized a defiant, assertive attitude.[16]

> La aparición de Lucha Reyes marcó el surgimiento del estilo de interpretación femenina de la canción ranchera. En 1927, después de una gira en Europa con la típica del maestro Torreblanca, la cantante había quedado afónica durante más de un año. Al recuperar la voz pudo entonar con un color de contralto y un matiz enronquecido y bronco la naciente canción ranchera-citadina. La personalidad y la neurosis hicieron el resto. Prodigaba su voz hasta desgarrarla, gemía, lloraba, reía e imprecaba. Nunca antes se habían escuchado interpretaciones de ese estilo. Sobreponiendose a las críticas que no aceptaban su falta de refinamiento, pronto Lucha Reyes simbolizaba y personificaba a la mujer bravia y temperamental a la mexicana.

> (The appearance of Lucha Reyes marked the emergence of a female style of singing the ranchera. In 1927, after a tour in Europe with the regional orchestra directed by Torreblanca, the singer lost her voice for almost a year. On recovery, she gained the ability to sing the nascent urban ranchera song in a contralto voice with a hoarse and rough quality. Her personality and neurosis did the rest. She exhausted her voice to the breaking point, she grunted, she cried, she laughed, and she cursed. Never before had this kind of interpretation been heard. Overcoming the critics who did not accept her lack of refinement, Lucha Reyes came to symbolize and personify the Mexican version of the fierce and temperamental woman.) (Moreno Rivas 1989, 190)

By incorporating a range of qualities culturally regarded as masculine, Reyes challenged sexist division of emotions, making it possible for women to access both male and female qualities. In so doing, Reyes also challenged the idea that women were confined to being sweet, proper, and innocent. As the music critic Yolanda Moreno Rivas observes, "Habia quedado atrás la dulce e ingenua rancherita encargada de confeccionar los 'calzones de cuero del ranchero.' Ahora, 'la flor más bella del ejido' gritaría, se emborracharía y experimentaría terribles pasiones y abandonos dignos de una verdadera citadina" (The idea of the sweet and innocent country girl in charge of "making the leather pants for the cowboy" was left behind. Now, the "most beautiful woman of the village" would scream, get drunk, and experience terrible passions and wild abandon worthy of the true urban woman) (1989, 191).[17] Reyes's style has since been emulated by many of the great ranchera singers including Lola Beltrán, Lucha Villa, Irma Serrano, Alicia Juaréz, and Beatriz Adriana. As performers of the ranchera, women portray variegated images of the Mexican woman: she is mean and tough, sweet, loving, forgiving or vengeful. By offering multiple ways of being a woman, the women ranchera singers help expand the idea of what constitutes womanhood.

Costume choices for performing ranchera songs provide women another opportunity to break out of a strictly gendered code. The classic female ranchera singer either exaggerates her femininity by wearing some version of the Adelita outfit—a long, lacy, and often low-cut dress—or wears a female version of the charro outfit, where long skirts (and, more recently, a short skirt or short shorts) substitute for pants. In contrast to female participants of the *charreada* (Mexican rodeo), whose use of the Adelita outfit and the charro costume is strictly regulated to ensure a wholesome appearance, the ranchera singer enjoys much more flexibility concerning what kind of image she wishes to display.[18] Indeed, some women singers have opted to break out of the traditional folkloric image altogether by wearing modern apparel such as evening gowns and pantsuits.[19] Through costuming, ranchera singers manipulate a range of images that expand the dualistic category of male-female to recuperate sexuality, agency, and independence as qualities available to women, not just men (see figures 1–3).

The sites of performance also suggest another domain in which female ranchera singers are transgressive of gender conventions. While some performances occur at family-oriented spaces such as charreadas, fairs, restaurants, and theaters, most are held in adult-oriented sites, including nightclubs, bars, cockfights, large concert halls, and dance halls. For women to sing outside of domestic spaces is already a transgression of traditional gender roles, but to sing in adult-oriented sites is especially defiant. Lydia Mendoza openly disclosed to me that her husband disapproved of her performances in night-

1. Nydia Rojas in ranchera dress. Photo courtesy of Gilbert Martinez, personal collection.

2. Lucero Hogaza León de Mijares in a white charro outfit. Photo courtesy of Gilbert Martinez, personal collection.

3. Rosenda Bernal in a hotpants-style charro outfit on the cover of her 1980 album, *Rosenda Bernal con Mariachi Mexico de Pepe Villa*. Courtesy of EMI-Capitol of Mexico.

clubs and bars. A club owner made a similar observation about Mendoza's husband.

> I remember when she used to come to the *salon* and perform. She was excellent. She would give a command performance. Her only setback was her husband, I can't quite remember his name. Anyway, he would drink a lot. This would affect her because many times he would cause scenes there at the dance hall. She would get extremely embarrassed and ashamed of what he would do. In addition to that, he would get very jealous with her and he would take it out on her. There were times that they would argue out in the back and I had to calm him down. It would take a while to explain to him that everything was going to be all right and that Lydia was doing this for him as well. It's very hard to explain things to a drunk! If she would have had a better husband or would have been single, things would have been so much better. (Valdez and Halley 1996, 157)

Noting that *los vicios* (the vices, i.e., drugs, alcohol, and sex) pose serious occupational hazards for anyone in show business, Mendoza emphasized that these dangers—along with scandalous cases of women who succumbed to them—have made it especially difficult for women to pursue a singing career and remain respectable.

Fully aware of the risks, real and exaggerated, that a public singing career poses for women, experienced ranchera singers negotiate performance spaces by skillfully weaving a narrative between each song, explaining the special meaning that a particular song holds for them.[20] Some have opted to strategically exploit the power of scandal and spectacle. The ranchera singer Irma Serrano, known as La tigresa (the tigress), provides a fascinating case in point.[21] Working in several genres, including books, films, theater, and politics, Serrano takes full advantage of the power of performance. Using sarcasm and tongue-in-cheek humor, she powerfully questions many social conventions regarding women, sexuality, pleasure, and authority. Whether on stage, in the courtroom, or in a political campaign, Serrano purposefully wears the most scandalously sexy outfits, thereby calling attention to herself as an object of beauty and desire, and at the same time confirming the powerful hold she has on the public.

> Her rhetorical strategy is to keep this parodic character constantly in motion, to amuse and to ironize, taking nothing seriously: not her sometimes disturbing revelations, not even her own ironic and amused commentaries on severe social problems. From her first exposure to the

> Mexican film industry, Serrano learned the lesson of accommodation: "*[Y]o quería llevar una carrera limpia, digna, honesta, pero era inútil*" [I wanted to have a clean, dignified, honest career but it was useless]. . . . Of the three writers studied here, Serrano is the most consistently and consciously aware of the value of a hardheaded exploitation of apparent frivolity for extremely businesslike ends. (Castillo 1998, 197)

Alert to the power of spectacle, Irma Serrano has cultivated a flamboyant image to fascinate, shock, disgust, or mock. By so doing, she remains in the public eye, assured of captivating an audience for personal gain as well as for political ends. In 1991 she ran unsuccessfully for senator in the state of Chiapas, but in 1994 she was elected to the national congress as a state representative.

Not only are women performers and composers of ranchera songs, they are also consumers of rancheras. While a detailed ethnographic investigation focusing on how women experience and interpret the ranchera is beyond the scope of this essay, I offer a few initial observations based on extensive interviews I conducted with an elderly Mexican woman who had been an avid consumer of ranchera music for most of her life. My informant told me that her earliest recollection of hearing rancheras performed by women dated back to the 1930s in her family home, when, at the request of her father, two teenaged female cousins sang for the family. (This was before radio was available in her hometown in Mexico.) At public community dances, she explained, only men were allowed to perform as singers, while women could not even attend a dance except under the careful supervision of a chaperone (usually their father).

By the 1940s, as radio—and, later, films and record players—became more accessible (especially when her family moved to the city), ranchera music took on greater meaning in my informant's life. Surrounded by ranchera music, she came to associate certain songs with specific events in her life. She recalled, for instance, how, after the breakup of a romance between her brother and his girlfriend, her brother played a particular ranchera, which evoked tears from their mother, who grieved for and with her son. Rancheras have likewise served to chronicle many significant moments in my informant's own personal life. To this day her eyes fill with tears when she listens to certain songs. "El amor de la paloma" (The Love of the Dove), popularized by Irma Serrano in 1964, powerfully evokes memories of the tragic death of her husband in that same year. Although "El amor de la paloma" speaks about how a female dove struggles to survive after her male partner abandons her, what my informant appreciated most about the song was that Serrano sang it with so much passion and sadness. By articulating her own sense of grief, this ranchera song provided a means through which my informant could give expression to, and even wallow in, her own sadness. Faced with the daunting task of raising a large family by herself, my informant had to focus on the practical matters of securing employment and maintaining a strong front for her children; she continuously struggled to keep her emotions in check. But while listening to the ranchera, she could at least momentarily release her pent-up emotions. Similarly, the song "Una lagrima" (A Teardrop) reminded her of when her eldest son joined the armed forces. Again, it was the emotional response to abandonment expressed in the song, rather than the literal narrative, that engaged her. She confided, "¡Cómo lloraba con esa canción!" (How I cried with that song!)

Listening to ranchera music on a transistor radio also helped reduce the monotony my informant experienced while working in the agricultural fields. She laughed, recalling how one of her co-workers, tired of the numerous commercial advertisements, would turn off the radio to "cantar más a gusto" (sing more comfortably). Even though Spanish-language radio stations remain the most important vehicle for disseminating ranchera music internationally, televised musical variety programs such as *Al fin de la semana*, *Sabado gigante*, and music specials on the Spanish-language television networks also reach a broad audience.[22] According to one report, female artists—including ranchera singers Ana Gabriel, Aída Cuevas, and, more recently, Nydia Rojas and Graciela Beltrán—currently contribute significantly to the Mexican music industry (Burr 1996b).

Although my informant did not frequent bars, nightclubs, dancehalls, or even restaurants, she remained an avid consumer of ranchera music via Spanish-language radio stations, Spanish-language television programs, compact discs, and occasionally a concert.[23] Having spent most of her adult life in the United States, she listened to the ranchera to stay connected to her Mexican roots.

Women engage the ranchera as consumers to give expression to and cope with, confront, and even remember their concerns, desires, losses, disappointments, and joys. Further study would expand understanding of the strategies women employ as consumers of the ranchera and, in turn, show how women consumers affect the marketing strategies of ranchera music.

Conclusion

The ranchera is a sophisticated art form that requires equally sophisticated analytical tools to avoid essentialist explications. Its use of emotional excess is evidence of its melodramatic form, rather than, as some have claimed, of an essential and in some cases negative attribute of Mexican culture and identity. Furthermore, as a melodramatic form, the ranchera provides a discursive space for contemplating personal, national, and global crises or anxieties in culturally appropriate ways. An examination of the situated use of the ranchera—the performance context—enables more specificity regarding issues of class, gender, ethnicity, and nationality. As performers, producers and consumers of the ranchera, women have increasingly taken a once predominantly male expressive form to give expression to their own desires, needs, and experiences. Indeed, women have employed the ranchera to expand that which is deemed culturally appropriate for both women and men. Therefore, the ranchera may speak to women's quotidian struggles in contemporary Greater Mexico even as it retains its nationalist, pastoral sensibility. Only in and through situated renderings can one see displayed, and therefore understand, certain cultural preoccupations expressed in the rancheras.

Notes

An earlier version of this paper was presented at the 1998 National Association for Chicana and Chicano Studies (NACCS) conference in Mexico City. I wish to thank Pat Zavella, Aída Hurtado, Norma Klahn, Russell Rodriguez, and Gabriela Arredondo for their thoughtful critiques and suggestions on earlier drafts of this paper. While I alone am responsible for all claims made in this paper, I recognize that my understanding of the ranchera has been significantly enriched by the numerous conversations I have had with close friends and family members over the years, in particular, Mrs. E. Nájera, Alicia, Elena and John Nájera, Becky Silva, Rosita Ruíz, and Josie Méndez Negrete, and my two mariachi friends, Laura Sobrino and Russell Rodriguez.

All translations from the Spanish are by the author.

1 The majority of the studies focus on the historical roots of the ranchera, offering various definitions and trajectories (Grial 1973; Geijerstam 1976; Mayer-Serra 1941; Reuter 1983; Saldívar 1934). Among the most complete studies are those offered in Mendoza 1988; Garrido 1974; Moreno Rivas 1989. Interpretative studies of the ranchera are provided in Fogelquist 1975; Gradante 1982; Gradante 1983; Lamas 1978; Monsiváis 1994a and 1994b [1977]. Manuel Peña also offers important insights on the ranchera in his important work on *conjunto* music (1985).
2 However, see also Broyles-González 2002.
3 I had the opportunity of interviewing Lydia Mendoza in 1984 in Houston, Texas, when I was conducting fieldwork for the Folk Art and Texas Agricultural Heritage Project sponsored by the Texas Department of Agriculture.
4 Indeed, claiming that "country music, if you listen, is filled with the sounds of Mexico," George H. Lewis notes the influences of the ranchera song on country music (1993, 94).

5 For a good discussion of the concept of *lo ranchero* in English, see Peña 1985 (10–12).
6 Mexican musicologist Juan S. Garrido explains that the term *canción ranchera* did not emerge until the twentieth century, when this type of music became associated with Mexican sound film (1974, 70).
7 In her insightful work on the blues and feminism, Angela Y. Davis makes a similar claim, stating, "The realism of the blues does not confine us to literal interpretations. On the contrary, blues contain many layers of meanings and are often astounding in their complexity and profundity" (1998, 24).
8 For a similar argument regarding country music, see Stewart 1993.
9 Lydia Mendoza, interview by author, Houston, Texas, 30 July 1984.
10 For discussions of the Mexican movie industry, see Aurelio de los Reyes 1988; Mora 1982. For a gender analysis of the charro in Mexican films, see Nájera-Ramírez 1994.
11 Many laborers migrate without their children and/or spouses to reduce the expense of relocation and to reduce the risk to the family. Typically, the laborer plans to send remittances to the family until they have accumulated sufficient resources to reunite as a family. Studies indicate, however, that instead of permanent reunification, families are increasingly constructing binational kin relations (see, for example, Zavella 1997b and Rouse 1992).
12 Juan Gabriel's songs commonly avoid the use of gendered pronouns making them subject to a range of uses and interpretations; that is, he doesn't privilege a heterosexual male point of view. Yvonne Yarbro-Bejarano (1997) makes a similar point in her discussion of Chabela Vargas.
13 Note, for example, how the second verse, taken from the song "Cuando viva conmigo," has been radically changed from the original text, which reads as follows.

De mis ojos esta brotanto llanto	From my eyes a cry is erupting
a mis años estoy enamorado	At my (old) age, I am in love
tengo el pelo completamente blanco	My hair is completely white
pero voy a sacar juventud de mi pasado	But I'm going to extract youth from my past
Y te voy a enseñar a querer	And I'm going to teach you to love
porque tu no has querido	Because you have not yet loved
ya verás lo que vas a aprender	You'll see how much you'll learn
cuando vivas conmigo	When you live with me

14 Even when women possess very deep, low voices, as does Lucha Villa, the singers are recognized as female.
15 The topic of gestures and other theatrical devices employed by the ranchera singers in this essay clearly merits further attention and analysis. The importance of the dynamics of performance has been taken up by scholars in numerous fields, including anthropology, folklore, ethnomusicology, and cultural studies. I have been particularly influenced by the "performance-oriented" approach to folkloristics as developed by Américo Paredes and Richard Bauman. Paredes's work on the subversive uses of performance by minorities in ethnographic encounters has been especially important in my own work.

16 See also Nájera-Ramírez 1994, 9.
17 These lyrics make reference to the classic ranchera song "Allá en el rancho grande," which portrays the *rancherita* (little country gal) as one who gladly offers to sew clothing for her cowboy.
18 The charro rulebook dictates the appropriate costume for all charreada participants.
19 According to the mariachi musician Russell Rodriguez, ranchera singers often change costumes several times during a performance.
20 I thank Russell Rodriguez for reminding me of this point.
21 For two provocative discussions of Irma Serrano see Monsiváis 1994a [1977] and Castillo 1998.
22 Onda Max features interviews with and musical videos of Latin singers, including ranchera singers. Ranchera singers are also sometimes featured on talk shows such as *Cristina* or morning shows like *Despierta America*.
23 Anonymous informant, interviews by author, Santa Cruz, California, November and December 1998.

Becoming Selena, Becoming Latina
DEBORAH PAREDEZ

[When I heard the news about Selena's murder] I was like, "Not Selena!" I said, "It can't be!" Selena had gotten so popular. Everybody just loved her to death and the way I felt—I felt like—it had been like—maybe part of—like—as if it happened to me.
—Lucia Orea Chapa, qtd. in *Corpus: A Home Movie for Selena*

✷ Selena Quintanilla Pérez achieved worldwide recognition for her interventions in and reinvention of the historically male-dominated Tejano music genre before her untimely death at the age of twenty-three. Her performances, which highlighted both her mastery of a range of musical styles and her racially and sexually marked Tejana body, drew audiences from Texas and from across its borders throughout the United States, Mexico, South America, and the Caribbean. Evidence of her transnational success was revealed in Texas Senate Resolution No. 619, which was adopted days after Selena's murder and included the following statement: "Whereas, Selena was equally as popular in Mexico as in Texas, having been featured as one of the Giants of Latin Music in one of Latin America's most watched shows, '*Siempre en Domingo*,' and appearing in the internationally watched [Mexican] soap opera, '*Dos Mujeres, Un Camino*,' . . . [it has been resolved] that the Senate of the State of Texas, 74th Legislature, hereby honor the life . . . of this self-made international star."[1]

Thus, while Selena represented and ultimately redefined Texas-Mexico border culture, she simultaneously succeeded in crossing over aesthetic, cultural, and national borders. This feat was engineered in part by the transnational corporate operations of Latin EMI Records, with which Selena had secured a contract when she was eighteen years old. During her tenure with Latin EMI,

Selena promotional photo. Courtesy of Q Productions.

Selena's concert tours and television appearances throughout Latin America and her musical collaborations with Honduran pop singer Alvaro Torres and the Nuyorican boy band Barrio Boyzz further facilitated her Latina/o American appeal. But recording-industry engineering did not solely account for Selena's inter-Latino popularity. Selena's remarkable stage charisma, vocal power, and deft inter-Latino choreographic moves during her live performances contributed substantially to her widespread acclaim.[2] Furthermore, Selena's frequently discussed body—specifically, her ample rear end (a trait often associated with Afro-Caribbean Latinas rather than with Mexicanas and Tejanas)—also emerged as a site of both obsessive racialized sexual fantasies and of identification by many women from across the Latina spectrum.[3]

Selena's popularity among a range of Latina/os and her promotion (both corporate and personal) as a Latina star conspicuously occurred even as she cultivated a proud Tejana persona through her style, linguistic markings, and decision to continue residing in the working-class Tejano neighborhood in which she was raised.[4] Selena's simultaneous maintenance of her Tejana identity and her claims to the space of *Latinidad* "defy the linear conceptions of identity shifts" which have often pervaded discussions of Latino identity formation (Aparicio 2003, 97). The Selena phenomenon raises critically productive questions about the tensions that disrupt and the affiliations that enable Latinidad. Indeed, by most accounts, Selena set in motion the Latin Music boom that exploded in the 1990s—an ironic fact, given the erasure of Mexicans and Tejanos within both dominant representations and within the Latina/o music industry itself, as the controversy over the first annual Latin Grammys made clear.[5] Given that Tejana/os historically have been (dis)regarded as unhip, blue-collar, country cousins within larger Latina/o imaginaries, how and why did Selena, with her proudly proclaimed Tejana markings (see figure), become a transnational Latina icon among often divided Latina/o communities across the Americas during the 1990s?[6] While this question underscores the "fractured and fraught" possibilities for Latinidad (De Genova and Ramos-Zayas 2003b, 45), it also points toward the ways the Selena phenomenon provides a critical map with which many Latina/os navigated and continue to navigate these inter-Latino tensions. Young Latinas, in particular, have created imaginative cartographies of identification though their participation in the Selena phenomenon. This essay investigates moments of young Latina contact with and commemoration of Selena in an effort to explore the makings of Latina identity within the "fractured and fraught" context of Latinidad.

Lost on La Brea: Selena in Hollywood

The morning after I had attended the short-lived touring musical *Selena: A Musical Celebration of Life* in Los Angeles in May 2001, I turned on the rental-car radio and scanned the stations in search of promotional announcements or discussions of the musical.[7] Intent on my research task, I soon found myself lost in West Hollywood. Unable to negotiate roadmap, radio dial, and steering wheel, I pulled out of the flow of traffic and parked the car at the corner of Santa Monica and La Brea. As I scoured the map for this intersection, I let the radio dial pause for a while on KCRW, the local National Public Radio affiliate. A familiar voice soon wafted out from the airwaves. While this mollifying moment of recognition is a common occurrence for avid listeners of public radio, the familiarity of this particular voice did not arise because it belonged to one of the regularly featured reporters or commentators on National Public Radio. Rather, this voice belonged to a young Latina named Claudia Pérez, who was speaking on an episode of the nationally syndicated show *This American Life*. The episode, entitled "From a Distance," which had first aired on 19 April 1996, included a segment that depicted the Chicago auditions for the movie *Selena*.[8] Claudia, eighteen years old at the time, had auditioned for the role and had agreed to report on the event as a guest correspondent for *This American Life*.[9] I recognized Claudia's voice because, in addition to having listened to the episode numerous times, I had interviewed her in Chicago two years before, in February 1999. Captivated by this continued circulation of Selena's spectral body, I abandoned my travel plans—unfolded map flung to the back seat—and tuned in, transfixed by the stories recounted by Claudia and other young Latinas who had sought to become Selena.

This essay emerges from my desire to understand this scene at the intersection where I was momentarily lost, as it were, transfixed by young Latinas' engagements with Selena. How do Latinas participate in the Selena phenomenon, and what are the implications for notions of racialized sexuality and sociopolitical identity formation resulting from their participation? The relationship between Selena commemorations and the production of a specifically Latina subjectivity both undergirds and destabilizes prevailing concepts of Latinidad. This forging of Latina identity as facilitated by engagements with Selena is especially notable in light of hegemonic impositions of Latinidad and of inter-Latina/o disidentifications that have marked the last decade, as Arlene Dávila (2001), Gina Pérez (2003), and others have persuasively argued.[10] To examine how the Selena phenomenon operated as a fraught but nonetheless powerfully effective and affective site for the production and negotiation of Latina identity, I rely on interviews with Latinas drawn from a range of sources that include newspaper accounts, television and radio reports, documentary film, and field research.[11] Guided by Eric Lott's theories about Elvis impersonations and by Joseph Roach's notion of surrogation, I pay particular attention to the ideological work enabled and disabled by the commemorative act of becoming Selena, countering the scholar Ilan Stavans's claim that the "countless imitators [who] mimic [Selena's] style" uncritically lose themselves in their attempts to become her (2000, 177). Young Latinas perform Selena, not as a way to lose themselves, but as a means of self-discovery and as a collective articulation of Latina identity within the contested terrains of Latinidad and larger (trans)national imaginaries. "Becoming" Selena is not simply reducible to "performing like" or "wanting to be" Selena, despite Stavans's and others' conflation of the acts. Rather, the act of becoming Selena reveals "the radical power of identification to override the constraints of identity" (Diamond 1997, 126). That is, identification with Selena provides a discursive and material space wherein many Latinas may momentarily seek to "override the constraints" that often circumscribe prevailing constructions of Latina identity. Latinas perform Selena with a critical difference.

Navigating the Theoretical Neighborhood

Two years before the incident on the corner of Santa Monica and La Brea, I displayed yet another instance of my navigational shortcomings when driving Claudia Pérez home after our lunch in Pilsen, Chicago's predominantly

Mexican immigrant and Mexican American neighborhood. Absorbed in my questions about her audition experience, I made a series of wrong turns. She guided me back to the right street, commenting, "I tell people: there's three things that make me mad. One is when you stereotype Mexican people. Can't stand that. And two, when they say Selena had a fake butt. That makes me *real* mad. Or, three, when they pass laws, all these crazy laws against Latino people."[12]

Claudia's statement emphasized the relationships among three phenomena that marked the 1990s: the struggles over representations of Latina/o identity, the conspicuous celebration—or, more precisely, surveillance—of the performing Latina body (part), and the enactment of the most restrictive immigration legislation in U.S. history.[13] By embedding her sentence concerning Selena's butt within comments about the circulation of stereotypes about "Mexican people" and legislation against "Latino people," Claudia pointed toward ways that constructions of Latina racialized sexuality figured centrally in the creation and maintenance of national nativist projects that shape U.S. political and cultural landscapes.

Claudia's tactical statement also reveals the dynamic and situational identity negotiations often deployed by Latinas/os within this hostile climate. Like Selena's identity shifts, Claudia's claim to both the space of Mexicanidad and Latinidad reveals the "dual sense of identity" shared by many Latina/os (De Genova and Ramos-Zayas 2003a, 7). Claudia—a first-generation Mexican American—begins by alluding to a national and ethnic self-identification, then highlights how the battles over racial or ethnic authenticity are often enacted on the terrain of the sexualized female body, and finally hints at how and when a counterhegemonic Latina/o subjectivity can emerge. Within the United States, and often in response to the legislative acts Claudia indicts, a Mexican American may momentarily prioritize a political (that is, a Latina/o) affiliation over a national (Mexican) identification. These shifts reveal the "politically efficacious" potential of Latinidad, wherein "people from quite distinct cultural backgrounds and ideological positions [can] meet and organize under the label Latina/o in order to register an oppositional stance to majoritarian institutions" (Román 1997, 151–52). Through her syntactic shifts, Claudia articulates an oppositional Latinidad by condemning the regulation of Latina bodies and the policing of American borders "against Latino people" that reproduce and circulate bureaucratic and corporate constructions of Latina/os. Latinidad emerges not as the strategically homogenizing construct of corporate industries or census measures, but as a momentary alliance based on a shared sense of injury or "of convergences and divergences in the formation of Latino/a (post)colonial subjectivities" (Aparicio 2003, 93). More precisely, Claudia's affirmation of a politically oppositional identity affirmation conspicuously follows from her reclamation of Selena's butt, revealing her awareness and disdain of the fetishization of Selena's butt and her nuanced understanding of how the racialized and sexualized female body is often deployed as a synecdoche for a subjugated community.

Claudia's indignant protection of Selena's butt articulates with the film scholar Frances Negrón-Muntaner's claim that for some Latinas, the rear end "proved to be the most compelling way . . . to speak about how 'Latinas' are constituted as racialized bodies" (1997, 195). This focus arises in response to the history of racialized discourses inscribed on the Latina butt. As Negrón-Muntaner writes, "A big *culo* [ass] does not only upset hegemonic (white) notions of beauty and good taste, it is a sign for the dark, incomprehensible excess of 'Latino' and other African diaspora cultures. Excess of food (unrestrained), excess of shitting (dirty), and excess of sex (heathen) are its three vital signs" (189).[14]

Indeed, the Spanish and U.S. colonialist projects throughout the Americas have historically relied on the violation of Latinas and the construction of Latina (excessive) sexuality to enable their maintenance.[15] These practices have figured prominently in recent nativist discourse concerning the "threat" of Latina/o immigration and in post-NAFTA constructions of Mexican women wherein "an old colonialist (and now neo-colonialist) narrative [constructs] *Mexicanas* on the border in terms of sexual excess and chaos" (Fregoso 2000, 146). Fregoso argues that this construction strategically relocates the burden of responsibility for violence against female laborers on the border onto the Mexicana body rather than on the operations of transnational capitalism and state-sanctioned patriarchy. Racialized female bodies are thus revealed as the location at which history, memory, colonial struggles, nationalist projects, and racial desire repeatedly converge.

Claudia foregrounds the connections between the discursive constructions of the Latina body and the obstacles to citizenship and social justice for Latina/os bodies in the United States. Thus, her critique of the political economy of Latina/os necessarily includes the reclamation of the Latina body, represented here by Selena's butt. Yet Claudia's reclamation operates as well as a critique of both hegemonic forces, invested in reinscribing whiteness as normative, and the patriarchal confines within Latina/o communities wherein Latina sexuality has traditionally been severely policed.[16] Claudia's comments reinforce the argument that Selena circulated as part of larger struggles over claims to civic, national, and political identity, but her reclamation of Selena also foregrounds Latina agency in and against these appropriations. Claudia thus reveals how the Selena phenomenon provides a provocative and complex site for examining the negotiation of Latina agency within the numerous matrices of power in which it is embedded.

Crossing Over Selena's Body

As her legions of fans can attest, Selena engaged in—and her career was often narratively channeled within—a number of crossovers during her life.[17] Frances Negrón-Muntaner observes how Selena's record company transformed her from a regionally identified Tejana into a nationally marketable Latina, thereby revealing the ways in which Latinidad operated as a "technology to demand and deliver emotions, votes, markets, and resources" (1997, 184). And yet, throughout this "transformation," Selena consistently affirmed her Tejana identity, thereby revealing both the identifications and disidentifications that charge Latinidad. Selena "crosses over" the spectrum of Latina identity via processes whereby her explicit, localized Tejana-ness was simultaneously celebrated even as it was transformed into (and thereby at times effaced by) an emblem of transnational Latina identity. This production of Latina subjectivity emerges in what Latinas have to say about Selena. Latinas' memories of Selena not only take part in transforming Selena into a Latina icon but constitute a powerful vehicle for enabling their own process of becoming Latina. An examination of how Latinas remember Selena thus illuminates the ways in which the Latina body was produced and Latina subjectivity was remade at the close of the twentieth century.

For many Latinas, Selena's success, coupled with the particular racialized markings her body carried, provided an unprecedentedly visible site for the affirmation of bodily traits traditionally undervalued within hegemonic standards for feminine beauty. Furthermore, Selena provided a significant intervention in dominant portrayals of Latina sexuality. Prior to Selena, the tropes of Latina sexuality were characterized by Dolores Del Rio's "upper-class exoticism" juxtaposed against Lupe Vélez's sexually predatory "Mexican Spitfire" during the 1930s and 1940s, by Carmen Miranda's excessively adorned body promoting the samba (and the Good Neighbor Policy) in the 1940s, and by Rita Moreno's mastery of the mambo undercut by her assimilationist proclamation, "I Want to Live in Amer-ee-ca!" during the 1950s and 1960s.[18] One other notable trope was evidenced in the careers of Rita Hayworth and Raquel Welch, both of whom opted for the total erasure of their Latina identity as a means to secure acceptance as sexual icons, thereby revealing the ways that, as Negrón-Muntaner notes, "dominant culture obsessively prohibits [the] display [of an affirming Latina sexuality] and punishes transgressors" (Negrón-Muntaner 1997, 187). Throughout their discussions about Selena,

Latinas understood this double-bind by acknowledging and applauding the transgressive potentials of Selena's performances of racialized sexuality. Remembering Selena provided a way to speak out against and to expose the racism embedded in hegemonic standards circumscribing female bodies, as Jennifer Lopez, the Nuyorican actress who portrayed Selena in the biographical motion picture, suggests.

> Rita Hayworth and Raquel Welch could only become stars after they disguised themselves. Selena could be who she was and, as for me, for once, I could be proud of my big bottom.... In my movies, I've always had costume people looking at me a little weary and immediately fitting me out with things to hide my bottom. I know it. They didn't say it but I know it.... All other movies I've done [besides *Selena*], it always seemed like they're trying to hide [my butt] or they think I look fat. Or I'm not the American tradition of beauty. (Mal Vincent 1997, E8)

Lopez astutely positions Selena as an affirming corrective to both the kinds and the disguise of representations of Latinas in the entertainment industry's history. Specifically, like Claudia, Lopez uses her identification with Selena's "big bottom" to launch an attack on systemic racist practices. Claiming (an affinity) with Selena's rear end permits the affirmation of a Latina identity that is explicitly inclusive of nonwhite(ning) features, which is significant given the dramatic "whitening" of Lopez's body in recent years. Filmmaker Renée Tajima-Peña concurs with Lopez: "Selena, I really liked also because she looked *normal*. She was gorgeous, but she had a normal look. She was just beautiful, you know. When I was growing up, I wish I'd had someone like Selena to look up to, someone that looked like me [she pointed emphatically at her own face], that looked normal."[19] Tajima-Peña's memory of Selena tactically reinscribes the category of normal-ness as the traditionally undervalued dark-haired, olive-skinned face that both she and Selena share. Selena emerges as a way to expose the very constructedness of whiteness as normative—to mark whiteness—thereby intervening in its regulatory regimes.

Many other Latinas shared Tajima-Peña's identification with Selena's complexion, further underscoring how Selena provided an affirmative (re)vision of their own historically devalued bodies. In a scene at a Corpus Christi Tejano radio station depicted in Lourdes Portillo's documentary, *Corpus: A Home Movie for Selena*, a Latina calls into the radio show, asserting, "I wanted to say a little bit about Selena. She was a very beautiful person and, you know, that made me feel great because I'm brown, too, and you know [what] people tend to think [about] these features. I thought she was beautiful and not only that— her skin was so, was so soft and *brown*." This sentiment was especially prevalent among young Latinas, as evidenced by comments from the young women who auditioned for both the film and stage roles of Selena. In a report on the *Selena Forever* auditions held in Manhattan, the *New York Times* described "Paola Cubides, 20-year-old New Yorker of Colombian descent ... [who] said Selena was her role model—an American-born, English-speaking Latina with indigenous features like her own who did not stray from her cultural roots to be successful" (Navarro 1999, B1). Cubides echoes comments made by young women like Yesenia Santos, a Dominican teenager who had auditioned for the film three years earlier: "Mis amigos siempre me decían que me parecía a ella. Pienso que por eso yo la amaba tanto" (My friends always used to tell me that I looked like Selena. I think that's why I loved her so much) (Lydia Martin 1996a, A1). The self-affirmations expressed by both Cubides and Santos are particularly significant, as Latina youths have during the past decade reported the lowest self-esteem rates among teenage women in the nation (Cabrera 2000, 4; Fernández 1999, B3). Identifying with Selena acts as a critically urgent tool for combating this phenomenon.

Identification with Selena's complexion not only provides a way to speak out against mainstream representations of feminine ideals but also enables Latinas to expose how these hegemonic notions are internalized by Latina/o communities and are ultimately borne by Latina bodies in particular. Claudia Pérez observed,

> I liked [Selena] because she was *morenita* [dark-skinned], too. . . . Growing up, people used to be, "Aye m'ijo tiene ojos verdes" [Oh, my baby has green eyes!] and they always wanted to have a light-skinned baby, or something, you know? And it made me so happy to know that she was, like, my complexion, and she was beautiful, you know. 'Cause when I was growing up, [my family] they used to tell me, "Stay out [of] the sun, you're gonna get dark[er]. Like saying, like, dark was bad or something, you know? So that made me more like, "Yeah, you know, I love Selena; she has *my* complexion."

For Claudia, identifying with Selena's body provides a way to speak back against the internalized racist discourses that circumscribed her upbringing, highlighting how the dark Latina body is repeatedly racialized and subsequently policed by multiple forces. Claudia's identification with Selena includes not simply a shared complexion but a shared sense of injury resulting from their racialized and gendered status within a range of power structures.

This identification with Selena as an icon of shared struggle is most evocatively expressed in Portillo's documentary by Lucia Orea Chapa, a Tejana who responded to Selena's tragedy "as if it happened to me." Chapa's reaction does not reflect a fanatical obsession; on the contrary, it reveals how Selena provides a site not only for affirming a historically maligned beauty but also for reflecting on the shared oppression Latina bodies have suffered. Chapa's connection with Selena's tragedy underscores how "it"—not so much Selena's murder, as a literal reading of the quote would suggest, but rather the devaluation of the Latina body, the struggle for affirming a Latina sexuality—"had happened" to her and to many other Latinas.

Whereas Claudia and others emphasize Selena's complexion as a site of identification, Negrón-Muntaner discusses how Selena's rear end enables a specifically Latina identity production: "For any Caribbean interlocutor, references to this part of the human anatomy are often a way of talking about Africa in(side) America. . . . And despite the fact that Selena was Chicana, an ethnicity not associated in the Caribbean popular imagination with big butts, she was definitely curvy. . . . Selena's butt was, from a Puerto Rican perspective, one of the elements that made her not specifically Chicana, but 'Latina,' and hence more easily embraced as one of our own" (1997, 185).

Negrón-Muntaner points out that, long before the fascination with "Jennifer's Butt," Selena's butt was well-known throughout the Latina diaspora. Moreover, her comments underscore how Selena's butt was used as site of identification wherein Puerto Ricans and other *afro-caribeñas* transformed themselves and not simply Selena into Latinas. Taken together, this range of Latina responses highlights how Selena's body became a site of recognition across the Latina spectrum because it signified toward both the often undervalued or ignored indigenous (*indígeno*) and the African presence within this spectrum. Selena's body sustains and indeed renders visible both the problematics—what José Esteban Muñoz calls the "incoherence" (2000, 67)—and the potentials of Latinidad.[20] That is, while Selena's body suggests the racial and sexual struggles that often foreclose Latinidad's potential for solidarity, it also provides a site wherein Mexican Americans, Dominicans, Colombians, Tejanas, and Puerto Ricans can come together momentarily to produce and reclaim the Latina body. This move emerges clearly in Jennifer Lopez's responses to some Chicana/o protests to the decision to cast her as Selena in Gregory Nava's film: "I'm all for Latinos playing Latinos, but saying a Puerto Rican couldn't play Selena, a Texas girl, is taking it a bit far. Selena looked like me. She was dark and she was, well, *curvy*" (Vincent 2000, E8). Certainly, the controversy over the casting of a Nuyorican in the role of a Tejana signaled another instance in which the Selena phenomenon reveals inter-Latino tensions between Puerto Ricans and Mexican Americans, tensions due in large part to the systematic erasure of Tejanos and Mexican Americans from representations in popular culture. But Lopez's quote also reveals how

Selena provides a space to fashion a Latina identity—based on shared racialized markings—that is deployed to overcome the "incoherence" of Latinidad not through facile essentialist claims, but rather through a pointed critique of prevailing notions of authenticity that invariably get played out on Latina bodies.

The Selena Phenomenon

One of the most prominent crossover narratives into which Selena and her ensuing phenomenon were often interpolated is evidenced by the frequent comparisons between her and that other American icon, Elvis Presley. Ilan Stavans referred to Selena as a "darker-complected Elvis" (2000, 181), and both Gregory Nava and Joe Nick Patoski, Selena's biographer, compared the tremendous outpouring of grief over Selena's death to the mourning that attended Elvis's death (Rohter 1997). Similar comparisons pervaded media coverage of the Selena phenomenon. For example, the *Minneapolis Star Tribune* reported that 30,000 mourners had filed by Selena's casket, noting that the same number had paid their respects to Elvis at his funeral (Burr 1996).[21]

Like Elvis, Selena became the subject of impersonation. Following Selena's death, young Latinas across the country often performed and/or dressed like Selena as a means of commemoration. In 1996 the *Corpus Christi Caller-Times* reported on young Selena impersonators in two separate articles (Berstein n.d.), while scholar Emma Pérez noted that "little girls who were dressed as Selena" crowded into a screening of the biographical motion picture about the star (1999, 19). I also witnessed this trend at the theatrical productions about Selena in San Antonio, Los Angeles, and Chicago. The episode of *This American Life* that depicts the auditions for the movie *Selena* features an interview with a young audition participant named Jessica, who, shortly after Selena's death, traveled to Corpus Christi and mourned Selena by performing "Como La Flor" at her gravesite, a scene that would be cannily restaged by the young actress Agina Alvarez at the close of *Selena: A Musical Celebration of Life* six years later.

In his insightful analysis of Elvis impersonations Eric Lott argues that "the art of impersonation is built on contradiction. . . . [E]ven as [Elvis impersonators] recognize the uniqueness and special power of Elvis Presley, these performers yearn in often unconscious ways to unseat the master" (1997, 198–99). His observations resonate with Joseph Roach's notion of surrogation (1996, 76), the process by which a community attempts to reproduce itself often through specially appointed mediums or surrogates. Roach notes how performers, in particular, provide such media—even in death.[22] Informed by the notion of performance as restored behavior, Roach asserts, "Much more happens by transmission through surrogacy than the reproduction of tradition. New traditions may be invented and others overturned. The paradox of the restoration of behavior resides in the phenomenon of repetition itself: no action or sequence of actions may be performed the same way twice" (28–29). Thus, precisely because performance is always "repetition with revision," the impersonator is frequently able to "unseat the master" by enacting something both more than and less than the original. The act of impersonation can thus be understood as not simply an uncritical practice of the unenlightened masses but as a self-conscious tool for the transmission of history and the refashioning of identity.

The act of becoming Selena is an example of surrogation that, as both Lott and Roach imply, registers a range of ambivalence and contradictions: that is, Latinas become Selena as a means to both revere and replace her. Thus, while Latinas embody Selena in an effort to emulate her as a model of affirming Latina sexuality, they ultimately unseat her precisely because through their enactments, they achieve the critically different Latina subjectivity originally represented by Selena. While this perpetual play of ambivalence certainly resonates with Elvis impersonations, the phenomenon of becoming Selena differs in one significant way: whereas Elvis impersonations, as Lott acknowledges, continue the tradition of effacing the black sources of Elvis's performances, Selena impersonations provide a space for revealing and affirming the "dark" roots of Latina identity. The act of becoming Selena is both determined by and productively disrupts the historical construction and performative displays of the racialized and sexualized Latina body, as the Chicana playwright and cultural critic Cherríe Moraga observes in Portillo's documentary:

> What's interesting is . . . it's like Selena gave these [teenaged girls] a way to have Chicana sexuality. . . . You know, they're in their bodies, *totally*. They're doing their little [she gestures with her hands, evoking a signature Selena move]. I mean, good dancers, really good dancers. And you know, like, there wasn't any of this typical—particularly at that age with that preteen stuff, you know—no *vergüenza* [shame]. They're like, *in* it, and doing it. . . . They're *being* a sexuality. And these songs, you know, I mean even the ones they sang that weren't Selena songs, were all these, like, tortured love songs kinda thing, and all about desire and everything.

Moraga's statement highlights how Selena impersonations provide a space wherein the policing of female sexuality that occurs within Latino families may be momentarily lessened or at least contested. This liminal space is especially critical for the young teenagers Moraga describes, who, given their economic dependency on their families, are most subjected to sexual policing by parental and school institutions. Furthermore, Moraga's comments pointedly foreground Selena as a Chicana who enables the affirmation of a specifically Chicana identity. As such, Moraga momentarily restores Selena's Mexicana identity as a countermove against its potential erasure in assertions of her as a Latina icon. The complex negotiations adopted by Latinas vis-à-vis patriarchal forces and vis-à-vis one another are made clear. As both Moraga and Negrón-Muntaner observe, becoming Selena provides a space for the articulation of a diverse array of Latina sexualities. Thus, the act of becoming Selena displays the resourceful ways in which Latinas negotiate their gendered and racialized subjection in and through the body.

The remainder of this essay focuses on the phenomenon of becoming Selena, using the widely publicized auditions for the motion picture *Selena* as a case study. Thousands of young Latinas impersonating Selena flocked to the auditions, as noted by a reporter for the *Houston Chronicle* who described the scene surrounding the auditions as "sort of like an Elvis look-alike convention, but prettier" (Stoeltje 1996, 1). Just as "a central fact of twentieth-century American social history is encoded in the odd practice of Elvis impersonation" (Lott 1997, 213), a central fact of resistance against the racialized and sexualized circumscriptions on the Latina performing body is encoded in the act of becoming Selena.

Becoming Selena

During our drive through Pilsen, Claudia Pérez continued to navigate me through the neighborhood, describing the Chicago auditions for the motion picture *Selena*: "[At the *Selena* auditions] there was everything. All [kinds of] Latinos. And there were even white girls there and there was a black guy I remember ... and he had a Selena shirt on. He started telling me about the songs and stuff. He was just watching. He had just come to watch beautiful Latina women, he was telling me. And there were other guys there [watching], too. And Jorge was there from Channel 66. And it was true. All there. They were all beautiful Latina women. All of 'em. You know. From all over."[23]

Claudia's description exposes the multiple communities present at the Selena auditions and hints at how the forms of their participation were contingent on gendered and racial identities. Claudia's comment that "there was everything" at the auditions underscores the richness of the *Selena* auditions as a case study of the ways in which competing vectors of power, invested in the (re)production of Latinidad, intersect and "cross over" publicly performing Latina bodies. Indeed, this idea is also reflected in an account of the Los Angeles auditions where, as *La Opinión* reporter Elena de la Cruz observed,

> Afuera el barullo era considerable.... La estación KMQA ... transmitío en vivo, emitiendo música de Selena por los altavoces, poniendo a bailar a muchas aspirantes y sus acompañentes, y convirtiendo el lugar en una fiesta. Había madres, padres, hermanos, abuelas, tíos y sobrinos de las candidatas que no se quisieron perder la oportunidad.
>
> (Outside the auditions, there was a considerable hubbub.... The Spanish-language radio station KMQA ... transmitted a live broadcast, playing Selena's music from loudspeakers, promoting dancing among the auditioners and their chaperones, and converting the place into a party. In attendance were mothers, fathers, siblings, grandmothers, uncles, and cousins of the aspirants who did not want to lose this opportunity.) (1996a, D1)

Coupled with Claudia's observations, this account suggests that the auditions provide a space sanctioned by the mainstream in which Latina/os could congregate to mourn and celebrate Selena and enact a fundamentally antihegemonic act directly under the dominant gaze. Thus, the *Selena* auditions did more than simply call on Latina bodies to stage Latinidad: they provided space for Latinas to navigate the terrain of what the performance scholar Peggy Phelan refers to as the "trap of visibility," wherein men "come to watch beautiful Latina women" (1993, 6).

In March 1996 Gregory Nava, the Latino director of *Selena*, along with Selena's father, Abraham Quintanilla, the film's executive producer, and executives from Warner Brothers Studios held a press conference announcing open-audition casting calls for the role of Selena. They invited girls between the ages of six and ten and young women between the ages of eighteen and twenty-three who were English-proficient to audition. Singing skills were not required, but dancing ability was taken into consideration. The auditions were to be held in San Antonio, Los Angeles, Miami, and Chicago—all cities with sizable Latina/o communities. Organizers set up a hotline to field questions. The overwhelming response created the largest open casting call in Hollywood history since the Scarlett O'Hara auditions for *Gone with the Wind*. Over 85,000 calls flooded the hotline, and nearly 24,000 young women and girls from across the Latina/o spectrum auditioned: 8,000 in San Antonio, 10,000 in Los Angeles, 3,000 in Miami, 3,000 in Chicago (*Phoenix Gazette*, 18 March 1996, A2; *Houston Chronicle*, 8 March 1996, 8; de la Cruz 1996b; Lydia Martin 1996b, A1).

Gregory Nava told the *Chicago Sun-Times*, "There's never been a casting call like this. About 600 boys showed up to be Dennis the Menace. We've had 24,000 Selenas. It shows how deeply she's touched a chord in this nation.... This is the story of the American dream.... She's a real hero to all of us" (Hoekstra 1996, 31). In the *New York Daily News* Nava proclaimed, "As it turned out, [the auditions] were a beautiful thing to have happened for our community. People felt they were a part of the process because Selena was so important to them" (Dominguez 1996, 49). In his first statement Nava juxtaposes 24,000 Selenas against 600 Caucasian, archetypal, all-American Dennis the Menaces, thereby asserting how "we" Latina/os are indeed a force to be reckoned with in America. When he equates Selena's story with the American Dream, wherein she is "a real hero to all of us," Nava invokes Selena as the vehicle through which "we" Latina/os become "us" Americans. For Nava, the auditions invited Latina/os to become "a part of the process." But, one might ask, part of what process? Was there only a single process in which participants engaged as part of these auditions? Claudia's thick description of her experience at the auditions offers some insights.

> They gave you a number, or something. They called you up and you went up there. And then you danced—you—they made you—well, [they said] "Just dance for me" and you see the girls dancing. And I was sitting down and I was watching the girls, you know, and the guys were not even looking at them.... [The casting people] didn't even know who Selena was. Some girl told me, "I didn't know who she was until she died." So that's what got me. It's like you don't get people like that. She was a *guera* [a white girl]. And then when I went up there, I went 'cause my sister was like, "Go! Go! Go! Go! Go!" And I was like, you know, I got to ... see what's going on here.... And um, I went up there and then for sure, he [the casting guy] didn't look at me. And I danced a little bit. Of course, I tried to imitate Selena, but you can't *be* Selena. There's only *one* Selena. And um, you know, I tried and he didn't look.... It was just, "Okay, bye, we'll call you." Shheeze call me, yeah right. How's he gonna remember me, you know? ... Well, I didn't really care. I knew it was a scam. To me it seemed like a scam.... Why I did it? Because, yeah, I wanted to see what it was about, you know. If they were really scammin'. And I wanted [to] watch how they watch me.

Considered alongside Nava's comments, Claudia's observations reveal ways in which the Selena auditions operated as an especially fraught and generative space wherein competing technologies (to evoke Negrón-Muntaner's term) of Latinidad were deployed and negotiated.[24] Claudia registers mistrust in the efficacy of these attempts at representation ("but you can't *be* Selena") and in the terms on which Latinas are let in on the process ("To me it seemed like a scam"). In fact, Claudia's hunch about and subsequent investigation of this scam suggest her politically astute belief that the auditions actually reflected the cooptation of Latina practices as a means for increasing publicity and revenues for the film. From her descriptions, the political economy of Latinas within this staging of Latinidad is made clear: Latino men and corporate executives (Nava, Quintanilla, Warner Brothers) do the inviting; uninformed *güeros* and *güeras* (the Anglo "girl" who did not know of Selena until after she died, "guys [who] were not even looking") do the judging; and Latinas perform the labor ("Just dance for me").

Now one could argue that this depersonalized setting is not unlike any large casting-call audition, but performed by these particular players within these roles and set within the surrounding discourses on Selena, the setup reinscribes invidious inter- and intracultural power dynamics among these groups along lines of race and gender. Publicly performing Latina bodies—or, more specifically, racially marked Latina bodies—perform the labor in both corporate attempts to increase their profits and to legitimize their foray into the Latina/o market and in Latino attempts to vie for a piece of the American pie. Yet Claudia's claims also emphasize that the auditions provide a space for at least one Latina to return the gaze. It is also a place to "watch how they watch me," a place where sisters encourage one another to perform ("Go! Go! Go! Go! Go!"), where fellow audition participants watch after one another, a space of incomplete surveillance where a young Latina can assert a subject position, where the watchers willfully choose not so see.

One Thousand Women Becoming Selena

In her report, "1000 Women Become Selena" (1996), compiled for the "From a Distance" episode of *This American Life*, Claudia focuses less on the auditions and more on the performances surrounding it—a framing that suggests with unequivocal irony that the phenomenon of and implications resulting from becoming Selena were best discerned from beyond the confines of the actual staged audition. Precisely because, as Claudia stated, "you can't *be* Selena," the object of study is directed toward how, through embodying Selena, young Latinas incorporate her into their own subjectivities. The segment consists largely of Claudia's interviews with young women and girls who convened at Roberto Clemente High School in the moments before and after their audition. Claudia also interviewed Gregory Nava, who assured her that chances were high that the young Selena would be chosen from the open auditions and that there was a "fifty-fifty chance" that the older Selena would be chosen from the auditions as well.

> *Claudia*: After a long day, the cars had cleared. Two cousins who flew in from Texas were sitting outside in the cold, eating pizza and waiting for a Chicago family friend to pick them up. They had arrived early in the morning and they didn't get much sleep. They weren't sure when their ride was coming, or where they were going to spend the night. I asked them what they thought of the auditions.
>
> *Young Woman #1*: I dunno, I don't think it went as great as I thought it would be.... Because you know, it's like, I don't think the producers were there when I got up to, you know, do my stuff. So, I dunno, they [are] look[ing] for something different.... They're not looking for a true Selena. They're just looking for appearances. And it's really bad, I mean, they might know who Selena was, but not truly what she meant to us, so....
>
> *Claudia*: They had spent $135 each, saved from babysitting to get to Chicago. But they didn't feel bad.
>
> *Young Woman #1*: No, it's fine, because we get [*sic*] to meet a lot of people and stuff. We just came and we knew we were not gonna get picked, you know, but we still came and took a chance because that's the thing that Selena would always say, you know: "You have a thing, you go for it. Don't let nobody put you down.... Give whatever you have." And that's what we did. So that's the reason why we came here.
>
> *Claudia*: They just sat there on the bench, waiting. They weren't really dressed for Chicago weather. They wore fishnet pantyhose, real short shorts, bustiers, and thin leather jackets. You could tell they were really cold. They were anxious for their ride to show up. A couple of weeks later, it was announced that none of the girls from the open auditions were chosen for the Selena part. Not them, not me, nobody....[25]

Clearly, Claudia is not the only one who suspects that the auditions were some sort of setup. This segment troubles Nava's construction of the auditions with its focus on the material negotiations (saving babysitting money) and the symbolic negotiations (evoking Selena in a way not represented by the audition organizers) that these Latinas engaged in to make possible their participation and continue to engage in as a result of their participation in the auditions. In particular, the experiences of these young women deflate Nava's promises by revealing that working hard and saving money do not guarantee access to the American Dream. In this segment, the young women reveal their motivations despite their foreknowledge of the setup; they claim they did it because Selena would have wanted it, not because they were invited by Latino men or a major studio. Participation in the auditions provides not simply a way to become American or even part of a cohesive Latina/o community but to assert a Latina subjectivity unrecognized by the inviter or the judges. In this performative context the assertion that "they're not looking for a true Selena" does not signal a facile assertion of authenticity but provides a way of exposing and countering the processes by which Latinas are encouraged to participate in the cooptation of Selena.

This is not to deny the allure of the potential financial rewards and recognition offered by the casting call, especially given the economic situation of many Latinas. But, notably, these incentives are never mentioned by the auditioners during the report or by Claudia during our conversations.[26] In fact, the discussions of mobility that surface among the participants do not suggest an uncritical yearning for the American Dream, as repeatedly evoked by Nava, but signal what Eric Lott calls a "trope of triumph" for young Latinas (1997, 218). Lott describes this trend among Elvis impersonators whose "fantasies about Elvisian excess" and rhetoric of mobility do not signal a longing to enter a higher class but rather a moment of "self-validation" (ibid.). Likewise, for many Latinas, to move like Selena in performance is also to acknowledge the ways in which many of them have been forced to move, like Selena, as a result of economic disparity.[27] Clearly, the auditions provided a culturally sanctioned physical mobility, as revealed by the young women who traveled from Texas and by Claudia whose intra-Chicago migrations required her to move beyond the borders of Pilsen into Humboldt Park, the predominately Puerto Rican neighborhood where the auditions took place.[28] Given the historical struggles in Chicago between the Mexicano/a and Puerto Rican communities, this migration signals how the Selena auditions both exposed the tensions undergirding Latinidad (i.e., intra-Latina/o conflicts) and simultaneously encouraged its creation. Most compelling in Claudia's report is its indictment of the audition's failure to crown a successor. While, as Nava would have it, the auditions sought to stage Latinidad as a cultural and economic force, this attempt ultimately staged the discursive formation of the failed crossovers prevalent in hegemonic portrayals of Latinas.

From a Distance

While Claudia's report certainly foregrounds the savvy among young Latinas who in the face of the audition "scam" attempt to forge a moment of community, one cannot ignore the frame in which the report is positioned. Ira Glass, the host of *This American Life*, begins this episode as he always does: "Back for another week documenting life in these United States." The week's title and theme, Ira says, is "From a Distance: Admiring Someone from Afar, Trying to Get Closer to Them." He then chronicles the four acts that the episode will comprise: a young female artist who becomes obsessed with a dead Dutch male artist; Miles Davis's biographer, Quincy Troupe, whose obsession with Davis eventually led to a friendship between the two men; an anonymous man who became obsessed with and began stalking the Snuggles bear featured on fabric-softener ads; and a thousand women who attempted to become Selena. Within this context, Selena fans are pathologized as obsessive fanatics despite the critically incisive, lucid, and rational responses they conveyed throughout the report. This framing device attempts to efface the complex ways in which Latinas participate in and theorize about the process of becoming Selena.

From a distance, then, it appears that within the circumscribed terms of racialized pathology, Latinas are granted space within the borders of this American life. From a distance, *This American Life* suggests that Selena and those who would be her have apparently, *por fín*, crossed over. But on closer scrutiny, the episode's frame appears, like the auditions, to offer false promises. Introducing the segment on the Selena auditions, Ira Glass distinguishes it from the others in the episode: "It's one thing to try to get close to someone. It's another thing to try to become them." Set within this frame, the girls' and young women's actions appear as inevitable failures—recall that none were selected to actually become Selena—as always and already futile attempts at crossing over into this American life. The frame and tone of the radio show implies that "it's one thing to try to get close" to a Latina who crossed over into American success—posthumously, no less—but that it's a pathological thing to try to become her. One thousand Selenas are transformed into one thousand simulacra who in the end still wait for their place on the American stage, who remain sitting on the bench, waiting for a ride home, a home that is far from here. Thus, in a performative move, the show enacts what the auditions promote: the circulation of the Latina failed crossover as the means by which to include Latina/os within the national imaginary.

Yet the story does not end here—and neither does this episode of *This American Life*. Following the "1000 Women Become Selena" segment, Ira speaks briefly with Claudia, who has chosen the episode's closing song, Selena's rendition of the mariachi song "Tú Solo Tú," which swells behind their voices.

> *Ira*: So, Claudia, so explain why this is the song you wanted us to play on our program after your story about Selena.

Claudia: I like it because she sings it with *mariachis*. And it's an old song, you know, from Mexico.

Ira: When I think of Selena, I don't think of her as a *mariachi* singer—

Claudia: Right, you don't. That's why—she didn't sing with *mariachis*. She was more of a beat-y person, you know, with a lot of beat. And that's why this song, this one and this other song that she sang—everybody sang it when she was . . . when she left.

Ira: Everybody sang when she left? You mean everybody sang [it] when she died?

Claudia: Yeah, yeah.

Ira: Listen to you. You sound like that girl in your story who's like, "She's not dead, she's just sleeping." The way you just said that.

Claudia: *(laughter)*

Ira: "When she left." She didn't just leave, honey—

Claudia: Well, I don't like saying death.[29]

The music swells again. Thus in the closing frame of the episode Claudia enacts a tactical refusal. By saying "I don't like saying death," she refuses the narrative that casts Selena, and the Latina, as a racialized Eurydice whose story begins and ends after her death, with a crossing over into another world, where she is promised freedom by a culture which cannot believe she is real until (indeed can assure its own realness only after) it has turned its gaze on her. Claudia intervenes in dominant crossover narratives about Selena and Latinas in general, saying no to death and instead, with her song selection, positioning Selena in an oppositional history.

One may argue that Claudia's choice of Selena's rendition of a mariachi song—a traditional Mexican genre—instead of a hybridized Tejano song "with a lot of beat" is merely an attempt at staging authenticity, an attempt at simplistically and sentimentally appropriating Selena to perform Mexicanness as opposed to Americanness. But within the performative context of the episode (and precisely because performance is never repetition without revision), Claudia's evocation of a Mexican *canción ranchera* locates Selena in a particular performance tradition that values voice over voluptuousness. The ranchera, as Olga Nájera-Ramirez argues in this volume, is a musical form that foregrounds the vocal skill of its singers and is "characterized by the intense expression of emotions" through which the "nostalgia, longing, and despair that Mexicans experience in all aspects of their lives is given expression." The ranchera shares much with melodrama in its self-conscious, emotionally excessive style, through which "issues of profound social concern are addressed" (Nájera-Ramírez in this volume). As such, the ranchera has emerged as a "culturally sanctioned site in which the ideas and values of a community are not merely displayed but, more important, are transmitted, produced, reproduced, and contested" (ibid.). As Nájera-Ramírez emphasizes, female performers and audiences have historically employed the ranchera's self-conscious stylings "as a site through which they make feminist interventions" (ibid.).[30] Claudia's evocation of Selena's version of a ranchera acts as one such intervention. By positioning Selena within a musical genealogy of powerfully affective singers, Claudia not only critiques the audition's devaluation of Latina voices—recall that no singing skills were required—but also counters dominant crossover rhetoric that constructs Selena as a "Tex-Mex Madonna" pop icon characterized by stylish costumes and dance moves rather than substantive talent.[31] Moreover, since the song Claudia selects does not have "a lot of beat," no one can summon her to dance. This choice not only refuses the failed crossover narrative but tactically speaks back to the casting personnel who can only say to her, "Just dance for me."

Claudia's choice to close the show with a ranchera does more than simply speak back to the radio producers or the film's casting personnel: it also explicitly carves out a space for grief on her own terms. Like other female consumers of rancheras who Nájera-Ramírez documents, Claudia uses the ranchera as a powerfully effective and affective means through which to perform grief. The very "excessiveness" of the ranchera's emotional tenor provides an expansive space for the articulation of multiple griefs. Claudia exploits this expansiveness, insisting on a moment of grieving for more than the loss of Selena. She refuses to say "death" because it cannot encompass the depth and contours of her mourning over a range of injustices: the ignorance about Selena expressed by casting agents; the framing of the radio show; the plight of the thousands of Latinas who were not offered the opportunity to become Selena; and the use of young Latinas by Latino filmmakers like Nava. Claudia's insistence on Selena's rendition of "an old song, you know, from Mexico" signifies a particularly Mexicana emotional register, whereby Claudia momentarily prioritizes an affiliation with Mexicanidad over Latinidad. By squarely positioning both herself and Selena within Mexicana performance traditions, Claudia recuperates Selena's Mexicana identity, which is often effaced in Latina appropriations of her. In this way, Claudia uses the complex poetics of the ranchera to speak back to other Latinas who honor Selena.

Navigating the Neighborhood: Reprise

Even if she's dead, it's like she's alive to me.
—Christina Vargas, nine-year-old audition participant

As I rounded the corner onto the street where Claudia lived and parked the car along the curb outside her house—unfolded map flung across the back seat—I, too, asked Claudia why she had chosen the song "Tú Solo Tú." She replied, "Because that song she sang more like *con ganas.*" To do something con ganas is to do so with great desire, gusto, or enthusiasm. To act con ganas is to express a self-conscious, unapologetic emotionality. Selena indeed sang "Tú Solo Tú" with ganas; like other female ranchera singers before her, Selena "lived what she sang" (Nájera-Ramírez in this volume). That is, she possessed the performative skill to embody—to live—what she sang as she performed, as opposed to singing what she lived. This distinction again foregrounds a self-conscious rather than an ontological emotionality expressed by Mexicana ranchera singers. Furthermore, Selena sang this song con ganas by altering the opening lyrics to "decenter the male perspective embedded in the narrative" (Nájera-Ramírez in this volume).[32] Claudia's return to the notion of the workings of desire and intense emotion within performance reflects how Selena is invoked and circulated not simply as a sexually consumable body on display but as an actively desiring agent through whom Latinas assert and refashion their own subjectivities. Claudia's comments underscore Emma Pérez's argument that "Selena represents decolonial desire," a desire that emerges "in that in-between space where Chicanas such as Selena exhibited an in-your-face, working-class sexuality and did so with pride, not inhibition" (1999, 116). Moreover, Claudia and her fellow auditioners recognize the ways in which the act of becoming Selena demonstrates not a pathologically affective Latina/o excess, but rather a critically generative one. This critically generative excess allows for a space wherein acts con ganas can emerge: the resignifying of ranchera lyrics, the refusal to say "death," the clandestine journeys taken by many young Latinas to the Selena auditions. When Claudia protests, "You can't *be* Selena," or when one of the Texas cousins asserts, "They're not looking for a true Selena. . . . They might know who Selena was, but not truly what she meant to us," they are not only indicting multinational capitalist industries for failing to acknowledge this distinction, but their very act of defiance signals a product of this enactment of Latina/o generative excess. That is, these young Latinas reveal that a worthy surrogate does not simply try to "be Selena," but rather tries to be "what Selena meant to us." For, as Claudia tactically suggested, there is "Tú Solo Tú," there is "you only you," Selena. The worthy Selena surrogate necessarily creates a generative excess of Selena wherein Latina desire can find a home even as the Latina body is consumed and circulated within the market. Thus, through their critical articulations and bold migrations, Claudia and the Texas cousins successfully become (more than) Selena, and in the space of "more than," of Latina generative excess, these young Latinas "watch how they watch me," watch after one another, refuse the closure of the death narrative, and, if only momentarily, effectively unseat the master. Con ganas, indeed.

Notes

I offer heartfelt appreciation to Frank Guridy, Heather McClure, Sandra Richards, and the participants at the Vassar College Women's Studies First Friday Speaker Series and at the City University of New York Center for Puerto Rican Studies, Hunter College, who offered critically incisive insights at various stages of this essay's completion. I also want to thank Denise Segura and Patricia Zavella for their generous editorial advice.

1 See "Selena Remembered" 1995. Following Selena's death, a staggering number of memorial tributes, public performances of grief, and Selena impersonations were enacted in her honor. These included feature-length and documentary films, video and magazine tributes, television specials, Web sites, commemorative Coca-Cola bottles, murals in her hometown and in New York City's Lower East Side, Selena dance contests, Selena Barbie dolls, biographies, monuments, musicals, a scholarship fund, a museum, and a display of one of her costumes at the Smithsonian. For a critical account of a diverse array of Selena commemorations see Paradez 2002.

2 For a popular biographical account of Selena's life and career, see Patoski 1996. For a Chicana feminist analysis of Selena's performances, see Vargas 2002a.

3 Joe Nick Patoski's biography certainly falls prey to the colonialist fascination with Selena's body: "Her lips had filled out voluptuously; so had her breasts and hips. Her rear was 'the kind you could place a beer glass on without spilling the foam,' as one admiring disc jockey put it. She was the total Latina" (1996, 115).

4 Selena's promotion and self-fashioning as the Tejana-in-touch-with-her-roots also point toward the demands of authenticity placed on minority communities and, in particular, on the racialized female's body.

5 For more on the controversy, see Navarro 2000. The second annual Latin Grammys were also rife with controversy, as Cuban exiles in Miami, where the awards were originally scheduled, protested the showcasing of Cuban performers from the island. In an effort to avoid a major disturbance, organizers moved the event to Los Angeles and rescheduled it for 11 September 2001. Given the national crisis that occurred that day, the Latin Grammys were again postponed, and the televised coverage was canceled. See Burr 2001; Canedy 2001.

6 In an interview by the ethnomusicologist Manuel Peña, Cameron Randle, an execu-

tive at Arista Records, commented, "We just came back from the *Billboard Magazine* Latin conference in Miami. And you go down and get a sobering reminder of Tejano's place within the Latino family, musically. It's still treated essentially as a blue-collar, secondary genre of music that is confined to a geographical area" (Manuel Peña 1999, 196).

7 The touring musical *Selena Forever* was launched in San Antonio in March 2000 to commemorate the five-year anniversary of Selena's death and was restaged in Los Angeles in May 2001 as *Selena: A Musical Celebration of Life*.

8 Following its April 1996 airing, the episode was rebroadcast on 27 December 1996, 6 November 1999, and 4 May 2001. This is common practice for all episodes of *This American Life*. See http://www.thislife.org.

9 Claudia was a high-school senior when she served as guest correspondent on *This American Life*. She became aware of and involved with the radio show through her participation in the outreach organization Street-Level Youth Media (Claudia Pérez, interview by author, Chicago, 8 May 1999). Street-Level regularly collaborates with a number of arts and media organizations in Chicago in an effort to "educate Chicago's inner-city youth in media arts and emerging technologies for use in self-expression, communication and social change" (see http://www.streetlevel.iit.edu/about/index.html).

10 See also De Genova and Ramos-Zayas 2003.

11 The documentary on which I rely is Lourdes Portillo's film, *Corpus: A Home Movie for Selena*, which is largely composed of interviews with Selena fans in Corpus Christi, Texas. The film premiered 12 November 1998 at the Chicago Mexican Fine Arts Museum as part of their "Tribute to Mexican Women" series and was broadcast nationally on the PBS series *POV* (*Point of View*) in 1999. Much controversy surrounded the film's editing and subsequent circulation, as Selena's father strove to control the image of his daughter. See Fregoso 2001.

12 Claudia Pérez, interview by author, Chicago, 26 February 1999. All subsequent quotes from my conversation with Claudia are drawn from the interview on this date.

13 The xenophobic hysteria that marked the decade was manifested in the passage of legislative acts that included California's Proposition 187 (1994), the immigrant provisions of the Personal Responsibility and Work Opportunity Act (1996), and the Illegal Immigration Reform and Immigrant Responsibility Act (1996). Proposition 187 denied access to public healthcare and schooling to all undocumented persons. Even though much of Proposition 187 was overturned by federal-court decisions (deemed unconstitutional), Congress ultimately enacted national legislation that enforced some of the proposition's provisions within the welfare and immigration-reform bills passed in 1996. The immigration-related provisions of the Work Opportunity Act sought drastic welfare cuts targeted at legal immigrants while the Immigration Reform Act further entrenched the border's status as a militarized zone with increased border patrols and fences, thereby constructing all Latina/os outside the borders of American citizenry. The draconian measures enforced by these acts severely disenfranchised many U.S. Latina/o communities, even while mainstream corporations celebrated the booming Latina/o market.

14 Negrón-Muntaner's observations echo Sander Gilman's and Paula Giddings's observations about how the buttocks have historically served as an emblem for racially marked sexual difference, whereby the racialized and sexualized "excessive" buttocks of black women were evoked by hegemonic forces as an emblem for the unrestrained threat of all black people and as the counterweight against which standards of white femininity were constructed (see Gilman 1985; Giddings 1992).

15 See, for example, Castañeda 1990; de la Torre and Pesquera 1993. In his discussion of Selena, Jose Limón (2000, 80–81) also notes the ways in which the construction of Latina sexuality is imbricated within colonial relationships in South Texas.

16 See, for example, Zavella 1997a.

17 For an astute analysis of the assimilationist crossover narratives into which Selena's career was discursively channeled, see Vargas 2002b.

18 Lopez (1991, 404–24) provides an insightful analysis of del Rio, Velez, and Miranda.

19 Quoted in Lourdes Portillo's *Corpus: A Home Movie for Selena*.

20 According to Muñoz, Latinidad is often rendered "politically incoherent" in its "inability to index with any regularity the central identity tropes that lead to our understandings of group identities in the United States" (2000, 67).

21 The *Chicago Sun-Times* commented, "It's not a stretch to put this weekend's tributes on an Elvis Presley level. Only 23 at her death, Selena—like Presley—sang in an inspiring range of musical styles.... And like Presley, Selena showed that dreams are not impossible to attain. Presley's spirit resounded within the working class South. Selena's music does the same with the Mexican-American community" (Hoekstra 1999b, 31). The *New York Times* echoed this sentiment three years later: "Selena achieved in death the celebrity of an Elvis Presley or a Marilyn Monroe among Latinos and others, even on the East Coast and in other areas where she was not as well known or Tejano music as popular as in Texas, her home state" (Navarro 1999, B1).

22 Roach writes, "Celebrity, performing in constitutional office even in death, holds open a space in collective memory while the process of surrogation nominates and eventually crowns successors" (1996, 76).

23 Claudia's comment about Jorge from Channel 66 refers to Jorge Barbosa, a news anchor for WGBO, the Univisión network affiliate in Chicago.

24 Certainly, given the appearance of his comments in the *Daily News*, Gregory Nava may have tactically targeted his comparisons to mainstream audiences unfamiliar with, or at least unconvinced by, Selena's popularity throughout the Latina/o world. However, it is important to note that in her narrated National Public Radio segment on the Selena auditions, Claudia chose not to appeal to mainstream sensibilities, but rather expressed the same bold and, indeed, risky skeptical stance she conveyed during my interview with her.

25 Transcribed by author from an audiotape of "From a Distance," *This American Life*, 19 April 1996.

26 I also listened to the unedited interview tapes that Claudia and the show's producer, Nancy Updike, gathered at the auditions. None of the young women and girls interviewed on these tapes mentioned potential financial rewards or recognition as motivations for their participation in the audition process.

27 The various relocations that marked Selena's childhood reflect the larger political economic plight of many Tejana/os as a result of the oil bust in the 1970s and 1980s. For a popular biographical chronicle of Selena's life, see Patoski 1996.

28 For nuanced analyses of inter-Latino relations in Chicago, see De Genova and Ramos-Zayas 2003a; Padilla 1985; Gina Pérez 2003; Rúa 2001.

29 Transcribed by author from an audiotape of "From a Distance," 19 April 1996. The girl to whom Ira Glass refers was eight years old; her understanding of Selena's murder as "Selena sleeping" is not entirely inconsistent with most children's conceptions of death.

30 Female ranchera singers make interventions not only by their mere presence and skill within a traditionally male-dominated genre but also through alteration of lyrics, costume, and bodily gestures (Nájera-Rámirez in this volume).

31 Immediately following Selena's death, numerous mainstream periodicals unfamiliar with Selena mislabeled her bustier-clad, dancing body as a Tex-Mex version of Madonna. For a critical analysis of this trend, see Willis and Gonzalez 1997.

32 As Nájera-Ramírez suggests in this volume, Selena's alterations were slight, but not insignificant. She changed the opening line from "Mira como ando mujer" (Look at the state I'm in, woman) to "Mira como ando mi amor" (Look at the state I'm in, my love).

Cyberbrides and Global Imaginaries:
Mexican Women's Turn from the National
to the Foreign
FELICITY SCHAEFFER-GRABIEL

✳ As I approached the glitzy Presidente hotel where I would interview men and women at the transnational single's party—otherwise known as the "Romance Vacation Tour"—the bus veered into Plaza del Sol, one of the wealthiest, most well-manicured, and most tourist-populated areas of Guadalajara, Mexico. As women began to arrive, I realized they were not your typical "mail-order brides," popularly thought to marry men from the United States out of poverty and desperation. On the contrary, the majority of women were well educated and from a small but burgeoning professional Mexican middle class. They were confident, savvy, and cosmopolitan in their familiarity with U.S. culture through film, television, the Internet, encounters with tourists, stories from family living in the United States, as well as through their own travel abroad. The owner of The Latina Connection (TLC) Worldwide gave me permission to attend the tour for research, because my bicultural identity set me apart from the "feminist type" who he assumed would write a scathing report on these interactions, whereas I spoke Spanish and was an offspring of a mixed Anglo-Mexican union.

The owner's distrust of feminist types had to do with critical activism by members of the National Organization for Women (NOW) and the Gabriela Network (Los Angeles) who have helped shut down mail-order-bride agencies that cater to the Philippines. While women's activism has helped to bring oftentimes abusive mail-order marriages into mainstream visibility, feminists and scholars alike have tended to situate all mail-order brides within the larger framework of the global trafficking of women, focusing on women's lack of agency or women's victimization in relation to global processes (Glodava and

Onizuka 1994; Ridenhour-Levitt 1999; Tolentino 1997; Gibbons and Pretlow 1999).[1] The trafficking of women has been defined as the underside of globalization that victimizes all Third World women's bodies as cheap labor for First World consumption—whether they are factory workers, domestics, sex workers, or "servile wives" in the Internet-bride industry. While it is important to make these gendered neocolonial and imperial legacies visible in terms of women's migration, scholarship and the media make certain assumptions about the ways in which globalization creates unequal gender, class, and racial norms across First and Third World countries: that women are the producers (and commodities) and men the consumers, that women travel as workers and men as pleasure seekers, that women are victims and men victimizers, and that U.S. culture dramatically alters local cultures, without taking into account the reverse phenomenon. In a growing trend, however, cosmopolitan middle-class women use global processes, such as the Internet and tourism circuits, to imagine and attain more stable and liberating lifestyles, equitable gender relations, and more opportunities than can be found in their local environments. Yet while scholars such as Arjun Appadurai (1996) celebrate the new postnational possibilities of the imagination that allow individuals throughout the world to imagine a wider set of possible lives than ever before, such imaginaries must be placed within structures of power at the local, national, and the transnational levels. While flexibility and mobility may be accelerated under current global flows, this "global imagination" plays out in uneven and even contradictory ways in the desires of women from Mexico.[2] Desire for Mexican women and U.S. men only makes sense when analyzed through the lens of two countries whose differences mark the site of desire.

As new accounts of women who seek out international lifestyles slowly surface, these women emerge not as mail-order brides escaping poverty, but as middle-class women impacted by global fantasies of the "American way of life." Women come to realize their gender and racial differences through a barrage of daily encounters with "foreign," U.S. culture. Mexican women turn to foreign men and lifestyles as a way to escape "traditional" value systems in the family, a corrupt and unstable government, and confining definitions of gender and womanhood. As women articulate their hopes to leave what is "oppressive" about Mexican men (and Mexico) for a seemingly more open and liberating journey with foreign men (and the United States), they demonstrate how powerful such a shift in their imaginary—from national to transnational citizenship—can be. The space of the foreign offers greater prospects for self-improvement and growth through a more intimate and equitable marriage partner, opportunities to travel, better education, and sometimes, careers (Kelsky 2001).

Yet, in the process of seeking love and marriage women do not completely detach themselves from the nation-state or traditional roles; instead, they accentuate these exact notions of tradition in an attempt to attract male clients. Mexican women are aware of the national and cultural differences between themselves and U.S. women, which they utilize as the basis to accentuate and "sell" a version of traditional Mexican femininity that is desired by U.S. men. Furthermore, the family is still the most important institution women use to enter into U.S. culture, preventing more radical critiques of the legacy of neocolonialism perpetuated through global policies such as North Atlantic Free Trade Agreement that create an atmosphere of dependency and disadvantage for Mexico. Not only is this new phenomenon of love and migration propelled by both contemporary local and global processes, but it also represents a rupture in traditional gender expectations that has reverberated across the Americas and beyond. Cosmopolitan women from Russia, Japan, Brazil, Colombia, Cuba, and Vietnam also utilize creative means to maintain and improve themselves and the lives of their children through global circuits of products, tourists, and imaginaries (Fusco 1997; O'Dougherty 2002; Kelsky 2001; Ong 1999; Kojima 2001; Thai 2002). Women's gender ideologies resonate with modern ideals of selfhood in the United States, as individuals seeking personal fulfillment (rather than adhering to social and familial commitments) through romantic encounters via the Internet or through matchmaking services. I interviewed women (and men) at the "Romance Vacation Tour," set up individual interviews with women whose e-mail addresses I bought from an Internet company, and translated and read e-mail correspondence shared with me by both men and women.[3]

Many Mexican women no longer feel bound by the futility of traditional gender roles that position men as head of the family. During the twentieth century, various changes in Guadalajara, Mexico—the rapid influx of people from rural to urban areas, industrialization, the secular and global expansion of commerce and services, an increase in mass communications—impacted women directly. As Guadalajara transformed from a rural to an urban economy, women enjoyed better employment, education, and healthcare (Oliveira 1990). The peso crisis of the 1980s affected single and middle-class women in particular. Because this widespread economic crisis resulted in a loss of jobs, large sectors of men migrated to the United States, opening up more job opportunities for the women left behind. Female work was no longer temporary or a rarity, but was incorporated into women's lives as a rite of passage through which women could escape isolation in the home (Hondagneu-Sotelo 1994, 13). When their newly found independence was coupled with higher levels of education, women began to want more equitable gender roles; they waited longer to marry, divorce rates increased, and a greater use of contraception resulted in fewer children.[4]

The peso crisis also shook the nation's faith (as well as that of the international community) in a stable and moral governmental body in Mexico. As women began to earn their own money, they depended less on patriarchal family figures, the state, and government. Yet the discrepancy between middle-class women's wages and their incorporation into the market as consumers of expensive goods and lifestyles imported through the global economy compromised their ability to attain new gender, family, and lifestyle goals. For example, Spanish-language teachers at the University of Guadalajara's foreign-language schools (with foreign-level tuition fees) made only $500 per month, and the professional class, including doctors and lawyers, were paid more in social prestige than in livable wages. In 1987 the minimum wage in urban areas fell to 58 percent of levels found in 1980, while the cost of living and food continued to rise.[5] Similar to what Maureen O'Dougherty has documented among the middle class in Brazil, Mexicans turned to symbolic markers of class standing, such as foreign products and lifestyles, education, careers, as well as cultural and moral standing, to distinguish themselves from the lower classes as well as to claim an affinity with a global cosmopolitan class (2002, 22–23).

I conducted interviews with thirty-two women at "Romance Vacation Tours" in Guadalajara and through e-mail correspondence. I worked with two marriage organizations with full Web-site services. Mexican Matchmakers, a small agency owned by a North American, was located in one of the most affluent neighborhoods of Guadalajara.[6] TLC Worldwide, based in Houston, Texas, offered tours to Mexico usually four times a year. These companies attracted hundreds of women through radio announcements, by placing ads in the back of *Cosmopolitan*, and by word of mouth. More than twenty-five Internet companies offered matchmaking services and marriage with women in Mexico.[7] On signing up with an agency, women provided a photograph, e-mail or mail addresses, and a physical and personal description that the companies then sold to men for varying prices. In exchange, women were invited to the vacation tours for free, while men paid between $500 and $1,000. The women varied in age from eighteen to fifty-five, most were well educated, and they worked in an array of professional jobs: doctors, accountants, teachers, business owners, secretaries, beauticians, and models. Some attended tours out of curiosity, to practice their English, to enjoy a free night out, while others were serious about finding true love and, eventually, a husband.

Many accounts of women's involvement in these industries assume the women are objectified by company Web sites and catalogs wherein Mexican women are advertised as superior commodities (compared to U.S. feminists) to be consumed by men in the global marketplace (Tolentino 1997; Glodava and Onizuka 1994). Such accounts are, in fact, accurate on the representational level, demonstrating companies' complicity in shaping men's expectations for docile, feminine, and sexualized Latinas. An analysis of the Web pages alone, however, cannot explain these relationships at the level of complexity that ethnographic methods provide. At the tours, for example, women show up with girlfriends and family members, and they display confidence and professional attire. The roles are also reversed at the tours: men's bodies are on display for women to consume, as they have to get up in front of a rowdy audience and describe themselves in idealized ways. Furthermore, TLC Worldwide often circulates small catalogs of men's photos and descriptions for women to peruse; the women are then prompted to initiate e-mail letters and courtship.

Mexican women might want to marry a man from the United States for many reasons, yet these desires often conflict with the types of men the agencies attract. Women in their late twenties and beyond hope to escape the stigma of being "older" and single in Mexican society, a society that generally assumes they are past their prime. While marriage symbolizes positive qualities such as happiness, achievement, opportunity, and advancement, the state of being single symbolizes the exact opposite: lack of achievement, solitude, stagnation, and failure (Salazar 2001, 147). U.S. men, however, are told on Web sites that they can expect to date and/or marry women who are twenty to thirty years younger than themselves—which accentuates the market for younger women. The majority of Mexican women who use matchmaking services are attractive, intelligent, and express feeling undervalued by local men. They idealize men from the United States as being appreciative of their commitment to the family, their femininity, and their intelligence, while they accuse local men of taking for granted their domestic labor and of being threatened by smart and beautiful women.

The majority of women I interviewed came from a small but privileged middle class. In Mexico middle-class status is based not merely on one's economic level. Other factors designating class status include higher levels of education, owning a car or home, having a job with a stable income, residence, having children in private schooling, technological access, and social and cultural expectations such as the desire for self-improvement. The acquisition of a tourist visa is also critical for traveling across the U.S.-Mexico border. Reviewing information collected at Mexican Matchmakers, I found that two-thirds of the women signed up with the agency had university or postgraduate levels of education. Almost half of the women had visas, while another one-fifth had had one in the past.[8] These women were not interested in merely migrating to the United States to work; they repeatedly described wanting to find a good, hardworking, and compatible partner with whom they could share their ideas and feelings. And most were not interested in migrating at a lower-class level, so they sought marriages that could protect and hopefully augment their way of life in Mexico and the United States.

Women and (Trans)Nationalism

As women described why they wanted to marry a man from the United States, it became difficult to distinguish their accounts of Mexican men from the body of the Mexican nation. They looked to men from the United States to embody utopian marriages and lifestyles—egalitarian relationships with men who would share in household chores and offer a better way of life, more economic stability, and opportunities—qualities Mexico and Mexican men lacked. In interviews I conducted and in written accounts from agency books, women stated that they wanted a man who was loyal, understanding of and responsive to their needs, and hardworking. When I asked why they could not find a man like that in Guadalajara, they shook their heads and voiced their dislike for "macho men."

Anna was a thirty-four-year-old widowed mother who worked part time as an accountant.[9] Her children attended a private school, and she told me she juggled working and taking care of them on her own with the support of her family. According to Anna, men in Mexico are more *machista*—than, presumably, U.S. men—because they are threatened by the fact that women earn more than they do. She said, "Economically, they [Mexican women] are more stable than the men . . . they already have their own house, car and luxuries that many men cannot give them. And, even more curious, what angers men here in Mexico is that the woman—and for this reason they are more macho—that women are more successful than them. But, the good thing about people from other countries is that they admire this kind of woman."

While Anna's conception that Mexican men's machismo stems from threats to their power in the home and workplace, she considers foreign men from First World countries to be the kind of men who respect strong and successful women. Anna keenly asserted that men in Mexico need to subordinate women in order to feel like a man. Machismo, according to Anna, is a defensive state against women's elevated social and economic positions. Yet the majority of men from the United States come to Mexico to find a traditional-minded woman in the hope of reasserting their masculinity and power in the home and workplace, which complicates this image of the foreign "feminist man."

When I asked women why they thought men from the United States differed from men in Mexico, they responded that Mexican men were coddled in the home by their mothers and expected the same from their wives. On the other hand, Anna explained,

> I have noticed that men from over there [United States] are well-disposed to share in the chores.... I've seen something that almost never occurs here ... over there they have told me, "I will cook for you," not like what they say here, "What do you mean I'm going to cook for you? [She laughs.] Over there men are more independent from a younger age, I think that they learn to value all of these aspects, you know ... and this gives them a little more maturity. It's liberating that they themselves feel this way and that they have fewer prejudices than men here.

For Anna, U.S. men's willingness to participate in "women's work" is liberating, as it opens relationships up to negotiation, flexibility, and communication. While processes such as urbanization and increases in education and employment for women contribute to changing gender roles, I observed that women are changing faster than men.[10] For example, Guadalajara is a city in motion, as men cross into the United States to find work. Among those who remain, said Josefina, a fifty-two-year-old divorced doctor with two grown children, "many want sex without commitment or sex in exchange for going out to eat or for going with him to the cinema." Josefina does not see a fair exchange between men whose earnings, lifestyles, and cosmopolitan outlook do not match her own. Like Anna, she characterizes machismo as a juvenile or childlike state when compared to the paternal father-husband to the north.

Women's complaints about machismo reveal contradictory critiques of men that are both problematic and significant. First, women reveal racial and class biases in associating all Mexican men with negative macho qualities, characterizations that also serve to critique an irresponsible, abusive, and overly patriarchal government and nation-state. Furthermore, women creatively verbalize dissatisfaction with their subordinate gender position in the patriarchal family, culture, and society in general. There is little support of women's new professional careers, nor are there more flexible and equitable gender roles in the family. Mexican feminists have recently brought attention to a backlash in television shows, newspapers, and even a popular talk-radio show in Monterrey. The host of this show, Oscar Muzquiz, solicits men to call in with stories of neglectful wives—in search of the "Female Slob of the Year"—or wives who are channeling their energy into careers rather than their families. Muzquiz attributes this shift to the "Americanization" of family values: "Mexican women are increasingly confusing 'liberty with licentiousness' and that Mexican women are turning us into '*mandelones*' [slang for browbeaten wimps or feminized men]."[11] These popular discourses and images of women out of control are meant to morally pressure or discipline women's bodies back into the home and into traditional gender roles.

Recent feminist scholarship on gender and nationalism focuses on the ways in which women are marginally positioned within national agendas as well as how their reproductive roles are both biological and ideological.[12] Women have historically garnered value for their reproductive role in populating the nation as well as for serving as teachers so youth will learn how to be good citizens. Thus, women's roles as wives and mothers in the heterosexual family have been mythically narrated to guard women's placement within the private spheres of the home. Women who stepped out of these roles were marked as outcasts, prostitutes, whores, or *mujeres mala* (bad women).

While national projects have historically targeted women's bodies as the focus of disciplinary control (Foucault 1978; McClintock 1995), few accounts take seriously how women themselves disrupt the moral body of the nation through negative characterizations of men. Conversant with global scripts of family behaviors and structures, women pollute the boundaries of their own nation by characterizing it as an overly macho male body. Women naturalize their defection from their own nation and highlight their affinity to another. They reverse the gender hierarchy by polluting the body of Mexico as a "spectacle of men out of control" (Kaplan, Alarcón, and Moallem 1999). Women see themselves as having to defect from Mexico, a nation they equate with immature, restless, noncommittal, and backward men.

Las Malinchistas

In characterizing Mexico as a machista or macho nation, women respond to negative reactions from mainstream Mexican society toward their involvement with foreign men. For this reason, many women keep secret from friends and family their interactions with the tours, e-mail exchanges, and dates. Lacking other outlets, many of the women I approached eagerly talked to me as a cultural outsider, yet my biracial identity reinforced their belief that I could relate to them as a woman who understood Mexican culture. Alicia, a single thirty-three-year-old with green eyes and light skin, owned her own photography studio and had traveled to the United States through a previous career with American Airlines. She asked that we meet in one of the new Guadalajara hot spots, El Centro Magno, a hip, cosmopolitan, and expensive mall with a Hard Rock Café, a Chili's (with higher prices than in the States), Italian restaurants and cafés, clothing stores with trendy styles from around the world, and a multiplex cinema that primarily featured films from the United States. Alicia mentioned that most of her friends call her a *Malinchista*, "'Cause I only date foreign men—Europeans, Canadians, and Americans.... I just don't like the men here—short, fat and dark-skinned ... no-o— I like them tall, slender, and well-dressed."

The term *Malinchista* has deep historical roots in Mexico. The union between the Spanish conquistador Hernán Cortés and his indigenous concubine, Malintzin, or La Malinche, has been mythologized as leading to the birth of the first mestizo, or mixed-race Mexicano. La Malinche has been narrated through Mexican and Chicano literature as the one who "sold out" her people to the colonizer, the enemy. This historical narrative of the origins of Mexico and Mexico's mixed racial heritage continues to infiltrate popular memory through colloquial language.[13] A Malinchista is popularly known as a traitor, or *la chingada*, literally the one who has been "fucked over," sexually or figuratively, by the penetration of foreign imperialism and policies.[14] Thus, the consumption of foreignness or foreign products is particularly intertwined with gender, race, and class, placing nationalism and Mexico's turn to modernity in constant conflict. The lighter one's skin color, the more one is associated with the upper class, the conqueror, modernity, wealth, and culture. While middle-class women equate freedoms and opportunities with foreign culture, those who benefit less—especially poor men and the indigenous—internalize the phallic intrusion of imperialist and global capital as an emasculating and neocolonial process. For the elite of Mexico, the United States and "things foreign" connote culture, professionalization, and status. This idea of boosting the economy of Mexico through foreign culture is further complicated by contemporary popular Mexican filmmakers, musicians, and artists who speak for the voiceless and condemn elite culture for selling out the country to foreign companies and buying into foreign cultures of taste. Contestation over the national image varies depending on one's gender, race, sexuality, class, and vision for the future.

Alicia characterized men from Mexico as short, balding, dark-skinned, and overweight (and thus lazy); they were therefore lower class, uneducated, and more likely indigenous. Conversely, she associated foreign men—tall, slender, well dressed, and light-skinned—with education, culture, and suit-wearing professionalism. Alicia internalized this dichotomy between First and Third World countries, between the United States and Mexico, as modern versus traditional, and she aligned herself with a more cosmopolitan class that extended national borders.

By describing men in Mexico as macho, women turned the moralizing discourse away from their own bodies, from the accusation that they are the Malinchistas. They instead degraded the national body with images of poor, uneducated, and emotionally abusive men. It is not that the women I interviewed had not suffered from a macho culture—their stories of neglect and abuse attest otherwise—yet they conflated their individual experiences with abusive, insensitive, immature, and adulterous men with popular images of the Mexican nation. Women from Colombia, Asia, Russia, and Japan similarly justified their searches for foreign men by degrading local men, which reveals how far the "personal" gender revolution has spread (Glodava and Onizuka 1994; Kelsky 2001; Del Rosario 1994). In an e-mail letter, a woman from Colombia wrote to her U.S. suitor, "But, thanks to GOD there are good people who work hard, not like the bad people of Colombia." Men who work hard are moral and upright citizens, unlike those men in Latin America, who women envision as drug dealers, unemployed, or lazy. While women turn this discourse onto men as unfit fathers, husbands, providers, and role models, they do not discuss the lack of economic opportunities for men in Mexico, which limits their ability to be as economically stable, well-traveled, and experienced as men from the United States.

It is inaccurate to say that all Mexican men are macho, but this stereotype has been widely perpetuated by popular culture and scholarship. As Matthew C. Gutmann demonstrates (1996), what is considered manly or macho must be understood as changing alongside history and across region, gender, and class. While Gutmann finds that many of his male interviewees highlight positive qualities of machismo—such as men's sense of caring and duty toward their children and families—he attributes some of the negative descriptions of abuse by women as practices exacerbated by the peso crisis in Mexico, which contributed to men's loss of status, worth, and identity.[15] Women's opposing constructions of men from Mexico and the United States demonstrate the power of their increasing interpellation as consumers, where commodities—including men—become fetish objects or signs that promise a new self and alternative lifestyles. As Pierrette Hondagneu-Sotelo and Michael Messner argue (1994), the image of the sensitive Anglo man in U.S. media is internalized as a softer and more open expression of masculinity constructed against the more aggressive display of masculinity expressed by racialized men such as Mexican immigrants and African American males.

How ironic that what women want and the types of men these services attract are almost always at odds. Many U.S. men are looking for the traditional wife and family relationship they believe existed during the 1950s, before the breakdown of the nuclear family due to the social movements of the 1960s and mainstream feminism. Men also idealize love as outside rational time and space: they must look outside the bounds of the nation, outside capitalism, to find true love. Likewise, women in Mexico must leave the Mexican nation, what one woman characterizes as the "cradle of machismo" (Biemann 2000). They equate marriage and relationships in the United States with utopian ideals of capitalism, democracy, and freedom in the First World.

Love, Work, and the "New Self"

Transnational marriages offer women dual citizenship and the flexibility to combine Mexican traditions of the importance of the family and a strong work ethic, and to enact their citizenship as consumers of the global marketplace. Women's commitment to their difference from norms within Mexican culture and society serves to mark their symbolic move away from the Mexican nation-state toward being a citizen and consumer in the transnational family. Néstor García Canclini (2001) argues that through consumption, most Latin Americans experience sentiments of belonging and citizenship by forging similar taste cultures across national, rather than regional, borders. As more and more women join the professional workforce in Mexico and realize that through hard work they can buy what they need, they are less dependent on men to embody this role.

Laura is a hardworking single woman in her early thirties who works five to six days a week for a company that imports and exports goods to and from Mexico and the United States. She lives with a relative and still has a hard time making the payments on a small new car she recently bought. In an e-mail she wrote to a wealthy man from Texas, who she is dating, she describes her view on relationships: "I'm not looking for a man to take care of me, I am looking for a man that is ready to share his life with me, that knows how to work and who desires to grow alongside his partner. For me, it would not be pleasant to live with a man that sits around and hopes for good luck so that things go well. . . . I like to work and I would like to work together with my partner so that between the two of us we could make something together for our future."

The kind of marriage Laura describes sounds more like a partnership wherein two people contribute equally to build an empire and to grow together. She does not make a distinction between love and the economy, the public and private, the individual and the collective. In bed and in the workplace, a couple should contribute equally and work hard toward uplifting themselves and the relationship. This understanding of love as work echoes the discourse promoted by U.S. magazines and psychological research on love. Eva Illouz's study on the parallels between love and capitalism looks to popular culture to trace these interconnections: "Women's magazines suggest that instead of being 'stricken' or 'smitten' by love, a woman is responsible for her romantic successes and failures, that she must 'work hard' to secure a comfortable emotional future for herself, and that she should guarantee that a relationship will provide an equitable exchange" (1997, 195).

Magazines such as *Cosmopolitan* are very popular with middle- to upper-class women in Mexico. The Mexican publication of *Cosmopolitan* mixes articles written in the United States with articles that are locally produced. Through this mixture of discourses, elite readers are asked to "vicariously" participate in emancipation even though editors know that women are expected to abide by more traditional norms (Illouz 1997, 30). The middle-class women I interviewed are not satisfied with vicarious participation in new ideas of womanhood and marriage. Instead, they see themselves as active participants in new flexible identities between the traditional and the modern, and between Mexico and the United States.

In her study of women and marriage in Guadalajara (2001, 185), T. R. Salazar concludes that the older women she interviewed based marriage on luck and destiny—ideas that coincide with appropriate gender roles for women as defined by Catholicism. Women are encouraged to be spiritually strong, like La Virgen de Guadalupe, and to be passive recipients of God's will. A woman should not actively seek a partner, but merely happen to be in the right place at the right time. The women I interviewed, however, describe themselves within modern ideas of the self as individuals actively seeking self-fulfillment and happiness through their use of the Internet and matchmaking services. Explaining her philosophy on love and life, Anna says, "I know from personal experience that if I need something I can achieve it if I go and look for it, if I save in order to buy it or if I work very carefully I can earn it . . . but I never wait for things to fall from the sky. . . . What's more, I think that happiness is found in the search and not in wait."

Anna bases her ideas of love and marriage less on destiny than on capitalist relations in which hardworking individuals achieve success. The fact that Anna is Protestant rather than Catholic also shapes her understanding of women's role in the world. The Protestant version of Christianity, intertwined with Puritan ideals of hard work as well as with capitalist relationships, asks followers not to be passive bystanders but hardworking participants. Women base love and marriage less on a Catholic interpretation that teaches people to be passive recipients of God's will than on capitalist relations in which people who work hard succeed.

Mexican women look to the United States to be freed from cultural norms and hope to become architects of their own lives. This is a liberating prospect and has the potential for subverting the gender hierarchy in Mexico. As women garner confidence and independence through professional careers and exposure to stories of love and marriages from abroad, they begin to imagine new possibilities for themselves. Yet women also do not accept everything about American culture or the capitalist framework. Aware that women in the United States are more liberal, that families are nuclear rather than extended, and that many U.S. women are more materialistic, most Mexican women state the importance of holding onto spiritual and family traditions. Many of them, especially those with children, know that they will have to "sacrifice" their professions and families in order to find happiness with a foreigner.

Internet Encounters

Fantasies, stereotypes, and utopian desires commingle on the screen through the act of Internet letter writing. The Mexican woman writes herself into a script in which she finds a loving, supportive, and gentle husband in a far-away land. Popular stories and images of the United States as a land of opportunity—where men respect feminism and love strong, yet family-oriented, women—make their way into this script. The act of writing to a faceless man from the privacy of one's home or workplace adds an element of mystery. Away from strict families, the gossip of friends, and Catholic teachings of respectable codes of behavior, the Mexican woman finds herself alone and able to explore her new role with an audience that she hopes will interact with her with fresh eyes. With the spread of the Internet in Mexico, women can participate in the creation of new gender identities not only as consumers of images but also as actors forging new personas. Part of the lure of the Internet is that women can express themselves outside of local norms and customs and explore new aspects of themselves as their audience extends across national, cultural, and racial boundaries. The Internet is a springboard for acting out changing times, sexual desires, and new identities. Sherry Turkle describes the computer screen as the place where "we project ourselves into our own dramas, dramas in which we are producer, director and star. . . . Computer screens are the new location for our fantasies, both erotic and intellectual" (1995, 26). Women turn to the Internet to express their hopes, dreams, and intimate desires, and in the process, access information about other people and their lives.

The use of the Internet and matchmaking agencies rather than social networks to find relationships also marks a new way of thinking about love, courtship, and marriage. According to Mexican family traditions, a woman is expected to wait patiently and passively for a man to make the first move. Once a man publicly claims his desire for a woman, she is marked as his territory, and she may not see anyone else. The courtship period may last a couple of years or longer. During this time, the woman, called a *novia*, must not appear in places where she might be a sexual target for another man's desire. On the other hand, because masculinity depends on expressions of independence and fraternity with other males, men are afforded the liberty to frequent bars, clubs, and other social spaces. Furthermore, the man (*novio*) can have numerous sexual adventures with a variety of available women (Carrier 1995).

For women, the Internet proves to be an ideal place for less-restrictive forms of courtship. While women's bodies are guarded and watched closely, the Internet affords them the opportunity to communicate or date multiple people and to develop sexual intimacy in a society that heavily moralizes women's sexual activities outside of marriage.

I interviewed Blanca in her beautiful home, which is tucked away in a heavily guarded, gated community in one of the nicer areas of Guadalajara. She was an attractive and fit fifty-two-year-old who had divorced her husband after discovering that he had cheated on her with one of their neighbors. As she showed me around her home, she mentioned that the many large-screen televisions were gifts from a Mexican doctor she had dated. In order to maintain her lifestyle and put her son through one of the more prestigious universities in the area, she had taken on various jobs, from working in the United States as a nanny to inviting foreign students to reside with her while they attended school. She explained how restricted she felt: "Right now I am very confined, I almost never go out. I go out once in a while into the street and they follow me, people speak to me, but I don't like to get to know people off the street because I think, I *think* that they think that I am easy, and I'm not easy, I'm not an easy kind of woman." When asked whether it was also difficult for women to meet people at bars, she responded, "Well, look . . . another time I went out with some friends, only one time, we went out at night. It's not difficult, they had come up to me, but in reality they are people that are drinking, that think that if a woman goes to a bar . . . the men think that if one goes to a bar alone, she is looking for a sexual encounter."

Opportunities for women to meet a partner are limited to introductions by family and friends, and thus it is extremely difficult for older women who do not have strong social or family networks to meet someone. Blanca had tried various e-mail dating services and had even hosted matchmaking events at her home. When I last spoke to her, she had given up on foreign men and was dating another doctor from Mexico.

Anna also described a sense of isolation and the difficulty of finding a partner: "The truth is I've parted from my friendships and all social contacts that I could have had. But time has gone by and apart from feeling alone—in spite of having my kids and family—I felt the need to have someone else who I could express my feelings to and my thoughts about what is going on in my daily life. I realized that I couldn't have a life as a hermit. Men that I have known, I had only known through work relations. And the truth is that due to my job, my work as a mother and as the head of the household, I don't have much time to have a social life."

Even though Anna lives at home and has the support and care of her family, she does not have the time or energy to build a social world that would allow her to meet and date people. In fact, almost all of the women I interviewed had weak social networks because of obligations to their families, children, and jobs. Not only is a woman's presence in public space questioned, but she may have little time outside work and family to develop close relationships with others.

Women also enjoy having more control over the selection process through Internet dating. Teresa and I met at a traditional outdoor café in downtown Guadalajara. She was a single and confident forty-two-year-old, taking a break from a stressful life as a journalist to nurture and develop herself and her personal life. She said, "At the bar, most people select each other by their looks rather than on intelligence. The atmosphere of the bar does not allow for more in-depth conversations where you really get to know a person. . . . Yet on the Internet I can specify the man I want. I ask them personal and political questions and if they are not interested in responding in this way, I know that they don't want a woman who is intelligent."

Rather than adhering to the concept of love at first sight, many women want to get to know the inner life of a prospective partner before delving into an emotional relationship. Teresa told me she would be playful and witty to see how men responded to her playful intelligence. She could read between the lines in Internet conversations and quickly judge whether someone was open-minded and whether they respected a woman's confidence and intelligence. Interestingly, through various e-mail relationships, Teresa came to find Europeans more cultured, liberal, and open-minded than U.S. men and opted to use various online dating agencies rather than attend the vacation-tour parties. Similar to the motives that inspire online dating in the United States, Mexican use of Internet dating draws from modern ideas of intimacy and selfhood based on talk, rather than from passion and the desire for the advancement of the self through contact with others.[16]

Having a larger cultural context in which women can assess themselves contributes to the rising number of women who feel that they do not have to settle for traditional patterns of marriage. Through conversations with men on the tours and through Internet e-mails and chat rooms, women gather ammunition for constructing norms around love, relationships, and marriage not as natural but as culturally determined. Regarding her experiences with TLC Tours and e-mail conversations, Anna said, "I think my country is renowned for having people and customs very deep-rooted . . . and from here that machismo still remains to this day very strongly rooted in the values of men . . . but, at the same time, I like to know other people who already consider this as a lack of maturity and that it gives guidelines so the woman has her place in society and in her life with men."

According to Anna, her discussions with men who did not abide by the same cultural norms strengthened her convictions that men benefit from machismo while women do not. Anna also said that she had received good advice from people with whom she had been communicating. Because many women condone and perpetuate machista behavior, Anna was often unable to find others with whom she could share her inner thoughts and feelings.

Yet, women are not entirely free to create themselves in these cyber-exchanges. Men often write to multiple women, an expensive process given that it involves not just e-mail access and translating fees but also the cost of sending flowers and gifts, and even of visiting a select few. And because many men send women between $500 and $1,000 to take English classes, women feel they must give the man what he wants, to be the ideally docile and appreciative woman who is available when he needs her. Monica wrote an e-mail to a man who had sent her $500 for English lessons: "Regarding my English classes, I'm very proud because they named me as the honor student. . . . I still don't know much but as I told you before, I'm doing my best to learn fast . . . and also I don't want to disappoint you." Women can be constricted by the consumer's wants and needs and codes of reciprocity.

Conclusion

Such searches for U.S. husbands demonstrate how global imaginaries affect women's intimate lives. Global processes, by bringing people from unevenly developed areas into greater contact with one another, provide middle-class women from Third World countries new scenarios with which to reimagine gender roles and thus to extend what is possible in their local culture. Recent studies locate the "female underside of globalization" as the process whereby millions of women from "poor countries in the south migrate to do the 'women's work' of the north—work that affluent women (and men) are no longer able or willing to do" (Ehrenreich and Hochschild 2002, 3). Rather than extract raw resources from Third World countries, wealthy nations hope to import workers who provide better care, love, and sex. In a similar slant, U.S. men look to Mexican women as more capable wives and mothers—that is, more dedicated, feminine, and willing to serve their husbands—and to take on the role they say feminist, career-driven women no longer want. And Mexican women likewise look to U.S. men as better husbands and fathers than Mexican men and culture. Their perceptions of foreign men coincide with the image of the globetrotter—the sensitive, loyal businessman who is economically savvy, successful, and hardworking—an image that is not always realized. Contrasting expectations produce uneven results, especially because U.S. men hope to replace traditional family and gender arrangements, while some women hope to transcend them. As women increasingly create communities of belonging through consumption in a global marketplace, they see these marriages as an opportunity to solidify a transborder middle-class identity. While Mexican women may turn to global circuits (such as tourism and Internet communication) and Western culture to express modern notions of the individual and of relationships, as well as liberal capitalist notions of consumer power, women incorporate these ideas unevenly and alongside traditional notions of family unity and codes of femininity. Thus, these intimate exchanges produced by the Internet and matchmaking services complicate an easy binary between the United States and Mexico, between the traditional and the modern, and between the global and the national.

Cyberbride industries target increasingly diverse populations of women as Internet matchmaking services become a more accepted, accessible, and widespread means (mostly for the middle class in Mexico) of finding a partner that fulfills one's individual needs and desires. I hope to have disrupted an easy equation of the cyberbride industry, a global broker of love and marriage, as an institution that exploits poor, desperate, and unsuspecting women. Along with this is a hope for a more nuanced understanding of the ways emerging sectors of educated and misplaced women from the "third world" turn to foreign men to step outside the limits of what is possible at home. Women are savvy excavators of opportunities that offer more stable, open, and exciting relationships, marriages, and futures.

Notes

1 For an exception, see Constable 2003.
2 Aihwa Ong (1999) argues that scholars have tended to overlook complicated negotiations between the nation-state and transnational processes such as mobile capital and migration. While cultural studies scholars have celebrated agency and hybridity for those who move between nation-states, Ong demonstrates that "flexible citizens" are often complicit actors in processes of liberal capitalism.
3 For an account of the men involved in this industry, see Schaeffer-Grabiel 2006.

4 Sarah Levine and Clara Sunderland Correa find that the national fertility rates declined in the 1970s and 1980s; the average number of children Mexican women bore decreased from 6.7 in 1970 to 3.46 in 1989 (1993, 197).
5 See Hondagneu-Sotelo 1994, which quotes Cordera Campos and Tiburcio 1989 (114).
6 Mexican Matchmakers, although a legitimate introduction agency, was recently closed down because they owed money in back taxes. The media in Guadalajara, however, forged a different story about the closing down of this company. In an attempt to ruin the company's reputation and to prevent women from joining affiliated agencies in Guadalajara, media and radio programs incorrectly reported it was involved in the trafficking of prostitutes from Mexico to Russia. The company has reopened under the name Mexican Brides.
7 It is difficult to say how many women are signed up with these agencies, because some are members of more than one agency and the numbers of women change quickly. Mexican Matchmakers has anywhere from 200 to 500 female participants, although the numbers of active members may be lower. There are also over 300 Internet companies advertising women from Asia, Russia, the Caribbean, and Latin America.
8 The middle to upper classes in Mexico are more likely to hold visas because they can prove their return to Mexico through stable jobs, bank accounts, and the ownership of cars and/or property. In order to move to the United States, women must obtain a fiancée visa. Matchmaking agencies provide detailed information on their Web sites or at the actual agency and sometimes even sell "immigration kits" with all of the relevant paperwork and information.
9 I have changed the names of all of the women interviewed. Unless specified, quotes are from personal interviews that were transcribed. All translations from Spanish into English are my own.
10 See Hondagneu-Sotelo 1994. Arlie Hochschild and Anne Machung (1989) make a similar argument in their U.S.-based study.
11 See "Shock Jock Rails against Mexico's Modern Women," 2003.
12 On how women are marginally positioned within national agendas, see Yuval-Davis 1997; McClintock 1995; Kaplan, Alarcón, and Moallem 1999; Enloe 1989; Mayer 2000. On how their reproductive roles are both biological and ideological, see Yuval-Davis 1997; Kaplan, Alarcón, and Moallem 1999; Mayer 2000.
13 This offspring was later coined by José Vasconcelos (1997) to be the turbulent beginnings of the "la raza cósmica."
14 See Paz 1961.
15 Also see Hirsch 2003 for a more nuanced discussion of machismo in Mexican relationships and marriarge.
16 In his discussion of Internet relationships Michael Hardy (2004) refers to Anthony Giddens's idea of modern intimacy (1992) to understand the broader contexts of Internet dating.

Bibliography

Abu-Lughod, Abu. 1991. "Writing Against Culture." In *Recapturing Anthropology*, edited by Richard D. Fox, 137–62. Albuquerque, N.M.: School of American Research Press.

———. 1996. "Honor and Shame." In *Things As They Are: New Directions in Phenomenological Anthropology*, edited by Michael Jackson, 50–69. Bloomington: Indiana University Press.

Acuña, Beatriz. 1988. "Transmigración legal en la frontera México-Estados Unidos." *Revista Mexicana de Sociología* no. 4 (October–December): 277–322.

Acuña, Rodolfo. 1981. *Occupied America: A History of Chicanos*. 2d ed. New York: Harper and Row.

Adorno, Theodor. 1976. *Introduction to the Sociology of Music*. New York: Seabury Press.

Agamben, Giorgio. 1998. *Homo Sacer: Sovereign Power and Bare Life*. Stanford, Calif.: Stanford University Press.

———. 2000. *Form-of-Life*. Translated by Vincenzo Binetti and Cesare Casarino. Minneapolis: University of Minnesota Press.

Alegría, Tito. 1989. "La ciudad y los procesos transfronterizos entre México y Estados Unidos." *Frontera Norte* 1, no. 2: 53–90.

Alexander, M. Jacqui, and Chandra Talpade Mohanty. 1997. *Feminist Genealogies, Colonial Legacies, Democratic Futures*. New York: Routledge.

Allen, Beverly. 1996. *Rape Warfare: The Hidden Genocide in Bosnia-Herzegovina and Croatia*. Minneapolis: University of Minnesota Press.

Almaguer, Tomás. 1975. "Class, Race, and Chicano Oppression." *Socialist Revolution* 5: 71–99.

———. 1991. "Chicano Men: A Cartography of Homosexual Identity and Behavior." *Differences* 3: 75–100.

———. 1993. "Chicano Men: A Cartography of Homosexual Identity and Behavior." In *The Lesbian and Gay Studies Reader*, edited by Henry Abelove, Michéle Aina Barale, and David M. Halperin, 255–73. New York: Routledge.

Alonso, Ana María. 1995. *Thread of Blood: Colonialism, Revolution, and Gender on Mexico's Northern Frontier*. Tucson: University of Arizona.

Alonso, Ana María, and María Teresa Koreck. 1993. "Silences: 'Hispanics,' AIDS, and Sexual Practices." In *The Lesbian and Gay Studies Reader*, edited by Henry Abelove, Michéle Aina Barale, and David M. Halperin, 110–26. New York: Routledge.

Althusser, Louis. 1971. "Ideology and Ideological State Apparatuses (Notes toward an Investigation)." In *Lenin and Philosophy and Other Essays*, edited by Louis Althusser, 127–86. New York: Monthly Review Press.

Álvarez, Robert. *Familia: Migration and Adaptation in Baja and Alta California*. Berkeley: University of California Press, 1987.

Alvirez, David, and Frank D. Bean. 1976. "The Mexican American Family." In *Ethnic Families in America: Patterns and Variations*, edited by Charles H. Mindel and Robert W. Habenstein, 271–92. New York: Elsevier.

Amaro, Hortensia. 1988a. "Considerations for Prevention of HIV Infection among Hispanic Women." *Psychology of Women Quarterly* 12, no. 4: 429–44.

―――. 1988b. "Women in the Mexican-American Community: Religion, Culture, and Reproductive Attitudes and Experiences." *Community Psychology* 16: 6–20.

American Friends Service Committee. 1992. *Sealing Our Borders: The Human Toll*. Third Report of the Immigration Law Enforcement Monitoring Project. Philadelphia. February.

Americas Watch Committee. 1992. *Brutality Unchecked: Human Rights Abuses along the U.S. Border with Mexico*. New York: Human Rights Watch.

Amin, Samir. 1974. *Accumulation on a World Scale: A Critique of the Theory of Underdevelopment*. Translated by Brian Pearce. New York: Monthly Review Press.

Amnesty International. 1998. *United States of America: Human Rights Concerns in the Border Region with Mexico*. New York: Amnesty International.

Amott, Teresa, and Julie Matthei. 1996. *Race, Gender, and Work: A Multi-Cultural Economic History of Women in the United States*. Rev. ed. Boston: South End Press.

Amuchástegui, Ana. 1994. "La primera vez. El significado de la virginidad y la iniciación sexual para jóvenes mexicanos." Mexico City: Population Council.

―――. 2001. *Virginidad e Iniciación Sexual en México: Experiencias y Significados*. Mexico City: Edamex and Population Council.

Anderson, Joan B., and Martín De la Rosa. 1990. "Estrategias de sobrevivencia entre las familias pobres de la frontera." *La Ranura del Ojo*, October, 14–26.

Anderson, Michelle J. 1993. "A License to Abuse: The Impact of Conditional Status on Female Immigrants." *Yale Law Journal* 102, no. 6: 1401–30.

Andreas, Peter. 1998. "The U.S. Immigration Control Offensive: Constructing an Image of Order at the Southwest Border." In *Crossings: Mexican Immigration in Interdisciplinary Perspective*, edited by Marcelo Suárez-Orozco, 341–56. Cambridge, Mass.: Harvard University Press.

―――. 2000. *Border Games: Policing the US-Mexico Divide*. Ithaca, N.Y.: Cornell University Press.

Anglin, Mary K. 1998. "Feminist Perspectives on Structural Violence." *Identities* 5, no. 2: 145–51.

Anzaldúa, Gloria. 1987. *Borderlands, La Frontera: The New Mestiza*. San Francisco: Spinsters/Aunt Lute Book.

―――, ed. 1990. *Making Face, Making Soul/Haciendo Caras: Creative and Critical Perspectives by Feminists of Color*. San Francisco: Aunt Lute Books.

Aparicio, Frances R. 2003. "Jennifer as Selena: Rethinking Latinidad in Media and Popular Culture." *Latino Studies* 1, no. 1: 90–105.

———. 2004. "U.S. Latino Expressive Cultures." In *The Columbia History of Latinos in the United States Since 1960*, edited by David G. Gutiérrez, 355–90. New York: Columbia University Press.

Appadurai, Arjun. 1996. *Modernity at Large: Cultural Dimensions of Globalization*. Minneapolis: Minnesota University Press.

Applebaum, Richard, and Edna Bonacich. 2000. *Behind the Label: Inequality in the Los Angeles Apparel Industry*. Berkeley: University of California Press.

Ardener, Shirley. 1982. "Ground Rules and Social Maps for Women." In *Women and Space*, edited by Shirley Ardener, 11–32. New York: St. Martin's Press.

Arendt, Hannah. 1951. *The Origins of Totalitarianism*. New York: Harcourt, Brace.

Argüelles, Lourdes, and B. Ruby Rich. 1984. "Homosexuality, Homophobia, and Revolution: Notes toward an Understanding of the Cuban Lesbian and Gay Male Experience, part 1." *Signs* 9: 683–99.

———. 1985. "Homosexuality, Homophobia, and Revolution: Notes toward an Understanding of the Cuban Lesbian and Gay Male Experience, part 2." *Signs* 11: 120–35.

Argüelles, Lourdes, and Ann M. Rivero. 1988. "HIV Infection/AIDS and Latinas in Los Angeles County: Considerations for Prevention Treatment and Research Practice." *California Sociologist* 11: 69–89.

———. 1993. "Gender/Sexual Orientation Violence and Transnational Migration: Conversations with Some Latinas We Think We Know." *Urban Anthropology* 22, nos. 3–4: 259–75.

Arias, Patricia. 1985. *Guadalajara: La gran ciudad de la pequeña industria*. Zamora: El Colegio de Michoacan.

Arias, Patricia, and Fiona Wilson. 1997. *La aguja y el surco: Cambio regional, consumo y relaciones de género en la industria de la ropa en México*. Guadalajara: Universidad de Guadalajara.

Arizpe, Lourdes. 1979. *Indígenas en la ciudad de México: El caso de las "Marías."* Mexico City: Setentas, Diana.

———. 1982. *Etnicismo, Migración y Cambio Económico*. Mexico City: El Colegio de México.

———. 1994. *La mujer en el desarollo de Mexico y de America Latina*. Mexico City: Universidad Nacional Autónoma de México.

Arredondo, María Luisa. 2001. "Siempre hay una mañana: La Comisión de Los Angeles Contra los Asaltos a las Mujeres (LACAAW) tiene una línea de ayuda en español que atiende las 24 horas del día." *La Opinión*, 18 March, sec. Vida y Estilo, 1.

Arrow, Kenneth. 1987. "Economic Dimensions of Occupational Segregation: Comment I." *Signs* 1: 233–37.

Associated Press. 1999. "Women Raped by Border Patrol Agent Awarded $753,000." 14 October.

Axtman, Kris. 2002. "Border Mystery: 274 Murders in Nine Years." *Christian Science Monitor*, 2 May, 3.

Baca, Reynaldo, and Bryan Dexter. 1985. "Mexican Women, Migration and Sex Roles." *Migration Today* 13: 14–18.

Baker, Ross K., Laurily K. Epstein, and Rodney O. Forth. 1981. "Matters of Life and Death: Social, Political, Religious Correlates of Attitudes on Abortion." *American Politics Quarterly* 9: 89–102.

Balibar, Etienne. 1991. "Is There a Neo-Racism?" In *Race, Nation, Class: Ambiguous Identities*, edited by Etienne Balibar and Immanuel Wallerstein, 17–28. London: Verso.

Balls, Pamela, Kurt C. Organista, and Pearl R. Soloff. 1998. "Exploring AIDS-related Knowledge, Attitudes, and Behaviors of Female Migrant Workers." *Health and Social Work* 23, no. 2: 96–104.

Banks, Andy. 1991. "The Power and Promise of Community Unionism." *Labor Research Review* 18: 17–31.

Barber, Bob. 1994. "Overview: The Minority Communities of the South Coast." Santa Barbara, Calif.: Multicultural Community Partnership.

Barkley, B. H., and Enedina Salazar-Mosher. 1995. "Sexuality and Hispanic Culture: Counseling with Children and Their Parents." *Sex Education and Therapy* 21, no. 4: 255–67.

Barrera, D. Bassols, and C. Oehmichen Bazán. 2000. *Migración y relaciones de género en México*. Mexico City: Grupo Interdisciplinario sobre Mujer, Trabajo y Pobreza, A.C., and Universidad Nacional Autónoma de México.

Barrera, Mario. 1979. *Race and Class in the Southwest: A Theory of Racial Inequality*. Notre Dame, Ind.: University of Notre Dame Press.

Barrett, Michele. 1980. *Women's Oppression Today: Problems in Marxist Feminist Analysis*. London: Verso.

Basch, Linda, Nina Glick Schiller, and Cristina Szanton Blanc. 1994. *Nations Unbound: Transnational Projects, Postcolonial Predicaments and Deterritorialized Nation-states*. Amsterdam: Gordon and Breach.

Bauman, Richard, and Charles Briggs. 1990. "Poetics and Performance as Critical Perspectives on Language and Social Life." *Annual Review of Anthropology* 19: 59–88.

Bauman, Zygmunt. 1998. *Globalization: The Human Consequence*. New York: Columbia University Press.

———. 1989. *Modernity and the Holocaust*. Ithaca, N.Y.: Cornell University Press.

Bayer, Ronald. 1987. *Homosexuality and American Psychiatry: The Politics of Diagnosis*. 2nd ed. Princeton, N.J.: Princeton University Press.

Bean, Frank D., C. Gray Swicegood, and Ruth Berg. 2000. "Mexican-Origin Fertility: New Patterns and Interpretations." *Social Science Quarterly* 81: 404–20.

Bean, Frank D., C. Gray Swicegood, and Allan G. King. 1985. "Role Incompatibility and the Relationship between Fertility and Labor Supply among Hispanic Women." In *Hispanics in the U.S. Economy*, edited by George J. Borjas and Marta Tienda, 221–41. New York: Academic Press.

Becker, Gary S. 1975. *Human Capital*. Chicago: University of Chicago Press.

———. 1981. *A Treatise on the Family*. Cambridge, Mass.: Harvard University Press.

———. 1985. "Human Capital, Effort, and the Sexual Division of Labor." *Labor Economics* 3 (supplement): S33–S58.

Behar, Ruth. 1993. *Translated Women: Crossing the Border with Esperanza's Story*. Boston: Beacon Press.

Bejarano, Cynthia. 2002. "Las Super Madres de Latino América: Transforming Motherhood and Houseskirts by Challenging Violence in Juárez, Mexico, Argentina, and El Salvador." *Frontiers* 23, no. 1: 126–50.

Benería, Lourdes, and Shelley Feldman, eds. 1992. *Unequal Burden: Economic Crises, Persistent Poverty, and Women's Work*. Boulder, Colo.: Westview Press.

Benería, Lourdes, and Martha Roldán. 1987. *The Crossroads of Class and Gender: Industrial Homework, Subcontracting, and Household Dynamics in Mexico City*. Chicago: University of Chicago Press.

Benería, Lourdes, and Gita Sen. 1986. "Accumulation, Reproduction, and Women's Role in Economic Development: Boserup Revisited." In *Women's Work: Development and the Division of Labor by Gender*, edited by Eleanor Leacock and Helen I. Safa, 141–57. Massachusetts: Bergin and Garvey.

Benítez, Rohry, and Adriana Candia. 1999. *El silencio que la voz de todas quiebra: Mujeres y victimas de Ciudad Juarez*. Chihuahua, Mexico: Ediciones del Araz.

Benjamin, Walter. 1969a. *Reflections: Essays, Aphorisms, Autobiographical Writings*. Translated by Edmund Jephcott. Edited by Peter Demetz. New York: Harcourt Brace Jovanovich.

———. 1969b. "Theses on the Philosophy of History." In *Illuminations*, edited by Hannah Arendt, 257–58. New York: Schocken.

———. 1969c. "The Work of Art in the Age of Mechanical Reproduction." In *Illuminations*, edited by Hannah Arendt, 223. New York: Schocken.

Bensinger, Richard. 1991. "Committed to Organizing: An Interview with Richard Bensinger, Director, AFL-CIO Organizing Institute." *Labor Research Review* 18: 82–91.

Berg, Barbara J. 1986. *The Crisis of the Working Mother: Resolving the Conflict between Family and Work*. New York: Summit Books.

Berger, John. 1972. *Ways of Seeing*. Middlesex: British Broadcasting Corporation.

Bergman, Lowell, and Tim Golden. 1999. "Investigators Dig for Mass Graves at Mexico Border." *New York Times*, 30 November, A1.

Berlant, Lauren, and Elizabeth Freeman. 1992. "Queer Nationality." *Boundary* 2: 149–80.

Bernard, Jessie. 1974. *The Future of Motherhood*. New York: Penguin Books.

———. 1981. "The Rise and Fall of the Good Provider Role." *American Psychologist* 36: 1–12.

Bernstein, Ellen. n.d. "Impersonators Show Their Love through Imitation." *Corpus Christi Caller Times*, Interactive Online Selena Tribute. http://caller-times.com.

Bérubé, Allan. 1990. *Coming Out under Fire: The History of Gay Men and Women in World War II*. New York: Free Press.

Beruvides, Mario G., J. René Villalobos, and Scott T. Hutchinson. 1997. "High Turnover: Reduce the Impact." *Twin Plant News* 13, no. 3: 37–40.

Besserer, Federico. 1988. "Internacionalización de la fuerza de trabajo y conciencia de clase en la comunidad mixteca migrante de San Juan Mixtepec: Análisis de la historia de vida de Moisés Cruz. Tesis para acreditar las asignaturas 'Investigación de campo' y

'Seminario de investigación.'" Master's thesis, Universidad Autónoma Metropolitana, Unidad Iztapalapa.

Bhachu, Parminder. 1993. "Identities Constructed and Reconstructed: Representation of Asian Women in Britain." In *Migrant Women: Crossing Boundaries and Changing Identities*, edited by Gina Buijs, 99–113. Oxford: Berg Publishers.

Bielby, William T., and James N. Baron. 1987. "Undoing Discrimination: Job Integration and Comparable Worth." In *Ingredients for Women's Employment Policy*, edited by Christine Bose and Glenna Spitze, 211–29. New York: State University of New York Press.

Biemann, Ursula, director. 2000. *Writing Desire*. Film. New York: Women Make Movies.

Binion, Gayle. 1995. "Human Rights: A Feminist Perspective." *Human Rights Quarterly* 17: 509–26.

Biola, Heather. 1992. "The Black Washerwoman in Southern Tradition." In *History of Women in the United States: Domestic Ideology and Domestic Work*, edited by Nancy Cott, 307–16. Munich: K. G. Sauer.

Biron, Rebecca E. 1996. "Feminist Periodicals and Political Crisis in Mexico: *Fem, Debate Feminista*, and *La Correa Feminista* in the 1990s." *Feminist Studies* 22, no. 1: 151–69.

Bluestone, Barry, and Bennett Harrison. 1986. *The Deindustrialization of America*. Boston: Basic Books.

Blum, Linda, and Theresa Deussen. 1996. "Negotiating Independent Motherhood: Working-class African American Women Talk about Marriage and Motherhood." *Gender and Society* 10: 199–211.

Blumberg, Rae. 1991. "Income Under Female Versus Male Control: Hypotheses from a Theory of Gender Stratification and Data from the Third World." In *Gender, Family and Economy*, edited by Rae Blumberg, 97–127. Newbury Park: Sage Publications.

Bonacich, Edna. 2000. "Intense Challenges, Tentative Possibilities, Organizing Immigrant Garment Workers in Los Angeles." In *Organizing Immigrants: The Challenge for Unions in Contemporary California*, edited by Ruth Milkman, 130–49. Ithaca, N.Y.: ILR Press/Cornell University Press.

"Border Agent Pleads No Contest in Rape of Illegal Immigrant." 1994. *Arizona Republic*, 28 July, B2.

Borrego, John, and Patricia Zavella. 2000. *Policy Implications of the Restructuring of Frozen Food Production in North America and Its Impact on Watsonville, California*. Santa Cruz: University of California, Chicano/Latino Research Center.

Bourdieu, Pierre. 1999. *Acts of Resistance against the Tyranny of the Market*. Translated by Richard Nice. New York: New Press.

Bowden, Charles. 1996. "While You Were Sleeping: In Juárez, Mexico, Photographers Expose the Violent Realities of Free Trade." *Harper's*, December, 44–52.

———. 1998. *Juárez: The Laboratory of Our Future*. New York: Aperture.

———. 1999. "I Wanna Dance with the Strawberry Girl." *Talk*, September, 114–18.

Boyer, Richard. 1989. "Women, 'La Mala Vida,' and the Politics of Marriage." In *Sexuality and Marriage in Colonial Latin America*, edited by Asunción Lavrin, 252–86. Lincoln: University of Nebraska Press.

Bradley, Robert H., and Bettye M. Caldwell. 1984. "The Relation of Infants' Home Environments to Achievement Test Performance in First Grade: A Follow-up Study." *Child Development* 5: 803-9.

"Brain School." 1997. *Twin Plant News Staff Report* 12, no. 8: 39-41.

Breecher, Jeremy, and Tim Costello, eds. 1990. *Building Bridges: The Emerging Grassroots Coalition of Labor and Community.* New York: Monthly Review Press.

Brettel, Caroline, and Patricia Berjeois. 1992. "Anthropologists and the Study of Immigrant Women." In *Seeking Common Ground: Multidisciplinary Studies of Immigrant Women in the United States*, edited by Donna Gabaccia, 40-63. Westport, Conn.: Greenwood Press.

Bridges, Thomas. 1994. *The Culture of Citizenship: Inventing Postmodern Civic Culture.* Albany: State University of New York Press.

Brimelow, Peter. 1992. "Time to Rethink Immigration?" *National Review*, 22 June, 30-46.

———. 1996. *Alien Nation: Common Sense about America's Immigration Disaster.* New York: Harper Perennial.

Bronfenbrenner, Kate, Sheldon Friedman, Richard M. Hurd, Rudolph A. Oswald, and Ronald L. Seebers, eds. 1998. *Organizing to Win: New Research on Union Strategies.* Ithaca, N.Y.: ILR Press/Cornell University Press.

Bronfman, Mario, and Sergio López Moreno. 1996. "Perspectives on HIV/AIDS Prevention among Immigrants on the U.S.-Mexico Border." In *AIDS Crossing Borders*, edited by Shiraz Mishra, Ross F. Conner, and Raúl Magaña, 49-76. Boulder, Colo.: Westview Press.

Brooks, Peter. 1976. *The Melodramatic Imagination: Balzac, Henry James, Melodrama, and the Mode of Excess.* New Haven, Conn.: Yale University Press.

Brown, Robin. 1994. *Children in Crisis.* New York: H. W. Wilson.

Browner, Carole H. 1986. "The Politics of Reproduction in a Mexican Village." *Signs* 11: 710-24.

———. 2000. "Situating Women's Reproductive Activities." *American Anthropologist* 102: 773-88.

Browning, Harley L., and Rodolfo O. de la Garza, eds. 1986. *Mexican Immigrants and Mexican Americans: An Evolving Relation.* Austin: University of Texas, Center for Mexican American Studies.

Brownmiller, Susan. 1975. *Against Our Will: Men, Women and Rape.* New York: Simon and Schuster.

———. 1993. "Making Female Bodies the Battlefield." *Newsweek*, 4 January, 37.

Broyles-Gonzalez, Yolanda. 2002. "Ranchera Music(s) and the Legendary Lydia Mendoza: Performing Social Location and Relations." In *Chicana Traditions: Continuity and Change*, edited by Norma E. Cantú and Olga Nájera-Ramírez, 183-206. Champagne: University of Illinois Press.

Brubaker, William R. 1989. *Immigration and the Politics of Citizenship in Europe and North America.* Lanham, Md.: University Press of America.

Buchanan, Patrick J. 1994. "What Will America Be in 2050?" *Los Angeles Times*, 28 October, B7.

Buck-Morss, Susan. 1989. *The Dialectics of Seeing: Walter Benjamin and the Arcades Project.* Cambridge: MIT Press.

Buijs, Gina. 1993. *Migrant Women: Crossing Boundaries and Changing Identities: Cross Cultural Perspectives on Women*. Oxford, U.K.: Berg Publishers.

Burawoy, Michael. 1976. "The Functions and Reproduction of Migrant Labor: Comparative Material from Southern Africa and the United States." *American Journal of Sociology* 81: 1050–87.

———. 1979. *Manufacturing Consent: Changes in the Labor Process under Monopoly Capitalism*. Chicago: University of Chicago Press, 1979.

———. 1985. *The Politics of Production*. New York: Verso.

———. 2001. "Grounding Globalization." In *Global Ethnography: Forces, Connections, and Imaginations in a Post-modern World*, edited by Michael Burawoy, Joseph A. Blum, Sheba George, Zuzsa Gille, and Millie Thayer, 337–50. Berkeley: University of California Press.

Buriel, Raymond. 1984. "Integration with Traditional Mexican-American Culture and Sociocultural Adjustment." In *Chicano Psychology*, edited by Joseph L. Martinez Jr. and Richard H. Mendoza, 95–130. New York: Academic Press.

Buriel, Raymond, Silverio Caldaza, and Richard Vasquez. 1982. "The Relationship of Traditional Mexican American Culture to Adjustment and Delinquency among Three Generations of Mexican American Adolescents." *Hispanic Journal of Behavioral Sciences* 4: 50.

Burns, Melinda. 1994. "Issue Hits Home in Montecito." *Santa Barbara News Press*, 29 October, A1.

Burr, Ramiro. 1996a. "Selena's Impact Still Felt." *Minneapolis Star Tribune*, 31 March, F9.

———. 1996b. "Women Helping Drive Thriving Mexican Market." *Billboard* 108, no. 1: 93, 101.

———. 2001. "Sanz, Juanes Top Latin Grammys: TV Coverage Was Canceled Due to Attacks." *San Antonio Express*, 31 October, 2A.

Buss, Fran Leeper, ed. 1993. *Forged under the Sun/Forjado bajo el sol: The Life of Maria Elena Lucas*. Ann Arbor: University of Michigan Press.

Bustamante, Jorge A. 1989. "Medición del flujo de inmigrantes indocumentados." In *Retos de las relactiones entre México y Estados Unidos*, edited by Jorge A. Bustamante and Wayne A. Cornelius, 115–30. Mexico City: Fondo de Cultura Económica.

———. 1991. "Reporte de los resultados preliminares del proyecto de investigación 'Cañon Zapata.'" Mimeograph. Tijuana: El Colegio de la Frontera Norte.

Bustamante, Jorge A., and James D. Cockroft. 1983. "Unequal Exchange in the Binational Relationship: The Case of Immigrant Labor." In *Mexican-U.S. Relations: Conflict and Convergence*, edited by Carlos Vásquez and Manuel García, 309–23. Los Angeles: University of California, Chicano Studies Research Center and Latin American Center.

Butler, Judith. 1993. *Bodies That Matter: On the Discursive Limits of "Sex."* New York: Routledge.

———. 1997. "Merely Cultural." *Social Text* 52, no. 53: 265–77.

Cabrera, Cloe. 2000. "Latina Teens Help Each Other Deal with Problem Issues." *Tampa Tribune*, 20 July, 4.

Calavita, Kitty. 1992. *Inside the State: The Bracero Program, Immigration, and the I.N.S.* New York: Routledge.

———. 1996. "The New Politics of Immigration: 'Balanced-budget Conservatism' and the Symbolism of Proposition 187." *Social Problems* 43, no. 3: 284–305.

California Department of Health Services. 2000a. "AIDS Cases among the Mexican Origin Populations in California." California Office of AIDS. http://www.dhs.ca.gov/aids/.

———. 2000b. "An Epidemiologic Profile of Women and Children with HIV/AIDS in California." http://www.dhs.cahwnet.gov.

California Primary Care Association. 1999. "Position Statement on Prenatal Care Funding for Non-Citizens." http://www.cpca.org (accessed 13 January 1999).

California Program on Access to Care. 2001. "Access to Health Care for California's Hired Farm Workers: A Baseline Report." Berkeley: University of California.

California Rural Legal Assistance Foundation. 2004. "Stop Gatekeeper! Migrant Deaths." www.stopgatekeeper.org (accessed 15 November 2004).

California State Data Center. 1995. "1990 Census of the Population and Housing." Summary Tape File 4. Sacramento: California Data Center.

Cancian, Frank. 1965. *Economics and Prestige in a Maya Community: The Religious Cargo System in Zinacantán*. Stanford, Calif.: Stanford University Press.

Canedy, Dana. 2001. "Discord over Miami's Bid for Latin Grammys." *New York Times*, 30 March, A14.

Cantú, Lionel. 1999. "Border Crossings: Mexican Men and the Sexuality of Migration." Ph.D. diss., University of California, Irvine.

Cardenas, Gilberto, and Estevan T. Flores. 1986. *The Migration and Settlement of Undocumented Women*. Austin: University of Texas, Center for Mexican American Studies.

Carens, Joseph H. 1987. "Aliens and Citizens: The Case for Open Borders." *The Review of Politics* 49, no. 2: 251–73.

———. 1989. "Membership and Morality: Admission to Citizenship in Liberal Democratic States." In *Immigration and the Politics of Citizenship in Europe and North America*, edited by William R. Brubaker, 31–49. Lanham, Md.: University Press of America.

Carrier, Joseph M. 1995. *De los otros: Intimacy and Homosexuality among Mexican Men*. New York: Columbia University Press.

Carrillo, Jorge V., ed. 1990. *La nueva era de la industria automotriz en México*. Tijuana: Colegio de la Frontera Norte (COLEF).

Carillo, Teresa. 1990. "Women, Trade Unions, and New Social Movements in Mexico: The Case of the 'Nineteenth of September' Garment Workers Union." Unpublished paper.

———. 1998. "Cross-Border Talk: Transnational Perspectives on Labor, Race, and Sexuality." In *Talking Visions: Multicultural Feminism in a Transnational Age*, edited by Ella Habiba Shohat, 391–411. Cambridge: MIT Press.

Caspi, Avshalom, and Glen H. Elder Jr. 1988. "Emergent Family Patterns: The Intergenerational Construction of Problem Behaviour and Relationships." In *Relationships within Families: Mutual Influences*, edited by Robert A. Hinde and Joan Stevenson-Hinde, 218–40. New York: Oxford University Press.

Castañeda, Antonia I. 1990. "Anglo Images of Nineteenth Century Californianas." In *Between Borders: Essays on Mexicana/Chicano History*, edited by Adelaida Del Castillo, 213–36. Los Angeles: Floricanto Press.

———. 1993. "Sexual Violence in the Politics and Policies of Conquest." In *Building with our Hands: New Directions in Chicana Studies*, edited by Adela de la Torre and Beatríz Pesquera, 13–33. Berkeley: University of California Press.

Castañeda, Xóchitl, Claire Brindis, and Itza Castañeda. 2001. "Nebulous Margins: Sexuality and Social Constructions of Risks in Rural Areas of Central Mexico." In *Culture, Health and Sexuality*, edited by Peter Aggleton, 203–19. London: Taylor and Francis Health Sciences.

Castañeda, Xóchitl, Victor Ortiz, Betania Allen, Cecilia García, and Mauricio Hernández-Avila. 1996. "Sex Masks: The Double Life of Female Commercial Sex Workers in Mexico City." *Culture Medicine and Psychiatry* 20: 229–47.

Castañon, Araly. 1998. "Buscan igualdad laboral." *El Diario de Ciudad Juárez*, 10 October, C3.

———. 2002. "Exige ONG salvaguardar integridad de mujeres." *El Diario*. http://www.diario.com.mx.

Castells, Manuel, and Alejandro Portes. 1989. "World Underneath: The Origins, Dynamics, and Effects of the Informal Economy." In *The Informal Economy: Studies in Advanced and Less Developed Countries*, edited by Alejandro Portes, Manuel Castells, and Lauren Benton, 11–27. Baltimore: Johns Hopkins University Press.

Castillo, Debra A. 1998. *Easy Women: Sex and Gender in Modern Mexican Fiction*. Minneapolis: University of Minnesota Press.

Castro, Felipe G., Gloria J. Romero, and Richard C. Cervantes. 1987. "Long Term Stress among Latino Women after a Plant Closure." *Sociology and Social Research* 71, no. 2: 85–87.

Catanzarite, Lisa. 2000. "'Brown Collar Jobs': Occupational Segregation and Earnings of Recent-immigrant Latinos." *Sociological Perspectives* 43, no. 1: 45–75.

Center for AIDS Prevention Studies. 2001a. "Fact Sheet for Latinos." University of California San Francisco AIDS Research Institute. http://www.caps.ucsf.edu.

———. 2001b. "What Are Latinos' HIV Prevention Needs?" University of California San Francisco AIDS Research Institute. http://www.caps.ucsf.edu.

Centers for Disease Control and Prevention. 1994. *HIV/AIDS Surveillance Report*. Vol. 6. Atlanta: Centers for Disease Control and Prevention.

Cerrutti, Marcela, and Douglas S. Massey. 2001. "On the Auspices of Female Migration from Mexico to the United States." *Demography* 38, no. 2: 187–200.

Cesarani, David, and Mary Fulbrook. 1996. *Citizenship, Nationality and Migration in Europe*. New York: Routledge.

Chancer, Lynn. 1998. "The Beauty Context: Looks, Social Theory and Feminism." In *Reconcilable Differences: Confronting Beauty, Pornography and the Future of Feminism*, 82–172. Berkeley: University of California Press.

Chaney, Elsa, and María García Castro. 1989. *Muchachas No More, Household Workers in Latin America and the Caribbean*. Philadelphia: Temple University Press.

Chang, Grace. 1994. "Undocumented Latinas: Welfare Burdens or Beasts of Burden?" *Socialist Review* 23: 151–85.

Chant, Sylvia. 1985. "Family Formation and Female Roles in Querétaro, Mexico." *Bulletin of Latin American Research* 4, no. 1: 17–32.

———. 1991. *Women and Survival in Mexican Cities: Perspectives on Gender, Labor Markets and Low-Income Households*. Manchester, U.K.: Manchester University Press.

———. 1992. *Gender and Migration in Developing Countries*. London: Belhaven Press.

———. 1994. "Women, Work and Household Survival Strategies in Mexico, 1982-1992: Past Trends, Current Tendencies and Future Research." *Bulletin of Latin American Research* 13, no. 2: 203-33.

Chapin, Jessica. 1998. "Closing America's 'Back Door.'" *GLQ* 4, no. 3: 403-22.

Chapman, Leonard F., Jr. 1974. "'Silent Invasion' that Takes Millions of Americans' Jobs." *U.S. News and World Report*, 9 December, 77-78.

Chavez, John M., and Raymond Buriel. 1986. "Reinforcing Children's Effort: A Comparison of Immigrant, Native-Born Mexican American and Euro-American Mothers." *Hispanic Journal of Behavioral Sciences* 8: 127-42.

Chavez, Leo R. 1985. "Households, Migration, and Labor Market Participation: The Adaptation of Mexicans to Life in the United States." *Urban Anthropology* 14, no. 4: 301-46.

———. 1988. "Settlers and Sojourners: The Case of Mexicans in California." *Human Organization* 47, no. 2: 95-108.

———. 1990. "Coresidence and Residence: Strategies for Survival Among Undocumented Mexicans and Central Americans in the United States." *Urban Anthropology* 19, nos. 1 and 2: 31-62.

———. 1991. "Outside the Imagined Community: Undocumented Settlers and Experiences of Incorporation." *American Ethnologist* 18: 257-78.

———. 1997. "Immigration Reform and Nativism: The Nationalist Response to the Transnationalist Challenge." In *Immigrants Out! The New Nativism and the Anti-Immigrant Impulse in the United States*, edited by Juan F. Perea, 61-77. New York: New York University Press.

———. 1998. *Shadowed Lives: Undocumented Immigrants in American Society*. 2d ed. Fort Worth, Tex.: Harcourt, Brace, Jovanovich.

———. 2001. *Covering Immigration: Popular Images and the Politics of the Nation*. Berkeley: University of California Press.

Chavez, Leo R., F. Allan Hubbell, Juliet M. McMullin, Rebecca G. Martinez, and Shiraz I. Mishra. 1995. "Structure and Meaning in Models of Breast and Cervical Cancer Risk Factors: A Comparison of Perceptions among Latinas, Anglo Women, and Physicians." *Medical Anthropology Quarterly* 9: 40-74.

Chavez, Leo R., F. Allan Hubbell, Shiraz I. Mishra, and R. Burciaga Valdez. 1997. "Undocumented Immigrants in Orange County, California: A Comparative Analysis." *International Migration Review* 31: 88-107.

Chavez, Leo R., Juliet M. McMullin, Shiraz I. Mishra, and F. Allan Hubbell. 2001. "Beliefs Matter: Cultural Beliefs and the Use of Cervical Cancer Screening Tests." *American Anthropologist* 103: 1114-29.

Chavira, Alicia. 1988. "Tienes que ser valiente! Mexican Migrants in a Midwestern Farm Labor Camp." In *Mexicanas at Work in the United States*, edited by Margarita B. Melville, 64-74. Houston: University of Texas, Houston, Mexican American Studies Program.

Chavira-Prado, Alicia. 1992. "Work, Health, and the Family: Gender Structure and Women's Status in a Mexican Undocumented Migrant Population." *Human Organization* 51, no. 1: 53–64.

———. n.d. "Gender Difference and Marginalized Immigrants: Tarascan Women as Household Providers and Settlers." Unpublished manuscript.

Cheng, Lucie, and Edna Bonacich. 1984. *Labor Immigration under Capitalism: Asian Workers in the United States Before World War II*. Berkeley: University of California Press.

Childress, Alice. 1986. *Like One of the Family: Conversations from a Domestic's Life*. Boston: Beacon.

Chiñas, Beverly. 1973. *The Isthmus Zapotecs: Women's Roles in Cultural Context*. New York: Holt, Rinehart, and Wilson.

Chinchilla, Norma Stoltz, and Nora Hamilton. 1996. "Negotiating Urban Space: Latina Workers in Domestic Work and Street Vending in Los Angeles." *Humbolt Journal of Social Relations* 22: 25–35.

Chock, Phyllis Pease. 1996. "No New Women: Gender, 'Alien,' and 'Citizen' in the Congressional Debate on Immigration." *Political and Legal Anthropology Review* 19: 1–9.

Chodorow, Nancy. 1979. *The Reproduction of Mothering*. Berkeley: University of California Press.

Chomsky, Noam. 1998. "Notes on NAFTA: The Masters of Mankind." Preface to *Juárez: The Laboratory of our Future*, edited by Charles Bowden, 13–20. New York: Aperture.

Citizens for Legal Immigration/Save Our State. n.d. "Proposition 187: The 'Save Our State' Initiative: The Questions and the Answers." Orange County, Calif.: Citizens for Legal Immigration/Save Our State.

Clark, Eugene E., and William Ramsey. 1990. "The Importance of Family and Network of Other Relationships in Children's Success in School." *International Journal of Sociology of the Family* 20: 237–54.

Clark-Lewis, Elizabeth. 1994. *Living-In, Living-Out: African-American Domestics in Washington, D.C., 1900–1940*. Washington: Smithsonian Institution Press.

Cleeland, and Rabin. 2000. "Gore's Presence at Rally Boosts Janitors' Spirits." *Los Angeles Times*, 17 April, B1, 4.

Cleeland, Nancy. 1997. "Making Santa Ana Home." *Los Angeles Times*, 4 August, A22.

Cobble, Dorothy Sue. 1994. "The Prospects for Unionism in a Service Society." In *Working in the Service Society*, edited by Cameron Lynne Macdonald and Carmen Sirianni, 333–58. Philadelphia: Temple University Press.

Cock, Jacklyn. 1980. *Maids and Madams*. Johannesburg: Ravan Press.

Cockburn, Cynthia. 1985. *Machinery of Dominance*. London: Pluto Press.

Colen, Shellee. 1986. "With Respect and Feelings: Voices of West Indian Domestic Workers in New York City." In *All-American Women*, edited by Johnetta Cole, 46–70. New York: Free Press.

———. 1989. "Just a Little Respect: West Indian Domestic Workers in New York City." In *Muchachas No More: Household Workers in Latin America and the Caribbean*, edited by Elsa Chaney and María García Castro, 171–96. Philadelphia: Temple University Press.

———. 1990. "'Housekeeping' for the Green Card: West Indian Household Workers, the State, and Stratified Reproduction in New York." In *At Work in Homes: Household Workers in World Perspective*, edited by Roger Sanjek and Shellee Colen, 89–118. Washington: American Anthropological Association.

———. 1995. "Like a Mother to Them: Stratified Reproduction and West Indian Child Care Workers and Employers in New York." In *Conceiving the New World Order*, edited by Faye Ginsburg and Rayna Rapp, 78–102. Berkeley: University of California Press.

Coley, Soraya Moore. 1981. "'And Still I Rise': An Exploratory Study of Contemporary Black Private Household Workers." Bryn Mawr, Penn.: Bryn Mawr College.

Collier, Jane Fishburne, and Sylvia Junko Yanagisako. 1987. *Gender and Kinship: Essays toward a Unified Analysis*. Stanford, Calif.: Stanford University Press.

Collins, Patrica Hill. 1990. *Black Feminist Thought: Knowledge, Consciousness and the Politics of Empowerment*. New York: Routledge.

———. 1994. "Shifting the Center: Race, Class, and Feminist Theorizing About Motherhood." In *Mothering: Ideology, Experience, and Agency*, edited by Evelyn Nakano Glenn, Grace Chang, and Linda Rennie Forcey, 45–65. New York: Routledge.

———. 1999. "Will the 'Real' Mother Please Stand Up? The Logic of Eugenics and American Family Planning." In *Revisioning Women, Health, and Healing: Feminist, Cultural, and Technoscience Perspectives*, edited by Adele E. Clarke and Virginia L. Olesen, 266–82. New York: Routledge.

Committee of the Judiciary, Subcommittee no. 1, House of Representatives. 1963. "Inquiry into the Alien Medical Examination Program of the U.S. Public Health Service, Special Series no. 12." In *Study of Immigration and Population Problems*. Washington: Government Printing Office.

Compa, Lance. 2000. *Unfair Advantage: Workers' Freedom of Association in the United States under International Human Rights Standards*. Ithaca, N.Y. ILR Press/Cornell University Press.

Concha, Miguel. 2001. "Contra la violencia familiar." *La Jornada*, 7 April, 19.

Connell, Robert W. 1987. *Gender and Power*. Stanford: Stanford University Press.

———. 1995a. *Masculinities*. Berkeley: University of California Press.

———. 1995b. "Sociology and Human Rights." *Australian and New Zealand Journal of Sociology* 31: 25–29.

Connelly, Michael. 1992. "Jury Acquits INS Officer in Rapes." *Los Angeles Times*, 28 February, B1.

Connelly, Michael, and Patricia Klein Lerner. 1990. "INS Agent Faces More Sex Charges." *Los Angeles Times*, 15 June, B3.

Conniff, Ruth. 1993. "The War on Aliens: The Right Calls the Shots." *Progressive* 54, no. 10: 22–29.

Consejo Nacional de Población. 2000. "Reporte sobre migración México-Estados Unidos, present y future." Mexico City: Consejo Nacional de Población.

———. 2003. "(Mexican) National Fertility Rates, 1960–2000." A Report of the Mexican Government, Federal Institute for Access to Public Information. http://www.conapo.gob.mx.

Constable, Nicole. 1997. *Maid to Order in Hong Kong*. Ithaca, N.Y.: Cornell University Press.

———. 2003. *Romance on a Global Stage: Pen Pals, Virtual Ethnography, and "Mail-Order" Marriages*. Berkeley: University of California Press.

Cordera Campos, Rolando, and Enrique González Tiburcio. 1989. "Percances y damnificados de la crisis económica." In *México: El Reclamo Democratico*, edited by Cordera Campos Rolando, Raúl Trejo Delarbre, and Juan Enrique Vega. Mexico City: Siglo Veintiuno Editores.

Cornelius, Wayne A. 1989. "The U.S. Demand for Mexican Labor." In *Mexican Migration to the United States: Origins, Consequences, and Policy Options*, edited by Wayne A. Cornelius and Jorge A. Bustamante, 25–47. La Jolla, Calif.: Bilateral Commission on the Future of U.S.-Mexican Relations.

———. 1991. "Los migrantes de la crisis: The Changing Profile of Mexican Migration to the United States." In *Social Responses to Mexico's Economic Crisis*, edited by M. González de la Rocha and A. Escobar Latapí, 155–94. San Diego: Center for U.S.-Mexican Studies.

———. 1992. "From Soujourners to Settlers: The Changing Profile of Mexican Immigration to the United States." In *US-Mexico Relations: Labor Market Interdependence*, edited by Jorge Bustamante, Clark Reynolds, and Raul Hinojosa Ojeda, 155–95. Stanford, Calif.: Stanford University Press.

———. 2001. "Death at the Border: Efficacy and Unintended Consequences of US Immigration Control Policy." *Population and Development Review* 27, no. 4: 661.

Corona, Rodolfo. 1991. "Principales características demográficas de la zona fronteriza del norte de México." *Frontera Norte* 3, no. 5: 141–56.

Cott, Nancy. 1992. *History of Women in the United States: Domestic Ideology and Domestic Work*. Munich: K. G. Sauer.

Coutin, Susan Bibler, and Phyllis Pease Chock. 1995. "'Your Friend, the Illegal': Definition and Paradox in Newspaper Accounts of US Immigration Reform." *Identities* 2, nos. 1 and 2: 123–48.

Cowan, Ruth Schwartz. 1987. "Women's Work, Housework, and History: The Historical Roots of Inequality in Work-Force Participation." In *Families and Work*, edited by Naomi Gerstel and Harriet Engel Gross, 164–77. Philadelphia: Temple University.

Cranford, Cynthia. 1998. "Gender and Citizenship in the Restructuring of Janitorial Work in Los Angeles." *Gender Issues* 16, no. 4: 25–51.

———. 2001. "Labor, Gender and the Politics of Citizenship: Organizing Justice for Janitors in Los Angeles." Ph.D. diss., Department of Sociology, University of Southern California, Los Angeles.

Cravey, Altha J. 1998. *Women and Work in Mexico's Maquiladoras*. Lanham, Md.: Rowman and Littlefield.

Crawley, Heaven. 2000. "Engendering the State in Refugee Women's Claims for Asylum." In *States of Conflict*, edited by Susie Jacobs, Ruth Jacobson, and Jennifer Marchbank, 87–104. New York: Zed Books.

Crummett, María de los Ángeles. 1986. "La mujer rural y la migración en América Latina: 1986: Investigación, políticas y perspectivas." In *La mujer y la política agraria en*

América Latina, edited by Carmen Diana Deere and Magdalena León de Leal, 209–27. Bogotá, Colombia: Asociación Colombiana para el Estudio de la Población; Mexico City: Siglo Veintiuno Editores.

Crump, Joe. 1991. "The Pressure Is On: Organizing Without the NLRB." *Labor Research Review* 18: 33–43.

Cruz, Angeles. 2002. "Letra muerta, ley contra violencia interfamiliar." *La Jornada*, 26 May, 43.

Cruz, Angeles, and Roberto Garduño. 2001. "Fox: La mujer, nuevo actor político 'indispensable': promete igualdad." *La Jornada*, 9 March, 41.

"Cutoff of Prenatal Care for Illegal Immigrants Allowed." 1994. *Los Angeles Times*, 13 November, A28.

Dávila, Arlene. 2001. *Latinos, Inc.: The Marketing and Making of a People*. Berkeley: University of California Press.

Davis, Angela Y. 1998. *Blues Legacies and Black Feminism*. New York: Pantheon Books.

Davis, Mike. 1987. "Chinatown Part 2? The Internationalization of Downtown Los Angeles." *New Left Review* 164: 65–86.

Dawson, Deborah A., and Ann M. Hardy. 1989. "AIDS Knowledge and Attitudes of Hispanic Americans." National Center for Health Statistics Advance Data.

Deacon, Mitch. 2001. "Juárez Groups Demand Justice as Murders Continue." *News Staff*, 15 November. http://www.us-mex.org.

Decierdo, Margarita. 1991. "A Mexican Migrant Family in North Carolina." *Aztlán* 20, nos. 1 and 2: 183–94.

De Genova, Nicholas P. 2002. "Migrant 'Illegality' and Deportability in Everyday Life." *Annual Review in Anthropology* 31, no. 4: 19–47.

De Genova, Nicholas P., and Ana Y. Ramos-Zayas. 2003a. "Latino Racial Formations in the United States: An Introduction." *Latin American Anthropology* 8, no. 2: 2–17.

———. 2003b. "Latino Rehearsals: Racialization and the Politics of Citizenship between Mexicans and Puerto Ricans in Chicago." *Journal of Latin American Anthropology* 8, no. 2: 18–57.

de la Cruz, Elena. 1996a. "En busca de Selena." *La Opinión*, 15 March, D1.

———. 1996b. "Quién quiere ser Selena?" *La Opinión*, 18 March, D1.

de la O Martínez, María Eugenia. 1995. "Maquila, mujer y cambios productivos: Estudio de caso en la industria maquiladora de Ciudad Juárez." In *Mujeres, migración y maquila en la frontera norte*, edited by Soledad González Montes, Olivia Ruiz, Laura Velasco, and Ofelia Woo, 241–70. Mexico City: El Colegio de la Frontera Norte and El Colegio de México.

de la Rocha, Mercedes Gonzalez. 1986. *Los recursos de la pobreza: Familias de bajo ingresos de Guadalajara*. Guadalajara: El Colegio de Jalisco.

de la Torre, Adela. 1993. "Hard Choices and Changing Roles among Mexican Migrant Campesinas." In *Building with Our Hands: New Directions in Chicana Studies*, edited by Adela De la Torre and Beatríz M. Pesquera, 168–80. Berkeley: University of California Press.

de la Torre, Adela, and Beatríz M. Pesquera, eds. 1993. *Building with Our Hands: New Directions in Chicana Studies*. Berkeley: University of California Press.

Delauney, Daniel. 1995. "Mujeres migrantes: Las Mexicanas en los Estados Unidos." *Estudios Demograficos y Urbanos* 10, no. 3: 607–51.

del Carmen de Lara, María, director. 2000. *La Vida Sigue*. Film. Mexico City: CONSIDA (Consejo Nacional para la Prevención y Control del Síndrome de la Immunodeficiencia Adquirida).

Del Castillo, Adelaida R. 1993. "Covert Cultural Norms and Sex/Gender Meaning: A Mexico City Case." *Urban Anthropology* 22, nos. 3–4: 237–58.

———. 1997. "Postnational Citizenship in Los Angeles." Paper presented at conference, Women and Migration in Latin America and the Caribbean, Princeton University, Princeton, N.J., 1–2 March.

DeLey, Margo, and Rita J. Simon. 1987. "The Work Experiences of Undocumented Mexican Women Migrants in LA." *International Migration Review* 18, no. 4: 1212–29.

Delgado-Gaitan, Concha. 2001. *The Power of Community: Mobilizing for Family and Schooling*. Lanham, Md.: Rowman and Littlefield.

Del Rosario, Virginia. 1994. "Lifting the Smoke Screen: Dynamics of Mail-Order Bride Migration from the Philippines." Ph.D. diss., Institute of Social Studies, The Hague, Netherlands.

Denman, Catalina A., Janice Monk, and Norma Ojeda de la Peña, eds. 2004. *Compartiendo historias de fronteras: Cuerpos, géneros, generaciones y salud*. Hermosillo, Mexico: El Colegio de Sonora.

Deutsch, Sarah. 1987. *No Separate Refuge: Culture, Class, and Gender on an Anglo-Hispanic Frontier in the American Southwest, 1880–1940*. New York: Oxford University Press.

Dever, G. E. Allen. 1991. *Profile of a Population with Complex Health Problems*. Austin: National Migrant Resource Program.

Diamond, Elin. 1997. *Unmaking Mimesis*. New York: Routledge.

Diaz, May N. 1966. *Tonalá: Conservatism, Responsibility, and Authority in a Mexican Town*. Berkeley: University of California Press.

Díaz, Rafael M. 1998. *Latino Gay Men and HIV: Culture, Sexuality, and Risk Behavior*. New York: Routledge.

Diaz Barriga, Miguel. 1996. "Necesidad: Notes on the Discourses of Urban Politics in the Ajusco Foothills of Mexico City." *American Ethnologist* 23, no. 2: 291–310.

Díaz Olavarrieta, Claudia, and Julio Sotelo. 1996. "Domestic Violence in Mexico (Letter from Mexico City)." *Journal of the American Medical Association* 275, no. 24: 1937–41.

DiClemente, Ralph J., Cherrie B. Boyer, and Edward S. Morales. 1988. "Minorities and AIDS: Knowledge, Attitudes, and Misconceptions among Black and Latino Adolescents." *Public Health Briefs* 78, no. 1: 55–57.

di Leonardo, Micaela. 1984. *The Varieties of Ethnic Experience: Kinship, Class, and Gender among California Italian-Americans*. Ithaca, N.Y.: Cornell University Press.

———. 1991. Introduction. In *Gender at the Crossroads of Knowledge: Feminist Anthropology in the Postmodern Era*, edited by Micaela di Leonardo, 1–48. Berkeley: University of California Press.

Dill, Bonnie Thornton. 1988. "Our Mothers' Grief: Racial-ethnic Women and the Maintenance of Families." *Family History* 13: 415–31.

———. 1994a. *Across the Boundaries of Race and Class: An Exploration of Work and Family among Black Female Domestic Servants.* New York: Garland Press.

———. 1994b. "Fictive Kin, Paper Sons and Compadrazgo: Women of Color and the Struggle for Family Survival." In *Women of Color in U.S. Society*, edited by Maxine Baca Zinn and Bonnie Thornton Dill, 149–69. Philadelphia: Temple University Press.

Dill, Bonnie Thornton, Lynn Weber Cannon, and Reeve Vanneman. 1987. *Pay Equity: An Issue of Race, Ethnicity and Sex.* Washington: National Commission on Pay Equity.

Dinerman, Ina R. 1978. "Patterns of Adaptation among Households of U.S.-Bound Migrants From Michoacán, Mexico." *International Migration Review* 12, no. 4: 485–501.

Doherty, William J., and Richard H. Needle. 1991. "Psychological Adjustment and Substance Use among Adolescents before and after a Parental Divorce." *Child Development* 62: 328–37.

Dominguez, Robert. 1996. "Biopic Tryouts Had to Be Selena to Be Believed." *New York Daily News*, 22 March, 49.

Donato, Katherine. 1993. "Current Trends and Patterns of Female Migration: Evidence from Mexico." *International Migration Review* 24: 748–71.

Donnelly, Jack. 2001. "Ethics and International Human Rights." In *Ethics and International Affairs: Extent and Limits*, edited by Jean-Marc Coicaud and Daniel Warner, 128–60. Tokyo: United Nations University Press.

Downing, Theodore E., and Gilbert Kushner, eds. 1988. *Human Rights and Anthropology*. Cambridge, Mass.: Cultural Survival.

Dudden, Faye. 1983. *Serving Women: Household Service in 19th Century America.* Middletown, Conn.: Wesleyan University Press.

Dunn, Timothy. 1996. *The Militarization of the U.S.-Mexico Border 1978–1992: Low-Intensity Conflict Doctrine Comes Home.* Austin: University of Texas, Center for Mexican American Studies.

Duque, Joaquín, and Ernesto Pastrana. 1973. *Las estrategias de supervivencia de las unidades familiares del sector popular urbano: Una investigación exploratoria.* Santiago: Programa ELAS (Europe and Latin America Section)/Celade.

Durand, Jorge. 1992. "Mas Alla de la Linea: Patrones migratorios entre México y Estados Unidos." Ph.D. diss., Departamento de Antropología, Colegio de Michoacán, Zamora.

———. 2004. "From Traitors to Heroes: 100 Years of Mexican Migration Policies." Migration Information Source. http://www.migrationinformation.org (accessed on 28 October 2004).

Dutt, Mallika. 1994. *With Liberty and Justice for All: Women's Human's Rights in the United States.* New York: Center for Women's Global Leadership.

Economic Research Associates. 1981. *Economic Base Update: With Market Demand Projections for Selected Land Uses.* Santa Barbara: City of Santa Barbara, Community Development Department.

Edin, Kathryn, and Laura Lein. 1997. *Making Ends Meet: How Single Mothers Survive Welfare and Low-Wage Work.* New York: Russell Sage Foundation.

Ehrenreich, Barbara, and Arlie R. Hochschild, eds. 2002. *Global Woman: Nannies, Maids, and Sex Workers in the New Global Economy.* New York: Metropolitan.

Elder, Glen. 1985. *Life Course Dynamics: Trajectories and Transformations, 1968–1980*: Cornell University Press.

Ellingwood, Ken. 1999a. "Border Policy Violates Rights, Groups Charge." *Los Angeles Times*, 11 February, A3.

———. 1999b. "Data on Border Arrests Raise Gatekeeper Debate." *Los Angeles Times*, 1 October, A3.

Elmendorf, Mary. 1977. "Mexico: The Many Worlds of Women." In *Women: Roles and Status in Eight Countries*, edited by Janet Zollinger Giele and Audrey Chapman Stock, 127–72. New York: John Wiley.

Elson, Diane, and Ruth Pearson. 1981. "Nimble Fingers Make Cheap Workers: An Analysis of Women's Employment in Third World Export Manufacturing." *Feminist Review* 8: 87–107.

———. 1986. "'Third World Manufacturing.'" In *Waged Work*, edited by Feminist Review, 67–92. London: Virago.

Elson, Diane, and Ruth Pearson, eds. 1989. *Women's Employment and Multinationals in Europe*. Basingstoke, U.K.: Macmillan.

Elton, Charlotte. 1978. *Migración femenina en América Latina: Factores determinantes*. Santiago de Chile: Centro Latinoamericano de Demografía.

England, Paula, and George Farkas. 1986. *Households, Employment, and Gender*. New York: Aldine.

Enloe, Cynthia. 1990. *Bananas, Beaches, and Bases: Making Feminist Sense of International Politics*. Berkeley: University of California Press.

———. 2000. *Maneuvers: The International Politics of Militarizing Women's Lives*. Berkeley: University of California Press.

Environmental Work Group. 1987. *Report on Farmworker Health*. Rockville, Md.: Office of Migrant Health, Bureau of Health Case Delivery and Assistance, U.S. Department of Health and Human Services.

Epstein, Aaron. 1994. "GOP Targets Legal Noncitizens." *Orange County Register*, 27 December, A1.

Eschbach, Karl, Jacqueline Hagan, Nestor Rodriguez, Ruben Hernandez-Leon, and Stanley Bailey. 1999. "Death at the Border." *International Migration Review* 33, no. 2: 431–54.

Escobar, Javier I., and E. T. Randolph. 1982. "The Hispanic and Social Networks." In *Mental Health and Hispanic Americans: Clinical Perspectives*, edited by Rosina Marvin Becerra, M. Karno, and Javier I. Escobar, 41–57. New York: Grune and Stratton.

Espín, Oliva. 1986. "Cultural and Historical Influences on Sexuality in Hispanic/Latin Women." In *All American Women: Lines that Divide, Ties That Bind*, edited by Johnnette B. Cole, 272–84. New York: Free Press.

———. 1996. "The Immigrant Experience in Lesbian Studies." In *The New Lesbian Studies: Toward the Twenty-First Century*, edited by Bonnie Zimmerman and Toni McNaron, 145–52. New York: Feminist Press.

Espinoza, Guadalupe. 1978. "El contexto de la migración rural in México." In *Investigación demográfica en México*, 237–51. Mexico City: Consejo Nacional de Ciencia y Tecnología.

———. 1984. "Historia migratoria y fecundidad en la Encuesta Mexicana de Fecundidad." In *Los factores del cambio demográfico en México*, 328–55: Mexico City: Instituto de Investigaciones Sociales de la Universidad Nacional Autónoma de México, Siglo XXI.

"Ex-Border Guard Indicted on Federal Charges." 1995. *Phoenix Gazette*, 6 April.

Facultad de psicología. 1981. *Encuesta Regional en los siete exdistritos de la Mixteca Alta y Baja de Oaxaca*. Mexico City: Universidad Autónoma de México.

Fantasia, Mark. 1998. *Cultures of Solidarity: Consciousness, Action and Contemporary American Workers*. Berkeley: University of California Press.

Farmer, Paul. 1996. *Infections and Inequalities: the Modern Plagues*. Berkeley: University of California Press.

Federation for American Immigration Reform. 2000. *Immigration 101: A Primer on Immigration and the Need for Reform*. Washington: Federation for American Immigration Reform.

Ferguson, Roderick. 2000. "The Nightmares of the Heteronormative." *Cultural Values* 4, no. 4: 419–44.

Fernandez, Maria Elena. 1999. "Cultural Conflict: Latina Teens Caught Between Two Worlds Are Often Depressed." *Los Angeles Times*, 13 December, B3.

Fernández-Kelly, María Patricia. 1983a. *For We Are Sold, I and My People: Women and Industry in Mexico's Frontier*. Albany: State University of New York Press.

———. 1983b. "Maquiladora, desarrollo e inversión transnacional." *Migración y problemas fronterizos* 4, no. 8: 153–77.

———. 1983c. "Mexican Border Industrialization, Female Labor-Force Participation and Migration." In *Women, Men, and the International Division of Labor*, edited by June Nash and Maria Patricia Fernández-Kelly, 205–23. Albany: State University of New York Press.

Fernández-Kelly, María Patricia, and Anna M. García. 1988. "Economic Restructuring in the United States: Hispanic Women in the Garment and Electronics Industries." *Women and Work* 3: 49–65.

———. 1990. "Power Surrendered, Power Restored: The Politics of Work and Family among Hispanic Garment Workers in California and Florida." In *Women, Politics and Change*, edited by Louise A. Tilly and Patricia Gurin, 130–49. New York: Russell Sage Foundation.

———. 1997. "Power Surrendered, Power Restored: The Politics of Work and Family among Hispanic Garment Workers in California and Florida." In *Challenging Fronteras: Structuring Latina and Latino Lives in the U.S.*, edited by Mary Romero, Pierrette Hondagneu-Sotelo, and Vilma Ortiz, 215–28. New York: Routledge.

Fernández-Kelly, María Patricia, and Saskia Sassen. 1995. "Recasting Women in the Global Economy: Internationalization and Changing Definitions of Gender." In *Women in the Latin American Development Process*, edited by Christine Bose and Edna Acosta Belén, 99–124. Philadelphia: Temple University Press.

Ferrer, Aldo. 1996. "Mercosur: Trayectoría, situación actual y perspectivas." *Desarrollo Económico* 35, no. 140 (January–March): 563–83.

Figueroa Perea, Juan Guillermo. 1997. "Algunas reflexiones sobre el enfoque de género y la representación de la sexualidad." *Estudios Demográficos y Urbanos* 12, nos. 1 and 2: 201–44.

Finkler, Kaja. 1994. *Women in Pain: Gender and Morbidity in Mexico*. Philadelphia: University of Pennsylvania Press.

Firestore, Shulamith. 1970. *The Dialectic of Sex*. New York: Bantam Books.

Fisk, Catherine L., Daniel J. B. Mitchell, and Christopher Erickson. 2000. "Union Representation of Immigrant Janitors in Southern California: Economic and Legal Challenges." In *Organizing Immigrants: The Challenge for Unions and Contemporary California*, edited by Ruth Milkman, 199–224. Ithaca, N.Y.: ILR Press/Cornell University Press.

Fitzgerald, Lovise F., Suzanne Swan, and Vicki J. Magley. 1997. "But Was It Really Sexual Harassment? Legal, Behavioral and Psychological Definitions of the Workplace Victimization of Women." In *Sexual Harassment: Theory, Research and Treatment*, edited by William O'Donohue, 5–28. New York: Allyn and Bacon.

Fix, Michael E., and Jeffrey S. Passel. 1999. *Trends in Noncitizens' and Citizens' Use of Public Benefits Following Welfare Reform: 1994–1997*. Washington: Urban Institute.

Flores, Sara María Lara, ed. 1995. *Jornaleras, Temporeras y Bóias-Frias: El rostro femenino del mercado de trabajo rural en América Latina*. United Nations Research Institute for Social Development. Caracas: Nueva Sociedad.

Flores, William V. 1997. "*Mujeres en Huelga*: Cultural Citizenship and Gender Empowerment in a Cannery Strike." In *Latino Cultural Citizenship: Claiming Identity, Space, and Rights*, edited by William V. Flores and Rina Benmayor, 210–54. Boston: Beacon Press.

Flores, Yvette, and Enriqueta Valdez Curiel. Forthcoming. "Conflict Resolution and Intimate Partner Violence among Mexicans on Both Sides of the Border." In *Latinos in the United States: Challenges and Transformations*, edited by Patricia Zavella and Ramón Gutiérrez, with Denise Segura, Dolores Trevino, and Juan Vicente Palerm.

Flores-Ortiz, Yvette. 1993. "La Mujer y la Violencia: A Culturally Based Model for Understanding and Treatment of Domestic Violence in Chicana/Latina Communities." In *Chicana Critical Issues*, edited by Norma Alarcón et al., 168–82. Berkeley, Calif.: Third Woman Press.

Florida Council Against Sexual Violence. 2002. http://www.fcasv.org.

Fogelquist, Mark. 1975. Rhythm and Form in the Contemporary Son Jalisciense. Master's thesis, University of California, Los Angeles.

Folbre, Nancy. 1984. "The Pauperization of Motherhood: Patriarchy and Public Policy in the United States." *Review of Radical Political Economics* 16: 72–88.

———. 1991. *Women on Their Own: Global Patterns of Female Headship*. Washington: International Center for Research on women.

Foner, Nancy. 1997. "The Immigrant Family: Cultural Legacies and Cultural Changes." *International Migration Review* 31, no. 4: 961–74.

———. 1998. "Benefits and Burdens: Immigrant Women and Work in New York City." *Gender Issues* 16: 5–24.

Foster, George. 1967. *Tzintzuntzan: Mexican Peasants in a Changing World*. Boston: Little Brown.

Foucault, Michel. 1977. *Discipline and Punish: The Birth of the Prison*. London: Tavistock.

---. 1979. *Discipline and Punish: The Birth of the Prison.* New York: Vintage Books.

---. 1980a. *The History of Sexuality.* Translated from the French by Robert Hurley. New York: Vintage Books.

---. 1980b. "Body/Power." In *Power/Knowledge: Selected Interviews and Other Writings, 1972–1979,* edited by Colin Gordon, 55–62. New York: Pantheon Books.

---. 1990. *The History of Sexuality.* Translated by Robert Hurley. New York: Vintage Books.

---. 1991a. "Faire vivre et laisser lourir: La naissance du racisme." *Les Temps Modernes* 46, no. 535: 37–61.

---. 1991b. "Governmentality." In *The Foucault Effect: Studies in Governmentality,* edited by Graham Burchell, Colin Gordon, and Peter Miller, 87–104. London: Harvester/Wheatsheaf.

Fowler-Salamini, Heather, and Mary Kay Vaughan, eds. 1994. *Women of the Mexican Countryside 1850–1990: Creating Spaces, Shaping Transitions.* Tucson: University of Arizona Press.

Fox, Jonathan, and Gaspar Rivera-Salgado, eds. 2004. *Indigenous Mexican Migrants in the United States.* La Jolla: Center for U.S.-Mexican Studies and Center for Comparative Immigration Studies.

Fox, Linda C. 1983. "Obedience and Rebellion: Re-Vision of Chicana Myths of Motherhood." *Women's Studies Quarterly* (winter): 20–22.

Franco, Jean. 1999. *Critical Passions: Selected Essays by Jean Franco.* Edited by Mary Louise Pratt and Kathleen Newman. Durham, N.C.: Duke University Press.

---. 2002. *The Decline and Fall of the Lettered State.* Cambridge, Mass.: Harvard University Press.

Fraser, Nancy, and Linda Gordon. 1994. "A Genealogy of Dependency: Tracing a Keyword of the U.S. Welfare State." *Signs* 19: 309–35.

Freeman, Richard B. 1985. "Why Are Unions Faring Poorly in NLRB Representation Elections?" In *Challenges and Choices Facing American Labor,* edited by Thomas A. Kochran, 45–64. Cambridge: Massachusetts Institute of Technology Press.

Fregoso, Rosa Linda. 2000. "Voices without Echo: The Global Gendered Apartheid." *Emergences* 10, no. 1: 137–55.

---. 2001. *Lourdes Portillo: The Devil Never Sleeps.* Austin: University of Texas Press.

---. 2003. *meXicana Encounters: The Making of Social Identities on the Borderlands.* Berkeley: University of Californa Press.

Fregoso, Rosa Linda, and Angie Chabram. 1990. "Chicana/o Cultural Representations: Reframing Alternative Critical Discourses." *Cultural Studies* 4, no. 3: 203–12.

French, Howard W. 2000. "Japan Fails to Cope with Its Declining Population." *Orange County Register,* 14 March, 19.

Friaz, Guadalupe. 1991. "'I Want To Be Treated as an Equal': Testimony from a Latino Union Activist." *Aztlán* 20, nos. 1 and 2: 195–202.

Frobel, F., J. Heinrichs, and Otto Kreye. 1981. *The New International Division of Labor: Structural Unemployment in Industrialized Counties and Industrialization in Developing Countries.* Cambridge: Cambridge University Press.

Fromm, Erich. 1959. "Sex and Character." In *The Family: Its Function and Destiny*, edited by Ruth Nanda Anshen, 399–419. New York: Harper and Row.

Fry, Richard. 2002. *Latinos in Higher Education: Many Enroll, Too Few Graduate*. Washington: Pew Hispanic Center.

Fuentes, Annette, and Barbara Ehrenreich. 1983. *Women in the Global Factory*. Boston: South End Press.

Fulbrook, Mary. 1996. "Germany for the Germans? Citizenship and Nationality in a Divided Nation." In *Citizenship, Nationality and Migration in Europe*, edited by David Cesarani and Mary Fulbrook, 88–105. New York: Routledge.

Fusco, Coco. 1997. "Adventures in the Skin Trade." *Utne Reader*, July–August, 67–69, 107–109.

Gabaccia, Donna. 1992. *Seeking Common Ground: Multidisciplinary Studies of Immigrant Women in the United States*. Westport, Conn.: Greenwood Press.

Galán, José. 2001. "Tres milliones de hogares mexicanos son dirigidos por mujeres: Experta." *La Jornada*, 12 April, 28.

Gamio, Manuel. 1930. *The Mexican Immigrant: His Life Story*. Chicago: University of Chicago Press.

Gándara, Patricia. 1996. "Chicanas in Higher Education: Implications for Policy." In *Strategic Interventions in Education: Expanding the Latina/Latino Pipeline*, edited by Aída Hurtado, Richard Figueroa, and Eugene Garcia, 167–97. Santa Cruz: University of California, Latino Eligibility Study.

García, Alma. 1989. "The Development of Chicana Feminist Discourse, 1970–1980." *Gender and Society* 3, no. 2: 217–38.

———. 1997. *Chicana Feminist Thought: The Basic Historical Writings*. New York: Routledge.

García, Brígida, Humberto Muñoz, and Orlandina de Oliveira. 1982. *Hogares y trabajadores en la ciudad de México*. Universidad Nacional Autónoma de México, El Colegio de México.

García, Gustavo Castillo. 2001. "Ordenó Fox a PGR investigar a fondo los asesinatos de mujeres en Ciudad Juárez." *La Jornada*, 23 December, 17.

García, John A. 1981. "Yo Soy Mexicano . . . : Self-identity and Sociodemographic Correlates." *Social Science Quarterly* 62: 88–98.

Garcia, Mario. 1981. *Desert Immigrants*. New Haven, Conn.: Yale University Press.

García Canclini, Néstor. 2001. *Consumers and Citizens: Globalization and Multicultural Conflicts*. Minneapolis: University of Minnesota Press.

Gardetta, Dave. 1991. "True Grit: Clocking Time with Janitors' Organizer Rocio Saenz." *Los Angeles Weekly* 14: 35.

Garrido, Juan S. 1974. *Historia de la música popular de México*. Mexico City: Editorial Extemporaneos.

Geijerstam, Claes. 1976. *Popular Music in México*. Albuquerque: University of México Press.

Gerson, Kathleen. 1985. *Hard Choices*. Berkeley: University of California Press.

Gerstel, Naomi, and Harriet Engel Gross. 1987. Introduction. In *Families and Work*, edited by Naomi Gerstel and Harriet Engel Gross, 1–12. Philadelphia: Temple University Press.

Gianaris, Nicholas V. 1998. *The North American Free Trade Agreement and the European Union.* Westport: Praeger.

Gibbons, Leeza, and Jose Pretlow, prods. 1999. "The Trafficking of Philipino Mail-Order Brides." *Leeza Gibbons Show.* New York: NBC.

Gibson, Margaret A. 1988. "Punjabi Orchard Farmers: An Immigrant Enclave in Rural California." *International Migration Review* 22, no. 1: 28–50.

Giddens, Anthony. 1992. *The Transformation of Intimacy.* Stanford, Calif.: Stanford University Press.

Giddings, Paula. 1992. "The Last Taboo." In *Race-ing Justice, Engendering Power: Essays on Anita Hill, Clarence Thomas and the Construction of Social Reality*, edited by Toni Morrison. New York: Pantheon Books.

Gill, Lesley. 1994. *Precarious Dependencies: Gender, Class and Domestic Service in Bolivia.* New York: Columbia University Press.

Gillis, John R., Louise A. Tilly, and David Levine. 1992. *The European Experience of Declining Fertility, 1850–1970.* Cambridge, U.K.: Blackwell, 1992.

Gilman, Sander. 1985. "Black Bodies, White Bodies: Toward an Iconography of Female Sexuality in Late Nineteenth-Century Art, Medicine, and Literature." *Critical Inquiry* 12: 204–42.

Ginsburg, Faye D., and Rayna Rapp. 1991. "The Politics of Reproduction." *Annual Review of Anthropology* 20: 311–43.

———. 1995a. *Conceiving the New World Order: The Global Politics of Reproduction.* Berkeley: University of California Press.

———. 1995b. Introduction. In *Conceiving the New World Order: The Global Politics of Reproduction*, edited by Faye D. Ginsburg and Rayna Rapp, 1–18. Berkeley: University of California Press.

Glazer, Nona. 1984. "Servants to Capital: Unpaid Domestic Labor and Paid Work." *Review of Radical Economics* 16: 61–87.

Gledhill, Christine. 1987. Introduction. In *Home Is Where the Heart Is: Studies in Melodrama and the Woman's Film*, edited by Christine Gledhill, 1–39. London: British Film Institute.

Glenn, Evelyn Nakano. 1986. *Issei, Nisei, War Bride: Three Generations of Japanese American Women in Domestic Service.* Philadelphia: Temple University Press.

———. 1992. "From Servitude to Service Work: Historical Continuities in the Racial Division of Paid Reproductive Labor." *Signs* 18: 1–43.

———. 1994. "Social Constructions of Mothering: A Thematic Overview." In *Mothering: Ideology, Experience, and Agency*, edited by Evelyn Nakano Glenn, Grace Chang, and Linda Rennie Forcey, 1–29. New York: Routledge.

———. 2000. "Citizenship and Inequality: Historical and Global Perspectives." *Social Problems* 47, no. 1: 1–20.

Glick Schiller, Nina, Linda Basch, and Cristina Blanc-Szanton. 1995. "From Immigrant to Transmigrant: Theorizing Transnational Migration." *Anthropological Quarterly* 68, no. 1: 48–63.

———, eds. 1992. *Towards a Transnational Perspective on Migration: Race, Class, Ethnicity, and Nationalism Reconsidered*. New York: New York Academy of Sciences.

Glick Schiller, Nina, and George Eugene Fouron. 2001. *Georges Woke Up Laughing: Long-Distance Nationalism and the Search for Home*. Durham, N.C.: Duke University Press.

Glodava, M., and R. Onizuka. 1994. *Mail-order Brides: Women for Sale*. Fort Collins, Colo.: Alaken.

Gobierno Constitucional del Estado de Oaxaca. n.d. "Programa de Desarrollo Rural Integral de las Mixtecas Oaxaqueñas Alta y Baja, 1984 y 1988."

Gold, Scott. 2004. "Illegal Crossing Rising Sharply: Some Blame Rumors of Future Amnesty." *San Jose Mercury News*, 16 May, A23.

González, Deena. 1985. *Spanish-Mexican Women on the Santa Fe Frontier: Patterns of Their Resistance and Accommodation, 1820–1880*. Berkeley: University of California Press.

González de la Rocha, Mercedes. 1984. "Urban Households and Domestic Cycles in Guadalajara, Mexico." Ph.D. diss., Faculty of Social and Economic Studies, University of Manchester.

———. 1994. *The Resources of Poverty: Women and Survival in Mexico City*. Oxford, U.K.: Blackwell.

González-López, Gloria. 2000. "Beyond the Bed Sheets, Beyond the Borders: Mexican Immigrant Women and Their Sex Lives." Ph.D. diss., Department of Sociology, University of Southern California, Los Angeles.

———. 2005. *Erotic Journeys: Mexican Immigrants and Their Sex Lives*. Berkeley: University of California Press.

González Marín, María Luisa, ed. 1998. *Los mercados de trabajo femeninos: tendencias recientes*. Mexico City: M. A. Porrúa.

González Montes, Soledad. 1993. *Mujeres y relaciones de género en la antropología latinoamericana*. Mexico City: El Colegio de México.

González Montes, Soledad, and Vania Salles, eds. 1995. *Relaciones de género y transformaciones agrarias: Estudios sobre el campo*. Mexico City: El Colegio de México, Programa Interdisciplinario de Estudios de la Mujer.

González Montes, Soledad, and Julia Tuñon. 1997. *Familias y mujeres en México: Del modelo a la diversidad*. Mexico City: El Colegio de México, Programa Interdisciplinario de Estudios de la Mujer.

Goode, William J. 1963. *World Revolution and Family Patterns*. New York: Free Press.

Goodson-Lawes, Julie. 1992. "La decisión de ir o regresar: Una familia migrante de Mezquitic." *Estudios Jaliciense*, May, 37–50.

———. 1993. "Feminine Authority and Migration: The Case of One Family from Mexico." *Urban Anthropology* 22, nos. 3–4: 277–97.

Gordon, Margaret T., and Stephanie Riger. 1989. *The Female Fear*. New York: Free Press.

Gould, Stephen J. 1981. *The Mismeasure of Man*. New York: Norton.

Gradante, William. 1982. "El hijo del pueblo: José Alfredo Jimenez and the Mexican Canción Ranchera." *Latin American Music Review* 3, no. 1: 36–59.

———. 1983. "Mexican Popular Music at Mid-Century: The Role of José Alfredo Jimenez and the Canción Ranchera." *Studies in Latin American Popular Culture* 2: 99–114.

Grange, Mariette. 2001. "Elements for a Draft Declaration and Programme of Action for the World Conference Versus the 1978 and 1983 World Conferences: Final Documents." http://www.december18.net (accessed on 3 March 2002).

Grasmuck, Sherri, and Patricia R. Pessar. 1991. *Between Two Islands: Dominican International Migration.* Berkeley: University of California Press.

Gray, Lorraine, Anne Bohlen, María Patricia Fernández-Kelly, directors. 1986. *The Global Assembly Line.* Film. Harriman, N.H.: New Day Films.

Green, Richard. 1987. "'Give Me Your Tired, Your Poor, Your Huddled Masses' of Heterosexuals: An Analysis of American and Canadian Immigration Policy." *Anglo American Law Review* 16: 140–43.

Greenhalgh, Susan. 1995. "Anthropology Theorizes Reproduction: Integrating Practice, Political Economic, and Feminist Perspectives." In *Situating Fertility: Anthropology and Demographic Inquiry*, edited by Susan Greenhalgh, 3–28. Cambridge: Cambridge University Press.

Grial, Hugo de. 1973. *Músicos Mexicanos.* Mexico City: Editorial Diana.

Griffin, Susan. 1979. *Rape: The Power of Consciousness.* San Francisco: Harper and Row.

Griffith, David, Ed Kissam, Jeromino Camposeco, Anna García, David Runsten, and Manuel Valdes Pizzini. 1995. *Working Poor: Farmworkers in the United States.* Philadelphia: Temple University Press.

Griswold del Castillo, Richard. 1984. *La Familia: Chicano Families in the Urban Southwest, 1848 to the Present.* Notre Dame, Ind.: University of Notre Dame Press.

Grossman, Allyson Sherman. 1982. "More than Half of All Children Have Working Mothers: Special Labor Force Reports—Summaries." *Monthly Labor Review* 105, no. 2: 41–43.

Gruber, James. 1998. "The Impact of Male Work Environments and Organizational Policies on Women's Experiences of Sexual Harassment." *Gender and Society* 12, no. 3: 301–20.

Gruber, James, Michael Smith, and Kaisa Kauppinen-Toropainen. 1996. "Sexual Harassment Types and Severity: Linking Research and Policy." In *Sexual Harassment in the Workplace: Perspectives, Frontiers, and Response Strategies*, edited by Margaret Stockdale, 151–73. London: Sage Publications.

Guendelman, Sylvia R. 1987. "The Incorporation of Mexican Women in Seasonal Migration: A Study of Gender Differences." *Hispanic Journal of Behavioral Sciences* 9: 245–64.

Guendelman, Sylvia R., and Auristela Perez-Itriago. 1987. "Double Lives: The Changing Role of Women in Seasonal Migration." *Women's Studies* 13: 249–71.

Guendelman, Sylvia, Christina Malin, Barbara Herr-Harthorn, and Patricia Noemi Vargas. 2001. "Orientations to Motherhood and Male Partner Support among Women in Mexico and Mexican-origin Women in the United States." *Social Science and Medicine* 52: 1805–13.

Guidi, Marta. 1988. Estigma o prestigio: La tradición de migrar en San Juan Mixtepec." Master's thesis, Escuela Nacional de Antropología e Historia, Mexico.

Guiffre, Patti, and Christine Williams. 1994. "Boundary Lines: Labeling Sexual Harassment in Restaurants." *Gender and Society* 8, no. 3: 378–401.

Guillermoprieto, Alma. 1992. "Serenading the Future." *New Yorker*, 9 November, 96–104.

Gutiérrez, David G. 1995. *Walls and Mirrors: Mexican Americans, Mexican Immigrants, and the Politics of Ethnicity*. Berkeley: University of California Press.

———. 1998. "Ethnic Mexicans and the Transformation of 'American' Social Space: Reflections on Recent History." In *Crossings: Mexican Immigration in Interdisciplinary Perspectives*, edited by Marcelo Suárez-Orozco, 3070–40. Cambridge: Harvard University Press.

Gutiérrez, Elena Rebeca. 1999. "The Racial Politics of Reproduction: The Social Construction of Mexican-Origin Women's Fertility." Ph.D. diss., Department of Sociology, University of Michigan, Ann Arbor.

Gutiérrez, Ramón A. 1984. "From Honor to Love: Transformations of the Meaning of Sexuality in New Mexico." In *Kinship Ideology and Practice in Latin America*, edited by Raymond T. Smith, 237–63. Chapel Hill: University of North Carolina Press.

Gutmann, Matthew C. 1996. *The Meanings of Macho: Being a Man in Mexico City*. Berkeley: University of California Press.

Guzmán, Laura, and Cristina Zeledón. 1994. "Why Do Mexican and Central American Women Migrate? Inter-American Institute on Human Rights." *Houston Catholic Worker*. http://www.cjd.org.

Guzmán, R. 1998. "Empresas Maquiladoras Buscan Mano de Obra en Colonias." *El Diario de Ciudad Juárez*, 24 July, 5.

Habermas, Jürgen. 1992. "Citizenship and National Identity: Some Reflections on the Future of Europe." *Praxis International* 12, no. 1: 16.

Hall, Stuart, ed. 1997. *Representation: Cultural Representations and Signifying Practices*. Thousand Oaks, Calif.: Sage Publications.

Halley, Janet. 1996. "The Status/Conduct Distinction in the 1993 Revisions to Military Anti-Gay Policy: A Legal Archaeology." *GLQ* 3: 179–251.

Halperin, David M. 1995. *Saint Foucault: Towards a Gay Hagiography*. New York: Oxford University Press.

Hanisch, Kathy. 1996. "An Integrated Framework for Studying the Outcomes of Sexual Harassment: Consequences for Individuals and Organizations." In *Sexual Harassment in the Workplace: Perspectives, Frontiers, and Response Strategies*, edited by Margaret Stockdale, 174–98. London: Sage Publications.

Hanson, Susan, and Geraldine Pratt. 1995. *Gender, Work and Space*. New York: Routledge.

Hardey, Michael. 2002. "Life Beyond the Screen: Embodiment and Identity through the Internet." *Sociological Review* 50, no. 4: 570–85.

Hareven, Tamara. 1977. "Family Time and Historical Time." *Daedalus* 106, no. 2: 57–70.

Harris, Olivia, ed. 1982. *Latin American Women*. London: Minority Rights Group.

Hartmann, Heidi. 1976. "Capitalism, Patriarchy and Job Segregation by Sex." In *Women and the Work Place*, edited by Martha Blaxall and Barbara Reagan, 137–69. Chicago: University of Chicago Press.

———. 1981. "The Family as the Locus of Gender, Class, and Political Struggle: The Example of Housework." *Signs* 6: 366–94.

Harvey, David. 1982. *The Limits to Capital*. Oxford: Basil Blackwell.

———. 1989. *The Condition of Postmodernity: An Enquiry into the Origins of Cultural Change*. Cambridge, Mass.: Blackwell.

———. 2000. *Spaces of Hope*. Berkeley: University of California Press.

Harvey, S. Marie, Linda J. Beckman, Carole Browner, Helen Rodriguez-Trias, Silvia Balzano, Michelle Doty, and Sarah J. Satre. 1997. *Context and Meaning of Reproductive Decision-Making among Inner City Couples: Executive Summary: Report to Contraceptive Research and Development Program/Centers for Disease Control*. Los Angeles: Pacific Institute for Women's Health.

Hayden, Dolores. 1981. *The Grand Domestic Revolution: A History of Feminist Designs for American Homes, Neighborhoods and Cities*. Cambridge: Massachusetts Institute of Technology Press.

Hayes-Bautista, David E., Aída Hurtado, R. Burciaga Valdez, and Anthony C. R. Hernández. 1992. *No Longer a Minority: Latinos and Social Policy in California*. Los Angeles: University of California, Chicano Studies Research Center Publications.

Hayes-Bautista, David E., Warner Schink, and Jorge Chapa. 1988. *The Burden of Support*. Stanford, Calif.: Stanford University Press.

Hayghe, Howard. 1984. "Working Mothers Reach Record Number in 1984." *Monthly Labor Review* 107: 31–34.

Haynes, Karima A. 2000. "Janitors Draw Parallels Between Strike, Passover." *Los Angeles Times*, 20 April, B1.

Hearn, Jeff, and Wendy Parkin. 1995. *"Sex at Work": The Power and Paradox of Organisation Sexuality*. New York: St. Martin's Press.

Hennigg, Paulsdorff. 1985. *Cultura indígena y su adaptación al medio urbano: La organización social de los mixtecos residentes en la colonia Obrera*. Berlin: Fundación Carl-Duisberg.

Hernández-Castillo, Rosalva Aída. 2001. *Histories and Stories from Chiapas: Border Identities in Southern Mexico*. Translated by Martha Pou. Foreword by Renato Rosaldo. Austin: University of Texas Press.

Herr Harthorn, Barbara. 2003. "Safe Exposure? Perceptions of Health Risks from Agricultural Chemicals among California Farmworkers." In *Risk, Culture, and Health Inequality: Shifting Perceptions of Danger and Blame*, edited by Barbara Herr Harthorn and Laury Oaks, 142–62. Westport, Conn.: Praeger.

Herzog, Lawrence A. 1991. *Where North Meets South: Cities, Space, and Politics on the U.S.-Mexico Border*. Austin: University of Texas, Center for Mexican American Studies.

Hill, Sarah. 1998. "Purity and Danger on the U.S.-Mexico Border." Discussion paper. San Diego: Center for U.S.-Mexican Studies.

Hing, Bill Ong. 2004. *Defining America through Immigration Policy*. Philadelphia: Temple University Press.

Hirsch, Jennifer S. 1998a. "Migration, Modernity and Mexican Marriage: A Comparative Study of Gender, Sexuality and Reproductive Health in a Transnational Community." Ph.D. diss., Department of Anthropology and Population Dynamics, Johns Hopkins University, Baltimore.

———. 1998b. "'Que, pues, con el pinche NAFTA?' Gender, Power and Migration Between Western Mexico and Atlanta." Unpublished manuscript.

———. 2003. *A Courtship after Marriage: Sexuality and Love in Mexican Transnational Families*. Berkeley: University of California Press.

Hirsch, Jennifer S., and C. A. Nathanson. 1997. "Demografía informal: Cómo utilizar las redes sociales para construir una muestra etnográfica sistemática de mujeres mexicanas en ambos lados de la frontera." *Estudios Demograficos y de Desarollo Urbano* 12, nos. 1 and 2: 177–99.

"HIV as a Grounds of Inadmissibility: How It Works." 1996. In *Asylum Based on Sexual Orientation: A Resource Guide*, edited by Sydney Levy, 25. San Francisco: International Gay and Lesbian Human Rights Commission and Lambda Legal Defense and Education Fund.

Hochschild, Arlie. 1983. *The Managed Heart: The Commercialization of Human Feeling*. Berkeley: University of California Press.

———. 1990. "Ideology and Emotion Management: A Perspective and Path for Future Research." In *Research Agendas in the Sociology of Emotions*, edited by Theodore Kemper, 117–42. Albany: State University of New York Press.

Hochschild, Arlie, with Anne Machung. 1989. *The Second Shift: Working Parents and the Revolution at Home*. New York: Viking Penguin.

Hoekstra, Dave. 1996. "Selena Search: Thousands Vie for Role as Tejano Star." *Chicago Sun Times*, 28 March, 31.

Hofferth, Sandra. 1999. "Childcare, Maternal Employment, and Public Policy." *Annals of the American Academy of Political and Social Science* 563 (May): 20–39.

Hollway, Wendy, and Tony Jefferson. 1996. "PC or Not PC: Sexual Harassment and the Question of Ambivalence." *Human Relations* 49, no. 3: 373–93.

Hom, Sharon K. 2000. "Female Infanticide in China." In *Global Critical Race Feminism*, edited by Adrien Katherine Wing, 251–59. New York: New York University Press.

"Hombres por una vida sin violencia." October 1998. http://www.forum-global.de.

Hondagneu-Sotelo, Pierrette. 1994. *Gendered Transitions: Mexican Experiences of Immigration*. Berkeley: University of California Press.

———. 1995. "Women and Children First: New Directions in Anti-Immigrant Politics." *Socialist Review* 25, no. 1: 169–90.

———. 1998. "Latina Immigrant Women and Paid Domestic Work: Upgrading the Occupation." In *Community Activism and Feminist Politics: Organizing Across Race, Class, and Gender*, edited by Nancy Naples, 199–211. New York: Routledge.

———. 2001. *Doméstica: Immigrant Workers Cleaning and Caring in the Shadows of Affluence*. Berkeley: University of California Press.

Hondagneu-Sotelo, Pierrette, and Ernestine Avila. 1997. "I'm Here, but I'm There: The Meaning of Latina Transnational Motherhood." *Gender and Society* 11, no. 5: 548–71.

Hondagneu-Sotelo, Pierrette, and Michael A. Messner. 1994. "Gender Displays and Men's Power: The 'New' Man and the Mexican Immigrant Man." In *Theorizing Masculinities*, edited by Harry Brod and Michael Kaufman, 200–218. Thousand Oaks, Calif.: Sage Publications.

Hondagneu-Sotelo, Pierrette, and Cristina Riegos. 1997. "Sin organización, no hay solución: Latina Domestic Workers and Non-traditional Labor Organizing." *Latino Studies Journal* 8: 54–81.

Hood, Jane C. 1986. "The Provider Role: Its Meaning and Measurement." *Marriage and the Family* 48: 349–59.

hooks, bell. 1989. "Homophobia in Black Communities." In *Talking Back: Thinking Feminist, Thinking Black*, 120–26. Boston: South End Press.

"Hoping for Stardom: 3,000 Selena Look-Alikes Turn Out for Casting Call." 1996. *Phoenix Gazette*, 18 March, A2.

Horn, David G. 1994. *Social Bodies: Science, Reproduction, and Italian Modernity*. Princeton, N.J.: Princeton University Press.

Hossfeld, Karen. 1994. "Hiring Immigrant Women: Silicon Valley's 'Simple Formula.'" In *Women of Color in U.S. Society*, edited by Maxine Baca Zinn and Bonnie Thornton Dill, 1–14. Philadelphia: Temple University Press.

Howard, Bob. 2000. "L.A. Office Ownership Shifts to Funds, REITS." *Los Angeles Times*, 4 April, C1, 13.

"How Millions of Illegal Aliens Sneak into U.S.: Interview with Leonard Chapman Jr." 1974. *U.S. News and World Report*, 22 June, 27–30.

Hubbell, F. Allan, Leo R. Chavez, Shiraz I. Mishra, and R. Burciaga Valdez. 1995a. "Beliefs about Sexual Behavior and Other Predictors of Pap Smear Screening among Latinas and Anglo Women." *Archives of Internal Medicine* 156: 2353–58.

———. 1995b. "Differing Beliefs about Breast Cancer among Latinas and Anglo Women." *Western Journal of Medicine* 164: 405–9.

———. 1997. "The Influence of Knowledge and Attitudes about Breast Cancer on Mammography Use among Latinas and Anglo Women: Brief Report." *General Internal Medicine* 12: 505–8.

Hulin, Charles, Louise Fitzgerald, and Fritz Drasgow. 1996. "Organizational Influences on Sexual Harassment." In *Sexual Harassment in the Workplace: Perspectives, Frontiers, and Response Strategies*, edited by Margaret Stockdale, 127–50. London: Sage Publications.

Human Rights Watch. 1992. *Brutality Unchecked: Human Rights Abuses along the U.S. Border with Mexico*. New York: Human Rights Watch.

———. 1993. *Frontier Injustice: Human Rights Abuses along the U.S. Border with Mexico Persist amid Climate of Impunity*. New York: Human Rights Watch.

———. 1995a. *Crossing the Line: Human Rights Abuses along the U.S. Border with Mexico Persist amid Climate of Impunity*. New York: Human Rights Watch.

———. 1995b. *The Human Rights Global Watch Report on Women's Human Rights*. New York: Human Rights Watch.

Huntington, Samuel P. 2000. "Why Mexico Is a Problem." *American Enterprise*, December, 20–22.

———. 2004. "The Hispanic Challenge." *Foreign Policy*, March–April, 30–44.

Hurtado, Aída. 1994a. "Understanding Multiple Group Identities: Inserting Women into Cultural Transformations." *Social Sciences Issues* 53, no. 2: 299–328.

———. 1994b. "Variations, Combinations, and Evolutions: Latino Families in the United States." In *Latino Families: Developing a Paradigm for Research, Practice, and Policy*, edited by Ruth E. Zambrana and Maxine Baca Zinn, 40–61. Thousand Oaks, Calif.: Sage Publications.

Hurtado, Aída, David E. Hayes-Bautista, R. Burciaga Valdez, and Anthony R. C. Hernandez. 1992. *Redefining California: Latino Social Engagement in a Multicultural Society*. Los Angeles: University of California, Chicano Studies Research Center.

Hutter, Mark. 1981. *The Changing Family: Comparative Perspectives*. New York: John Wiley.

Ibarra, María de la Luz. 1998. "'Creen que no tenemos vidas': Mexicana Household Workers in Santa Barbara, California." In *More Than Class: Looking at Power in U.S. Workplaces*, edited by Ann Kingsolver, 148–72. Albany: State University of New York Press.

———. 2002. "Emotional Proletarians in a Global Economy: Mexican Immigrant Women and Elder Care Work." *Urban Anthropology* 31, nos. 3 and 4: 317–51.

———. 2003a. "*Buscando La Vida*: Mexican Immigrant Women's Memories of Home, Yearning, and Border Crossings." *Frontiers* 24, nos. 2 and 3: 261–81.

———. 2003b. "The Tender Trap: Mexican Immigrant Women and the Ethics of Elder Care Work." *Aztlán* 28: 87–113.

Ickovics, Jeannette R., and Judith Rodin. 1992. "Women and AIDS in the US: Epidemiology, Natural History and Mediating Mechanisms." *Health Psychology* 11: 1–16.

Iglesias Prieto, Norma. 1987. *La flor más bella de la maquiladora*. Mexico City: Secretaría de Educación Pública.

———. 1997. *Beautiful Flowers of the Maquiliadora: Life Histories of Women Workers in Tijuana*. Austin: University of Texas Press.

Iglesias Prieto, Norma, and Rosa Linda Fregoso, eds. 1998. *Miradas de mujer: Encuentro de cineastas y videoastas mexicanas y chicanas*. Tijuana: El Colegio de la Frontera Norte.

Illouz, Eva. 1997. *Consuming the Romantic Utopia: Love and the Cultural Contradictions of Capitalism*. Berkeley: University of California Press.

Immigration and Naturalization Service. 1996. *Illegal Alien Resident Population*. San Diego: Immigration and Naturalization Service.

Inda, Jonathan Xavier. 2002. "Biopower, Reproduction, and the Migrant Woman's Body." In *Decolonial Voices: Chicana and Chicano Cultural Studies in the 21st Century*, edited by Arturo J. Aldama and Naomi H. Quinones, 98–112. Bloomington: Indiana University Press.

Inhorn, Marcia C. 1996. *Infertility and Patriarchy: The Cultural Politics of Gender and Family Life in Egypt*. Philadelphia: University of Pennsylvania Press.

"INS Officer Pleads Not Guilty in Rape, Kidnapping." 1990. *Los Angeles Times*, 16 May, B2.

Islas, Francisco Cervantes. 1999. "Helping Men Overcome Violent Behavior toward Women." In *Too Close to Home: Domestic Violence in the Americas*, edited by Andrew R. Morrison and María Loreto Biehl, 143–47. Washington: Inter-American Development Bank.

Jacobs, Susie, Ruth Jacobson, and Jennifer Marchbank. 2000. "Introduction: States of Conflict." In *States of Conflict*, edited by Susie Jacobs, Ruth Jacobson, and Jennifer Marchbank, 1–19. London and New York: Zed Books.

Jacobson, David. 1996. *Rights across Borders: Immigration and the Decline of Citizenship*. Baltimore: Johns Hopkins University Press.

Javiedes, L. 1981. *La migración en la Mixteca de Oaxaca*. Chapingo, Mexico: Ponencia presentada al II seminario Nacional de Sociología y Desarrollo Rural.

Jelin, Elizabeth. 1984. "Familia, unidad doméstica y división del trabajo (Qué sabemos y hacia dónde vamos)." In *Memorias del Congreso Latino-americano de Población y Desarrollo*. Pispal, Mexico: Universidad Nacional Autónoma de México, El Colegio de México.

Jelin, Elizabeth, and María del Carmen Feijoo. 1980. *Trabajo y familia en el ciclo de vida femenino: El case de los sectores populares de Buenos Aires*. Estudios Cedes 3, nos. 8 and 9.

Jiminéz, María. 1992. "War in the Borderlands." *Report on the Americas* 26: 29–33.

Johnson, Hans P., Laura Hill, and Mary Heim. 2001. "New Trends in Newborns: Fertility Rates and Patterns in California." *California Counts: Population Trends and Profiles* 3, no. 1: 1–11.

Jonas, Susanne. 1996. "Rethinking Immigration Policy and Citizenship in the Americas: A Regional Framework." *Social Justice* 23: 68–85.

Jones, Jacqueline. 1985. *Labor of Love, Labor of Sorrow: Black Women, Work, and the Family from Slavery to the Present*. New York: Basic Books.

Joseph, Miranda. 1998. "The Performance of Production and Consumption." *Social Text* 54: 25–62.

Kadetsky, Elizabeth. 1994. "'Save Our State' Initiative: Bashing Illegals in California." *Nation*, 17 October, 416–22.

Kamel, Rachel. 1990. *The Global Factory: Analysis and Action for a New Economic Era*. Philadelphia: American Friends Service Committee.

Kanaaneh, Rhoda Ann. 2002. *Birthing the Nation: Strategies of Palestinian Women in Israel*. Berkeley: University of California Press.

Kanaiaupuni, Shawn Malia. 2000. "Reframing the Migration Questions: An Analysis of Men, Women, and Gender in Mexico." *Social Forces* 78, no. 4: 1311–47.

Kang, Laura Hyun Yi. 1997. "Si(gh)ting Asian/American Women as Transnational Labor." *Positions* 5, no. 2 (fall): 403–37.

Kanter, Rosabeth Moss. 1977. *Men and Women of the Corporation*. New York: Basic Books.

Kaplan, Caren, Norma Alarcón, and Minoo Moallem, eds. 1992. *Between Woman and Nation*: Nationalisms, Transnational Feminisms, and the State. Durham, N.C.: Duke University Press.

Kaplan, E. Ann. 1992. *Motherhood and Representation: The Mother in Popular Culture and Melodrama*. New York: Routledge.

Kaplan, Robert D. 1993. "The Coming Anarchy." *Atlantic Monthly*, February, 44–76.

Katzman, David. 1978. *Seven Days a Week: Women and Domestic Service in Industrializing America*. New York: Oxford University Press.

Kearney, Michael. 1972. *The Winds of Ixtepeji: World View and Society in a Zapotec Town*. New York: Holt, Rinehart, and Winston.

———. 1986. "From Invisible Hand to Visible Feet: Anthropological Studies of Migration and Development." *Annual Review in Anthropology* 15: 331–61.

———. 1991. "Borders and Boundaries of State and Self at the End of Empire." *Historical Sociology* 4, no. 1: 52–74.

———. 1995a. "The Effects of Transnational Culture, Economy and Migration on Mixtec Identity in Oaxacalifornia." In *The Bubbling Cauldron: Race, Ethnicity and the Urban Crisis*, edited by Michael Peter Smith and Joseph R. Feagin, 226–43. Minneapolis: University of Minnesota Press.

———. 1995b. "The Local and the Global: The Anthropology of Globalization and Transnationalism." *Annual Review of Anthropology* 24: 547–65.

Kearney, Michael, and James Stuart. 1981. "Causes and Effects of Agricultural Labor Migration from the Mixteca of Oaxaca to California." In *Working Papers in U.S. Mexican Studies*. San Diego: Program in United States-Mexican Studies, University of California.

Keefe, Susan E., and Amado M. Padilla. 1987. *Chicano Ethnicity*. Albuquerque: University of New Mexico Press.

Kegeles, Susan M., Robert B. Hays, Lance M. Pollack, and Thomas J. Coates. 1999. "Mobilizing Young Gay and Bisexual Men for HIV Prevention." *AIDS* 12: 1753–62.

Keil, Roger. 1998. *Los Angeles: Globalization, Urbanization and Social Struggles*. Chichester, N.Y.: John Wiley.

Kelly, Jeff, A. M. Somlai, W. J. Difranceisco, L. L. Otto-Salaj, T. L. Mcauliffe, K. L. Hackl, T. G. Heckman, D. R. Holtgrave, and D. Rompa. 2000. "Bridging the Gap between the Science and Service of HIV Prevention." *American Journal of Public Health* 90: 1082–88.

Kelly, Karen. 2001. *Women on the Verge: Japanese Women, Western Dreams*. Durham, N.C.: Duke University Press.

Kelly, Orr. 1977. "Border Crisis: Illegal Aliens Out of Control?" *U.S. News and World Report* 82: 33–39.

Kemper, Robert V. 1977. *Migration and Adaptation: Tzintzuntzan Peasants in Mexico City*. Beverly Hills: Sage Publications.

Kimmel, Michael, and Michael A. Messner, eds. 2001. *Men's Lives*. 5th ed. Boston: Allyn and Bacon.

King, Katie. 1992. "Local and Global: AIDS Activism and Feminist Theory." *Camera Obscura* 28: 70–100.

Klahn, Norma. 1997. "Writing the Border: The Languages and Limits of Representation." *Travesia* 3, nos. 1 and 2 (special issue): 29–55.

Knapp, Deborah, and Gary Gustis. 1996. "The Real 'Disclosure': Sexual Harassment and the Bottom Line." In *Sexual Harassment in the Workplace: Perspectives, Frontiers, and Response Strategies*, edited by Margaret Stockdale, 199–213. London: Sage Publications.

Kojima, Yu. 2001. "In the Business of Cultural Reproduction: Theoretical Implications of the Mail-order-bride Phenomenon." *Women's Studies International Forum* 24: 199–210.

Kondo, Dorinne. 1990. *Crafting Selves: Power, Gender, and Discourses of Identity in a Japanese Workplace*. Chicago: University of Chicago Press.

Kopinak, Katheryn. 1995. "Gender as a Vehicle for the Subordination of Women Maquila Workers in Mexico." *Latin American Perspectives* 22, no. 1: 30–48.

Kranau, Edgar J., Vicki Green, and Valencia-Weber. 1982. "Acculturation and the Hispanic Woman: Attitudes Toward Women, Sex-Role Attribution, Sex-Role Behavior, and Demographics." *Hispanic Journal of Behavioral Sciences* 4: 21–40.

Kuhn, Annette. 1978. "Structure of Patriarchy and Capital in the Family." In *Feminism and Materialism: Women and Modes of Production*, edited by Annette Kuhn and Ann Marie Wolfe, 42–66. London: Routledge and Kegan Paul.

Laclau, Ernesto, and Chantal Mouffe. 1985. *Hegemony and Socialist Strategy: Towards a Radical Democratic Politics*. London: Verso.

Lagarde, Marcela. 1997. *Los cautiverios de las mujeres: Madresposas, monjas, putas, presas y locas*. Edited by Tercera Edición. Mexico City: Universidad Nacional Autónoma de México.

Lamas, Marta. 1978. "De abandonada a leona: La imagen de la mujer en la canción ranchera." *Fem* 2, no. 6: 20–28.

———. 1996. "Trabajadoras sexuales: Del estigma a la consciencia política." *Estudios Sociológicos* 14, no. 40: 33–52.

———. 1998. "Scenes from a Mexican Battlefield: Report on Sexual Politics." NACLA *Report on the Americas* 31, no. 4: 17–21.

Lamphere, Louise, Alex Stepick, and Guillermo Grenier, eds. 1994. *Newcomers in the Workplace: Immigrants and the Restructuring of the U.S. Economy*. Philadelphia: Temple University Press.

Lamphere, Louise, and Patricia Zavella. 1997. "Women's Resistance in the Sunbelt: Anglos and Hispanas Respond to Managerial Control." In *Women and Work: Exploring Race, Ethnicity, and Class*, edited by Elizabeth Higginbotham and Mary Romero, 337–54. Thousand Oaks, Calif.: Sage Publications.

Lamphere, Louise, Patricia Zavella, Felipe González, and Peter B. Evans. 1993. *Sunbelt Working Mothers: Reconciling Family and Factory*. Ithaca, N.Y.: Cornell University Press.

Landau, Saul. 2002. "A Report on NAFTA and the State of Health of Maquilas." *Progreso Weekly*, 22 July. http://www.progreso.com.

Landau, Saul, and Sonia Angulo, directors. 2000. *Maquila: A Tale of Two Mexicos*. Film. New York: MediaRights.

Landy, Marcia. 1991. Introduction. In *Imitations of Life: A Reader on Film and Television Melodrama*, edited by Marcia Landy, 13–30. Detroit: Wayne State University Press.

Lang, John S., and Jeannye Thornton. 1985. "The Disappearing Border." *U.S. News and World Report*, 30.

Latin American Data Base. 2004. "Increasing Number of Rural Women Migrating to U.S." *Economic and Political News on Mexico* 15, no. 9.

Lauretis, Teresa de. 1987. "The Technology of Gender." In *Technologies of Gender: Essays on Theory, Film and Fiction*, 1–30. Bloomington: Indiana University Press.

Lerner, Stephen. 1991. "Let's Get Moving: Labor's Survival Depends on Organizing Industry-wide for Justice and Power." *Labor Research Review* 18: 1–15.

Lesher, Dave, and Patrick McDonnell. 1996. "Wilson Calls Halt to Much Aid for Illegal Immigrants." *Los Angeles Times*, 28 August, A1.

Levine, Sarah, and Clara Sunderland Correa. 1993. *Dolor y Algria: Women and Social Change in Urban Mexico*. Madison: University of Wisconsin Press.

Levitt, Peggy. 2001. *The Transnational Villagers*. Berkeley: University of California Press.

———. 2003. "Transnational Migration and the Redefinition of the State: Variations and Explanations." *Ethnic and Racial Studies* 26: 587–611.

Levitt, Peggy, and Rafael de la Dehesa. 2003. "Transnational Migration and the Redefinition of the State: Variations and Explanations." *Ethnic and Racial Studies* 26, no. 4: 587–611.

Levy, Sydney, ed. 1996. *Asylum Based on Sexual Orientation: A Resource Guide*. San Francisco: International Gay and Lesbian Human Rights Commission and Lambda Legal Defense and Education Fund.

Lewis, George H. 1993. "Mexican Musical Influences on Country Songs and Styles." In *All That Glitters: Country Music in America*, edited by George Lewis, 94–101. Bowling Green, Ind.: Bowling Green University Popular Press.

Lewis, Oscar. 1951. *Life in a Mexican Village: Tepoztlán Restudied*. Urbana: University of Illinois Press.

———. 1961. *The Children of Sanchez: Autobiography of a Mexican Family*. New York: Random House.

LexisNexis. 1995. "Bill Tracking Report: H.R. 2119." http://www.lexisnexis.com.

Leyva, Yolanda Chavez. 1996. "Breaking the Silence: Putting Latina Lesbian History at the Center." In *The New Lesbian Studies: Toward the Twenty-First Century*, edited by Bonnie Zimmerman and Toni McNaron, 145–52. New York: Routledge.

Limas Hernández, A. 1998. "Desproteción ciudadana." *El Diario de Ciudad Juárez*, 16 July, A11.

Limón, José. 2000. *American Encounters: Greater Mexico, the United States, and the Politics of Culture*. New York: Beacon Press.

Linares, Jesse J. 2000. "Arestan a tres asambleístas." *La Opinión*, 15 April, A6.

Link, Jürgen. 1991. "Fanatics, Fundamentalists, Lunatics, and Drug Traffickers: The New Southern Enemy Image." *Cultural Critique* 19: 33–53.

Little, Jo, Linda Peake, and Pat Richardson, eds. 1988. *Women in Cities: Gender and the Urban Environment*. London: Macmillan Education.

Lock, Margaret, and Patricia A. Kaufert, eds. 1998. *Pragmatic Women and Body Politics*. Cambridge: Cambridge University Press.

Loe, Meika. 1996. "Working for Men: At the Intersection of Power, Gender, and Sexuality." *Sociological Inquiry* 66, no. 4: 399–421.

Lomnitz, Larissa Adler. 1975. *Cómo sobreviven los marginados*. Mexico City: Siglo XXI.

———. 1977. *Networks and Marginality: Life in a Mexican Shanty Town*. New York: Academic Press.

López, Ana M. 1991a. "Are All Latins from Manhattan? Hollywood, Ethnography, and Cultural Colonialism." In *Unspeakable Images: Ethnicity and the American Cinema*, edited by Lester D. Friedman, 404–24. Urbana: University of Illinois Press.

———. 1991b. "Celluloid Tears: Melodrama in the 'Old' Mexican Cinema." *Iris* 13: 29–51.

López, Ann Aurelia. 2002. "From the Farms of West Central Mexico to California's Corporate Agribusiness: The Social Transformation of Two Binational Farming Regions." Ph.D. diss., Environmental Studies Department, University of California, Santa Cruz.

Lopez, Iris. 1998. "An Ethnography of the Medicalization of Puerto Rican Women's Reproduction." In *Pragmatic Women and Body Politics*, edited by Margaret Lock and Patricia A. Kaufert, 240–59. Cambridge: Cambridge University Press.

López Estrada, Raúl Eduardo. 2002. *La pobreza en Monterrey: Los recursos económicos de las unidades domésticas*. Monterrey, Mexico: Universidad Autónoma de Nuevo León.

Los Angeles Commission on Assaults Against Women. 1999. *Training Workshop for Counselors and Advocates*. Los Angeles: The Los Angeles Commission on Assaults Against Women.

Lott, Eric. 1997. "All the King's Men: Elvis Impersonators and White Working Class Masculinity." In *Race and the Subject of Masculinities*, edited by Harry Stecopoulous and Michael Uebel, 192–227. Durham, N.C.: Duke University Press.

Low, Georgiana, and Kurt C. Organista. 2000. "Latinas and Sexual Assault: Towards Culturally Sensitive Assessment and Intervention." *Multicultural Social Work* 8, nos. 1 and 2: 131–57.

Lucker, G. William, and A. Alvarez. 1985. "Controlling Maquiladora Turnover through Personnel Selection." *Southwest Journal of Business and Economics* 2, no. 3: 1–10.

Macaulay, Fiona. 2000. "Tackling Violence against Women in Brazil: Converting International Principles into Effective Local Policy." In *States of Conflict: Gender, Violence and Resistance*, edited by Susie Jacobs, Ruth Jacobson, and Jennifer Marchbank, 144–62. New York: Zed Books.

MacKinnon, Catherine. 1982. "Feminism, Marxism, Method and the State: An Agenda for Theory." *Signs* 7, no. 3: 515–44.

———. 1991. "Reflections on Sex Equality Under the Law." *Yale Law Journal* 100: 1281–1328.

Mackler, Anne Marie. 1998. "Another Expert Explains Murders of Women." *Frontera Norte Sur*. http://frontera.nmsu.edu.

Magis-Rodríguez, Carlos, Enrique Bravo, and Pilar Rivera. 2001. "El SIDA en México en el año 2000." Paper presented at the Binational Forum on Migrant Health, sponsored by the California Policy Research Center at the University of California, Berkeley, 19 October.

Magis-Rodríguez, Carlos, Aurora del Río-Zolezzi, José Luis Valdespino-Gómez, and María de Lourdes García-García. 1995. "Casos de Sida en el área rural de México." *Salud Pública de México* 37, no. 6: 615–23.

Mahler, Sarah J. 1995. *American Dreaming: Immigrant Life on the Margins*. Princeton, N.J.: Princeton University Press.

———. 1996. "Bringing Gender to a Transnational Focus: Theoretical and Empirical Ideas." Unpublished manuscript.

Malkin, Victoria. 1997. "Gender, Status, and Modernity in a Transnational Migrant Circuit." Paper presented at the conference on Transnationalism: An Exchange of Theoretical Perspectives from Latin American, Africanist and Asian Anthropology, sponsored by the Wenner-Gren Foundation for Anthropological Research, University of Manchester and University of Keele, 16–18 May. http://les1.man.ac.uk.

———. 1998. *Gender and Family in Transmigrant Circuits.* London: University College.
———. 2001. "Narcotrafficking, Migration and Modernity." *Latin American Perspectives* 28, no. 4: 101–28.
———. 2004. "We Go to Get Ahead: Gender and Status in Two Mexican Migrant Communities." *Latin American Perspectives* 31, no. 5: 75–99.
Mallon, Florencia. 1984. "Exploring the Origins of Democratic Patriarchy in Mexico: Gender and Popular Resistance in the Puebla Highlands." In *Women of the Mexican Countryside 1985–1990,* edited by Heather Fowler-Salamini and Mary Kay Vaughan, 3–26. Tucson: University of Arizona Press.
Malveaux, Julianne, and Phyllis Wallace. 1987. "Minority Women in the Workplace." In *Women and Work: Industrial Relations Research Association Research Volume,* edited by Karen S. Koziara, Michael H. Moskow, and Lucretia D. Tanner, 265–98. Washington: Bureau of National Affairs.
Marchi, Kristen, and Sylvia R. Guendelman. 1994. "Gender Differences in the Sexual Behavior of Latino Adolescents: An Exploratory Study in a Public High School in the San Francisco Bay Area." *International Quarterly of Community Health Education* 15: 209–26.
Margulis, Mario, and Rodolfo Tuirán. 1986. *Desarrollo y población en la frontera norte: El caso de Reynosa.* Mexico City: Centro de Estudios Demográficos y de Desarrollo Urbano, El Colegio de México.
Marin, Gerardo, Fabio Sabogal, Barbara Vanóss Marin, Regina Otero-Sabogal, and Eliseo J. Perez-Stáble. 1987. "Development of a Short Acculturation Scale for Hispanics." *Hispanic Journal of Behavioral Sciences* 9: 183–205.
Marks, Jonathan. 2002. *What It Means to be 98% Chimpanzee: Apes, People, and their Genes.* Berkeley: University of California Press.
Marshall, T. H. 1950. *Citizenship and Social Class and Other Essays.* Cambridge: Cambridge University Press.
Martin, Emily. 1995. *Flexible Bodies: Tracking Immunity in American Culture: From the Days of Polio to the Age of AIDS.* New York: Beacon.
Martin, Joanne. 1990. "Motherhood and Power. The Production of a Women's Culture of Politics in a Mexican Community." *American Ethnologist* 17, no. 3: 470–91.
Martin, Linda, and Kerry Segrave. 1985. *The Servant Problem: Domestic Workers in North America.* Jefferson: McFarland.
Martin, Lydia. 1996a. "Aspiran las chicas de Miami." *El Nuevo Herald,* 18 March, A1.
———. 1996b. "2,000 Try Out to Play Slain Tejano Singer." *Miami Herald,* 18 March, A1.
Martínez, Elizabeth. 1998. *De Colores Means All of Us: Latina Views for a Multi-Colored Century.* Cambridge, Mass.: South End Press.
Marx, Karl. 1977. *Capital: A Critique of Political Economy.* Vol. 2. New York: Vintage.
Massey, Doreen. 1994. *Space, Place and Gender.* Minneapolis: University of Minnesota Press.
Massey, Douglas S., Jorge Durand, and Nolan J. Malone. 2002. *Beyond Smoke and Mirrors: Mexican Immigration in an Era of Economic Integration.* New York: Russell Sage Foundation.
Mattingly, Doreen. 1997. "The Gender of Economic Restructuring: Paid Household Work

in San Diego, California." Unpublished manuscript, Department of Women's Studies, San Diego State University.

Mauricio Gastón Institute for Latino Community Development and Public Policy. 1994. "Barriers to Employment and Work-Place Advancement of Latinos: Report to the Glass Ceiling Commission, U.S. Department of Labor." Unpublished report, University of Massachusetts, Boston.

Mayer, T. 2000. *Gender Ironies of Nationalism: Sexing the Nation*. London: Routledge.

Mayer-Serra, Otto. 1941. *Panorama de la música mexicana desde la independencia hasta la actualidad*. Mexico City: El Colegio de México.

Mays, Vickie, and Susan Cochran. 1988. "Issues in the Perception of AIDS Risk and Risk Reduction Activities by Black and Hispanic/Latina Women." *American Psychologist* 43, no. 11: 949–56.

McCarthy, Kevin, and George Vernez. 1997. *Immigration in a Changing Economy: California's Experience*. Santa Monica, Calif.: RAND.

———. 1998. *Immigration in a Changing Economy: California's Experience: Questions and Answers*. Santa Monica, Calif.: RAND.

McClintock, Anne. 1995. *Imperial Leather: Race, Gender, and Sexuality in the Colonial Conquest*. New York: Routledge.

McDonnell, Patrick J. 1995. "Study Disputes Immigrant Stereotypes, Cites Gains." *Los Angeles Times*, 3 November, A1.

———. 1996. "Plan to End Funding for Prenatal Care Is Assailed." *Los Angeles Times*, 17 October, A3.

———. 1997a. "Judge Upholds Wilson Ban on Prenatal Care." *Los Angeles Times*, 18 December, A3.

———. 1997b. "State Delays Ban on Prenatal Care for Immigrants." *Los Angeles Times*, 10 July, A3.

———. 1998. "Ruling Delays Prenatal Care Ban Decision." *Los Angeles Times*, 12 June, A3.

McDonnell, Patrick J., and Sebastian Rotella. 1993. "Crossing the Line: Turmoil in the U.S. Border Patrol." *Los Angeles Times*, 23 April, A1.

McDowell, Linda. 1991. "Life without Father and Ford: The New Gender Order of Post-Fordism." *Transactions of the Institute of British Geographers* 16: 400–419.

———. 1997. *Capital Culture: Gender at Work in the City*. Oxford: Basil Blackwell.

Melhuus, Marit. 1992. "Morality, Meaning and Change in a Mexican Context." Ph.D. diss., Department of Museum and Anthropology, University of Oslo.

———. 1996. "Power, Value and the Ambiguous Meanings of Gender." In *Machos, Mistresses and Madonnas: Contesting the Power of Latin American Gender Imagery*, edited by Marit Melhuus and Kristi Anne Stolen, 230–59. London: Verso.

———. 1997. "The Troubles of Virtue-Values of Violence and Suffering in a Mexican Context." In *The Ethnography of Moralities*, edited by Signe Howell, 74–97. London: Routledge.

Melville, Margarita B. 1978. "Mexican Women Adapt to Migration." *International Migration Review* 12, no. 2: 225–35.

———. 1980a. "Introduction: Matrascence." In *Twice a Minority: Mexican American Women*, edited by Margarita B. Melville, 1–16. St. Louis: C.V. Mosby.

———, ed. 1980b. *Twice a Minority: Mexican American Women*. St. Louis: C.V. Mosby Company.

———. 1981. "Mexican Women Adapt to Migration." In *Mexican Immigrant Workers in the U.S.*, edited by Antonio Ríos Bustamante, 225–35. Los Angeles: Chicano Studies Research Center, University of California.

———. 1988. *Mexicanas at Work in the United States*. Houston: University of Houston, Mexican American Studies Monograph No. 5.

Mena, Jennifer. 2000a. "Creating the New Macho Man: To the Men in these Latino Discussion Groups, Machismo Is about Strength, Love, Family and Respect." *Los Angeles Times*, 12 December, E1, 3.

———. 2000b. "Cruel Memento: Mexican Immigrant Workers Come Back from the North with HIV." *San Francisco Chronicle*, 29 September, 18–19.

Mendoza, Richard H. 1984. "Acculturation and Sociocultural Variability." In *Chicano Psychology*, 2d ed., edited by Joe L. Martinez Jr. and Richard H. Mendoza, 61–75. New York: Academic Press.

Mendoza, Vicente T. 1988 [1961]. *La Canción Mexicana*. Mexico City: Fondo de Cultura Económica.

Michaelsen, Scott, and David E. Johnson. 1997. *Border Theory: The Limits of Cultural Politics*. Minneapolis: University of Minnesota Press.

Mies, Maria. 1982. *The Lace Makers of Narsapur: Indian Housewives Produce for the World Market*. London: Zed Press.

Milkman, Ruth, Ellen Reese, and Benita Roth. 1998. "The Macro-Sociology of Housework." *Work and Occupations* 25: 483–510.

Miller, Neil. 1995. *Out of the Past: Gay and Lesbian History from 1869 to the Present*. New York: Vintage Books.

Mills, Mary Beth. 1997. "Contesting the Margins of Modernity: Women, Migration and Consumption in Thailand." *American Ethnologist* 24, no. 1: 37–61.

Mindiola, Tatcho, Jr., Yolanda Flores Niemann, and Nestor Rodriguez. 2002. *Black-Brown Relations and Stereotypes*. Austin: University of Texas Press.

Mines, Richard, and Jeffrey Avina. 1992. "Immigrants and Labor Standards: The Case of California Janitors." In *U.S.-Mexico Relations: Labor Market Interdependence*, edited by Jorge Bustamante, Clark W. Reynolds, and Raul A. Hinojosa Ojeda, 429–48. Stanford, Calif.: Stanford University Press.

Minter, Shannon. 1993. "Sodomy and Public Morality Offenses under U.S. Immigration Law: Penalizing Lesbian and Gay Identity." *Cornell International Law Journal* 26: 780–99.

Mirande, Alfredo, and Evangelina Enriquez. 1979. *La Chicana: The Mexican American Woman*. Chicago: University of Chicago Press.

Mishra, Shiraz I., Ross F. Conner, and J. Raúl Magaña. 1996. *AIDS Crossing Borders*. Boulder, Colo.: Westview Press.

Mohanty, Chandra Talpade. 1997. "Women Workers and Capitalist Script: Ideologies of Domination, Common Interests, and the Politics of Solidarity." In *Feminist Geneologies, Colonial Legacies, Democratic Futures*, edited by M. Jacqui Alexander and Chandra Talpade Mohanty, 3–29. New York: Routledge.

Monárrez, Julia Estela. 2000. "La cultura del feminicidio en Ciudad Juárez, 1993–1999." *Frontera Norte* 12, no. 23: 87–117.

Monsiváis, Carlos. 1992. "Las mitologies del cine mexicano." *Intermedios* 2: 12–23.

———.1994a [1977]. "Irma Serrano: Entra apariciones de la venus de fuego." In *Amor perdido*, 297–318. Mexico City: Ediciones Era.

———. 1994b [1977]. "José Alfredo Jiménez: No vengo a pedir lectores (Se repite el disco por mi puritita gana)." In *Amor perdido*, 87–97. Mexico City: Ediciones Era.

———. 1994c. "Se sufre, pero se aprende el melodrama y las reglas de la falta de limites." In *A través del espejo: El cine mexicano y su público*, edited by Carlos Monsiváis and Carlos Bonfil, 99–224. Mexico City: Ediciones el Milagro, Instituto Mexicano de Cinematografia.

Moore, Henrietta. 1988. *Feminism and Anthropology*. Cambridge: Polity Press.

Moore, Joan, and Raquel Pinderhughes, eds. 1993. *In the Barrios: Latinos and the Underclass Debate*. New York: Russell Sage Foundation.

Mora, Carlos. 1982. *Mexican Cinema*. Berkeley: University of California Press.

Moraga, Cherríe. 1983. *Loving in the War Years: Lo que nunca pasó por sus labios*. Boston: South End Press.

Morales, Rebecca, and Frank Bonilla, eds. 1993. *Latinos in a Changing U.S. Economy: Comparative Perspectives on Growing Inequality*. Newbury Park, Calif.: Sage Publications.

Morales, Rebecca, and Paul Ong. 1991. "Immigrant Women in Los Angeles." *Economic and Industrial Democracy* 12: 65–81.

Moreno Rivas, Yolanda. 1989. *Historia de la música popular mexicana*. Mexico City: Alianza Editorial Mexicana, Consejo Nacional para la Cultura y las Artes.

Morgan, David L., ed. 1993. *Successful Focus Groups: Advancing the State of the Art*. Newbury Park, Calif.: Sage Publications.

Moser, Caroline O. N. 1988. *Housing Policy and Women: Towards a Gender Aware Approach: DPU Gender and Planning Work Paper No. 7*. London: Development Planning Unit, University College London, 1988.

Mulvey, Laura. 1975. "Visual Pleasure and Narrative Cinema." *Screen* 16, no. 3: 6–18.

Mummert, Gail, ed. 1999. *Fronteras fragmentadas*. Zamora: El Colegio de Michoacán, Centro de Investigaciónes y Desarrollo del Estado de Michoacán.

Muñoz, José Esteban. 2000. "Feeling Brown: Ethnicity and Affect in Ricardo Bracho's *The Sweetest Hangover (and Other STDs)*." *Theatre Journal* 52: 67–79.

Nagengast, Carol, and Michael Kearney. 1990. "Mixtec Ethnicity: Social Identity, Political Consciousness, and Political Activism." *Latin American Research Review* 25, no. 2; 61–91.

Nagengast, Carol, and Carlos G. Vélez-Ibañez. 2004. *Human Rights: The Scholar as Activist*. Washington: Publications of the Society of Applied Anthropology.

Nájera-Ramírez, Olga. 1994. "Engendering Nationalism: Identity, Discourse, and the Mexican Charro." *Anthropology Quarterly* 67, no. 1: 1–14.

———. 1999. "La Escaramuza Charra." Paper presented at the conference, Mexican Women in Transnational Context, Center for Chicano/Latino Studies, University of California, Santa Cruz, April.

Nakano-Glenn, Evelyn. 1986. *Issei, Nissei, War Bride: Three Generations of Japanese American Women in Domestic Service*. Philadelphia: Temple University Press.

Naples, Nancy A. 1991. "A Socialist Feminist Analysis of the Family Support Act of 1988." *Affilia* 6: 23–38.

Napolitano, Valentina. 1995. *Self and Identity in a Colonia Popular of Guadalajara, Mexico*. London: School of Oriental and African Studies, University of London.

Narayan, Uma. 1997. *Dis-locating Cultures: Identities, Traditions and Third World Feminism*. New York: Routledge.

Nash, June, and María Patricia Fernández-Kelly, eds. 1983. *Women, Men, and the International Division of Labor*. Albany: State University of New York Press.

Nathan, Debbie. 1991. *Women and Other Aliens*. El Paso: Cinco Puntos Press.

———. 1997. "Death Comes to the Maquilas: A Border Story." *The Nation*, 13 January, 18–22.

———. 1999. "Work, Sex, and Danger in Ciudad Juárez." *North American Congress on Latin America* 33, no. 3: 26–30.

National Defense Authorization Act of 1982 (Public Law 97-86). 1981. *United States Statutes at Large Containing the Laws and Concurrent Resolutions of the 97th Congress of the United States of America*. Washington: U.S. Government Printing Office.

Navarro, Mireya. 1999. "Inspired By Selena, They Seek Her Role." *New York Times*, 8 November, B1.

———. 2000. "Latin Grammys' Border Skirmish: New Awards Face Complaints About Slighting a Mexican Genre." *New York Times*, 30 September, E1.

Neft, Naomi, and Ann D. Levine. 1997. *Where Women Stand: An International Report of the Status of Women in 140 Countries*. New York: Random House.

Negrón-Muntaner, Frances. 1997. "Jennifer's Butt." *Aztlán* 22, no. 2: 184–95.

Nelson, Diane M. 1999. *A Finger in the Wound: Body Politics in Quincentennial Guatemala*. Berkeley: University of California Press.

Nesiah, Vasuki. 2000. "Toward a Feminist Intersectionality: A Critique of U.S. Feminist Legal Scholarship." In *Global Critical Race Feminism: An International Reader*, edited by Adrien Katherine Wing, 42–52. New York: New York University Press.

Nevins, Joseph. 2002. *Operation Gatekeeper: The Rise of the "Illegal Alien" and the Making of the US-Mexico Boundary*. New York: Routledge.

Newman, Katherine. 1998. *No Shame in My Game*. New York: Random House.

Nielsen, Francois, and Roberto M. Fernandez. 1981. *Hispanic Students in American High Schools: Background Characteristics and Achievement*. Washington: U.S. Government Printing Office.

Nieves, Evelyn. 2002. "To Work and Die in Juárez." *Mother Jones*, June, 50–55.

Nuttin, Joseph, ed. 1982. *Teoría de la motivación humana (de la necesidad al proyecto de acción*. Buenos Aires: Editorial Paidos Barcelona.

Nyamathi, Adeline, and Rose Vasquez. 1989. "Impact of Poverty, Homelessness, and Drugs on Hispanic Women at Risk for HIV Infection." *Hispanic Journal of Behavioral Sciences* 11, no. 4: 299–314.

O'Connor, Anne-Marie. 1996. "Border Agent Gets 10 Years for Sexual Assault." *Los Angeles Times*, 20 November, A3.

O'Connor, Mary. 1990. "Women's Networks and the Social Needs of Mexican Immigrants." *Urban Anthropology* 19, nos. 1 and 2: 81–98.

O'Dougherty, Maureen. 2002. *Consumption Intensified: The Politics of Middle-Class Daily Life in Brazil*. Durham, N.C.: Duke University Press.

Office of Minority Health Resource Center. 1988. *Closing the Gap: Wide Health Disparities Continue*. Washington: Health Resources and Services Administration.

Ojeda de la Peña, Norma. 1990. "Hogares transfronterizos." Paper presented at the Cuarta Reunión Nacional de la Investigación Demográfica en México, Mexico City, 25–27 April.

———. 1992. "Migración y trabajo en la formación de las familias transfronterizas en el norte de México." Paper presented at the Conferencia Sobre el Poblamiento de las Américas, Veracruz, Mexico, 18–23 May.

Ojeda de la Peña, Norma, and Roberto Ham Chande. 1989. "Estudio de las interrelaciones demográficas en la frontera de México con Estadoes Unidos." In *Fronteras en Iberoamérica ayer y hoy*, 47–58. Tijuana: Universidad Autónoma de Baja California.

Oliveira, Orlandina de. 1984. "Migración femenina, organización laboral y mercados laborales en México." *Comercio Exterior* 34, no. 7: 676–87.

———. 1987. "Presencías y ausencias femeninas. Consideraciones acerca de la investigación social sobre las mujeres." Paper presented at El Coloquio sobre Estudios de la Mujer, Encuentro de Talleres, Mexico, 10–13 March.

———. 1990. "Empleo feminino en México en tiempos de recesión económica: Tendencia recientes." In *Mujeres y Crisis: Respuestas Ante la Recession*, edited by L. G. Ortega et al. Caracas, Venezuela: Editorial Nueva Sociedad.

———. 2000. "Quality of Life and Marital Experiences in Mexico." In *Women, Poverty and Demographic Change*, edited by Brígida García, 75–94. Oxford: Oxford University Press.

Oliveira, Orlandina de, and Vania Salles. 1988. "Reflexiones teóricas para el estudio de la reproducción de la fuerza de trabajo." *Argumentos: Estudios Críticas de la Sociedad*, no. 4: 19–43.

———. 1989. "Acerca del estudio de los grupos domésticos: Un enfoque sociodemográfico." In *Grupos domésticos y reproducción cotidiana*, edited by Orlandina de Oliveira, Pepin Lehalleur, and Vania Salles, 11–36. Mexico City: Universidad Nacional Autónoma de México/Porrúa.

Omi, Michael, and Howard Winant. 1994. *Racial Formation in the United States*. New York: Routledge.

Ong, Aihwa. 1991. "The Gender and Labour Politics of Postmodernity." *Annual Review in Anthropology* 20: 279–309.

———. 1999. *Flexible Citizenship: The Cultural Logics of Transnationality*. Durham, N.C.: Duke University Press.

Ono, Kent A., and John M. Sloop. 2002. *Shifting Borders: Rhetoric, Immigration, and California's Proposition 187*. Philadelphia: Temple University Press.

Organista, Kurt C., Pamela Balls Organista, G. J. Garcia De Alba, and M. A. Castillo. 1996. "AIDS and Condom-Related Knowledge, Beliefs, and Behaviors in Mexican Migrant Laborers." *Hispanic Journal of Behavioral Sciences* 18, no. 3: 392–406.

Orlansky, Dora, and Silvia Dubrovsky. 1976. *The Effects of Rural-Urban Migration on Women's Role and Status in Latin America*. Reports and Papers in the Social Sciences, no. 41. Paris: UNICEF.

Orquiz, M. 1998. "Asesinatos de Mujeres: 'Como Dejar un Dulce en u Colegio.'" *El Diario de Ciudad Juárez*, 2 August, C3.

Ortiz, Vilma. 1994. "Women of Color: A Demographic Overview." In *Women of Color in U.S. Society*, edited by Maxine Baca Zinn and Bonnie Thornton Dill, 13–40. Philadelphia: Temple University Press.

———. 1996. "The Mexican Origin Population: Permanent Working Class or Emerging Middle Class?" In *Ethnic Los Angeles*, edited by Roger Waldinger and Mehdi Bozorgmehr, 247–48. New York: Russell Sage Foundation.

Ortiz, Vilma, and Rosemary Santana Cooney. 1984. "Sex-Role Attitudes and Labor Force Participation among Young Hispanic Females and Non-Hispanic White Females." *Social Science Quarterly* 65: 392–400.

Padilla, Felix. 1985. *Latino Ethnic Consciousness: The Case of Mexican Americans and Puerto Ricans in Chicago*. Notre Dame, Ind.: University of Notre Dame Press.

Paglia, Camille. 1992. *Sexual Personae*. New York: Vintage Books.

Palafox, Jose. 2000. "Opening up Borderland Studies: A Review of U.S.-Mexico Border Militarization Discourse." *Social Justice* 27: 56–72.

Palerm, Juan-Vicente. 1991. *Farm Labor Needs and Farm Workers in California, 1970–1989*. Sacramento: California Employment Development Department, Labor Market Information Division, California Agricultural Studies.

———. 1994. *Immigrant and Migrant Farmworkers in the Santa Maria Valley of California*. Washington: Center for Survey Methods Research, Bureau of the Census.

Palerm, Juan-Vicente, and José Ignacio Urquiola. 1993. "A Binational System of Agricultural Production: The Case of the Mexican Bajío and California." In *Mexico and the United States: Neighbors in Crisis*, edited by Daniel G. Aldrich Jr. and Lorenzo Meyer, 311–36. San Bernardino: Borgo Press.

Palmer, Phyllis. 1984. "Housework and Domestic Labor: Racial and Technological Change." In *My Troubles Are Going to Have Trouble With Me: Everyday Trials and Triumphs of Women Workers*, edited by Karen Brodkin Sacks and Dorothy Remy, 89–94. New Brunswick: Rutgers University Press.

———. 1989. *Domesticity and Dirt: Housewives and Domestic Servants in the United States, 1920–1945*. Philadelphia: Temple University Press.

Parcel, Toby L., and Elizabeth G. Menaghan. 1990. "Maternal Working Conditions and Child Verbal Facility: Studying the Intergenerational Transmission of Inequality from Mothers to Young Children." *Social Psychology Quarterly* 53: 132–47.

Pardo, Mary S. 1990. "Mexican American Women Grassroots Community Activists: Mothers of East Los Angeles." *Frontiers* 11, no. 1: 1–7.

———. 1998a. "Creating Community: Mexican American Women in Eastside Los Angeles." In *Community Activism and Feminist Politics: Organizing Across Race, Class, and Gender*, edited by Nancy A. Naples, 275–300. New York: Routledge.

———. 1998b. *Mexican American Women Activists: Identity and Resistance in Two Los Angeles Communities*. Philadelphia: Temple University Press.

Paredes, Américo. 1977. "On Ethnographic Work among Minorities: A Folklorist's Perspective." *New Scholar* 6: 1–32.

———. 1982. "Folklore, Lo Mexicano and Proverbs." *Aztlán* 13: 1–11.

———. 1993. "The Folklore of Groups of Mexican Origin in the United States." In *Folklore and Culture on the Texas-Mexican Border*, edited by Richard Bauman, 3–18. Austin: University of Texas at Austin, Center for Mexican American Studies.

Paredez, Deborah. 2002. "Remembering Selena, Re-membering Latinidad." *Theatre Journal* 54, no. 1: 63–84.

Parsons, Talcott, and Robert Bales. 1995. *Family, Socialization, and Interaction Processes*. New York: Free Press.

Pastor, Manuel, Jr. 2003. "Rising Tides and Sinking Boats: The Economic Challenge for California's Latinos." In *Latinos and Public Policy in California: an Agenda for Opportunity*, edited by David Lopez and Andrés Jimenez, 35–64. Berkeley: University of California, Institute of Governmental Studies.

———. Forthcoming. "Poverty, Work, and Public Policy: Latino Futures in California's New Economy." In *Latinos in the United States: Challenges and Transformation*, edited by Patricia Zavella, Ramón Gutiérrez, with Denise Segura, Dolores Trevizo, and Juan Vicente Palerm.

Patoski, Joe Nick. 1996. *Selena: Como la flor*. Boston: Little, Brown.

Paz, Octavio. 1961. *The Labyrinth of Solitutude: Life and Thought in Mexico*. Translated by Lysander Kemp. New York: Grove Press.

Peck, Robert F., and Rogelio Diaz-Guerrero. 1967. "Two Core-Culture Patterns and the Diffusion of Values across Their Borders." *International Journal of Psychology* 2: 272–82.

Pedraza, Silvia. 1991. "Women and Migration: The Social Consequences of Gender." *Annual Review of Sociology* 17: 303–25.

Peek, Charles E., and Sharon Brown. 1980. "Sex Prejudice among White Protestants: Like or Unlike Ethnic Prejudice?" *Social Forces* 59: 169–85.

Peña, Devon G. 1997. *The Terror of the Machine: Technology, Work, Gender, and Ecology on the U.S.-Mexico Border*. Austin: University of Texas Press.

Peña, Manuel. 1985. *The Texas-Mexican Conjunto: History of a Working-class Music*. Austin: University of Texas.

———. 1999. *Música Tejana: The Cultural Economy of Artistic Transformation*. College Station: Texas A&M Press.

Perez, Claudia, narrator. 1996. "1000 Women Become Selena." Report compiled for the "From a Distance" episode of *This American Life*, National Public Radio, 19 April.

Pérez, Emma. 1999. *The Decolonial Imaginary: Writing Chicanas into History*. Bloomington: Indiana University Press.

Pérez, Gina. 2003. "Puertorriqueñas Rencorosas y Mejicanas Sufridas: Gendered Ethnic Identity Formation in Chicago's Latino Communities." *Latin American Anthropology* 8, no. 2: 96–125.

———. 2004. *The Near Northwest Side Story: Puerto Rican Families and Transnational Politics of Belonging*. Berkeley: University of California Press.

Pérez, Sonia M., and Deirdre Martínez. 1993. *State of Hispanic America 1993: Toward a Latino Anti-Poverty Agenda*. Washington: National Council of La Raza.

Perilla, Julia L. 1999. "Domestic Violence as a Human Rights Issue: The Case of Immigrant Latinos." *Hispanic Journal of Behavioral Sciences* 21, no. 2: 107–33.

Pessar, Patricia. 1995. "On the Homefront and in the Workplace: Integrating Immigrant Women into Feminist Discourse." *Anthropological Quarterly* 68, no. 1: 37–47.

———. 1998. "The Role of Gender, Household and Social Networks in the Migration Process: A Review and Appraisal." In *Becoming American/America Becoming*, edited by Josh DeWind, Charles Hirschman, and Philip Kasinitz, 53–70. New York: Russell Sage Foundation.

Phelan, Peggy. 1993. *Unmarked: The Politics of Performance*. New York: Routledge.

Phelps, Edmund. 1980. "The Statistical Theory of Racism and Sexism." In *The Economics of Women and Work*, edited by Alice H. Amsden, 206–10. New York: St. Martin's Press.

Philipose, Liz. 1996. "The Laws of War and Women's Human Rights." *Hypatia* 11: 46–62.

Podalsky, Laura. 1993. "Disjointed Frames: Melodrama, Nationalism and Representation in 1940s México." *Studies in Latin American Popular Culture* 12: 57–73.

Podnanski, Robert. 1983–1984. "The Propriety of Denying Entry to Homosexual Aliens: Examining the Public Health Service's Authority over Medical Exclusions." *University of Michigan Journal of Law Reform* 17: 331–59.

Polacheck, Solomon W. 1975. "Discontinuous Labor Force Participation and Its Effect on Women's Market Earnings." In *Sex Discrimination and the Division of Labor*, edited by Cynthia B. Lloyd, 90–122. New York: Columbia University Press.

———. 1981a. "Occupational Segregation among Women: Theory, Evidence, and a Prognosis." In *Women in the Labor Market*, edited by Cynthia B. Lloyd, Emily Andrews, and Curtis Gilroy, 137–57. New York: Columbia University Press.

———. 1981b. "Occupational Self-Selection: A Human Capital Approach to Sex Differences in Occupational Structure." *Review of Economics and Statistics* 63: 60–69.

Poniatowska, Elena. 2000. *Las mil y una . . . (la herida de Paulina)*. Mexico City: Plaza and Janés Editores.

Population Reference Bureau. 2004. *World Population Data Sheet: Total Births per Woman, Mexico 2003*. Population Reference Bureau, 3 March. http://www.prb.org.

Porter, Dorothy. 1999. *Health, Civilization, and the State: A History of Public Health from Ancient to Modern Times*. London: Routledge.

Portes, Alejandro, Manuel Castells, and Lauren Benton, eds. 1989. *The Informal Economy: Studies in Advanced and Less Developed Countries*. Tucson: University of Arizona Press.

Portes, Alejandro, Luis E. Guarnizo, and Patricia Landolt. 1999. "The Study of Transnationalism: Pitfalls and Promise of an Emergent Research Field." *Ethnic and Racial Studies* 22: 217–23.

Portes, Alejandro, and Rubén G. Rumbaut, eds. 2001. *Legacies: the Story of the Immigrant Second Generation*. Berkeley: University of California Press.

Portillo, Lourdes, director. 1999. *Corpus: A Home Movie for Selena*. Hohokus, N.J.: Xóchitl Productions.

"A Portrait of America: Lands of Our Fathers." 1983. *Newsweek*, 17 January, 22.

Proctor, Robert N. 1995. "The Destruction of 'Lives Not Worth Living.'" In *Deviant Bodies:*

Critical Perspectives on Difference in Science and Popular Culture, edited by Jennifer Terry and Jacqueline Urla, 170–96. Bloomington: Indiana University Press.

Puig, Claudia. 1996. "Audition for Selena Roles Turns into Celebration." *Los Angeles Times*, 18 March, B1.

Quintana, Victor M. 2001a. "Los feminicidios de Ciudad Juárez." *La Jornada*, 23 November.

———. 2001b. "Ciudad Juárez: Parar los homicidios." *La Jornada*, 13 December.

Radcliffe, Sarah. 1986. "Gender Relations, Peasant Livelihood, Strategies and Migration: A Case Study from Cuzo, Peru." *Bulletin of Latin American Studies* 5, no. 2: 29–47.

Ramirez, David Piñera. 1985. *Historia de Tijuana: Semblanza general*. Tijuana: Universidad Autónoma de Baja California.

Ramirez III, Manuel, and Alfredo Castaneda. 1974. *Cultural Democracy Bicognitive Development and Education*. New York: Academic Press.

Ramos Lira, Luciana, Mary P. Koss, and Nancy Felipe Russo. 1999. "Mexican American Women's Definitions of Rape and Sexual Abuse." *Hispanic Journal of Behavioral Sciences* 21, no. 3: 236–65.

Rapp, Rayna. 2000a. "Family and Class in Contemporary America: Notes towards an Understanding of Ideology." In *Household and Gender Relations in Latin America*, edited by Elizabeth Gallein, 197–215. London: Keegan Paul.

———. 2000b. *Testing Women, Testing the Fetus: The Social Impact of Amniocentesis in America*. New York: Routledge.

Redfield, Robert. 1930. *Tepoztlán, A Mexican Village: A Study of Folk Life*. Chicago: University of Chicago Press.

Reeves Sanday, Peggy, and Ruth Gallagher Goodenough, eds. 1990. *Beyond the Second Sex: New Directions in the Anthropology of Gender*. Philadelphia: University of Pennsylvania Press.

Repak, Terri. 1995. *Waiting on Washington*. Philadelphia: Temple University Press.

Repard, Pauline, and Leonel Sanchez. 1995. "Border Agent Accused of Rape, Federal Officer Join Police in Probe." *San Diego Union Tribune*, 2 December, B1, 3.

Reuter, Jas. 1983. *La música popular de México: Origen e historia de la música que canta y toca el pueblo mexicano*. Mexico City: Panorama Editorial.

Reyes, Aurelio de los. 1988. *Medio siglo de cine mexicano (1896–1947)*. Mexico City: Editorial Trillas.

Reyes, Belinda I. 1997. "Dynamics of Immigration: Return Migration to Western Mexico." San Francisco: Public Policy Institute of California.

Rich, Adrienne. 1977. *Of Woman Born*. London: Virago.

Richardson, Chad, and Cruz Torres. 1999. "Only a Maid: Undocumented Domestic Workers in South Texas." In *Batos, Bolillos, Pochos, and Pelados: Class and Culture on the South Texas Border*, edited by Chad Richardson, 69–94. Austin: University of Texas Press.

Richwald, Gary A., Margarita Schneider-Muñoz, and Robert Burciaga Valdez. 1989. "Are Condom Instructions in Spanish Readable? Implications for AIDS Prevention Activities for Hispanics." *Hispanic Journal of Behavioral Sciences* 11, no. 1: 70–82.

Riddenhour-Levitt, Jennifer. 1999. "Constructing Gender, Race, and Ethnicity in a Globalized Context: The 'Mail-order Bride' Trade." *Critica: A Journal of Critical Essays*, Spring, 51–56.

Roach, Joseph. 1996. *Cities of the Dead: Circum-Atlantic Performance*. New York: Columbia University Press.

Roberts, Bryan R. 1989. "Employment Structure, Life Cycle, and Life Chances: Formal and Informal Sectors in Guadalajara." In *The Informal Economy: Studies in Advanced and Less Developed Countries*, edited by Alejandro Portes, Manuel Castells, and Lauren Benton, 41–59. Baltimore: Johns Hopkins University Press.

Roberts, Dorothy E. 1997a. *Killing the Black Body: Race, Reproduction, and the Meaning of Liberty*. New York: Pantheon Books.

———. 1997b. "Who May Give Birth to Citizens? Reproduction, Eugenics, and Immigration." In *Immigrants Out! The New Nativism and the Anti-Immigrant Impulse in the United States*, edited by Juan F. Perea, 205–19. New York: New York University Press.

Rocco, Raymond. 1992. "Citizenship, Culture, and Community: Restructuring in Southeast Los Angeles." In *Latino Cultural Citizenship: Claiming Identity, Space, and Rights*, edited by William V. Flores and Rina Benmayor, 97–124. Boston: Beacon Press.

Roche, Maurice. 1992. *Rethinking Citizenship: Welfare, Ideology, and Change in Modern Society*. Cambridge, U.K.: Polity Press.

Rodebaugh, D. 1999. "Settlement Reached in Harassment Suit." *San Jose Mercury News*, 24 February, B1.

Rodríguez, Daniel. 1981. "Discusiones en torno al concepto de estrategias de sobrevivencia." *Demografía y Economía* 15, no. 2: 238–52.

Rodríguez, Gabriela. 2001. "Señoritas asesinadas en Juárez." *La Jornada*, 13 December, 22.

Rodríguez, Marta, and Jorge Silva, directors. 1988. *Love, Women, and Flowers*. Film. New York: Women Make Movies.

Rodríguez, Néstor. 1996. "The Battle for the Border: Notes on Autonomous Migration, Transnational Communities and the State." *Social Justice* 23: 21–37.

———. 1997. "The Social Construction of the US-Mexico Border." In *Immigrants Out! The New Nativism and the Anti-Immigrant Impulse in the United States*, edited by Juan F. Perea, 223–43. New York: New York University Press.

Rodriguez, Nice. 1992. "Big Nipple of the North." In *Piece of My Heart: A Lesbian of Colour Anthology*, edited by Makeda Silvera, 33–36. Toronto.

Rogers, Jackie, and Kevin Henson. 1997. "'Hey, Why Don't You Wear a Shorter Skirt?': Structural Vulnerability and the Organization of Sexual Harassment in Temporary Clerical Employment." *Gender and Society* 11, no. 2: 215–37.

Rohter, Larry. 1997. "A Legend Grows, and So Does an Industry." *New York Times*, 12 January, H39.

Rollins, Judith. 1985. *Between Women: Domestics and Their Employers*. Philadelphia: Temple University Press.

Román, David. 1997. "Latino Performance and Identity." *Aztlán* 22, no. 2: 151–52.

Romanucci-Ross, Lola. 1973. *Conflict, Violence, and Morality in a Mexican Village*. Chicago: University of Chicago Press.

Romany, Celina. 2000. "Themes for a Conversation on Race and Gender in International

Human Rights Law." In *Global Critical Race Feminism: An International Reader*, edited by Adrien Katherine Wing, 53–66. New York: New York University Press.

Romero, Gloria J., and Lourdes Argüelles. 1993. "AIDS Knowledge and Beliefs of Citizen and Non-Citizen Chicanas/Mexicanas." *Latino Studies Journal*, September, 79–94.

Romero, Gloria J., Felipe G. Castro, and Richard C. Cervantes. 1988. "Latinas Without Work: Family, Occupational, and Economic Stress Following Unemployment." *Psychology of Women Quarterly* 12, no. 3: 281–97.

Romero, Mary. 1988. "Sisterhood and Domestic Service: Race, Class and Gender in the Mistress-Maid Relationship." *Humanity and Society* 12: 318–46.

———. 1992. *Maid in the USA*. New York: Routledge.

———. 1996. "Life as the Maid's Daughter: An Exploration of the Everyday Boundaries of Race, Class and Gender." In *Feminisms in the Academy: Rethinking the Disciplines*, edited by Abigail J. Steward and Donna Stanon, 195–213. Ann Arbor: University of Michigan Press.

———. 1997. "Who Takes Care of the Maid's Children? Exploring the Costs of Domestic Service." In *Feminism and Families*, edited by Hilde L. Nelson, 151–69. New York: Routledge.

Ronquillo, Víctor. 1999. *Las muertas de Juárez*. Mexico City: Editorial Planeta.

Root, Maria P. P., ed. 1992. *Racially Mixed People in America*. Newbury Park, Calif.: Sage Publications.

Rosaldo, Michelle Z., and Louise Lamphere. 1974. Introduction. In *Women, Culture and Society*, 1–15. Stanford, Calif.: Stanford University Press.

Rosaldo, Renato. 1997. "Cultural Citizenship, Inequality, and Multiculturalism." In *Latino Cultural Citizenship*, edited by William V. Flores and Rina Benmayor, 27–38. Boston: Beacon Press.

Rose, Kieran. 1995. "The Tenderness of the Peoples." In *Lesbian and Gay Visions of Ireland: Towards the Twenty-First Century*, edited by Íde O'Carroll and Eoin Collins, 71–85. London: Cassell.

Rotella, Sebastian. 1994. "Agents Begin Massive Sweep along Border." *Los Angeles Times*, 2 October, A3.

Rothstein, Frances. 1983. "Women and Men in the Family Economy: An Analysis of the Relations Between the Sexes in Three Peasant Communities." *Anthropological Quarterly* 56: 10–23.

Rouse, Roger. 1989. "Mexican Migration to the United States: Family Relations in the Development of a Transnational Migrant Circuit." Ph.D. diss., Department of Anthropology, Stanford University, California.

———. 1991. "Mexican Migration and the Social Space of Postmodernism." *Diaspora* 1, no. 1: 8–23.

———. 1992. "Making Sense of Settlement: Class Transformation, Cultural Struggle and Transnationalism among Mexican Migrants in the United States." *Annals of the New York Academy of Sciences* 645: 25–52.

———. 1995a. "Questions of Identity: Personhood and Collectivity in Transnational Migration to the United States." *Critique of Anthropology* 15, no. 4: 351–80.

———. 1995b. "Thinking through Transnationalism: Notes on the Cultural Politics of Class Relations in the Contemporary United States." *Public Culture* 7, no. 2: 353–402.

Rúa, Mérida. 2001. "Colao Subjectivities: PortoMex and MexiRican Perspectives on Language and Identity." *Centro* 2: 116–33.

Rubin, Lillian B. 1983. *Intimate Strangers: Men and Women Together*. New York: Harper and Row.

Ruddick, Sara. 1989. *Maternal Thinking: Toward a Politics of Peace*. Boston: Beacon Press.

Ruiz, Vicki L. 1987. "By the Day or the Week: Mexicana Domestic Workers in El Paso." In *Women on the U.S.-Mexico Border: Responses to Change*, edited by Vicki L. Ruiz and Susan Tiano, 61–76. Boston: Allen and Unwin.

———. 1988. "'And Miles to Go . . .': Mexican Women and Work, 1930–1985." In *Western Women: Their Land, Their Lives*, edited by Lillian Schlissel, Vicky L. Ruiz, and Janice Monk, 117–36. Albuquerque: University of New Mexico Press.

———. 1998. *From Out of the Shadows: Mexican Women in Twentieth-Century America*. New York: Oxford University Press.

Ruiz, Vicki L., and Ellen Carol DuBois. 1994. *Unequal Sisters: A Multicultural Reader in U.S. Women's History*. New York: Routledge.

Ruiz, Vicki L., and Susan Tiano, eds. 1987. *Women on the U.S.-Mexico Border: Responses to Change*. Boston: Allen and Unwin.

Rumberger, Russell W., and Brenda Arellano Anguiano. Forthcoming. "Understanding and Addressing the Latino Achievement Gap in California." In *Latinos in the United States: Challenges and Transformation*, edited by Patricia Zavella and Ramón Gutiérrez, with Denise Segura, Dolores Trevizo, and Juan Vicente Palerm.

Russell, Dianna, and Jill Radford. 1992. *Feminicide: The Politics of Woman Killing*. New York: Twayne.

Russell, Sabin. 1993. "Racism Blamed for AIDS Rise in Minorities." *San Francisco Chronicle*, 12 January, 11.

Ryan, R., D. Foulk, J. Lafferty, and A. Robertson. 1988. *Health Knowledge and Practices of Georgia's Migrant and Seasonal Workers Relative to AIDS: A Comparison of Two Groups*. Statesboro: Georgia Southern College, Center for Rural Health.

Salazar, Tania Rodríguez. 2001. *Las razones del matrimonio: Representaciones, relatos de vida y sociedad*. Guadalajara: University of Guadalajara Press.

Saldívar, Gabriel. 1934. *Historia de la música en México*. Mexico City: Secretaría de Educación Pública.

Salgado de Snyder, V. Nelly, Andrea Acevedo, María de Jesús Díaz-Pérez, and Alicia Garduño-Saldívar. 2000. "Understanding the Sexuality of Mexican-born Women and their Risk for HIV/AIDS." *Psychology of Women Quarterly* 24, no. 1: 100–109.

Salgado de Snyder, V. Nelly, María de Jesús Díaz-Pérez, and Margarita Maldonado. 1996. "AIDS: Risk Behaviors among Rural Mexican Women Married to Migrant Workers in the United States." *AIDS Education and Prevention* 8, no. 2: 134–42.

Salmon, Lucy. 1897. *Domestic Service*. London: Macmillan.

Salzinger, Leslie. 1991. "A Maid By Any Other Name: The Transformation of 'Dirty Work' by Central American Immigrants." In *Ethnography Unbound: Power and Resistance in the Modern Metropolis*, edited by Michael Burawoy, Alice Burton, Ann Arnett Ferguson, and Kathryn J. Fox, 139–60. Berkeley: University of California Press.

———. 1997. "From High Heels to Swathed Bodies: Gendered Meanings Under Production in Mexico's Export-Processing Industry." *Feminist Studies* 23: 549–74.

———. 2003. *Genders in Production: Making Workers in Mexico's Global Factories*. Berkeley: University of California Press.

———. Forthcoming. *Gender under Production: Making Subjects in Mexico's Global Factories*. Berkeley: University of California Press.

Sampaio, Anna. 2002. "Transforming Chicana/o and Latina/o Politics: Globalization and the Formation of Transnational Resistance in the United States and Chiapas." In *Transnational Latina/o Communities: Politics, Processes, and Cultures*, edited by Carlos Vélez-Ibañez, Anna Sampaio, with Manolo González-Estay, 47–72. Lanham, Md.: Rowman and Littlefield.

———. 2004. "Transnational Feminisms in a New Global Matrix: *Hermanas en la Lucha*." *International Feminist Journal of Politics* 6, no. 2: 181–206.

Sánchez, Gabriela Romero. 2001. "Presentan iniciativa de reforma para castigar explotación sexual contra menores de edad." *La Jornada*, 2 May, 48.

Sanchez, George. 1984. "'Go After the Women': Americanization and the Mexican Immigrant Woman, 1915–1929." Stanford, Calif.: Stanford University, Stanford Center for Chicano Research.

Sanjek, Roger, and Shellee Colen, eds. 1990. *At Work in Homes: Household Workers in World Perspective*. American Ethnological Society Monograph No. 63.

Santa Cruz County Farmworker Housing Committee. 1993. "Santa Cruz County Farm Worker Housing Needs." Unpublished report.

Santos Preciado, José Ignacio. 2001. "Migration and Health: The New Mexican Strategy to Address Migrant Health Issues: Vete Sano, Regresa Sano Program." Paper presented at the Binational Forum on Migrant Health, sponsored by the California Policy Research Center at the University of California, Berkeley, 19 October.

Sassen, Saskia. 1988. *The Mobility of Labor and Capital: A Study in International Investment and Labor Flow*. Cambridge: Cambridge University Press.

———. 1996. *Losing Control? Sovereignty in an Age of Globalization*. New York: Columbia University Press.

———. 1998. *Globalization and Its Discontents: Essays on the New Mobility of People and Money*. New York: New Press.

Sassen-Koob, Saskia. 1982. "Recomposition and Peripheralization at the Core." In *The New Nomads*, edited by Marlene Dixon and Susanne Jonas, 88–100. San Francisco: Synthesis Publications.

Schaeffer-Grabiel, Felicity. 2006. "Planet-Love.com: Cyberbrides in the Americas and the Transnational Routes of U.S. Masculinity." *Signs* 30, no. 2 (winter): forthcoming.

Scheper-Hughes, Nancy. 1992. *Death Without Weeping: The Violence of Everyday Life in Brazil*. Berkeley: University of California Press.

———. 1994. "AIDS and the Social Body." *Social Science and Medicine* 39, no. 7: 991–1003.

Schmidt Camacho, Alicia. 2004a. "Body Counts on the Mexico-US Border: Feminicidio,

Reification, and the Theft of Mexicana Subjectivity." *Chicana/Latina Studies*: 4, no. 1: 23–60.

———. 2004b. "Ciudadana X: Gender Violence and the Denationalization of Women's Rights in Ciudad Juárez, Mexico." *New Centennial Review*, Spring, 255–92.

Schmitter, Barbara. 1979. "Immigration and Citizenship in West Germany and Switzerland." Ph.D. diss., University of Chicago.

Schneider, Dorothee. 1998. "'I Know All about Emma Lazarus': Nationalism and Its Contradictions in Congressional Rhetoric of Immigration Restriction." *Cultural Anthropology* 13, no. 1: 82–99.

Schniepp, Mark. 1997. "Economic Outlook: Santa Barbara County." Santa Barbara: University of California Economic Forecasting Project, Department of Economics.

Schrader, Ester, and James F. Smith. 1999. "2 Mass Graves in Mexico May Hold Hundreds." *Los Angeles Times*, 30 November, A1.

Schuck, Peter H. 1989. "Membership in the Liberal Polity: The Devaluation of American Citizenship." In *Immigration and the Politics of Citizenship in Europe and North America*, edited by William R. Brubaker, 51–65. Lanham, Md.: University Press of America.

Schuck, Peter H., and Rogers M. Smith. 1985. *Citizenship without Consent: Illegal Aliens in the American Polity*. New Haven, Conn.: Yale University Press.

Schwartz, Stacey M. 1997. "Beaten before They Are Born: Immigrants, Their Children, and a Right to Prenatal Care." *Annual Survey of American Law* 3: 695–730.

Scott, James C. 1985. *Weapons of the Weak: Everyday Forms of Peasant Resistance*. New Haven, Conn.: Yale University Press, 1985.

Secretaría de Educación Pública. 1984. *Problemática educativa de la población migrante en los municipios de Ensenada y Tijuana*. Mexicali, Baja California: Subdirección General de Planeación.

Sedgwick, Eve Kosofsky. 1990. *Epistemology of the Closet*. Berkeley: University of California Press.

Segura, Denise A. 1984. "Labor Market Stratification: The Chicano Experience." *Berkeley Journal of Sociology* 29: 57–91.

———. 1986. "Chicanas and Mexican Immigrant Women in the Labor Market: A Study of Occupational Mobility and Stratification." Ph.D. diss., Department of Sociology, University of California, Berkeley.

———. 1989a. "Chicana and the Mexican Immigrant Women at Work: The Impact of Class, Race, and Gender on Occupational Mobility." *Gender and Society* 3, no. 1: 37–52.

———. 1989b. "The Interplay of Familism and Patriarchy on Employment among Chicana and Mexican Immigrant Women." In *Renato Rosaldo Lecture Series Monograph*, edited by Ignacio M. Garcia, 35–53. Tucson: University of Arizona Center for Mexican American Studies.

———. 1991. "Ambivalence or Continuity? Motherhood and Employment among Chicanas and Mexican Immigrant Women Workers." *Aztlán* 20, nos. 1 and 2: 119–50.

———. 1992. "Walking on Eggshells: Chicanas in the Labor Force." In *Hispanics in the*

Workplace, edited by Stephen B. Krause, Paul Rosenfeld, and Amy L. Culberston, 173–93. Beverly Hills, Calif.: Sage Publications, 1992.

———. 2001. "Challenging the ChicanO text: Towards a more inclusive contemporary '*causa*.'" *Signs* 26, no. 2: 541–50.

Segura, Denise A., and Jennifer L. Pierce. 1993. "Chicana/o Family Structure and Gender Personality: Chodorow, Familism, and Psychoanalytic Sociology Revisited." *Signs* 19: 62–79.

Seifert, Ruth. 1994. "War and Rape: A Preliminary Analysis." In *Mass Rape: The War against Women in Bosnia-Herzegovina*, edited by Alexandra Stiglmeyer, 54–72. Lincoln: University of Nebraska Press.

"Selena Remembered." 1995. Texas State Senate Resolution, 3 April. http://www.homestead.com/SelenaRemembered/TexasSenateResolution.html.

Selik, Richard, Kenneth G. Castro, and Marguerite Pappaioanou. 1989. "Racial/Ethnic Differences in the Risk of AIDS in the United States." *American Journal of Public Health* 78, no. 12: 1539–45.

Sen, Amartya. 1990. "Gender and Cooperative Conflicts." In *Persistent Inequalities: Women and World Development*, edited by Irene Tinker, 123–49. New York: Oxford University Press.

Senado de la República. 1983. "Informe de la Comisión de Asuntos Indígenas: Mixteca Oaxaqueña." *Cuadernos del Senado* 28.

Shah, Nayan. 2001. *Contagious Divides: Epidemics and Race in San Francisco's Chinatown*. Berkeley: University of California Press.

Shapiro, Michael. 1994. "Moral Geographies and the Ethics of Post-Sovereignty." *Public Culture* 3: 479–502.

Sherman, Rachel, and Kim Voss. 2000. "'Organize or Die': Labor's New Tactics and Immigrant Workers." In *Organizing Immigrants: The Challenge for Unions in Contemporary California*, edited by Ruth Milkman, 81–108. Ithaca, N.Y.: Cornell University Press.

"Shock Jock Rails against Mexico's Modern Women." 2003. *Christian Science Monitor*, 18 February. http://www.csmonitor.com.

Shohat, Ella, ed. 1998. *Talking Visions: Multicultural Feminism in a Transnational Age*. Cambridge, Mass.: MIT Press.

Shore, Cris, and Annabel Black. 1996. "Citizens' Europe and the Construction of European Identity." In *The Anthropology of Europe: Identities and Boundaries in Conflict*, edited by Victoria A. Goddard, Josep R. Llobera, and Cris Shore, 275–98. Oxford, U.K.: Berg.

Simison, Robert L., and Gregory L. White. 1998. "Mexico's Growth May Explain GM Buildup There." *Wall Street Journal*, 13 July, 1.

Simmons, Christina. 1979. "Companionate Marriage and the Lesbian Threat." *Frontiers* 4, no. 3: 54–59.

Simon, Rita J. 1985. *Public Opinion and the Immigrant: Print Media Coverage*. Lexington, Mass.: Lexington Books.

Simon, Rita J., and Carolyn B. Brettel. 1986. *International Migration: The Female Experience*. Totowa, N.J.: Rowman and Allenheld.

Simon, Rita J., and Margo C. DeLey. 1986. "Undocumented Mexican Women: Their Work and Personal Experiences." In *International Migration: The Female Experience*, edited by Rita J. Simon and Caroline B. Brettel, 113–32. Totowa, N.J.: Rowan and Allenheld.

Simon, Rita J., and Jean M. Landis. 1989. "Women's and Men's Attitudes about a Woman's Place and Role." *Public Opinion Quarterly* 53: 265–76.

Singer, Merrill, Flores Candída, Lani Davison, Georgine Burke, Zaida Castillo, Kelley Scanlon, and Migdalia Rivera. 1990. "SIDA: The Economic, Social, and Cultural Context of AIDS among Latinos." *Medical Anthropology Quarterly* 4, no. 1: 72–114.

Singer, Paul, ed. 1974. "Migraciones internas: Consideraciones téoricas sobre su estudio." In *Las migraciones internas en América Latina: Consideraciones teóricas*, edited by Muñoz, Oliveira, Singer, and Stern, 51–67. Buenos Aires: Nueva Visión.

Skerry, Peter, and Stephen J. Rockwell. 1998. "The Cost of a Tighter Border: People-Smuggling Networks." *Los Angeles Times*, 3 May, M2.

Sklair, Leslie. 1993. *Assembling for Development: The Maquila Industry in Mexico and the United States*. San Diego: University of California, Center for U.S.-Mexican Studies.

Skolnick, Arlene S. 1991. *Embattled Paradise: The American Family in an Age of Uncertainty*. New York: Basic Books.

Smith, Anthony D. 1990. "Toward a Global Culture?" *Theory, Culture and Society* 7, nos. 2 and 3: 171–92.

Smith, D. n.d. "Sexual Relationships and Social Change: Linking Fertility Preferences and Contraceptive Use to the Social (Re)construciton of Gender and the Individual." Unpublished manuscript, Department of Anthropology, Emory University.

Smith, Dorothy. 1987. "Women's Inequality and the Family." In *Families and Work*, edited by Naomi Gerstel and Harriet Gross, 23–54. Philadelphia: Temple University Press.

Smith, Michael Peter. 2001. *Transnational Urbanism*. Malden: Blackwell.

Snitow, Ann, Christine Stansell, and Sharon Thompson, eds. 1983. *Powers of Desire: The Politics of Sexuality*. New York: Monthly Review Press.

Soldatenko, María Angelina. 1991. "Organizing Latina Garment Workers in Los Angeles." *Las Obreras* 20, nos. 1 and 2: 73–96.

Solis, J. M., G. Marks, M. Garcia, and D. Shelton. 1990. "Acculturation, Access to Care, and Use of Preventative Services by Hispanics: Findings from HHANES 1992–1984." *American Journal of Public Health* (supplement), December, 11–19.

Sólorzano-Torres, Rosalía. 1987. "Female Mexican Immigrants in San Diego County." In *Women on the U.S.-Mexico Border: Responses to Change*, edited by Vicki L. Ruiz and Susan Tiano, 41–60. Boston: Allen and Unwin.

———. 1988. "Women, Labor and the US-Mexico Border: Mexican Maids in El Paso, Texas." In *Mexicanas at Work in the United States*, edited by Margarita B. Melville, 75–83. Mexican American Studies Program Monograph No. 5. Houston: University of Houston Press.

Soto, Shirlene. 1986. "Tres modelos culturales: La virgin de Guadalupe, la malinche, y la llorona." *Fem* 48: 13–16.

Soysal, Yasemin Nuhoglu. 1994. *Limits of Citizenship: Migrants and Postnational Membership in Europe*. Chicago: University of Chicago Press.

———. 1996. "Changing Citizenship in Europe: Remarks on Postnational Membership and the National State." In *Citizenship, Nationality and Migration in Europe*, edited by David Cesarani and Mary Fulbrook, 17–29. New York and London: Routledge.

Stacey, Judith. 1996. *In the Name of the Family: Rethinking Family Values in the Postmodern Age*. Boston: Beacon Press.

Stack, Carol B., and Linda M. Burton. 1994. "Kinscripts: Reflections on Family, Generation, and Culture." In *Mothering: Ideology, Experience, and Agency*, edited by Evelyn Nakano Glenn, Grace Chang, and Linda Rennie Forcey, 33–44. New York: Routledge.

Stack, Megan, and Diana Washington Valdez. 1999. "Juárez Girl Accuses Driver in Attack." *El Paso Times*, 19 March, 1A.

Standing, Guy. 1989. "Global Feminization through Flexible Labor." *World Development* 17: 1077–95.

Stansell, Christine. 1987. *City of Women*. Urbana: University of Illinois Press.

Stanton-Salazar, Ricardo D. 2001. *Manufacturing Hope and Despair: The School and Kin Support Networks of U.S.-Mexico Youth*. New York: Teachers College Press.

State Advisory Committees to the United States Commission on Civil Rights (Arizona, California, New Mexico, and Texas). 1997. *Federal Immigration Law Enforcement in the Southwest: Civil Rights Impacts on Border Communities*. Washington: U.S. Government Printing Office.

Stavans, Ilan. 2000. "Santa Selena." In *The Essential Ilan Stavans*, 181. New York: Routledge.

Steele, Valerie. 1985. *Fashion and Eroticism: Ideals of Feminine Beauty from the Victorian Era to the Jazz Age*. New York: Oxford University Press.

Steinberg, Ronnie J, and Deborah M. Figart. 1999. "Emotional Labor Since *The Managed Heart*." *Annals of the American Academy of Political and Social Science* 561: 8–26.

Stephen, Lynn. 2005. *Zapotec Women: Gender, Class, and Ethnicity in globalized Oaxaca*. Durham, N.C.: Duke University Press.

Stern, Steve. 1995. *The Secret History of Gender: Women, Men and Power in Late Colonial Mexico*. Chapel Hill: University of North Carolina Press.

Stewart, Kathleen. 1993. "Engendering Narratives of Lament in Country Music." In *All That Glitters: Country Music in America*, edited by George Lewis, 221–25. Bowling Green, Ind.: Bowling Green University Popular Press.

Stigler, George J. 1961. "The Economics of Information." *Political Economy* 69, no. 3: 213–25.

Stockdale, Margaret. 1996a. "What We Know and What We Need to Learn about Sexual Harassment." In *Sexual Harassment in the Workplace: Perspectives, Frontiers, and Response Strategies*, edited by Margaret Stockdale, 3–25. London: Sage Publications.

———, ed. 1996b. *Sexual Harassment in the Workplace: Perspectives, Frontiers, and Response Strategies*. London: Sage Publications.

Stoeltje, Melissa Fletcher. 1996. "Searching for the Perfect Selena." *Houston Chronicle*, 18 March, 1.

Stolcke, Verena. 1995. "Talking Culture: New Boundaries, New Rhetorics of Exclusion in Europe." *Current Anthropology* 36: 1–24.

Stoler, Laura Ann. 1995. *Race and the Education of Desire: Foucault's History of Sexuality and the Colonial Order of Things*. Durham, N.C.: Duke University Press.

Stroup-Benham, Christine A., and Fernando M. Trevino. 1991. "Reproductive Characteristics of Mexican-American, Mainland Puerto Rican, and Cuban-American Women." *Journal of the American Medical Association* 265: 222–26.

Stull, Donald D., Michael J. Broadway, and Ken Erickson. 1992. "The Price of a Good Steak: Beef Packing and Its Consequences for Garden City, Kansas." In *Structuring Diversity: Ethnographic Perspectives on the New Immigration*, edited by Louise Lamphere, 35–64. Chicago: University of Chicago Press.

Suárez-Orozco, Marcelo M., ed. 1998. *Crossings: Mexican Immigration in Interdisciplinary Perspectives*. Cambridge, Mass.: Harvard University Press.

Sullivan, Teresa. 1987. "The Occupational Prestige of Women Immigrants: A Comparison of Cubans and Mexicans." *International Migration Review* 18, no. 4: 1045–62.

Survey Sampling. 1990. "Statistical Analysis of Sample." Fairfield, Conn.: Survey Sampling.

Sutherland, David. 1981. *Americans and Their Servants: Domestic Service in the United States from 1800–1920*. Baton Rouge: Louisiana University Press.

Tabuenca Córdoba, Maria-Socorro. 1995–1996. "Viewing the Border: Perspectives from the 'Open Wound.'" *Discourse* 18: 146–68.

———. 1998. *Mujeres y fronteras: Una perspectiva de género*. Chihuahua, Mexico: Instituto Chihuahuense de al Cultura, Fondo Estatal para la Cultural y las Artes.

Takacs, Stacy. 1999. "Alien-Nation: Immigration, National Identity and Transnationalism." *Cultural Studies* 13, no. 4: 591–620.

Takaki, Ronald. 1993. *A Different Mirror: A History of Multicultural America*. Boston: Little, Brown.

Tapia, Javier. 1995. "Microeconomics of US-Mexican Households." *Urban Anthropology* 24, no. 3: 255–80.

Task Force on Diagnostic and Statistical Manual, American Psychiatric Association. 1952. *Diagnostic and Statistical Manual of Mental Disorders*. Arlington, Va.: American Psychiatric Publications.

Taussig, Michael. 1987. *Shamanism, Colonialism, and the Wild Man*. Chicago: University of Chicago Press.

———. 1999. *Defacement*. Stanford, Calif.: Stanford University Press.

Taylor, Charles. 1990. "Modes of Civil Society." *Public Culture* 1: 95–118.

Terry, Jennifer. 1989. "Medical Surveillance of Women as Reproducers." *Socialist Review* 19, no. 2: 13–43.

———. 1990. "Lesbians under the Medical Gaze: Scientists Search for Remarkable Differences." *Sex Research* 27: 317–39.

Texas State Data Center. 1998. "Projections of the Population of Texas and Counties in Texas by Age, Sex and Race/Ethnicity, for 2000–2030." http://txsdc.tamu.edu.

Thai, Hung Cam. 2002. "Clashing Dreams: Highly Educated Overseas Brides and Low-wage U.S. Husbands." In *Global Woman: Nannies, Maids, and Sex Workers in the New Global Economy*, edited by Barara Ehrenreich and Arlie R. Hochschild, 230–53. New York: Metropolitan.

Thompson, Ginger. 2005. "Mexico's Migrants Profit From Dollars Sent Home." *New York Times*, 23 February, A1, 8.

Thorne, Barrie, and Marilyn Yalom. 1992. *Rethinking the Family: Some Feminist Questions.* Boston: Northeastern University Press.

Tiano, Susan. 1986. "Women and Industrial Development in Latin America." *Latin American Research Review* 21, no. 3: 157–71.

Tienda, Marta, and Karen Booth. 1991. "Gender, Migration and Social Change." *International Sociology* 6: 51–72.

Tienda, Marta, and P. Guhleman. 1985. "The Occupational Position of Employed Hispanic Women." In *Hispanics in the U.S. Economy*, edited by George J. Borjas and Marta Tienda, 243–73. New York: Academic Press.

Tilly, Louise A., and Joan W. Scott. 1978. *Women, Work, and Family.* New York: Holt, Rinehart, and Winston.

"Time Bomb in Mexico: Why There'll be No End to the Invasion by 'Illegals.'" 1977. *U.S. News and World Report*, 4 July, 27.

Tirado, Silvia. 1994. "Weaving Dreams, Constructing Realities: The Nineteenth of September National Union of Garment Workers in Mexico." In *Dignity and Daily Bread: New Forms of Economic Organizing among Poor Women in the Third World and the First*, edited by Sheila Rowbotham and Swasti Mitter, 100–113. London: Routledge.

Todaro, Michael, and Veena Thadani. 1979. *Female Migration in Developing Countries: A Framework for Analysis.* Center for Policy Studies, Policy Council, Working Paper No. 47. New York: Population Council.

Tolentino, Roland B. 1997. "Bodies, Letters, Catalogs: Filipinas in Transnational Space." *Social Text* 48, no. 14: 3.

Torrado, Susana. 1981. "El foque de las estrategias familiares de vida en América Latina: orientaciones teórico-metadológicas." Paper presented at the Conferencia de la Unión Internacional para el Estudio Científico de la Población, Manila, Philippines, 9–16 December.

———. 1983. *La familia como unidad de análisis en censos y encuestas de hogares: Metodología actual prospectiva en América Latina.* Buenos Aires: Centro de Estudios Urbanos y Regionales.

Tostado Gutiérrez, Marcela. 1991. *El álbum de la mujer: Antología ilustrada de las mexicanas.* Vol. 2. Mexico City: Instituto Nacional de Antropología e Historia.

Treviño, Fernando M., Christine A. Troup, and Laura Ray. 1988. "The Feminization of Poverty among Hispanic Households." Working paper, Tomás Rivera Center, San Antonio, Texas.

Tucker, Susan. 1994. *Telling Memories among Southern Women and Their Employers in the Segregated South.* Baton Rouge: Louisiana State University.

Tuñon Pablos, Esperanza, ed. 2001. *Mujeres en las fronteras: Trabajo, salud y migración: Belice, Guatemala, Estados Unidos y México.* Mexico City: El Colegio de Frontera Sur (ECOSUR) and El Colegio de Sonora (COISON).

Turkle, Sherry. 1995. *Life on the Screen: Identity in the Age of the Internet.* New York: Touchstone.

Turner, Bryan S. 1986. "Personhood and Citizenship." *Theory, Culture and Society* 3, no. 1: 1–16.

Twinam, Ann. 1989. "Honor, Sexuality, and Illegitimacy in Colonial Spanish America." In

Sexuality and Marriage in Latin America, edited by Asunción Lavrin, 118–55. Lincoln: University of Nebraska Press.

Twine, Fred. 1994. *Citizenship and Social Rights: The Interdependence of Self and Society.* London: Sage Publications.

United Nations. 1978. *Report of the World Conference to Combat Racism and Racial Discrimination.* Geneva, 14–25 August, A/CONF.92/40.

———. 1983. *Report of the Second World Conference to Combat Racism and Racial Discrimination.* Geneva, 1–12 August, A/CONF.119/26.

———. 1990. *Domestic Violence against Women in Latin America and the Caribbean: Series on Women and Development.* Santiago, Chile: Social Development Division.

United Nations Economic and Social Council. 1993a. *Question of the Violation of Human Rights and Fundamental Freedoms in Any Part of the World, with Particular Reference to Colonial and Other Dependent Countries and Territories: Rape and Abuse of Women in the Territory of the Former Yugoslavia.* New York: UNESCO.

———. 1993b. *Situation of Human Rights in the Territory of the Former Yugoslavia: Report on the Situation of Human Rights in the Territory of the Former Yugoslavia.* New York: UNESCO.

United Nations General Assembly. 1948. *Universal Declaration of Human Rights.* New York: UNESCO.

United Nations High Commissioner for Human Rights. 1990. "International Convention on the Protection of the Rights of all Migrant Workers and Members of Their Families." 18 December. http://www.unhchr.ch.

United Nations Population Fund. 1993. *The State of World Population.* New York: United Nations.

United Press International. 1982. "Jury Finds Two Border Patrol Guilty of Rape," 23 July.

Urzúa, Raúl. 1979. *El desarrollo y la población en América Latina.* Mexico City: Programa de Investigaciones Sociales sobre Población en América Latina, Siglo XXI.

U.S. Border Patrol. 1994. *Border Patrol Strategic Plan 1994 and Beyond: National Strategy.* Washington: U.S. Border Patrol.

U.S. Bureau of the Census. 1980. *Population and Housing Report: Standard Metropolitan Statistical Area: Santa Barbara, Santa Maria, Lompoc.* Washington: U.S. Government Printing Office.

———. 1987. "Fertility of American Women: June 1986." In *Current Population Report*, Series P-20, No. 421. Washington: U.S. Government Printing Office.

———. 1990. *Population and Housing Report: Standard Metropolitan Statistical Area: Santa Barbara, Santa Maria, Lompoc.* Washington: U.S. Government Printing Office.

———. 1991. "Fertility of American Women: June 1990." In *Current Population Report*, Series P-20, No. 454. Washington: U.S. Government Printing Office.

———. 2000. *Summary File 1: Table 3: Female Population by Age, Race, and Hispanic or Latino Origin for the United States: 2000.* Washington: U.S. Government Printing Office.

———. 2001a. "Demographic Analysis." http://www.census.gov.

———. 2001b. *Statistical Abstract of the United States, 2001: Table No. 292: Crimes and Crime Rates by Type and Area: 1999.* Washington: U.S. Government Printing Office.

———. 2003. *The Hispanic Population in the United States: March 2002*, Series P-20, No. 545. Washington: U.S. Government Printing Office.

———. 2004. State and County Quickfacts: Orange County, California. Electronic document. http://quickfacts.census.gov (accessed on 18 February 2004).

———. 2005. State and County QuickFacts: California. Electronic document. http://quickfacts.census.gov (accessed on 22 November 2005).

U.S. Congress. House. 1952. *Public Health Service Report*. 82d. Cong., 2d sess. H. Rep. 1365.

———. House. 1984. *Exclusion and Deportation Amendments of 1983: Hearing before the Subcommittee on Immigration, Refugees, and International Law of the Committee of the Judiciary*. 98th Cong., 2d sess., 28 June, H. Rep. 4509 and H. Rep. 5227, ser. no. 98–72. Washington: U.S. Government Printing Office.

———. House. 1989. *Military Role in Drug Interdiction*. Committee on the Armed Services, pt. 2, 101st Cong., 2d sess. Washington: U.S. Government Printing Office.

———. House. 1993. *The Immigration and Naturalization Service: Overwhelmed and Unprepared for the Future*. Committee on Government Operations, 193d Cong., 1st sess., H.R. Rep. 216. Washington: U.S. Government Printing Office.

———. House. 1996. *U.S. Border Patrol's Implementation of "Operation Gatekeeper."* Committee on Government Reform and Oversight, 104th Cong., 2d session. Washington: U.S. Government Printing Office.

U.S. Congress. Senate. Committee of the Judiciary. 1950. *The Immigration and Naturalization Systems of the United States*. 81st Cong., 2d sess. S. Rep. 1515.

———. Senate. 1952. *Revision of the Immigration and Nationality Laws*. 82d Cong., 2d. sess. S. Rep. 1137. 29 January.

U.S. Department of Homeland Security. 2005. *Yearbook of Immigration Statistics, 2004*. Washington: U.S. Government Printing Office.

U.S. Department of Justice. 1997a. *INS Releases Updated Estimates of U.S. Illegal Population*. Washington: U.S. Government Printing Office.

———. 1997b. *Office of the Inspector General's Semiannual Report to Congress*. Washington: U.S. Government Printing Office.

U.S. Department of Labor. 1998. *Public Report of Review of NAO Submission No. 9701*. Washington: U.S. Government Printing Office.

U.S. Department of State. 2000. *Mexico-1999: Country Reports on Human Rights Practices*. Washington: U.S. Government Printing Office.

U.S. General Accounting Office. 2001. *INS' Southwest Border Strategy: Resource and Impact Issues Remain After Seven Years*. Washington: Government Printing Office.

U.S. Immigration and Naturalization Service. 1997. *Citizens' Advisory Panel Report to the Attorney General*. Washington: U.S. Government Printing Office.

_____. 1998. *Operation Gatekeeper: New Resources, Enhanced Results—Fact Sheet*. Washington: Immigration and Naturalization Service.

_____. 1999. *INS Recruiting Update: Spotlight on San Diego Sector Recruitment Efforts—Comminiqué*. Washington: Immigration and Naturalization Service.

Uttal, Lynet. 1996. "Custodial Care, Surrogate Care, and Coordinated Care: Employed Mothers and the Meaning of Child Care." *Gender and Society* 10: 291–311.

Valdez, Avelardo, and Jeffrey A. Halley. 1996. "Gender in the Culture of Mexican American Conjunto Music." *Gender and Society* 10, no. 2: 148–67.

Valdez, Luz María, and Teresa Menéndez. 1987. *Dinámica de la población indígena 1900–1980*. Serie Demografía Etnica. Mexico City: Instituto Nacional de Antropologia e Historia.

Vance, Carole S. 1991. "Anthropology Rediscovers Sexuality: A Theoretical Comment." *Social Science and Medicine* 33: 875–84.

———, ed. 1984. *Pleasure and Danger: Exploring Female Sexuality*. Boston: Routledge and Kegan Paul.

Vargas, Deborah R. 2002a. "Bidi Bidi Bom Bom: Selena and Tejano Music in the Making of *Tejas*." In *Latina/o Popular Culture*, edited by Michelle Habell-Pállan and Mary Romero, 117–26. New York: New York University Press.

———. 2002b. "Cruzando Frontejas: Remapping Selena's Tejano Music Crossover." In *Chicana Traditions: Continuity and Change*, edited by Norma Cantú and Olga Nájera-Ramírez, 234–46. Urbana: University of Illinois Press.

Vasconcelos, José. 1997. *The Cosmic Race*. Translated and annotated by Didier T. Jaén. Baltimore: Johns Hopkins Press.

Vásquez, Daniel. 1989. *Guadalajara: Ensayos de interpretación*. Guadalajara: El Colegio de Jalisco.

Vega, Carlos Alba, and D. Kruijt. 1988. *Los Empresarios y la Industria de Guadalajara*. Guadalajara: El Colegio de Jalisco.

Vega, William A., Bohdan Kolody, and Juan Ramon Valle. 1990. "Migration and Mental Health: An Empirical Test of Depression Risk Factors among Immigrant Women." *International Migration Review* 21, no. 3: 512–29.

Velasco, Elizabeth C. 2001. "Milenio Femenista anuncia que pedirá a la CIDH pesquisa sobre las 258 asesinadas en Juárez." *La Jornada*, 10 December, 11.

Velasco Ortiz, Laura. 1986. "Los motivos de la mujer migrante en la Mixteca de Oaxaca." Ph.D. diss., Facultad de Psicología, Universidad Nacional Autónoma de México.

Vélez-Ibañez, Carlos G. 1980. "The Non-Consenting Sterilization of Mexican Women in Los Angeles: Issues of Psychocultural Rupture and Legal Redress in Paternalistic Behavioral Environments." In *Twice a Minority: Mexican American Women*, edited by Margarita B. Melville, 235–48. St. Louis: C. V. Mosby Press.

———. 1983. *Rituals of Marginality: Politics, Process, and Culture Change in Central Urban Mexico, 1969–1974*. Berkeley: University of California Press.

———. 1988. "Networks of Exchange among Mexicans in the United States and Mexico." *Urban Anthropology* 17, no. 1: 27–53.

———. 1993. "U.S. Mexicans in the Borderlands: Being Poor Without the Underclass." In *In The Barrios: Latinos and the Underclass Debate*, edited by Joan Moore and Raquel Pinderhughes, 195–210. New York: Russell Sage Foundation.

———. 1999. "Se me Acabó la Canción: An Ethnography of Non-Consenting Sterilizations among Mexican Women in Los Angeles." In *Latina Issues: Fragments of Historia (Ella) (Herstory)*, edited by Antoinette S. Lopez, 71–91. New York: Garland Press.

———. 2004. "The Human Rights Issues of the Commoditization and Devalorization of the Mexican Population of the Southwest United States." In *Human Rights: The*

Scholar as Activist, edited by Carole Nagengast and Carlos G. Vélez-Ibañez, 153–68. Oklahoma City: Society of Applied Anthropology.

Vélez-Ibañez, Carlos G., and James B. Greenberg. 1992. "Formation and Transformation of Funds of Knowledge among U.S.-Mexican Households." *Anthropology and Education Quarterly* 23, no. 4: 313–34.

Ventura, Stephanie J., William D. Mosher, Sally C. Curtin, and Joyce C. Abma. 2001. "Trends in Pregnancy Rates for the United States, 1976–1997: An Update." In *National Vital Statistics Reports*, 1–10. Atlanta: Centers for Disease Control.

Vieth, Warren, and Edward Chen. 2004. "Bush Supports Shift of Jobs Overseas." *Los Angeles Times*, 10 February, A14.

Villalobos, René, M. G. Beruvides, and S. T. Hutchinson. 1997. "High Turnover: What It Does to Production." *Twin Plant News* 3, no. 2: 41–44.

Villalpando, Ruben. 2001. "Hallan en Juárez los cuerpos de tres mujeres asesinadas." *La Jornada*, 7 November, 34.

———. 2002. "Surgen en Chihuahua casos similares a los de las jovenes en Juárez." *La Jornada*, 6 April, 35.

Villalpando, Ruben, and Miroslava Breach. 2001. "Hallan 5 cadáveres más de jovencitas en Juárez." *La Jornada*, 8 November, 27.

———. 2002a. "Arribó a Ciudad Juárez el éxodo por la vida." *La Jornada*, 14 March, 47.

———. 2002b. "'Pasional,' la majoría de crímenes contra mujeres en Juárez: Procurador." *La Jornada*, 13 March, 47.

Villar, Maria de Lourdes. 1990. "Rethinking Settlement Process among Mexican Migrants in Chicago." *Urban Anthropology* 19, nos. 1 and 2: 63–79.

———. 1994. "Hindrances to the Development of an Ethnic Economy among Mexican Migrants." *Human Organization* 53, no. 3: 263–68.

Villareal, Magdalena. 1996. "Power and Self-Identity: The Beekeepers of Ayuquila." In *Machos, Mistresses and Madonnas*, edited by Marit Melhuus and Kristi Anne Stolen, 184–206. London: Verso.

Villarejo, Don, David Lighthall, Daniel Williams, Ann Souter, Richard Mines, Bonnie Bade, Steve Sarnules, and Stephen A. Mccurdy. 2000. *Suffering in Silence: A Report on the Health of California's Agricultural Workers*. Davis: California Institute for Rural Studies.

Vincent, Mal. 1997. "Lopez Is Bursting into Hollywood Spotlight." *Virginian Pilot*, 22 March, E8.

Vincent, R. J. 1992. "The Idea of Right in International Ethics." In *Traditions of International Ethics*, edited by Terry Nardin and David Mapel, 250–69. Cambridge: Cambridge University Press.

Vosko, Leah F. 2000. *Temporary Work: The Gendered Rise of a Precarious Employment Relationship*. Toronto: University of Toronto Press.

Wade, Peter. 1994. "Man the Hunter: Gender and Violence in Music and Drinking Contexts in Colombia." In *Sex and Violence: Issues in Representation and Experience*, edited by Peter Gow and Penelope Harvey, 115–37. New York: Routledge.

Waldinger, Roger, Chris Erickson, Ruth Milkman, Daniel J. B. Mitchell, Abel Valenzuela, Kent Wong, and Maurice Zeitlin. 1998. "Helots No More: A Case Study of the Justice for Janitors Campaign in Los Angeles." In *Organizing to Win: New Research on Union Strategies*, edited by Kate Bronfenbrenner, Sheldon Friedman, Richard W. Hurd, Rudolph A. Oswald, and Ronald L. Seeber, 102–19. Ithaca, N.Y.: ILR Press/Cornell University Press.

Walker, Lorraine O., and Mary Ann Best. 1991. "Well-Being of Mothers with Infant Children: A Preliminary Comparison of Employed Women and Homemakers." *Women and Health* 17: 71–88.

Wallace, William. 1990. *The Transformation of Western Europe*. London: Pinter.

Wallerstein, Immanuel M. 1976. *The Modern World System*. New York: Academic Press.

"Wanted: Actress for Selena Role." 1996. *Houston Chronicle*, 8 March, 1.

Wayne, Cornelius. 1989. "La demanda de fuerza de trabajo mexicana a Estados Unidos." In *Retos de las relaciones entre México y Estados Unidos*, edited by Jorge A. Bustamante and Wayne A. Cornelius, 39–66. Mexico City: Fondo de Cultura Económix.

Wearing, Betsy. 1984. *The Ideology of Motherhood: A Study of Sydney Suburban Mothers*. Sydney: George Allen and Unwin.

Weaver, Thomas. 1988. "The Human Rights of Undocumented Workers in the United States–Mexico Border Region." In *Human Rights and Anthropology*, edited by Theodore E. Downing and Gilbert Kushner, 73–90. Cambridge, Mass.: Cultural Survival.

Weintraub, Daniel M. 1994. "Wilson Sues US Over Immigrants' 'Invasion.'" *Los Angeles Times*, 23 September, A3.

Wekerle, Gerda, Rebecca Peterson, and David Morley, eds. 1980. *New Space for Women*. Boulder, Colo.: Westview Press.

Welsh, Sandy. 1999. "Gender and Sexual Harassment." *Annual Review of Sociology* 25: 169–90.

Werbach, Adam. 2004. "Anti-Immigration Coalition Seeks Control of Sierra Club." *In These Times*, 9 March. http://www.groundswellsierra.org/in_these_times.php (accessed on 31 July 2006).

Weston, Kath. 1991. *Families We Choose: Lesbians, Gays, Kinship*. New York: Columbia University Press.

Wilcox, Clyde. 1987. "Religious Attitudes and Anti-Feminism: An Analysis of the Ohio Moral Majority." *Women and Politics* 48: 1041–51.

Wilcox, Clyde, and Elizabeth Adell Cook. 1989. "Evangelical Women and Feminism: Some Additional Evidence." *Women and Politics* 9: 27–49.

Williams, Christine. 1993. *Doing Women's Work*. Newbury Park, Calif.: Sage Publications.

———. 1997. "Sexual Harassment in Organizations: A Critique of Current Research and Policy." *Sexuality and Culture* 1: 19–43.

Williams, Christine, Patti Guiffre, and Kirsten Dellinger. 1999. "Sexuality in the Workplace: Organizational Control, Sexual Harassment, and the Pursuit of Pleasure." *Annual Review of Sociology* 25: 73–93.

Williams, Linda. 1991. "Film Bodies: Gender, Genre and Excess." *Film Quarterly* 44, no. 4: 3–13.

Willis, Jennifer L., and Alberto Gonzalez. 1997. "Reconceptualizing Gender Through Dialogue: The Case of the Tex-Mex Madonna." *Women and Language* 20, no. 1: 9–12.

Wilson, Elizabeth. 1995. "The Rhetoric of Urban Space." *New Leftist Review* 209: 146–60.

Wilson, Fiona. 1990. *De la casa al taller: Mujeres, trabajo y clase social en la industria textil y del vestido*. Santiago Tangamandapio, Zamore: El Colegio de Michoacán.

———. 1991. *Sweaters: Gender, Class, and Workshop-Based Industry in Mexico*. New York: St. Martin's Press.

Wilson, Sandra. 1994. "Huffington Concedes He Broke Law in Hiring Alien." *Santa Barbara News Press*, 28 October, A1.

Wilson, Tamar D. 2000. "Anti-Immigrant Sentiment and the Problem of Reproduction/Maintenance in Mexican Immigration to the United States." *Critique of Anthropology* 20: 191–213.

Wise, Carolyn, ed. 1998. *The Post-NAFTA Political Economy: Mexico and the Western Hemisphere*. University Park: Pennsylvania State University Press.

Wolf, Diane L. 1992. *Factory Daughters: Gender, Household Dynamics and Rural Industrialization in Java*. Berkeley: University of California Press.

Woo Morales, Ofelia. 1995. "Las mujeres mexicanas indocumentadas en la migración internacional y la movilidad transfronteriza." In *Mujeres, Migración y Maquila en la Frontera*, edited by Soledad González, Olivia Ruiz, Laura Velasco, and Ofelia Woo, 65–87. Tijuana: El Colegio de la Frontera Norte.

———.1997. "La migración de las mujeres mexicanas hacia Estados Unidos." Ph.D. diss., Universidad de Guadalajara, Guadalajara, Mexico.

Woodhull, Winifred. 1988. "Sexuality, Power, and the Question of Rape." In *Feminism and Foucault: Reflections on Resistance*. Boston: Northeastern University Press.

Wools, Daniel. 2000. "Spain Is Running Short on Babies." *Orange County Register*, 5 March, 47.

Wright, Melissa W. 1998. "Maquiladora Mestizas and a Feminist Border Politics: Revisiting Anzaldúa." *Hypatia* 13, no. 3: 114–31.

———. 2001. "Desire and the Prosthetics of Supervision: A Case of Maquiladora Flexibility." *Cultural Anthropology* 16, no. 3: 354–73.

———. 2006. *Disposable Women and Other Myths of Global Capitalism*. New York: Routledge.

Wrigley, Julia. 1995. *Other People's Children*. New York: Basic Books.

Yáñez, Raúl. 1985. "Puntos de encuentro en una comunidad mixteca en Tijuana: Migración de los mixtecos de Oaxaca a Baja, California." *Educación de Adultos* 3, no. 2 (April-June).

Yarbro-Bejarano, Yvonne. 1991. "De-constructing the Lesbian Body: Cherríe Moraga's *Loving in the War Years*." In *Chicana Lesbians: The Girls Our Mothers Warned Us About*, edited by Carla Trujillo, 143–55. Berkeley: University of California Press.

———. 1997. "Crossing the Border with Chabela Vargas: A Chicano Femme's Tribute." In *Sex and Sexuality in Latin America*, edited by Daniel Balderston and Donna J. Guy, 33–43. New York: New York University Press.

Yelvington, Kevin. 1996. "Flirting in the Factory." *Royal Anthropology* 2, no. 2: 313–33.

Young, Kate. 1978. "Economía campesina, unidad doméstica y migración." *América Indígena*, no. 2: 279–301.

Yuval-Davis, Nira. 1997. *Gender and Nation*. London: Sage Publications.

Zabin, Carol, Michael Kearney, Anna García, David Runsten, and Carol Nagengast. 1993.

    Mixtec Migrants in California Agriculture: A New Cycle of Poverty. Davis: California Institute for Rural Studies.

Zaretsky, Eli. 1976. *Capitalism, The Family and Personal Life*. New York: Harper Colphon Books.

Zavella, Patricia. 1984. "The Impact of 'Sun Belt Industrialization' on Chicanas." *Frontiers* 8, no. 1: 21–27.

———. 1987. *Women's Work and Chicano Families: Cannery Workers of the Santa Clara Valley*. Ithaca, N.Y.: Cornell University Press.

———. 1988. "The Politics of Race and Gender: Organizing Chicana Cannery Workers in Northern California." In *Women and the Politics of Empowerment: Perspectives from the Workplace and the Community*, edited by Ann Bookman and Sandra Morgen, 202–24. Philadelphia: Temple University Press.

———. 1991a. "Mujeres in Factories: Race and Class Perspectives on Women, Work, and Family." In *Gender at the Crossroads of Knowledge: Feminist Anthropology in the Postmodern Era*, edited by Micaela di Leonardo, 312–36. Los Angeles: University of California Press.

———. 1991b. "Reflections on Diversity among Chicanos." *Frontiers* 2: 75.

———. 1997a. "Playing with Fire: The Gendered Construction of Chicana/Mexicana Sexuality." In *Gender/Sexuality Reader: Culture, History, Political Economy*, edited by Roger N. Lancaster and Micaela di Leonardo, 342–408. New York: Routledge.

———. 1997b. "The Tables Are Turned: Immigration, Poverty, and Social Conflict in California Communities." In *Immigrants Out! The New Nativism and the Anti-Immigrant Impulse in the United States*, edited by Juan F. Perea, 136–61. New York: New York University Press.

———. 2000. "Engendering Transnationalism in Food Processing: Peripheral Vision on Both Sides of the U.S.-Mexico Border." In *Las Nuevas Fronteras del Siglo XXI: Dimensiones culturales, políticas y socioeconómicas de las relaciones México-Estados Unidos*, edited by Norma Klahn, Pedro Castillo, Alejandro Alvarez and Federico Manchón, 397–424. Mexico City: La Jornada Ediciones, Centro de Investigaciones Colección, La Democracia en México.

———. 2002. "Engendering Transnationalism in Food Processing: Peripheral Vision on Both Sides of the U.S.-Mexico Border." In *Transnational Latina/o Communities: Politics, Processes and Cultures*, edited by Carlos G. Vélez-Ibañez and Ann Sampaio, with Manolo González-Estay, 397–424. Lanham, Md.: Rowman and Littlefield.

———. 2003. "Talkin' Sex: Chicanas and Mexicanas Theorize about Silences and Sexual Pleasures." In *Chicano Feminisms: A Critical Reader*, edited by Gabriela Arredondo, Aída Hurtado, Norma Klahn, Olga Nájera-Ramírez, and Patricia Zavella, 228–53. Durham, N.C.: Duke University Press.

Zelizer, Viviana. 1994. *Pricing the Priceless Child: The Social Value of Children*. Princeton, N.J.: Princeton University Press.

Zinn, Deborah K., and Rosemary C. Sarri. 1984. "Turning Back the Clock on Public Welfare." *Signs* 10: 355–70.

Zinn, Maxine Baca. 1979. "Chicano Family Research: Conceptual Distortions and Alternative Directions." *Ethnic Studies* 7: 59–71.

———. 1980. "Employment and Education of Mexican-American Women: The Interplay of Modernity and Ethnicity in Eight Families." *Harvard Educational Review* 50: 47–62.

———. 1982. "Mexican-American Women in the Social Sciences." *Signs* 8: 259–72.

———. 1989. "Family, Race and Poverty in the Eighties." *Signs* 14: 856–69.

Zitner, Aaron. 2003. "Nation's Birthrate Drops to Its Lowest Level Since 1909." *Los Angeles Times*, 26 June, A1.

Zlolniski, Christian. 1998. "In the Shadow of the Silicon Valley: Mexican Immigrant Workers in a Low-Income Barrio in San Jose." Ph.D. diss., University of California, Santa Barbara.

Zlotnik, Hania. 1995. "The South to North Migration of Women." *International Migration Review* 29: 229–54.

Zúñiga, Víctor. 1992. "Tradiciones migratorias internacionales y socialización familiar: Expectativas migratorieas de los alumnos de secundaria de cuatro municipios del norte de Nuevo León." *Frontera Norte* 4, no. 7: 45–74.

Contributors

Ernestine Avila teaches in the Department of Sociology at the University of Southern California.

Xóchitl Castañeda is the director of the California-Mexico Health Initiative, University of California Office of the President, California Policy Research Center.

Sylvia Chant teaches in the Department of Development Geography at the London School of Economics and Political Science.

Leo R. Chavez teaches in the Anthropology Department and Chicano Latino Studies Program at the University of California, Irvine.

Cynthia Cranford teaches in the Department of Sociology at the University of Toronto.

Adelaida R. Del Castillo teaches in the Department of Chicana and Chicano Studies at San Diego State University.

Sylvanna M. Falcón teaches in the Sociology Department at the University of California, Santa Barbara.

Rosa Linda Fregoso teaches in the Latin American and Latino Studies Department at the University of California, Santa Cruz.

Gloria González-López teaches in the Sociology Department at the University of Texas, Austin.

Jennifer S. Hirsch teaches in the Department of Sociomedical Sciences at Columbia University.

Pierrette Hondagneu-Sotelo teaches in the Department of Sociology at the University of Southern California.

María de la Luz Ibarra teaches in the Department of Chicana and Chicano Studies at San Diego State University.

Jonathan Xavier Inda teaches in the Chicana/o Studies Department at the University of California, Santa Barbara.

Eithne Luibhéid teaches in Lesbian, Gay, Bisexual, Transgender, and Women's Studies at the University of Arizona, Tucson.

Victoria Malkin is the anthropologist and information coordinator at the Wenner Gren Foundation for Anthropological Research.

Faranak Miraftab teaches in the Department of Urban and Regional Planning at the University of Illinois, Urbana-Champaign.

Olga Nájera-Ramírez teaches in the Anthropology Department at the University of California, Santa Cruz.

Norma Ojeda de la Peña teaches in the Department of Chicana and Chicano Studies and the Department of Sociology at San Diego State University.

Deborah Paredez teaches in the Department of Theatre and Dance at the University of Texas, Austin.

Leslie Salzinger teaches in the Sociology Department at the University of Chicago.

Felicity Schaeffer-Grabiel teaches in the Feminist Studies Department at the University of California, Santa Cruz.

Denise A. Segura teaches in the Sociology Department at the University of California, Santa Barbara.

Laura Velasco Ortiz teaches in the Departamento de Sociología at the Colegio de la Frontera Norte, Tijuana.

Melissa W. Wright teaches in the Geography Department and the Department of Women's Studies at Pennsylvania State University.

Patricia Zavella teaches in the Department of Latin American and Latino Studies at the University of California, Santa Cruz.

Index

Acculturation, 78, 369–370; language, 79, 86; models, 384
Activism: cross-border, 56; political, 323; women's, 503
Ademanes, 459
Affirmative Action, 8
AFL-CIO, 309
Agamben, Giorgio, 52
Agency, 291, 293; human, 15, 29; migrant, 1; social, 27; women's, 2, 427, 467, 469
AIDS. *See* HIV/AIDS
American Psychiatric Association (APA), 115, 123, 126
Amnesty, 6, 317, 417
Amnesty International, 216
Anzaldúa, Gloria, 2, 4,
Assimilation, 15; model, 389, 438
Association of Maquiladoras (AMAC), 188–189, 201 n.6

Banda, 47
Benjamin, Walter, 49, 51, 184–185, 200, 201 n.3
Bilingual education, 141
Bilingual programs, 99
Binationality: approaches to, 1–2; binational households, 15, 253; dialogue, 5; research teams on, 19; social structures, 20
Biomedical-environmental policies, 5
Biopolitical rationality, 139, 144, 150

Biopolitics, 21, 138–139, 143, 148–149, 151, 153–154, 155 n.2
Biopower, 134–139, 154, 155 n.2
Board of Immigration Appeals (BIA), 118, 120, 122
Body, 113; dangerous, 139; devalued, 484; exploited, 46; exterminated, 46, 139; female, 1, 48, 67, 203–204, 207, 221, 233, 237, 258, 484; gendered, 37; homosexual and heterosexual, 110; illegal immigrant, 135; Latina, 308, 485, 499; macho male, 510–511; objectification, 24; performing, 481, 489, 492; productive, 161–181, 196, 260; racialized, 37, 264, 482; reproductive, 11; sexualized, 168, 239, 260, 264–265; sexually consumable, 498; social, 21, 134–136, 139–141, 250, 260; spectral, 479; Tejana, 477; territorial, 48; Third World white, 67; of women, 504, 510, 516
Body politic, 134–135, 139–140, 143, 149
Border Industrialization Program (BIP), 12, 30 n.16, 62 n.1
Borderlands, 1–3, 4, 7, 20, 29, 36, 44, 56–57, 93, 410; death in, 147–149; militarization of, 19; politics of, 5
Border Patrol, 8, 113, 146–149, 156 n.13, 203, 204, 207–217, 222 n.11, 294
Bowden, Charles, 47–50
Bracero Program (1942–64), 6–7, 301, 305 n.9, 348, 392–393
Buchanan, Patrick, 140

Buck v. Bell (on involuntary sterilization law), 152
"Burials on the Border" conference, 37, 44, 57, 60, 63 n.13, 65 n.43

Cacique, 421
California Rural Legal Assistance Foundation (CLRA), 148
Capital, 5, 17, 95, 199, 69; human, 13, 292; variable, 185, 190
Capitalism, 12, 25, 40, 52, 56, 60, 95, 385 n.4, 388, 512–513, 519 n.2; consumer power and, 519; global, 46–47, 482; relations, 514
Capitalist development, 288
Cartographies of identification, 29
Casa Amiga, 50
Catholicism, 256, 264, 269, 319, 364, 391, 416, 448. *See also* Religion
Charreada, 469
Chicana/o Studies, 11, 15–16, 18, 369
Chisme, 423
Círculos de Hombres (against domestic violence), 243
Citizens Advisory Panel (of INS), 216
Citizenship, 27, 73, 104, 253, 307–309, 312–313, 317, 320–323, 482, 513; civic education, 93; consensual, 94; legal, 21, 102; political, 94, 99–100, 102; postnational, 93–94, 96; rights, 51–52, 56, 64 n. 37, 98–99; social, 21, 92–95, 97, 100–101, 103; transnational, 29, 504; U.S., 94; world, 92; 103
Ciudad Juarez, 62 n.1, 106, 163; and face of terror, 49; maquiladora industry in, 40, 42–45, 46–47, 163–168, 170–176, 184–189, 191–193, 197–198; and violence against women, 35–37, 39, 40, 41, 42–43, 46–47, 52–54, 56–60, 46–49, 52–61, 186, 199
Civic identity, 92–93
Civil disobedience, 319
Civil rights, 207–209, 217
Civil society, 37, 39, 57; planetary, 56, 58
Climate of fear, 394

Code of silence, 217–218, 221
Colonia, 12, 36, 341, 352, 358 n.2
Colonialism, 23, 203, 482
Colonialist gaze, 49
Colonization, 204, 220
Collective of Men for Egalitarian Relations in Mexico City, 243
Comadre, 427, 448
Comisión Nacional de Derechos Humans (National Human Rights Commission), 37
Comite Independiente de Chihuaha de Derechos Humanos, 35
Compadrazgo, 431, 448
Confianza, 28, 98, 441–446, 452–453, 455
Conjunto, 457
Conquistadors, 75, 231
Convention to Eliminate All Forms of Discrimination Against Women, 51
Corporate death, 186, 190, 197–199
Corporate space, 309, 316
Corridos, 45, 459
Cortés, Hernán, 511
Courtship, 439, 446, 515
Coyotes, 224, 298, 446
Criadas, 398
Cult of domesticity, 390
Culture: border, 477; of care, 304; corporate, 316; death by, 188–189, 197–199; differences, 140; expressions of, 8, 18–19; representations of, 57; of solidarity, 312; transformation of, 15, 18; values of, 28; Western, 519

Day laborers, 419
Democratic Party, 320–321
Department of Homeland Security, 21
Desire, 170, 176–177, 504; decolonial, 498; poetics of, 24, 254; as productive force, 180
Diagnostic and Statistical Manual of Mental Disorders, 115
Dialectical image, 184–185, 190, 197, 201
Diaspora, and subjectivity, 253

"Diffuse causality," 118
Discourse, 186; anti-immigrant, 21, 139; Chicano, 16; civic, 97; countervailing, 253; economy of, 118, 131; gender, 22, 24, 429, 435, 461–462, 512; global, 188; hegemonic, 254, 266; heterosexual, 175; homophobic, 114–115, 124, 126, 128; human rights, 92; immigration, 1, 67, 149; on Latina reproduction, 87; on love, 513; misogynist, 22; moralizing, 62 n.7, 511; nation-bound, 2; nativist, 1, 19–20, 22, 95, 142–143, 482; patriarchal, 264, 428; political, 308; popular, 68; public, 99; racist, 485; of religiosity, 59; on sexuality, 24, 174, 445; silencing, 29
Domestic work, 23, 26, 273, 281, 354–357, 419; labor market for, 303; as model of labor relations, 273; workers, 106, 286, 288, 290–291, 294–295, 392–410, 504
Don Eduardo (community leader in new Rochelle), 420
"Double day," 362
Double life, 37, 44, 46, 65 n.46, 186–187

Economy of discourses (Foucault), 117–118
El mando (power to give orders), 450. *See also* Patriarchy
Emasculation, 176; of work, 221
Embodiment of availability, 161
Emotional work, 402, 446
Empowerment, 1, 18, 225, 433, 439, 453
Encuentros, 14, 30 n.28
English as a Second Language, 261, 394, 419
English-only initiative, 206
Enmascarada, 259. *See also* Mask
Envidia, 421
Ethnic cleansing, 218
Ethnicity, 345, 486
Eugenics, 152–153, 155 n.5, 157 n.17, 157 n.18; policies, 69
Eurocentric victimology, 46
Euro-masculine representation, 316, 322

Exclusion: of immigrants, 134–135; of lesbian and gay immigrants, 106–107, 114, 125, 128
Exodus for Life campaign, 55
Extermination, 40, 52, 139; of gendered bodies, 40–41; sexual politics of, 60; systematic, 36

Familism, 25–27, 309, 313; immigrant, 313
Family Unity and Employment Opportunity Immigration Act of 1990, 133 n.49
Family wage, 306
Federation for American Immigration Reform (FAIR), 73, 142–143
Feinstein, Dianne, 144, 146
Female-headed households, 360–361, 363, 366, 428
Feminicide, 23, 35–37, 39–42, 46–47, 49, 53, 56–57, 59–60, 62 n.2, 63 n.18; culture of, 50; social, 54
Femininity, 18, 22, 43, 45–46, 259; codes of, 519; in maquiladoras, 174, 177–178; Mexican, 186, 192, 194; in rancheras, 468; recodifications of, 61; sexualized, 161; and untrainability, 192
Feminists: activism of, 56–57; Chicana, 287; distrust of, 503; First World, 47; interventions of, 456; mainstream, 512; politics of, 46, 314; scholars, 370, 390, 392, 429, 510; Western model of, 433–434
Feminization: of labor market, 12; of migrant streams, 7, 12; of occupations, 5, 30 n.13, 221, 289; of proletariat, 41
Fertility, 10–11, 20, 67–89, 136; age and, 84; ethnicity and, 87–88; normative levels, 69; "problem," 89; as threat to U.S. society, 67, 72;
Flexibility of labor, 306–307, 312, 314; gendered and racialized, 308, 323
Foucault, Michel, 107,115, 117–118, 129, 131, 134–139, 149, 155 n.2, 157 n.18, 182 n.5, 183 n.15
Fox, Vicente, 35

INDEX 589

Gabriela Network, 503
Gays, 57, 108, 111–113, 124
Gender, 6, 12, 56, 109, 111, 169, 185, 192, 287, 438, 443, 453; analysis, 17; boundaries, 24, 27; as construction, 390, 451; differences, 173–174, 333, 336; and division of labor, 13, 24, 168, 193, 256, 279–280, 286; extermination, 20, 35, 41; ideologies, 505; inequality, 243; male, and maquilas, 193; norms, 98; notions, 29, 241; performative demands, 448; in production, 161–181; relations, 22, 27, 192, 257; roles, 111, 270, 283, 463, 505, 509; transgressions, 448; of transnational migrants, 7. *See also* Violence
Genocide, 137
Globalism, 40, 41, 42, 46–48, 50, 52; fallacy of, 63 n.17
Globalization, 15, 17, 20–21, 29, 40, 47, 51, 60, 410, 504, 518
Golpe, 314
Grassroots activism, 14, 31 n.28, 39, 51, 54–56, 58–59, 142, 314, 319–320, 322–323
Grupo de 8 de Marzo, 35–36
Guest-worker program, 8, 30 n.9

Harassment, 203, 259, 261; of pregnant women, 196–197. *See also* Sexual harassment
Heteronormative structures, 19
Heterosexuality, 192, 225; excessive female, 187; relations, 265; standards, 128
Heterosociality, 443
Hierarchy of sight (in maquiladoras), 169
Hispanics, 30, n.10, 73, 75
HIV/AIDS, 5, 127, 133 n.56, 211, 225, 244 n.4, 251–253, 255, 263, 265, 267 n.8, 267 n.9, 267 n.11
Holocaust, 21, 135, 138–139, 154
Home-based work, 270–271, 274–275, 281, 284; congestion phase, 276; expansion phase, 276; self-exploitation in, 283
Homemakers (*amas de casa*), 78
Hometown associations, 9, 390, 420

Homeworkers, 271; female, 272, 275, 279, 282; male, 274 281
Homophobia, 17, 111–112, 114, 120, 127, 255; discourse, 114–115, 124, 126, 128; practices demonstrating, 116, 124
Homosexuality, 38, 107–128; and sociopathic personality, 115
Households: female-headed, 13; binational, 15
Huffington, Michael, 144, 294
Human-care providers, 296, 304
Human rights, 36, 51, 93, 95, 96, 100–103, 206, 214–219, 221; activists, 39, 57; advocacy, 94; discourse, 92; ethics, 102; framework, 56; groups, 35, 59; work, 35
Human Rights Watch, 216
Huntington, Samuel, 74–75
Hymen reconstruction, 229
Hyperfemininity, 44
Hypermasculinity, 23, 203, 208, 221
Hypersexuality and hypersexualization, 43–44, 64 n.28

Identity, 5, 29, 488; civic, 482; construction, 3, 28, 417; differentiation by region, 45; dual sense of, 481 (*see also* Latinidad); ethnic, 17, 357; fluid, 29; formation, 4, 56, 478, 480; gender, 176, 179, 433–436 n.5; indigenous, 10; intersectional, 54, 56; Latina, 479–480, 484, 487; lesbian, 123, 126; masculinist, 227, 243; Mexicana, 489; moral, 433; national, 482; negotiations, 481; political, 17, 482; queer, 108; reconfigured, 19; sexual, 123, 176; social, 6, 11, 17–18, 418, 420, 423, 426–427, 432, 436 n.8, Tejana, 478, 483; transnational, 17, 483; tropes, 501 n.20; U.S., 74, 145
Illegal Immigration Reform and Immigrant Responsibility Act, 8, 134, 555 n.13
Imaginary: Mexican popular, 45; national, 46
Immigration Act of 1924, 113
Immigration Act of 1990, 126
Immigration and Nationality Act, 119

Immigration and Naturalization Service (INS), 21, 23, 72, 107–110, 112–113, 116–123, 125–127, 130–132, 143, 145–147, 203, 206–210, 214–217, 222 n.11, 445. *See also* U.S. Citizenship and Immigration Services
Immigration Law of 1965, 6–7
Immigration Reform and Control Act of 1986 (IRCA), 6–7, 10, 210, 308, 312, 417, 436 n.2
Incest, 23, 51, 224, 229, 237, 241, *See also* Survivors
Indigenous people, 7, 10, 32 n.33, 53, 57, 60–61, 43, 345, 347, 352, 354, 357, 485–486, 511; languages, 16; life, 347; women, 19, 26. *See also* Mixtec
Interamerican Human Rights Commission, 62, n.4
International Monetary Fund (IMF), 41
Internet bride industry, 504

Juárez. *See* Ciudad Juárez
Juárez: The Laboratory of Our Future (Bowden), 48–49
Job-gendering, 165. *See also* Gender
Justice, social, 307, 313, 317, 322
Justice for Janitors, 25, 306, 309, 311–314, 322–323

Kin (kinship), 15, 249, 300, 408, 454; female, 388, 391; fictive, 13, 98; networks, 425, 431–432, 451
Kin-scription, 391

Labor. *See* Domestic work; Flexibility of labor; Homeworkers; Maquiladora
La doble vida, 37, 44, 46, 65 n.46, 186–187
La Llorona, 391
La Malinche, 391, 511
La Red Ciudadana contra la Violencia, 36
Las dos Vias, 44
La Vida Sigue (film), 255
Latina body, discursive construction of, 482, 492. *See also* Body

Latina Connection Worldwide (TLC), 503, 506–507
Latin American Studies, 11, 17–18
Latinidad, 28–29, 478–479, 481, 483, 486–487, 489–492, 494, 497, 501 n.20
Lesbianism, 37, 112, 123
Lesbians, 38, 108, 111–112, 123; and medical-exclusion certificate, 113–119, 122, 124–125, 128
Liberal democracy, 93–95, 100
Life-course analysis (as methodology), 328–329
Lopez, Jennifer, 484, 486
Los Angeles Commission on Assaults against Women (LACAAW), 242
Los Angeles Federation of Labor, 319
Low-intensity conflict (LIC), 23, 204–205, 218
Luz y Justicia (NGO), 50

Machismo (macho), 29, 229, 281, 366; culture, 512; Mexican, 421, 508–509, 511
Madres por la Paz, 255
Mahoney, Roger (cardinal), 319–320
Mail-order brides, 503
Male privilege, 383–384, 463. *See also* Patriarchy
Malinchista, 510–511
Mandelones, 281
Maquila. *See* Maquiladora
Maquila: A Tale of Two Mexicos (film), 42–43
Maquiladora, 12–13, 22, 41–42, 62, n.163 n.19, 161–162, 164–166, 168, 170, 181, 181 n.2, 184–187, 189–198, 200, 201 n.2, 221, 271–272, 275, 278, 282, 351, 353–354; narrative, 184; remasculinzation of labor in, 63 n.21
Maquiladora Association, 38
Marginalization, 1; in borderlands, 4; of dangerous bodies, 139; economic, 3; social and cultural, 3, 290
Mariachi, 169, 457, 495–496
Marriage, companionate, 445, 453

Marx, Karl, 185, 190–191, 200
Masculine subject, 186
Masculinity, 18, 443, 455, 508, 512, 516; image of, 273; in maquiladoras, 173–176, 179, 194; misogynist, 243; in rancheras, 468; redefinition of, 445; rituals of, 176; Western, 48
Mask, 49; of culture, 50; of democracy, 52; social, 253
Maternalism, 291
Matrifocal household, 360
McCarren-Walter Act, 106–107
Media, 36, 215, 294, 313, 457, 487, 504, 512; audiovisual, 54; campaign, 63 n.14; newspapers, 203, 318
Melodrama, 456, 459–461, 473
Mercado Común del Sur, 96
Mexican Revolution, 7
Mexican woman, 199–201
Microentrepreneurs, 271
Migrant Head Start program, 99
Migration patterns: gendered, 6; of women, 7
Militarization of the border, 19
Military culture, 203, 216–217
Misogyny, 20, 42, 47–48, 60, 220, 308; murder and, 62 n.2; racist, 54
Mixtec, 341, 343–345, 347–348, 350, 352, 354–356, 358 n.1, 358 n.5, 358 n.6
Motherhood. *See* Mothers
Mothers (motherhood), 15, 25–27, 31 n.29, 38, 57, 59, 186–187, 190, 228, 242, 271, 366, 438, 452; and employment, 321, 369, 373–374, 377–384; and guilt, 368–369, 373–384; self-sacrificing, 375; suffering, 364; transnational, 27, 292, 388–389, 390–406, 408–410, 411 n.1, 411 n.6

NAFTA (North American Free Trade Agreement), 2, 35, 40, 62 n.1, 96, 104, 195, 482, 505
Nannygate, 292, 294
Narcotraffick, 12, 64 n.34
Nathan, Debbie, 43–46

National Human Rights Commission, 37
National Labor Relations Act, 312
National Labor Relations Board (NLRB), 311
National Latino Alliance for the Elimination of Domestic Violence, 243
National Network for Immigrant and Refugee Rights, 206
National Organization for Women (NOW), 101, 503
Nativism, 9; arguments, 20, 140–141 (*see also* Discourse); groups, 93; politics, 29; projects, 28
Neoliberalism, 40–41, 313; and policies, 5, 52, 56, 60, 30
Nervios, 427
9/11, 8, 205
Ni Una Más, 20, 35, 55–56
Non-governmental organizations (NGOs), 35, 39, 51, 54, 203
Non(hetero)normative sexuality, 38, 46, 62 n.8
Nonnormativity, 38, 47–48

Ochoa, Digna, 38
Office of Inspector General (OIG), 207–208, 210, 214–215, 222 n.5
Operation Gatekeeper, 134, 145–146, 148–149, 156 n.12, 205
Organization of American States, 39
Orquesta, 457
"Other," 20, 70
Outsourcing of U.S. jobs, 5, 14

Paisano, 348
Panopticon, 163, 169, 172–173, 183 n.11
Partido Action Nacional (PAN), 51
Partido Revolucionario Internacional (PRI), 52
Patriarchy, 3, 12, 20, 36, 47, 52, 57, 204, 208, 225, 369–370, 377, 437 n.9, 482; assumptions, 281; family order and, 382–383; forms of control and domination, 46; and gender norms, 6, 38, 270; ideology,

371; notions, 224, 250, 257, 281; ownership of female body, 233; privilege, 372; roles, 428; state, 53–54, 59, 509; structure, 382; values, 278
Pedophilia, 51
Perez, Claudia, 479–480, 489, 491, 494, 497–499
Performance studies, 456
Performing the Border (film), 46
"Peripheral vision," 254, 264
Personal Responsibility and Work Opportunity Act, 500 n.13
Pláticas, 228
Poetics of desire, 24, 254
Political advocacy groups, 125
"Political economy of risk," 23–24, 250, 265
Political existence, 137
Popular culture, 9, 19, 29, 512
Poverty, 14; feminization of, 14
Prenatal care, 150–151, 153, 157 n.19
Presidential Office for Mexicans Abroad, 9
Principles for a Responsible Commercial Real Estate Industry, 315
Pro-choice advocates, 236
Programa de Desarrollo de las Mixtecas (Mixtec Development Program), 343
Proposition 54, 8
Proposition 63, 8
Proposition 187, 8, 68, 88, 95, 101, 103–104, 134, 142, 150–151, 252–253, 293, 308, 317, 394, 410, 412 n.9, 555 n.13
Proposition 209, 8
Proposition 227, 8, 308
Purity: cultural, 23; female, 228

"Quebec problem," 74
Queer subjects, 108, 112

Racialization, 12, 19, 250; gendered, 262
Racialized enemy, 207, 220
Ranchera, 28, 45, 456–474, 475 n.5, 475 n.6, 496–498; as feminist intervention,
Rape, 23, 184, 189, 203–221, 224–225, 227, 234–236, 238–242; interfamily, 229, 231; marital, 230
Rapto, 225, 230
Religion: Catholicism, 256, 264, 269, 319, 364, 391, 416, 448; discourse of religiosity, 59; and fertility, 70; groups, 98; involvement in, 390, 422, 424, 426, 449; and love, 514–515; subversive religiosity, 54
Remittances, 5, 30 n.8, 267 n.14, 343, 353, 406, 475 n.11
Representation: gender, 44; identity, 3; mechanics of, 200; regimes of, 1, 69; strategies of, 460
Reproduction (biological), 10, 21, 144, 234, 253, 370, 439, 510; African American, 69; Latina, 67–68; politics, 70, 76, 88; as reconquest, 71, 74, 87; stratified, 292. *See also* Social reproduction
Resistance, 1, 4, 18, 225, 269, 287; narratives, 25; organized, 13
Respeto, 28, 228, 233, 240, 424, 441–443, 453, 455
Rights: civil, 207–209, 217; social, 95, 98; of women, 58–60
Rituals of marginality, 13, 104
Robo, 225, 230–231

"Save Our State," 21. *See also* Proposition 187
Second shift, 371
Segregation, occupational, 13–14
Self-exploitation (in home-based work), 283
"Sending communities," 6, 17, 98–99, 439–440, 453
Señorita extraviada (film), 57–60
Service complex regime, 307–308
Sex: confession, 117–118; deviant, 110, 112, 124, 127; discrimination, 365; and division of family roles, 338; and division of labor, 342, 346, 362; intercourse, 79; intimacy, 444; objectification, 169, 173, 175–176, 179–181, 259; and "silence," 225,

Sex (*continued*)
228, 257; slavery, 224; surveillance, 180; transgressive, 171
Sex education, 236
Sexist social system, 220
Sexual assault, 214, 219, 224–225, 230, 236, 241, 257, *See also* Violence
Sexual harassment, 13, 22–23, 161–163, 179–181, 182 n.5, 249, 254, 258, 311. *See also* Harassment
Sexuality, 21, 234, 240, 250, 439–440, 471; of border females, 45, 189–190, 200; forbidden, 174; gay male, 109; gendered, 249–251; of immigrant women, 123; Latina, 486, 488; lesbian, 109, 122; marital, 444; in maquiladora production, 161–181; racialized, 28, 250–251, 257, 480–481; research, 452; transgressive, 38. *See also* Gays; Gender; Lesbians; Masculinity
Sexually transmitted infections (STI's), 249–251, 253–255, 264, 439
Sex work, 12
Shame, 228, 232, 239, 240, 252, 442
"Shared responsibility," 9
Silence, 232–233; as alternative to sexual confession, 123; code of, 217–218, 221
Social death, 139, 269
Social movements, 253, 309–310, 318, 512
Social networks, 6, 13–15, 18–19, 25, 99, 289, 304, 352, 421, 422, 426–427, 429, 440, 446, 515, 517; gendered construction of, 19; transnational, 18, 27, 265
Social reproduction, 3, 5, 18, 24, 30 n.7, 356, 68–69, 197, 199–200, 250, 288, 303, 308, 313, 316, 322, 327–328, 332, 346, 352, 441, 443, 450
Social rights, 95, 98
Sojourner (immigration model), 389
Space of death, 53, 60–61
State of exception, 52, 57, 60, 65 n.42
Sterilization, involuntary, 152
Structural-adjustment programs, 289
Structural dislocation, 19
Structural forces, 2, 14

Structures of power, 19, 42
Subcomandante Marcos, 43, 50
Surrogacy (of Selena), 488
Surveillance, 13, 21, 38, 43, 46, 84, 145, 151, 172, 196, 265; incomplete, 492; video, 146
Survival, 1, 18, 22, 27, 347, 352, 358 n.3, 365–366, 418; family, 353, 357; mechanisms, 24, 254; of social body, 154; strategies, 13, 26, 93, 96–97, 98, 270, 289, 341, 342, 351–353, 357
Survivors (of sexual violence), 203, 227, 233, 236–237, 239
Symbol: action of, 311, 313, 316; in gender construction, 416

Taller de Género de la Universidad Autónoma de Juárez, 35
Talleres familiares, 272
Tarascan, 97–99
Tequila, as image of masculinity, 227
Third World, 4, 14, 40, 63 n.21, 161, 188, 204, 288, 290, 360, 504, 511, 518–519; and female sexual drives, 189; and feminist activism, 56; health status, 251; immigrants, 134, 140; police force, 39; women, 41, 47, 49, 70, 222 n.13
Three for One, 9
TLC Worldwide. *See* Latina Connection Worldwide
Transborder area, 25–26, 330–339, 340 n.4
Transborder Consortium, 29 n.1
Transborder families, 25, 327–332, 335–337, 339
Transculturation, 5
Transmigration, 26, 327
Transnationalism, 1–2, 3, 15, 25, 30 n.5, 56, 93, 103, 105, 162, 181, 225, 243, 250, 309, 390, 394, 409, 417, 452, 480, 439, 503–504; capital, 40; communities, 225, 244 n.4, 389, 438–441, 447; context, 18, 99, 260; forces of, 253; framework of, 32 n.34, 389; and identity, 56; and migration, 2, 21, 29, 250, 266, 461; "new," 17; and political economy, 161; processes of, 250,

453, 519 n.2; transnational corporations, 40–41, 63 n. 21, 477, 163; and women, 107
Transvestis, 255
"Trap of visibility," 490
Trauma, social, 35, 54, 59
Trope of triumph (for young Latinas), 494
Turnover of workers, 22, 185, 189–190, 193, 195, 197–200
"Twin cities," 12

Uniones libres, 26
Unionization, 42, 291
United Farmworkers, 255
United Nations, 39; Seminar on Immigration, Racism, and Racial Discrimination, 101; World Conference of Human Rights, 56
Usar, 444
U.S. Citizenship and Immigration Services (formerly INS), 21, 204. *See also* Immigration and Naturalization Service (INS)
U.S. Commission on Civil Rights, 216

Vecindades, 274
Vendida, 123
Vergüenza, 228, 232, 239, 240, 252, 442
Villaraigosa, Antonio, 320
Violence, 12, 19, 22, 23, 25, 47, 53, 54, 57–58, 99, 189, 203, 231, 245 n.12, 253, 451; absence of, 365; climate of, 20, 50, 188; discursive, 61; domestic, 16, 40, 50, 52, 200, 221, 223 n.15, 244 n.3, 349, 442, 447, 449–450; emotional, 23; gender, 23, 37–38, 53–54, 56, 65 n.50, 200, 204, 209, 215, 219, 221, 221 n.1, 228, 482; institutional, 38; male, 51; sexual, 23, 36, 39, 52, 221, 224–229, 232, 237, 239–243, 243 n.2, n.3, 244 n.6 n.7; social, 13–15, 19, 21, 29; state-sanctioned, 11, 18, 52–53, 225; structural, 2–3, 5, 11–12, 29, 21, 29 n.2; symbolic, 47–48, 54; systemic, 124
Violence against Women Act (VAWA), 242, 246 n.13
Virgen de Guadalupe, 391, 514
Virginity, 229, 232, 236, 238–240; and virgin-whore discourse, 257
Visual rhetoric (in maquilas), 167
Voces Sin Eco (Voices without Echo), 54, 59, 62, 63 n.18, 62, 65 n.44, 65 n.46

War against Drugs, 12, 204
Welfare, 73, 75, 135, 137; economic, 365; law, 151; national, 140, 145, 149; of population, 138, 143, 151; social, 308, 322; state, 93, 95, 102, 366
Whiteness, 482, 484
Wilson, Pete, 68, 135, 141, 144, 150–151, 153, 308
Woman and race question, 56
Womanhood, 380, 467, 469. *See also* Mothers
Women of color, 112, 222 n.13, 391, 409
Women's rights activists, 58–60
World Bank, 41
World Conference against Racism, 101
World Trade Organization (WTO), 41

Zapatista, 43, 53
Zapotec, 343
Zedillo, Ernesto, 35
Zero population growth, 10, 20, 72, 89
Zero Population Growth (organization), 73

The following were published previously and are used with permission in this volume.

Rosa Linda Fregoso. 2003. "Toward a Planetary Civil Society." In meXicana Encounters: The Making of Social Identities on the Borderlands, 1–29. Berkeley: University of California Press.

Leo R. Chavez. 2004. "A Glass Half Empty: Latina Reproduction and Public Discourse." Human Organization 63, no. 2: 173–88.

Adelaida R. Del Castillo. 2002. "Illegal Status and Social Citizenship: Thoughts on Mexican Immigrants in a Postnational World." Aztlán 27, no. 2 (fall): 11–32.

Eithne Luibheid. 1998. "'Looking Like a Lesbian': The Organization of Sexual Monitoring at the United States-Mexican Border." Journal of the History of Sexuality 8, no. 3: 477–506.

Leslie Salzinger. 2000. "Manufacturing Sexual Subjects: 'Harassment,' Desire and Discipline on a Maquiladora Shopfloor." Ethnography 1, no. 1: 67–92.

Melissa W. Wright. 1999. "The Dialectics of Still Life: Murder, Women and Maquiladoras." Public Culture 11, no. 3: 453–74.

Sylvanna M. Falcón, 2001. "Rape as a Weapon of War: Advancing Human Rights for Women at the U.S.-Mexico Border." Social Justice 28, no. 2: 31–50.

Xóchitl Castañeda and Patricia Zavella. 2003. "Changing Constructions of Sexuality and Risk: Migrant Mexican Women Farmworkers in California." Latin American Anthropology 8, no. 2: 126–51.

Faranak Miraftab. 1996. "Space, Gender, and Work: Home-Based Workers in Mexico." In Homeworkers in Global Perspective: Invisible No More, edited by Eileen Boris and Elisabeth Prügl, 63–80. New York: Routledge.

María de la Luz Ibarra. 2000. "Mexican Immigrant Women and the New Domestic Labor." Human Organization 59, no. 4: 452–64.

Norma Ojeda de la Peña. 1995. "Familias transfronterizas y trayectorias de migración y trabajo." In Mujeres, Migración y Maquila en la Frontera Norte, edited by Soledad González Montes, Olivia Ruiz, Laura Velasco, and Ofelia Woo, 89–112. Mexico City: El Colegio de la Frontera Norte.

Laura Velasco Ortiz. 1995. "Migración femenina y estrategias de sobrevivencia de la unidad doméstica: Un caso de estudio de mujeres mixtecas en Tijuana." In Mujeres, Migración y Maquila en la Frontera Norte, edited by Soledad González Montes, Olivia Ruiz, Laura Velasco, and Ofelia Woo, 37–64. Mexico City: El Colegio de la Frontera Norte.

Sylvia Chant. 1997. "Single-Parent Families: Choice or Constraint? The Formation of Female-Headed Households in Mexican Shanty Towns." In The Women, Gender and Development Reader, edited by Nalini Visvanathan, Lynn Duggan, Laurie Nisonoff, and Nan Wiegersma, 155–62, 165. London: Zed Books Ltd.

Denise A. Segura. 1994. "Working at Motherhood: Chicana and Mexican Immigrant Mothers and Employment." In Mothering: Ideology, Experience, and Agency, edited by Evelyn Nakano Glenn, Grace Chang, and Linda Rennie Forcey, 211–36. New York: Routledge.

Pierrette Hondagneu-Sotelo and Ernestine Avila. 1997. "'I'm Here, But I'm There': The Meanings of Latina Transnational Motherhood." *Gender and Society* 11, no. 5: 548–71.

Jennifer S. Hirsch. 1999. "'En el Norte la Mujer Manda': Gender, Generation, and Geography in a Mexican Transnational Community." *American Behavioral Scientist* 42, no. 9: 1332–49.

Olga Nájera-Ramírez. 2003. "Unruly Passions: Poetics, Performance, and Gender in the Ranchera Song." In *Chicana Feminisms: A Critical Reader*, edited by Gabriela Arredondo, Aída Hurtado, Norma Klahn, Olga Nájera-Ramírez, and Patricia Zavella, 184–210. Durham, N.C.: Duke University Press.

Felicity Schaeffer-Grabiel. 2004. "Cyberbrides and Global Imaginaries: Mexican Women's Turn from the National to the Foreign." *Space and Culture* 7, no. 1: 33–48.

Denise A. Segura teaches in the Sociology Department at the University of California, Santa Barbara. Patricia Zavella teaches in the Department of Latin American and Latino Studies at the University of California, Santa Cruz.

Library of Congress Cataloging-in-Publication Data
Women and migration in the U.S.-Mexico borderlands :
a reader / edited by Denise A. Segura and Patricia Zavella.
p. cm. — (Latin America otherwise)
Includes bibliographical references and index.
ISBN 978-0-8223-4097-3 (cloth : alk. paper)
ISBN 978-0-8223-4118-5 (pbk. : alk. paper)
1. Women immigrants—Mexican-American Border
Region—Social conditions. 2. Mexican American women—
Mexican-American Border Region—Social conditions.
3. Mexicans—Mexican-American Border Region—Social
conditions. 4. Social change—Mexican-American Border
Region. 5. Mexican-American Border Region—Emigration
and immigration—Social aspects. I. Segura, Denise A.
II. Zavella, Patricia.
JV6602.W66 2007
305.40972'1—dc22   2006036829